6TH EDITION

Invitation
to Computer
Science

LEVEL SIX

Social Issues
chapter 17

LEVEL FIVE

Applications
chapters 13,14,15,16

LEVEL FOUR

The Software World
chapters 9,10,11,12

LEVEL THREE

The Virtual Machine
chapters 6,7,8

LEVEL TWO

The Hardware World
chapters 4,5

LEVEL ONE

The Algorithmic Foundations of
Computer Science
chapters 2,3

6TH EDITION

Invitation to Computer Science

G. Michael Schneider
Macalester College

Judith L. Gersting
Indiana University-Purdue University
at Indianapolis

Contributing author:
Bo Brinkman
Miami University

CENGAGE
Learning·

Australia • Brazil • Japan• Korea • Mexico• Singapore • Spain• United Kingdom• United States

CENGAGE
Learning®

Invitation to Computer Science, Sixth Edition

G. Michael Schneider and Judith L. Gersting

Executive Editor: Marie Lee

Acquisitions Editor: Brandi Shailer

Senior Product Manager: Alyssa Pratt

Development Editor: Deb Kaufmann

Associate Product Manager:
Stephanie Lorenz

Associate Marketing Manager:
Shanna Shelton

Senior Content Project Managers: Jill Braiewa,
Jennifer Goguen McGrail

Associate Art Director: Faith Brosnan

Cover Designer: Roycroft Design|
roycroftdesign.com

Cover Image: iStockphoto.com/
Dmitry Pistrov

Compositor: Integra

> For product information and technology assistance, contact us at
> **Cengage Learning Customer & Sales Support, www.cengage.com/support**
>
> For permission to use material from this text or product, submit all requests online at **cengage.com/permissions**
> Further permissions questions can be emailed to
> **permissionrequest@cengage.com**

Library of Congress Control Number: 2011943942

ISBN-13: 978-1-133-19082-0

ISBN-10: 1-133-19082-0

Cengage Learning
20 Channel Center Street
Boston, MA 02210
USA

Cengage Learning is a leading provider of customized learning solutions with office locations around the globe, including Singapore, the United Kingdom, Australia, Mexico, Brazil, and Japan. Locate your local office at:
international.cengage.com/region

Cengage Learning products are represented in Canada by Nelson Education, Ltd.

For your lifelong learning solutions, visit **course.cengage.com**

Visit our corporate website at **cengage.com.**

Printed in Canada
1 2 3 4 5 6 7 16 15 14 13 12

To my wife, Ruthann, our children, Benjamin, Rebecca, and Trevor, grandson, Liam, and granddaughter, Sena.

G. M. S.

To my husband, John, and to: Adam and Francine; Jason, Cathryn, Sammie, and Johnny

J. L. G.

Brief Contents

Online Chapters

This text includes five language-specific online-only downloadable chapters on Ada, C++, C#, Java, and Python, available at **www.cengagebrain.com** (search for the ISBN of this book) and on the CourseMate for this text.

Contents

Chapter 3   The Efficiency of Algorithms   90

LEVEL 3   The Virtual Machine   274

Chapter 6   An Introduction to System Software and Virtual Machines   276

LEVEL 4   The Software World   422

Chapter 9   Introduction to High-Level Language Programming   424

Online Chapters

This text includes five language-specific online-only downloadable chapters on Ada, C++, C#, Java, and Python, available at **www.cengagebrain.com** (search for the ISBN of this book) and on the CourseMate for this text.

LEVEL 5   Applications   620

Chapter 13   Simulation and Modeling   622

Chapter 14   Electronic Commerce and Databases   654

Preface

Overview

This text is intended for use in a one-semester introductory course in computer science. It presents a breadth-first overview of the discipline that assumes no prior background in computer science, programming, or mathematics. It is appropriate for a service course for students not majoring in computer science, as well as for schools that implement their introductory sequence for majors using the breadth-first model described in the ACM/IEEE Computing Curricula 2001 Report. It would be quite suitable for a high school computer science course as well. Previous editions of this text have been used in all these types of courses.

The Non-Majors Course

The introductory computer science service course has undergone many changes over the years. In the 1970s and early 1980s, it was usually a course in FOR-TRAN, BASIC, or Pascal. At that time it was felt that the most important skill a student could acquire was learning to program in a high-level language. In the mid-to-late '80s, a rapid increase in computer use caused the course to evolve into something called "computer literacy" in which students learned about new applications of computing in such fields as business, medicine, law, and education. With the growth of personal computers and productivity software, a typical early to mid-1990s version of this course would spend a semester teaching students to use word processors, databases, spreadsheets, presentation software, and electronic mail. The most recent change has been its evolution into a Web-centric course where students learn to design and implement Web pages using technology such as HTML, XML, ASP, and Java applets.

In many institutions the computer science service course has evolved yet again. There are two reasons for this. First, virtually all students in college today are familiar with personal computers and productivity software. They have been using word processors and presentation systems since elementary school and are quite familiar with social networks, online retailing, e-mail, and chat rooms. Many have designed Web pages and even manage their own Web sites and blogs. In this day and age, a course that focuses on applications of computing will be of little or no interest.

But a more important reason for rethinking the structure of this course, and the primary reason why we authored this book, is the following observation:

> *Most computer science service courses do not teach students the foundations and fundamentals of computer science!*

We believe quite strongly that students in a computer science service course should receive a solid grounding in the fundamental intellectual concepts of computer science in addition to important uses of computing and information technology. This parallels the introductory course in biology, physics, or geology, where the central underpinnings of the respective fields are introduced. The topics in such a computer science course would not be limited to "fun" applications such as Web page design, social networking, and interactive graphics, but would also cover issues such as algorithms, hardware design, computer organization, system software, language models, theory of computation, and social and ethical issues of computing. An introduction to these core ideas exposes students to the overall richness and beauty of the field, and it allows them to not only use computers and software effectively but to understand and appreciate the basic ideas underlying their creation and implementation.

The CS1 Course

The design of a first course for computer science majors has also come in for a great deal of discussion. Since the emergence of computer science as a distinct academic discipline in the 1960s, the first course has always been an introduction to programming—from BASIC to FORTRAN to Pascal, to C++, Java, and Python today. Some new programming-related topics have been added to the syllabus (e.g., object-oriented design), but the central focus has remained high-level language programming. However, the most recent ACM/IEEE curriculum report proposed a number of alternative models for the first course, including a breadth-first overview, an approach that has gained in popularity over time.

A first course for computer science majors using the breadth-first model emphasizes early exposure to the sub-disciplines of the field rather than placing exclusive emphasis on programming. This gives new majors a more complete and well-rounded understanding of their chosen field of study. As stated in the Curriculum Report, "[introductory] courses that emphasize only this one aspect [programming] fail to let students experience the many other areas and styles of thought that are part of computer science as a whole." Our book—intended for either majors or non-majors—is organized around this breadth-first approach, and it presents a wide range of subject matter drawn from many areas of computer science. However, to avoid drowning students in a sea of seemingly unrelated facts and details, a breadth-first presentation must be carefully woven into a cohesive fabric, a theme, a "big picture" that ties together these topics and presents computer science as a unified and integrated discipline. To achieve this we have divided the study of computer science into a hierarchy of topics, with each layer in the hierarchy building on and expanding upon concepts presented in earlier chapters.

A Hierarchy of Abstractions

The central theme of this book is that *computer science is the study of algorithms*. Our hierarchy utilizes this definition by first looking at the algorithmic basis of computer science and then moving upward from this central theme to higher-level issues such as hardware, software, applications, and ethics. Just as the chemist starts from protons, neutrons, and electrons and builds up to atoms, molecules, and compounds, so, too, does our text build from elementary concepts such as algorithms, binary arithmetic, gates, and circuits to higher-level ideas such as computer organization, operating systems, high-level languages, applications, and the social, legal, and ethical problems of information technology.

The six levels in our computer science hierarchy are as follows:

Level 1. The Algorithmic Foundations of Computer Science
Level 2. The Hardware World
Level 3. The Virtual Machine
Level 4. The Software World
Level 5. Applications
Level 6. Social Issues in Computing

Following an introductory chapter, **Level 1** (Chapters 2–3) introduces "The Algorithmic Foundations of Computer Science," the bedrock on which all other aspects of the discipline are built. It presents fundamental ideas such as the design of algorithms, algorithmic problem solving, abstraction, pseudocode, iteration, and efficiency. It illustrates these ideas using well-known examples such as searching a list, finding maxima and minima, sorting a list, and matching patterns. It also introduces the concepts of algorithm efficiency and asymptotic growth and demonstrates that not all algorithms are, at least in terms of running time, created equal.

The discussions in Level 1 assume that our algorithms are executed by something called a "computing agent," an abstract concept for any entity that can effectively carry out the instructions contained in our solution. However, in **Level 2** (Chapters 4–5), "The Hardware World," we now want our algorithms to be executed by "real" computers to produce "real" results. Thus begins our discussion of hardware, logic design, and computer organization. The initial discussion introduces the basic building blocks of computer systems—binary numbers, Boolean logic, gates, and circuits. It then shows how these elementary concepts can be used to construct a real computer using the classic Von Neumann architecture, including processors, memory, buses, and input/output. It presents a typical machine language instruction set and explains how the algorithmic primitives of Level 1 can be represented in machine language and run on the Von Neumann hardware of Level 2, conceptually tying together these two areas. It ends with a discussion of important new directions in hardware design—multicore processors and massively parallel machines.

By the end of Level 2 students have been introduced to some basic concepts in logic design and computer organization, and they understand and appreciate the enormous complexity of these ideas. This complexity is the motivation for the material contained in **Level 3** (Chapters 6–8), "The Virtual Machine." This section describes how system software produces a more friendly, user-oriented problem-solving environment that hides many of the ugly hardware details just described. Level 3 looks at the same problems discussed in Level 2, encoding and executing algorithms, but shows how much easier this is in a virtual environment containing helpful software tools like editors, translators, debuggers, and loaders. This section also discusses the services and responsibilities of operating systems and how operating systems have evolved. It investigates one of the most important virtual environments in current use—networks of computers. It shows how systems such as the Ethernet, Internet, and the Web are created from computers linked together via transmission media and communications software. This linkage creates a virtual environment in which we seamlessly use not only the computer on our desk or in our hand but computers located practically anywhere in the world. Level 3 concludes with a look at one of the most important services provided by a virtual machine, information security, and describes algorithms for protecting the user and the system from accidental or malicious damage.

Once we have created this user-oriented virtual environment, what do we want to do with it? Most likely we want to write programs to solve interesting problems. This is the motivation for **Level 4** (Chapters 9–12), "The Software World." Although this book should not be viewed as a programming text, it contains an overview of the features found in modern programming languages. This gives students an appreciation for the interesting and challenging task of the computer programmer and the power of the problem-solving environment created by a modern high-level language. (Detailed introductions to five important high-level programming languages are available via online, downloadable chapters accessible through the CourseMate for this text, as well as at *www.cengagebrain.com.*) There are many different programming language models, so this level includes a discussion of other language types, including special-purpose languages such as SQL, HTML, and JavaScript, as well as the functional, logic, and parallel language paradigms. This level also describes the design and construction of a compiler and shows how high-level languages can be translated into machine language for execution. This latter discussion ties together ideas presented in earlier chapters, as we show how an algorithm (Level 1) is translated into a high-level language (Level 4), compiled and executed on a typical Von Neumann machine (Level 2), which makes use of the system software tools of Level 3. These "recurring themes" and frequent references to earlier concepts help reinforce the idea of computer science as an integrated set of related topics. At the conclusion of Level 4, we introduce the idea of computability and unsolvability. A formal model of computing (the Turing machine) is used to prove that problems exist for which no general algorithmic solution can be found. This shows students that there are provable limits to what computers and computer science can achieve.

We now have a high-level programming environment in which it is possible to write programs to solve important problems. In **Level 5** (Chapters 13–16),

"Applications," we take a look at a few important uses of computers in our modern society. There is no way to cover even a tiny fraction of the many applications of computers and information technology in a single section. Indeed, there is hardly a field of study, from Art to Zoology, that has not been significantly impacted by the advances in computation and communication. Instead, we focus on a relatively small set of applications that demonstrate important concepts, tools, and techniques of computer science. This includes applications drawn from the sciences and engineering (simulation and modeling), business and finance (e-commerce, databases), the social sciences (artificial intelligence), and everyday life (computer generated imagery, video gaming, virtual communities). Our goal is not to provide "encyclopedic coverage" of modern computing usage; instead, it is to show students that these applications are not "magic boxes" whose inner workings are totally unfathomable. Rather, they are the direct result of utilizing and building upon core computer science concepts—e.g., algorithms, hardware, languages—presented in earlier chapters. We hope that the discussions in this section will encourage readers to seek out information on applications and software packages specific to their own areas of interest.

Finally, we reach the highest level of study, **Level 6** (Chapter 17), "Social Issues in Computing," which addresses the social, ethical, and legal issues raised by the applications presented in Level 5. This section (written by contributing author Professor Bo Brinkman of Miami University) examines such thorny problems as the theft of intellectual property, national security concerns aggravated by information technology, and problems caused by the unauthorized access to online databases. It also discusses erosions to our personal privacy caused by the growing popularity of social networks. This chapter does not attempt to provide quick solutions to these complex problems. Instead, it focuses on techniques that students can use to think about these ethical issues and reach their own conclusions. Our goal in this final section is to make students aware of the enormous impact that information technology is having on everyone's lives and to give them tools that will allow them to make more informed decisions.

This, then, is the hierarchical structure of our text. It begins with the algorithmic foundations of the discipline and works its way from low-level hardware concepts through virtual machine environments, languages, software, and applications to the social issues raised by computer technology. This organizational structure, along with the use of recurring themes, enables students to view computer science as a unified, integrated, and coherent field of study. While the social issues material in Chapter 17 can be presented at any time, the rest of the material is intended to be covered sequentially.

What's New

This sixth edition of *Invitation to Computer Science* contains a number of new features on emerging issues in computer science. We have added material on topics such as multicore and parallel systems, cloud computing, wireless communications, embedded computing and its security vulnerabilities, agile software development, emerging programming languages (Go and F#), new models of e-commerce, database integrity rules, and the progress of artificial intelligence in game playing.

There are many new in-chapter Practice Problems (with answers provided at the end of the text) as well as numerous new End of Chapter Exercises. There are also new additions to the end-of-chapter Challenge Problems; these more complex questions can be used for longer assignments done either individually or by teams of students. Many new or updated Special Interest Boxes highlight historical information, new developments in computing, or interesting news items that show how computing affects everyday life.

One of the most important new features in this edition is the rewrite of Chapter 17, *Making Decisions about Computers, Information, and Society*, authored by Bo Brinkman of Miami University, a recognized expert on the topic of social and ethical issues in computing. In addition to new Case Studies, this chapter contains a completely new section entitled "Personal Privacy and Social Networks," which addresses the real and growing problems of cyberbullying and the threats to our personal privacy caused by the enormous popularity of Web sites such as Facebook, Twitter, and YouTube.

An Interactive Experience - CourseMate

This edition offers significantly enhanced supplementary material and additional resources available online through a new CourseMate. Course-Mate is a valuable Web resource containing an eBook with highlighting and note-taking capabilities, supplementary readings that correspond to each chapter, a glossary and flashcards of key technical terms, and links to interesting articles, helpful references, and relevant videos from across the Web. The CourseMate encourages a truly interactive experience with study games, objective- and application-based quizzing, and hands-on exploration projects that speak students' language.

Instructors may add CourseMate to the textbook package, or students may purchase CourseMate directly through *www.cengagebrain.com*.

An Experimental Science - Laboratory Manual

Another important aspect of computer science education is the realization that, like physics, chemistry, and biology, computer science is an empirical, laboratory-based discipline in which learning comes not only from watching and listening but from doing and trying. Many complex ideas in computer science cannot be fully understood and appreciated until they are visualized, manipulated, and tested. Today, most computer science faculty consider formal laboratories to be an essential part of any introductory course. We concur, and this development is fully reflected in our approach to the material.

Associated with this text is a laboratory manual and custom-designed laboratory software that enables students to experiment with the concepts we present. The manual contains 20 laboratory experiences, closely coordinated with the main text, that cover all levels except Level 6. These labs give students the chance to observe, study, analyze, and/or modify an important idea or concept. For example, associated with Level 1 (the algorithmic foundations of computer science) are experiments that animate the algorithms in Chapters 2 and 3 and ask students to observe and discuss what is happening in these animations. There are also labs that allow students to measure the running time of these algorithms for different-sized data sets and discuss their behavior, thus providing concrete observations of an abstract concept like algorithmic efficiency. Associated with Level 2 (the hardware world) are projects to design and analyze logic circuits as well as program a simulated Von Neumann machine that is identical to the one presented in the text. There are similar labs available for Levels 3, 4, and 5 that highlight and clarify the material presented in the text.

Each of the lab manual experiments includes an explanation of how to use the software, a description of exactly how to conduct the experiment, and discussion questions and problems for students to complete and hand in. When doing these projects, students could work on their own or in teams, and the course may utilize either a closed-lab (formal, scheduled) or an open-lab (informal, unscheduled) setting. The manual and software will work well in any of these laboratory models. The text contains 20 boxes labeled "Laboratory Exercise" that describe each lab and identify the point in the text where it is most appropriate.

Instructors may add the Laboratory Manual and accompanying software to the textbook package. The Laboratory Manual and CourseMate may also be bundled together for the optimal experience; contact your sales representative for more information. Students may purchase the Laboratory Manual directly through www.cengagebrain.com.

Summary

Computer science is a young and exciting discipline, and we hope that the material in this text, along with the laboratory projects and online modules, will convey this feeling of excitement. By presenting the field in all its richness—algorithms, hardware, software, systems, applications, and social issues—we hope to give students a deeper appreciation for the many diverse and interesting areas of research and study within the discipline of computer science. We hope that you will enjoy reading and learning from this latest edition of our text.

Instructor Resources

The following supplemental teaching tools are available when this book is used in a classroom setting. All of the teaching tools available with this book are provided to the instructor on a single CD-ROM. Many are also available for download at *login.cengage.com*.

Electronic Instructor's Manual

The Instructor's Manual follows the text chapter-by-chapter and includes material to assist in planning and organizing an effective, engaging course. The Manual includes Overviews, Chapter Objectives, Teaching Tips, Quick Quizzes, Class Discussion Topics, Additional Projects, Additional Resources, and Key Terms. A **Sample Syllabus** is also available.

Solutions

Complete solutions to chapter Review Questions, Discussion Questions, and quantitative hands-on work are provided.

ExamView®

This textbook is accompanied by ExamView, a powerful testing software package that allows instructors to create and administer printed, LAN-based, and Internet exams. ExamView includes hundreds of questions that correspond to the text, enabling students to generate detailed study guides that include page references for further review. The computer-based and Internet testing components allow students to take exams at their computers and save the instructor time by grading each exam automatically. These test banks are also available in **Blackboard, Web CT, and Angel** compatible formats.

PowerPoint Presentations

This text provides Microsoft PowerPoint slides to accompany each chapter. Slides may be used to guide classroom presentation, to make available to students for chapter review, or to print as classroom handouts. Instructors may customize the slides to best suit their course with the complete **Figure Files** from the text.

—G. Michael Schneider
Macalester College
schneider@macalester.edu

—Judith L. Gersting
Indiana University-Purdue University at Indianapolis
gersting@iupui.edu

An Introduction to Computer Science

1.1 Introduction

This text is an invitation to learn about one of the youngest and most exciting of scientific disciplines—*computer science*. Almost every day our newspapers, televisions, and electronic media carry reports of significant advances in computing, such as high-speed supercomputers that perform over 8 quadrillion (10^{15}) mathematical operations per second; networks that transmit high-definition images and movies anywhere in the world in fractions of a second; minute computer chips that can be embedded into our appliances, clothing, and even our bodies; and artificial intelligence systems that answer English language questions faster and more accurately than humans. The next few years will see technological breakthroughs that, until a few years ago, existed only in the minds of dreamers and science fiction writers. These are exciting times in computing, and our goal in this text is to provide you with an understanding of computer science and an appreciation for the diverse areas of research and study within this important field.

Although the average person can produce a reasonably accurate description of most scientific fields, even if he or she did not study the subject in school, many people do not have an intuitive understanding of the types of problems studied by computer science professionals. For example, you probably know that biology is the study of living organisms and that chemistry deals with the structure and composition of matter. However, you might not have the same fundamental understanding of the work that goes on in computer science. In fact, many people harbor one or more of the following common misconceptions about this field.

MISCONCEPTION 1: *Computer science is the study of computers.*

This apparently obvious definition is actually incorrect or, to put it more precisely, incomplete. For example, some of the earliest and most fundamental theoretical work in computer science took place from 1920 to 1940, years before the development of the first computer system. (This pioneering work was initially considered a branch of logic and applied mathematics. Computer science did not come to be recognized as a separate and independent field of scientific study until the late 1950s to early 1960s.) Even today, there are branches of computer science quite distinct from the study of "real" machines. In *theoretical computer science*, for example, researchers study the logical and mathematical properties of problems and their solutions. Frequently, these researchers investigate problems not with actual computers but rather with *formal models* of computation, which are easier to study and analyze mathematically. Their work involves pencil and paper, not circuit boards and disks.

This distinction between computers and computer science was beautifully expressed by computer scientists Michael R. Fellows and Ian Parberry in an article in the journal *Computing Research News*:

> Computer science is no more about computers than astronomy is about telescopes, biology is about microscopes, or chemistry is about beakers and test tubes. Science is not about tools. It is about how we use them and what we find out when we do.[1]

MISCONCEPTION 2: *Computer science is the study of how to write computer programs.*

Many people are introduced to computer science when learning to write programs in a language such as C++, Python, or Java. This almost universal use of programming as the entry to the discipline can create the misunderstanding that computer science is equivalent to computer programming.

Programming is extremely important to the discipline—researchers use it to study new ideas and build and test new solutions—but like the computer itself, it is a tool. When computer scientists design and analyze a new approach to solving a problem or create new ways to represent information, they often implement their ideas as programs to test them on an actual computer system. This enables researchers to see how well these new ideas work and whether they perform better than previous methods.

---

[1]Fellows, M. R., and Parberry, I. "Getting Children Excited About Computer Science," *Computing Research News*, vol. 5, no. 1 (January 1993).

For example, searching a list is one of the most common applications of computers, and it is frequently applied to huge problems, such as finding one name among the approximately 20,000,000 listings in the New York City telephone directory. (We will solve this problem in Chapter 2.) A more efficient lookup method could significantly reduce the time that customers must wait for directory assistance. Assume that we have designed what we believe to be a "new and improved" search technique. After analyzing it theoretically, we would study it empirically by writing a program to implement our new method, executing it on our computer, and measuring its performance. These tests would demonstrate under what conditions our new method is or is not faster than the directory search procedures currently in use.

In computer science, it is not simply the construction of a high-quality program that is important but also the methods it embodies, the services it provides, and the results it produces. It is possible to become so enmeshed in writing code and getting it to run that we forget that a program is only a means to an end, not an end in itself.

MISCONCEPTION 3: *Computer science is the study of the uses and applications of computers and software.*

If one's introduction to computer science is not programming, then it may be a course on the application of computers and software. Such a course typically teaches the use of a number of popular packages, such as word processors, search engines, database systems, imaging software, mapping packages, smartphone apps, and Web browsers.

These packages are widely used by professionals in all fields. However, learning to use a software package is no more a part of computer science than driver's education is a branch of automotive engineering. A wide range of people *use* computer software, but it is the computer scientist who is responsible for *specifying*, *designing*, *building*, and *testing* software packages as well as the computer systems on which they run.

These three misconceptions about computer science are not entirely wrong; they are just woefully incomplete. Computers, programming languages, software, and applications *are* part of the discipline of computer science, but neither individually nor combined do they capture the richness and diversity of this field.

We have spent a good deal of time saying what computer science is *not*. What, then, is it? What are its basic concepts? What are the fundamental questions studied by professionals in this field? Is it possible to capture the breadth and scope of the discipline in a single definition? We answer these fundamental questions in the next section and, indeed, in the remainder of the text.

In the Beginning...

There is no single date that marks the beginning of computer science. Indeed, there are many "firsts" that could be used to mark this event. For example, some of the earliest theoretical work on the logical foundations of computer science occurred in the 1930s. The first general-purpose, electronic computers appeared during the period 1940–1946. (We will discuss the history of these early machines in Section 1.4.) These first computers were one-of-a-kind experimental systems that never moved outside the research laboratory. The first commercial machine, the UNIVAC I, did not make its appearance until March 1951, a date that marks the real beginning of the computer industry. The first high-level (i.e., based on natural language) programming language was FORTRAN. Some people mark its debut in 1957 as the beginning of the "software" industry. The appearance of these new machines and languages created new occupations, such as programmer, numerical analyst, and computer engineer. To address the intellectual needs of these workers, the first professional society for people in the field of computing, the Association for Computing Machinery (ACM), was established in 1947. (The ACM has almost 100,000 members and is the largest professional computer science society in the world. Its Web page is located at *www.acm.org*.) To help meet the rapidly growing need for computer professionals, the first Department of Computer Science was established at Purdue University in October 1962. It awarded its first M.Sc. degree in 1964 and its first Ph.D. in computer science in 1966. An undergraduate program was established in 1968.

Thus, depending on what you consider the most important "first," the field of computer science is somewhere between 45 and 80 years old. Compared with such classic scientific disciplines as mathematics, physics, chemistry, and biology, computer science is the new kid on the block.

1.2 The Definition of Computer Science

There are many definitions of computer science, but the one that best captures the richness and breadth of ideas embodied in this branch of science was first proposed by professors Norman Gibbs and Allen Tucker.[2] According to their definition, the central concept in computer science is the algorithm. It is not possible to understand the field without a thorough understanding of this critically important idea.

---

[2]Gibbs, N. E., and Tucker, A. B. "A Model Curriculum for a Liberal Arts Degree in Computer Science," *Comm. of the ACM*, vol. 29, no. 3 (March 1986).

DEFINITION

Computer science: the study of algorithms, including

1. Their formal and mathematical properties
2. Their hardware realizations
3. Their linguistic realizations
4. Their applications

The Gibbs and Tucker definition says that it is the task of the computer scientist to design and develop algorithms to solve a range of important problems. This design process includes the following operations:

- Studying the behavior of algorithms to determine if they are correct and efficient (their formal and mathematical properties)

- Designing and building computer systems that are able to execute algorithms (their hardware realizations)

- Designing programming languages and translating algorithms into these languages so that they can be executed by the hardware (their linguistic realizations)

- Identifying important problems and designing correct and efficient software packages to solve these problems (their applications)

Because it is impossible to appreciate this definition fully without knowing what an algorithm is, let's look more closely at this term. The dictionary defines the word *algorithm* as follows:

al • go • rithm n. A procedure for solving a mathematical problem in a finite number of steps that frequently involves repetition of an operation; broadly: a step-by-step method for accomplishing some task.

Informally, an algorithm is an ordered sequence of instructions that is guaranteed to solve a specific problem. It is a list that looks something like this:

Step 1:   Do something

Step 2:   Do something

Step 3:   Do something

.   .

.   .

.   .

Step N: Stop, you are finished

If you are handed this list and carefully follow its instructions in the order specified, when you reach the end you will have solved the task at hand.

All the operations used to construct algorithms belong to one of only three categories:

1. **Sequential operations** A sequential instruction carries out a single well-defined task. When that task is finished, the algorithm moves on to the next operation. Sequential operations are usually expressed as simple declarative sentences.
   - Add 1 cup of butter to the mixture in the bowl.
   - Subtract the amount of the check from the current account balance.
   - Set the value of x to 1.

2. **Conditional operations** These are the "question-asking" instructions of an algorithm. They ask a question, and the next operation is selected on the basis of the answer to that question.
   - If the mixture is too dry, then add one-half cup of water to the bowl.
   - If the amount of the check is less than or equal to the current account balance, then cash the check; otherwise, tell the person there are insufficient funds.
   - If x is not equal to 0, then set y equal to $1/x$; otherwise, print an error message that says you cannot perform division by 0.

3. **Iterative operations** These are the "looping" instructions of an algorithm. They tell us not to go on to the next instruction but, instead, to go back and repeat the execution of a previous block of instructions.
   - Repeat the previous two operations until the mixture has thickened.
   - While there are still more checks to be processed, do the following five steps.
   - Repeat Steps 1, 2, and 3 until the value of y is equal to $+1$.

We use algorithms (although we don't call them that) all the time—whenever we follow a set of instructions to assemble a child's toy, bake a cake, balance a checkbook, or go through the college registration process. A good example of an algorithm used in everyday life is the set of instructions shown in Figure 1.1 for programming a DVR to record a sequence of television shows. Note the three types of instructions in this algorithm: sequential (Steps 2, 4, 5, 6, and 8), conditional (Steps 1 and 7), and iterative (Step 3).

Mathematicians use algorithms all the time, and much of the work done by early Greek, Roman, Persian, and Indian mathematicians involved the discovery of algorithms for important problems in geometry and arithmetic; an example is *Euclid's algorithm* for finding the greatest common divisor of two positive integers. (Exercise 10 at the end of the chapter presents this

---

FIGURE 1.1

Step 1	If the clock and calendar are not correctly set, then go to page 9 of the instruction manual and follow the instructions there before proceeding to Step 2
Step 2	Place a blank disc into the DVR disc slot
Step 3	Repeat Steps 4 through 7 for each program that you want to record
Step 4	Enter the channel number that you want to record and press the button labeled CHAN
Step 5	Enter the time that you want recording to start and press the button labeled TIME-START
Step 6	Enter the time that you want recording to stop and press the button labeled TIME-FINISH. This completes the programming of one show
Step 7	If you do not want to record anything else, press the button labeled END-PROG
Step 8	Turn off your DVR. Your DVR is now in TIMER mode, ready to record

Programming your DVR: An example of an algorithm

FIGURE 1.2

Given: $m \geq 1$ and two positive numbers each containing m digits, $a_{m-1} \, a_{m-2} \ldots a_0$ and $b_{m-1} \, b_{m-2} \ldots b_0$

Wanted: $c_m \, c_{m-1} \, c_{m-2} \ldots c_0$, where $c_m \, c_{m-1} \, c_{m-2} \ldots c_0 = (a_{m-1} \, a_{m-2} \ldots a_0) + (b_{m-1} \, b_{m-2} \ldots b_0)$

Algorithm:

Step 1	Set the value of *carry* to 0
Step 2	Set the value of *i* to 0
Step 3	While the value of *i* is less than or equal to $m - 1$, repeat the instructions in Steps 4 through 6
Step 4	Add the two digits a_i and b_i to the current value of *carry* to get c_i
Step 5	If $c_i \geq 10$, then reset c_i to $(c_i - 10)$ and reset the value of *carry* to 1; otherwise, set the new value of *carry* to 0
Step 6	Add 1 to *i*, effectively moving one column to the left
Step 7	Set c_m to the value of *carry*
Step 8	Print out the final answer, $c_m \, c_{m-1} \, c_{m-2} \ldots c_0$
Step 9	Stop

Algorithm for adding two *m*-digit numbers

2,300-year-old algorithm.) We also studied algorithms in elementary school, even if we didn't know it. For example, in the first grade we learned an algorithm for adding two numbers such as

$$\begin{array}{r} 47 \\ +25 \\ \hline 72 \end{array}$$

The instructions our teachers gave were as follows: First add the rightmost column of numbers (7 + 5), getting the value 12. Write down the 2 under the line and carry the 1 to the next column. Now move left to the next column, adding (4 + 2) and the previous carry value of 1 to get 7. Write this value under the line, producing the correct answer 72.

Although as children we learned this algorithm informally, it can, like the DVR instructions in Figure 1.1, be written formally as an explicit sequence of instructions. Figure 1.2 shows an algorithm for adding two positive *m*-digit numbers. It expresses formally the operations informally described previously. Again, note the three types of instructions used to construct the algorithm: sequential (Steps 1, 2, 4, 6, 7, 8, and 9), conditional (Step 5), and iterative (Step 3).

Even though it might not appear so, this is the same "decimal addition algorithm" that you learned in grade school; if you follow it rigorously, it is guaranteed to produce the correct result. Let's watch it work.

$$\begin{array}{lll}
Add & (47 + 25) & \\
& m = 2 & \\
& a_1 = 4 & a_0 = 7 \\
& b_1 = 2 & b_0 = 5
\end{array} \left. \rule{0pt}{40pt} \right\} \quad \text{The input}$$

STEP 1: $carry = 0$

STEP 2: $i = 0$

STEP 3: We now repeat Steps 4 through 6 while i is less than or equal to 1

First repetition of the loop (i has the value 0)

STEP 4: Add ($a_0 + b_0 + carry$), which is $7 + 5 + 0$, so $c_0 = 12$

STEP 5: Because $c_0 \geq 10$, we reset **c_0 to 2** and reset $carry$ to 1

STEP 6: Reset i to $(0 + 1) = 1$. Because i is less than or equal to 1, go back to Step 4

Second repetition of the loop (i has the value 1)

STEP 4: Add ($a_1 + b_1 + carry$), which is $4 + 2 + 1$, so **$c_1 = 7$**

STEP 5: Because $c_1 < 10$, we reset $carry$ to 0

STEP 6: Reset i to $(1 + 1) = 2$. Because i is greater than 1, we do not repeat the loop but instead go to Step 7

STEP 7: Set **$c_2 = 0$**

STEP 8: Print out the answer $c_2\, c_1\, c_0 = 072$ (see the **boldface** values)

STEP 9: Stop

Abu Ja'far Muhammad ibn Musa Al-Khowarizmi (AD 780–850?)

The word *algorithm* is derived from the last name of Muhammad ibn Musa Al-Khowarizmi, a famous Persian mathematician and author from the eighth and ninth centuries. Al-Khowarizmi was a teacher at the House of Wisdom in Baghdad and the author of the book *Kitab al jabr w'al muqabala*, which in English means "The Concise Book of Calculation by Reduction." Written in AD 820, it is one of the earliest mathematical textbooks, and its title gives us the word *algebra* (the Arabic word *al jabr* means "reduction").

In AD 825, Al-Khowarizmi wrote another book about the base-10 positional numbering system that had recently been developed in India. In this book, he described formalized, step-by-step procedures for doing arithmetic operations, such as addition, subtraction, and multiplication, on numbers represented in this new decimal system, much like the addition algorithm diagrammed in Figure 1.2. In the twelfth century, this book was translated into Latin, introducing the base-10 Hindu-Arabic numbering system to Europe, and Al-Khowarizmi's name became closely associated with these formal numerical techniques. His last name was rendered as Algoritmi in Latin characters, and eventually the formalized procedures that he pioneered and developed became known as *algorithms* in his honor.

We have reached the end of the algorithm, and it has correctly produced the sum of the two numbers 47 and 25, the three-digit result 072. (A more clever algorithm would omit the unnecessary leading zero at the beginning of the number if the last carry value is a zero. That modification is an exercise—Exercise 6—at the end of the chapter.) Try working through the algorithm shown in Figure 1.2 with another pair of numbers to be sure that you understand exactly how it functions.

The addition algorithm shown in Figure 1.2 is a highly formalized representation of a technique that most people learned in the first or second grade and that virtually everyone knows how to do informally. Why would we take such a simple task as adding two numbers and express it in so complicated a fashion? Why are formal algorithms so important in computer science? Because of the following fundamental idea:

If we can specify an algorithm to solve a problem, then we can automate its solution.

Once we have formally specified an algorithm, we can build a machine (or write a program or hire a person) to carry out the steps contained in the algorithm. The machine (or program or person) does not need to understand the concepts or ideas underlying the solution. It merely has to do Step 1, Step 2, Step 3, …exactly as written. In computer science terminology, the machine, robot, person, or thing carrying out the steps of the algorithm is called a computing agent.

Thus computer science can also be viewed as the *science of algorithmic problem solving.* Much of the research and development work in computer science involves discovering correct and efficient algorithms for a wide range of interesting problems, studying their properties, designing programming languages into which those algorithms can be encoded, and designing and building computer systems that can automatically execute these algorithms in an efficient manner.

At first glance, it might seem that every problem can be solved algorithmically. However, you will learn in Chapter 12 the startling fact (first proved by the German logician Kurt Gödel in the early 1930s) that there are problems for which no generalized algorithmic solution can possibly exist. These problems are, in a sense, *unsolvable.* No matter how much time and effort is put into obtaining a solution, none will ever be found. Gödel's discovery, which staggered the mathematical world, effectively places a limit on the ultimate capabilities of computers and computer scientists.

There are also problems for which it is possible to specify an algorithm but a computing agent would take so long to execute it that the solution is essentially useless. For example, to get a computer to play winning chess, we could adopt a *brute force* approach. Given a board position as input, the computer would examine every legal move it could possibly make, then every legal response an opponent could make to each initial move, then every response it could select to that move, and so on. This analysis would continue until the game reached a win, lose, or draw position. With that information, the computer would be able to optimally choose its next move. If, for simplicity's sake, we assume that there are 40 legal moves from any given position on a chessboard, and it takes about 30 moves to reach a final conclusion, then the total number of board positions that our brute force program would need to evaluate in deciding its first move is

$$\underbrace{40 \times 40 \times 40 \times \ldots \times 40}_{30 \text{ times}} = 40^{30}, \text{ which is roughly } 10^{48}$$

If we use a supercomputer that evaluates 1 quadrillion (10^{15}) board positions per second, it would take about 30,000,000,000,000,000,000,000,000 years for the computer to make its first move! Obviously, a computer could not use a brute force technique to play a real chess game.

There also exist problems that we do not yet know *how* to solve algorithmically. Many of these involve tasks that require a degree of what we term "intelligence." For example, after only a few days a baby recognizes the face of its mother from among the many faces it sees. In a few months, it begins to develop coordinated sensory and motor control skills and can efficiently plan how to use them—how to get from the playpen to the toy on the floor without bumping into either the chair or the desk that is in the way. After a few years, the child begins to develop powerful language skills and abstract reasoning capabilities.

We take these abilities for granted, but the operations just mentioned—sophisticated visual discrimination, high-level problem solving, abstract reasoning, sophisticated natural language understanding—cannot be done well (or even at all) using the computer systems and software packages currently available. The primary reason is that researchers do not yet know how to specify these operations algorithmically. That is, they do not yet know how to specify a solution formally in a detailed step-by-step fashion. As humans, we are able to do them simply by using the "algorithms" in our heads. To appreciate this problem, imagine trying to describe algorithmically exactly what steps you follow when you are painting a picture, composing a love poem, or formulating a business plan.

Thus, algorithmic problem solving has many variations. Sometimes solutions do not exist; sometimes a solution is too inefficient to be of any use; sometimes a solution is not yet known. However, discovering an algorithmic solution has enormously important consequences. As we noted earlier, if we can create a correct and efficient algorithm to solve a problem, and if we encode it into a programming language, then we can take advantage of the speed and power of a computer system to automate the solution and produce the desired result. This is what computer science is all about.

1.3 Algorithms

1.3.1 The Formal Definition of an Algorithm

The formal definition of an algorithm is rather imposing and contains a number of important ideas. Let's take it apart, piece by piece, and analyze each of its separate points.

…a well-ordered collection…

DEFINITION
Algorithm: a well-ordered collection of unambiguous and effectively computable operations that, when executed, produces a result and halts in a finite amount of time.

An algorithm is a collection of operations, and there must be a clear and unambiguous *ordering* to these operations. Ordering means that we know which operation to do first and precisely which operation to do next as each step is successfully completed. After all, we cannot expect a computing agent to carry out our instructions correctly if it is confused about which instruction it should be doing next.

Consider the following "algorithm" that was taken from the back of a shampoo bottle and is intended to be instructions on how to use the product.

Step 1:   Wet hair

Step 2:   Lather

Step 3:   Rinse

Step 4:   Repeat

At Step 4, what operations should be repeated? If we go back to Step 1, we will be unnecessarily wetting our hair. (It is presumably still wet from the previous operations.) If we go back to Step 3 instead, we will not be getting our hair any cleaner because we have not reused the shampoo. The Repeat instruction in Step 4 is ambiguous in that it does not clearly specify what to do next. Therefore, it violates the well-ordered requirement of an algorithm. (It also has a second and even more serious problem—it never stops! We will have more to say about this second problem shortly.) Statements such as

- Go back and do it again. (Do *what* again?)

- Start over. (From *where*?)

- If you understand this material, you may skip ahead. (How *far*?)

- Do either Part 1 or Part 2. (How do I decide *which* one to do?)

are ambiguous and can leave us confused and unsure about what operation to do next. We must be extremely precise in specifying the order in which operations are to be carried out. One possible way is to number the steps of the algorithm and use these numbers to specify the proper order of execution. For example, the ambiguous operations just shown could be made more precise as follows:

- Go back to Step 3 and continue execution from that point.

- Start over from Step 1.

- If you understand this material, skip ahead to Line 21.

- If you are 18 years of age or older, do Part 1 beginning with Step 9; otherwise, do Part 2 beginning with Step 40.

. . . of unambiguous and effectively computable operations . . .

Algorithms are composed of things called "operations," but what do those operations look like? What types of building blocks can be used to construct an algorithm? The answer to these questions is that the operations used in an algorithm must meet two criteria—they must be *unambiguous,* and they must be *effectively computable.*

Here is a possible "algorithm" for making a cherry pie:

STEP 1:   Make the crust

STEP 2:   Make the cherry filling

STEP 3:   Pour the filling into the crust

STEP 4:   Bake at 350°F for 45 minutes

For a professional baker, this algorithm would be fine. He or she would understand how to carry out each of the operations listed. Novice cooks, like most of us, would probably understand the meaning of Steps 3 and 4. However, we would probably look at Steps 1 and 2, throw up our hands in confusion, and ask for clarification. We might then be given more detailed instructions.

STEP 1:   Make the crust
       1.1   Take one and one-third cups flour
       1.2   Sift the flour
       1.3   Mix the sifted flour with one-half cup butter and one-fourth cup water
       1.4   Roll into two 9-inch pie crusts

STEP 2:   Make the cherry filling
       2.1   Open a 16-ounce can of cherry pie filling and pour into bowl
       2.2   Add a dash of cinnamon and nutmeg, and stir

With this additional information, most people—even inexperienced cooks—would understand what to do, and they could successfully carry out this baking algorithm. However, there might be some people, perhaps young children, who still do not fully understand each and every line. For those people, we must go through the simplification process again and describe the ambiguous steps in even more elementary terms.

For example, the computing agent executing the algorithm might not know the meaning of the instruction "Sift the flour" in Step 1.2, and we would have to explain it further.

       1.2   Sift the flour
           1.2.1   Get out the sifter, which is the device shown on page A-9 of your cookbook, and place it directly on top of a 2-quart bowl
           1.2.2   Pour the flour into the top of the sifter and turn the crank in a counterclockwise direction
           1.2.3   Let all the flour fall through the sifter into the bowl

Now, even a child should be able to carry out these operations. But if that were not the case, then we would go through the simplification process yet one more time, until every operation, every sentence, every word was clearly understood.

An unambiguous operation is one that can be understood and carried out directly by the computing agent without further simplification or explanation. When an operation is unambiguous, we call it a *primitive operation,* or simply a **primitive** of the computing agent carrying out the algorithm. An algorithm must be composed entirely of primitives. Naturally, the primitive operations of different individuals (or machines) vary depending on their sophistication, experience, and intelligence, as is the case with the cherry pie recipe, which varies with the baking experience of the person following the instructions. Hence, an algorithm for one computing agent may not be an algorithm for another.

One of the most important questions we will answer in this text is, *What are the primitive operations of a typical modern computer system?* What operations can a hardware processor "understand" in the sense of being able to carry out directly, and what operations must be further refined and simplified?

However, it is not enough for an operation to be understandable. It must also be *doable* by the computing agent. If an algorithm tells me to flap my arms really quickly and fly, I understand perfectly well what it is asking me to do. However, I am incapable of doing it. "Doable" means there exists a computational process that allows the computing agent to complete that operation successfully. The formal term for "doable" is **effectively computable**.

For example, the following is an incorrect technique for finding and printing the 100th prime number. (A prime number is a whole number not evenly divisible by any numbers other than 1 and itself, such as 2, 3, 5, 7, 11, 13,....)

Step 1:   Generate a list L of all the prime numbers: $L_1, L_2, L_3, \ldots$

Step 2:   Sort the list L in ascending order

Step 3:   Print out the 100th element in the list, L_{100}

Step 4:   Stop

The problem with these instructions is in Step 1, "Generate a list L of *all* the prime numbers...." That operation cannot be completed. There are an infinite number of prime numbers, and it is not possible in a finite amount of time to generate the desired list L. No such computational process exists, and the operation described in Step 1 is not effectively computable. Here are some other examples of operations that may not be effectively computable:

Write out the exact decimal value of π. (π cannot be represented exactly.)

Set number to 0.
Set *average* to (*sum* ÷ *number*). (Division by 0 is not permitted.)

Set N to −1.
Set the value of *result* to $\sqrt{N}$. (You cannot take the square root of negative values using real numbers.)

Add 1 to the current value of *x*. (What if *x* currently has no value?)

This last example explains why we had to initialize the value of the variable called *carry* to 0 in Step 1 of Figure 1.2. In Step 4, the algorithm says, "Add the two digits a_i and b_i to the current value of *carry* to get c_i." If *carry* has no current value, then when the computing agent tries to perform the instruction in Step 4, it will not know what to do, and this operation is not effectively computable.

...that produces a result...

Algorithms solve problems. To know whether a solution is correct, an algorithm must produce a result that is observable to a user, such as a numerical answer, a new object, or a change to its environment. Without some observable result, we would not be able to say whether the algorithm is right or wrong. In the case of the DVR algorithm (Figure 1.1), the result will be a disc containing recorded TV programs. The addition algorithm (Figure 1.2) produces an *m*-digit sum.

Note that we use the word *result* rather than *answer*. Sometimes it is not possible for an algorithm to produce the correct answer because for a given set of input, a correct answer does not exist. In those cases, the algorithm may produce something else, such as an error message, a red warning light, or an approximation to the correct answer. Error messages, lights, and approximations, though not necessarily what we wanted, are all observable results.

...and halts in a finite amount of time.

Another important characteristic of algorithms is that the result must be produced after the execution of a finite number of operations, and we must guarantee that the algorithm eventually reaches a statement that says, "Stop, you are done" or something equivalent. We have already pointed out that the shampooing algorithm was not well ordered because we did not know which statements to repeat in Step 4. However, even if we knew which block of statements to repeat, the algorithm would still be incorrect because it makes no provision to terminate. It will essentially run forever, or until we run out of hot water, soap, or patience. This is called an infinite loop, and it is a common error in the design of algorithms.

Figure 1.3 shows an algorithmic solution to the shampooing problem that meets all the criteria discussed in this section if we assume

---

FIGURE 1.3

Step	Operation
1	Wet your hair
2	Set the value of *WashCount* to 0
3	Repeat Steps 4 through 6 until the value of *WashCount* equals 2
4	Lather your hair
5	Rinse your hair
6	Add 1 to the value of *WashCount*
7	Stop, you have finished shampooing your hair

A correct solution to the shampooing problem

FIGURE 1.4

Step	Operation
1	Wet your hair
2	Lather your hair
3	Rinse your hair
4	Lather your hair
5	Rinse your hair
6	Stop, you have finished shampooing your hair

Another correct solution to the shampooing problem

---

that you want to wash your hair twice. The algorithm of Figure 1.3 is well ordered. Each step is numbered, and the execution of the algorithm unfolds sequentially, beginning at Step 1 and proceeding from instruction i to instruction $i + 1$, unless the operation specifies otherwise. (For example, the iterative instruction in Step 3 says that after completing Step 6, you should go back and start again at Step 4 until the value of *WashCount* equals 2.) The intent of each operation is (we assume) clear, unambiguous, and doable by the person washing his or her hair. Finally, the algorithm will halt. This is confirmed by observing that *WashCount* is initially set to 0 in Step 2. Step 6 says to add 1 to *WashCount* each time we lather and rinse our hair, so it will take on the values 0, 1, 2, ... However, the iterative statement in Step 3 says stop lathering and rinsing when the value of *WashCount* reaches 2. At that point, the algorithm goes to Step 7 and terminates execution with the desired result: clean hair. (Although it is correct, do not expect to see this algorithm on the back of a shampoo bottle in the near future.)

As is true for any recipe or set of instructions, there is always more than a single way to write a correct solution. For example, the algorithm of Figure 1.3 could also be written as shown in Figure 1.4. Both of these are correct solutions to the shampooing problem. (Although they are both correct, they are not necessarily equally elegant. This point is addressed in Exercise 9 at the end of the chapter.)

1.3.2 The Importance of Algorithmic Problem Solving

The instruction sequences in Figures 1.1, 1.2, 1.3, and 1.4 are examples of the types of algorithmic solutions designed, analyzed, implemented, and tested by computer scientists, although they are much shorter and simpler. The operations shown in these figures could be encoded into some appropriate language and given to a computing agent (such as a personal computer or a robot) to execute. The device would mechanically follow these instructions and successfully complete the task. This device could do this without having to understand the creative processes that went into the discovery of the solution and without knowing the principles and concepts that underlie the problem. The robot simply follows the steps in the specified order (a required characteristic of algorithms), successfully completing each operation (another required characteristic), and ultimately producing the desired result after a finite amount of time (also required).

Just as the Industrial Revolution of the nineteenth century allowed machines to take over the drudgery of repetitive physical tasks, the "computer revolution" of the twentieth and twenty-first centuries has enabled us to implement algorithms that mechanize and automate the drudgery of repetitive mental tasks, such as adding long columns of numbers, finding names in a telephone book, sorting student records by course number, and retrieving hotel or airline reservations from a file containing millions of pieces of data. This mechanization process offers the prospect of enormous increases in productivity. It also frees people to do those things that humans do much better than computers, such as creating new ideas, setting policy, doing high-level planning, and determining the significance of the results produced by a computer. Certainly, these operations are a much more effective use of that unique computing agent called the human brain.

Practice Problems

Get a copy of the instructions that describe how to do the following:

1. Register for classes at the beginning of the semester.

2. Use the online computer catalog to see what is available in the college library on a given subject.

3. Use the copying machine in your building.

4. Log on to the World Wide Web.

5. Add someone as a friend to your Facebook account.

Look over the instructions and decide whether they meet the definition of an algorithm given in this section. If not, explain why, and rewrite each set of instructions so that it constitutes a valid algorithm. Also state whether each instruction is a sequential, conditional, or iterative operation.

1.4 A Brief History of Computing

Although computer science is not simply a study of computers, there is no doubt that the field was formed and grew in popularity as a direct response to their creation and widespread use. This section takes a brief look at the historical development of computer systems.

The appearance of some technologies, such as the telephone, the light-bulb, and the first heavier-than-air flight, can be traced directly to a single place, a specific individual, and an exact instant in time. Examples include the flight of Orville and Wilbur Wright on December 17, 1903, in Kitty Hawk, North Carolina, and the famous phrase "Mr. Watson, come here, I want to see you." uttered by Alexander Graham Bell over the first telephone on March 12, 1876.

Computers are not like that. They did not appear in a specific room on a given day as the creation of some individual genius. The ideas that led to the design of the first computers evolved over hundreds of years, with con-tributions coming from many people, each building on and extending the work of earlier discoverers.

1.4.1 The Early Period: Up to 1940

If this were a discussion of the history of mathematics and arithmetic instead of computer science, it would begin 3,000 years ago with the early work of the Greeks, Egyptians, Babylonians, Indians, Chinese, and Persians. All these cultures were interested in and made important contributions to the fields of mathematics, logic, and numerical computation. For example, the Greeks developed the fields of geometry and logic; the Babylonians and Egyptians developed numerical methods for generating square roots, multiplication tables, and trigonometric tables used by early sailors; Indian mathemati-cians developed both the base-10 decimal numbering system and the con-cept of zero; and in the ninth century, the Persians developed algorithmic problem solving (as you learned in the Abu Ja'far Muhammad ibn Musa Al-Khowarizmi Special Interest Box earlier in the chapter).

The first half of the seventeenth century saw a number of important developments related to automating and simplifying the drudgery of arith-metic computation. (The motivation for this work appears to be the sudden increase in scientific research during the sixteenth and seventeenth centu-ries in the areas of astronomy, chemistry, and medicine. This work required the solution of larger and more complex mathematical problems.) In 1614, the Scotsman John Napier invented *logarithms* as a way to simplify dif-ficult mathematical computations. The early seventeenth century also wit-nessed the development of a number of new and quite powerful mechanical devices designed to help reduce the burden of arithmetic. The first *slide rule* appeared around 1622. In 1672, the French philosopher and mathemati-cian Blaise Pascal designed and built one of the first *mechanical calculators* (named the *Pascaline*) that could do addition and subtraction. A model of this early calculating device is shown in Figure 1.5.

FIGURE 1.5

The Pascaline, one of the earliest mechanical calculators
Source: Alamy/© Interfoto

The famous German mathematician Gottfried Leibnitz (who, along with Isaac Newton, was one of the inventors of calculus) was also excited by the idea of automatic computation. He studied the work of Pascal and others, and in 1674, he constructed a mechanical calculator called *Leibnitz's Wheel* that could do not only addition and subtraction but multiplication and division as well. Both Pascal's and Leibnitz's machines used interlocking mechanical cogs and gears to store numbers and perform basic arithmetic operations. Considering the state of technology available to Pascal, Leibnitz, and others in the seventeenth century, these first calculating machines were truly mechanical wonders.

These early developments in mathematics and arithmetic were important milestones because they demonstrated how mechanization could simplify and speed up numerical computation. For example, Leibnitz's Wheel enabled seventeenth-century mathematicians to generate tables of mathematical functions many times faster than was possible by hand. (It is hard to believe in our modern high-tech society, but in the seventeenth century the generation of a table of logarithms could represent a *lifetime's* effort of one person!) However, the slide rule and mechanical calculators of Pascal and Leibnitz, though certainly impressive devices, were not computers. Specifically, they lacked two fundamental characteristics:

- They did not have a *memory* where information could be stored in machine-readable form.

- They were not *programmable*. A person could not provide *in advance* a sequence of instructions that could be executed by the device without manual intervention.

Surprisingly, the first actual "computing device" to include both of these features was not created for the purposes of mathematical computations. Rather, it was a loom used for the manufacture of rugs and clothing. It was developed in 1801 by the Frenchman Joseph Jacquard. Jacquard wanted to automate the weaving process, at the time a painfully slow and cumbersome task in which each separate row of the pattern had to be set up by the weaver and an apprentice. Because of this, anything but the most basic style of clothing was beyond the means of most people.

Jacquard designed an automated loom that used *punched cards* to create the desired pattern (Figure 1.6). If there was a hole in the card in a particular location, then a hook could pass through the card, grasp a warp thread, and raise it to allow a second thread to pass underneath. If there was no hole in the card, then the hook could not pass through, and the thread would pass over the warp. Depending on whether the thread passed above or below the warp, a specific design was created. Each punched card described one row of the pattern. Jacquard connected the cards and fed them through his loom, and

FIGURE 1.6

Drawing of the Jacquard loom

Source: © Bettmann/CORBIS

The Original "Technophobia"

The development of the automated Jacquard loom and other technological advances in the weaving industry was so frightening to the craft guilds of the early nineteenth century that in 1811 it led to the formation of a group called the Luddites. The Luddites, named after their leader Ned Ludd of Nottingham, England, were violently opposed to this new manufacturing technology, and they burned down factories that attempted to use it. The movement lasted only a few years and its leaders were all jailed, but their name lives on today as a pejorative term for any group that is frightened and angered by the latest developments in any branch of science and technology, including computers.

it automatically sequenced from card to card, weaving the desired pattern. The rows of connected punched cards can be seen at the top of the device.

Jacquard's loom represented an enormously important stage in the development of computers. Not only was it the first programmable device, but it also showed how the knowledge of a human expert (in this case, a master weaver) could be captured in machine-readable form and used to control a machine that accomplished the same task automatically. Once the program was created, the expert was no longer needed. The lowliest apprentice could load the cards into the loom, turn it on, and produce a finished, high-quality product over and over again.

These pioneers had enormous influence on the designers and inventors who came after them, among them a mathematics professor at Cambridge University named Charles Babbage. Babbage was interested in automatic computation. In 1823, he extended the ideas of Pascal and Leibnitz and constructed a working model of the largest and most sophisticated mechanical calculator of its time. This machine, called the *Difference Engine*, could do addition, subtraction, multiplication, and division to 6 significant digits, and it could solve polynomial equations and other complex mathematical problems as well. Babbage tried to construct a larger model of the Difference Engine that would be capable of working to an accuracy of 20 significant digits, but after 12 years of work he had to give up his quest. The technology available in the 1820s and 1830s was not sufficiently advanced to manufacture cogs and gears to the precise tolerances his design required. Like Galileo's helicopter or Jules Verne's atomic submarine, Babbage's ideas were fundamentally sound but years ahead of their time. (In 1991, the London Museum of Science, using Babbage's original plans, built an actual working model of the Difference Engine. It was 7 feet high, 11 feet wide, weighed 3 tons, and had 4,000 moving parts. It worked exactly as Babbage had planned.)

Babbage did not stop his investigations with the Difference Engine. In the 1830s, he designed a more powerful and general-purpose computational machine that could be configured to solve a much wider range of numerical problems. His machine had four basic components: a *mill* to perform the arithmetic manipulation of data, a *store* to hold the data, an *operator* to process the instructions contained on punched cards, and an *output unit* to put the results onto separate punched cards. Although it would be about 110 years before a "real" computer would be built, Babbage's proposed machine, called the Analytic Engine, is amazingly similar in design to a modern computer. The four components of the Analytic Engine are virtually identical in function to the four major components of today's computer systems:

Babbage's Term	Modern Terminology
mill	arithmetic/logic unit
store	memory
operator	processor
output unit	input/output

Babbage died before a working steam-powered model of his Analytic Engine could be completed, but his ideas lived on to influence others, and many computer scientists consider the Analytic Engine the first "true" computer system, even if it existed only on paper and in Babbage's dreams.

Another person influenced by the work of Pascal, Jacquard, and Babbage was a young statistician at the U.S. Census Bureau named Herman Hollerith. Because of the rapid increase in immigration to America at the end of the nineteenth century, officials estimated that doing the 1890 enumeration manually would take from 10 to 12 years. The 1900 census would begin before the previous one was finished. Something had to be done.

Hollerith designed and built programmable card-processing machines that could automatically read, tally, and sort data entered on punched cards. Census data were coded onto cards using a machine called a *keypunch*. The cards were taken either to a *tabulator* for counting and tallying or to a *sorter* for ordering alphabetically or numerically. Both of these machines were programmable (via wires and plugs) so that the user could specify such things as which card columns should be tallied and in what order the cards should be sorted. In addition, the machines had a small amount of memory to store results. Thus, they had all four components of Babbage's Analytic Engine.

Hollerith's machines were enormously successful, and they were one of the first examples of the use of automated information processing to solve large-scale, real-world problems. Whereas the 1880 census required 8 years to be completed, the 1890 census was finished in about 2 years, even though there was a 30% increase in the U.S. population during that decade.

Although they were not really general-purpose computers, Hollerith's card machines were a very clear and very successful demonstration of the enormous advantages of automated information processing. This fact was not lost on Hollerith, who left the Census Bureau in 1902 to found the Computer Tabulating Recording Company to build and sell these machines.

He planned to market his new product to a country that was just entering the Industrial Revolution and that, like the Census Bureau, would be generating and processing enormous volumes of inventory, production, accounting, and sales data. His punched card machines became the dominant form of data-processing equipment during the first half of the twentieth century, well into the 1950s and 1960s. During this period, virtually every major U.S. corporation had data-processing rooms filled with keypunches, sorters, and tabulators, as well as drawer upon drawer of punched cards. In 1924, Hollerith's tabulating machine company changed its name to IBM, and it eventually evolved into the largest computing company in the world.

Charles Babbage (1791–1871) Ada Augusta Byron, Countess of Lovelace (1815–1852)

Charles Babbage, the son of a banker, was born into a life of wealth and comfort in eighteenth-century England. He attended Cambridge University and displayed an aptitude for mathematics and science. He was also an inventor and "tinkerer" who loved to build all sorts of devices. Among the devices he constructed were unpickable locks, skeleton keys, speedometers, and even the first cow catcher for trains. His first and greatest love, though, was mathematics, and he spent the better part of his life creating machines to do automatic computation. Babbage was enormously impressed by the work of Jacquard in France. (In fact, Babbage had on the wall of his home a woven portrait of Jacquard that was created using 24,000 punched cards.) He spent the last 30 to 40 years of his life trying to build a computing device, the Analytic Engine, based on Jacquard's ideas.

In that quest, he was helped by Countess Ada Augusta Byron, daughter of the famous English poet, Lord Byron. The countess was introduced to Babbage and was enormously impressed by his ideas about the Analytic Engine. As she put it, "We may say most aptly that the Analytic Engine weaves algebraic patterns just as the Jacquard Loom weaves flowers and leaves." Lady Lovelace worked closely with Babbage to specify how to organize instructions for the Analytic Engine to solve a particular mathematical problem. Because of that pioneering work, she is generally regarded as history's first computer programmer.

Babbage died in 1871 without realizing his dream. He also died quite poor because the Analytic Engine ate up virtually all of his personal fortune. His work was generally forgotten until the twentieth century when it became instrumental in moving the world into the computer age.

We have come a long way from the 1640s and the Pascaline, the early adding machine constructed by Pascal. We have seen the development of more powerful mechanical calculators (Leibnitz), automated programmable manufacturing devices (Jacquard), a design for the first computing device (Babbage), and the initial applications of information processing on a massive scale (Hollerith). However, we still have not yet entered the "computer age." That did not happen until about 1940, and it was motivated by an event that, unfortunately, has fueled many of the important technological advances in human history—the outbreak of war.

1.4.2 The Birth of Computers: 1940–1950

World War II created another, quite different set of information-based problems. Instead of inventory, sales, and payroll, the concerns became ballistics tables, troop deployment data, and secret codes. A number of research projects were started, funded largely by the military, to build automatic computing machines to perform these tasks and assist the Allies in the war effort.

Beginning in 1931, the U.S. Navy and IBM jointly funded a project at Harvard University under Professor Howard Aiken to build a computing device called Mark I. This was a general-purpose, electromechanical programmable computer that used a mix of relays, magnets, and gears to process and store data. The Mark I was the first computing device to use the base-2 binary numbering system, which we will discuss in Chapter 4. It used vacuum tubes and electric current to represent the two binary values, off for 0, on for 1. Until then, computing machines had used decimal representation, typically using a 10-toothed gear, each tooth representing a digit from 0 to 9. The Mark I was completed in 1944, about 110 years after Babbage's dream of the Analytic Engine, and is generally considered one of the first working general-purpose computers. The Mark I had a memory capacity of 72 numbers, and it could be programmed to perform a 23-digit multiplication in the lightning-like time of 4 seconds. Although laughably slow by modern standards, the Mark I was operational for almost 15 years, and it carried out a good deal of important and useful mathematical work for the U.S. Navy during the war.

At about the same time, a much more powerful machine was taking shape at the University of Pennsylvania in conjunction with the U.S. Army. During the early days of World War II, the Army was producing many new artillery pieces, but it found that it could not produce the firing tables equally as fast. These tables told the gunner how to aim the gun on the basis of such input as distance to the target and current temperature, wind, and elevation. Because of the enormous number of variables and the complexity of the computations (which use both trigonometry and calculus), these firing tables were taking more time to construct than the gun itself—a skilled person with a desk calculator required about 20 hours to analyze a single 60-second trajectory.

To help solve this problem, in 1943 the Army initiated a research project with J. Presper Eckert and John Mauchly of the University of Pennsylvania to build a completely electronic computing device. The machine, dubbed the ENIAC (Electronic Numerical Integrator and Calculator), was completed

FIGURE 1.7

Photograph of the ENIAC computer

Source: From the Collections of the University of Pennsylvania Archives (U.S. Army photo)

in 1946 (too late to assist in the war effort) and was the first fully electronic general-purpose programmable computer. This pioneering machine is shown in Figure 1.7.

ENIAC contained 18,000 vacuum tubes and nearly filled a building; it was 100 feet long, 10 feet high, and weighed 30 tons. Because it was fully electronic, it did not contain any of the slow mechanical components found in Mark I, and it executed instructions much more rapidly. The ENIAC could add two 10-digit numbers in about 1/5,000 of a second and could multiply two numbers in 1/300 of a second, a thousand times faster than the Mark I.

The Mark I and ENIAC are two well-known examples of early computers, but they are by no means the only ones of that era. For example, the ABC system (Atanasoff-Berry Computer), designed and built by Professor John Atanasoff and his graduate student Clifford Berry at Iowa State University, was actually the first electronic computer, constructed during the period 1939–1942. However, it never received equal recognition because it was useful for only one task, solving systems of simultaneous linear equations. In England, a computer called Colossus was built in 1943 under the direction of Alan Turing, a famous mathematician and computer scientist whom we will meet again in Chapter 12. This machine, one of the first computers built outside the United States, was used to crack the famous German Enigma code that the Nazis believed to be unbreakable. Colossus has also not received as much recognition as ENIAC because of the secrecy that shrouded the Enigma project. Its very existence was not widely known until many years after the end of the war.

At about the same time that Colossus was taking form in England, a German engineer named Konrad Zuse was working on a computing device for the German army. The machine, code named Z1, was similar in design to the ENIAC—a programmable, general-purpose, fully electronic computing device. Fortunately for the Allied forces, the Z1 project was not completed before the end of World War II.

Although the machines just described—ABC, Mark I, ENIAC, Colossus, and Z1—were computers in the fullest sense of the word (they had memory and were programmable), they did not yet look like modern computer systems. One more step was necessary, and that step was taken in 1946 by the individual who was most instrumental in creating the computer as we know it today, John Von Neumann.

Von Neumann was not only one of the most brilliant mathematicians who ever lived, he was also a genius in many other areas as well, including experimental physics, chemistry, economics, and computer science. Von Neumann, who taught at Princeton University, had worked with Eckert and Mauchly on the ENIAC project at the University of Pennsylvania. Even though that project was successful, he recognized a number of fundamental shortcomings in ENIAC. In 1946, he proposed a radically different computer design based on a model called the stored program computer. Until then, all computers were programmed *externally* using wires, connectors, and plugboards. The memory unit stored only data, not instructions. For each different problem, users had to rewire virtually the entire computer. For example, the plugboards on the ENIAC contained 6,000 separate switches, and reprogramming the ENIAC involved specifying the new settings for all these switches—not a trivial task.

Von Neumann proposed that the instructions that control the operation of the computer be encoded as binary values and stored internally in the memory unit along with the data. To solve a new problem, instead of rewiring the machine, you would rewrite the sequence of instructions—that is, create a new program. Von Neumann invented programming as it is known today.

The model of computing proposed by Von Neumann included many other important features found on all modern computing systems, and to honor him this model of computation has come to be known as the Von Neumann architecture. We will study this architecture in great detail in Chapters 4 and 5.

Von Neumann's research group at the University of Pennsylvania implemented his ideas, and they built one of the first stored program computers, called EDVAC, in 1951. At about the same time, a stored program computer called EDSAC was built at Cambridge University in England under the direction of Professor Maurice Wilkes. The appearance of these machines and others like them ushered in the modern computer age. Even though they were much slower, bulkier, and less powerful than our current machines, EDVAC and EDSAC executed programs in a fashion surprisingly similar to the miniaturized and immensely more powerful computers of the twenty-first

John Von Neumann
(1903–1957)

John Von Neumann was born in Budapest, Hungary. He was a child prodigy who could divide 8-digit numbers in his head by the age of 6. He was a genius in virtually every field that he studied, including physics, economics, engineering, and mathematics. At 18 he received an award as the best mathematician in Hungary, a country known for excellence in the field, and he received his Ph.D., summa cum laude, at 21. He came to the United States in 1930 as a guest lecturer at Princeton University and taught there for 3 years. Then, in 1933 he became one of the founding members (along with Albert Einstein) of the Institute for Advanced Studies, where he worked for 20 years.

Source: Los Alamos National Laboratory

He was one of the most brilliant minds of the twentieth century, a true genius in every sense, both good and bad. He could do prodigious mental feats in his head, and his thought processes usually raced way ahead of "ordinary" mortals who found him quite difficult to work with. One of his colleagues described him as possessing the most fearsome technical intellect of the century. Another joked that "Johnny wasn't really human, but after living among them for so long, he learned to do a remarkably good imitation of one."

Von Neumann was a brilliant theoretician who did pioneering work in pure mathematics, operations research, game theory, and theoretical physics. He was also an engineer, concerned about practicalities and real-world problems, and it was this interest in applied issues that led Von Neumann to design and construct the first stored program computer. One of the early computers built by the RAND Corp. in 1953 was affectionately called "Johnniac" in his honor, although Von Neumann detested that name. Like the UNIVAC I, it has a place of honor at the Smithsonian Institution.

century. A commercial model of the EDVAC, called UNIVAC I—the first computer actually sold—was built by Eckert and Mauchly and delivered to the U.S. Bureau of the Census on March 31, 1951. (It ran for 12 years before it was retired, shut off for the last time, and moved to the Smithsonian Institution.) This date marks the true beginning of the "computer age."

The importance of Von Neumann's contributions to computer systems development cannot be overstated. Although his original proposals are at least 65 years old, virtually every computer built today is a Von Neumann machine in its basic design. A lot has changed in computing, and the sleek iPad and the slow and bulky EDVAC would appear to have little in common. However, the basic principles on which these two very disparate machines are constructed are virtually identical, and the same theoretical model underlies their operation. There is an old saying in computer science that "There is nothing new since Von Neumann!" This saying is certainly not true (much *has* happened), but it demonstrates the importance and amazing staying power of Von Neumann's original design.

1.4.3 The Modern Era: 1950 to the Present

The last 60 or so years of computer development have involved taking the Von Neumann architecture and improving it in terms of hardware and software.

And the Verdict Is...

Our discussion of what was happening in computing from 1939 to 1946 showed that many groups were involved in designing and building the first computers. Therefore, it would seem that no single individual can be credited with the title Inventor of the Electronic Digital Computer.

Surprisingly, that is not true. In February 1964, the Sperry Rand Corp. (now UNISYS) was granted a U.S. patent on the ENIAC computer as the first fully electronic computing device, J. Presper Eckert and John Mauchly being its designers and builders. However, in 1967 a suit was filed in U.S. District Court in Minneapolis, Minnesota, to overturn that patent. The suit, *Honeywell v. Sperry Rand*, was heard before U.S. Federal Judge Earl Larson, and on October 19, 1973, his verdict was handed down. (This enormously important verdict was never given the media coverage it deserved because it happened in the middle of the Watergate hearings and on the very day that Vice President Spiro Agnew resigned in disgrace for tax fraud.) Judge Larson overturned the ENIAC patent on the basis that Eckert and Mauchly had been significantly influenced in their 1943–1944 work on ENIAC by earlier research and development work by John Atanasoff at Iowa State University. During the period 1939–1943, Mauchly had communicated extensively with Atanasoff and had even traveled to Iowa to see the ABC machine in person. In a sense, the verdict declared that Atanasoff is really the inventor of the first computer. This decision was never appealed. Therefore, the official honor of having designed and built the first electronic computer, at least in U.S. District Court, goes to Professor John Vincent Atanasoff.

On November 13, 1990, in a formal ceremony at the White House, Professor Atanasoff was awarded the National Medal of Technology by President George H. W. Bush for his pioneering contributions to the development of the computer.

Since 1950, computer systems development has been primarily an *evolutionary* process, not a revolutionary one. The enormous number of changes in computers in recent decades has made them faster, smaller, cheaper, more reliable, and easier to use, but has not drastically altered their basic underlying structure.

The period 1950–1957 (these dates are rough approximations) is often called the *first generation* of computing. This era saw the appearance of UNIVAC I, the first computer built for sale, and the IBM 701, the first computer built by the company that would soon become a leader in this new field. These early systems were similar in design to EDVAC, and they were bulky, expensive, slow, and unreliable. They used vacuum tubes for processing and storage, and they were extremely difficult to maintain. The simple act of turning the machine on could blow out a dozen tubes! For this reason, first-generation machines were used only by trained personnel and only in specialized locations such as large corporations, government and university research labs, and military installations, which could provide this expensive support environment.

The *second generation* of computing, roughly 1957–1965, heralded a major change in the size and complexity of computers. In the late 1950s, the bulky vacuum tube was replaced by a single transistor only a few millimeters in size, and memory was now constructed using tiny magnetic cores only 1/50 of an inch in diameter. (We will introduce and describe both of these devices in Chapter 4.) These technologies not only dramatically reduced the size of computers but also increased their reliability and reduced costs. Suddenly, buying and using a computer became a real possibility for some small- and medium-sized businesses, colleges, and government agencies. This was also the era of the appearance of FORTRAN and COBOL, the first high-level (English-like) programming languages. (We will study this type of programming language in Chapters 9 and 10.) Now it was no longer necessary to be an electrical engineer to solve a problem on a computer. One simply needed to learn how to write commands in a high-level language. The occupation called *programmer* was born.

This miniaturization process continued into the *third generation* of computing, which lasted from about 1965 to 1975. This was the era of the *integrated circuit*. Rather than using discrete electronic components, integrated circuits with transistors, resistors, and capacitors were photographically etched onto a piece of silicon, which further reduced the size and cost of computers. From building-sized to room-sized, computers now became desk-sized, and this period saw the birth of the first minicomputer—the PDP-1 manufactured by the Digital Equipment Corp. It also saw the birth of the *software industry*, as companies sprang up to provide programs such as accounting packages and statistical programs to the ever-increasing numbers of computer users. By the mid-1970s, computers were no longer a rarity. They were being widely used throughout industry, government, the military, and education.

The *fourth generation*, 1975–1985, saw the appearance of the first microcomputer. Integrated circuit technology had advanced to the point that a complete computer system could be contained on a single circuit board that you could hold in your hand. The desk-sized machine of the early 1970s now became a desktop machine, shrinking to the size of a typewriter. The Altair 8800, the world's first microcomputer, appeared in January 1975 (see the Special Interest Box on the next page).

The World's First Microcomputer

The Altair 8800, shown below, was the first microcomputer and made its debut on the cover of *Popular Electronics* in January 1975. Its developer, Ed Roberts, owned a tiny electronics store in Albuquerque, New Mexico. His company was in desperate financial shape when he read about a new microprocessor from Intel, the Intel 8080. Roberts reasoned that this new chip could be used to sell a complete personal computer in kit form. He bought these new chips from Intel at the bargain basement price of $75 each and packaged them in a kit called the Altair 8800 (named after a location in the TV series Star Trek), which he offered to hobbyists for $397. Roberts figured he might sell a few hundred kits a year, enough to keep his company afloat temporarily. He ended up selling hundreds of them a day! The Altair microcomputer kits were so popular that he could not keep them in stock, and legend has it that people even drove to New Mexico and camped out in the parking lot to buy their computers.

This is particularly amazing in view of the fact that the original Altair was difficult to assemble and had only 256 memory cells, no I/O devices, and no software support. To program it, the user had to enter binary machine language instructions directly from the console switches. But even though it could do very little, people loved it because it was a real computer, and it was theirs.

The Intel 8080 chip did have the capability of running programs written in the language called BASIC that had been developed at Dartmouth in the early 1960s. A small software company located in Washington State wrote Ed Roberts a letter telling him that it had a BASIC compiler that could run on his Altair, making it much easier to use. That company was called Microsoft—and the rest, as they say, is history.

Source: University of Hawai'i at Hilo Graphics Services

It soon became unusual *not* to see a computer on someone's desk. The software industry poured forth all types of new packages—spreadsheets, databases, word processors, and drawing programs—to meet the needs of the burgeoning user population. This era saw the appearance of the first *computer networks*, as users realized that much of the power of computers lies in their facilitation of communication with other users. (We will look at networking in great detail in Chapter 7.) *Electronic mail* became an important application. Because so many users were computer novices, the concept of *user-friendly systems* emerged. This included new *graphical user interfaces* with pull-down menus, icons, and other visual aids to make computing easier and more fun. *Embedded systems*—devices that contain a computer to control their internal operation—first appeared during this generation. Computers were becoming small enough to be placed inside cars, thermostats, microwave ovens, and wristwatches.

The *fifth generation*, 1985–?, is where we are today. However, so much is changing so fast that most computer scientists believe that the concept of distinct generations has outlived its usefulness. In computer science, change is now a constant companion. Some of the recent developments in computer systems include the following:

- Massively parallel processors capable of quadrillions (10^{15}) of computations per second

- Smartphones, tablets, and other types of handheld digital devices

- High-resolution graphics for imaging, animation, movie making, video games, and virtual reality

- Powerful multimedia user interfaces incorporating sound, voice recognition, touch, photography, video, and television

- Integrated digital devices incorporating data, television, telephone, camera, fax, the Internet, and the World Wide Web

- Wireless communications

- Massive storage devices capable of holding 100 petabytes (10^{17}) of data

- Ubiquitous computing, in which miniature computers are embedded into our cars, cameras, kitchen appliances, home heating systems, clothing, and even our bodies

In only a few decades, computers have progressed from the UNIVAC I, which cost millions of dollars, had a few thousand memory locations, and was capable of only a few thousand operations per second, to today's top-of-the-line graphics workstation with a high-resolution flat panel monitor, trillions of memory cells, massive amounts of external storage, and enough processing power to execute tens of billions of instructions per second, all for about $1,000. Changes of this magnitude have never occurred so quickly in any other technology. If the same rate of change had occurred in the auto industry, beginning with the 1909 Model-T, today's cars would be capable

Good Evening, This Is Walter Cronkite

In the earliest days of computing (1951–1952), few people knew what a computer was, and even fewer had seen or worked with one. Computers were the tool of a very small group of highly trained technical specialists in such fields as mathematics, physics, and engineering. In those days, the general public's knowledge of computer science was limited to the robots and alien computers of science fiction movies.

This all changed in November 1952, when millions of Americans turned on their television sets (also a relatively new technology) to watch returns from the 1952 presidential election between Dwight D. Eisenhower and Adlai Stevenson. In addition to seeing Walter Cronkite and TV reporters and analysts, viewers were treated to an unexpected member of the news staff—a UNIVAC I. CBS executives had rented a computer and installed it in the very center of their set, where it sat, lights blinking and tape drives spinning. They planned to use UNIVAC to produce election predictions quickly and scoop rival stations that did their analyses by hand. Ironically, UNIVAC correctly predicted early that evening, on the basis of well-known statistical sampling techniques, that Eisenhower would win the election, but nervous CBS executives were so skeptical about this new technology that they did not go on the air with the computer's prediction until it had been confirmed by old-fashioned manual methods.

It was the first time that millions of TV viewers had actually seen this thing called an electronic digital computer. The CBS staff, who were also quite inexperienced in computer technology, treated the computer as though it were human. They would turn toward the computer console and utter phrases like "UNIVAC, can you tell me who is currently ahead in Ohio?" or "UNIVAC, do you have any prediction on the final electoral vote total?" In actuality, the statistical algorithms had been programmed in, days earlier, by the Remington Rand staff, but it looked great on TV! This first public appearance of a computer was so well received that computers were used many more times in the early days of TV, primarily on quiz shows, where they reinforced the public's image of the computer as a "giant electronic brain."

of traveling at a speed of 20,000 miles per hour, would get about a million miles per gallon, and would cost about $1.00!

Figure 1.8 summarizes the major developments that occurred during each of the five generations of computer development discussed in this section. And underlying all of these amazing improvements, the theoretical model describing the design and construction of computers has not changed significantly in the last 65 years.

However, many people feel that significant and important structural changes are on the way. At the end of Chapter 5, we will introduce models of computing that are fundamentally quite different from the Von Neumann architecture in use today. These totally new approaches (e.g., quantum computing) may be the models used in the twenty-second century and beyond.

FIGURE 1.8

Generation	Approximate Dates	Major Advances
First	1950–1957	First commercial computers
		First symbolic programming languages
		Use of binary arithmetic, vacuum tubes for storage
		Punched card input/output
Second	1957–1965	Transistors and core memories
		First disks for mass storage
		Size reduction, increased reliability, lower costs
		First high-level programming languages
		First operating systems
Third	1965–1975	Integrated circuits
		Further reduction in size and cost, increased reliability
		First minicomputers
		Time-shared operating systems
		Appearance of the software industry
		First set of computing standards for compatibility between systems
Fourth	1975–1985	Large-scale and very-large-scale integrated circuits
		Further reduction in size and cost, increased reliability
		First microcomputers
		Growth of new types of software and of the software industry
		Computer networks
		Graphical user interfaces
Fifth	1985–?	Ultra-large-scale integrated circuits
		Supercomputers and parallel processors
		Laptops, tablets, smartphones, and handheld digital devices
		Wireless computing
		Massive external data storage devices
		Ubiquitous computing
		High-resolution graphics, visualization, virtual reality
		Worldwide networks and cloud computing
		Multimedia user interfaces
		Widespread use of digitized sound, images, and movies

Some of the major advancements in computing

1.5 Organization of the Text

This book is divided into six separate sections, called levels, each of which addresses one aspect of the definition of computer science that appears at the beginning of this chapter. Let's repeat the definition and see how it maps into the sequence of topics to be presented.

Computer science is the study of algorithms, including

1. *Their formal and mathematical properties* Level 1 of the text (Chapters 2 and 3) is titled "The Algorithmic Foundations of Computer Science." It continues the discussion of algorithmic problem solving begun in Sections 1.2 and 1.3 by introducing important mathematical and logical properties of algorithms. Chapter 2 presents the development of a number of algorithms that solve important technical problems—certainly more "technical" than shampooing your hair. It also looks at concepts related to the problem-solving process, such as how we discover and create good algorithms, what notation we can use to express our solutions, and how we can check to see whether our proposed algorithm correctly solves the desired problem.

   Our brute force chess example illustrates that it is not enough simply to develop a correct algorithm; we also want a solution that is efficient and that produces the desired result in a reasonable amount of time. (Would you want to market a chess-playing program that takes 10^{25} years to make its first move?) Chapter 3 describes ways to compare the efficiency of different algorithms and select the best one to solve a given problem. The material in Level 1 provides the necessary foundation for a study of the discipline of computer science.

2. *Their hardware realizations* Although our initial look at computer science investigated how an algorithm behaved when executed by some abstract "computing agent," we ultimately want to execute our algorithms on "real" machines to get "real" answers. Level 2 of the text (Chapters 4 and 5) is titled "The Hardware World," and it looks at how to design and construct computer systems. It approaches this topic from two quite different viewpoints.

   Chapter 4 presents a detailed discussion of the underlying hardware. It introduces the basic building blocks of computers—binary numbers, transistors, logic gates, and circuits—and shows how these elementary electronic devices can be used to construct components to perform arithmetic and logic functions such as addition, subtraction, comparison, and sequencing. Although it is both interesting and important, this perspective produces a rather low-level view of a computer system. It is difficult to understand how a computer works by studying only these elementary components, just as it would be difficult to understand human behavior by investigating the behavior of individual cells. Therefore, Chapter 5 takes a higher-level view of computer hardware. It looks at computers not as a bunch of wires and circuits but as an integrated collection of subsystems called memory, processor, storage, input/output, and communications. It will explain in great detail the principles of the Von Neumann architecture introduced in Section 1.4.

A study of computer systems can be done at an even higher level. To understand how a computer works, we do not need to examine the functioning of every one of the thousands of components inside a machine. Instead, we need only be aware of a few critical pieces that are essential to our work. From the user's perspective, everything else is superfluous. This "user-oriented" view of a computer system and its resources is called a virtual machine or a virtual environment. A virtual machine is composed only of the resources that the user perceives rather than of all the hardware resources that actually exist.

This viewpoint is analogous to our level of understanding of what happens under the hood of our car. There may be thousands of mechanical components inside an automobile engine, but most of us concern ourselves only with the items reported on the dashboard—for example, oil pressure, fuel level, engine temperature. This is our "virtual engine," and that is all we need or want to know. We are all too happy to leave the remaining details about engine design to our friendly neighborhood mechanic.

Level 3 (Chapters 6, 7, and 8), titled "The Virtual Machine," describes how a virtual environment is created using a component called *system software*. Chapter 6 takes a look at the most important and widely used piece of system software on a modern computer system, the *operating system*, which controls the overall operation of a computer and makes it easier for users to access. Chapter 7 then goes on to describe how this virtual environment can extend beyond the boundaries of a single system as it examines how to interconnect individual machines into *computer networks* and *distributed systems* that provide users with access to a huge collection of computer systems and information as well as an enormous number of other users. It is the system software, and the virtual machine it creates, that makes computer hardware manageable and usable. Finally, Chapter 8 discusses a critically important component of a virtual machine—the *security system* that validates who you are and ensures that you are not attempting to carry out an improper, illegal, or unsafe operation. As computers become central to the management of such sensitive data as medical records, military information, and financial data, this aspect of system software is taking on even greater importance.

3. *Their linguistic realizations* After studying hardware design, computer organization, and virtual machines, you will have a good idea of the techniques used to design and build computers. In the next section of the text, we ask the question, How can this hardware be used to solve important and interesting problems? Level 4, titled "The Software World" (Chapters 9–12), takes a look at what is involved in designing and implementing computer software. It investigates the programs and instruction sequences executed by the hardware, rather than the hardware itself.

Chapter 9 compares several high-level programming languages and introduces fundamental concepts related to the topic of computer programming regardless of the particular language being studied. This single chapter is certainly not intended to make you a proficient programmer, and this book is not meant to be a programming text. Instead, its purpose is to illustrate some basic features of modern programming languages and give you an appreciation for the interesting and challenging task of the computer programmer. Rather than print a separate version of this text for each programming language, the textual material specific to each language can be found on the Web site for this text, and you can download the pages for the language specified by your instructor and used in your class. See the Preface of this text for instructions on accessing these Web pages.

There are many programming languages such as C++, Python, Java, and Perl that can be used to encode algorithms. Chapter 10 provides an overview of a number of different languages and language models in current use, including the functional and parallel models. Chapter 11 describes how a program written in a high-level programming language can be translated into the low-level machine language codes first described in Chapter 5. Finally, Chapter 12 shows that, even when we marshal all the powerful hardware and software ideas described in the first 11 chapters, problems exist that cannot be solved algorithmically. Chapter 12 demonstrates that there are, indeed, limits to computing.

4. *Their applications* Most people are concerned not with creating programs but with using programs, just as there are few automotive engineers but many, many drivers. Level 5, titled "Applications" (Chapters 13–16), moves on from *how* to write a program to *what* these programs can do.

Chapters 13 through 16 explore just a few of the many important and rapidly growing applications of computers, such as simulation, visualization, e-commerce, databases, artificial intelligence, computer graphics, and entertainment. This section cannot possibly survey all the ways in which computers are being used today or will be used in the future. Indeed, there is hardly an area in our modern, complex society that is not affected in some important way by information technology. Readers interested in applications not discussed should seek readings specific to their own areas of interest.

Some computer science professionals are not concerned with building computers, creating programs, or using any of the applications just described. Instead, they are interested in the social and cultural impact—both positive and negative—of this ever-changing technology. The sixth level of this text addresses this important perspective on computer science. This is not part of the original definition of computer science but has become an important area of study. In Level 6, titled "Social Issues" (Chapter 17), we move to the highest level of abstraction—the view furthest removed from the computer itself—to discuss social, ethical, legal, and professional issues related to computer and information technology. These issues are critically important because even individuals not directly involved in developing or using computers are deeply affected by them, just as society has been drastically and permanently altered by such technological developments as the telephone, television, automobile, and nuclear power. This last chapter takes a look at such thorny and difficult topics as computer crime, information privacy, and intellectual property. It also looks at one of the most important phenomena supported by this new technology, the creation of social networks such as Facebook and Twitter. Because it's impossible to resolve all the complex questions that arise in these areas, our intent is simply to raise your awareness and provide some decision-making tools to help you reach your own conclusions.

The overall six-layer hierarchy of this text is summarized in Figure 1.9. The organizational structure diagrammed in Figure 1.9 is one of

FIGURE 1.9

Organization of the text into a six-layer hierarchy

the most important aspects of this text. To describe a field of study, it is not enough to present a mass of facts and explanations. For learners to absorb, understand, and integrate this information, there must be a theme, a relationship, a thread that ties together the various parts of the narrative—in essence, a "big picture." Our big picture is Figure 1.9.

We first lay out the basic foundations of computer science (Level 1). We then proceed upward through five distinct layers of abstraction, from extremely low-level machine details such as electronic circuits and computer hardware (Level 2), through intermediate levels that address virtual machines (Level 3), programming languages and software development (Level 4), to higher levels that investigate computer applications (Level 5), and address the use and misuse of information technology (Level 6). The material in each level provides a foundation to reveal the beauty and complexity of a higher and more abstract view of the discipline of computer science.

Laboratory Experience 1

Associated with this text is a laboratory manual that includes software packages and a collection of formal laboratory exercises. These Laboratory Experiences are designed to give you a chance to build on, modify, and experiment with the ideas discussed in the text. You are strongly encouraged to carry out these laboratories to gain a deeper understanding of the concepts presented in the chapters. Learning computer science involves not just reading and listening but also doing and trying. Our laboratory exercises will give you that chance. (In addition, we hope that you will find them fun.)

Laboratory Experience 1, titled "Building A Glossary," introduces the fundamental operations that you will need in all future labs—operations such as using menus, buttons, and windows. In addition, the lab provides a useful tool that you may use during your study of computer science and in other courses as well. You will learn how to build a *glossary* of important technical terms along with their definitions and locations in the text.

Please open Laboratory Experience 1 and try it now.

EXERCISES

1. Identify some algorithms, apart from DVR instructions and cooking recipes, that you encounter in your everyday life. Write them out in any convenient notation, and explain how they meet all of the criteria for algorithms presented in this chapter.

2. A concept related to, but not identical to, an algorithm is the idea of a *heuristic*. Read about heuristics (Wikipedia is a good place to start) and identify differences between the two. Describe a heuristic for obtaining an approximate answer to the sum of two 3-digit numbers and show how this "addition heuristic" differs from the addition algorithm of Figure 1.2.

3. In the DVR instructions in Figure 1.1, Step 4 says, "Enter the channel number that you want to record and press the button labeled CHAN." Is that an unambiguous and well-defined operation? Explain why or why not.

4. Identify which type of algorithmic operation each one of the following steps belongs to:

   a. Get a value for x from the user.

   b. Test to determine if x is positive. If not, tell the user that he or she has made a mistake.

   c. Take the cube root of x.

   d. Do Steps 1.1, 1.2, and 1.3 x times.

5. Trace through the decimal addition algorithm of Figure 1.2 using the following input values:

   $$m = 3 \quad a_2 = 1 \quad a_1 = 4 \quad a_0 = 9$$
   $$b_2 = 0 \quad b_1 = 2 \quad b_0 = 9$$

   At each step, show the values for c_3, c_2, c_1, c_0, and *carry*.

6. Modify the decimal addition algorithm of Figure 1.2 so that it does not print out nonsignificant leading zeroes; that is, the answer to Exercise 5 would appear as 178 rather than 0178.

7. Modify the decimal addition algorithm of Figure 1.2 so that the two numbers being added do not have to have the same number of digits. That is, the algorithm should be able to add a value a containing m digits to a value b containing n digits, where m may or may not be equal to n.

8. Under what conditions would the well-known quadratic formula

   $$Roots = \frac{-b \pm \sqrt{b^2 - 4ac}}{2a}$$

   not be effectively computable? (Assume that you are working with real numbers.)

9. Compare the two solutions to the shampooing algorithm shown in Figures 1.3 and 1.4. Which do you think is a better general-purpose solution? Why? (*Hint:* What if you wanted to wash your hair 1,000 times?)

10. The following is Euclid's 2,300-year-old algorithm for finding the greatest common divisor of two positive integers I and J.

Step	Operation
1	Get two positive integers as input; call the larger value I and the smaller value J
2	Divide I by J, and call the remainder R
3	If R is *not* 0, then reset I to the value of J, reset J to the value of R, and go back to Step 2
4	Print out the answer, which is the value of J
5	Stop

   a. Go through this algorithm using the input values 20 and 32. After each step of the algorithm is completed, give the values of I, J, and R. Determine the final output of the algorithm.

   b. Does the algorithm work correctly when the two inputs are 0 and 32? Describe exactly what happens, and modify the algorithm so that it gives an appropriate error message.

11. A salesperson wants to visit 25 cities while minimizing the total number of miles she has to drive. Because she has studied computer science, she decides to design an algorithm to determine the optimal order in

which to visit the cities to (1) keep her driving distance to a minimum, and (2) visit each city exactly once. The algorithm that she has devised is the following:

> The computer first lists *all* possible ways to visit the 25 cities and then, for each one, determines the total mileage associated with that particular ordering. (Assume that the computer has access to data that gives the distances between all cities.) After determining the total mileage for each possible trip, the computer searches for the ordering with the minimum mileage and prints out the list of cities on that optimal route, that is, the order in which the sales-person should visit her destinations.

If a computer could analyze 10,000,000 separate paths per second, how long would it take to determine the optimal route for visiting these 25 cities? On the basis of your answer, do you think this is a feasible algorithm? If it is not, can you think of a way to obtain a reasonable solution to this problem?

12. One way to do multiplication is by repeated addition. For example, 47 × 25 can be evaluated as 47 + 47 + 47 + ... + 47 (25 times). Sketch out an algorithm for multiplying two positive numbers a and b using this technique.

13. A student was asked to develop an algorithm to find and output the largest of three numerical values x, y, and z that are provided as input. Here is what was produced:

Input: x, y, z

Algorithm: Check if $(x > y)$ and $(x > z)$. If it is, then output the value of x and stop. Otherwise, continue to the next line.

Check if $(y > x)$ and $(y > z)$. If it is, then output the value of y and stop. Otherwise, continue to the next line.

Check if $(z > x)$ and $(z > y)$. If it is, then output the value of z and stop.

Is this a correct solution to the problem? Explain why or why not. If it is incorrect, fix the algorithm so that it is a correct solution.

14. Read about one of the early pioneers mentioned in this chapter—Pascal, Liebnitz, Jacquard, Babbage, Lovelace, Hollerith, Eckert, Mauchly, Aiken, Zuse, Atanasoff, Turing, or Von Neumann. Write a paper describing in detail that person's contribution to computing and computer science.

15. Get the technical specifications of the computer on which you are working (either from a technical manual or from your computer center staff). Determine its cost, its processing speed (in MIPS, millions of instructions per second), its computational speed (in GFlops, billions of floating point operations per second), and the size of its primary memory.

Compare those values with what was typically available on first-, second-, and third-generation computer systems, and calculate the percentage improvement between your computer and the first commercial machines of the early 1950s.

16. A new and growing area of computer science is *ubiquitous computing*, in which a number of computers automatically provide services for a user without that user's knowledge or awareness. For example, a computer located in your car contacts the garage door opener and tells it to open the garage door when the car is close to home. Read about this new model of computing and write a paper describing some of its applications. What are some of the possible problems that could be created?

17. Another important new area of computer science is *cloud computing*, which relies on a computer network, along with networking software, to provide transparent access to remote data and applications. Read about this new model of data and software access and write a paper describing some of the important uses, as well as potential risks, of this new information structure.

18. A standard computer DVD holds approximately 5 billion characters. Estimate how many linear feet of shelf space would be required to house 5 billion characters encoded as printed bound books rather than as electronic media. Assume there are 5 characters per word, 300 words per page, and 300 pages/inch of shelf.

CHALLENGE WORK

1. Assume we have a "computing agent" that knows how to do one-digit subtraction where the first digit is at least as large as the second (i.e., we do not end up with a negative number). Thus, our computing agent can do such operations as $7 - 3 = 4$, $9 - 1 = 8$, and $5 - 5 = 0$. It can also subtract a one-digit value from a two-digit value in the range 10–18 as long as the final result has only a single digit. This capability enables it to do such operations as $13 - 7 = 6$, $10 - 2 = 8$, and $18 - 9 = 9$.

   Using these primitive capabilities, design an algorithm to do *decimal subtraction* on two m-digit numbers, where $m \geq 1$. You will be given two unsigned whole numbers $a_{m-1} a_{m-2} \ldots a_0$ and $b_{m-1} b_{m-2} \ldots b_0$. Your algorithm must compute the value $c_{m-1} c_{m-2} \ldots c_0$, the difference of these two values.

$$\begin{array}{r} a_{m-1}a_{m-2} \cdots a_0 \\ - b_{m-1}b_{m-2} \cdots b_0 \\ \hline c_{m-1}c_{m-2} \cdots c_0 \end{array}$$

   You may assume that the top number ($a_{m-1} a_{m-2} \ldots a_0$) is greater than or equal to the bottom number ($b_{m-1} b_{m-2} \ldots b_0$) so that the result is not a negative value. However, do not assume that each individual digit a_i is greater than or equal to b_i. If the digit on the bottom is larger than the digit on the top, then you must implement a *borrowing scheme* to allow the subtraction to continue. (*Caution:* It may have been easy to learn subtraction as a first grader, but it is devilishly difficult to tell a computer how to do it!)

2. Our definition of the field of computer science is only one of many that have been proposed. Because it is so young, people working in the field are still debating how best to define exactly what they do. Review the literature of computer science (see the CourseMate for this text and chapter for some ideas) and browse the Web to locate other definitions of computer science. Compare these definitions with the one presented in this chapter and discuss the differences among them. Discuss how different definitions may give you a vastly different perspective on the field and what people in this field do. [*Note:* A very well-known and widely used definition of computer science was presented in "Report of the ACM Task Force on the Core of Computer Science," reprinted in the journal *Communications of the ACM*, vol. 32, no. 1 (January 1989).]

ADDITIONAL RESOURCES

CourseMate **For additional print and/or online resources relevant to this chapter, visit the Computer Science CourseMate at login.cengagebrain.com.**

Level 1 of the text continues our exploration of algorithms and algorithmic problem solving—essential material for studying any branch of computer science. It first introduces methods for designing and representing algorithms. It then uses these ideas to develop solutions to some real-world problems, including an important application in medicine and biology.

When judging the quality of an essay or book report, we do not look only at sentence structure, spelling, and punctuation. Although grammatical issues are important, we also evaluate the work's style, for it is a combination of correctness and expressiveness that produces a written document of high quality. So, too, for algorithms: Correctness is not the only measure of excellence. This section will present criteria for evaluating the quality and elegance of the algorithmic solutions that you develop.

Algorithm Discovery and Design

2.1 Introduction

Chapter 1 introduced algorithms and algorithmic problem solving, two of the most fundamental concepts in computer science. Our introduction used examples drawn from everyday life, such as programming a DVR (Figure 1.1) and washing your hair (Figures 1.3 and 1.4). Although these are perfectly valid examples of algorithms, they are not of much interest to computer scientists. This chapter develops more fully the notions of algorithms and algorithmic problem solving and applies these ideas to problems that *are* of interest to computer scientists: searching lists, finding maxima and minima, and matching patterns.

2.2 Representing Algorithms

2.2.1 Pseudocode

Before presenting any algorithms, we must first make an important decision. How should we represent them? What notation should we use to express our algorithms so that they are clear, precise, and unambiguous?

One possibility is *natural language*, the language we speak and write in our everyday lives. (This could be English, Spanish, Arabic, Japanese, Swahili, or any language.) This is an obvious choice because it is the language with which we are most familiar. If we use natural language, then our algorithms read much the same as a term paper or an essay. For example, when expressed in natural language, the addition algorithm in Figure 1.2 might look something like the paragraph shown in Figure 2.1.

Comparing Figure 1.2 with Figure 2.1 illustrates the problems of using natural language to represent algorithms. Natural language can be extremely verbose, causing the resulting algorithms to be rambling, unstructured, and hard to follow. (Imagine reading 5, 10, or even 100 pages of text like Figure 2.1.) An unstructured, "free-flowing" writing style might be wonderful for novels and essays, but it is horrible for algorithms. The lack of structure makes it difficult for the reader to locate specific sections of the algorithm because they are buried inside the text. For example, on the eighth line of Figure 2.1 is the phrase, "... and begin the loop all over again." To

FIGURE 2.1

Initially, set the value of the variable *carry* to 0 and the value of the variable *i* to 0. When these initializations have been completed, begin looping as long as the value of the variable *i* is less than or equal to $(m - 1)$. First, add together the values of the two digits a_i and b_i and the current value of the carry digit to get the result called c_i. Now check the value of c_i to see whether it is greater than or equal to 10. If c_i is greater than or equal to 10, then reset the value of *carry* to 1 and reduce the value of c_i by 10; otherwise, set the value of *carry* to 0. When you are finished with that operation, add 1 to *i* and begin the loop all over again. When the loop has completed execution, set the leftmost digit of the result c_m to the value of *carry* and print out the final result, which consists of the digits $c_m\ c_{m-1} \ldots c_0$. After printing the result, the algorithm is finished, and it terminates.

The addition algorithm of Figure 1.2 expressed in natural language

what part of the algorithm does this refer? Without any clues to guide us, such as indentation, line numbering, or highlighting, locating the beginning of that loop can be a daunting and time-consuming task. (For the record, the beginning of the loop corresponds to the sentence that starts, "When these initializations have been completed … ." It is certainly not easy to determine this from a casual reading of the text.)

A second problem is that natural language is too "rich" in interpretation and meaning. Natural language frequently relies on either context or a reader's experiences to give precise meaning to a word or phrase. This permits different readers to interpret the same sentence in totally different ways. This may be acceptable, even desirable, when writing poetry or fiction, but it is disastrous when creating algorithms that must always execute in the same way and produce identical results. We can see an example of this problem in the sentence on Lines 7 and 8 of Figure 2.1 that starts with "When you are finished with that operation … ." When we are finished with *which* operation? It is not at all clear from the text, and individuals might interpret the phrase *that operation* in different ways, producing radically different behavior. Similarly, the statement "Determine the shortest path between the source and destination" is ambiguous until we know the precise meaning of the phrase "shortest path." Does it mean shortest in terms of travel time, distance, or something else?

Because natural languages are not sufficiently precise to represent algorithms, we might be tempted to go to the other extreme. If we are ultimately going to execute our algorithm on a computer, why not write it out as a computer program using a *high-level programming language* such as C++ or Java? If we adopt that approach, the addition algorithm of Figure 1.2 might start out looking like the program fragment shown in Figure 2.2.

As an algorithmic design language, this notation is also seriously flawed. During the initial phases of design, we should be thinking and writing at a highly abstract level. Using a programming language to express our design forces us to deal immediately with detailed language issues, such as punctuation, grammar, and syntax. For example, the algorithm in Figure 1.2 contains an operation that says, "Set the value of *carry* to 0." This is an easy statement to understand. However, when translated into a language like C++ or Java, that statement becomes

```
carry = 0;
```

FIGURE 2.2

```
{
Scanner inp = new Scanner(System.in);
int i, m, carry;
int[] a = new int[100];
int[] b = new int[100];
int[] c = new int[100];
m = inp.nextInt();
for (int j = 0;j <= m-1;j++) {
        a[j] = inp.nextInt();
        b[j] = inp.nextInt();
}
carry = 0;
i = 0;
while (i < m) {
    c[i] = a[i] + b[i] + carry;
    if (c[i] >= 10)
                .
                .
                .
```

The beginning of the addition algorithm of Figure 1.2 expressed in a high-level programming language

Is this operation setting *carry* to 0 or asking if *carry* is equal to 0? Why does a semicolon appear at the end of the line? Would the statement

    Carry = 0;

mean the same thing? Similarly, what is meant by the utterly cryptic statement on Line 4: int[]a = new int[100];? These technical details clutter our thoughts and at this point in the solution process are totally out of place. When creating algorithms, a programmer should no more worry about semicolons and capitalization than a novelist should worry about typography and cover design when writing the first draft!

If the two extremes of natural languages and high-level programming languages are both less than ideal, what notation should we use? What is the best way to represent the solutions shown in this chapter and the rest of the book?

Most computer scientists use a notation called **pseudocode** to design and represent algorithms. This is a set of English language constructs designed to resemble statements in a programming language but that do not actually run on a computer. Pseudocode represents a compromise between the two extremes of natural and formal languages. It is simple, highly readable, and has virtually no grammatical rules. (In fact, pseudocode is sometimes called a programming language without the details.) However, because it contains only statements that have a well-defined structure, it is easier to visualize the organization of a pseudocode algorithm than one represented as long, rambling natural-language paragraphs. In addition, because pseudocode closely resembles many popular programming languages, the subsequent translation of the algorithm into a computer program is relatively simple. The algorithms shown in Figures 1.1, 1.2, 1.3, and 1.4, and Exercise 10 of Chapter 1 are all written in pseudocode.

In the following sections, we will introduce a set of popular and easy-to-understand constructs for the three types of algorithmic operations introduced in Chapter 1: sequential, conditional, and iterative. Keep in mind, however, that pseudocode is *not* a formal language with rigidly standardized syntactic and semantic rules and regulations. On the contrary, it is an informal design notation used solely to express algorithms. If you do not like the constructs presented in the next two sections, feel free to modify them or select others that are more helpful to you. One of the nice features of pseudocode is that you can adapt it to your own personal way of thinking and problem solving.

2.2.2 Sequential Operations

Our pseudocode must include instructions to carry out the three basic *sequential operations* called computation, input, and output.

The instruction for performing a **computation** and saving the result looks like the following. (Words and phrases inside quotation marks represent specific elements that you must insert when writing an algorithm.)

    Set the value of "variable" to "arithmetic expression"

This operation evaluates the "arithmetic expression," gets a result, and stores that result in the "variable." A variable is simply a named storage location that can hold a data value. A variable is often compared with a mailbox into which you can place a value and from which you can retrieve a value. Let's look at an example.

Set the value of *carry* to 0

First, evaluate the arithmetic expression, which in this case is the constant value 0. Then store that result in the variable called *carry*. If *carry* had a previous value, say 1, it is discarded and replaced by the new value 0. You can visualize the result of this operation as follows:

carry | 0 |

Here is another example:

Set the value of *Area* to (πr^2)

Assuming that the variable *r* has been given a value by a previous instruction in the algorithm, this statement evaluates the arithmetic expression πr^2 to produce a numerical result. This result is then stored in the variable called *Area*. If *r* does not have a value, an error condition occurs because this instruction is not effectively computable, and it cannot be completed.

We can see additional examples of computational operations in Steps 4, 6, and 7 of the addition algorithm of Figure 1.2:

Step 4: Add the two digits a_i and b_i to the current value of *carry* to get c_i

Step 6: Add 1 to *i*, effectively moving one column to the left

Step 7: Set c_m to the value of *carry*

Note that these three steps are not written in exactly the format just described. If we had used that notation, they would have looked like this:

Step 4: Set the value of c_i to ($a_i + b_i +$ *carry*)

Step 6: Set the value of *i* to ($i + 1$)

Step 7: Set the value of c_m to *carry*

However, in pseudocode it doesn't matter exactly how you choose to write your instructions as long as the intent is clear, effectively computable, and unambiguous. At this point in the design of a solution, we do not really care about the minor linguistic differences between

Add *a* and *b* to get *c*

and

Set the value of *c* to ($a + b$)

Remember that pseudocode is not a precise set of notational rules to be memorized and rigidly followed. It is a flexible notation that can be adjusted to fit your own view about how best to express ideas and algorithms.

When writing arithmetic expressions, you may assume that the computing agent executing your algorithm has all the capabilities of a typical calculator. Therefore, it "knows" how to do all basic arithmetic operations such as $+$, $-$, $\times$, $\div$, $\sqrt{}$, absolute value, sine, cosine, and tangent. It also knows the value of important constants such as π.

The remaining two sequential operations enable our computing agent to communicate with "the outside world," which means everything other than the computing agent itself:

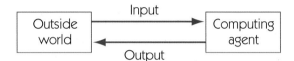

Input operations provide the computing agent with data values from the outside world that it may then use in later instructions. Output operations send results from the computing agent to the outside world. When the computing agent is a computer, communications with the outside world are done via the input/output equipment available on a typical system (e.g., keyboard, screen, mouse, printer, hard drive, CD/DVD, flash drive, camera, touch screen). However, when designing algorithms, we generally do not concern ourselves with such details. We care only that data is provided when we request it, and that results are issued for presentation.

Our pseudocode instructions for input and output are expressed as follows:

Input: Get values for "variable", "variable", …

Output: Print the values of "variable", "variable", …

For example,

Get a value for *r*, the radius of the circle

When the algorithm reaches this input operation, it waits until someone or something provides it with a value for the variable *r*. (In a computer, this may be done by entering a value at the keyboard.) When the algorithm has received and stored a value for *r*, it continues on to the next instruction.

Here is an example of an output operation:

Print the value of *Area*

Assuming that the algorithm has already computed the area of the circle, this instruction says to display that value to the outside world. This display may be viewed on a screen or printed on paper by a printer.

Sometimes we use an output instruction to display a message in place of the desired results. If, for example, the computing agent cannot complete a computation because of an error condition, we might have it execute something like the following operation. (We will use 'single quotes' to enclose messages so as to distinguish them from such pseudocode constructs as "variable" and "arithmetic expression," which are enclosed in double quotes.)

Print the message 'Sorry, no answers were computed.'

FIGURE 2.3

Step	Operation
1	Get values for *gallons used, starting mileage, ending mileage*
2	Set value of *distance driven* to (*ending mileage − starting mileage*)
3	Set value of *average miles per gallon* to (*distance driven ÷ gallons used*)
4	Print the value of *average miles per gallon*
5	Stop

Algorithm for computing average miles per gallon (version 1)

Using these three sequential operations—computation, input, and output—we can now write some simple but useful algorithms. Figure 2.3 presents an algorithm to compute the average miles per gallon on a trip, when given as input the number of gallons used and the starting and ending mileage readings on the odometer.

Practice Problems

Write pseudocode versions of the following:

1. An algorithm that gets three data values x, y, and z as input and outputs the average of those three values.

2. An algorithm that gets the radius r of a circle as input. Its output is both the circumference and the area of a circle of radius r.

3. An algorithm that gets the amount of electricity used in kilowatt-hours and the cost of electricity per kilowatt-hour. Its output is the total amount of the electric bill, including an 8% sales tax.

4. An algorithm that inputs your current credit card balance, the total dollar amount of new purchases, and the total dollar amount of all payments. The algorithm computes the new balance, which includes a 12% interest charge on any unpaid balance.

5. An algorithm that is given the length and width, in feet, of a rectangular carpet and determines its total cost given that the material cost is $23/square yard.

2.2.3 Conditional and Iterative Operations

The average miles per gallon algorithm in Figure 2.3 performs a set of operations once and then stops. It cannot select among alternative operations or perform a block of instructions more than once. A purely sequential algorithm of the type shown in Figure 2.3 is sometimes termed a *straight-line algorithm* because it executes its instructions in a straight line from top to bottom and then stops. Unfortunately, virtually all real-world problems are not straight-line in nature. They involve nonsequential operations such as branching and repetition.

To allow us to address these more interesting problems, our pseudo-code needs two additional statements to implement conditional and iterative operations. Together, these two types of operations are called control operations; they allow us to alter the normal sequential flow of control in an algorithm. As we saw in Chapter 1, control operations are an essential part of all but the very simplest of algorithms.

Conditional statements are the "question-asking" operations of an algorithm. They allow an algorithm to ask a question and select the next operation to perform on the basis of the answer to that question. There are a number of ways to phrase a question, but the most common conditional statement is the *if/then/else* statement, which has the following format:

If "a true/false condition" is true then
　　first set of algorithmic operations
Else (or otherwise)
　　second set of algorithmic operations

The meaning of this statement is as follows:

1. Evaluate the true/false condition on the first line to determine whether it is true or false.

2. If the condition is true, then do the first set of algorithmic operations and skip the second set entirely.

3. If the condition is false, then skip the first set of operations and do the second set.

4. Once the appropriate set of operations has been completed, continue executing the algorithm with the operation that follows the if/then/else instruction.

Figure 2.4 is a visual model of the execution of the if/then/else statement. We evaluate the condition shown in the diamond. If the condition is true, we execute the sequence of operations labeled T1, T2, T3, ... If the condition is false, we execute the sequence labeled F1, F2, F3, ... In either case, however, execution continues with statement S, which is the one that immediately follows the if/then/else statement.

Basically, the if/then/else statement allows you to select exactly one of two alternatives—either/or, this or that. We saw an example of this statement in Step 5 of the addition algorithm shown in Figure 1.2. (The statement has been reformatted slightly to highlight the two alternatives clearly, but it has not been changed.)

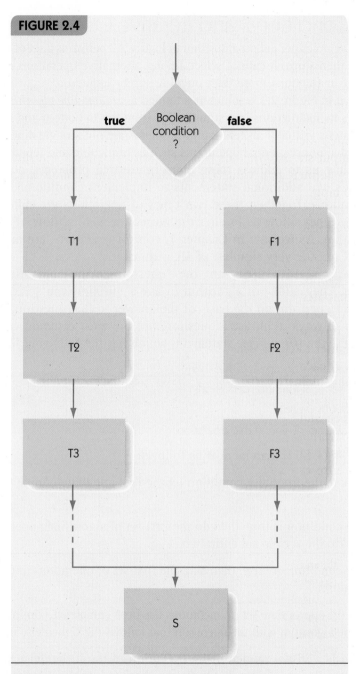

FIGURE 2.4

The if/then/else pseudocode statement

If ($c_i \geq 10$) then

Set the value of c_i to ($c_i - 10$)

Set the value of *carry* to 1

Else

Set the value of *carry* to 0

The condition ($c_i \geq 10$) can be only true or false. If it is true, then there is a carry into the next column, and we must do the first set of instructions—subtracting 10 from c_i and setting *carry* to 1. If the condition is false, then there is no carry—we skip over these two operations, and perform the second block of operations, which simply sets the value of *carry* to 0.

Figure 2.5 shows another example of the if/then/else statement. It extends the miles per gallon algorithm of Figure 2.3 to include a second line of output stating whether you are getting good gas mileage. Good gas mileage is defined as a value for average miles per gallon strictly greater than 25.0 mpg.

The last algorithmic statement to be introduced allows us to implement a *loop*—the repetition of a block of instructions. The real power of a computer comes not from doing a calculation once but from doing it many, many times. If, for example, we need to compute a single value of average miles per gallon, it would be foolish to convert an algorithm like Figure 2.5 into a computer program and execute it on a computer—it would be far faster to use a calculator, which could complete the job in a few seconds. However, if we need to do the same computation 1 million times, the power of a computer to repetitively execute a block of statements becomes quite apparent. If each computation of average miles per gallon takes 5 seconds on a hand calculator, then 1 million of them would require about 2 months, not allowing for such luxuries as sleeping and eating. Once the algorithm is developed and the program written, a computer can carry out that same task in a fraction of a second!

The first algorithmic statement that we will use to express the idea of iteration, also called *looping*, is the *while* statement:

FIGURE 2.5

Step	Operation
1	Get values for *gallons used, starting mileage, ending mileage*
2	Set value of *distance driven* to (*ending mileage – starting mileage*)
3	Set value of *average miles per gallon* to (*distance driven ÷ gallons used*)
4	Print the value of *average miles per gallon*
5	If *average miles per gallon* is greater than 25.0 then
6	Print the message 'You are getting good gas mileage'
	Else
7	Print the message 'You are NOT getting good gas mileage'
8	Stop

Second version of the average miles per gallon algorithm

While ("a true/false condition") do Step i to Step j

> Step i: operation
>
> Step i + 1: operation
>
> .
>
> .
>
> .
>
> Step j: operation

This instruction initially evaluates the "true/false condition"—called the continuation condition—to determine if it is true or false. If the condition is true, all operations from Step i to Step j, inclusive, are executed. This block of operations is called the loop body. (Operations within the loop body should be indented so that it is clear to the reader of the algorithm which operations belong inside the loop.) When the entire loop body has finished executing, the algorithm again evaluates the continuation condition. If it is still true, then the algorithm executes the entire loop body, statements i through j, again. This looping process continues until the continuation condition evaluates to false, at which point execution of the loop body terminates and the algorithm proceeds to the statement immediately following the loop—Step $j + 1$ in the above pseudocode. If for some reason the continuation condition never becomes false, then we have violated one of the fundamental properties of an algorithm, and we have the error, first mentioned in Chapter 1, called an *infinite loop*.

Figure 2.6 is a visual model of the execution of a while loop. The algorithm first evaluates the continuation condition inside the diamond-shaped symbol. If it is true, then it executes the sequence of operations labeled S1, S2, S3, … , which are the operations of the loop body. Then the algorithm returns to the top of the loop and reevaluates the condition. If the condition is false, then the loop has ended, and the algorithm continues executing with the statement after the loop, the one labeled S_n in Figure 2.6.

Here is a simple example of a loop:

Step	Operation
1	Set the value of *count* to 1
2	While (*count* ≤ 100) do Step 3 to Step 5
3	Set *square* to (*count* × *count*)
4	Print the values of *count* and *square*
5	Add 1 to *count*

Step 1 initializes *count* to 1, the next operation determines that (*count* ≤ 100), and then the loop body is executed, which in this case includes the three statements in Steps 3, 4, and 5. Those statements compute the value of *count* squared (Step 3) and print the value of both *count* and *square* (Step 4). The last operation inside the loop body (Step 5) adds 1 to *count* so that it

FIGURE 2.6

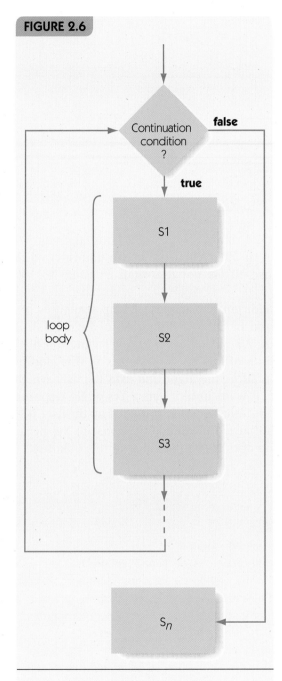

Execution of the while loop

now has the value 2. At the end of the loop, the algorithm must determine whether it should be executed again. Because *count* is 2, the continuation condition (*count* ≤ 100) is still true, and the algorithm must perform the loop body again. Looking at the entire loop, we can see that it will execute 100 times, producing the following output, which is a table of numbers and their squares from 1 to 100.

1	1
2	4
3	9
.	
.	
.	
100	10,000

At the end of the 100th pass through the loop, the value of *count* is incremented in Step 5 to 101. When the continuation condition is evaluated, it is false (because 101 is not less than or equal to 100), and the loop terminates.

We can see additional examples of loop structures in Steps 3 through 6 of Figure 1.2 and in Steps 3 through 6 of Figure 1.3. Another example is shown in Figure 2.7, which is yet another variation of the average miles per gallon algorithm of Figures 2.3 and 2.5. In this modification, after finishing one computation, the algorithm asks the user whether to repeat this calculation again. It waits until it gets a Yes or No response and repeats the entire algorithm until the response provided by the user is No. (Note that the algorithm must initialize the value of *response* to Yes because the very first thing that the loop does is test the value of this quantity.)

FIGURE 2.7

Step	Operation
1	*response* = Yes
2	While (*response* = Yes) do Steps 3 through 11
3	Get values for *gallons used, starting mileage, ending mileage*
4	Set value of *distance driven* to (*ending mileage* – *starting mileage*)
5	Set value of *average miles per gallon* to (*distance driven* ÷ *gallons used*)
6	Print the value of *average miles per gallon*
7	If average miles per gallon > 25.0 then
8	Print the message 'You are getting good gas mileage'
	Else
9	Print the message 'You are NOT getting good gas mileage'
10	Print the message 'Do you want to do this again? Enter Yes or No'
11	Get a new value for *response* from the user
12	Stop

Third version of the average miles per gallon algorithm

There are many variations of this particular looping construct in addition to the while statement just described. For example, it is common to omit the line numbers from algorithms and simply execute them in order, from top to bottom. In that case, we could use an End of Loop construct (or something similar) to mark the end of the loop rather than explicitly stating which steps are contained in the loop body. Using this approach, our loops would be written something like this:

While ("a true/false condition") do

    operation

      .

      .

      .

    operation

End of the loop

In this case, the loop body is delimited not by explicit step numbers but by the two lines that read, "While ..." and "End of the loop".

The type of loop just described is called a *pretest loop* because the continuation condition is tested at the *beginning* of each pass through the loop, and therefore it is possible for the loop body never to be executed. (This would happen if the continuation condition were *initially* false.) Sometimes this can be inconvenient, as we see in Figure 2.7. In that algorithm, the value of the variable called *response* is tested for the first time long before we ask the user if he or she wants to solve the problem again. Therefore, we had to give *response* a "dummy" value of Yes so that the test would be meaningful when the loop was initially entered.

A useful variation of the looping structure is called a *posttest loop*, which also uses a true/false continuation condition to control execution of the loop. However, now the test is done at the *end* of the loop body, not the beginning. The loop is typically expressed using the *do/while* statement, which is usually written as follows:

Do

  operation

  operation

   .

   .

   .

While ("a true/false condition")

This type of iteration performs all the algorithmic operations contained in the loop body before it evaluates the true/false condition specified at the end of the loop. If this condition is false, the loop is terminated and execution continues with the operation following the loop. If it is true, then the entire loop body is executed again. Note that in the do/while variation, the loop body is always executed at least once, whereas the while loop can execute 0, 1, or more times. Figure 2.8 diagrams the execution of the post-test do/while looping structure.

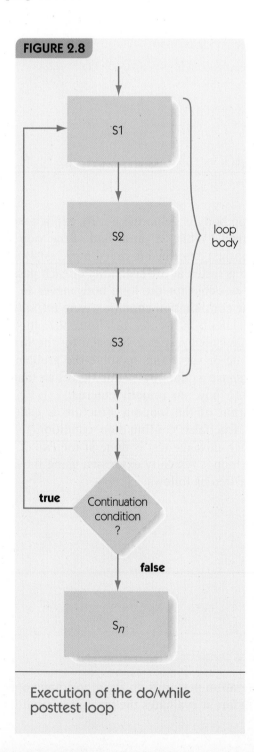

FIGURE 2.8

Execution of the do/while posttest loop

Figure 2.9 summarizes the algorithmic operations introduced in this section. These represent the primitive operations of our computing agent. These are the instructions that we assume our computing agent understands and is capable of executing without further explanation or simplification. In the next section, we will use these operations to design algorithms that solve some interesting and important problems.

FIGURE 2.9

Computation:

Set the value of "variable" to "arithmetic expression"

Input/Output:

Get a value for "variable", "variable"…

Print the value of "variable", "variable", …

Print the message 'message'

Conditional:

If "a true/false condition" is true then

first set of algorithmic operations

Else

second set of algorithmic operations

Iterative:

While ("a true/false condition") do Step i through Step j

Step i: operation

.

.

.

Step j: operation

While ("a true/false condition") do

operation

.

.

operation

End of the loop

Do

operation

operation

.

.

.

While ("a true/false condition")

Summary of pseudocode language instructions

From Little Primitives Mighty Algorithms Do Grow

Although the set of algorithmic primitives shown in Figure 2.9 might seem quite puny, it is anything but! In fact, an important theorem in theoretical computer science proves that the operations shown in Figure 2.9 are sufficient to represent *any* valid algorithm. No matter how complicated it might be, if a problem can be solved algorithmically, it can be expressed using only the sequential, conditional, and iterative operations just discussed. This includes not only the simple addition algorithm of Figure 1.2 but also the exceedingly complex algorithms needed to operate the International Space Station, manage billions of Internet and Web users, and describe all the Internal Revenue Service's tax rules and regulations.

In many ways, building algorithms is akin to constructing essays or novels using only the 26 letters of the English alphabet, plus a few punctuation symbols. Expressive power does not always come from a huge set of primitives. It can also arise from a small number of simple building blocks combined in interesting ways. This is the real secret of building algorithms.

2.3 Examples of Algorithmic Problem Solving

2.3.1 Example 1: Go Forth and Multiply

Our first example of algorithmic problem solving addresses a problem originally posed in Chapter 1 (Exercise 12). That problem asked you to implement an algorithm to multiply two numbers using repeated addition. This problem can be formally expressed as follows:

Given two nonnegative integer values, $a \geq 0$, $b \geq 0$, compute and output the product $(a \times b)$ using the technique of repeated addition. That is, determine the value of the sum $a + a + a + \ldots + a$ (b times).

Obviously, we need to create a loop that executes exactly b times, with each execution of the loop adding the value of a to a running total. These operations will not make any sense (that is, they will not be effectively

Practice Problems

1. Write an if/then/else statement that sets the variable y to the value 1 if $x \geq 0$. If $x < 0$, then the statement should set y to the value 2. (Assume x already has a value.)

2. Write an algorithm that gets as input three data values x, y, and z and outputs the average of these values if the value of x is positive. If the value of x is either 0 or negative, your algorithm should not compute the average but should print the error message 'Bad Data' instead.

3. Write an algorithm that gets as input your current credit card balance, the total dollar amount of new purchases, and the total dollar amount of all payments. The algorithm computes the new balance, which this time includes an 8% interest charge on any unpaid balance below $100, 12% interest on any unpaid balance between $100 and $500, inclusive, and 16% on any unpaid balance above $500.

4. Write an algorithm that gets as input a single data value x and outputs the three values x^2, $\sin x$, and $1/x$. This process is repeated until the input value for x is equal to 999, at which time the algorithm terminates.

5. Write an algorithm that inputs the length and width, in feet, of a rectangular carpet and the price of the carpet in $/square yard. It then determines if we can afford to purchase this carpet, given that our total budget for carpeting is $500.

6. Add the following feature to the algorithm created in the previous Practice Problem: If the cost of the carpet is less than or equal to $250, output a message that this is a particularly good deal.

computable) until we have explicit values for a and b. So one of the first operations in our algorithm must be to input these two values.

Get values for a and b

To create a loop that executes exactly b times, we create a counter, let's call it *count*, initialized to 0 and incremented by (increased by) 1 after each pass through the loop. This means that when we have completed the loop once, the value of *count* is 1; when we have completed the loop twice, the value of *count* is 2, and so forth. Because we want to stop when we have completed the loop b times, we want to stop when (*count* = b). Therefore, the condition for continuing execution of the loop is (*count* < b). Putting all these pieces together produces the following algorithmic structure, which is a loop that executes exactly *b* times as the variable *count* ranges from 0 up to (*b* – 1).

Get values for *a* and *b*

Set the value of *count* to 0

While (*count* < *b*) do

    … the rest of the loop body will go here …

    Set the value of *count* to (*count* + 1)

End of loop

The purpose of the loop body is to add the value of *a* to a running total, which we will call *product*. We express that operation in the following manner:

Set the value of *product* to (*product* + *a*)

This statement says the new value of *product* is to be reset to the current value of *product* added to *a*.

What is the current value of *product* the first time this operation is encountered? Unless we initialize it, it has no value, and this operation is not effectively computable. Before starting the loop, we must be sure to include the following step:

Set the value of *product* to 0

Now our solution is starting to take shape. Here is what we have developed so far:

Get values for *a* and *b*

Set the value of *count* to 0

Set the value of *product* to 0

While (*count* < *b*) do

        Set the value of *product* to (*product* + *a*)

        Set the value of *count* to (*count* + 1)

End of loop

There are only a few minor "tweaks" left to make this a correct solution to our problem.

When the while loop completes, we have computed the desired result, namely (*a* × *b*), and stored it in *product*. However, we have not displayed that result, and as it stands, this algorithm produces no output. Remember from Chapter 1 that one of the fundamental characteristics of an algorithm is that it produces an observable result. In this case, the desired result is the final value of *product*, which we can display using our output primitive:

Print the value of *product*

The original statement of the problem said that the two inputs *a* and *b* must satisfy the following conditions: $a \geq 0$ and $b \geq 0$. The previous algorithm works for positive values of *a* and *b*, but what happens when either $a = 0$ or $b = 0$? Does it still function correctly?

If $b = 0$, there is no problem. If you look at the while loop, you see that it continues executing so long as (*count* < *b*). The variable *count* is initialized to 0. If the input variable *b* also has the value 0, then the test $(0 < 0)$ is initially false, and the loop is *never* executed. The variable *product* keeps its initial value of 0, and that is the output that is printed, which is the correct answer.

Now let's look at what happens when $a = 0$ and *b* is any nonzero value, say 5,386. Of course we know immediately that the correct result is 0, but the algorithm does not. Instead, the loop will execute 5,386 times, the value of *b*, each time adding the value of *a*, which is 0, to *product*. Because adding 0 to anything has no effect, *product* remains at 0, and that is the output that is printed. In this case, we do get the right answer, and our algorithm does work correctly. However, it gets that correct answer only after doing 5,386 unnecessary and time-wasting repetitions of the loop.

In Chapter 1, we stated that it is not only algorithmic correctness we are after but efficiency and elegance as well. The algorithms designed and implemented by computer scientists are intended to solve important real-world problems, and they must accomplish that task in a correct and reasonably efficient manner. Otherwise they are not of much use to their intended audience.

In this case, we can eliminate those needless repetitions of the loop by using our if/then/else conditional primitive. Right at the start of the algorithm, we ask if either *a* or *b* is equal to 0. If the answer is yes, we can immediately set the result to 0 without requiring any further computations:

If (either $a = 0$ or $b = 0$) then

        Set the value of *product* to 0

Else

        … solve the problem as described above …

We will have much more to say about the critically important concepts of algorithmic efficiency and elegance in Chapter 3.

This completes the development of our multiplication algorithm, and the finished solution is shown in Figure 2.10.

This first example needed only two integer values, *a* and *b*, as input. That is a bit unrealistic, as most interesting computational problems deal not with a few numbers but with huge collections of data, such as lists of

FIGURE 2.10

Get values for *a* and *b*
If (either *a* = 0 or *b* = 0) then
    Set the value of *product* to 0
Else
    Set the value of *count* to 0
    Set the value of *product* to 0
    While (*count* < *b*) do
        Set the value of *product* to (*product* + *a*)
        Set the value of *count* to (*count* + 1)
    End of loop
Print the value of *product*
Stop

Algorithm for multiplication of nonnegative values via repeated addition

Practice Problems

1. Manually work through the algorithm in Figure 2.10 using the input values
   a = 2, *b* = 4. After each completed pass through the loop, write down the
   current value of the four variables *a*, *b*, *count*, and *product*.

2. Trace the execution of the algorithm in Figure 2.10 using the "special" input values
   a = 0, *b* = 0. Does the algorithm produce the result you expect?

3. Describe exactly what would be output by the algorithm in Figure 2.10 for each
   of the following two cases, and state whether that output is or is not correct.
   (*Note:* Because one of the two inputs is negative, these values violate the basic
   conditions of the problem.)

   case 1: *a* = −2, *b* = 4
   case 2: *a* = 2, *b* = −4

4. If the algorithm of Figure 2.10 produced the wrong answer for either case 1 or
   case 2 of Practice Problem 3, explain exactly how you could fix the algorithm so it
   works correctly and produces the correct answer.

5. Explain why the multiplication algorithm shown in Figure 2.10 is or is not an
   efficient way to do multiplication. Justify and explain your answer.

names, sequences of characters, or sets of experimental data. In the following sections, we will show examples of the types of processing—searching, reordering, comparing—often done on these large collections of information.

2.3.2 Example 2: Looking, Looking, Looking

Finding a solution to a given problem is called algorithm discovery, and it is the most challenging and creative part of the problem-solving process. We developed an algorithm for a fairly simple problem (multiplication by repeated addition) in Example 1. Discovering a correct and efficient algorithm to solve a complicated problem can be difficult and can involve equal parts of intelligence, hard work, past experience, technical skill, and plain good luck. In the remaining examples, we will develop solutions to a range of problems to give you more experience in working with algorithms. Studying these examples, together with lots of practice, is by far the best way to learn creative problem solving, just as experience and practice are the best ways to learn how to write essays, hit a golf ball, or repair cars.

The next problem we will solve was also mentioned in Chapter 1—locating a particular person's name in a telephone directory. This is just the type of simple and rather uninteresting repetitive task so well suited to computerization. (Many large telephone companies have implemented such an application. Most of us have dialed directory assistance and heard the desired telephone number spoken in an automated, computer-generated voice.)

Assume that we have a list of 10,000 names that we define as N_1, N_2, $N_3, \ldots, N_{10,000}$, along with the 10,000 telephone numbers of those individuals, denoted as $T_1, T_2, T_3, \ldots, T_{10,000}$. To simplify the problem, we initially assume that all names in the book are unique and that the names need not be in alphabetical order. Essentially what we have described is a nonalphabetized telephone book of the following form:

Name	Telephone Number	
N_1	T_1	
N_2	T_2	
N_3	T_3	
.	.	10,000 (name, phone number) pairs
.	.	
.	.	
$N_{10,000}$	$T_{10,000}$	

Let's create an algorithm that allows us to input the name of a specific person, which we will denote as *NAME*. The algorithm will check to see if *NAME* matches any of the 10,000 names contained in our telephone book. If *NAME* matches the value N_j, where j is a value between 1 and 10,000, then the output of our algorithm will be the telephone number of that person: the value T_j. If *NAME* is not contained in our telephone book, then the output of our algorithm will be the message 'I am sorry but this name is not in the directory.' This type of lookup algorithm has many additional uses. For example, it could be used to locate the zip code of a particular city, the seat number of a specific airline passenger, or the room number of a hotel guest.

Because the names in our telephone book are not in alphabetical order, there is no clever way to speed up the search. With a random collection of names, there is no method more efficient than starting at the beginning and looking at each name in the list, one at a time, until we either find the one we are looking for or come to the end of the list. This rather simple and straightforward technique is called *sequential search*, and it is the standard algorithm for searching an *unordered* list of values. For example, this is how we would search a telephone book to see who lives at 123 Elm Street because a telephone book is not sorted by address. It is also the way that we look through a shuffled deck of cards trying to locate one particular card. A first attempt at designing a sequential search algorithm to solve our search problem might look something like Figure 2.11.

The solution shown in Figure 2.11 is extremely long. At 66 lines per page, it would require about 150 pages to write out the 10,002 steps in the completed solution. It would also be unnecessarily slow. If we are lucky enough to find *NAME* in the very first position of the telephone book, N_1, then we get the answer T_1 almost immediately. However, the algorithm does not stop at that point. Even though it has already found the correct answer, it foolishly asks 9,999 more questions looking for *NAME* in positions $N_2, \ldots, N_{10,000}$. Of course, humans have enough "common sense" to know that when they find the answer they are searching for, they can stop. However, we cannot assume common sense in a computer system. On the contrary, a computer will mechanically execute the entire algorithm from the first step to the last.

Not only is the algorithm excessively long and highly inefficient, it is also wrong. If the desired *NAME* is not in the list, this algorithm simply

FIGURE 2.11

Step	Operation
1	Get values for *NAME*, $N_1, \ldots, N_{10,000}$, and $T_1, \ldots, T_{10,000}$
2	If *NAME* = N_1 then print the value of T_1
3	If *NAME* = N_2 then print the value of T_2
4	If *NAME* = N_3 then print the value of T_3
.	.
.	.
.	.
10,000	If *NAME* = $N_{9,999}$ then print the value of $T_{9,999}$
10,001	If *NAME* = $N_{10,000}$ then print the value of $T_{10,000}$
10,002	Stop

First attempt at designing a sequential search algorithm

stops (at Step 10,002) rather than providing the desired result, a message that the name you requested is not in the directory. An algorithm is deemed correct only when it produces the correct result for *all* possible cases.

The problem with this first attempt is that it does not use the powerful algorithmic concept of *iteration*. Instead of writing an instruction 10,000 separate times, it is far better to write it only once and indicate that it is to be repetitively *executed* 10,000 times, or however many times it takes to obtain the answer. As you learned in the previous section, much of the power of a computer comes from being able to perform a *loop*–the repetitive execution of a block of statements a large number of times. Virtually every algorithm developed in this text contains at least one loop and most contain many. (This is the difference between the two shampooing algorithms shown in Figures 1.3 and 1.4. The algorithm in the former contains a loop; that in the latter does not.)

The algorithm in Figure 2.12 shows how we might write a loop to implement the sequential search technique. It uses a variable called i as an *index*, or *pointer*, into the list of all names. That is, N_i refers to the ith name in the list. The algorithm then repeatedly executes a group of statements using different values of i. The variable i can be thought of as a "moving finger" scanning the list of names and pointing to the one on which the algorithm is currently working.

The first time through the loop, the value of the index i is 1, so the algorithm checks (in Step 4) to see whether *NAME* is equal to N_1, the first name on the list. If it is, then the algorithm writes out the result and sets the variable *Found* to YES, which causes the loop in Steps 4 through 7 to terminate. If it is not the desired *NAME*, then i is incremented by 1 (in Step 7) so that it now has the value 2, and the loop is executed again. The algorithm now checks to see whether *NAME* is equal to N_2, the second name on the list. In this way, the algorithm uses the single conditional statement "If *NAME* is equal to the ith name on the list ..." to check up to 10,000 names. It executes that one line over and over, each time with a different value of i. This is the advantage of using iteration.

FIGURE 2.12

Step	Operation
1	Get values for *NAME*, $N_1, \ldots, N_{10,000}$, and $T_1, \ldots, T_{10,000}$
2	Set the value of i to 1 and set the value of *Found* to NO
3	While (*Found* = NO) do Steps 4 through 7
4	If *NAME* is equal to the ith name on the list N_i then
5	Print the telephone number of that person, T_i
6	Set the value of *Found* to YES
	Else (*NAME* is not equal to N_i)
7	Add 1 to the value of i
8	Stop

Second attempt at designing a sequential search algorithm

However, the attempt shown in Figure 2.12 is not yet a complete and correct algorithm because it still does not work correctly when the desired *NAME* does not appear anywhere on the list. This final problem can be solved by terminating the loop either when the desired name is found or the end of the list is reached. The algorithm can determine exactly what happened by checking the value of *Found* when the loop terminates. If the value of *Found* is NO, then the loop terminated because the index i exceeded 10,000, and we searched the entire list without finding the desired *NAME*. The algorithm should then produce an appropriate message.

An iterative solution to the sequential search algorithm that incorporates this feature is shown in Figure 2.13. The sequential search algorithm shown in Figure 2.13 is a correct solution to our telephone book lookup problem. It meets all the requirements listed in Section 1.3.1: It is well ordered, each of the operations is clearly defined and effectively computable, and it is certain to halt with the desired result after a finite number of operations. (In Exercise 12 at the end of this chapter, you will develop a formal argument that proves that this algorithm will always halt.) Furthermore, this algorithm requires only 10 steps to write out fully, rather than the 10,002 steps of the first attempt in Figure 2.11. As you can see, not all algorithms are created equal.

Looking at the algorithm in Figure 2.13, our first thought might be that this is not at all how people manually search a telephone book. When looking for a particular telephone number, we would never turn to page 1, column 1, and scan all names beginning with Aardvark, Alan. Certainly, a telephone company in New York City would not be satisfied with the performance of a directory search algorithm that always began on page 1 of its 2,000-page telephone book.

FIGURE 2.13

Step	Operation
1	Get values for *NAME*, $N_1, \ldots, N_{10,000}$, and $T_1, \ldots, T_{10,000}$
2	Set the value of i to 1 and set the value of *Found* to NO
3	While both (*Found* = NO) and ($i \leq 10,000$) do Steps 4 through 7
4	If *NAME* is equal to the ith name on the list N_i then
5	Print the telephone number of that person, T_i
6	Set the value of *Found* to YES
	Else (*NAME* is not equal to N_i)
7	Add 1 to the value of i
8	If (*Found* = NO) then
9	Print the message 'Sorry, this name is not in the directory'
10	Stop

The sequential search algorithm

Because our telephone book was not alphabetized, we really had no choice in the design of a search algorithm. However, in real life we can do much better than sequential search, because telephone books *are* alphabetized, and we can exploit this fact during the search process. For example, we know that *M* is about halfway through the alphabet, so when looking for the name Samuel Miller, we open the telephone book somewhere in the middle rather than to the first page. We then see exactly where we are by looking at the first letter of the names on the current page, and then we move forward or backward toward names beginning with *M*. This approach allows us to find the desired name much more quickly than searching sequentially beginning with the letter *A*.

This use of different search techniques points out a very important concept in the design of algorithms:

> *The selection of an algorithm to solve a problem is greatly influenced by the way the input data for that problem are organized.*

An algorithm is a method for processing some data to produce a result, and the way the data are organized has an enormous influence both on the algorithm we select and on how speedily that algorithm can produce the desired result.

Laboratory Experience 2

Computer science is an empirical discipline as well as a theoretical one. Learning comes not just from reading about concepts like algorithms, but also from manipulating and observing them. The laboratory manual for this text includes laboratory exercises that enable you to engage the ideas and concepts presented on these pages. Laboratory Experience 2 introduces the concept of *algorithm animation,* in which you can observe an algorithm being executed and watch as data values are dynamically transformed into final results.

Bringing an algorithm to life in this way can help you understand what the algorithm does and how it works. The first animation that you will work with is the sequential search algorithm shown in Figure 2.13. The laboratory software allows you to create a list of data values and to watch as the algorithm searches this list to determine whether a special target value occurs.

We strongly encourage you to work through these Laboratory Experiences to deepen your understanding of the ideas presented in this and the following chapters.

In Chapter 3, we will expand on the concept of the efficiency and quality of algorithms, and we will present an algorithm for searching *alphabetized* telephone books that is far superior to the one shown in Figure 2.13.

2.3.3 Example 3: Big, Bigger, Biggest

The third algorithm we will develop is similar to the sequential search in Figure 2.13 in that it also searches a list of values. However, this time the algorithm will search not for a particular value supplied by the user but for the numerically largest value in a list of numbers. This type of "find largest" algorithm could be used to answer a number of important questions. (With only a single trivial change, the same algorithm also finds the smallest value, so a better name for it might be "find extreme values.") For example, given a list of examinations, which student received the highest (or lowest) score? Given a list of annual salaries, which employee earns the most (or least) money? Given a list of grocery prices from different stores, where should I shop to find the lowest price? All these questions could be answered by executing this type of algorithm.

In addition to being important in its own right, such an algorithm can also be used as a "building block" for the construction of solutions to other problems. For example, the Find Largest algorithm that we will develop could be used to implement a *sorting algorithm* that puts an unordered list of numbers in ascending order. (Find and remove the largest item in list A and move it to the last position of list B. Now repeat these operations, each time moving the largest remaining number in list A to the last unfilled slot of list B. We will develop and write this algorithm in Chapter 3.)

The use of a "building-block" component is a very important concept in computer science. The examples in this chapter might lead you to believe that every algorithm you write must be built from only the most elementary and basic of primitives—the sequential, conditional, and iterative operations shown in Figure 2.9. However, once an algorithm has been developed, it may itself be used in the construction of other, more complex algorithms, just as we will use "find largest" in the design of a sorting algorithm. This is similar to what a builder does when constructing a home from prefabricated units rather than bricks and boards. Our problem-solving task need not always begin at the beginning but can instead build on ideas and results that have come before. Every algorithm that we create becomes, in a sense, a primitive operation of our computing agent and can be used as part of the solution to other problems. That is why a collection of useful, prewritten algorithms, called a library, is such an important tool in the design and development of algorithms.

Formally, the problem we will be solving in this section is defined as follows:

> Given a value $n \geq 1$ and a list containing exactly n unique numbers called $A_1, A_2, \ldots, A_n$, find and print out both the largest value in the list and the position in the list where that largest value occurred.

For example, if our list contained the five values

19, 41, 12, 63, 22   ($n = 5$)

then our algorithm should locate the largest value, 63, and print that value together with the fact that it occurred in the fourth position of the list. (*Note:* Our definition of the problem states that all numbers in the list are unique, so there can be only a single occurrence of the largest number. Exercise 15 at the end of the chapter asks how our algorithm would behave if the numbers in the list were not unique and the largest number could occur two or more times.)

When faced with a problem statement like the one just given, how do we go about creating a solution? What strategies can we employ to discover a correct and efficient answer to the problem? One way to begin is to ask ourselves how the same problem might be solved by hand. If we can understand and explain how we would approach the problem manually, we might be able to express that manual solution as a formal algorithm.

For example, suppose we were given a pile of papers, each of which contains a single number, and were asked to locate the largest number in the pile. (The following diagrams assume the papers contain the five values 19, 41, 12, 63, and 22.)

The pile

We might start off by saying that the first number in the pile (the top one) is the largest one that we have seen so far, and then putting it off to the side where we are keeping the largest value.

The pile

The largest so far

Now we compare the top number in the pile with the one that we have called the largest one so far. In this case, the top number in the pile, 41, is larger than our current largest, 19, so we make it the new largest. To do this, we throw the value 19 into the wastebasket (or, better, into the recycle bin) and put the number 41 off to the side because it is the largest value encountered so far.

The pile   The largest so far   The previous largest so far

We now repeat this comparison operation, asking whether the number on top of the pile is larger than the largest value seen so far, now 41. This time the value on top of the pile, 12, is not larger, so we do not want to save it. We simply throw it away and move on to the next number in the pile.

The pile   The largest so far   The value 12, which was not used

This compare-and-save-or-discard process continues until our original pile of numbers is empty, at which time the largest so far is the largest value in the entire list.

Let's see how we can convert this informal, pictorial solution into a formal algorithm that is built from the primitive operations shown in Figure 2.9.

We certainly cannot begin to search a list for a largest value until we have a list to search. Therefore, our first operation must be to get a value for n, the size of the list, followed by values for the n-element list $A_1, A_2, \ldots,$ A_n. This can be done using our input primitive:

Get a value for n, the size of the list

Get values for $A_1, A_2, \ldots, A_n$, the list to be searched

Now that we have the data, we can begin to implement a solution.

Our informal description of the algorithm stated that we should begin by calling the first item in the list, A_1, the largest value so far. (We know that this operation is meaningful because we stated that the list must always have at least one element.) We can express this formally as

Set the value of *largest so far* to A_1

Our solution must also determine where that largest value occurs. To remember this value, let's create a variable called *location* to keep track of the position in the list where the largest value occurs. Because we have initialized *largest so far* to the first element in the list, we should initialize *location* to 1.

Set the value of *location* to 1

We are now ready to begin looking through the remaining items in list A to find the largest one. However, if we write something like the following instruction:

If the second item in the list is greater than *largest so far* then …

we will have made exactly the same mistake that occurred in the initial version of the sequential search algorithm shown in Figure 2.11. This instruction explicitly checks only the second item of the list. We would need to rewrite that statement to check the third item, the fourth item, and so on. Again, we are failing to use the idea of *iteration*, where we repetitively execute a loop as many times as it takes to produce the desired result.

To solve this problem, let's use the same technique used in the sequential search algorithm. Let's not talk about the second, third, fourth, … item in the list but about the *i*th item in the list, where *i* is a variable that takes on different values during the execution of the algorithm. Using this idea, a statement such as

If A_i > *largest so far* then …

can be executed with different values for *i*. This allows us to check all *n* values in the list with a single statement. Initially, *i* should be given the value 2 because the first item in the list was automatically set to the largest value. Therefore, we want to begin our search with the second item in the list.

.

.

.

Set the value of *i* to 2

.

.

.

If A_i > *largest so far* then …

What operations should appear after the word *then*? A check of our earlier discussion shows that the algorithm must reset the values of both *largest so far* and *location.*

If A_i > *largest so far* then
    Set *largest so far* to A_i
    Set *location* to *i*

If A_i is not larger than *largest so far*, then we do not want the algorithm to do anything. To indicate this, the if/then instruction can include an else clause that looks something like

Else

Don't do anything at all to *largest so far* and *location*

This is certainly correct, but instructions that tell us not to do anything are usually omitted from an algorithm because they do not carry any meaningful information.

Regardless of whether the algorithm does or does not reset the values of *largest so far* and *location*, it needs to move on to the next item in the list. Our algorithm refers to A_i, the *i*th item in the list, so it can move to the next item by simply adding 1 to the value of *i* and repeating the if/then statement. The outline of this iteration can be sketched as follows:

> If A_i > *largest so far* then
>
> Set *largest so far* to A_i
>
> Set *location* to *i*
>
> Add 1 to the value of *i*
>
> .
>
> .
>
> .

However, we do not want the loop to repeat forever. (Remember that one of the properties of an algorithm is that it must eventually halt.) What stops this iterative process? When does the algorithm display an answer and terminate execution?

The conditional operation "If A_i > *largest so far* then …" is meaningful only if A_i represents an actual element of list *A*. Because *A* contains *n* elements numbered 1 to *n*, the value of *i* must be in the range 1 to *n*. If *i* > *n*, then the loop has searched the entire list, and it is finished. Therefore, our continuation condition should be expressed as ($i \leq n$). When this condition becomes false, the algorithm can stop looping and print the values of both *largest so far* and *location*. Using our looping primitive, we can describe this iteration as follows:

While ($i \leq n$) do

If A_i > *largest so far* then

Set *largest so far* to A_i

Set *location* to *i*

Add 1 to the value of *i*

End of the loop

We have now developed all the pieces of the algorithm and can finally put them together. Figure 2.14 shows the completed Find Largest algorithm. Note that the steps are not numbered. This omission is quite common, especially as algorithms get larger and more complex.

FIGURE 2.14

Get a value for n, the size of the list
Get values for $A_1, A_2, \ldots, A_n$, the list to be searched
Set the value of *largest so far* to A_1
Set the value of *location* to 1
Set the value of i to 2
While $(i \leq n)$ do
    If A_i > *largest so far* then
        Set *largest so far* to A_i
        Set *location* to i
    Add 1 to the value of i
End of the loop
Print out the values of *largest so far* and *location*
Stop

Algorithm to find the largest value in a list

Practice Problems

1. What part(s) of the sequential search algorithm of Figure 2.13 would need to be changed if our phone book contained 1 million names rather than 10,000?

2. Rewrite the sequential search algorithm to use the do/while looping structure shown in Figure 2.9 in place of the while structure.

3. Modify the algorithm of Figure 2.14 so that it finds the smallest value in a list rather than the largest. Describe exactly what changes were necessary.

4. Describe exactly what would happen to the algorithm in Figure 2.14 if you tried to apply it to an empty list of length $n = 0$. Describe exactly how you could fix this problem.

5. Describe exactly what happens to the algorithm in Figure 2.14 when it is presented with a list with exactly one item, i.e., $n = 1$.

6. Would the *Find Largest* algorithm of Figure 2.14 still work correctly if the test on Line 7 were written as $(A_i \geq$ *largest so far*$)$? Explain why or why not.

Laboratory Experience 3

Like Laboratory Experience 2, this laboratory also uses animation to help you better understand the concept of algorithm design and execution. It presents an animation of the Find Largest algorithm discussed in the text and shown in Figure 2.14.

This Laboratory Experience allows you to create a list of data and watch as the algorithm attempts to determine the largest numerical value contained in that list. You will be able to observe dynamic changes to the variables *index*, *location*, and *maximum*, and will be able to see how values are set and discarded as the algorithm executes. Like the previous Laboratory Experience, it is intended to give you a deeper understanding of how this algorithm works by allowing you to observe its behavior.

2.3.4 Example 4: Meeting Your Match

The last algorithm we develop in this chapter solves a common problem in computer science called *pattern matching*. For example, imagine that you have a collection of Civil War data files that you want to use as resource material for an article on Abraham Lincoln. Your first step would probably be to search these files to locate every occurrence of the text patterns "Abraham Lincoln," "A. Lincoln," and "Lincoln." The process of searching for a special pattern of symbols within a larger collection of information is called *pattern matching*. Most good word processors provide this service as a menu item called *Find* or something similar. Furthermore, most Web search engines try to match your search keys to the keywords that appear on a Web page.

Pattern matching can be applied to almost any kind of information, including graphics, sound, and pictures. For example, an important medical application of pattern matching is to input an X-ray or CT scan image into a computer and then have the computer search for special patterns, such as dark spots, which represent conditions that should be brought to the attention of a physician. This can help speed up the interpretation of X-rays and avoid the problem of human error caused by fatigue or oversight. (Computers do not get tired or bored!)

One of the most interesting and exciting applications of pattern matching is assisting microbiologists and geneticists studying and mapping the *human genome*, the basis for all human life. The human genome is composed of a sequence of approximately 3.5 billion *nucleotides*, each of which can be one of only four different chemical compounds. These compounds (adenine, cytosine, thymine, guanine) are usually referred to by the first letter of their chemical names: A, C, T, and G. Thus, the basis for our existence can be rendered in a very large "text file" written in a four-letter alphabet.

... T C G G A C T A A C A T C G G G A T C G A G A T G ...

Sequences of these nucleotides are called *genes*. There are about 25,000 genes in the human genome, and they determine virtually all of our physical characteristics—sex, race, eye color, hair color, and height, to name just a few. Genes are also an important factor in the occurrence of certain diseases. A missing or flawed nucleotide can result in one of a number of serious genetic disorders, such as Down syndrome or Tay-Sachs disease. To help find a cure for these diseases, researchers are attempting to locate individual genes that, when exhibiting a certain defect, cause a specific malady. A gene is typically composed of thousands of nucleotides, and researchers generally do not know the entire sequence. However, they may know what a small portion of the gene—say, a few hundred nucleotides—looks like. Therefore, to search for one particular gene, they must match the sequence of nucleotides that they do know, called a *probe*, against the entire 3.5 billion-element genome to locate every occurrence of that probe. From this matching information, researchers hope to isolate specific genes. For example,

Genome:	... T C A G G C	T A A T C	G T A G G ...	
Probe:		T A A T C		a match

When a match is found, researchers examine the nucleotides located before and after the probe to see whether they have located the desired gene and, if so, to see whether the gene is defective. Physicians hope someday to be able to "clip out" a bad sequence and insert in its place a correct sequence.

This application of pattern matching dispels any notion that the algorithms discussed here—sequential search (Figure 2.13), Find Largest (Figure 2.14), and pattern matching—are nothing more than academic exercises that serve as examples for introductory classes but have absolutely no role in solving real-world problems. The algorithms that we have presented (or will present) *are* important, either in their own right or as building blocks for algorithms used by physical scientists, mathematicians, engineers, and social scientists.

Let's formally define the pattern-matching problem as follows:

You will be given some *text* composed of n characters that will be referred to as $T_1 T_2 \ldots T_n$. You will also be given a *pattern* of m characters, $m \le n$, that will be represented as $P_1 P_2 \ldots P_m$. The algorithm must locate every occurrence of the given pattern within the text. The output of the algorithm is the location in the text where each match occurred. For this problem, the location of a match is defined to be the index position in the text where the match begins.

For example, if our text is the phrase "to be or not to be, that is the question" and the pattern for which we are searching is the word *to*, then our algorithm produces the following output:

Text: **to** *be or not to be, that is the question*

Pattern: **to**

Output: *Match starting at position 1.*

Text: *to be or not* **to** *be, that is the question*

Pattern: **to**

Output: *Match starting at position 14. (The t is in position 14, including blanks.)*

The pattern-matching algorithm that we will implement is composed of two parts. In the first part, the pattern is aligned under a specific position of the text, and the algorithm determines whether there is a match at that given position. The second part of the algorithm "slides" the entire pattern ahead one character position. Assuming that we have not gone beyond the end of the text, the algorithm returns to the first part to check for a match at this new position. Pictorially, this algorithm can be represented as follows:

Repeat the following two steps.

Step 1: The matching process: $T_1\ T_2\ T_3\ T_4\ T_5 \ldots$

                                                 $P_1\ P_2\ P_3$

Step 2: The slide forward: $T_1\ T_2\ T_3\ T_4\ T_5 \ldots$

        one-character slide → $P_1\ P_2\ P_3$

The algorithm involves repetition of these two steps beginning at position 1 of the text and continuing until the pattern has slid off the right-hand end of the text.

A first draft of an algorithm that implements these ideas is shown in Figure 2.15, in which not all of the operations are expressed in terms of the basic algorithmic primitives of Figure 2.9. Although statements like "Set k, the starting location for the attempted match, to 1" and "Print the value of k, the starting location of the match" are just fine, the instructions "Attempt to match every character in the pattern beginning at position k of the text" and "Keep going until we have fallen off the end of the text" are certainly not primitives. On the contrary, they are both high-level operations that, if written out using only the operations in Figure 2.9, would expand into many instructions.

Is it okay to use high-level statements like this in our algorithm? Wouldn't their use violate the requirement stated in Chapter 1 that algorithms be constructed only from unambiguous operations that can be directly executed by our computing agent?

In fact, it is perfectly acceptable, and quite useful, to use high-level statements like this during the *initial phase* of the algorithm design process.

FIGURE 2.15

Get values for n and m, the size of the text and the pattern, respectively
Get values for both the text $T_1 T_2 \ldots T_n$ and the pattern $P_1 P_2 \ldots P_m$
Set k, the starting location for the attempted match, to 1
Keep going until we have fallen off the end of the text
    Attempt to match every character in the pattern beginning at
        position k of the text (this is Step 1 from the previous page)
    If there was a match then
        Print the value of k, the starting location of the match
    Add 1 to k, which slides the pattern forward one position (this is Step 2)
End of the loop
Stop

First draft of the pattern-matching algorithm

When starting to design an algorithm, we might not want to think only in terms of elementary operations such as input, computation, output, conditional, and iteration. Instead, we might want to express our proposed solution in terms of high-level and broadly defined operations that represent dozens or even hundreds of primitive instructions. Here are some examples of these higher-level constructs:

- Sort the entire list into ascending order.

- Attempt to match the entire pattern against the text.

- Find a root of the equation.

Using instructions like these in an algorithm allows us to postpone worrying about how to implement that operation and lets us focus instead on other aspects of the problem. Eventually, we will come back to these statements and either express them in terms of our available primitives or use existing "building-block" algorithms taken from a program library. However, we can do this at our convenience.

The use of high-level instructions during the design process is an example of one of the most important intellectual tools in computer science—abstraction. Abstraction refers to the separation of the high-level view of an entity or an operation from the low-level details of its implementation. It is abstraction that allows us to understand and intellectually manage any large, complex system, whether it is a mammoth corporation, a complex piece of machinery, or an intricate and very detailed algorithm. For example, the president of General Motors views the company in terms of its major corporate divisions and very high-level policy issues, not in terms of every worker, every supplier, and every car. Attempting to manage the company at that level of detail would drown the president in a sea of detail.

In computer science, we frequently use abstraction because of the complexity of hardware and software. For example, abstraction allows us to view the hardware component called "memory" as a single, indivisible high-level entity without paying heed to the billions of electronic devices that go into constructing a memory unit. (Chapter 4 examines how computer memories are built, and it makes extensive use of abstraction.) In algorithm design and software development, we use abstraction whenever we think of an operation at a high level and temporarily ignore how we might actually implement that operation. This allows us to decide which details to address now and which to postpone until later. Viewing an operation at a high level of abstraction and fleshing out the details of its implementation at a later time constitute an important computer science problem-solving strategy called **top-down design**.

Ultimately, however, we do have to describe how each of these high-level abstractions can be represented using the available algorithmic primitives. The fifth line of the first draft of the pattern-matching algorithm shown in Figure 2.15 reads:

Attempt to match every character in the pattern beginning at position *k* of the text

When this statement is reached, the pattern is aligned under the text beginning with the *k*th character. Pictorially, we are in the following situation:

Text: $T_1 \, T_2 \, T_3 \, \cdots$ $T_k \, T_{k+1} \, T_{k+2} \, \cdots \, T_{k+(m-1)} \, \cdots$

Pattern: $P_1 \, P_2 \, P_3 \, \cdots \, P_m$

The algorithm must now perform the following comparisons:

Compare P_1 to T_k

Compare P_2 to T_{k+1}

Compare P_3 to T_{k+2}

.

.

.

Compare P_m to $T_{k+(m-1)}$

If the members of every single one of these pairs are equal, then there is a match starting at position *k*. However, if even one pair is not equal, then there is no match, and the algorithm can immediately cease making comparisons at this location. Thus, we must construct a loop that executes until one of two things happens—it has either completed *m* successful comparisons (i.e., we have matched the entire pattern) or it has detected a mismatch. When either of these conditions occurs, the loop stops; however, if neither condition has occurred, the loop must keep going. Algorithmically, this iteration can be expressed in the following way. (Remember that *k* is the starting location in the text.)

Set the value of i to 1

Set the value of *Mismatch* to NO

While both ($i \leq m$) and (*Mismatch* = NO)

    If $P_i \neq T_{k+(i-1)}$ then

        Set *Mismatch* to YES

    Else

        Increment i by 1 (to move to the next character)

End of the loop

When the loop has finished, we can determine whether there was a match by examining the current value of the variable *Mismatch*. If *Mismatch* is YES, then there was not a match because at least one of the characters was out of place. If *Mismatch* is NO, then every character in the pattern matched its corresponding character in the text, and there is a match starting at position k.

If *Mismatch* = NO then

    Print the message 'There is a match at position '

    Print the value of k

Regardless of whether there was a match at position k, we must add 1 to k to begin searching for a match at the next position. This is the "sliding forward" step diagrammed earlier.

The final high-level statement in Figure 2.15 that needs to be expanded is the loop on Line 4.

Keep going until we have fallen off the end of the text

What does it mean to "fall off the end of the text"? Where is the last possible place that a match can occur? To answer these questions, let's draw a diagram in which the last character of the pattern, P_m, lines up directly under T_n, the last character of the text.

Text:	$T_1\ T_2\ T_3\ \ldots$	$T_{n-m+1}\ \ldots$	T_{n-2}	T_{n-1}	T_n
Pattern:		$P_1\ \ldots$	P_{m-2}	P_{m-1}	P_m

This diagram illustrates that the last possible place a match could occur is when the first character of the pattern is aligned under the character at position T_{n-m+1} of the text because P_m is aligned under T_n, P_{m-1} is under T_{n-1}, P_{m-2} is aligned under T_{n-2}, and so on. Thus, P_1, which can be written as $P_{m-(m-1)}$, is aligned under $T_{n-(m-1)}$, which is T_{n-m+1}. If we tried to slide the pattern forward any further, we would truly "fall off" the right-hand end of the text. Therefore, our loop must terminate when k, the starting point for the match, strictly exceeds the value of $n - m + 1$. We can express this as follows:

While ($k \leq (n - m + 1)$) do

FIGURE 2.16

Get values for n and m, the size of the text and the pattern, respectively

Get values for both the text $T_1 T_2 \ldots T_n$ and the pattern $P_1 P_2 \ldots P_m$

Set k, the starting location for the attempted match, to 1

While $(k \leq (n - m + 1))$ do

    Set the value of i to 1

    Set the value of Mismatch to NO

    While both $(i \leq m)$ and (Mismatch = NO) do

        If $P_i \neq T_{k+(i-1)}$ then

          Set Mismatch to YES

        Else

          Increment i by 1 (to move to the next character)

    End of the loop

    If Mismatch = NO then

        Print the message 'There is a match at position'

        Print the value of k

    Increment k by 1

End of the loop

Stop, we are finished

Final draft of the pattern-matching algorithm

Now we have all the pieces of our algorithm in place. We have expressed every statement in Figure 2.15 in terms of our basic algorithmic primitives and are ready to put it all together. The final draft of the pattern-matching algorithm is shown in Figure 2.16.

2.4 Conclusion

You have now had a chance to see the step-by-step design and development of some interesting, nontrivial algorithms. You have also been introduced to a number of important concepts related to problem solving, including algorithm design and discovery, pseudocode, control statements, iteration, libraries, abstraction, and top-down design. However, this by no means marks the end of our discussion of algorithms. The development of a correct solution to a problem is only the first step in creating a useful solution.

Designing a technically correct algorithm to solve a given problem is only part of what computer scientists do. They must also ensure that they have created an *efficient* algorithm that generates results quickly enough for its intended users. Chapter 1 described a brute force chess algorithm that would, at least theoretically, play perfect chess but that would be unusable because it would take millions of centuries to make its first move. Similarly, a directory

Practice Problems

1. Consider the following "telephone book."

Name	Number
Smith	555-1212
Jones	834-6543
Adams	921-5281
Doe	327-8900

   Trace the sequential search algorithm of Figure 2.13 using each of the following *NAME*s and show the output produced.

   a. Adams

   b. Schneider

2. Consider the following list of seven data values.

   22, 18, 23, 17, 25, 30, 2

   Trace the Find Largest algorithm of Figure 2.14 and show the output produced.

3. Consider the following text.

   Text: A man and a woman

   Trace the pattern-matching algorithm of Figure 2.16 using the two-character pattern *an* and show the output produced.

4. Explain exactly what would happen to the algorithm of Figure 2.16 if m, the length of the pattern, were greater than n, the length of the text.

5. Explain exactly what would happen to the algorithm of Figure 2.16 if Line 5 had been incorrectly written as "set the value of i to 0".

assistance program that takes 10 minutes to locate a telephone number would be of little or no use. A caller would surely hang up long before the answer was found. This practical concern for efficiency and usefulness, in addition to correctness, is one of the hallmarks of computer science.

Therefore, after developing a correct algorithm, we must analyze it thoroughly and study its efficiency properties and operating characteristics. We must ask ourselves how quickly it will give us the desired results and whether it is better than other algorithms that solve the same problem. This analysis, which is the central topic of Chapter 3, enables us to create algorithms that are not only correct, but elegant, efficient, and useful as well.

EXERCISES

1. Write pseudocode instructions to carry out each of the following computational operations:

   a. Determine the area of a triangle given values for the base *b* and the height *h*.

   b. Compute the interest earned in 1 year given the starting account balance *B* and the annual interest rate *I* and assuming simple interest, that is, no compounding. Also determine the final balance at the end of the year.

   c. Determine the flying time between two cities given the mileage *M* between them and the average speed of the airplane.

2. Using only the sequential operations described in Section 2.2.2, write an algorithm that gets values for the starting account balance *B*, annual interest rate *I*, and annual service charge *S*. Your algorithm should output the amount of interest earned during the year and the final account balance at the end of the year. Assume that interest is compounded monthly and the service charge is deducted once, at the end of the year.

3. Using only the sequential operations described in Section 2.2.2, write an algorithm that gets four numbers corresponding to scores received on three semester tests and a final examination. Your algorithm should compute and display the average of all four tests, weighting the final exam twice as heavily as a regular test.

4. Write an algorithm that gets the price for item A plus the quantity purchased. The algorithm prints the total cost, including a 6% sales tax.

5. Write an if/then/else primitive to do each of the following operations:

   a. Compute and display the value $x \div y$ if the value of *y* is not 0. If *y* does have the value 0, then display the message 'Unable to perform the division.'

   b. Compute the area and circumference of a circle given the radius *r* if the radius is greater than or equal to 1.0; otherwise, you should compute only the circumference.

6. Modify the algorithm of Exercise 2 to include the annual service charge only if the starting account balance at the beginning of the year is less than $1,000. If it is greater than or equal to $1,000, then there is no annual service charge.

7. Write an algorithm that uses a loop (1) to input 10 pairs of numbers, where each pair represents the score of a football game with the Computer State University (CSU) score listed first, and (2) for each pair of numbers, determine whether CSU won or lost. After reading in these 10 pairs of values, print out the won/lost/tie record of CSU. In addition, if this record is a perfect 10-0, then print out the message 'Congratulations on your undefeated season.'

8. Modify the test-averaging algorithm of Exercise 3 so that it reads in 15 test scores rather than 4. There are 14 regular tests and a final examination, which counts twice as much as a regular test. Use a loop to input and sum the scores.

9. Modify the sales computation algorithm of Exercise 4 so that after finishing the computation for one item, it starts on the computation for the next. This iterative process is repeated until the total cost exceeds $1,000.

10. Write an algorithm that is given your electric meter readings (in kilowatt-hours) at the beginning and end of each month of the year. The algorithm determines your annual cost of electricity on the basis of a charge of 6 cents per kilowatt-hour for the first 1,000 kilowatt-hours of each month and 8 cents per kilowatt-hour beyond 1,000. After printing out your total annual charge, the algorithm also determines whether you used less than 500 kilowatt-hours for the entire year and, if so, prints out a message thanking you for conserving electricity.

11. Develop an algorithm to compute gross pay. The inputs to your algorithm are the hours worked per week and the hourly pay rate. The rule for determining gross pay is to pay the regular pay rate for all hours worked up to 40, time-and-a-half for all hours over 40 up to 54, and double time for all hours over 54. Compute and display the value for gross pay using this rule. After displaying one value, ask the user whether he or she wants to do another computation. Repeat the entire set of operations until the user says no.

12. Develop a formal argument that "proves" that the sequential search algorithm shown in Figure 2.13 cannot have an infinite loop; that is, prove that it will always stop after a finite number of operations.

13. Modify the sequential search algorithm of Figure 2.13 so that it works correctly even if the names in the directory are not unique, that is, if the desired name occurs more than once. Your modified algorithm should find *every* occurrence of *NAME* in the directory and print out the telephone number corresponding to *every* match. In addition, after all the numbers have been displayed, your algorithm should print out how many occurrences of *NAME* were located. For example, if *NAME* occurred three times, the output of the algorithm might look something like this:

    528-5638

    922-7874

    488-2020

    A total of three occurrences were located.

14. Use the Find Largest algorithm of Figure 2.14 to help you develop an algorithm to find the median value in a list containing *N* unique numbers. The median of *N* numbers is defined as the value in the list in which approximately half the values are larger than it and half the values are smaller than it. For example, consider the following list of seven numbers.

    26, 50, 83, 44, 91, 20, 55

    The median value is 50 because three values (20, 26, and 44) are smaller and three values (55, 83, and 91) are larger. If *N* is an even value, then the number of values larger than the median will be one greater than the number of values smaller than the median.

15. With regard to the Find Largest algorithm of Figure 2.14, if the numbers in our list were not unique and therefore the largest number could occur more than once, would the algorithm find the first occurrence? The last occurrence? Every occurrence? Explain precisely how this algorithm would behave when presented with this new condition.

16. On the sixth line of the Find Largest algorithm of Figure 2.14, there is an instruction that reads,

    While ($i \le n$) do

    Explain exactly what would happen if we changed that instruction to read as follows:

    a. While ($i \ge n$) do

    b. While ($i < n$) do

    c. While ($i = n$) do

17. On the seventh line of the Find Largest algorithm of Figure 2.14, there is an instruction that reads,

    If A_i > largest so far then …

    Explain exactly what would happen if we changed that instruction to read as follows:

    a. If $A_i \ge$ largest so far then …

    b. If $A_i <$ largest so far then …

    Looking back at your answers in Exercises 16 and 17, what do they say about the importance of using the correct relational operation ($<, =, >, \ge, \le, \ne$) when writing out either an iterative or conditional algorithmic primitive?

18. Refer to the pattern-matching algorithm in Figure 2.16.

    a. What is the output of the algorithm as it currently stands if our text is

    Text: We must band together and handle adversity

    and we search for the pattern "and"?

    b. How could we modify the algorithm so that it finds only the complete word *and* rather than the occurrence of the character sequence a, n, and d that is contained within another word, such as *band*?

19. Refer to the pattern-matching algorithm in Figure 2.16. Explain how the algorithm would behave if we accidentally omitted the statement on Line 16 that says,

    Increment k by 1

20. Design an algorithm that is given a positive integer N and determines whether N is a prime number, that is, not evenly divisible by any value other than 1 and itself. The output of your algorithm is either the message 'not prime,' along with a factor of N, or the message 'prime.'

21. Write an algorithm that generates a Caesar cipher—a secret message in which each letter is replaced by the one that is k letters ahead of it in the alphabet, in a circular fashion. For example, if $k = 5$, then the letter a would be replaced by the letter f, and the letter x would be replaced by the letter c. (We'll talk more about the Caesar cipher and other encryption algorithms in Chapter 8.) The input to your algorithm is the text to be encoded, ending with the special symbol "$", and the value k. (You may assume that, except for the special ending character, the text contains only the 26 letters $a \ldots z$.) The output of your algorithm is the encoded text.

22. Design and implement an algorithm that is given as input an integer value $k \geq 0$ and a list of k numbers $N_1, N_2, \ldots, N_k$. Your algorithm should reverse the order of the numbers in the list. That is, if the original list contained:

    $$N_1 = 5, N_2 = 13, N_3 = 8, N_4 = 27, N_5 = 10 \, (k = 5)$$

    then when your algorithm has completed, the values stored in the list will be:

    $$N_1 = 10, N_2 = 27, N_3 = 8, N_4 = 13, N_5 = 5$$

23. Design and implement an algorithm that gets as input a list of k integer values $N_1, N_2, \ldots, N_k$ as well as a special value SUM. Your algorithm must locate a pair of values in the list N that sum to the value SUM. For example, if your list of values is 3, 8, 13, 2, 17, 18, 10, and the value of SUM is 20, then your algorithm would output either the two values (2, 18) or (3, 17). If your algorithm cannot find any pair of values that sum to the value SUM, then it should print out the message 'Sorry, there is no such pair of values.'

24. Instead of reading in an entire list $N_1, N_2, \ldots$ all at once, some algorithms (depending on the task to be done) can read in only one element at a time and process that single element completely before inputting the next one. This can be a useful technique when the list is very big (e.g., billions of elements) and there might not be enough memory in the computer to store it in its entirety. Write an algorithm that reads in a sequence of values $V \geq 0$, one at a time, and computes the average of all the numbers. You should stop the computation when you input a value of $V = -1$. Do *not* include this negative value in your computations; it is not a piece of data but only a marker to identify the end of the list.

25. Write an algorithm to read in a sequence of values $V \geq 0$, one at a time, and determine if the list contains at least one adjacent pair of values that are identical. The end of the entire list is marked by the special value $V = -1$. For example, if you were given the following input:

    14, 3, 7, 7, 9, 1, 804, 22, −1

    the output of your algorithm should be a 'Yes' because there is at least one pair of adjacent numbers that are equal (the 7s). However, given the following input:

    14, 3, 7, 77, 9, 1, 804, 22, −1

    the output of your algorithm should be a 'No' because there are no adjacent pairs that are equal. You may assume in your solution that there are at least two numbers in the list.

26. Modify the algorithm that you developed in Exercise 25 so that if there is a pair of identical adjacent values, your algorithm also outputs, in addition to the phrase 'Yes,' the value of the identical numbers. So, given the first list of numbers shown in Exercise 25, the output of your algorithm would be something like 'Yes, the numbers 7 and 7 are adjacent to each other in the list.'

CHALLENGE WORK

1. Design an algorithm to find the *root* of a function $f(x)$, where the root is defined as a point x such that $f(x) = 0$. Pictorially, the root of a function is the point where the graph of that function crosses the x-axis.

Your algorithm should operate as follows. Initially it will be given three values:

1. A starting point for the search

2. A step size

3. The accuracy desired

Your algorithm should begin at the specified starting point and begin to "walk up" the x-axis in units of step size. After taking a step, it should ask the question "Have I passed a root?" It can determine the answer to this question by seeing whether the sign of the function has changed from the previous point to the current point. (Note that below the axis, the sign of $f(x)$ is negative; above the axis, it is positive. If it crosses the x-axis, it must change its sign.) If the algorithm has not passed a root, it should keep walking up the x-axis until it does. This is expressed pictorially as:

When the algorithm passes a root, it must do two things. First, it changes the sign of step size so that it starts walking in the reverse direction because it is now past the root. Second, it multiplies step size by 0.1, so our steps are 1/10 as big as they were before. We now repeat the operation described previously, walking down the x-axis until we pass the root.

Again, the algorithm changes the sign of step size to reverse direction and reduces it to 1/10 its previous size. As the diagrams show, we are slowly zeroing in on the root—going past it, turning around, going past it, turning around, and so forth. This iterative process stops when the algorithm passes a root and the step size is smaller than the desired accuracy. It has now bracketed the root within an interval that is smaller than the accuracy we want. At this point, it should print out the midpoint of the interval and terminate.

There are many special cases that this algorithm must deal with, but in your solution you may disregard them. Assume that you will always encounter a root in your "travels" along the x-axis. After creating a solution, you might want to look at some of these special cases, such as a function that has no real roots, a starting point that is to the right of all the roots, and two roots so close together that they fall within the same step.

2. One of the most important and widely used classes of algorithms in computer science is *sorting*, the process of putting a list of elements into a predefined order, usually numeric or alphabetic. There are many different sorting

algorithms, and we will look at some of them in Chapter 3. One of the simplest sorting algorithms is called *selection sort*, and it can be implemented using the tools that you have learned in this chapter. It is also one of the easiest to understand as it mimics how we often sort collections of values when we must do it by hand.

Assume that we are given a list named A, containing eight values that we want to sort into ascending order, from smallest to largest:

A:	23	18	66	9	21	90	32	4
Position:	1	2	3	4	5	6	7	8

We first look for the largest value contained in positions 1 to 8 of list A. We can do this using something like the Find Largest algorithm that appears in Figure 2.14. In this case, the largest value is 90, and it appears in position 6. Because this is the largest value in list A, we swap it with the value in position 8 so that it is in its correct place at the back of the list. The list is now partially sorted from position 8 to position 8:

A:	23	18	66	9	21	4	32	90
Position:	1	2	3	4	5	6	7	8

We now search the array for the second largest value. Because we know that the largest value is contained in position 8, we need to search only positions 1 to 7 of list A to find the second largest value. In this case, the second largest value is 66, and it appears in position 3. We now swap the value in position 3 with the value in position 7 to get the second largest value into its correct location. This produces the following:

A:	23	18	32	9	21	4	66	90
Position:	1	2	3	4	5	6	7	8

The list is now partially sorted from position 7 to position 8, with those two locations holding the two largest values. The next search goes from position 1 to position 6 of list A, this time trying to locate the third largest value, and we swap that value with the number in position 6. After repeating this process seven times, the list is completely sorted. (That is because if the last seven items are in their correct place, the item in position 1 must also be in its correct place.)

Using the Find Largest algorithm shown in Figure 2.14 (which may have to be slightly modified) and the primitive pseudocode operations listed in Figure 2.9, implement the selection sort algorithm that we have just described. Assume that *n*, the size of the list, and the *n*-element list A are input to your algorithm. The output of your algorithm should be the sorted list.

3. Most people are familiar with the work of the great mathematicians of ancient Greece and Rome, such as Archimedes, Euclid, Pythagoras, and Plato. However, a great deal of important work in arithmetic, geometry, algebra, number theory, and logic was carried out by scholars working in Egypt, Persia, India, and China. For example, the concept of zero was first developed in India, and positional numbering systems (like our own decimal system) were developed and used in China, India, and the Middle East long before they made their way to Europe. Read about the work of some mathematician (such as Al-Khowarizmi) from these or other places, and write a paper describing his or her contributions to mathematics, logic, and (ultimately) computer science.

ADDITIONAL RESOURCES

CourseMate For additional print and/or online resources relevant to this chapter, visit the Computer Science CourseMate at login.cengagebrain.com.

The Efficiency of Algorithms

3.1 Introduction

Finding algorithms to solve problems of interest is an important part of computer science. Any algorithm that is developed to solve a specific problem has, by definition, certain required characteristics (see the formal definition in Chapter 1, Section 1.3.1), but are some algorithms better than others? That is, are there other desirable but nonessential characteristics of algorithms?

Consider the automobile: There are certain features that are part of the "definition" of a car, such as four wheels and an engine. These are the basics. However, when purchasing a car, we almost certainly take into account other things, such as ease of handling, style, and fuel efficiency. This analogy is not as superficial as it seems—the properties that make better algorithms are in fact very similar.

3.2 Attributes of Algorithms

First and foremost, we expect *correctness* from our algorithms. An algorithm intended to solve a problem must, again by formal definition, give a result and then halt. But this is not enough; we also demand that the result be a correct solution to the problem. You could consider this an inherent property of the definition of an algorithm (like a car being capable of transporting us where we want to go), but it bears emphasizing. An elegant and efficient algorithm that gives wrong results for the problem at hand is worse than useless. It can lead to mistakes that are enormously expensive or even fatal.

Determining that an algorithm gives correct results might not be as straightforward as it seems. For one thing, our algorithm might indeed be providing correct results—but to the wrong problem. This can happen when we design an algorithm without a thorough understanding of the real problem we are trying to solve, and it is one of the most common causes of "incorrect" algorithms. Also, once we understand the problem, the algorithm must provide correct results for all possible input values, not just for those values that are the most likely to occur. Do we know what all those correct results are? Probably not, or we would not be writing an algorithm to solve this problem. But there may be a certain standard against which we can check the result for reasonableness, thus giving us a way to determine when a result is obviously incorrect. In some cases, as noted in Chapter 1, the correct result may be an error message saying that there is no correct answer. There may also be an issue of the accuracy of the result we are willing to accept as correct. If the "real" answer is π, for example, then we can only approximate its decimal value. Is 3.14159 close enough to "correct"? Is 3.1416 close enough? What about 3.14? Computer scientists often summarize these two views of correctness by asking, "Are we solving the right problem? Are we solving the problem right?"

If an algorithm to solve a problem exists and has been determined, after all the considerations of the previous paragraph, to give correct results, what more can we ask? To many mathematicians, this would be the end of the matter. After all, once a solution has been obtained and shown to be correct, it is no longer of interest (except possibly for use in obtaining solutions to other problems). This is where computer science differs significantly from theoretical disciplines such as pure mathematics and begins to take on an "applied" character more closely related to engineering or applied mathematics. The algorithms developed by computer scientists are not merely of academic interest. They are also intended to be *used*.

Suppose, for example, that a road to the top of a mountain is to be built. An algorithmic solution exists that gives a correct answer for this problem in the sense that a road is produced: Just build the road straight up the mountain. Problem solved. But the highway engineer knows that the road must be usable by real traffic and that this constraint limits the grade of the road. The existence and correctness of the algorithm is not enough; there are practical considerations as well.

The practical considerations for computer science arise because the algorithms developed are executed in the form of computer programs running on real computers to solve problems of interest to real people. Let's consider the "people aspect" first. A computer program is seldom written to be used only once to solve a single instance of a problem. It is written to solve many instances of that problem with many different input values, just as the sequential search algorithm of Chapter 2 would be used many times with different lists of names and different target *NAME* values. Furthermore, the problem itself does not usually "stand still." If the program is successful, people will want to use it for slightly different versions of the problem, which means they will want the program slightly enhanced to do more things. Therefore, after a program is written, it needs to be maintained, both to fix any errors that are uncovered through repeated usage with different input values, and to extend the program to meet new requirements. A great deal of time and money are devoted to *program maintenance*. The person who has to modify a program, either to correct errors or to expand its functionality, often is not the person who wrote the original program. To make program maintenance as easy as possible, the algorithm the program uses should be easy to understand. *Ease of understanding*, clarity, "ease of handling"—whatever you want to call it—is a highly desirable characteristic of an algorithm.

On the other hand, there is a certain satisfaction in having an "elegant" solution to a problem. *Elegance* is the algorithmic equivalent of style. The classic example, in mathematical folklore, is the story of the German mathematician Karl Frederick Gauss (1777–1855) who was asked as a schoolchild to add up the numbers from 1 to 100. The straightforward algorithm of adding $1 + 2 + 3 + 4 + \ldots + 100$ by adding one number at a time can be expressed in pseudocode as follows:

1. Set the value of *sum* to 0

2. Set the value of *x* to 1

3. While *x* is less than or equal to 100, do Steps 4 and 5

4.   Add *x* to sum

5.   Add 1 to the value of *x*

6. Print the value of *sum*

7. Stop

This algorithm can be executed to find that the sum has the value 5,050. It is fairly easy to read this pseudocode and understand how the algorithm works. It is also fairly clear that if we want to change this algorithm to one that adds the numbers from 1 to 1,000, we only have to change the loop condition to

3. While *x* is less than or equal to 1,000, do Steps 4 and 5

However, Gauss noticed that the numbers from 1 to 100 could be grouped into 50 pairs of the form

1 + 100 = 101
2 + 99 = 101

.
.
.

50 + 51 = 101

so that the sum equals 50 × 101 = 5,050. This is certainly an elegant and clever solution, but is it easy to understand? If a computer program just said to multiply

$$\left(\frac{100}{2}\right) 101$$

with no further explanation, we might guess how to modify the program to add up the first 1,000 numbers, but would we really grasp what was happening enough to be sure the modification would work? (The Practice Problems at the end of this section discuss this.) Sometimes elegance and ease of understanding work at cross-purposes; the more elegant the solution, the more difficult it may be to understand. Do we win or lose if we have to trade ease of understanding for elegance? Of course, if an algorithm has both characteristics—ease of understanding and elegance—that's a plus.

Now let's consider the real computers on which programs run. Although these computers can execute instructions very rapidly and have some memory in which to store information, time and space are not unlimited resources. The computer scientist must be conscious of the resources consumed by a given algorithm, and if there is a choice between two (correct) algorithms that perform the same task, the one that uses fewer resources is preferable. Efficiency is the term used to describe an algorithm's careful use of resources. In addition to *correctness*, *ease of understanding*, and *elegance*, *efficiency* is an extremely desirable attribute of an algorithm.

Because of the rapid advances in computer technology, today's computers have much more memory capacity and execute instructions much more rapidly than computers of just a few years ago. Efficiency in algorithms might seem to be a moot point; we can just wait for the next generation of technology and it won't matter how much time or space is required. There is some truth to this, but as computer memory capacity and processing speed increase, people find more complex problems to be solved, so the boundaries of the computer's resources continue to be pushed. Furthermore, we will see in this chapter that there are algorithms that consume so many resources that they will never be practical, no matter what advances in computer technology occur.

How shall we measure the time and space consumed by an algorithm to determine whether it is efficient? Space efficiency can be judged by the amount of information the algorithm must store in the computer's memory to do its job, in addition to the initial data on which the algorithm is operating. If it uses only a few extra memory locations while processing the input data, the algorithm is relatively space efficient. If the algorithm requires almost as much additional storage as the input data itself takes up, or even more, then it is relatively space inefficient.

How can we measure the time efficiency of an algorithm? Consider the sequential search algorithm shown in Figure 2.13, which looks up a name in a telephone directory where the names are not arranged in alphabetical order. How about running the algorithm on a real computer and timing it to see how many seconds (or maybe what small fraction of a second) it takes to find a name or announce that the name is not present? The difficulty with this approach is that there are three factors involved, each of which can affect the answer to such a degree as to make whatever number of seconds we come up with rather meaningless.

1. On what computer will we run the algorithm? Shall we use a modest laptop or a supercomputer capable of doing many trillions of calculations per second?

2. What telephone book (list of names) will we use: New York City or Yeehaw Junction, Florida?

3. What name will we try to find? What if we pick a name that happens to be first in the list? What if it happens to be last in the list?

Simply timing the running of an algorithm is more likely to reflect machine speed or variations in input data than the efficiency (or lack thereof) of the algorithm itself.

This is not to say that you can't obtain meaningful information by timing an algorithm. For example, using the same input data (searching for Karlenski, say, in the New York City phone book) and timing the algorithm on different machines gives a comparison of machine speeds because the task is identical. Using the same machine and the same list of names, but searching for different names, gives an indication of how the choice of *NAME* affects the algorithm's running time on that particular machine. This type of comparative timing is called benchmarking. Benchmarks are useful for rating one machine against another and for rating how sensitive a particular algorithm is with respect to variations in input on one particular machine.

However, what we mean by an algorithm's time efficiency is an indication of the amount of "work" required by the algorithm itself. It is a measure of the inherent efficiency of the method, independent of the speed of the machine on which it executes or the specific input data being processed. Is the amount of work an algorithm does the same as the number of instructions it executes? Not all instructions do the same things, so perhaps they should not all be "counted" equally. Some instructions are carrying out work that is fundamental to the way the algorithm operates, whereas other instructions are carrying out peripheral tasks that must be done in support of the fundamental work. To measure time efficiency, we identify the fundamental unit (or units) of work of an algorithm and count how many times the work unit is executed. Later in this chapter, we will see why we can ignore peripheral tasks.

Practice Problems

1. Use Gauss's approach to find a formula for the sum of the numbers from 1 to n,

   $1 + 2 + 3 + \ldots + n$

   where n is an even number. Your formula will be an expression involving n.

2. Test your formula from Practice Problem 1 for the following sums:

   a. $1 + 2$

   b. $1 + 2 + \ldots + 6$

   c. $1 + 2 + \ldots + 10$

   d. $1 + 2 + \ldots + 100$

   e. $1 + 2 + \ldots + 1000$

3. Now see if the same formula from Practice Problem 1 works when n is odd; try it on the following sums:

   a. $1 + 2 + 3$

   b. $1 + 2 + \ldots + 5$

   c. $1 + 2 + \ldots + 9$

3.3 Measuring Efficiency

The study of the efficiency of algorithms is called the **analysis of algorithms**, and it is an important part of computer science. As a first example of the analysis of an algorithm, we'll look at the sequential search algorithm.

3.3.1 Sequential Search

The pseudocode description of the **sequential search algorithm** from Chapter 2 appears in Figure 3.1, where we have assumed that the list contains n entries instead of 10,000 entries.

The central unit of work is the comparison of the *NAME* being searched for against a name in the list. The essence of the algorithm is the repetition of this task against successive names in the list until *NAME* is found or the list is exhausted. The comparison takes place at Step 4, within the loop body composed of Steps 4 through 7. Peripheral tasks include setting the initial value of the index i and the initial value of *Found*, writing the output, adjusting *Found*, and moving the index forward in the list of names. Why are these considered peripheral tasks?

FIGURE 3.1

1. Get values for *NAME*, *n*, $N_1, \ldots, N_n$ and $T_1, \ldots, T_n$
2. Set the value of *i* to 1 and set the value of *Found* to NO
3. While (*Found* = NO) and (*i* ≤ *n*) do Steps 4 through 7
4.   If *NAME* is equal to the *i*th name on the list, N_i, then
5.   Print the telephone number of that person, T_i
6.   Set the value of *Found* to YES
       Else (*NAME* is not equal to N_i)
7.   Add 1 to the value of *i*
8. If (*Found* = NO) then
9.   Print the message 'Sorry, this name is not in the directory'
10. Stop

Sequential search algorithm

Setting the initial value of the index and the initial value of *Found* requires executing a single instruction, done at Step 2. Writing output requires executing a single instruction, either at Step 5 if *NAME* is in the list or at Step 9 if *NAME* is not in the list. Note that instruction 5, although it is part of the loop, writes output at most once (if *NAME* equals N_i). Similarly, setting *Found* to YES occurs at most once (if *NAME* equals N_i) at Step 6. We can ignore the small contribution of these single-instruction executions to the total work done by the algorithm.

Moving the index forward is done once for each comparison, at Step 7. We can get a good idea of the total amount of work the algorithm does by simply counting the number of comparisons and then multiplying by some constant factor to account for the index-moving task. The constant factor could be 2 because we do one index move for each comparison, so we would double the work. It could be less because it is less work to add 1 to *i* than it is to compare *NAME* letter by letter against N_i. As we will see later, the precise value of this constant factor is not very important.

So again, the basic unit of work in this algorithm is the comparison of *NAME* against a list element. One comparison is done at each pass through the loop in Steps 4 through 7, so we must ask how many times the loop is executed. Of course, this depends on when, or if, we find *NAME* in the list.

The minimum amount of work is done if *NAME* is the very first name in the list. This requires only one comparison because *NAME* has then been found and the algorithm exits the loop after only one pass. This is the *best case*, requiring the least work. The *worst case*, requiring the maximum amount of work, occurs if *NAME* is the very last name in the list or is absent. In either of these situations, *NAME* must be compared against all *n* names in the list before the loop terminates because *FOUND* gets set to YES (if *NAME* is the last name in the list) or because the value of the index *i* exceeds *n* (if *NAME* is not in the list).

When *NAME* occurs somewhere in the middle of the list, it requires somewhere between 1 (the best case) and *n* (the worst case) comparisons. If we were to run the sequential search algorithm many times with random *NAME*s occurring at various places in the list and count the number of comparisons done each time, we would find that the average number of comparisons done is about $n/2$. (The exact average is actually slightly higher than $n/2$; see Exercise 5 at the end of the chapter.) It is not hard to explain why an average of approximately $n/2$ comparisons are done (or the loop is executed approximately $n/2$ times) when *NAME* is in the list. If *NAME* occurs halfway down the list, then roughly $n/2$ comparisons are required; random *NAME*s in the list occur before the halfway point about half the time and after the halfway point about half the time, and these cases of less work and more work balance out.

This means that the average number of comparisons needed to find a *NAME* that occurs in a 10-element list is about 5, in a 100-element list about 50, and in a 1,000-element list about 500. On small values of n—say, a few hundred or a few thousand names—the values of $n/2$ (the average case) or n (the worst case) are small enough that a computer could execute the algorithm quickly and get the desired answer in a fraction of a second. However, computers are generally used to solve not tiny problems but very large ones. Therefore, we are usually interested in the behavior of an algorithm as the size of a problem (n) gets very, very large. For example, in the New York City telephone directory, n may be as large as 20,000,000. If the sequential search algorithm were executed on a computer that could do 50,000 comparisons per second, it would require on the average about

$$\frac{20,000,000}{2} \text{ comparisons} \times \frac{1}{50,000} \text{ seconds/comparison} = 200 \text{ seconds}$$

or 3-1/3 minutes just to do the comparisons necessary to locate a specific name. Including the constant factor for advancing the index, the actual time needed would be even greater. It would require almost 7 minutes just to do the comparisons required to determine that a name was not in the directory! Sequential search is not sufficiently time efficient for large values of n to be useful as a telephone directory lookup algorithm.

Information about the number of comparisons required to perform the sequential search algorithm on a list of n names is summarized in Figure 3.2. Note that the values for both the worst case and the average case depend on n, the number of names in the list. The bigger the list, the more work must be done to search it. Few algorithms do the same amount of work on large inputs as on small inputs, simply because most algorithms process the input data, and more data to process means more work. The work an algorithm does can usually be expressed in terms of a formula that depends on the size of the problem input. In the case of searching a list of names, the input size is the length of the list.

FIGURE 3.2

Best Case	Worst Case	Average Case
1	n	$n/2$

Number of comparisons to find NAME in a list of n names using sequential search

Let's say a word about the space efficiency of sequential search. The algorithm stores the list of names and the target *NAME* as part of the input. The only additional memory required is storage for the index value i and the *Found* indicator. Two single additional memory locations are insignificant compared with the size of the list of names, just as executing a single instruction to initialize the value of i and *Found* is insignificant beside the repetitive comparison task. Therefore, sequential search uses essentially no more memory storage than the original input requires, so it is very space efficient.

3.3.2 Order of Magnitude—Order *n*

When we analyzed the time efficiency of the sequential search algorithm, we glossed over the contribution of the constant factor for the peripheral work. To see why this constant factor doesn't particularly matter, we need to understand a concept called *order of magnitude*.

The worst-case behavior of the sequential search algorithm on a list of n names requires n comparisons, and if c is a constant factor representing the peripheral work, it requires cn total work. Suppose that c has the value 2. Then the values of n and $2n$ are

n	$2n$
1	2
2	4
3	6

and so on

These values are shown in Figure 3.3, which illustrates how the value of $2n$, which is the total work, changes as n changes. We can add to this graph to

FIGURE 3.3

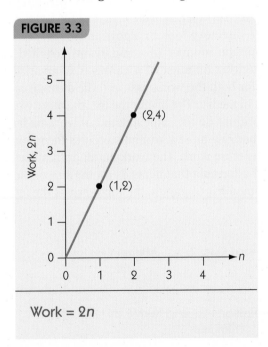

Work = $2n$

show how the value of *cn* changes as *n* changes, where $c = 1$ or $c = 1/2$ as well as $c = 2$ (see Figure 3.4; these values of *c* are completely arbitrary). Figure 3.5 presents a different view of the growth rate of *cn* as *n* changes for these three values of *c*.

Both Figure 3.4 and Figure 3.5 show that the amount of work *cn* increases as *n* increases, but at different rates. The work grows at the same

FIGURE 3.4

Work = *cn* for various values of *c*

FIGURE 3.5

Growth of work = *cn* for various values of *c*

Flipping Pancakes

(a)

(b)

(c)

A problem posed in the *American Mathematical Monthly* in 1975 by Jacob Goodman concerned a waiter in a café where the cook produced a stack of pancakes of varying sizes. The waiter, on the way to delivering the stack to the customer, attempted to arrange the pancakes in order by size, with the largest on the bottom. The only action available was to stick a spatula into the stack at some point and flip the entire stack above that point. The question is: What is the maximum number of flips ever needed for any stack of n pancakes? This number, P_n, is known as the *nth pancake number*.

Here's a fairly simple algorithm to arrange the pancakes. Put the spatula under the largest pancake, as shown in (a) in the figure, and flip. This puts the largest pancake on top [(b) in the figure]. Put the spatula at the bottom of the unordered section (in this case at the bottom) and flip. This puts the largest pancake on the bottom [(c) in the figure], where it belongs. Repeat with the rest of the pancakes. Each pancake therefore requires two flips, which would give a total of $2n$ flips required. But the last two pancakes require at most one flip; if they are already in order, no flips are needed, and if they are out of order, only one flip is needed. So this algorithm requires at most $2(n-2) + 1 = 2n - 3$ flips in the worst case, which means that $P_n \leq 2n - 3$. Are there other algorithms that require fewer flips in the worst case?

A faculty member at Harvard University posed this question to his class; several days later, a sophomore from the class came to his office with a better algorithm. This algorithm, which requires at most $(5n + 5) / 3$ flips, was published in the journal *Discrete Mathematics* in 1979. The authors were William Gates (the student) and Christos Papadimitriou.

Yes, *that* William Gates!

rate as n when $c = 1$, at twice the rate of n when $c = 2$, and at half the rate of n when $c = 1/2$. However, Figure 3.4 also shows that all of these graphs follow the same basic straight-line shape of n. Anything that varies as a constant times n (and whose graph follows the basic shape of n) is said to be of **order of magnitude** n, written $\Theta(n)$. We will classify algorithms according to the order of magnitude of their time efficiency. Sequential search is therefore an $\Theta(n)$ algorithm (an order-n algorithm) in both the worst case and the average case.

Practice Problem

Using the information in Figure 3.2, fill in the following table for the number of comparisons required in the sequential search algorithm.

n	Best Case	Worst Case	Average Case
10			
50			
100			
1,000			
10,000			
100,000			

3.3.3 Selection Sort

The sequential search algorithm solves a very common problem: searching a list of items (such as the names in a telephone directory) for a particular item. Another very common problem is that of sorting a list of items into order—either alphabetical or numerical order. The registrar at your institution sorts students in a class by name, a mail-order business sorts its customer list by name, and the IRS sorts its tax records by Social Security number. In this section, we'll examine a sorting algorithm and analyze its efficiency.

Suppose we have a list of numbers to sort into ascending order—for example, 5, 7, 2, 8, 3. The result of sorting this list is the new list 2, 3, 5, 7, 8. The selection sort algorithm performs this task. The selection sort "grows" a sorted subsection of the list from the back to the front. We can look at "snapshots" of the progress of the algorithm on our sample list, using a vertical line as the marker between the unsorted section at the front of the list and the sorted section at the back of the list in each case. At first the sorted subsection is empty; that is, the entire list is unsorted. This is how the list looks when the algorithm begins.

5, 7, 2, 8, 3 |

Unsorted subsection (entire list)   Sorted subsection (empty)

Later, the sorted subsection of the list has grown from the back so that some of the list members are in the right place.

5, 3, 2, | 7, 8

Unsorted subsection   Sorted subsection

FIGURE 3.6

1. Get values for *n* and the *n* list items
2. Set the marker for the unsorted section at the end of the list
3. While the unsorted section of the list is not empty, do Steps 4 through 6
4.   Select the largest number in the unsorted section of the list
5.   Exchange this number with the last number in the unsorted section of the list
6.   Move the marker for the unsorted section left one position
7. Stop

Selection sort algorithm

Finally, the sorted subsection of the list contains the entire list; there are no unsorted numbers, and the algorithm stops.

$$| \ 2, \ 3, \ 5, \ 7, \ 8$$

Unsorted subsection (empty)   *Sorted subsection (entire list)*

At any point, then, there is both a sorted and an unsorted section of the list. A pseudocode version of the algorithm is shown in Figure 3.6.

Before we illustrate this algorithm at work, take a look at Step 4, which finds the largest number in some list of numbers. We developed an algorithm for this task in Chapter 2 (Figure 2.14). A detailed version of the selection sort algorithm would replace Step 4 with the instructions from this existing algorithm. New algorithms can be built up from "parts" consisting of previous algorithms, just as a recipe for pumpkin pie might begin with the instruction, "Prepare crust for a one-crust pie." The recipe for pie crust is a previous algorithm that is now being used as one of the steps in the pumpkin pie algorithm.

Let's follow the selection sort algorithm. Initially, the unsorted section is the entire list, so Step 2 sets the marker at the end of the list.

5, 7, 2, 8, 3 |

Step 4 says to select the largest number in the unsorted section—that is, in the entire list. This number is 8. Step 5 says to exchange 8 with the last number in the unsorted section (the whole list). To accomplish this exchange, the algorithm must determine not only that 8 is the largest value but also the location in the list where 8 occurs. The Find Largest algorithm from Chapter 2 provides both these pieces of information. The exchange to be done is

5, 7, 2, 8, 3 |

After this exchange and after the marker is moved left as instructed in Step 6, the list looks like

5, 7, 2, 3 | 8

The number 8 is now in its correct position at the end of the list. It becomes the sorted section of the list, and the first four numbers are the unsorted section.

The unsorted section is not empty, so the algorithm repeats Step 4 (find the largest number in the unsorted section); it is 7. Step 5 exchanges 7 with the last number in the unsorted section, which is 3.

5, 7, 2, 3 | 8

After the marker is moved, the result is

5, 3, 2 | 7, 8

The sorted section is now 7, 8 and the unsorted section is 5, 3, 2.

Repeating the loop of Steps 4 through 6 again, the algorithm determines that the largest number in the unsorted section is 5, and exchanges it with 2, the last number in the unsorted section.

5, 3, 2 | 7, 8

After the marker is moved, we get

2, 3 | 5, 7, 8

Now the unsorted section (as far as the algorithm knows) is 2, 3. The largest number here is 3. Exchanging 3 with the last number of the unsorted section (that is, with itself) produces no change in the list ordering. The marker is moved, giving

2 | 3, 5, 7, 8

When the only part of the list that is unsorted is the single number 2, there is also no change in the list ordering produced by carrying out the exchange. The marker is moved, giving

| 2, 3, 5, 7, 8

The unsorted section of the list is empty, and the algorithm terminates.

To analyze the amount of work the selection sort algorithm does, we must first decide on the unit of work to count. When we analyzed sequential search, the unit of work that we measured was the comparison between the name being searched for and the names in the list. At first glance, there seem to be no comparisons of any kind going on in the selection sort. Remember, however, that there is a subtask within the selection sort: the task of finding the largest number in a list. The algorithm from Chapter 2 for finding the largest value in a list begins by taking the first number in the list as the largest so far. The largest-so-far value is compared against successive numbers in the list; if a larger value is found, it becomes the largest so far.

When the selection sort algorithm begins, the largest-so-far value, initially the first number, must be compared with all the other numbers in the list. If there are n numbers in the list, $n - 1$ comparisons must be done. The next time through the loop, the last number is already in its proper place, so it is never again involved in a comparison. The largest-so-far value, again initially the first number, must be compared with all the other numbers in the unsorted part of the list, which will require $n - 2$ comparisons.

The number of comparisons keeps decreasing as the length of the unsorted section of the list gets smaller, until finally only one comparison is needed. The total number of comparisons is

$$(n - 1) + (n - 2) + (n - 3) + \ldots + 3 + 2 + 1$$

Reviewing our sample problem, we can see that the following comparisons are done:

- To put 8 in place in the list 5, 7, 2, 8, 3 |

  Compare 5 (largest so far) to 7

     7 becomes largest so far

  Compare 7 (largest so far) to 2

  Compare 7 (largest so far) to 8

     8 becomes largest so far

  Compare 8 to 3

  8 is the largest

  Total number of comparisons: 4 (which is 5 − 1)

- To put 7 in place in the list 5, 7, 2, 3 | 8

  Compare 5 (largest so far) to 7

     7 becomes largest so far

  Compare 7 to 2

  Compare 7 to 3

  7 is the largest

  Total number of comparisons: 3 (which is 5 − 2)

- To put 5 in place in the list 5, 3, 2 | 7, 8

  Compare 5 (largest so far) to 3

  Compare 5 to 2

  5 is the largest

  Total number of comparisons: 2 (which is 5 − 3)

- To put 3 in place in the list 2, 3 | 5, 7, 8

  Compare 2 (largest so far) to 3

  3 is the largest

  Total number of comparisons: 1 (which is 5 − 4)

To put 2 in place requires no comparisons; there is only one number in the unsorted section of the list, so it is of course the largest number. It gets exchanged with itself, which produces no effect. The total number of comparisons is $4 + 3 + 2 + 1 = 10$.

The sum

$$(n - 1) + (n - 2) + (n - 3) + \ldots + 3 + 2 + 1$$

turns out to be equal to

$$\left(\frac{n-1}{2}\right)n = \frac{1}{2}n^2 - \frac{1}{2}n$$

(Recall from earlier in this chapter how Gauss computed a similar sum.) For our example with five numbers, this formula says that the total number of comparisons is (using the first version of the formula):

$$\left(\frac{5-1}{2}\right)5 = \left(\frac{4}{2}\right)5 = (2)5 = 10$$

which is the number of comparisons we had counted.

Figure 3.7 uses this same formula

$$\frac{1}{2}n^2 - \frac{1}{2}n$$

to compute the comparisons required for larger values of n. Remember that n is the size of the list we are sorting. If the list becomes 10 times longer, the work increases by much more than a factor of 10; it increases by a factor closer to 100, which is 10^2.

The selection sort algorithm not only does comparisons, it also does exchanges. Even if the largest number in the unsorted section of the list is already at the end of the unsorted section, the algorithm exchanges this number with itself. Therefore, the algorithm does n exchanges, one for each position in the list to put the correct value in that position. With every exchange, the marker gets moved. However, the work contributed by exchanges and marker moving is so much less than the amount contributed by comparisons that it can be ignored.

We haven't talked here about a best case, a worst case, or an average case for the selection sort. This algorithm does the same amount of work no matter how the numbers are initially arranged. It has no way to recognize, for example, that the list might already be sorted at the outset.

A word about the space efficiency of the selection sort: The original list occupies n memory locations, and this is the major space requirement. Some storage is needed for the marker between the unsorted and sorted sections and for keeping track of the largest-so-far value and its location in the list, used in Step 4. Surprisingly, the process of exchanging two values at Step 5

FIGURE 3.7

Length n of List to Sort	n^2	Number of Comparisons Required
10	100	45
100	10,000	4,950
1,000	1,000,000	499,500

Comparisons required by selection sort

also requires an extra storage location. Here's why. If the two numbers to be exchanged are at position X and position Y in the list, we might think the following two steps will exchange these values:

1. Copy the current value at position Y into position X
2. Copy the current value at position X into position Y

The problem is that after Step 1, the value at position X is the same as that at position Y. Step 2 does not put the original value of X into position Y. In fact, we don't even have the original value of position X anymore. In Figure 3.8(a), we see the original X and Y values. At Figure 3.8(b), after execution of Step 1, the current value of position Y has been copied into position X, writing over what was there originally. At Figure 3.8(c), after execution of Step 2, the current value at position X (which is the original Y value) has been copied into position Y, but the picture looks the same as Figure 3.8(b).

Here's the correct algorithm, which makes use of one extra temporary storage location that we'll call T.

1. Copy the current value at position X into location T
2. Copy the current value at position Y into position X
3. Copy the current value at location T into position Y

Figure 3.9 illustrates that this algorithm does the job. In Figure 3.9(a), the temporary location contains an unknown value. After execution of Step 1 (Figure 3.9b), it holds the current value of X. When Y's current value is put into X at Step 2 (Figure 3.9c), T still holds the original X value. After Step 3 (Figure 3.9d), the current value of T goes into position Y, and the original values of X and Y have been exchanged. (Step 5 of the selection sort algorithm is thus performed by another algorithm, just as Step 4 is.)

All in all, the extra storage required for the selection sort, over and above that required to store the original list, is slight. Selection sort is space efficient.

FIGURE 3.8

X [3]   Y [5]

(a)

X [5]   Y [5]

(b)

X [5]   Y [5]

(c)

An attempt to exchange the values at X and Y

Practice Problems

1. For each of the following lists, perform a selection sort and show the list after each exchange that has an effect on the list ordering:

   a. 4, 8, 2, 6

   b. 12, 3, 6, 8, 2, 5, 7

   c. D, B, G, F, A, C, E, H

2. How many comparisons are required to sort each of the three lists shown in Practice Problem 1? How many exchanges?

FIGURE 3.9

Exchanging the values at X and Y

3.3.4 Order of Magnitude—Order n^2

We saw that the number of comparisons done by the selection sort algorithm does not grow at the same rate as the problem size n; it grows at approximately the *square* of that rate. An algorithm that does cn^2 work for any constant c is **order of magnitude** n^2, or $\Theta(n^2)$. Figure 3.10 shows how cn^2 changes as n changes, where $c = 1, 2,$ and $1/2$. The work grows at the same rate as n^2 when $c = 1$, at twice that rate when $c = 2$, and at half that rate when $c = 1/2$. But all three graphs in Figure 3.10 follow the basic shape of n^2, which is different from all of the straight-line graphs that are of $\Theta(n)$. Thus, we have come up with two different "shape classifications": one including all graphs that are $\Theta(n)$ and the other including all graphs that are $\Theta(n^2)$.

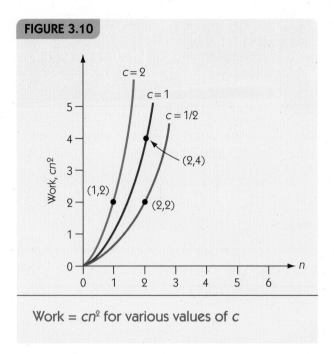

FIGURE 3.10

Work = cn^2 for various values of c

If it is not important to distinguish among the various graphs that make up a given order of magnitude, why is it important to distinguish between the two different orders of magnitude n and n^2? We can find the answer by comparing the two basic shapes n and n^2, as is done in Figure 3.11.

Figure 3.11 illustrates that n^2 grows at a much faster rate than n. The two curves cross at the point (1,1), and for any value of n larger than 1, n^2 has

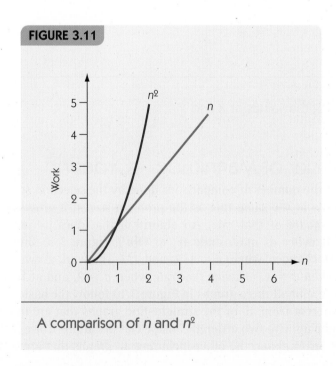

FIGURE 3.11

A comparison of n and n^2

FIGURE 3.12

For large enough n, $0.25n^2$ has larger values than $10n$

a value increasingly greater than n. Furthermore, anything that is order of magnitude n^2 eventually has larger values than anything that is of order n, no matter what the constant factors are. For example, Figure 3.12 shows that if we choose a graph that is $\Theta(n^2)$ but has a small constant factor (to keep the values low), say $0.25n^2$, and a graph that is $\Theta(n)$ but has a larger constant factor (to pump the values up), say $10n$, it is still true that the $\Theta(n^2)$ graph eventually has larger values. (Note that the vertical scale and the horizontal scale are different.)

Selection sort is an $\Theta(n^2)$ algorithm (in all cases) and sequential search is an $\Theta(n)$ algorithm (in the worst case), so these two algorithms are different orders of magnitude. Because these algorithms solve two different problems, this is somewhat like comparing apples and oranges—what does it mean? But suppose we have two different algorithms that solve the same problem and count the same units of work, but have different orders of magnitude. Suppose that algorithm A does $0.0001n^2$ units of work to solve a problem with input size n and that algorithm B does $100n$ of the same units of work to solve the same problem. Here algorithm B's factor of 100 is *1 million times larger* than algorithm A's factor of 0.0001. Nonetheless, when the problem gets large enough, the inherent inefficiency of algorithm A causes it to do more work than algorithm B. Figure 3.13 shows that the "crossover" point occurs at a value of 1,000,000 for n. At this point, the two algorithms do the same amount of work and therefore take the same amount of time to run. For larger values of n, the order-n^2 algorithm A runs increasingly

FIGURE 3.13

| | Number of Work Units Required | |
| | Algorithm A | Algorithm B |
n	$0.0001n^2$	$100n$
1,000	100	100,000
10,000	10,000	1,000,000
100,000	1,000,000	10,000,000
1,000,000	100,000,000	100,000,000
10,000,000	10,000,000,000	1,000,000,000

A comparison of two extreme $\Theta(n^2)$ and $\Theta(n)$ algorithms

slower than the order-n algorithm B. (Input sizes of 1,000,000 are not that uncommon—think of the New York City telephone list.)

As we have seen, if an $\Theta(n^2)$ algorithm and an $\Theta(n)$ algorithm exist for the same task, then for large enough n, the $\Theta(n^2)$ algorithm does more work and takes longer to execute, regardless of the constant factors for peripheral work. *This is the rationale for ignoring constant factors and concentrating on the basic order of magnitude of algorithms.*

As an analogy, the two shape classifications $\Theta(n^2)$ and $\Theta(n)$ may be thought of as two different classes of transportation, the "walking" class and the "driving" class, respectively. The walking class is fundamentally more time consuming than the driving class. Walking can include jogging, running, and leisurely strolling (which correspond to different values for c), but compared with any form of driving, these all proceed at roughly the same speed. The driving class can include driving a MINI Cooper and driving a Ferrari (which correspond to different values for c), but compared with any form of walking, these proceed at roughly the same speed. In other words, varying c can make modest changes within a class, but changing to a different class is a quantum leap.

Given two algorithms for the same task, we should usually choose the algorithm of the lesser order of magnitude because for large enough n, it always "wins out." It is for large values of n that we need to be concerned about the time resources being used and, as we noted earlier, it is often for large values of n that we are seeking a computerized solution in the first place.

Note, however, that for smaller values of n, the size of the constant factor is significant. In Figure 3.12, the $10n$ line stayed above the $0.25n^2$ curve up to the crossover point of $n = 40$ because it had a large constant factor relative to the factor for n^2. Varying the factors changes the crossover point. If $10n$ and $0.25n^2$ represented the work of two different algorithms for the same task, and if we are sure that the size of the input is never going to

The Tortoise and the Hare

One way to compare performance among different makes of automobiles is to give the number of seconds it takes each car to go from 0 to 60 miles per hour. One way to compare performance among different makes of computers is to give the number of arithmetic operations, such as additions or subtractions of real numbers, that each one can do in 1 second. These operations are called *floating-point operations*, and computers are often compared in terms of the number of **flops** (floating-point operations per second) they can crank out. This is only one measure of a computer's performance, primarily related to processing power for "number-crunching" applications. Whereas this is the measure we use here, other measures include the ability of the machine to handle multimedia, graphics, or multitasking. (For example, how well can the machine run a virus checker in the background while you are playing a video game?)

The fastest desktop computer as of 2011 uses a six-core processor, meaning there are six individual processors bundled into a single chip package. The chip is the Intel Core i7 980 XE, which, before its release, was known within Intel by the codename Gulftown. This chip contains 1.17 billion transistors. If all six cores can be efficiently put to use, the top performance is about 100 *gigaflops* (100 billion floating-point operations per second). In June, 2011, the 'K' system at the RIKEN Advanced Institute for Computational Science in Japan was declared the world's top-speed supercomputer. Built by Fujitsu, this machine is a parallel processor system containing 548,352 cores bundled in 68,544 eight-core chip packages housed in 672 separate cabinets. It can perform at the rate of about 8.2 *petaflops* (which is 8.2 quadrillion floating-point operations per second). The supercomputer is almost 82,000 times faster than the desktop computer. The stage is set for the race between the tortoise and the hare.

Not fair, you say? We'll see. Let's suppose the desktop machine is assigned to run an $\Theta(n)$ algorithm, whereas the supercomputer gets an $\Theta(n^2)$ algorithm for the same task. The work units are floating-point operations, and for simplicity, we'll take the constant factor to be 1 in each case. Here are the timing results:

n	Desktop	Supercomputer
1,000	0.00000001 sec	0.00000000012 sec
100,000	0.000001 sec	0.00000121951 sec
10,000,000	0.0001 sec	0.01219512195 sec
1,000,000,000	0.01 sec	121.95 sec = 2.03 min
100,000,000,000	1 sec	1,219,512 sec = 14 days
10,000,000,000,000	100 sec = 1.67 min	12,195,121,951 sec = 387 years

(Continued)

Out of the gate—that is, for relatively small values of n such as 1,000—the supercomputer has the advantage and takes less time. When n reaches 100,000, however, the supercomputer is falling a tiny bit behind, taking about 0.00000122 sec as opposed to the desktop's 0.000001 sec. And for the largest value of n, the desktop has left the supercomputer in the dust. The difference in order of magnitude between the algorithms was enough to slow down the mighty supercomputer and let the desktop pull ahead, chugging along doing its more efficient $\Theta(n)$ algorithm. Where would one need to perform 10,000,000,000,000 operations? Complex problems involving weather simulations, biomedical research, and economic modeling might utilize such number-crunching applications.

The point of this little tale is not to say that supercomputers will be readily replaced by desktop computers! It is to demonstrate that the order of magnitude of the algorithm being executed can play a more important role than the raw speed of the computer.

Future Speculation: Desktops will give ever faster performance. In early 2011, Intel began producing a new chip, code-named Sandy Bridge, that is expected to produce 32 gigaflops per core, more than three times the per-core performance of Gulftown. And supercomputers will also improve their performance. IBM is planning to build a 750,000 core supercomputer in 2012 to support the research of the Argonne National Laboratory near Chicago, Illinois. IBM expects this system will run at 10 *petaflops* (that's 10 million gigaflops). It is estimated that if every man, woman, and child in the United States performed one calculation each second, it would take them almost a year to do as many calculations as this machine will do in one second.

exceed 40, then the $0.25n^2$ algorithm is preferable in terms of time resources used. (To continue the transportation analogy, for traveling short distances—say, to the end of the driveway—walking is faster than driving because of the overhead of getting the car started, and so on. But for longer distances, driving is faster.)

However, making assumptions about the size of the input on which an algorithm will run can be dangerous. A program that runs quickly on small input size may at some point be selected (perhaps because it seems efficient) to solve instances of the problem with large input size, at which point the efficiency may go down the drain! Sequential search may serve for directory assistance in Yeehaw Junction, Florida, but it won't translate satisfactorily to New York City. Part of the job of program documentation is to make clear any assumptions or restrictions about the input size the program was designed to handle.

Comparing algorithm efficiency only makes sense if there is a choice of algorithms for the task at hand. Are there any tasks for which a choice of algorithms exists? Yes; because sorting a list is such a common task, a lot of research has gone into finding good sorting algorithms. Selection sort is

Laboratory Experience 4

This Laboratory Experience allows you to step through animations of various sorting algorithms to understand how they work. The sorting algorithms available in the laboratory software include selection sort and bubble sort—which are described in this text—as well as insertion sort and quicksort, which are described in the laboratory manual. You'll be able to see values being switched around according to the various algorithms, and see how lists eventually settle into sorted order.

You'll also do some experiments to measure the amount of work the various algorithms perform.

one sorting algorithm, but there are many others, including the bubble sort, described in Exercises 9–12 at the end of this chapter. You might wonder why people don't simply use the one "best" sorting algorithm. It's not that simple. Some algorithms (unlike the selection sort) are sensitive to what the original input looks like. One algorithm might work well if the input is already close to being sorted, whereas another algorithm might work better if the input is random. An algorithm like selection sort has the advantage of being relatively easy to understand. If the size of the list, n, is fairly small, then an easy-to-understand algorithm might be preferable to one that is more efficient but more obscure.

Practice Problem

An algorithm does $14n^2 + 5n + 1$ units of work on input of size n. Explain why this is considered an $\Theta(n^2)$ algorithm even though there is a term that involves just n.

3.4 Analysis of Algorithms

3.4.1 Data Cleanup Algorithms

In this section, we'll look at three different algorithms that solve the same problem—the *data cleanup problem*—and then do an analysis of each. Suppose a survey includes a question about the age of the person filling out the survey, and that some people choose not to answer this question. When data from the survey are entered into the computer, an entry of 0 is used to denote "no response" because a legitimate value for age would have to be a positive number. For example, assume that the age data from 10 people who completed the survey are stored in the computer as the following 10-entry list, where the positions in the list range from 1 (far left) to 10 (far right).

0	24	16	0	36	42	23	21	0	27
1	2	3	4	5	6	7	8	9	10

Eventually, the average age of the survey respondents is to be computed. Because the 0 values are not legitimate data—including them in the average would produce too low a value—we want to perform a "data cleanup" and remove them from the list before the average is computed. In our example, the cleaned data could consist of a 10-element list, where the seven legitimate elements are the first seven entries of the list, and some quantity—let's call it *legit*—has the value 7 to indicate that only the first seven entries are legitimate. An alternative acceptable result would be a seven-element list consisting of the seven legitimate data items, in which case there is no need for a *legit* quantity.

The Shuffle-Left Algorithm. Algorithm 1 to solve the data cleanup problem works in the way we might solve this problem using a pencil and paper (and an eraser) to modify the list. We proceed through the list from left to right, pointing with a finger on the left hand to keep our place, and passing over nonzero values. Every time we encounter a 0 value, we squeeze it out of the list by copying each remaining data item in the list one cell to the left. We could use a finger on the right hand to move along the list and point at what to copy next. The value of *legit*, originally set to the length of the list, is reduced by 1 every time a 0 is encountered. (Sounds complicated, but you'll see that it is easy.)

The original configuration is

legit = *10*

Because the first cell on the left contains a 0, the value of *legit* is reduced by 1, and all of the items to the right of the 0 must be copied one cell left. After the first such copy (of the 24), the scenario looks like

legit = 9

| 24 | 24 | 16 | 0 | 36 | 42 | 23 | 21 | 0 | 27 |

↑ ↑

After the second copy (of the 16), we get

legit = 9

| 24 | 16 | 16 | 0 | 36 | 42 | 23 | 21 | 0 | 27 |

↑ ↑

And after the third copy (of the 0), we get

legit = 9

| 24 | 16 | 0 | 0 | 36 | 42 | 23 | 21 | 0 | 27 |

↑ ↑

Proceeding in this fashion, we find that after we copy the last item (the 27), the result is

legit = 9

| 24 | 16 | 0 | 36 | 42 | 23 | 21 | 0 | 27 | 27 |

↑ ↑

Because the right hand finger has moved past the end of the list, one entire shuffle-left process has been completed. It required copying nine items. We reset the right hand finger to start again.

legit = 9

| 24 | 16 | 0 | 36 | 42 | 23 | 21 | 0 | 27 | 27 |

↑ ↑

We must again examine position 1 for a 0 value because if the original list contained 0 in position 2, it would have been copied into position 1. If the value is not 0, as is the case here, both the left hand finger and the right hand finger move forward.

legit = 9

| 24 | 16 | 0 | 36 | 42 | 23 | 21 | 0 | 27 | 27 |

↑ ↑

Moving along, we pass over the 16.

legit = 9

24	16	0	36	42	23	21	0	27	27

↑   ↑

Another cycle of seven copies takes place to squeeze out the 0; the result is

legit = 8

24	16	36	42	23	21	0	27	27	27

↑   ↑

The 36, 42, 23, and 21 are passed over, which results in

legit = 8

24	16	36	42	23	21	0	27	27	27

↑   ↑

and then copying three items to squeeze out the final 0 gives

legit = 7

24	16	36	42	23	21	27	27	27	27

↑   ↑

The left hand finger is pointing at a nonzero element, so another advance of both fingers gives

legit = 7

24	16	36	42	23	21	27	27	27	27

↑   ↑

At this point, we can stop because the left hand finger is past the number of legitimate data items (*legit* = 7). In total, this algorithm (on this list) examined all 10 data items, to see which ones were 0, and copied 9 + 7 + 3 = 19 items.

A pseudocode version of the shuffle-left algorithm to act on a list of *n* items appears in Figure 3.14. The quantities *left* and *right* correspond to the positions where the left hand and right hand fingers point, respectively. You should trace through this algorithm for the preceding example to see that it does what we described.

To analyze the time efficiency of an algorithm, you begin by identifying the fundamental units of work the algorithm performs. For the data cleanup problem, any algorithm must examine each of the *n* elements in the list to see whether they are 0. This gives a base of at least $\Theta(n)$ work units.

FIGURE 3.14

1. Get values for *n* and the *n* data items
2. Set the value of *legit* to *n*
3. Set the value of *left* to *1*
4. Set the value of *right* to *2*
5. While *left* is less than or equal to *legit* do Steps 6 through 14
6.   If the item at position *left* is not 0 then do Steps 7 and 8
7.   Increase *left* by 1
8.   Increase *right* by 1
9.   Else (the item at position *left* is 0) do Steps 10 through 14
10.   Reduce *legit* by 1
11.   While *right* is less than or equal to *n* do Steps 12 and 13
12.   Copy the item at position *right* into position (*right* − 1)
13.   Increase *right* by 1
14.   Set the value of *right* to (*left* + 1)
15. Stop

The shuffle-left algorithm for data cleanup

The other unit of work in the shuffle-left algorithm is copying numbers. The best case occurs when the list has no 0 values because no copying is required. The worst case occurs when the list has all 0 values. Because the first element is 0, the remaining $n - 1$ elements are copied one cell left and *legit* is reduced from *n* to $n - 1$. After the 0 in position 2 gets copied into position 1, the first element is again 0, which again requires $n - 1$ copies and reduces *legit* from $n - 1$ to $n - 2$. This repeats until *legit* is reduced to 0, a total of *n* times. Thus there are *n* passes, during each of which $n - 1$ copies are done. The algorithm does

$$n(n - 1) = n^2 - n$$

copies. If we were to draw a graph of $n^2 - n$, we would see that for large *n*, the curve follows the shape of n^2. The second term can be disregarded because as *n* increases, the n^2 term grows much larger than the *n* term; the n^2 term dominates and determines the shape of the curve. The shuffle-left algorithm is thus an $\Theta(n^2)$ algorithm in the worst case.

The shuffle-left algorithm is space efficient because it only requires four memory locations to store the quantities *n*, *legit*, *left*, and *right* in addition to the memory required to store the list itself.

The Copy-Over Algorithm. The second algorithm for solving the data cleanup problem also works as we might if we decided to write a new list using a pencil and paper. It scans the list from left to right, copying every legitimate (nonzero) value into a new list that it creates. After this algorithm is finished, the original list still exists, but so does a new list that contains only nonzero values.

For our example, the result would be

0	24	16	0	36	42	23	21	0	27

24	16	36	42	23	21	27

Every list entry is examined to see whether it is 0 (as in the shuffle-left algorithm), and every nonzero list entry is copied once (into the new list), so a total of seven copies are done for this example. This is fewer copies than the shuffle-left algorithm requires, but a lot of extra memory space is required because an almost complete second copy of the list is stored. Figure 3.15 shows the pseudocode for this copy-over algorithm.

The best case for this algorithm occurs if all elements are 0; no copies are done so the work is just the $\Theta(n)$ work to examine each list element and see that it is 0. No extra space is used. The worst case occurs if there are no 0 values in the list. The algorithm copies all n nonzero elements into the new list and doubles the space required. Combining the two types of work units, we find that the copy-over algorithm is only $\Theta(n)$ in time efficiency even in the worst case because $\Theta(n)$ examinations and $\Theta(n)$ copies still equal $\Theta(n)$ steps.

Comparing the shuffle-left algorithm and the copy-over algorithm, we see that no 0 elements is the best case of the first algorithm and the worst case of the second, whereas all 0 elements is the worst case of the first and the best case of the second. The second algorithm is more time efficient and less space efficient. This choice is called the *time/space trade-off*—you gain something by giving up something else. Seldom is it possible to improve both dimensions at once, but our next algorithm accomplishes just that.

The Converging-Pointers Algorithm. For the third algorithm, imagine that we move one finger along the list from left to right and another finger from right to left. The left finger slides to the right over nonzero

---

FIGURE 3.15

1. Get values for *n* and the *n* data items
2. Set the value of *left* to 1
3. Set the value of *newposition* to 1
4. While *left* is less than or equal to *n* do Steps 5 through 8
5.   If the item at position *left* is not 0 then do Steps 6 and 7
6.   Copy the item at position *left* into position *newposition* in new list
7.   Increase *newposition* by 1
8.   Increase *left* by 1
9. Stop

The copy-over algorithm for data cleanup

values. Whenever the left finger encounters a 0 item, we reduce the value of *legit* by 1, copy whatever item is at the right finger into the left-finger position, and slide the right finger one cell left. Initially in our example

And because a 0 is encountered at position *left*, the item at position *right* is copied into its place, and both *legit* and *right* are reduced by 1. This results in

The value of *left* increases until the next 0 is reached.

Again, the item at position *right* is copied into position *left*, and *legit* and *right* are reduced by 1.

The item at position left is still 0, so another copy takes place.

From this point, the left finger advances until it meets the right finger, which is pointing to a nonzero element, and the algorithm stops. Once again, each element is examined to see whether it equals 0. For this example, only three copies are needed—fewer even than for algorithm 2, but this algorithm requires no more memory space than algorithm 1. The pseudocode version of the converging-pointers algorithm is given in Figure 3.16.

FIGURE 3.16

1. Get values for *n* and the *n* data items
2. Set the value of *legit* to *n*
3. Set the value of *left* to 1
4. Set the value of *right* to *n*
5. While *left* is less than *right* do Steps 6 through 10
6.   If the item at position *left* is not 0 then increase *left* by 1
7.   Else (the item at position *left* is 0) do Steps 8 through 10
8.   Reduce *legit* by 1
9.   Copy the item at position *right* into position *left*
10.   Reduce *right* by 1
11. If the item at position *left* is 0, then reduce *legit* by 1
12. Stop

The converging-pointers algorithm for data cleanup

The best case for this algorithm, as for the shuffle-left algorithm, is a list containing no 0 elements. The worst case, as for the shuffle-left algorithm, is a list of all 0 entries. With such a list, the converging-pointers algorithm repeatedly copies the element at position *right* into the first position, each time reducing the value of *right*. *Right* goes from *n* to 1, with one copy done at each step, resulting in *n* – 1 copies. This algorithm is $\Theta(n)$ in the worst case. Like the shuffle-left algorithm, it is space efficient. It is possible in this case to beat the time space trade-off, in part because the data cleanup problem requires no particular ordering of the nonzero elements in the "clean" list; the converging-pointers algorithm moves these elements out of their original order.

It is hard to define what an "average" case is for any of these algorithms; the amount of work done depends on how many 0 values there are in the list and perhaps on where in the list they occur. If we assume, however, that the number of 0 values is some percentage of *n* and that these values are scattered throughout the list, then it can be shown that the shuffle-left algorithm will still do $\Theta(n^2)$ work, whereas the converging-pointers algorithm will do $\Theta(n)$. Figure 3.17 summarizes our analysis, although it doesn't reflect the three or four extra memory cells needed to store other quantities used in the algorithms, such as *legit*, *left*, and *right*.

Let's emphasize again the difference between an algorithm that is $\Theta(n)$ in the amount of work it does and one that is $\Theta(n^2)$. In an $\Theta(n)$ algorithm, the work is proportional to *n*. Hence if you double *n*, you double the amount of work; if you multiply *n* by 10, you multiply the work by 10. But in an $\Theta(n^2)$ algorithm, the work is proportional to the *square* of *n*. Hence if you double *n*, you multiply the amount of work by 4; if you multiply *n* by 10, you multiply the work by 100.

FIGURE 3.17

	1. Shuffle-left		2. Copy-over		3. Converging-pointers	
	Time	Space	Time	Space	Time	Space
Best case	$\Theta(n)$	n	$\Theta(n)$	n	$\Theta(n)$	n
Worst case	$\Theta(n^2)$	n	$\Theta(n)$	$2n$	$\Theta(n)$	n
Average case	$\Theta(n^2)$	n	$\Theta(n)$	$n \leq x \leq 2n$	$\Theta(n)$	n

Analysis of three data cleanup algorithms

This is probably a good place to explain why the distinction between n and $2n$ is important when we are talking about space, but we simply classify n and $8000n$ as $\Theta(n)$ when we are talking about units of work. Units of work translate into time when the algorithm is executed, and time is a much more elastic resource than space. Whereas we want an algorithm to run in the shortest possible time, in many cases there is no fixed limit to the amount of time that can be expended. There is, however, always a fixed upper bound on the amount of memory that the computer has available to use while executing an algorithm, so we track space consumption more closely.

3.4.2 Binary Search

The sequential search algorithm searches a list of n items for a particular item; it is an $\Theta(n)$ algorithm. Another algorithm, the **binary search algorithm**, is more efficient but it works only when the search list is already sorted.

Practice Problems

In the data cleanup problem, suppose the original data are

2	0	4	1

1. Write the data list after completion of algorithm 1, the shuffle-left algorithm.

2. Write the two data lists after completion of algorithm 2, the copy-over algorithm.

3. Write the data list after completion of algorithm 3, the converging-pointers algorithm.

4. Make up a data list such that Step 11 of the converging-pointers algorithm (Figure 3.16) is needed.

To understand how binary search operates, let us go back to the problem of searching for *NAME* in a telephone directory. When you look up the name Miranda in the telephone book, you do not do a sequential search beginning with the very first name in the directory and looking at each name in succession until you come to Miranda or the end of the directory! Instead you make use of the fact that the names in the directory have already been sorted into ascending order. You open the phone book in a place somewhere near the middle. If the name you see is Miranda, your search is over. If the name you see begins with *P*, you look closer to the front of the book; if the name you see begins with *L*, you move farther toward the back of the book.

The binary search algorithm works in a similar fashion on a sorted list. It first looks for *NAME* at roughly the halfway point in the list. If the name there equals *NAME*, the search is over. If *NAME* comes alphabetically before the name at the halfway point, then the search is narrowed to the front half of the list, and the process begins again on this smaller list. If *NAME* comes alphabetically after the name at the halfway point, then the search is narrowed to the back half of the list, and the process begins again on *this* smaller list. The algorithm halts when *NAME* is found or when the sublist becomes empty.

Figure 3.18 gives a pseudocode version of the binary search algorithm on a sorted *n*-element list. Here *beginning* and *end* mark the beginning and end of the section of the list under consideration. Initially the whole list is considered, so at first *beginning* is 1 and *end* is *n*. If *NAME* is not found at the midpoint *m* of the current section of the list, then setting *end* equal to one less than the midpoint (Step 9) means that at the next pass through the loop, the front half of the current section is searched. Setting

---

FIGURE 3.18

1. Get values for *NAME, n, N_1, ... , N_n* and *T_1, ... , T_n*
2. Set the value of *beginning* to 1 and set the value of *Found* to NO
3. Set the value of *end* to *n*
4. While *Found* = NO and *beginning* is less than or equal to *end* do Steps 5 through 10
5.   Set the value of *m* to the middle value between *beginning* and *end*
6.   If *NAME* is equal to N_m, the name found at the midpoint between *beginning* and *end*, then do Steps 7 and 8
7.   Print the telephone number of that person, T_m
8.   Set the value of *Found* to YES
9.   Else if *NAME* precedes N_m alphabetically, then set *end* = *m* − 1
10.   Else (*NAME* follows N_m alphabetically) set *beginning* = *m* + 1
11. If (*Found* = NO) then print the message 'I am sorry but that name is not in the directory'
12. Stop

Binary search algorithm (list must be sorted)

beginning equal to one more than the midpoint (Step 10) means that at the next pass through the loop, the back half of the current section is searched. Thus, as the algorithm proceeds, the *beginning* marker can move toward the back of the list, and the *end* marker can move toward the front of the list. If the *beginning* marker and the *end* marker cross over—that is, *end* becomes less than *beginning*—then the current section of the list is empty and the search terminates. Of course it also terminates if the name is found.

Let's do an example, using seven names sorted into ascending order. The following list shows not only the names in the list but also their locations in the list.

Ann	Bob	Cora	Devi	Grant	Nathan	Sue
1	2	3	4	5	6	7

Suppose we search this list for the name Cora. We set *beginning* to 1 and *end* to 7; the midpoint between 1 and 7 is 4. We compare the name at position number 4, Devi, with Cora. Cora precedes Devi alphabetically, so the algorithm sets *end* to 4 − 1 = 3 (Step 9) to continue the search on the front half of the list,

Ann	Bob	Cora
1	2	3

The midpoint between *beginning* = 1 and *end* = 3 is 2, so we compare the name at position number 2, Bob, with Cora. Cora follows Bob alphabetically, so the algorithm sets *beginning* to 2 + 1 = 3 (Step 10) in order to continue the search on the back half of this list, namely

Cora
3

At the next pass through the loop, the midpoint between *beginning* = 3 and *end* = 3 is 3, so we compare the name at position number 3, Cora, with the target name, Cora. We have found the name; the appropriate telephone number can be printed and *Found* changed to YES. The loop terminates, and then the algorithm terminates.

Now suppose we search this same list for the name Maria. As before, the first midpoint is 4, so Devi is compared with Maria. Maria follows Devi, so the search continues with *beginning* = 5, *end* = 7 on the back half:

Grant	Nathan	Sue
5	6	7

The midpoint is 6, so Nathan is compared with Maria. Maria precedes Nathan, so the search continues with *beginning* = 5, *end* = 5 on the front half:

Grant
5

The midpoint is 5, so Grant is compared with Maria. Maria follows Grant, so *beginning* is set to 6 to continue the search on the back half of this list. The algorithm checks the condition at Step 4 to see whether to repeat the loop again and finds that *end* is less than *beginning* (*end* = 5, *beginning* = 6). The loop is abandoned, and the algorithm moves on to Step 11 and indicates that Maria is not in the list.

It is easier to see how the binary search algorithm operates if we list the locations of the names checked in a treelike structure. The tree in Figure 3.19 shows the possible search locations in a seven-element list. The search starts at the top of the tree, at location 4, the middle of the original list. If the name at location 4 is *NAME*, the search halts. If *NAME* comes after the name at location 4 (as Maria does in our example), the right branch is taken and the next location searched is location 6. If *NAME* comes before the name at location 4 (as Cora does in our example), the left branch is taken and the next location searched is location 2. If *NAME* is not found at location 2, the next location searched is either 1 or 3. Similarly, if *NAME* is not found at location 6, the next location searched is either 5 or 7.

In Figure 3.18, the binary search algorithm, we assume in Step 5 that there is a middle position between *beginning* and *end*. This happens only when there is an odd number of elements in the list. Let us agree to define the "middle" of an even number of entries as the end of the first half of the list. With eight elements, for example, the midpoint position is location 4.

1 2 3 4̲ 5 6 7 8

With this understanding, the binary search algorithm can be used on lists of any size.

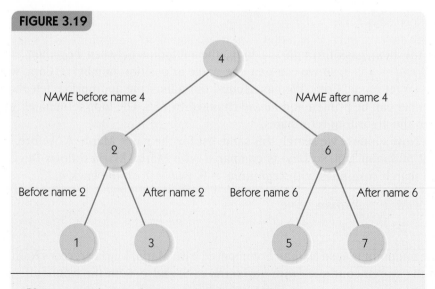

FIGURE 3.19

Binary search tree for a seven-element list

Like the sequential search algorithm, the binary search algorithm relies on comparisons, so to analyze the algorithm, we count the number of comparisons as an indication of the work done. The best case, as in sequential search, requires only one comparison—*NAME* is located on the first try. The worst case, as in sequential search, occurs when *NAME* is not in the list. However, we learn this much sooner in binary search than in sequential search. In our list of seven names, only three comparisons are needed to determine that Maria is not in the list. The number of comparisons needed is the number of circles in some branch from the top to the bottom of the tree in Figure 3.19. These circles represent searches at the midpoints of the whole list, half the list, one quarter of the list, and so on. This process continues as long as the sublists can be cut in half.

Let's do a minor mathematical digression here. The number of times a number *n* can be cut in half and not go below 1 is called the *logarithm of n to the base 2*, which is abbreviated lg *n* (also written in some texts as $\log_2 n$). For example, if *n* is 16, then we can do four such divisions by 2:

$$16 / 2 = 8$$
$$8 / 2 = 4$$
$$4 / 2 = 2$$
$$2 / 2 = 1$$

so lg 16 = 4. This is another way of saying that $2^4 = 16$. In general,

lg *n* = *m* is equivalent to $2^m = n$

Figure 3.20 shows a few values of *n* and lg *n*. From these, we can see that as *n* doubles, lg *n* increases by only 1, so lg *n* grows much more slowly than *n*. Figure 3.21 shows the two basic shapes of *n* and lg *n* and again conveys that lg *n* grows much more slowly than *n*.

Remember the analogy we suggested earlier about the difference in time consumed between $\Theta(n^2)$ algorithms, equivalent to various modes of walking, and $\Theta(n)$ algorithms, equivalent to various modes of driving? We carry

FIGURE 3.20

n	lg n
8	3
16	4
32	5
64	6
128	7

Values for *n* and lg *n*

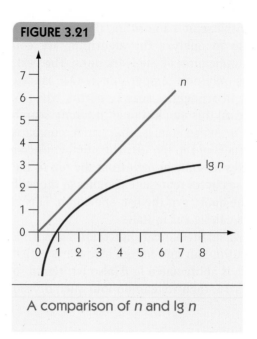

FIGURE 3.21

A comparison of *n* and lg *n*

that analogy further by saying that algorithms of order of magnitude lg *n*, Θ(lg *n*), are like various modes of flying. Changing the coefficients of lg *n* can mean that we go from a Piper cub to an F-22 Raptor but flying, in any form, is still a fundamentally different—and much faster—mode of travel than walking or driving.

Suppose we are doing a binary search on *n* names. In the worst case, as we have seen, the number of comparisons is related to the number of times the list of length *n* can be halved. Binary search does Θ(lg *n*) comparisons in the worst case (see Exercise 26 at the end of the chapter for an exact formula for the worst case). As a matter of fact, it also does Θ(lg *n*) comparisons in the average case (although the exact value is a smaller number than in the worst case). This is because most of the names in the list occur at or near the bottom of the tree, where the maximum amount of work must be done; recall that it also took three comparisons to find that Cora was in the list. As Figure 3.19 shows, relatively few locations (where *NAME* might be found and the algorithm terminate sooner) are higher in the tree.

Both binary search and sequential search solve the telephone book search problem, but these algorithms differ in the order of magnitude of the work they do. Binary search is an Θ(lg *n*) algorithm, whereas sequential search is an Θ(*n*) algorithm, in both the worst case and the average case. To compare the binary search algorithm with the sequential search algorithm, suppose there are 100 elements in the list. In the worst case, sequential search requires 100 comparisons, and binary search requires 7 ($2^7 = 128$). In the average case, sequential search requires about 50 comparisons, and binary search 6 or 7 (still much less work). The improvement in binary search becomes even more apparent as the search list gets longer. For example, if $n = 100{,}000$, then in the worst case sequential search requires 100,000 comparisons, whereas binary search requires 17 ($2^{17} = 131{,}072$). If we wrote two programs, one using sequential search and one using binary search, and ran them on a computer that can do 1,000 name comparisons per second, then to determine that a name is not in the list (the worst case) the sequential search program would use

$$100{,}000 \text{ comparisons} \times \frac{1}{1{,}000} \text{ seconds/comparison} = 100 \text{ seconds}$$

or 1.67 minutes, just to do the necessary comparisons, disregarding the constant factor for advancing the index. The binary search program would use

$$17 \text{ comparisons} \times \frac{1}{1{,}000} \text{ seconds/comparison} = 0.017 \text{ seconds}$$

to do the comparisons, disregarding a constant factor for updating the values of *beginning* and *end*. This is quite a difference.

Suppose our two programs are used with the 20,000,000 names we assume are in the New York City phone book. On the average, the sequential search program needs about

$$\frac{20{,}000{,}000}{2} \text{ comparisons} \times \frac{1}{1{,}000} \text{ seconds/comparison} = 10{,}000 \text{ seconds}$$

(about 2.78 hours!) just to do the comparisons to find a name in the list, whereas the binary search program needs (because $2^{25} \approx 33{,}000{,}000$) about

$$25 \text{ comparisons} \times \frac{1}{100} \text{ seconds/comparison} = 0.025 \text{ seconds}$$

This is an even more impressive difference. Furthermore, it's a difference due to the inherent inefficiency of an $\Theta(n)$ algorithm compared with an $\Theta(\lg n)$ algorithm; the difference can be mitigated but not eliminated by using a faster computer. If our computer does 50,000 comparisons per second, then the average times become about

$$\frac{20{,}000{,}000}{2} \text{ comparisons} \times \frac{1}{50{,}000} \text{ seconds/comparison} = 200 \text{ seconds}$$

or 3.33 minutes for sequential search and about

$$25 \text{ comparisons} \times \frac{1}{50{,}000} \text{ seconds/comparison} = 0.005 \text{ seconds}$$

for binary search. The sequential search alternative is simply not acceptable. That is why analyzing algorithms and choosing the best one can be so important. We also see, as we noted in Chapter 2, that the way the problem data are organized can greatly affect the best choice of algorithm.

The binary search algorithm works only on a list that has already been sorted. An unsorted list could be sorted before using a binary search, but sorting also takes a lot of work, as we have seen. If a list is to be searched only a few times for a few particular names, then it is more efficient to do sequential search on the unsorted list (a few $\Theta(n)$ tasks). But if the list is to be searched repeatedly—as in the daily use of an automated telephone directory for the

Practice Problems

1. Suppose that, using the list of seven names from this section, we try binary search to decide whether Grant is in the list. What names would be compared with Grant?

2. Suppose that, using the list of seven names from this section, we try binary search to decide whether Vernon is in the list. What names would be compared with Vernon?

3. In the worst case, how many comparisons will be required to find a single Social Security number (SSN) from among the approximately 350,000,000 numbers currently assigned if the data file is sorted numerically by SSN? How many will be required in the worst case if the data file is sorted alphabetically by the individual's last name? (Use a spreadsheet to help with the computations.)

foreseeable future—it is more efficient to sort it and then use binary search: one $\Theta(n^2)$ task and many $\Theta(\lg n)$ tasks, as opposed to many $\Theta(n)$ tasks.

As to space efficiency, binary search, like sequential search, requires only a small amount of additional storage to keep track of beginning, end, and midpoint positions in the list. Thus, it is space efficient; in this case,

Laboratory Experience 5

In this Laboratory Experience, you will be able to run animations of the shuffle-left algorithm and the converging-pointers algorithm for the data cleanup problem. You'll be able to see the left and right pointers take on different values, which represent changing positions in the data list. As the algorithms run on various lists, you can count the number of copies of data elements that are required and see how they relate to the original positions of any 0 items in the list.

You will also work with an animation of the binary search algorithm and see how the work done compares with the theoretical results we discovered in this section.

we did not have to sacrifice space efficiency to gain time efficiency. But we did have to sacrifice generality—binary search works only on a sorted list whereas sequential search works on any list.

3.4.3 Pattern Matching

The pattern-matching algorithm in Chapter 2 involves finding all occurrences of a pattern of the form $P_1P_2\ldots P_m$ within text of the form $T_1T_2\ldots T_n$. Recall that the algorithm simply does a "forward march" through the text, at each position attempting to match each pattern character against the text characters. The process stops only after text position $n - m + 1$, when the remaining text is not as long as the pattern so that there could not possibly be a match. This algorithm is interesting to analyze because it involves two measures of input size: n, the length of the text string, and m, the length of the pattern string. The unit of work is comparison of a pattern character with a text character.

Surprisingly, both the best case and the worst case of this algorithm can occur when the pattern is not in the text at all. The difference hinges on exactly *how* the pattern fails to be in the text. The best case occurs if the first character of the pattern is nowhere in the text, as in

Text: *KLMNPQRSTX*

Pattern: *ABC*

In this case, $n - m + 1$ comparisons are required, trying (unsuccessfully) to match P_1 with $T_1, T_2, \ldots, T_{n-m+1}$ in turn. Each comparison fails, and the algorithm slides the pattern forward to try again at the next position in the text.

The maximum amount of work is done if the pattern *almost* occurs everywhere in the text. Consider, for example, the following case:

Text: *AAAAAAAAA*

Pattern: *AAAB*

Starting with T_1, the first text character, the match with the first pattern character is successful. The match with the second text character and the second pattern character is also successful. Indeed $m - 1$ characters of the pattern match with the text before the mth comparison proves a failure. The process starts over from the second text character, T_2. Once again, m comparisons are required to find a mismatch. Altogether, m comparisons are required for each of the $n - m + 1$ starting positions in the text.

Another version of the worst case occurs when the pattern is found at each location in the text, as in

Text: *AAAAAAAAA*

Pattern: *AAAA*

This results in the same comparisons as are done for the other worst case, the only difference being that the comparison of the last pattern character is successful.

FIGURE 3.22

Problem	Unit of Work	Algorithm	Best Case	Worst Case	Average Case
Searching	Comparisons	Sequential search	1	$\Theta(n)$	$\Theta(n)$
		Binary search	1	$\Theta(\lg n)$	$\Theta(\lg n)$
Sorting	Comparisons and exchanges	Selection sort	$\Theta(n^2)$	$\Theta(n^2)$	$\Theta(n^2)$
Data cleanup	Examinations and copies	Shuffle-left	$\Theta(n)$	$\Theta(n^2)$	$\Theta(n^2)$
		Copy-over	$\Theta(n)$	$\Theta(n)$	$\Theta(n)$
		Converging-pointers	$\Theta(n)$	$\Theta(n)$	$\Theta(n)$
Pattern matching	Character comparisons	Forward march	$\Theta(n)$	$\Theta(m \times n)$	

Order-of-magnitude time efficiency summary

Unlike our simple examples, pattern matching usually involves a pattern length that is short compared with the text length, that is, when m is much less than n. In such cases, $n - m + 1$ is essentially n. The pattern-matching algorithm is therefore $\Theta(n)$ in the best case and $\Theta(m \times n)$ in the worst case.

It requires somewhat improbable situations to create the worst cases we have described. In general, the forward-march algorithm performs quite well on text and patterns consisting of ordinary words. Other pattern-matching algorithms are conceptually more complex but require less work in the worst case.

3.4.4 Summary
Figure 3.22 shows an order-of-magnitude summary of the time efficiency for the algorithms we have analyzed.

Practice Problem

Use the first sample pattern and text given in Section 3.4.3 for the worst case of the pattern-matching algorithm. What is m? What is n? What is $m \times n$? This algorithm is $\Theta(m \times n)$ in the worst case, but what is the exact number of comparisons done?

3.5 When Things Get Out of Hand

We have so far found examples of algorithms that are $\Theta(\lg n)$, $\Theta(n)$, and $\Theta(n^2)$ in time efficiency. Order of magnitude determines how quickly the values grow as n increases. An algorithm of order $\lg n$ does less work as n increases than does an algorithm of order n, which in turn does less work than one of order n^2. The work done by any of these algorithms is no worse than a constant multiple of n^2, which is a polynomial in n. Therefore, these algorithms are **polynomially bounded** in the amount of work they do as n increases.

Some algorithms must do work that is not polynomially bounded. Consider four cities, A, B, C, and D, that are connected as shown in Figure 3.23, and ask the following question: Is it possible to start at city A, go through every other city exactly once, and end up back at A? Of course, we as humans can immediately see in this small problem that the answer is Yes and that there are two such paths: A-B-D-C-A and A-C-D-B-A. However, an algorithm doesn't get to "see" the entire picture at once, as we can; it has available to it only isolated facts such as "A is connected to B and to C," "B is connected to A and to D," and so on. If the number of *nodes* and connecting *edges* is large, humans also might not "see" the solution immediately. A collection of nodes and connecting edges is called a *graph*. A path through a graph that begins and ends at the same node and goes through all other nodes exactly once is called a *Hamiltonian circuit*, named for the Irish mathematician William Rowan Hamilton (1805–1865). If there are n nodes in the graph, then a Hamiltonian circuit, if it exists, must have exactly n links. In the case of the four cities, for instance, if the path must go through exactly A, B, C, D, and A (in some order), then there are five nodes on the path (counting A twice) and four links.

Our problem is to determine whether an arbitrary graph has a Hamiltonian circuit. An algorithm to solve this problem examines all possible paths through the graph that are the appropriate length to see whether any of them are Hamiltonian circuits. The algorithm can trace all paths by beginning at the starting node and choosing at each node where to go next. Without going into the details of such an algorithm, let's represent the possible paths with four links in the graph of Figure 3.23. Again, we use a tree

FIGURE 3.23

A ●———————● B

C ●———————● D

Four connected cities

FIGURE 3.24

Hamiltonian circuits among all paths from A in
Figure 3.23 with four links

structure. In Figure 3.24, A is the tree "root," and at each node in the tree, the nodes directly below it are the choices for the next node. Thus, any time B appears in the tree, it has the two nodes A and D below it because edges exist from B to A and from B to D. The "branches" of the tree are all the possible paths from A with four links. Once the tree has been built, an examination of the paths shows that only the two dark paths in the figure represent Hamiltonian circuits.

The number of paths that must be examined is the number of nodes at the bottom level of the tree. There is one node at the top of the tree; we'll call the top of the tree level 0. The number of nodes is multiplied by 2 for each level down in the tree. At level 1, there are 2 nodes; at level 2, there are 2^2 nodes; at level 3, there are 2^3 nodes; and at level 4, the bottom of the tree, there are $2^4 = 16$ nodes.

Suppose we are looking for a Hamiltonian circuit in a graph with n nodes and two choices at each node. The bottom of the corresponding tree is at level n, and there are 2^n paths to examine. If we take the examination of a single path as a unit of work, then this algorithm must do 2^n units of work. This is more work than any polynomial in n. An $\Theta(2^n)$ algorithm is called an **exponential algorithm**. Hence the trial-and-error approach to solving the Hamiltonian circuit problem is an exponential algorithm. (We could improve on this algorithm by letting it stop tracing a path whenever a repeated node different from the starting node is encountered, but it is still exponential. If there are more than two choices at a node, the amount of work is even greater.)

FIGURE 3.25

Comparison of lg n, n, n^2, and 2^n

Figure 3.25 shows the four curves lg n, n, n^2, and 2^n. The rapid growth of 2^n is not really apparent here, however, because that curve is off the scale for values of n above 5. Figure 3.26 compares these four curves for values of n that are still small, but even so, 2^n is already far outdistancing the other values.

To appreciate fully why the order of magnitude of an algorithm is important, let's again imagine that we are running various algorithms as programs on a computer that can perform a single operation (unit of work) in 0.0001 second. Figure 3.27 shows the amount of time it takes for algorithms of $\Theta(\lg n)$, $\Theta(n)$, $\Theta(n^2)$, and $\Theta(2^n)$ to complete their work for various values of n.

The expression 2^n grows unbelievably fast. An algorithm of $\Theta(2^n)$ can take so long to solve even a small problem that it is of no practical value. Even if we greatly increase the speed of the computer, the results are much the same. We now see more than ever why we added *efficiency* as a desirable feature for an algorithm and why future advances in computer technology won't change this. No matter how fast computers get, they will not be able to solve a problem of size $n = 100$ using an algorithm of $\Theta(2^n)$ in any reasonable period of time.

FIGURE 3.26

Comparisons of lg n, n, n^2, and 2^n for larger values of n

The algorithm we have described here for testing an arbitrary graph for Hamiltonian circuits is an example of a *brute force algorithm*—one that beats the problem into submission by trying all possibilities. In Chapter 1, we described a brute force algorithm for winning a chess game; it consisted of looking at all possible game scenarios from any given point on and then picking a winning one. This is also an exponential algorithm. Some very practical problems have exponential solution algorithms. For example, an e-mail message that you send over the Internet is routed along the shortest possible path through intermediate computers from your mail server computer to the destination mail server computer. An exponential algorithm to solve this problem would examine all possible paths to the destination and then use the shortest one. As you can imagine, the Internet uses a better (more efficient) algorithm than this one!

Are there problems for which no polynomially bounded algorithm exists? Such problems are called intractable; they are solvable, but the

FIGURE 3.27

Order	n			
	10	50	100	1,000
lg n	0.0003 sec	0.0006 sec	0.0007 sec	0.001 sec
n	0.001 sec	0.005 sec	0.01 sec	0.1 sec
n^2	0.01 sec	0.25 sec	1 sec	1.67 min
2^n	0.1024 sec	3,570 years	4×10^{16} centuries	*Too big to compute!!*

A comparison of four orders of magnitude

solution algorithms all require so much work as to be virtually useless. The Hamiltonian circuit problem is suspected to be such a problem, but we don't really know for sure! No one has yet found a solution algorithm that works in polynomial time, but neither has anyone proved that such an algorithm does not exist. This is a problem of great interest in computer science. A surprising number of problems fall into this "suspected intractable" category. Here's another one, called the *bin-packing problem*: Given an unlimited number of bins of volume X units and given n objects, all of volume between 0 and X, find the minimum number of bins needed to store the n objects. A brute force algorithm would try all possibilities, which again is not a polynomial algorithm. Any manufacturer who ships sets of various items in standard-sized cartons or anyone who wants to store variable-length video clips on a set of DVDs in the most efficient way would be interested in a polynomial algorithm that solves this minimization problem.

Problems for which no known polynomial solution algorithm exists are sometimes approached via approximation algorithms. These algorithms don't solve the problem, but they provide a close approximation to a solution. (See Exercise 2 of Chapter 1.) For example, an approximation algorithm to solve the bin-packing problem is to take the objects in order, put the first one into bin 1, and stuff each remaining object into the first bin that can hold it. This (reasonable) approach may not give the absolute minimum number of bins needed, but it gives a first cut at the answer. (Anyone who has watched passengers stowing carry-on baggage in an airplane has seen this approximation algorithm at work.)

For example, suppose a sequence of four objects with volumes of 0.3, 0.4, 0.5, and 0.6 are stored using the "first-fit" algorithm described previously. The result requires three bins, which would be packed as shown in Figure 3.28. However, this is not the optimal solution (see Exercise 34 at the end of the chapter).

In Chapter 12, we will learn that there are problems that cannot be solved algorithmically, even if we are willing to accept an extremely inefficient solution.

FIGURE 3.28

A first-fit solution to a bin-packing problem

Practice Problems

1. Consider the following graph:

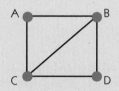

   Draw a tree similar to Figure 3.24 showing all paths from A and highlighting those that are Hamiltonian circuits (these are the same two circuits as before). How many paths have to be examined?

2. The following tree shows all paths with two links that begin at node A in some graph. Draw the graph.

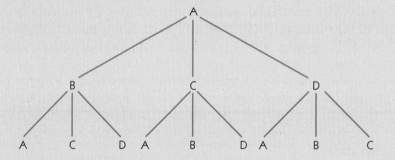

3. If an algorithm were determined to have an order of magnitude of n^n, do you think it would be classified as polynomial or exponential? Explain.

3.6 Summary of Level 1

We defined computer science as the study of algorithms, so it is appropriate that Level 1 was devoted to exploring algorithms in more detail. In Chapter 2, we discussed how to represent algorithms using pseudocode. Pseudocode provides us with a flexible language for expressing the building blocks from which algorithms can be constructed. These building blocks include assigning a particular value to a quantity, choosing one of two next steps on the basis of some condition, or repeating steps in a loop.

Laboratory Experience 6

The various sorting algorithms examined in Laboratory Experience 4 (selection sort, quicksort, etc.) do different amounts of work on the same data sets. But how do these various workloads affect the actual running time of the algorithms? In this Laboratory Experience, you can run these sorting algorithms and find their wall-clock running time on different sizes of input. In addition, because you can see the patterns of values falling into place in a large list while an algorithm runs, you will get a much better understanding of how each sorting algorithm moves values around to accomplish its task.

We developed algorithmic solutions to three very practical problems: searching for a name in a list of names, finding the largest number in a list of numbers, and searching for a particular pattern of characters within a segment of text. In Chapter 3, we noted that computer scientists develop algorithms to be *used* and thus there is a set of desirable properties for algorithms, including ease of understanding, elegance, and efficiency, in addition to correctness. Of these, efficiency—which may be either time efficiency or space efficiency—is the most easily quantifiable.

A convenient way to classify the time efficiency of algorithms is by examining the order of magnitude of the work they do. Algorithms that are of differing orders of magnitude do fundamentally different amounts of work. Regardless of the constant factor that reflects peripheral work or how fast the computer on which these algorithms execute, for problems with sufficiently large input, the algorithm of the lowest order of magnitude requires the least time.

We analyzed the time efficiency of the sequential search algorithm and discovered that it is an $\Theta(n)$ algorithm in both the worst case and the average case. We found a selection sort algorithm that is $\Theta(n^2)$, we found a binary search algorithm that is $\Theta(\lg n)$, and we analyzed the pattern-matching algorithm from Chapter 2. By examining the data cleanup problem, we learned that algorithms that solve the same task can indeed differ in the order of magnitude of the work they do, sometimes by employing a time/space trade-off. We also learned that there are algorithms that require more than polynomially bounded time to complete their work and that such algorithms may take so long to execute, regardless of the speed of the computer on which they are run, that they provide no practical solution. Some important problems may be intractable—that is, have no polynomially bounded solution algorithms.

Some computer scientists work on trying to decide whether a particular problem is intractable. Some work on finding more efficient algorithms for problems—such as searching and sorting—that are so common that a more efficient algorithm would greatly improve productivity. Still others seek to discover algorithms for new problems. Thus, as we said, the study of algorithms underlies much of computer science. But everything we have done so far has been a pencil-and-paper exercise. In terms of the definition of computer science that we gave in Chapter 1, we have been looking at the formal and mathematical properties of algorithms. It is time to move on to the next part of that definition: the hardware realizations of algorithms. When we execute real algorithms on real computers, those computers are electronic devices. How does an electronic device "understand" an algorithm and carry out its instructions? We begin to explore these questions in Chapter 4.

EXERCISES

1. a. Use Gauss's approach to find the following sum:

    $2 + 4 + 6 + \ldots + 100$

    b. Use Gauss's approach to find a formula for the sum of the even numbers from 2 to $2n$:

    $2 + 4 + 6 + \ldots + 2n$

    Your formula will be an expression involving n.

2. An English Christmas carol, "The Twelve Days of Christmas," dates from the late 1700s. The twelve verses in the song are cumulative, each verse adding an additional gift given by "my true love." The twelfth verse says "On the twelfth day of Christmas, my true love gave to me …"

    12 Drummers Drumming

    11 Pipers Piping

    10 Lords-a-Leaping

    … and so forth down to …

    3 French Hens

    2 Turtle Doves

    And a Partridge in a Pear Tree.

    a. Use Gauss's formula to find the total number of gifts given on Day 12.

    b. How many total gifts are given over all 12 days? *Hint:*

    $$1(2) + 2(3) + 3(4) + \ldots + n(n + 1) = \frac{n(n + 1)(n + 2)}{3}$$

3. The *Fibonacci sequence* of numbers is defined as follows: The first and second numbers are both 1. After that, each number in the sequence is the sum of the two preceding numbers. Thus, the Fibonacci sequence is as follows:

   1, 1, 2, 3, 5, 8, 13, 21, ...

   If $F(n)$ stands for the nth value in the sequence, then this definition can be expressed as

   $F(1) = 1$

   $F(2) = 1$

   $F(n) = F(n-1) + F(n-2)$ for $n > 2$

   a. Using the definition of the Fibonacci sequence, compute the value of $F(20)$.

   b. A formula for $F(n)$ is

   $$F(n) = \frac{\sqrt{5}}{5}\left(\frac{1+\sqrt{5}}{2}\right)^n - \frac{\sqrt{5}}{5}\left(\frac{1-\sqrt{5}}{2}\right)^n$$

   Using the formula (and a calculator), compute the value of $F(20)$.

   c. What are your opinions on the relative clarity, elegance, and efficiency of the two algorithms (using the definition and using the formula) to compute $F(20)$? Would your answer change if you considered $F(100)$?

4. A tennis tournament has 342 players. A single match involves 2 players. The winner of a match will play the winner of a match in the next round, whereas losers are eliminated from the tournament. The 2 players who have won all previous rounds play in the final game, and the winner wins the tournament. What is the total number of matches needed to determine the winner?

   a. Here is one algorithm to answer this question. Compute 342 / 2 = 171 to get the number of pairs (matches) in the first round, which results in 171 winners to go on to the second round. Compute 171 / 2 = 85 with 1 left over, which results in 85 matches in the second round and 85 winners, plus the 1 left over, to go on to the third round. For the third round compute 86 / 2 = 43, so the third round has 43 matches, and

   so on. The total number of matches is 171 + 85 + 43 + ... Finish this process to find the total number of matches.

   b. Here is another algorithm to solve this problem. Each match results in exactly one loser, so there must be the same number of matches as losers in the tournament. Compute the total number of losers in the entire tournament. (*Hint:* This isn't really a computation; it is a one-sentence argument.)

   c. What are your opinions on the relative clarity, elegance, and efficiency of the two algorithms?

5. We have said that the average number of comparisons needed to find a name in an n-element list using sequential search is slightly higher than $n/2$. In this problem, we find an exact expression for this average.

   a. Suppose a list of names has an odd number of names, say 15. At what position is the middle name? Using sequential search, how many comparisons are required to find the middle name? Repeat this exercise with a few more odd numbers until you can do the following: If there are n names in the list and n is an odd number, write an expression for the number of comparisons required to find the middle name.

   b. Suppose a list of names has an even number of names, say 16. At what positions are the two "middle" names? Using sequential search, how many comparisons are required to find each of these? What is the average of these two numbers? Repeat this exercise with a few more even numbers until you can do the following: If there are n names in the list and n is an even number, write an expression for the average number of comparisons required to find the two middle names.

   c. Noting that half the names in a list fall before the midpoint and half after the midpoint, use your answer to Parts a and b to write an exact expression for the average number of comparisons done using sequential search to find a name that occurs in an n-element list.

6. Here is a list of seven names:

   Sherman, Jane, Ted, Elise, Raul, Maki, John

   Search this list for each name in turn, using sequential search and counting the number of comparisons for each name. Now take the seven comparison counts and find their average. Did you get a number that you expected? Why?

7. Perform a selection sort on the list 7, 4, 2, 9, 6. Show the list after each exchange that has an effect on the list ordering.

8. The selection sort algorithm could be modified to stop when the unsorted section of the list contains only one number, because that one number must be in the correct position. Show that this modification would have no effect on the number of comparisons required to sort an n-element list.

Exercises 9–12 refer to another algorithm, called **bubble sort**, which sorts an n-element list. Bubble sort makes multiple passes through the list from front to back, each time exchanging pairs of entries that are out of order. Here is a pseudocode version:

1. Get values for n and the n list items

2. Set the marker U for the unsorted section at the end of the list

3. While the unsorted section has more than one element, do Steps 4 through 8

4.   Set the current element marker C at the second element of the list

5.   While C has not passed U, do Steps 6 and 7

6.   If the item at position C is less than the item to its left, then exchange these two items

7.   Move C to the right one position

8.   Move U left one position

9. Stop

9. For each of the following lists, perform a bubble sort, and show the list after each exchange. Compare the number of exchanges done here and in the Practice Problem at the end of Section 3.3.3.

   a. 4, 8, 2, 6

   b. 12, 3, 6, 8, 2, 5, 7

   c. D, B, G, F, A, C, E, H

10. Explain why the bubble sort algorithm does $\Theta(n^2)$ comparisons on an n-element list.

11. Suppose selection sort and bubble sort are both performed on a list that is already sorted. Does bubble sort do fewer exchanges than selection sort? Explain.

12. Bubble sort can be improved. **Smart bubble sort** keeps track of how many exchanges are done within any single pass through the unsorted section of the list. If no exchanges occur, then the list is sorted and the algorithm should stop.

   a. Write a pseudocode version of the smart bubble sort algorithm.

   b. Perform a smart bubble sort on the following list. How many comparisons are required?

      7, 4, 12, 9, 11

   c. Describe the best-case scenario for smart bubble sort on an n-element list. How many comparisons are required? How many exchanges are required?

   d. Under what circumstances does smart bubble sort do the same number of comparisons as regular bubble sort?

13. This exercise discusses a new algorithm to sort an n-element list.

   a. A permutation of a list is any arrangement of the list items. For example, 2, 4 and 4, 2 are the two permutations of the list 2, 4. Find all permutations of the list 4, 3, 7.

   b. Given an n-element list, the number of permutations can be counted as follows. There are n positions in the list. Any of the n items can occupy position 1:

      $n,$ ___, ___, ___, ... ___, ___, ___

      Once the item for position 1 has been chosen, any of the remaining $n-1$ items can occupy position 2:

      $n, \underline{n-1},$ ___, ___, ... ___, ___, ___

      There are then $n-2$ choices for position 3, etc., until there is only one choice left for the last position:

      $n, \underline{n-1}, \underline{n-2}, \underline{n-3}, ... 3, \underline{2}, \underline{1}$

The total number of permutations is the product

$$n(n-1)(n-2)(n-3)\cdots(3)(2)(1)$$

This value is called *n factorial* and is denoted by *n*!. Compute the value of 3!. How many permutations did you find in Part a?

c. Here is a pseudocode description of the new sorting algorithm. It first generates all possible permutations of the list elements and then looks for which of these is the sorted-order permutation.

   1. Get values for *n* and the *n* list items

   2. Set the value of permutation counter *i* to 1

   3. While ($i \leq n!$), do Steps 4 through 6

   4.   Create a new empty list of size *n*

   5.   Write the next permutation in this list

   6.   Increase the value of *i* by 1

   7. Set the value of list counter *j* to 1

   8. Set the value of Sorted to NO

   9. While ($j \leq n!$) and (Sorted = NO), do Steps 10 through 13

  10.   Check whether list *j* is sorted

  11.   If list *j* is sorted then

  12.   Set the value of Sorted to YES

  13.   Increase the value of *j* by 1

  14. Print list ($j - 1$)

  15. Stop

To write this algorithm in complete detail, we would need to explain Step 5:

    Write the next permutation in this list

and Step 10:

    Check whether list *j* is sorted

in terms of more primitive operations. For simplicity, assume that each execution of Step 5 is one work unit and that each execution of Step 10 is also one work unit. Explain the best case for this algorithm and give an expression for the total number of work units required. Explain the worst case and give an expression for the total number of work units required.

d. Selection sort is $\Theta(n^2)$ and the new sorting algorithm is $\Theta(n!)$. Fill in the following table, assuming a work rate of 0.0001 seconds per unit of work.

			n	
Order	3	5	10	20
n^2				
$n!$				

e. Comment on the space efficiency of the new algorithm.

14. Algorithms A and B perform the same task. On input of size *n*, algorithm A executes $0.003n^2$ instructions, and algorithm B executes $243n$ instructions. Find the approximate value of *n* above which algorithm B is more efficient. (You may use a calculator or spreadsheet.)

15. Suppose a metropolitan area is divided into four school districts: 1, 2, 3, 4. The State Board of Education keeps track of the number of student transfers from one district to another and the student transfers within a district. This information is recorded each year in a 4 × 4 table as shown here. The entry in row 1, column 3 (314), for example, shows the number of student transfers from district 1 to district 3 for the year. The entry in row 1, column 1 (243) shows the number of student transfers within district 1.

	1	2	3	4
1	243	187	314	244
2	215	420	345	172
3	197	352	385	261
4	340	135	217	344

Suppose there are *n* school districts, and the Board of Education maintains an $n \times n$ table.

a. Write a pseudocode algorithm to print out the table, that is, to print each of the entries in the table. Write an expression for the number of print statements the algorithm executes.

b. Write a pseudocode algorithm to print *n* copies of the table, one to give to each of the *n* school district supervisors. Write an expression for the number of print statements the algorithm executes.

c. What is the order of magnitude of the work done by the algorithm in Part b if the unit of work is printing a table element?

16. Write the data list that results from running the shuffle-left algorithm to clean up the following data. Find the exact number of copies done.

3	0	0	2	6	7	0	0	5	1

17. Write the resulting data list and find the exact number of copies done by the converging-pointers algorithm when it is executed on the data in Exercise 16.

18. Explain in words how to modify the shuffle-left data cleanup algorithm to slightly reduce the number of copies it makes. (*Hint:* Must item n always be copied?) If this modified algorithm is run on the data list of Exercise 16, exactly how many copies are done?

19. The shuffle-left algorithm for data cleanup is supposed to perform $n(n-1)$ copies on a list consisting of n 0s (zeros). Confirm this result for the following list:

0 0 0 0 0 0

20. Consider the following list of names.

Arturo, Elsa, JoAnn, John, Jose, Lee, Snyder, Tracy

a. Use binary search to decide whether Elsa is in this list. What names will be compared with Elsa?

b. Use binary search to decide whether Tracy is in this list. What names will be compared with Tracy?

c. Use binary search to decide whether Emile is in this list. What names will be compared with Emile?

21. Use the binary search algorithm to decide whether 35 is in the following list:

3, 6, 7, 9, 12, 14, 18, 21, 22, 31, 43

What numbers will be compared with 35?

22. If a list is already sorted in ascending order, a modified sequential search algorithm can be used that compares against each element in turn, stopping if a list element exceeds the target

value. Write a pseudocode version of this **short sequential search** algorithm.

23. This exercise refers to short sequential search (see Exercise 22).

a. What is the worst-case number of comparisons of short sequential search on a sorted n-element list?

b. What is the approximate average number of comparisons to find an element that is in a sorted list using short sequential search?

c. Is short sequential search ever more efficient than regular sequential search? Explain.

24. Draw the tree structure that describes binary search on the eight-element list in Exercise 20. What is the number of comparisons in the worst case? Give an example of a name to search for that requires that many comparisons.

25. Draw the tree structure that describes binary search on a list with 16 elements. What is the number of comparisons in the worst case?

26. We want to find an exact formula for the number of comparisons that binary search requires in the worst case on an n-element list. (We already know the formula is $\Theta(\lg n)$.)

a. If x is a number that is not an integer, then $\lfloor x \rfloor$, called the *floor function* of x, is defined to be the largest integer less than or equal to x. For example, $\lfloor 3.7 \rfloor = 3$ and $\lfloor 5 \rfloor = 5$. Find the following values: $\lfloor 1.2 \rfloor, \lfloor 2.3 \rfloor, \lfloor 8.9 \rfloor, \lfloor -4.6 \rfloor$.

b. If n is not a power of 2, then $\lg n$ is not an integer. If n is between 8 and 16, for example, then $\lg n$ is between 3 and 4 (because $\lg 8 = 3$ and $\lg 16 = 4$). Complete the following table of values:

n	$\lfloor \lg n \rfloor$
2	1
3	
4	2
5	
6	
7	
8	3

c. For $n = 2, 3, 4, 5, 6, 7, 8$, draw a tree structure similar to Figure 3.19 to describe the positions searched by binary search. For each value of n, use the tree structure to find the number of comparisons in the worst case, and complete the following table:

n	Number of Compares, Worst Case
2	
3	
4	3
5	
6	
7	3
8	

d. Comparing the tables of Parts b and c, find a formula involving $\lfloor \lg n \rfloor$ for the number of comparisons binary search requires in the worst case on an n-element list. Test your formula by drawing trees for other values of n.

27. Using the tree in Figure 3.19, find the number of comparisons to find each of items 1–7 in a seven-element list using binary search. Then find the average. Compare this with the worst case.

28. At the end of Section 3.4.2, we talked about the trade-off between using sequential search on an unsorted list as opposed to sorting the list and then using binary search. If the list size is $n = 100,000$, about how many worst-case searches must be done before the second alternative is better in terms of number of comparisons? (*Hint:* Let p represent the number of searches done.)

29. Suppose the pattern-matching problem is changed to require locating only the first instance, if any, of the pattern within the text.

a. Describe the worst case, give an example, and give the exact number of comparisons (of a pattern character with a text character) required.

b. Describe the best case, give an example, and give the exact number of comparisons required.

30. Suppose you use the brute force (unimproved) algorithm to search for a Hamiltonian circuit in the graph shown here.

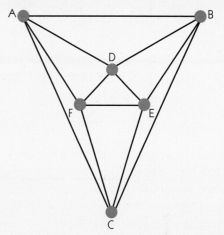

a. How many links would such a circuit have?

b. How many different paths would this algorithm examine?

c. If this algorithm is run on a computer where it takes 0.0001 seconds to examine a single path, what is the total time required to examine all paths?

d. On the same computer, what is the approximate total time required to examine all paths in a graph with 12 nodes, each of which has four choices for the next node?

31. An *Euler path* in a graph (named for the Swiss mathematician Leonhard Euler, 1707–1783) is a path that uses each edge of the graph exactly once. For example, this graph clearly has an Euler path A-B-D-C-A.

a. Decide which of the graphs on the following page have Euler paths, and write out such a path if one exists. (Unlike Hamiltonian circuits, an Euler path need not end at the same node from which it starts, and can go through a given node more than once.)

b. Like the Hamiltonian circuit problem, there is a brute force algorithm to determine whether a graph has an Euler path, again by testing all possibilities. You probably used a variation of this algorithm to solve Part a. But the Euler path problem has another solution. The *degree* of a node is the number of edges at that node. A node with odd degree is an *odd node* and a node with even degree is an *even node*. In the first graph of Part a, nodes A and D are even (degree 2) and nodes B and C are odd (degree 3). An Euler path exists in any graph with exactly 0 or 2 odd nodes. Which of the following graphs have Euler paths and why? Write out such a path if one exists.

3.   Set the value of node counter i to 1

4.   While ($i \leq n$), do Steps 5 through 13

5.   Set the value of node counter j to 1

6.   Set the value of *Degree* to 0

7.   While ($j \leq n$), do Steps 8 through 10

8.   If an edge i-j exists then

9.   Increase *Degree* by 1

10   Increase j by 1

11.   If *Degree* is an odd number then

12.   Increase *Odds* by 1

13.   Increase i by 1

14.   If *Odds* > 2 then

15.   Print the message 'No Euler path'

       Else

16.   Print the message 'Euler path exists'

17.   Stop

What is the order of magnitude of this algorithm where the "work unit" is checking whether an edge exists (Step 8)?

d. Is the Euler path problem intractable?

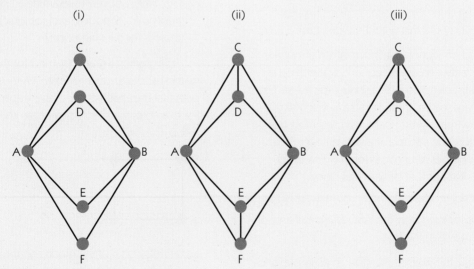

(i)   (ii)   (iii)

c. Here is a pseudocode version of this algorithm for a graph with *n* nodes labeled 1 to *n*:

   1.   Get values for *n* and all edges of the graph

   2.   Set the value of *Odds* to 0

32. At about what value of *n* does an algorithm that does $100n^2$ instructions become more efficient than one that does $0.01(2^n)$ instructions? (Use a calculator or spreadsheet.)

33. a. An algorithm that is $\Theta(n)$ takes 10 seconds to execute on a particular computer when $n = 100$. How long would you expect it to take when $n = 500$?

    b. An algorithm that is $\Theta(n^2)$ takes 10 seconds to execute on a particular computer when $n = 100$. How long would you expect it to take when $n = 500$?

34. Find an optimal solution to the bin-packing problem described in Section 3.5.

35. In the data cleanup problem, we assumed that the items were stored in a list with a fixed number of positions. Each item could be examined by giving its position in the list. This arrangement of data is called an *array*. Here is an array of four items:

43	13	55	39
1	2	3	4

Another way to arrange items is to have a way to locate the first item and then have each item "point to" the next item. This arrangement of data is called a *linked list*. Here are the same four items in a linked list arrangement:

43 → 13 → 55 → 39

To examine any item in a linked list, one must start with the first item and follow the pointers to the desired item.

Unlike arrays, which are fixed in size, linked lists can shrink and grow. An item can be eliminated from a linked list by changing the pointer to that item so that it points to the next item instead.

a. Draw the linked list that results when item 13 is eliminated from the foregoing linked list.

b. Draw the linked list that results when data cleanup is performed on the following linked list.

19 → 0 → 53 → 28 → 0 → 33

c. Describe (informally) an algorithm to do data cleanup on a linked list. You may assume that neither the first item nor the last item has a value of 0, and you may assume the existence of operations such as "follow pointer" and "change pointer." If these operations are the unit of work used, show that your algorithm is an $\Theta(n)$ algorithm, where n is the number of items in the list.

36. Below is a pseudocode algorithm that prints a set of output values:

1. Get value for n

2. Set the value of k to 1

3. While k is less than or equal to n, do Steps 4 through 8

4.   Set the value of j to one-half n

5.   While j is greater than or equal to 1, do Steps 6 through 7

6.   Print the value of j

7.   Set the value of j to one-half its former value

8.   Increase k by 1

9. Stop

a. Let n have the value 4. Write the values printed out by this algorithm.

b. Let n have the value 8. Write the values printed out by this algorithm.

c. Which of the following best describes the efficiency of this algorithm, where the "work unit" is printing a value?

$\Theta(n^2)$ $\Theta(n \lg n)$ $\Theta(n)$ $\Theta(\lg n)$

d. How many work units would you expect this algorithm to do if $n = 16$?

37. Chapter 2 contains an algorithm that finds the largest value in a list of n values.

a. What is the order of magnitude of the largest-value algorithm, where the work unit is comparisons of values from the list?

b. Suppose that you want to find the second-largest value in the list. Find the order of magnitude of the work done if you use the following algorithm: Sort the list, using selection sort, then directly get the second-largest value.

c. Suppose that you want to find the second-largest value in the list. Find the order of magnitude of the work done if you use the following algorithm: Run the largest-value algorithm twice, first to find (and eliminate from the list) the largest value, then to find the second-largest value.

CHALLENGE WORK

1. You are probably familiar with the children's song "Old MacDonald Had a Farm." The first verse is

> Old MacDonald had a farm, *eee-eye,*
>   *eee-eye,* oh.
>
> And on that farm he had a cow, *eee-eye,*
>   *eee-eye,* oh.
>
> > With a moo-moo here and a moo-moo there,
> >
> > Here a moo, there a moo,
> >
> > Everywhere a moo-moo,
>
> Old MacDonald had a farm, *eee-eye,*
>   *eee-eye,* oh.

In successive verses, more animals are added, and the middle refrain gets longer and longer. For example, the second verse is

> Old MacDonald had a farm, *eee-eye,*
>   *eee-eye,* oh.
>
> And on that farm he had a pig, *eee-eye,*
>   *eee-eye,* oh.
>
> > With an oink-oink here and an oink-oink there,
> >
> > Here an oink, there an oink,
> >
> > Everywhere an oink-oink,
> >
> > With a moo-moo here and a moo-moo there,
> >
> > Here a moo, there a moo,
> >
> > Everywhere a moo-moo,
>
> Old MacDonald had a farm, *eee-eye,*
>   *eee-eye,* oh.

a. Show that after *n* verses of this song have been sung, the total number of syllables sung would be given by the expression $22n(n + 1)/2 + 37n$

(You may assume that all animal names and all animal sounds consist of one syllable, as in cow, pig, moo, oink, and so on.)

b. If singing this song is the algorithm, and the work unit is singing one syllable, what is the order of magnitude of the algorithm?[1]

2. *Linear programming* involves selecting values for a large number of quantities so that they satisfy a set of inequalities (such as $x + y + z \leq 100$) while at the same time maximizing (or minimizing) some particular function of these variables. Linear programming has many applications in communications and manufacturing. A trial-and-error approach to a linear programming problem would involve guessing at values for these variables until all of the inequalities are satisfied, but this may not produce the desired maximum (or minimum) value. In addition, real-world problems may involve hundreds or thousands of variables. A common algorithm to solve linear programming problems is called the *simplex method.* Although the simplex method works well for many common applications, including those that involve thousands of variables, its worst-case order of magnitude is exponential. Find information on the work of N. Karmarkar of Bell Labs, who discovered another algorithm for linear programming that is of polynomial order in the worst case and is faster than the simplex method in average cases.

---

[1]This exercise is based on work found in Chavey, D., "Songs and the Analysis of Algorithms," *Proceedings of the Twenty-Seventh SIGCSE Technical Symposium* (1996), pp. 4–8.

ADDITIONAL RESOURCES

CourseMate For additional print and/or online resources relevant to this chapter, visit the Computer Science CourseMate at login.cengagebrain.com.

Chapter
17   Social Issues

Chapters
13, 14, 15, 16   Applications

Chapters
9, 10, 11, 12   The Software World

Chapters
6, 7, 8   The Virtual Machine

Chapters
4, 5   The Hardware World

Chapters
2, 3   The Algorithmic Foundations
                      of Computer Science

Some computer scientists are interested only in the logical and mathematical properties of algorithms—the material presented in Level 1. Others are interested in discovering and studying a solution and *using* that solution to produce results more efficiently than was previously possible. They want to execute algorithms on *real* computers.

Level 2 of the text takes us into a fascinating region of computer science, the hardware world. Chapter 4 examines the fundamental building blocks used to construct computers. It discusses how to represent and store information inside a computer, how to use the principles of symbolic logic to design *gates*, and how to use gates to construct *circuits* that perform operations such as adding numbers, comparing numbers, and fetching instructions. These ideas are part of the branch of computer science known as *hardware design*, also called *logic design*. The second part of Level 2, Chapter 5, investigates computer hardware from a higher-level perspective called *computer organization*. This chapter introduces the four major subsystems of a modern computer (memory, input/output, arithmetic/logic unit, and control unit), demonstrates how they are built from the elementary building blocks described in Chapter 4, and shows how these subsystems can be organized into a complete, functioning computer system.

The Building Blocks: Binary Numbers, Boolean Logic, and Gates

4.1 Introduction

Level 1 of the text investigated the algorithmic foundations of computer science. It developed algorithms for searching tables, finding largest and smallest values, locating patterns, sorting lists, and cleaning up bad data. It also showed how to analyze and evaluate algorithms to demonstrate that they are not only correct but efficient and useful as well.

Our discussion assumed that these algorithms would be executed by something called a *computing agent*, an abstract concept representing any object capable of understanding and executing our instructions. At the time we didn't care what that computing agent was—person, mathematical model, computer, or robot. However, in this section of the text we *do* care what our computing agent looks like and how it is able to execute instructions and produce results.

In this chapter, we introduce the fundamental building blocks of all computer systems—binary representation, Boolean logic, gates, and circuits.

4.2 The Binary Numbering System

Our first concern with learning how to build computers is understanding how computers represent information. Their internal storage techniques are quite different from the way you and I represent information when we write a note or do a quick calculation on paper.

4.2.1 Binary Representation of Numeric and Textual Information

People generally represent numeric and textual information (language differences aside) by using the following notational conventions:

a. The 10 decimal digits 0, 1, 2, 3, 4, 5, 6, 7, 8, 9 for numeric values such as 459.

b. *Sign/magnitude notation* for signed numbers—that is, a + or − sign placed immediately to the left of the digits; +31 and −789 are examples.

c. *Decimal notation* for real numbers, with a decimal point separating the whole number part from the fractional part; an example is 12.34.

d. The 26 letters A, B, C, ... , Z for textual information (as well as lowercase letters and a few special symbols for punctuation).

You might suppose that these well-known schemes are the same conventions that computers use to store information in memory. Surprisingly, this is not true.

There are two types of information representation: The *external* representation of information is the way information is represented by humans and the way it is entered at a keyboard or displayed on a printer or screen. The *internal* representation of information is the way it is stored in the memory of a computer. This difference is diagrammed in Figure 4.1.

Externally, computers do use decimal digits, sign/magnitude notation, and the 26-character alphabet. However, virtually every computer ever built stores data—numbers, letters, graphics, images, sound—internally using the binary numbering system.

Binary is a base-2 positional numbering system not unlike the more familiar decimal, or base-10, system used in everyday life. In these systems, the value or "worth" of a digit depends not only on its absolute value but also on its specific position within a number. In the decimal system, there are 10 unique digits (0, 1, 2, 3, 4, 5, 6, 7, 8, and 9), and the value of the positions in a decimal number is based on powers of 10. Moving from right to left in a number, the positions represent ones (10^0), tens (10^1), hundreds (10^2), thousands (10^3), and so on. Therefore, the decimal number 2,359 is evaluated as follows:

$$(2 \times 10^3) + (3 \times 10^2) + (5 \times 10^1) + (9 \times 10^0)$$
$$= 2{,}000 + 300 + 50 + 9$$
$$= 2{,}359$$

FIGURE 4.1

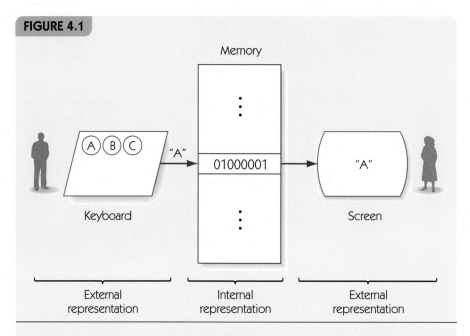

Distinction between external and internal representation of information

The same concepts apply to binary numbers except that there are only two digits, 0 and 1, and the value of the positions in a binary number is based on powers of 2. Moving from right to left, the positions represent ones (2^0), twos (2^1), fours (2^2), eights (2^3), sixteens (2^4), and so on. The two digits, 0 and 1, are frequently referred to as **bits**, a contraction of the two words *binary digits*.

For example, the six-digit binary number 111001 is evaluated as follows:

$$111001 = (1 \times 2^5) + (1 \times 2^4) + (1 \times 2^3) + (0 \times 2^2) + (0 \times 2^1) + (1 \times 2^0)$$
$$= 32 + 16 + 8 + 0 + 0 + 1$$
$$= 57$$

The five-digit binary quantity 10111 is evaluated in the following manner:

$$10111 = (1 \times 2^4) + (0 \times 2^3) + (1 \times 2^2) + (1 \times 2^1) + (1 \times 2^0)$$
$$= 16 + 0 + 4 + 2 + 1$$
$$= 23$$

Evaluating a binary number is quite easy, because 1 times any value is simply that value, and 0 times any value is always 0. Thus, when evaluating a binary number, use the following *binary-to-decimal algorithm*: Whenever there is a 1 in a column, add the positional value of that column to a running sum, and whenever there is a 0 in a column, add

FIGURE 4.2

Binary	Decimal	Binary	Decimal
0	0	10000	16
1	1	10001	17
10	2	10010	18
11	3	10011	19
100	4	10100	20
101	5	10101	21
110	6	10110	22
111	7	10111	23
1000	8	11000	24
1001	9	11001	25
1010	10	11010	26
1011	11	11011	27
1100	12	11100	28
1101	13	11101	29
1110	14	11110	30
1111	15	11111	31

Binary-to-decimal conversion table

nothing. The final sum is the decimal value of this binary number. This is the procedure we followed in the previous two examples.

A binary-to-decimal conversion table for the values 0–31 is shown in Figure 4.2. You might want to evaluate a few of the binary values using this algorithm to confirm their decimal equivalents.

Any whole number that can be represented in base 10 can also be represented in base 2, although it may take more digits because a single decimal digit contains more information than a single binary digit. Note that in the first example shown on the previous page it takes only two decimal digits (5 and 7) to represent the quantity 57 in base 10, but it takes six binary digits (1, 1, 1, 0, 0, and 1) to express the same value in base 2.

To go in the reverse direction—that is, to convert a decimal value into its binary equivalent—we use the *decimal-to-binary algorithm*, which is based on successive divisions by 2. Dividing the original decimal value by 2 produces a quotient and a remainder, which must be either a 0 or a 1. Record the remainder digit and then divide the quotient by 2, getting a new quotient and a second remainder digit. The process of dividing by 2, saving the quotient, and writing down the remainder is repeated until the quotient equals 0. The sequence of remainder digits, when written left to right from the last remainder digit to the first, is the binary representation of the original decimal value. For example, here is the conversion of the decimal value 19 into binary:

Convert the value 19 to binary:

$19 \div 2$	quotient $= 9$	remainder $= 1$	
$9 \div 2$	quotient $= 4$	remainder $= 1$	order for
$4 \div 2$	quotient $= 2$	remainder $= 0$	reading the
$2 \div 2$	quotient $= 1$	remainder $= 0$	remainder
$1 \div 2$	quotient $= 0$	remainder $= 1$	digits

Stop, because the quotient is now 0.

In this example, the remainder digits, when written left to right from the last one to the first, are 10011. This is the binary form of the decimal value 19. To confirm this, we can convert this value back to decimal form using the binary-to-decimal algorithm.

$$10011 = (1 \times 2^4) + (0 \times 2^3) + (0 \times 2^2) + (1 \times 2^1) + (1 \times 2^0)$$
$$= 16 + 0 + 0 + 2 + 1$$
$$= 19$$

In every computer, there is a maximum number of binary digits that can be used to store an integer. Typically, this value is 16, 32, or 64 bits. Once we have fixed this maximum number of bits (as part of the design of the computer), we also have fixed the largest unsigned whole number that can be represented in this computer. For example, Figure 4.2 used at most 5 bits to represent binary numbers. The largest value that could be represented is

A Not So Basic Base

The decimal system has been in use for so long that most people cannot imagine using a number system other than base 10. Tradition says it was chosen because we have 10 fingers and 10 toes. However, the discussion of the past few pages should convince you that there is nothing unique or special about decimal numbering, and the basic operations of arithmetic (addition, subtraction, multiplication, and division) work just fine in other bases, such as base 2. In addition to binary, computer science makes frequent use of *octal* (base 8) and *hexadecimal* (base 16). Furthermore, it is not only computers that utilize nondecimal bases. For example, the Native American Yuki tribe of northern California reportedly used base 4, or *quaternary* numbers, counting using the spaces between fingers rather than on the fingers themselves. The pre-Columbian Mayans of Mexico and Central America used a *vigesimal* system, or base 20, whereas ancient Babylonians employed *sexagesimal*, or base 60 (and we are quite sure that members of both cultures had the same number of fingers and toes as twenty-first-century human beings!).

11111, not unlike the number 99999, which is the maximum mileage value that can be represented on a five-digit decimal odometer. 11111 is the binary representation for the decimal integer 31. If there were 16 bits available, rather than 5, then the largest integer that could be represented is

1 1 1 1 1 1 1 1 1 1 1 1 1 1 1 1

This quantity is $2^{15} + 2^{14} + \ldots + 2^2 + 2^1 + 2^0 = 65,535$. Unsigned integers larger than this cannot be represented with 16 binary digits. Any operation on this computer that produces an unsigned value greater than 65,535 results in the error condition called **arithmetic overflow**. This is an attempt to represent an integer that exceeds the maximum allowable value. The computer could be designed to use more than 16 bits to represent integers, but no matter how many bits are ultimately used, there is always a maximum value beyond which the computer cannot correctly represent any integer. This characteristic is one of the major differences between the disciplines of mathematics and computer science. In mathematics, a quantity may usually take on any value, no matter how large. Computer science must deal with a finite—and sometimes quite limited—set of possible representations, and it must handle the errors that occur when those limits are exceeded.

Arithmetic in binary is quite easy because we have only 2 digits to deal with rather than 10. Therefore, the rules that define arithmetic operations such as addition and subtraction have only $2 \times 2 = 4$ entries, rather than the $10 \times 10 = 100$ entries for decimal digits. For example, here are the four rules that define binary addition:

```
   0     0     1     1
 + 0   + 1   + 0   + 1
 ───   ───   ───   ───
   0     1     1    10  (that is, 0 with a carry of 1.)
```

The last rule says that 1 + 1 = 10, which has the decimal value 2.

To add two binary numbers, you use the same technique first learned in grade school. Add each column one at a time from right to left, using the binary addition rules shown above. In the column being added, you write the sum digit under the line and any carry digit produced is written above the next column to the left. For example, addition of the two binary values 7 (00111) and 14 (01110) proceeds as follows:

```
   00111   (the binary value 7)
 + 01110   (the binary value 14)
```

Start by adding the two digits in the rightmost column—the 1 and 0. This produces a sum of 1 and a carry digit of 0; the carry digit gets "carried" to the second column.

```
        0        ← carry digit
    00111
  + 01110
        1
```

Now add the carry digit from the previous column to the two digits in the second column, which gives $0 + 1 + 1$. From the rules above, we see that the $(0 + 1)$ produces a 1. When this is added to the value 1, it produces a sum of 0 and a new carry digit of 1.

```
     1         ← carry digit
   00111
 + 01110
   ─────
      01
```

Adding the two digits in the third column plus the carry digit from the second column produces $1 + 1 + 1$, which is 11, or a sum of 1 and a new carry digit of 1.

```
     1         ← carry digit
   00111
 + 01110
   ─────
     101
```

Continuing in this right-to-left manner until we reach the leftmost column produces the final result, 10101 in binary, or 21 in decimal.

```
   00111
 + 01110
   ─────
   10101    (the value 21 = 16 + 4 + 1)
```

Signed Numbers. Binary digits can represent not only whole numbers but also other forms of data, including signed integers, decimal numbers, and characters. For example, to represent signed integers, we can use the leftmost bit of a number to represent the sign, with 0 meaning positive (+) and 1 meaning negative (–). The remaining bits are used to represent the magnitude of the value. This form of signed integer representation is termed **sign/magnitude notation**, and it is one of a number of different techniques for representing positive and negative whole numbers. For example, to represent the quantity –49 in sign/magnitude, we could use seven binary digits with 1 bit for the sign and 6 bits for the magnitude:

$$\underbrace{1}_{-} \; \underbrace{1\,1\,0\,0\,0\,1}_{49} \qquad (2^5 + 2^4 + 2^0 = 32 + 16 + 1 = 49)$$

The value +3 would be stored like this:

$$\underbrace{0}_{+} \; \underbrace{0\,0\,0\,0\,1\,1}_{3} \qquad (2^1 + 2^0 = 2 + 1 = 3)$$

You might wonder how a computer knows that the seven-digit binary number 1110001 in the first example above represents the signed integer value –49 rather than the unsigned whole number 113.

$$1110001 = (1 \times 2^6) + (1 \times 2^5) + (1 \times 2^4) + (1 \times 2^0)$$
$$= 64 + 32 + 16 + 1$$
$$= 113$$

The answer to this question is that a computer does *not* know. A sequence of binary digits can have many different interpretations, and there is no fixed, predetermined interpretation given to any binary value. A binary number stored in the memory of a computer takes on meaning only because it is used in a certain way. If we use the value 1110001 as though it were a signed integer, then it will be interpreted that way and will take on the value −49. If it is used, instead, as an unsigned whole number, then that is what it will become, and it will be interpreted as the value 113. The meaning of a binary number stored in memory is based solely on the context in which it is used.

Initially, this might seem strange, but we deal with this type of ambiguity all the time in natural languages. For example, in the Hebrew language, letters of the alphabet are also used as numbers. Thus the Hebrew character aleph (א) can stand for either the letter A or the number 1. The only way to tell which meaning is appropriate is to consider the context in which the character is used. Similarly, in English, the word *ball* can mean either a round object used to play games or an elegant formal party. Which interpretation is correct? We cannot say without knowing the context in which the word is used. The same is true for values stored in the memory of a computer system. It is the context that determines the meaning of a binary string.

Sign/magnitude notation is quite easy for people to work with and understand, but, surprisingly, it is used rather infrequently in real computer systems. The reason is the existence of the very "messy" and unwanted signed number: 10000 . . . 0000. Because the leftmost bit is a 1, this value is treated as negative. The magnitude is 0000 . . . 0000. Thus this bit pattern represents the numerical quantity "negative zero," a value that has no real mathematical meaning and should not be distinguished from the other representation for zero, 00000 . . . 0000. The existence of two distinct bit patterns for a single numerical quantity causes some significant problems for computer designers.

For example, assume we are executing the following algorithmic operation on two signed numbers *a* and *b*

```
if (a = b)
     do operation 1
else
     do operation 2
```

when *a* has the value 0000 . . . 0 and *b* has the value 1000 . . . 0. Should they be considered equal to each other? Numerically, the value −0 does equal +0, so maybe we should do operation 1. However, the two bit patterns are not identical, so maybe these two values are not equal, and we should do operation 2. This situation can result in programs that execute in different ways on different machines.

Therefore, computer designers tend to favor signed integer representations that do not suffer from the problem of two zeros. One of the most widely used is called **two's complement representation**. To understand how this method works, you need to write down, in circular form, all binary patterns from 000 . . . 0 to 111 . . . 1 in increasing order. Here is what that circle might look like using three-digit numbers:

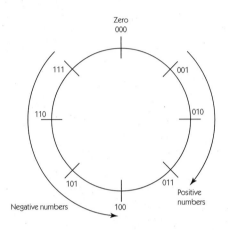

In this diagram, the positive numbers begin at 000 and proceed in order around the circle to the right. Negative numbers begin at 111 and proceed in order around the circle to the left. The leftmost digit specifies whether the number is to be given a positive interpretation (leftmost bit = 0) or a negative interpretation (leftmost bit = 1).

Bit Pattern	Decimal Value
000	0
001	+1
010	+2
011	+3
100	−4
101	−3
110	−2
111	−1

In this representation, if we add, for example, $3 + (-3)$, we get 0, as expected:

```
11    ← carry digits
011
101
───
000    (Note: The 1 that carries into column 4 can be discarded.)
```

Note that in the two's complement representation, there is only a single zero, the binary number 000 . . . 0. However, the existence of a single pattern for zero leads to another unusual situation. The total number of values that can be represented with n bits is 2^n, which is always an even number. In the previous example, $n = 3$, so there were $2^3 = 8$ possible values. One of these is used for 0, leaving seven remaining values, which is an odd number. It is impossible to divide these seven patterns equally between the positive and negative numbers, and in this example we ended up with four negative values but only three positive ones. The pattern that was previously "negative zero" (100) now represents the value -4, but there is no equivalent number on the positive side, that is, there is no binary pattern that represents $+4$. In the two's complement representation of signed integers, you can always represent one more negative number than positive. This is not as severe a problem as having two zeros, though, and two's complement is widely used for representing signed numbers inside a computer.

This has been only a brief introduction to the two's complement representation. A Challenge Work problem at the end of this chapter invites you to investigate further the underlying mathematical foundations of this interesting representational technique.

Fractional Numbers. Fractional numbers, such as 12.34 and -0.001275, can also be represented in binary by using the signed-integer techniques we have just described. To do that, however, we must first convert the number to **scientific notation**:

$$\pm M \times B^{\pm E}$$

where M is the *mantissa*, B is the *exponent base* (usually 2), and E is the *exponent*. For example, assume we want to represent the decimal quantity $+5.75$. In addition, assume that we will use 16 bits to represent the number, with 10 bits allocated for representing the mantissa and 6 bits for the exponent. (The exponent base B is assumed to be 2 and is not explicitly stored.) Both the mantissa and the exponent are signed integer numbers, so we can use either the sign/magnitude or two's complement notations that we just learned to represent each of these two fields. (In all the following examples, we have chosen to use sign/magnitude notation.)

In binary, the value 5 is 101. To represent the fractional quantity 0.75, we need to remember that the bits to the right of the decimal point (or binary point in our case) have the positional values r^{-1}, r^{-2}, r^{-3}, and so on, where r is the base of the numbering system used to represent the number. When using decimal notation, these position values are the tenths (10^{-1}), hundredths (10^{-2}), thousandths (10^{-3}), and so on. Because r is 2 in our case, the positional values of the digits to the right of the binary point are halves (2^{-1}), quarters (2^{-2}), eighths (2^{-3}), sixteenths (2^{-4}), and so on. Thus,

$0.75 = 1/2 + 1/4 = 2^{-1} + 2^{-2}$ (which in binary is 0.11)

Therefore, in binary $5.75 = 101.11$. Using scientific notation, and an exponent base $B = 2$, we can write this value as

$5.75 = 101.11 \times 2^0$

Next, we must *normalize* the number so that its first significant digit is immediately to the right of the binary point. As we move the binary point, we adjust the value of the exponent so that the overall value of the number remains unchanged. If we move the binary point to the left one place (which makes the value smaller by a factor of 2), then we add 1 to the exponent (which makes it larger by a factor of 2). We do the reverse when we move the binary point to the right.

$$5.75 = 101.11 \times 2^0$$
$$= 10.111 \times 2^1$$
$$= 1.0111 \times 2^2$$
$$= .10111 \times 2^3$$
$$\text{(which is } (1/2 + 1/8 + 1/16 + 1/32) \times 8 = 5.75)$$

We now have the number in the desired format and can put all the pieces together. We separately store the mantissa (excluding the binary point, which is assumed to be to the left of the first significant digit) and the exponent, both of which are signed integers and can be represented in sign/magnitude notation. The mantissa is stored with its sign—namely, 0, because it is a positive quantity—followed by the assumed binary point, followed by the magnitude of the mantissa, which in this case is 10111. Next we store the exponent, which is +3, or 000011 in sign/magnitude. The overall representation, using 16 bits, is

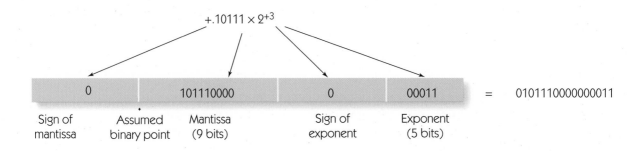

For another example, let's determine the internal representation of the fraction −5/16.

$$-5/16 = -(1/4 + 1/16)$$
$$= -.0101 \times 2^0 \quad \text{(this is the value } -5/16 \text{ in scientific notation)}$$
$$= -.101 \times 2^{-1} \quad \text{(after normalization)}$$

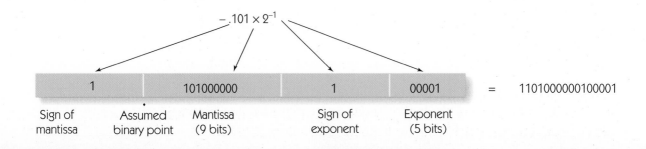

Textual Information. To represent textual material in binary, the system assigns to each printable letter or symbol in our alphabet a unique number (this assignment is called a *code mapping*), and then it stores that symbol internally using the binary equivalent of that number. For example, here is one possible mapping of characters to numbers, which uses 8 bits to represent each character.

Symbol	*Decimal Value*	*Binary (Using 8 Binary Digits)*
A	1	00000001
B	2	00000010
C	3	00000011
D	4	00000100
⋮	⋮	⋮
Z	26	00011010
⋮	⋮	⋮
@	128	10000000
!	129	10000001
⋮	⋮	⋮

To store the four-character string "BAD!" in memory, the computer would store the binary representation of each individual character using the above 8-bit code.

BAD! = 00000010   00000001   00000100   10000001

         B   A   D   !

We have indicated above that the 8-bit numeric quantity 10000001 is interpreted as the character "!". However, as we mentioned earlier, the only way a computer knows that the 8-bit value 10000001 represents the symbol "!" and not the unsigned integer value 129 (128 + 1) or the signed integer value −1 (sign bit = negative, magnitude is 1) is by the context in which it is used. If these 8 bits are sent to a display device that expects to be given characters, then this value will be interpreted as an "!". If, on the other hand, this 8-bit value is sent to an arithmetic unit that adds unsigned numbers, then it will be interpreted as a 129 in order to make the addition operation meaningful.

To facilitate the exchange of textual information, such as word-processing documents and electronic mail, between computer systems, it would be most helpful if everyone used the same code mapping. Fortunately, this is pretty much the case. Currently, the most widely used code for representing characters internally in a computer system is called ASCII, an acronym for the American Standard Code for Information Interchange. ASCII is an international standard for representing textual information in the majority of computers. It uses 8 bits to represent each character, so it is able to encode a total of $2^8 = 256$ different characters. These are assigned the integer values 0 to 255. However, only the numbers 32 to 126 have been assigned so far to printable characters. The remainder either are unassigned or are used for nonprinting control characters such as tab, form feed, and return. Figure 4.3 shows the ASCII conversion table for the numerical values 32–126.

FIGURE 4.3

Keyboard Character	Binary ASCII Code	Integer Equivalent	Keyboard Character	Binary ASCII Code	Integer Equivalent
(blank)	00100000	32	P	01010000	80
!	00100001	33	Q	01010001	81
"	00100010	34	R	01010010	82
#	00100011	35	S	01010011	83
$	00100100	36	T	01010100	84
%	00100101	37	U	01010101	85
&	00100110	38	V	01010110	86
'	00100111	39	W	01010111	87
(	00101000	40	X	01011000	88
)	00101001	41	Y	01011001	89
*	00101010	42	Z	01011010	90
+	00101011	43	[	01011011	91
'	00101100	44	\	01011100	92
−	00101101	45	]	01011101	93
.	00101110	46	^	01011110	94
/	00101111	47	_	01011111	95
0	00110000	48	`	01100000	96
1	00110001	49	a	01100001	97
2	00110010	50	b	01100010	98
3	00110011	51	c	01100011	99
4	00110100	52	d	01100100	100
5	00110101	53	e	01100101	101
6	00110110	54	f	01100110	102
7	00110111	55	g	01100111	103
8	00111000	56	h	01101000	104
9	00111001	57	i	01101001	105
:	00111010	58	j	01101010	106
;	00111011	59	k	01101011	107
<	00111100	60	l	01101100	108
=	00111101	61	m	01101101	109
>	00111110	62	n	01101110	110
?	00111111	63	o	01101111	111
@	01000000	64	p	01110000	112
A	01000001	65	q	01110001	113
B	01000010	66	r	01110010	114
C	01000011	67	s	01110011	115
D	01000100	68	t	01110100	116
E	01000101	69	u	01110101	117
F	01000110	70	v	01110110	118
G	01000111	71	w	01110111	119
H	01001000	72	x	01111000	120
I	01001001	73	y	01111001	121
J	01001010	74	z	01111010	122
K	01001011	75	{	01111011	123
L	01001100	76	:	01111100	124
M	01001101	77	]	01111101	125
N	01001110	78	~	01111110	126
O	01001111	79			

ASCII conversion table

However, a code set called Unicode has gained popularity because it uses a 16-bit representation for characters rather than the 8-bit format of ASCII. This means that it is able to represent $2^{16} = 65,536$ unique characters instead of the $2^8 = 256$ of ASCII. It might seem like 256 characters are more than enough to represent all the textual symbols that we would ever need—for example, 26 uppercase letters, 26 lowercase letters, 10 digits, and a few dozen special symbols, such as $+=-\{\}[\backslash:"?><.,;\%\$\#@$. Add that all together and it still totals only about 100 symbols, far less than the 256 that can be represented in ASCII. However, that is true only if we limit our work to Arabic numerals and the Roman alphabet. The world grows more connected all the time—helped along by computers, networks, and the Web—and it is critically important that computers represent and exchange textual information using alphabets in addition to these 26 letters and 10 digits. When we start assigning codes to symbols drawn from alphabets such as Russian, Arabic, Chinese, Hebrew, Greek, Thai, Bengali, and Braille, as well as mathematical symbols and special linguistic marks such as the tilde, umlaut, and accent grave, it becomes clear that ASCII does not have nearly enough room to represent them all. However, Unicode, with space for over 65,000 symbols, is large enough to accommodate all these symbols and many more to come. In fact, Unicode has defined standard code mappings for more than 50,000 symbols from literally hundreds of alphabets, and it is a way for users around the world to share textual information regardless of the language in which they are writing. The Unicode home page, which gives all the current standard mappings, is located at *www.unicode.org*.

4.2.2 Binary Representation of Sound and Images

During the first 30 to 40 years of computing, the overwhelming majority of applications, such as word processing and spreadsheets, were text-based and limited to the manipulation of characters, words, and numbers. However, sound and images are now as important a form of representation as text and numbers because of the rapid growth of the Web, the popularity of digitally encoded music, the emergence of digital photography, and the almost universal availability of digital DVD movies. Most of us, whether computer specialists or not, have had the experience of playing MP3 files, e-mailing vacation pictures to friends and family, or enjoying a YouTube video clip. In this section, we take a brief look at how sounds and images are represented in computers, using the same binary numbering system that we have been discussing.

Sound is analog information, unlike the digital format used to represent text and numbers discussed in the previous section. In a digital representation, the values for a given object are drawn from a finite set, such as letters {A, B, C, ... , Z} or a subset of integers {0, 1, 2, 3, ... , MAX}.

Practice Problems

1. What is the value of the 8-bit binary quantity 10101000 if it is interpreted (a) as an unsigned integer, and (b) as a signed integer represented in sign/magnitude notation?

2. What does the unsigned decimal value 99 look like in binary using 8 bits?

3. What do the signed integers −300 and +254 look like in binary using 10 bits and sign/magnitude integer representation?

4. What is the value of the 8-bit binary quantity 10010111 when it is interpreted as a sign/magnitude integer?

5. Using 4 bits and two's complement representation, what is the binary representation of the following signed decimal values:

   a. +6
   b. −3

6. Perform the following 5-bit binary addition showing the carry bit that propagates to each column. Assume the numbers are unsigned binary quantities:

   ```
     01110
   + 01011
   ```

7. What does the three-character string "X+Y" look like internally using the 8-bit ASCII code given in Figure 4.3? What does it look like in 16-bit Unicode? (Go to www.unicode.org to find the specific code mappings for these three characters.)

8. Using 10 bits to represent the mantissa (sign/magnitude) and 6 bits for the exponent (also sign/magnitude), show the internal representation of the following two values:

   a. + 0.25
   b. − 32 1/16

9. Explain exactly what happens when you add a 1 to the following 5-bit, two's complement value: 01111

10. Explain exactly what happens when you perform addition on the following two sign/magnitude integer values:

    ```
      00111 (+7)
    + 01110 (+14)
    ```

FIGURE 4.4

Example of sound represented as a waveform

In an analog representation, objects can take on any value. For example, in the case of sound, a tone is a continuous sinusoidal waveform that varies in a regular periodic fashion over time, as shown in Figure 4.4. (*Note:* This diagram shows only a single tone. Complex sounds, such as symphonic music, are composed of multiple overlapping waveforms. However, the basic ideas are the same.)

The amplitude (height) of the wave is a measure of its loudness—the greater the amplitude, the louder the sound. The period of the wave, designated as T, is the time it takes for the wave to make one complete cycle. The frequency f is the total number of cycles per unit time measured in cycles/second, also called *hertz*, and defined as $f = 1/T$. The frequency is a measure of the *pitch*, the highness or lowness of a sound. The higher the frequency, the higher the perceived tone. A human ear can generally detect sounds in the range of 20 to 20,000 hertz.

To store a waveform (such as the one in Figure 4.4) in a computer, the analog signal must first be digitized, that is, converted to a digital representation. This can be done using a technique known as sampling. At fixed time intervals, the amplitude of the signal is measured and stored as an integer value. The wave is thus represented in the computer in digital form as a sequence of sampled numerical amplitudes. For example, Figure 4.5(a) shows the sampling of the waveform of Figure 4.4.

This signal can now be stored inside the computer as the series of signed integer values 3, 7, 7, 5, 0, −3, −6, −6, ... , where each numerical value is encoded in binary using the techniques described in the previous section. From these stored digitized values, the computer can re-create an approximation to the original analog wave. It would first generate an amplitude level of 3, then an amplitude level of 7, then an amplitude level of 7, and so on, as shown in Figure 4.5(b). These values would be

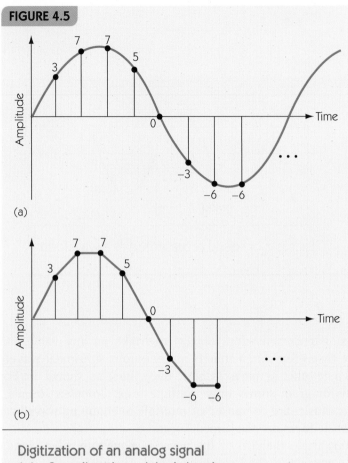

FIGURE 4.5

(a)

(b)

Digitization of an analog signal
(a)   Sampling the original signal
(b)   Recreating the signal from the sampled values

sent to a sound-generating device, like stereo speakers, which would produce the actual sounds based on the numerical values received.

The accuracy with which the original sound can be reproduced is
dependent on two key parameters—the sampling rate and the bit depth. The
sampling rate measures how many times per second we sample the amplitude of the sound wave. Obviously, the more often we sample, the more
accurate the reproduction. Note, for example, that the sampling shown in
Figure 4.5(a) appears to have missed the peak value of the wave because the
peak occurred between two sampling intervals. Furthermore, the more often
we sample, the greater the range of frequencies that can be captured; if the
frequency of a wave is greater than or equal to the sampling rate, we may
not sample any points whatsoever on an entire waveform. For example,
look at the following sampling interval t, which is exactly equal to the
period T of the wave being measured:

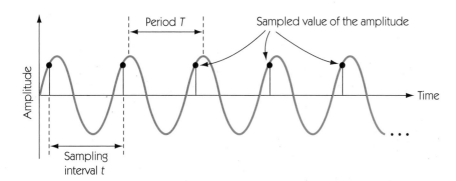

This rate of sampling produces a constant amplitude value, totally distorting the original sound. In general, a sampling rate of R samples/second allows you to reproduce all frequencies up to about R/2 hertz. Because the human ear can normally detect sound up to about 20,000 hertz, a sampling rate of at least 40,000 samples per second is necessary to capture all audible frequencies.

The **bit depth** is the number of bits used to encode each sample. In the previous section, you learned that ASCII is an 8-bit character code, allowing for 256 unique symbols. Unicode uses 16 bits, allowing for more than 65,000 symbols and greatly increasing the number of symbols that can be represented. The same trend can be seen in sound reproduction. Initially, 8 bits per sample was the standard, but the 256 levels of amplitude that could be represented turned out to be insufficient for the sophisticated high-end sound systems produced and marketed today. Most audio encoding schemes today use either 16 or 24 bits per sample level, allowing for either 65,000 or 16,000,000 distinct amplitude levels.

There are many audio-encoding formats in use today, including WAV (Waveform Audio File Format), AAC (Advanced Audio Coding), WMA (Windows Media Audio), and MIDI (Musical Instrument Digital Interface). Probably the most popular and widely used digital audio format is *MP3*, an acronym for MPEG-1, Audio Level 3 Encoding. This is a digital audio encoding standard established by the Motion Picture Experts Group (MPEG), a committee of the International Organization for Standardization (ISO) of the United Nations. MP3 samples sound signals at the rate of 44,100 samples/second, using 16 bits per sample. This produces high-quality sound reproduction, which is why MP3 is the most widely used format for rock, opera, and classical music.

An image, such as a photograph, is also analog data but can also be stored using binary representation. An image is a continuous set of intensity and color values that can be digitized by sampling the analog information, just as is done for sound. The sampling process, often called *scanning*, consists of measuring the intensity values of distinct points located at regular intervals across the image's surface. These points are called *pixels*, for picture elements, and the more pixels used, the more accurate the encoding of the image. The average human eye cannot accurately discern components closer together than about 0.05–0.1 mm, so if the pixels, or dots, are sufficiently dense, they appear to the human eye as a single, contiguous image. For example, a high-quality digital camera stores about 5–10 million pixels per photograph. For a 3 in. × 5 in. image, this is about 500,000 pixels/in.[2], or 700 pixels per linear inch. This means the individual pixels are separated by about 1/700th of an inch, or 0.03 mm—too close together to be individually visualized. Figure 4.6 enlarges a small section of a digitized photograph to better show how it is stored internally as a set of discrete picture elements.

One of the key questions we need to answer is how much information is stored for each pixel. Suppose we want to store a representation of a black-and-white image. The easiest and most space-efficient approach is to mark each pixel as either white, stored as a binary 0, or black, stored as a binary 1. The only problem is that this produces a stark *black-and-white image*, with a highly sharp and unpleasant visual contrast. A much better way, though it takes more storage, is to represent black-and-white images using a *gray scale* of varying intensity. For example, if we use 3 bits per pixel, we can represent $2^3 = 8$ shades of intensity from level 0, pure white, to level 7, pure black. An example of this eight-level gray scale is shown in Figure 4.7. If we wanted more detail than is shown there, we could use 8 bits per pixel, giving us $2^8 = 256$ distinct shades of gray.

We now can encode our image as a sequence of numerical pixel values, storing each row of pixels completely, from left to right, before moving down to store the next row. Each pixel is encoded as an unsigned binary

FIGURE 4.6

(a)

(b)

Example of a digitized photograph
(a) Individual pixels in the photograph
(b) Photograph

FIGURE 4.7

An eight-level gray scale

value representing its gray scale intensity. This form of image representation is called raster graphics, and it is used by such well-known graphics standards as JPEG (Joint Photographer Experts Group), GIF (Graphics Interchange Format), and BMP (bitmap).

Today, most images are not black and white, but are in color. To digitize color images, we still measure the intensity value of the image at a discrete set of points, but we need to store more information about each pixel. The most common format for storing color images is the RGB encoding scheme, RGB being an acronym for Red-Green-Blue. This technique describes a specific color by capturing the individual contribution to a pixel's color of each of the three colors, red, green, and blue. It uses one byte, or 8 bits, for each color, allowing us to represent an intensity range of 0 to 255. The value 0 means that there is no contribution from this color, whereas the value 255 means a full contribution of this color.

For example, the color magenta is an equal mix of pure red and blue, which would be RGB encoded as (255, 0, 255):

Red	Green	Blue
255	0	255

The color hot pink is produced by setting the three RGB values to

Red	Green	Blue
255	105	180

and harvest gold is rendered as

Red	Green	Blue
218	165	32

Using 3 bytes of information per pixel—24 bits—allows us to represent 2^{24} distinct colors, about 16.7 million. This 24-bit color-encoding scheme is often referred to as *True Color*, and it provides an enormous range of shades and an extremely accurate color image reproduction. That is why it is the encoding scheme used in the JPEG Color Imaging format. However, representing 16+ million colors requires a huge amount of memory space, and some image representation techniques reduce that value by using what is called a *color palette*. While theoretically supporting 16+ million different colors, they only allow you to use 256 (or some other small number) at any one time, just as a painter may have a lot of colors in his or her studio but puts only a few on the palette at a time. With a palette size of 256, we can encode each pixel using only 8 bits rather than 24, because $2^8 = 256$, thus reducing storage space demands by almost 67%. Each of these 256 values does not represent an explicit RGB color value but rather an index into a palette, or a color table. This index specifies which color on the palette is to be used to draw this pixel. This is the technique used, for example, in the Graphics Interchange Format (GIF), which uses a palette that can hold as few as 2 colors or as many as 256.

Sound and image data typically require huge amounts of storage, far more than is required for the numbers and text discussed in Section 4.2.1. For example, a 300-page novel contains about 100,000 words. Each word has on average about five characters and, as discussed in the previous section, each character can be encoded into the ASCII code set using 8 bits. Thus, the total number of bits needed to represent this book is roughly

100,000 words × 5 char/word × 8 bits/char = *4 million bits*

By comparison, 1 minute of sound recording encoded using the MP3 standard, which samples 44,100 times per second using a bit depth of 16 bits per sample, requires

44,100 samples/sec × 16 bits/sample × 60 sec/minute = *42 million bits*

It takes 10 times as much space to store the information in 1 minute of music as it does to store an entire 300-page book! Similarly, to store a single photograph taken using a digital camera with 5 million pixels using 24-bit True-Color raster graphics requires:

5,000,000 pixels/photograph × 24 bits/pixel = *120 million bits*

A single photograph could require as much as 30 times more storage than an entire novel.

As these examples clearly show, the storage of analog information, such as sound, images, voice, and video, is enormously space intensive, and an important area of computer science research—data compression—is directed at addressing just this issue. Data compression algorithms attempt to represent information in ways that preserve accuracy while using significantly less space.

For example, a simple compression technique that can be used on almost any form of data is *run-length encoding*. This method replaces a sequence of identical values $v_1, v_2, \dots, v_n$ by a pair of values (v, n), which indicates that the value v is replicated n times. If both v and n require 1 byte of storage, then we have reduced the total number of bytes required to store this sequence from n down to 2. Using this method, we could encode the following 5 × 3 image of the letter E, where 0 = white, 255 = black:

255	255	255
255	0	0
255	255	255
255	0	0
255	255	255

like this:

$(255, 4) (0, 2) (255, 4) (0, 2) (255, 3)$

Run-length encoding reduces the number of bytes needed to store this image from 15, using the raster graphics representation, to the 10 bytes shown above. Compression schemes are usually evaluated by their compression ratio, which measures how much they reduce the storage requirements of the data:

$$\text{compression ratio} = \frac{\text{size of the uncompressed data}}{\text{size of the compressed data}}$$

For the example shown above, this ratio is

$\text{ratio} = 15/10 = 1.5$

meaning the scheme reduces the amount of space needed to store the image by 33%. Applied to a larger image, this might mean that a 4-million-bit representation could be reduced to about 2.7 million bits, a significant savings.

Another popular compression technique is *variable-length code sets*, which are often used to compress text but can also be used with other forms of data. In Section 4.2.1, we showed that textual symbols, such as A, z, and #, are represented internally by a code mapping that uses exactly the same number of bits for every symbol, either 8 (ASCII) or 16 (Unicode). That is a wasteful approach as some symbols occur much more frequently than others. (For example, in English, the letters E and A are much more common than J, Q, X, and Z.) If the codes representing commonly used symbols were shorter than the codes representing the less-common symbols, this could result in a significant saving of space.

Assume that we want to encode the Hawaiian alphabet, which only contains the five vowels A, E, I, O, and U, and the seven consonants H, K, L, M, N, P, and W. If we were to store these characters using a fixed-length code set, we would need at least 4 bits/symbol, because $2^4 = 16$. Figure 4.8(a) shows one possible encoding of these 12 letters using a fixed-length, 4-bit encoding. However, if we know that A and I are the most commonly used letters in the Hawaiian alphabet, with H and W next, we could represent A and I using two bits, H and W using 3 bits, and the remaining letters using either 4, 5, 6, or 7 bits, depending on their frequency. However, we must be sure that if the 2-bit sequence $s_1 s_2$ is used to represent an A, for example, then no other symbol representation can start with the same 2-bit sequence. Otherwise, if we saw the sequence $s_1 s_2$, we would not know if it was an A or the beginning of another character.

One possible variable-length encoding for the Hawaiian alphabet is shown in Figure 4.8(b).

FIGURE 4.8

Letter	4-bit Encoding	Variable Length Encoding
A	0000	00
I	0001	10
H	0010	010
W	0011	110
E	0100	0110
O	0101	0111
M	0110	11100
K	0111	11101
U	1000	11110
N	1001	111110
P	1010	1111110
L	1011	1111111
	(a)	(b)

Using variable-length code sets

(a) Fixed length
(b) Variable length

Representing the six-character word HAWAII using the fixed-length 4-bit encoding scheme of Figure 4.8(a) requires 6 × 4 = 24 bits. Representing it with the variable-length encoding shown in Figure 4.8(b) produces the following:

H	A	W	A	I	I
010	00	110	00	10	10

This is a total of 14 bits, producing a compression ratio of 24/14 = 1.71, a reduction in storage demands of about 42%.

These two techniques are examples of what are called **lossless compression** schemes. This means that no information is lost in the compression, and it is possible to exactly reproduce the original data. **Lossy compression** schemes compress data in a way that does not guarantee that all of the information in the original data can be fully and completely re-created. They trade a possible loss of accuracy for a higher compression ratio because the small inaccuracies in sounds or images are often undetectable to the human ear or eye. Many of the compression schemes in widespread use today, including MP3 and JPEG, use lossy techniques, which permit significantly greater compression ratios than would otherwise be possible. Using lossy JPEG, for example, it is possible to achieve compression ratios of 10:1, 20:1, or more, depending on how much loss of detail we are willing to tolerate. This compares with the values of 1.5 and 1.7 in the earlier described lossless schemes. Using these lossy compression schemes, that

Practice Problems

1. Using MP3, how many bits are required to store a 3-minute song in uncompressed format? If the information is compressed with a ratio of 4:1, how many bits are required?

2. If we instead use a sampling rate of 66,000 samples per second and a bit depth of 24, how many bits are required to store that same 3-minute song?

3. How many bits are needed to store a single uncompressed RGB image from a 2.1 megapixel (millions of pixels) digital camera? How many bytes of memory is this?

4. If we want the image in Problem 3 to fit into 1 megabyte of memory, what compression ratio is needed? If we want it to fit into 256 kilobytes (thousands of bytes) of memory, what compression ratio is needed?

5. If we were able to reduce the storage space of an image to 3 megabits from its original size of 9.6 megabits, what would the compression ratio be?

6. How much space is saved by representing the Hawaiian word ALOHA in the variable-length code of Figure 4.8(b) as compared with the fixed-length representation of Figure 4.8(a)? What is the compression ratio?

120-megabit, high-resolution image mentioned earlier could be reduced to only 6 or 12 megabits, certainly a much more manageable value. Data compression schemes are an essential component in allowing us to represent multimedia information in a concise and manageable way.

4.2.3 The Reliability of Binary Representation

At this point, you might be wondering: Why are we bothering to use binary? Because we use a decimal numerical system for everyday tasks, wouldn't it be more convenient to use a base-10 representation for both the external and the internal representation of information? Then there would be no need to go through the time-consuming conversions diagrammed in Figure 4.1, or to learn the binary representation techniques discussed in the previous two sections.

As we stated in the Special Interest Box, "A Not So Basic Base," there is absolutely no theoretical reason why one could not build a "decimal" computer or, indeed, a computer that stored numbers using base 3 (*ternary*), base 8 (*octal*), or base 16 (*hexadecimal*). The techniques described in the previous two sections apply to information represented in *any* base of a positional numbering system, including base 10.

Computers use binary representation not for any theoretical reasons but for reasons of *reliability*. As we shall see shortly, computers store information using electronic devices, and the internal representation of information must be implemented in terms of electronic quantities such as currents and voltage levels.

Building a base-10 "decimal computer" requires finding a device with 10 distinct and stable energy states that can be used to represent the 10 unique digits (0, 1, ... , 9) of the decimal system. For example, assume there exists a device that can store electrical charges in the range from 0 to +45 volts. We could use it to build a decimal computer by letting certain voltage levels correspond to specific decimal digits:

Voltage Level	Corresponds to This Decimal Digit
+0	0
+5	1
+10	2
+15	3
+20	4
+25	5
+30	6
+35	7
+40	8
+45	9

Storing the two-digit decimal number 28 requires two of these devices, one for each of the digits in the number. The first device would be set to +10 volts to represent the digit 2, and the second would be set to +40 volts to represent the digit 8.

Although this is theoretically feasible, it is certainly not recommended. As electrical devices age, they become unreliable, and they may *drift*, or change their energy state, over time. What if the device representing the value 8 (the one set to +40 volts) lost 6% of its voltage (not a huge amount for an old, well-used piece of equipment)? The voltage would drop from +40 volts to about +37.5 volts. The question is whether the value +37.5 represents the digit 7 (+35) or the digit 8 (+40). It is impossible to say. If that same device lost another 6% of its voltage, it would drop from +37.5 volts to about +35 volts. Our 8 has now become a 7, and the original value of 28 has unexpectedly changed to 27. Building a reliable decimal machine would be an engineering nightmare.

The problem with a base-10 representation is that it needs to store 10 unique symbols, and, therefore, it needs devices that have 10 stable states. Such devices are extremely rare. Electrical systems tend to operate best in a *bistable environment*, in which there are only two (rather than 10) stable states separated by a huge energy barrier. Examples of these bistable states include the following:

- Full on/full off

- Fully charged/fully discharged

- Charged positively/charged negatively

- Magnetized/nonmagnetized

- Magnetized clockwise/magnetized counterclockwise

In the binary numbering system, there are only two symbols (0 and 1), so we can let one of the two stable states of our bistable device represent a 0 and the other a 1. This is a much more reliable way to represent information inside a computer.

For example, if we use binary rather than decimal to store data in our hypothetical electronic device that stores voltages in the range from 0 to +45 volts, the representational scheme becomes much simpler:

    0 volts   = 0 (full off)
    +45 volts   = 1 (full on)

Now a 6% or even a 12% drift doesn't affect the interpretation of the value being represented. In fact, it takes an almost 50% change in voltage level to create a problem in interpreting a stored value. The use of binary for the internal representation of data significantly increases the inherent reliability of a computer. This single advantage is worth all the time it takes to convert from decimal to binary for internal storage and from binary to decimal for the external display of results.

4.2.4 Binary Storage Devices

As you learned in the previous section, binary computers can be built out of any bistable device. This idea can be expressed more formally by saying that it is possible to construct a binary computer and its internal components using any hardware device that meets the following four criteria:

1. The device has two stable energy states (one for a 0, one for a 1).

2. These two states are separated by a large energy barrier (so that a 0 does not accidentally become a 1, or vice versa).

3. It is possible to sense which state the device is in (to see whether it is storing a 0 or a 1) without permanently destroying the stored value.

4. It is possible to switch the state from a 0 to a 1, or vice versa, by applying a sufficient amount of energy.

There are many devices that meet these conditions, including some surprising ones such as a light switch. A typical light switch has two stable states (ON and OFF). These two states are separated by a large energy barrier so that a switch that is in one state will not accidentally change to the other. We can determine what state the switch is in by looking to see whether the label says ON or OFF (or just by looking at the light), and we can change the state of the switch by applying a sufficient amount of energy via our fingertips. Thus it would be possible to build a reliable (albeit very slow and bulky) binary computing device out of ordinary light switches and fingertips!

FIGURE 4.9

Using magnetic cores to represent binary values

As you might imagine, computer systems are not built from light switches, but they have been built using a wide range of devices. This section describes two of these devices.

Magnetic cores were used to construct computer memories for about 20 years. From roughly 1955 to 1975, this was by far the most popular storage technology—even today, the memory unit of a computer is sometimes referred to as *core memory* even though it has been decades since magnetic cores have been used.

A *core* is a small, magnetizable, iron oxide-coated "doughnut," about 1/50 of an inch in inner diameter, with wires strung through its center hole. The two states used to represent the binary values 0 and 1 are based on the *direction* of the magnetic field of the core. When electric current is sent through the wire in one specific direction, say left to right, the core is magnetized in a counterclockwise direction.[1] This state could represent the binary value 0. Current sent in the opposite direction produces a clockwise magnetic field that could represent the binary value 1. These scenarios are diagrammed in Figure 4.9. Because magnetic fields do not change much over time, these two states are highly stable, and they form the basis for the construction of memory devices that store binary numbers.

In the early 1970s, core memories began to be replaced by smaller, cheaper technologies that required less power and were easier to manufacture. One-fiftieth of an inch in diameter and a few grams of weight might not seem like much, but it can produce a bulky and unworkable structure

---

[1]The righthand rule of physics says that if the thumb of your right hand is pointing in the direction of the electric current, then the fingers will be curled in the direction of the magnetic field.

when memory units must contain millions or billions of bits. For example, a typical core memory from the 1950s or 1960s had about 500 cores/in^2. The memory in a modern computer typically has at least 1 GB (1 gigabyte = 1 billion bytes), which is more than 8 billion bits. At the bit density of core memory, the memory unit would need about 16 million in^2, which is a square about 4,000 inches, or 330 feet, on a side. Built from cores, the memory unit would stand more than 30 stories high!

Today, the elementary building block for all modern computer systems is no longer the core but the transistor. A transistor is much like the light switch mentioned earlier. It can be in an OFF state, which does not allow electricity to flow, or in an ON state, in which electricity can pass unimpeded. However, unlike the light switch, a transistor is a solid-state device that has no mechanical or moving parts. The switching of a transistor from the OFF to the ON state, and vice versa, is done electronically rather than mechanically. This allows the transistor to be fast as well as extremely small. A typical transistor can switch states in a billionth of a second, and at current technology levels 1 billion transistors can fit into a space only 1 cm^2. Furthermore, hardware technology is changing so rapidly that both these numbers might be out of date by the time you read these words.

Transistors are constructed from special materials called *semiconductors*, such as silicon and gallium arsenide. A large number of transistors, as well as the electrical conducting paths that connect them, can be printed photographically on a wafer of silicon to produce a device known as an *integrated circuit* or, more commonly, a *chip*. The chip is mounted on a *circuit board*, which interconnects all the different chips (e.g., memory, processor, communications) needed to run a computer system. This circuit board is then plugged into the computer using a set of connectors located on the end of the board. The relationships among transistors, chips, and circuit boards are diagrammed in Figure 4.10. The use of photographic rather than mechanical production techniques has numerous advantages. Because light can be focused very sharply, these integrated circuits can be manufactured in very high densities—high numbers of transistors per square centimeter—and with a very high degree of accuracy. The more transistors that can be packed into a fixed amount of space, the greater the processing power of the computer and the greater the amount of information that can be stored in memory.

Another advantage of photographic production techniques is that it is possible to make a standard template, called a *mask*, which describes the circuit. This mask can be used to produce a virtually unlimited number of copies of that chip, much as a photographic negative can be used to produce an unlimited number of prints.

Together, these characteristics can result in very small and very inexpensive high-speed circuits. Whereas the first computers of the early 1940s (as seen in Chapter 1, Figure 1.6) filled huge rooms and cost millions of dollars, the processor inside a modern workstation contains hundreds of millions or billions of transistors on a tiny chip just a few centimeters square, is thousands of times more powerful than those early machines, and costs just a few hundred dollars.

FIGURE 4.10

Relationships among transistors, chips, and circuit boards

The theoretical concepts underlying the physical behavior of semi-conductors and transistors, as well as the details of chip manufacture, are well beyond the scope of this book. They are usually discussed in courses in physics or electrical engineering. Instead, we will examine a transistor in terms of the simplified model shown in Figure 4.11 and then use this model to explain its behavior. (Here is another example of the importance of abstraction in computer science.)

In the model shown in Figure 4.11, each transistor contains three lines—two input lines (collector and control) and one output line (emitter), with each line either in the 1-state, with a high positive voltage, or in the 0-state, with a voltage close to 0. The first input line, called the *control* or the *base*, is used to open or close the switch inside the transistor. If we set the control line to a 1 by applying a sufficiently high positive voltage, the switch closes

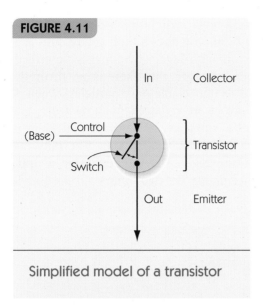

FIGURE 4.11

Simplified model of a transistor

and the transistor enters the ON state. In this state, current from the input line called the *collector* can flow directly to the single output line called the *emitter*, and the associated voltage can be detected by a measuring device. This ON state could be used to represent the binary value 1. If instead we set the control line to a 0 by applying a voltage close to zero, the switch opens, and the transistor enters the OFF state. In this state, the flow of current through the transistor is blocked and no voltage is detected on the emitter line. The OFF state could be used to represent the binary value 0. This is diagrammed as follows:

This type of solid-state switching device forms the basis for the construction of virtually all computers built today, and it is the fundamental building block for all high-level components described in the upcoming chapters. Remember, however, that there is no theoretical reason why we must use transistors as our "elementary particles" when designing computer systems. Just as cores were replaced by transistors, transistors may ultimately be replaced by some newer (perhaps molecular or biological) technology that is faster, smaller, and cheaper. The only requirements for our building blocks are those given in the beginning of this section—that they be able to represent reliably the two binary values 0 and 1.

Moore's Law and the Limits of Chip Design

Since the development of the first integrated circuits in the 1950s, the number of transistors on a circuit board has been doubling roughly every 24 months. This observation was first reported in a 1965 paper by Gordon E. Moore, the cofounder of Intel, and is now universally referred to as "Moore's law." This doubling has continued unabated for the last 40 years, and represents a rate of improvement unequaled in any other technical field. More transistors on a chip means more speed and more power, and is the reason for the enormous increase in performance (and decrease in size) of computers in the last 40–50 years. The following table details this growth from 1971, when chips held just a few thousand transistors, to today's microprocessors that hold billions.

Processor	Transistor Count	Date
Intel 404	2,300	1971
Intel 8080	4,500	1974
Intel 8088	29,000	1979
Intel 80286	134,000	1982
Intel 80386	275,000	1985
Intel 80486	1,200,000	1989
Pentium	3,100,000	1993
Pentium II	7,500,000	1997
Pentium 4	42,000,000	2000
Itanium 2	220,000,000	2003
Dual-Core Itanium 2	1,400,000,000	2006
Quad-Core Itanium Tukwila	2,000,000,000	2008
nVidiaGeForce 6800 Ultra	3,000,000,000	2011

It is impossible to maintain this type of exponential growth for an indefinitely extended period of time, and industry analysts have been predicting the demise of Moore's law for the last 10–15 years. However, the ongoing development of new materials and new manufacturing technologies has allowed the industry to continue this phenomenal rate of improvement. But there is a physical limit looming on the horizon that will be the most difficult hurdle yet. As more and more transistors are packed onto a single chip, distances between them get smaller and smaller, and experts estimate that in about 10–20 years intertransistor distances will approach the space between individual atoms. For example, transistors on today's chips are separated by 50–100 nanometers (1 nanometer = 10^{-9} meter), only about 500–1,000 times greater than the diameter of a single atom of silicon, which is about 10^{-10} meters. In a few generations, these atomic distances will be reached, and a totally new approach to computer design will be required, perhaps one based on the emerging fields of nanotechnology and quantum computing.

4.3 Boolean Logic and Gates

4.3.1 Boolean Logic

The construction of computer circuits is based on the branch of mathematics and symbolic logic called **Boolean logic**. This area of mathematics deals with rules for manipulating the two logical values *true* and *false*, and it is used to construct circuits that perform operations such as adding numbers, comparing numbers, and fetching instructions. These ideas are part of the branch of computer science known as **hardware design**, also called **logic design**.

It is easy to see the relationship between Boolean logic and computer design: The truth value *true* could represent the binary value 1, and the truth value *false* could represent the binary value 0. Thus anything stored internally as a sequence of binary digits (which, as we saw in earlier sections, is everything stored inside a computer) can also be viewed as a sequence of the logical values true and false, and these values can be manipulated by the operations of Boolean logic.

Let us define a **Boolean expression** as any expression that evaluates to either true or false. For example, the expression $(x = 1)$ is a Boolean expression because it is true if x is 1, and it is false if x has any other value. Similarly, both $(a \neq b)$ and $(c > 5.23)$ are Boolean expressions.

In "traditional" mathematics (the mathematics of real numbers), the operations used to construct arithmetic expressions are $+$, $-$, $\times$, $\div$, and a^b, which map real numbers into real numbers. In Boolean logic, the operations used to construct Boolean expressions are AND, OR, and NOT, and they map a set of (true, false) values into a single (true, false) result.

The rule for performing the AND operation is as follows: If *a* and *b* are Boolean expressions, then the value of the expression (*a* AND *b*), also written as (*a* · *b*), is *true* if and only if both *a* and *b* have the value *true*; otherwise, the expression (*a* AND *b*) has the value *false*. Informally, this rule says that the AND operation produces the value *true* if and only if both of its components are true. This idea can be expressed using a structure called a truth table, shown in Figure 4.12.

The two columns labeled Inputs in the truth table of Figure 4.12 list the four possible combinations of true/false values of *a* and *b*. The column labeled Output specifies the value of the expression (*a* AND *b*) for the corresponding values of *a* and *b*.

To illustrate the AND operation, imagine that we want to check whether a test score *S* is in the range 90 to 100 inclusive. We want to develop a Boolean expression that is true if the score is in the desired range and false otherwise. We cannot do this with a single comparison. If we test only that ($S \geq 90$), then a score of 105, which is greater than or equal to 90, will produce the result *true*, even though it is out of range. Similarly, if we test only that ($S \leq 100$), then a score of 85, which is less than or equal to 100, will also produce a *true*, even though it too is not in the range 90 to 100.

Instead, we need to determine whether the score *S* is greater than or equal to 90 *and* whether it is less than or equal to 100. Only if both conditions are true can we say that *S* is in the desired range. We can express this idea using the following Boolean expression:

$$(S \geq 90) \text{ AND } (S \leq 100)$$

Each of the two expressions in parentheses can be either true or false depending on the value of *S*. However, only if both conditions are true does the expression evaluate to *true*. For example, a score of *S* = 70 causes the first expression to be false (70 is not greater than or equal to 90), whereas the second expression is true (70 is less than or equal to 100). The truth table in Figure 4.12 shows that the result of evaluating (*false* AND *true*) is *false*. Thus, the overall expression is false, indicating (as expected) that 70 is not in the range 90 to 100.

FIGURE 4.12

Inputs		Output a AND b
a	b	(also written a · b)
False	False	False
False	True	False
True	False	False
True	True	True

Truth table for the AND operation

The second Boolean operation is OR. The rule for performing the OR operation is as follows: If *a* and *b* are Boolean expressions, then the value of the Boolean expression (*a* OR *b*), also written as (*a* + *b*), is *true* if *a* is *true*, if *b* is *true*, or if both are *true*. Otherwise, (*a* OR *b*) has the value *false*. The truth table for OR is shown in Figure 4.13.

To see the OR operation at work, imagine that a variable called *major* specifies a student's college major. If we want to know whether a student is majoring in either math or computer science, we cannot accomplish this with a single comparison. The test (*major* = math) omits computer science majors, whereas the test (*major* = computer science) leaves out the mathematicians. Instead, we need to determine whether the student is majoring in *either* math or computer science (or perhaps in both). This can be expressed as follows:

(*major* = math) OR (*major* = computer science)

If the student is majoring in either one or both of the two disciplines, then one or both of the two terms in the expression are true. Referring to the truth table in Figure 4.13, we see that (*true* OR *false*), (*false* OR *true*), and (*true* OR *true*) all produce the value *true*, which indicates that the student is majoring in at least one of these two fields. However, if the student is majoring in English, both conditions are false. As Figure 4.13 illustrates, the value of the expression (*false* OR *false*) is *false*, meaning that the student is not majoring in either math or computer science.

The final Boolean operator that we examine here is NOT. Unlike AND and OR, which require two operands and are, therefore, called *binary operators*, NOT requires only one operand and is called a *unary operator*, like the square root operation in arithmetic. The rule for evaluating the NOT operation is as follows: If *a* is a Boolean expression, then the value of the expression (NOT *a*), also written as $\bar{a}$, is *true* if *a* has the value *false*, and it is *false* if *a* has the value *true*. The truth table for NOT is shown in Figure 4.14.

Informally, we say that the NOT operation reverses, or *complements*, the value of a Boolean expression, making it true if currently false, and vice versa. For example, the expression (GPA > 3.5) is true if your grade point

FIGURE 4.13

Inputs		Output a OR b
a	b	(also written a + b)
False	False	False
False	True	True
True	False	True
True	True	True

Truth table for the OR operation

FIGURE 4.14

Input	Output NOT a
a	(also written $\bar{a}$)
False	True
True	False

Truth table for the NOT operation

average is greater than 3.5, and the expression NOT (GPA $>$ 3.5) is true only under the reverse conditions, that is when your grade point average is less than or equal to 3.5.

AND, OR, and NOT are the three operations of Boolean logic that we use in this chapter. (Later in this chapter we briefly mention other Boolean operators such as NAND, NOR, and XOR.) Why have we introduced these Boolean operations in the first place? The previous section discussed hardware concepts such as energy states, electrical currents, transistors, and integrated circuits. Now it appears that we have changed directions and are discussing highly abstract ideas drawn from the discipline of symbolic logic. However, as we hinted earlier and will see in detail in the next section, there is a very close relationship between the hardware concepts of Section 4.2.4 and the operations of Boolean logic. In fact, the fundamental building blocks of a modern computer system (the objects with which engineers actually design) are not the transistors introduced in Section 4.2.4 but the gates that implement the Boolean operations AND, OR, and NOT. Surprisingly, it is the rules of logic—a discipline developed by the Greeks 2,300 years ago and expanded by George Boole (see the Special Interest Box on page 189) 150 years ago—that provide the theoretical foundation for constructing modern computer hardware.

Practice Problems

1. Assuming that $x = 1$ and $y = 2$, determine the value of each of the following Boolean expressions:

   a. $(x = 1)$ AND $(y = 3)$

   b. $(x < y)$ OR $(x > 1)$

   c. NOT $[(x = 1)$ AND $(y = 2)]$

2. Assume that A, B, and C are Boolean variables that can take on the values true and false. Create a truth table to show all the possible values for the Boolean expression:

   ((NOT A) AND B) OR C

   (*Hint:* Your table will have eight rows.)

3. What is the value of the following Boolean expression:

   $(x = 5)$ AND $(y = 11)$ OR $([x + y] = z)$

   if $x = 5$, $y = 10$, and $z = 15$? Did you have to make some assumptions when you evaluated this expression?

4. Write a Boolean expression that is true if and only if x and y are both in the range 0 to 100 but x is not equal to y.

5. Write a Boolean expression that is true if and only if the variable *score* is *not* in the range 200–800, inclusive.

6. For what values of A and B will the value of the following Boolean expression be false?

   (A OR B) OR (NOT A)

4.3.2 Gates

A **gate** is an electronic device that operates on a collection of binary inputs to produce a binary output. That is, it transforms a set of (0,1) input values into a single (0,1) output value according to a specific transformation rule. Although gates can implement a wide range of different transformation rules, the ones we are concerned with in this section are those that implement the Boolean operations AND, OR, and NOT introduced in the previous section. As shown in Figure 4.15, these gates can be represented symbolically, along with the truth tables that define their transformation rules.

FIGURE 4.15

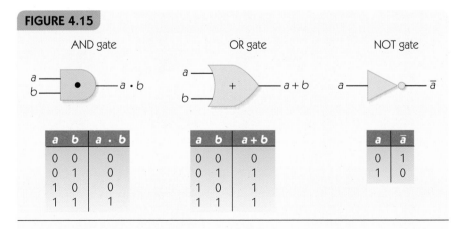

The three basic gates and their symbols

Comparing Figures 4.12 through 4.14 with Figure 4.15 shows that if the value 1 is equivalent to *true* and the value 0 is equivalent to *false*, then these three electronic gates directly implement the corresponding Boolean operation. For example, an AND gate has its output line set to 1 (set to some level of voltage that represents a binary 1) if and only if both of its inputs are 1. Otherwise, the output line is set to 0 (set to some level of voltage that represents a binary 0). This is functionally identical to the rule that says the result of (*a* AND *b*) is *true* if and only if both *a* and *b* are *true*; otherwise, (*a* AND *b*) is *false*. Similar arguments hold for the OR and NOT.

A NOT gate can be constructed from a single transistor, as shown in Figure 4.16, in which the collector is connected to the power supply (Logical-1) and the emitter is connected to the ground (Logical-0). If the control line of the transistor (labeled Input) is set to 1, then the transistor is in the ON state, and it passes current through to the ground. In this case, the output voltage of the gate is 0. However, if Input is set to 0, the transistor is in the OFF state, and it blocks passage of current to the ground. Instead, the current is transmitted to the line labeled Output, producing a value of 1. Thus, the value appearing on the output line of Figure 4.16 is the complement—the NOT—of the value appearing on the input line.

To construct an AND gate, we begin by connecting two transistors *in series*, as shown in Figure 4.17(a), with the collector line of transistor 1 connected to the power supply (Logical-1) and the emitter line of transistor 2 connected to ground (Logical-0). If both control lines, called Input-1 and Input-2 in Figure 4.17(a), are set to 1, then both transistors are in the ON state, and the current will be connected to ground, resulting in a value of 0 on the output line. If either (or both) Input-1 or Input-2 is 0, then the corresponding

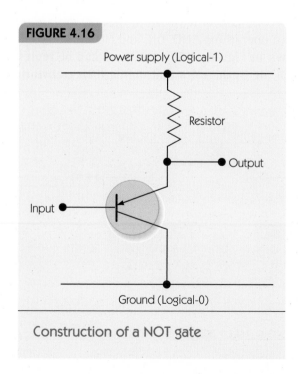

FIGURE 4.16

Power supply (Logical-1)

Resistor

Output

Input

Ground (Logical-0)

Construction of a NOT gate

FIGURE 4.17

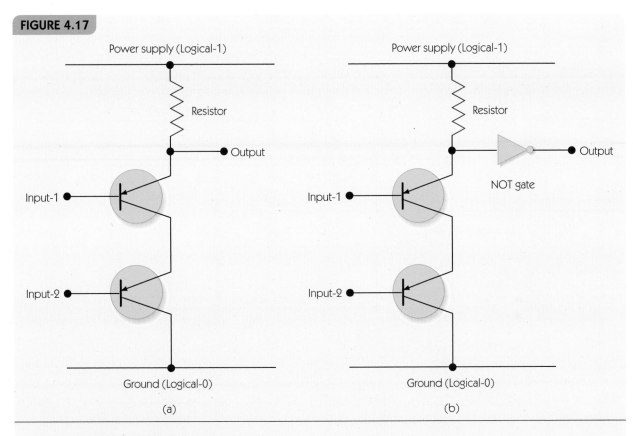

Construction of NAND and AND gates
(a) A two-transistor NAND gate
(b) A three-transistor AND gate

transistor is in the OFF state and does not allow current to pass, resulting in a 1 on the output line. Thus, the output of the gate in Figure 4.17(a) is a 0 if and only if both inputs are a 1; otherwise, it is a 1. This is the exact *opposite* of the definition of AND, and Figure 4.17(a) represents a gate called NAND, an acronym for *NOT AND*. It produces the complement of the AND operation, and it is an important and widely used gate in hardware design.

If, however, we want to build an AND gate, then all we have to do is add a NOT gate (of the type shown in Figure 4.16) to the output line. This complements the NAND output and produces the AND truth table of Figure 4.12. This gate is shown in Figure 4.17(b). Note that the NAND of Figure 4.17(a) requires two transistors, whereas the AND of Figure 4.17(b) requires three. This is one reason why NAND gates are widely used to build computer circuits.

To construct an OR gate, we again start with two transistors. However, this time they are connected *in parallel* rather than in series, as shown in Figure 4.18(a).

In Figure 4.18(a) if either, or both, of the lines Input-1 and Input-2 are set to 1, then the corresponding transistor is in the ON state, and the current

FIGURE 4.18

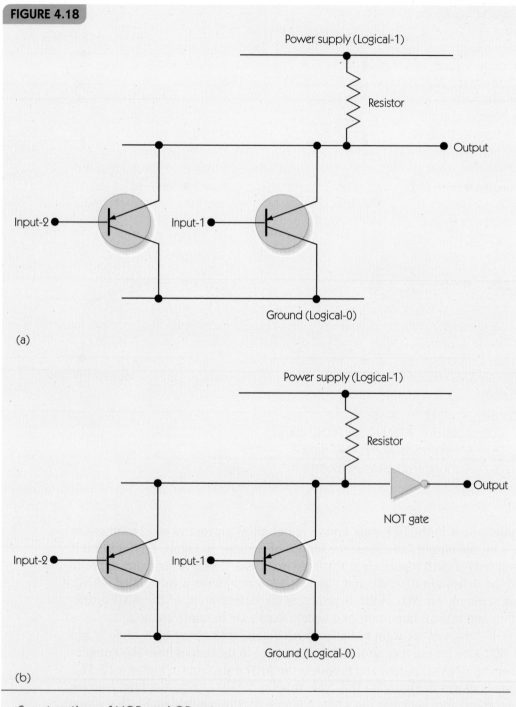

Construction of NOR and OR gates
(a)   A two-transistor NOR gate
(b)   A three-transistor OR gate

is connected to the ground, producing an output line value of 0. Only if both input lines are 0, effectively shutting off both transistors, will the output line contain a 1. Again, this is the exact opposite to the definition of OR given in Figure 4.13. Figure 4.18(a) is an implementation of a NOR gate, an acronym for *NOT OR*. To convert this to an OR gate, we do the same thing we did earlier—add a NOT gate to the output line. This gate is diagrammed in Figure 4.18(b).

Gates of the type shown in Figures 4.16 through 4.18 are not abstract entities that exist only in textbooks and classroom discussions. They are actual electronic devices that serve as the building blocks in the design and construction of modern computer systems. The reason for using gates rather than transistors is that a transistor is too elementary a device to act as the fundamental design component. It requires a designer to deal with such low-level issues as currents, voltages, and the laws of physics. Transistors, grouped together to form more powerful building blocks called gates, allow us to think and design at a higher level. Instead of dealing with the complex physical rules associated with discrete electrical devices, we can use the power and expressiveness of mathematics and logic to build computers.

This seemingly minor shift (from transistors to gates) has a profound effect on how computer hardware is designed and built. From this point on in our discussion of hardware design, we no longer need deal with anything electrical. Instead, our building blocks are AND, OR, and NOT gates, and our circuit construction rules are the rules of Boolean logic. This is another example of the importance of abstraction in computer science.

George Boole (1815–1864)

George Boole was a mid-nineteenth-century English mathematician and logician. He was the son of a shoemaker and had little formal education, having dropped out of school in the third grade. He taught himself mathematics and logic and mastered French, German, Italian, Latin, and Greek. He avidly studied the works of the great Greek and Roman philosophers such as Aristotle, Plato, and Euclid. He built on their work in logic, argumentation, and reasoning and, in 1854, produced a book titled *Introduction into the Laws of Thought*. This seminal work attempted to apply the formal laws of algebra and arithmetic to the principles of logic. That is, it treated reasoning as simply another branch of mathematics containing operators, variables, and transformation rules. He created a new form of logic containing the values *true* and *false* and the operators AND, OR, and NOT. He also developed a set of rules describing how to interpret and manipulate expressions that contain these values.

(Continued)

At the time of its development, the importance of this work was not apparent, and it languished in relative obscurity. However, 100 years later, Boole's ideas became the theoretical framework underlying the design of all computer systems. In his honor, these true/false expressions became known as *Boolean expressions*, and this branch of mathematics is called *Boolean logic* or *Boolean algebra*.

Even though he had very little formal schooling, Boole was eventually appointed Professor of Mathematics at Queens College in Cork, Ireland, and he received a gold medal from the Royal Mathematical Society. He is now universally recognized as one of the greatest mathematicians of the nineteenth century.

4.4 Building Computer Circuits

4.4.1 Introduction

A **circuit** is a collection of logic gates that transforms a set of binary inputs into a set of binary outputs and in which the values of the outputs depend only on the current values of the inputs. (Actually, this type of circuit is more properly called a *combinational circuit*. We use the simpler term *circuit* in this discussion.) A circuit C with m binary inputs and n binary outputs is represented as shown in Figure 4.19.

Internally, the circuit shown in Figure 4.19 is constructed from the AND, OR, and NOT gates introduced in the previous section. (*Note:* We do not use the NAND and NOR gates diagrammed in Figure 4.17(a) and 4.18(a).) These gates can be interconnected in any way so long as the connections do not violate the constraints on the proper number of inputs and outputs

FIGURE 4.19

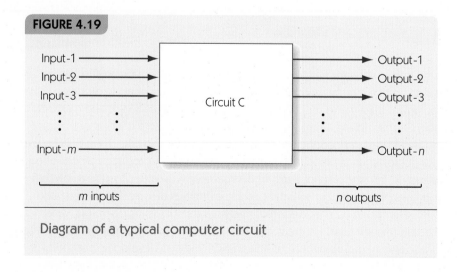

Diagram of a typical computer circuit

for each gate. Each AND and OR gate must have exactly two inputs and one output. (Multiple-input AND and OR gates do exist, but we do not use them in our examples.) Each NOT gate must have exactly one input and one output. For example, the following is the diagram of a circuit with two inputs labeled a and b and two outputs labeled c and d. It contains one AND gate, one OR gate, and two NOT gates.

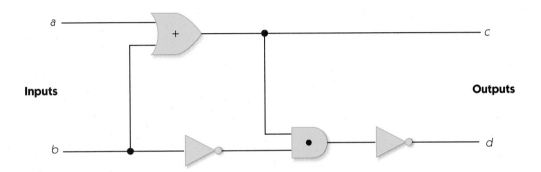

There is a direct relationship between Boolean expressions and *circuit diagrams* of this type. Every Boolean expression can be represented pictorially as a circuit diagram, and every output value in a circuit diagram can be written as a Boolean expression. For example, in the diagram shown, the two output values labeled c and d are equivalent to the following two Boolean expressions:

$c = (a \text{ OR } b)$
$d = \text{NOT} ((a \text{ OR } b) \text{ AND } (\text{NOT } b))$

The choice of which representation to use depends on what we want to do. The pictorial view better allows us to visualize the overall structure of the circuit, and is often used during the design stage. A Boolean expression may be better for performing mathematical or logical operations, such as verification and optimization, on the circuit. We use both representations in the following sections.

The value appearing on any output line of a circuit can be determined if we know the current input values and the transformations produced by each logic gate. (*Note:* There are circuits, called sequential circuits, which contain feedback loops in which the output of a gate is fed back as input to an earlier gate. The output of these circuits depends not only on the current input values but also on *previous* inputs. These circuits are typically used to build memory units because, in a sense, they can "remember" inputs. We do not discuss sequential circuits here.)

In the previous example, if $a = 1$ and $b = 0$, then the value on the c output line is 1, and the value on the d output line is 0. These values can be determined as follows:

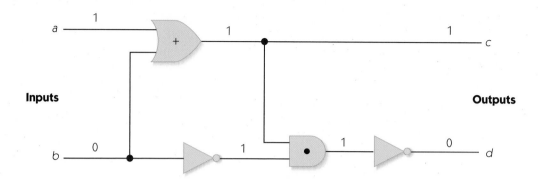

Note that it is perfectly permissible to "split" or "tap" a line and send its value to two different gates. Here the input value b was split and sent to two separate gates.

The next section presents an algorithm for designing and building circuits from the three fundamental gate types AND, OR, and NOT. This enables us to move to yet a higher level of abstraction. Instead of thinking in terms of transistors and electrical voltages (as in Section 4.2.4) or in terms of logic gates and truth values (as in Section 4.3.2), we can think and design in terms of circuits for high-level operations such as addition and comparison. This makes understanding computer hardware much more manageable.

4.4.2 A Circuit Construction Algorithm

The circuit shown at the end of the previous section is simply an example, and is not meant to carry out any meaningful operation. To create circuits that perform useful arithmetic and logical functions, we need a way to convert a description of a circuit's desired behavior into a circuit diagram, composed of AND, OR, and NOT gates, that does exactly what we want it to do.

There are a number of **circuit construction algorithms** to accomplish this task, and the remainder of this section describes one such technique, called the *sum-of-products algorithm*, that allows us to design circuits. Section 4.4.3 demonstrates how this algorithm works by constructing actual circuits that all computer systems need.

Step 1: Truth Table Construction. First, determine how the circuit should behave under all possible circumstances. That is, determine the binary value that should appear on each output line of the circuit for every possible combination of inputs. This information can be organized as a truth table. If a circuit has N input lines, and if each input line can be either a 0 or a 1, then there are 2^N combinations of input values, and the truth table has 2^N rows. For each output of the circuit, we must specify the desired output value for every row in the truth table.

For example, if a circuit has three inputs and two outputs, then a truth table for that circuit has $2^3 = 8$ input combinations and might look something like the following. (In this example, the output values are completely arbitrary.)

Inputs			Outputs	
a	b	c	Output-1	Output-2
0	0	0	0	1
0	0	1	0	0
0	1	0	1	1
0	1	1	0	1
1	0	0	0	0
1	0	1	0	0
1	1	0	1	1
1	1	1	0	0

$2^3 = 8$ input combinations

This circuit has two outputs labeled Output-1 and Output-2. The truth table specifies the value of each of these two output lines for every one of the eight possible combinations of inputs. We will use this example to illustrate the subsequent steps in the algorithm.

Step 2: Subexpression Construction Using AND and NOT Gates. Choose any one output column of the truth table built in Step 1 and scan down that column. Every place that you find a 1 in that output column, you build a Boolean *subexpression* that produces the value 1 (i.e., is true) for exactly that combination of input values and no other. To build this subexpression, you examine the value of each input for this specific case. If the input is a 1, use that input value directly in your subexpression. If the input is a 0, first take the NOT of that input, changing it from a 0 to a 1, and then use that *complemented* input value in your subexpression. You now have an input sequence of all 1s, and if all of these modified inputs are ANDed together (two at a time, of course), then the output value is a 1. For example, let's look at the output column labeled Output-1 in the truth table below.

Inputs			Output-1	
a	b	c	Output-1	
0	0	0	0	
0	0	1	0	
0	1	0	1	← case 1
0	1	1	0	
1	0	0	0	
1	0	1	0	
1	1	0	1	← case 2
1	1	1	0	

There are two 1s in the column labeled Output-1; they are referred to as case 1 and case 2. We thus need to construct two subexpressions, one for each of these two cases.

In case 1, the inputs a and c have the value 0 and the input b has the value 1. Thus we apply the NOT operator to both a and c, changing them from 0 to 1. Because the value of b is 1, we can use b directly. We now have three modified input values, all of which have the value 1. ANDing these three values together yields the Boolean expression $(\bar{a} \cdot b \cdot \bar{c})$. This expression produces a 1 only when the input is exactly $a = 0$, $b = 1$, $c = 0$. In any other case, at least one of the three factors in the expression is 0, and when the AND operation is carried out, it produces a 0. (Check this yourself by trying some other input values and seeing what is produced.) Thus the desired subexpression for case 1 is

$$(\bar{a} \cdot b \cdot \bar{c})$$

The subexpression for case 2 is developed in an identical manner, and it results in

$$(a \cdot b \cdot \bar{c})$$

This subexpression produces a 1 only when the input is exactly $a = 1$, $b = 1$, $c = 0$.

Step 3: Subexpression Combination Using OR Gates. Take each of the subexpressions produced in Step 2 and combine them, two at a time, using OR gates. Each of the individual subexpressions produces a 1 for exactly one particular case where the truth table output is a 1, so the OR of the output of all of them produces a 1 in each case where the truth table has a 1 and in no other case. Consequently, the Boolean expression produced in Step 3 implements exactly the function described in the output column of the truth table on which we are working. In the current example, the final Boolean expression produced during Step 3 is

$$(\bar{a} \cdot b \cdot \bar{c}) + (a \cdot b \cdot \bar{c})$$

Step 4: Circuit Diagram Production. Construct the final circuit diagram. To do this, convert the Boolean expression produced at the end of Step 3 into a circuit diagram, using AND, OR, and NOT gates to implement the AND, OR, and NOT operators appearing in the Boolean expression. This circuit diagram produces the output described in the corresponding column of the truth table created in Step 1. The circuit diagram for the Boolean expression developed in Step 3 is shown in Figure 4.20.

We have successfully built the part of the circuit that produces the output for the column labeled Output-1 in the truth table shown in Step 1. We now repeat Steps 2, 3, and 4 for any additional output columns contained in the truth table. (In this example, there is a second column labeled Output-2. We leave the construction of that circuit as a practice exercise.) When we have constructed a circuit diagram for every output of the circuit, we are finished. The sum-of-products algorithm is summarized in Figure 4.21.

FIGURE 4.20

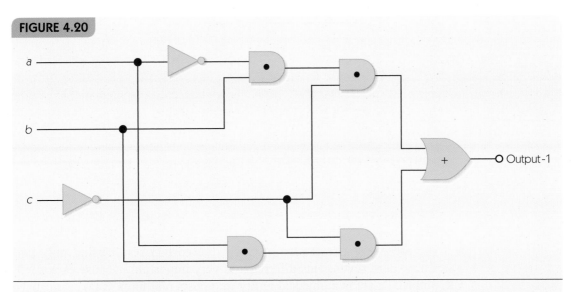

Circuit diagram for the output labeled Output-1

This has been a formal introduction to one particular circuit construction algorithm. The algorithm is not easy to comprehend in an abstract sense. The next section clarifies this technique by using it to design two circuits that perform the operations of comparison and addition. Seeing it used to design actual circuits will make the steps of the algorithm easier to understand and follow.

We end this section by noting that the circuit construction algorithm just described does not always produce an optimal circuit, where *optimal* means that the circuit accomplishes its desired function using the smallest number of logic gates. For example, using the truth table shown on the bottom of page 193, our sum-of-products algorithm produced the seven-gate circuit shown in Figure 4.20. This is a correct answer in the sense that the circuit does produce the correct values for Output-1 for all combinations of inputs. However, it is possible to do much better.

FIGURE 4.21

1. Construct the truth table describing the behavior of the desired circuit
2. While there is still an output column in the truth table, do Steps 3 through 6
3.   Select an output column
4.   Subexpression construction using AND and NOT gates
5.   Subexpression combination using OR gates
6.   Circuit diagram production
7. Done

The sum-of-products circuit construction algorithm

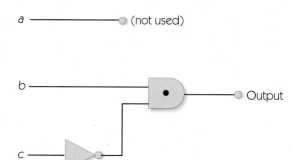

The preceding circuit also produces the correct result using only two gates instead of seven. This difference is very important because each AND, OR, and NOT gate is a physical entity that costs real money, takes up space on the chip, requires power to operate, and generates heat that must be dissipated. Eliminating five unnecessary gates produces a real savings. The fewer gates we use, the cheaper, more efficient, and more compact are our circuits and hence the resulting computer. Algorithms for circuit optimization—that is, for reducing the number of gates needed to implement a circuit—are an important part of hardware design. Challenge Work problem 1 at the end of the chapter invites you to investigate this interesting topic in more detail.

Practice Problems

1. Design the circuit to implement the output described in the column labeled Output-2 in the truth table on page 193.

2. Design a circuit using AND, OR, and NOT gates to implement the following truth table.

a	b	Output
0	0	0
0	1	1
1	0	1
1	1	0

This is the *exclusive-OR* operation, *XOR*. It is true if and only if a is 1 or b is 1, but not both.

3. Build a circuit using AND, OR, and NOT gates to implement the following truth table.

a	b	c	Output
0	0	0	1
0	0	1	0
0	1	0	0
0	1	1	0
1	0	0	0
1	0	1	0
1	1	0	0
1	1	1	1

This is called a *full-ON/full-OFF* circuit. It is true if and only if all three of its inputs are OFF (0) or all three are ON (1).

4. Design a circuit to implement the following truth table.

a	b	Output
0	0	1
0	1	1
1	0	0
1	1	0

After completing the design, count how many AND, OR, and NOT gates were required to build this circuit. Now take a careful look at the truth table above and see if you can come up with a more efficient way to build the same circuit, where efficient means using fewer gates. How many gates did your efficient circuit require?

4.4.3 Examples of Circuit Design and Construction

Let's use the algorithm described in Section 4.4.2 to construct two circuits important to the operation of any real-world computer: a compare-for-equality circuit and an addition circuit.

A Compare-for-Equality Circuit. The first circuit we will construct is a *compare-for-equality circuit*, or CE circuit, which tests two unsigned binary numbers for exact equality. The circuit produces the value 1 (*true*) if the two numbers are equal and the value 0 (*false*) if they are not. Such a circuit could be used in many situations. For example, in the shampooing algorithm in Chapter 1, Figure 1.3(a), there is an instruction that says,

Repeat Steps 4 through 6 until the value of *WashCount* equals 2

Laboratory Experience 7

To give you hands-on experience working with logic circuits, the first Laboratory Experience in this chapter introduces you to a software package called a *circuit simulator*. This is a program that enables you to construct logic circuits from the AND, OR, and NOT gates just described, and then test them by observing the outputs of the circuits using any desired inputs.

The output of each gate will be displayed on the screen, which allows you to determine if your circuit is or is not behaving correctly as the signals propagate from input lines to output lines.

Our CE circuit could accomplish the comparison between *WashCount* and 2 and return a true or false, depending on whether these two values were equal or not equal.

Let's start by using the sum-of-products algorithm in Figure 4.21 to construct a simpler circuit called 1-CE, short for *1*-bit compare for equality. A 1-CE circuit compares two 1-bit values *a* and *b* for equality. That is, the circuit 1-CE produces a 1 as output if both its inputs are 0 or both its inputs are 1. Otherwise, 1-CE produces a 0. After designing 1-CE, we will use it to create a "full-blown" comparison circuit that can handle numbers of any size.

Step 1 of the algorithm says to construct the truth table that describes the behavior of the desired circuit. The truth table for the 1-CE circuit is

a	*b*	*Output*
0	0	1 ← case 1 (both numbers equal to 0)
0	1	0
1	0	0
1	1	1 ← case 2 (both numbers equal to 1)

In the output column of the truth table, there are two 1 values, labeled case 1 and case 2, so Step 2 of the algorithm is to construct two subexpressions, one for each of these two cases. The subexpression for case 1 is $(\bar{a} \cdot \bar{b})$ because this produces the value 1 only when $a = 0$ and $b = 0$. The subexpression for case 2 is $(a \cdot b)$, which produces a 1 only when $a = 1$ and $b = 1$.

FIGURE 4.22

One-bit compare-for-equality circuit

We now combine the outputs of these two subexpressions with an OR gate, as described in Step 3, to produce the Boolean expression

$$(\bar{a} \cdot \bar{b}) + (a \cdot b)$$

Finally, in Step 4, we convert this expression to a circuit diagram, which is shown in Figure 4.22. The circuit shown in Figure 4.22 correctly compares two 1-bit quantities and determines if they are equal. If they are equal, it outputs a 1. If they are unequal, it outputs a 0.

The numbers compared for equality by a computer are usually much larger than a single binary digit. We want a circuit that correctly compares two numbers that contain N binary digits. To build this "N-bit compare-for-equality" circuit, we use N of the 1-CE circuits shown in Figure 4.22, one for each bit position in the numbers to be compared. Each 1-CE circuit produces a 1 if the two binary digits in its specific location are identical and produces a 0 if they are not. If every circuit produces a 1, then the two numbers are identical in every bit position, and they are equal. To check whether all our 1-CE circuits produce a 1, we simply AND together (two at a time) the outputs of all N 1-CE circuits. Remember that an AND gate produces a 1 if and only if both of its inputs are a 1. Thus the final output of the N-bit compare circuit is a 1 if and only if every pair of bits in the corresponding location of the two numbers is identical—that is, the two numbers are equal.

Figure 4.23 shows the design of a complete *N-bit compare-for-equality circuit* called CE. Each of the two numbers being compared, *a* and *b*, contains N bits, and they are labeled $a_{N-1} a_{N-2} \ldots a_0$ and $b_{N-1} b_{N-2} \ldots b_0$. The box labeled 1-CE in Figure 4.23 is the 1-bit compare-for-equality circuit shown in Figure 4.22. Looking at these figures, you can see that we have designed a very complex electrical circuit without the specification of a single electrical

FIGURE 4.23

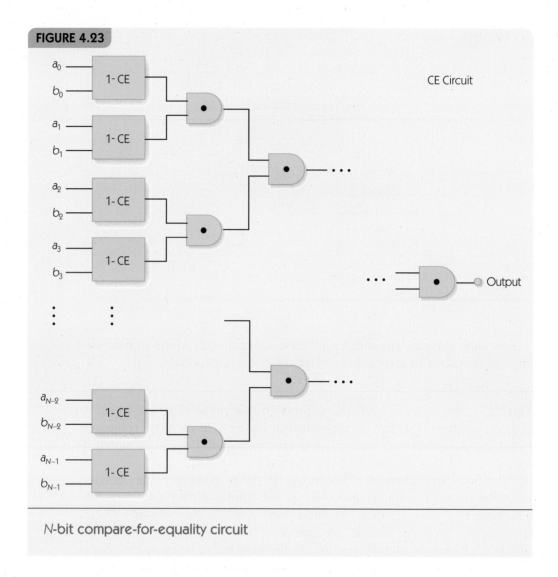

CE Circuit

N-bit compare-for-equality circuit

device. The only "devices" in those diagrams are gates to implement the logical operations AND, OR, and NOT, and the only "rules" we need to know to understand the diagrams are the transformation rules of Boolean logic. George Boole's "not very important" work is the starting point for the design of every circuit found inside a modern computer.

An Addition Circuit. Our second example of circuit construction is an addition circuit called ADD that performs binary addition on two unsigned N-bit integers. Typically, this type of circuit is called a *full adder*. For example, assuming $N = 6$, our ADD circuit would be able to perform the following 6-bit addition operation:

11	($\leftarrow$ the carry bit)
001101	(the binary value 13)
+ 001110	(the binary value 14)
011011	(the binary value 27, which is the correct sum)

Just as we did with the CE circuit, we carry out the design of the ADD circuit in two stages. First, we use the circuit construction algorithm of Figure 4.21 to build a circuit called 1-ADD that adds a single pair of binary digits, along with a carry digit. We then interconnect N of these 1-ADD circuits to produce the complete N-bit full adder circuit ADD.

Looking at the addition example just shown, we see that summing the values in any column i requires us to add three binary values—the two binary digits in that column, a_i and b_i, and the carry digit from the previous column, called c_i. Furthermore, the circuit must produce two binary outputs: a sum digit s_i and a new carry digit c_{i+1} that propagates to the next column. The pictorial representation of the 1-bit adder circuit 1-ADD and its accompanying truth table are shown in Figure 4.24.

Because the 1-ADD circuit being constructed has two outputs, s_i and c_{i+1}, we must use Steps 2, 3, and 4 of the circuit construction algorithm twice, once for each output. Let's work on the sum output s_i first.

The s_i output column of Figure 4.24 contains four 1s, so we need to construct four subexpressions. In accordance with the guidelines given in Step 2 of the construction algorithm, these four subexpressions are

Case 1: $\overline{a}_i \cdot \overline{b}_i \cdot c_i$

Case 2: $\overline{a}_i \cdot b_i \cdot \overline{c}_i$

Case 3: $a_i \cdot \overline{b}_i \cdot \overline{c}_i$

Case 4: $a_i \cdot b_i \cdot c_i$

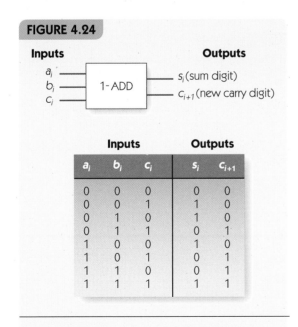

FIGURE 4.24

Inputs

a_i
b_i — 1-ADD
c_i

Outputs

s_i (sum digit)
c_{i+1} (new carry digit)

Inputs			Outputs	
a_i	b_i	c_i	s_i	c_{i+1}
0	0	0	0	0
0	0	1	1	0
0	1	0	1	0
0	1	1	0	1
1	0	0	1	0
1	0	1	0	1
1	1	0	0	1
1	1	1	1	1

The 1-ADD circuit and truth table

Step 3 says to combine the outputs of these four subexpressions using three OR gates to produce the output labeled s_i in the truth table of Figure 4.24. The final Boolean expression for the sum output is

$$s_i = (\overline{a}_i \cdot \overline{b}_i \cdot c_i) + (\overline{a}_i \cdot b_i \cdot \overline{c}_i) + (a_i \cdot \overline{b}_i \cdot \overline{c}_i) + (a_i \cdot b_i \cdot c_i)$$

The logic circuit to produce the output whose expression is given above is shown in Figure 4.25. (This circuit diagram has been labeled to highlight the four separate subexpressions created during Step 2, as well as the combining of the subexpressions in Step 3 of the construction algorithm.)

We are not yet finished, because the 1-ADD circuit in Figure 4.24 has a second output—the carry into the next column. That means the circuit construction algorithm must be repeated for the second output column, labeled c_{i+1}.

FIGURE 4.25

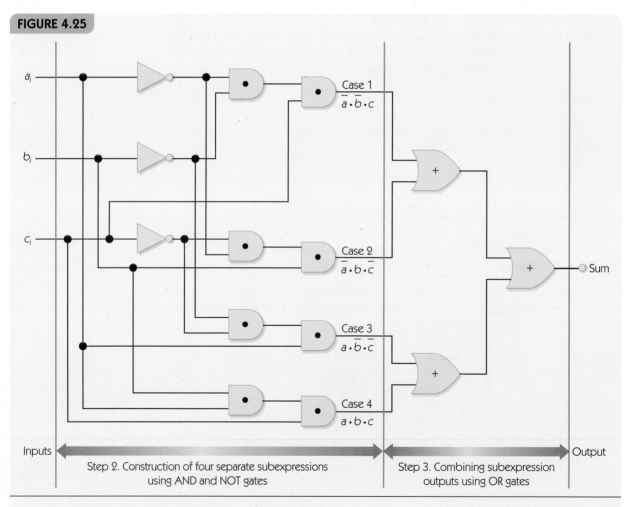

Sum output for the 1-ADD circuit

The c_{i+1} column also contains four 1s, so we again need to build four separate subcircuits, just as for the sum output, and combine them using OR gates. The construction proceeds in a fashion similar to the first part, so we leave the details as an exercise for the reader. The Boolean expression describing the carry output c_{i+1} of the 1-ADD circuit is

$$c_{i+1} = (\overline{a}_i \cdot b_i \cdot c_i) + (a_i \cdot \overline{b}_i \cdot c_i) + (a_i \cdot b_i \cdot \overline{c}_i) + (a_i \cdot b_i \cdot c_i)$$

We have now built the two parts of the 1-ADD circuit that produce the sum and the carry outputs. The complete 1-ADD circuit is constructed by simply putting these two pieces together. Figure 4.26 shows the complete (and admittedly quite complex) 1-ADD circuit to implement 1-bit addition. To keep the diagram from becoming an incomprehensible tangle of lines, we have drawn it in a slightly different orientation from Figures 4.22 and 4.25. Everything else is exactly the same.

When looking at this rather imposing diagram, do not become overly concerned with the details of every gate, every connection, and every operation. Figure 4.26 more importantly illustrates the *process* by which we design such a complex and intricate circuit: by transforming the idea of 1-bit binary addition into an electrical circuit using the tools of algorithmic problem solving and symbolic logic.

How is the 1-ADD circuit shown in Figure 4.26 used to add numbers that contain N binary digits rather than just one? The answer is simple if we think about the way numbers are added by hand. (We discussed exactly this topic when developing the addition algorithm of Figure 1.2 in Chapter 1.) We add numbers one column at a time, moving from right to left, generating the sum digit, writing it down, and sending any carry to the next column. The same thing can be done in hardware. We use N of the 1-ADD circuits shown in Figure 4.26, one for each column. Starting with the rightmost circuit, each 1-ADD circuit adds a single column of digits, generates a sum digit that is part of the final answer, and sends its carry digit to the 1-ADD circuit on its left, which replicates this process. After N repetitions of this process, all sum digits have been generated, and the N circuits have correctly added the two numbers.

The complete full adder circuit called ADD is shown in Figure 4.27. It adds the two N-bit numbers $a_{N-1} a_{N-2} \ldots a_0$ and $b_{N-1} b_{N-2} \ldots b_0$ to produce the $(N+1)$-bit sum $s_N s_{N-1} s_{N-2} \ldots s_0$. Because addition is one of the most common arithmetic operations, the circuit shown in Figure 4.27 (or something equivalent) is one of the most important and most frequently used arithmetic components. Addition circuits are found in every computer, workstation, and handheld calculator in the marketplace. They are even found in computer-controlled thermostats, clocks, and microwave ovens, where they enable us, for example, to add 30 minutes to the cooking time.

Figure 4.27 is, in a sense, the direct hardware implementation of the addition algorithm shown in Figure 1.2. Although Figure 1.2 and

FIGURE 4.26

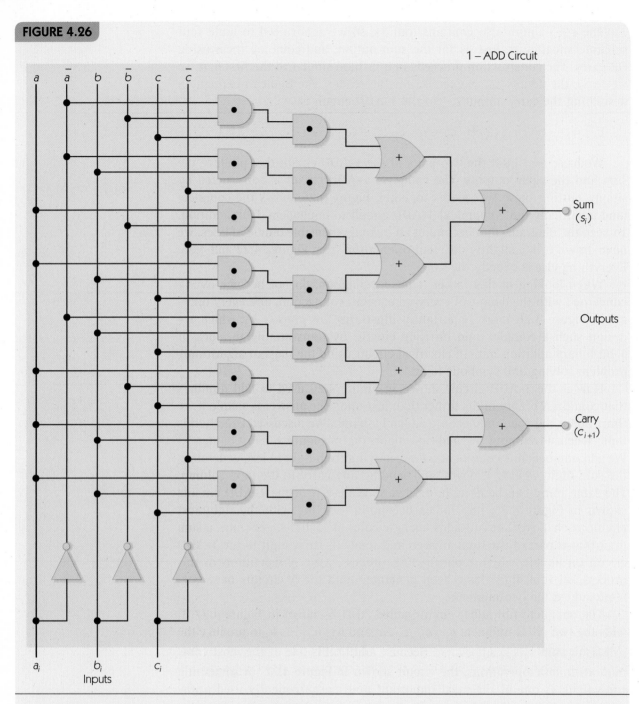

Complete 1-ADD circuit for 1-bit binary addition

Figure 4.27 are quite different, both represent essentially the same algorithm: the column-by-column addition of two N-bit numerical values. This demonstrates quite clearly that there are many different ways to express the same algorithm—in this case, pseudocode (Figure 1.2) and hardware circuits

FIGURE 4.27

The complete full adder ADD circuit

(Figure 4.27). Later chapters show additional ways to represent algorithms, such as machine language programs and high-level language programs. However, regardless of whether we use English, pseudocode, mathematics, or transistors to describe an algorithm, its fundamental properties are the same, and the central purpose of computer science—algorithmic problem solving—remains the same.

It may also be instructive to study the size and complexity of the ADD circuit just designed. Figure 4.27 shows that the addition of two N-bit integer values requires N separate 1-ADD circuits. Let's assume that $N = 32$, a typical value for modern computers. Referring to Figure 4.26, we see that each 1-ADD circuit uses 3 NOT gates, 16 AND gates, and 6 OR gates, a total of 25 logic gates. Thus the total number of logic gates used to implement 32-bit binary addition is $32 \times 25 = 800$ gates. Figures 4.16, 4.17(b), and 4.18(b) show that each AND and OR gate requires three transistors and each NOT gate requires one. Therefore, more than 2,200 transistors are needed to build a 32-bit adder circuit:

$$
\begin{aligned}
NOT\!: \ & 32 \times 3 \ = 96 \quad NOT \text{ gates} \times 1 \text{ transistor/gate} \ = \ \ \ \ 96 \\
AND\!: \ & 32 \times 16 = 512 \ AND \text{ gates} \times 3 \text{ transistors/gate} = 1{,}536 \\
OR\!: \ \ & 32 \times 6 \ = 192 \ OR \ \text{ gates} \times 3 \text{ transistors/gate} = \ \underline{\ \ 576} \\
& \hspace{6.5cm} \text{Total} = 2{,}208
\end{aligned}
$$

(*Note:* Optimized 32-bit addition circuits can be constructed using as few as 500 to 600 transistors. However, this does not change the fact that it takes many, many transistors to accomplish this addition task.)

Practice Problems

1. Determine how many transistors are required to build the N-bit compare-for-equality circuit of Figure 4.23. Assume $N = 32$.

2. Design a circuit that implements a 1-bit compare-for-greater-than (1-GT) operation. This circuit is given two 1-bit values, a and b. It outputs a 1 if $a > b$, and outputs a 0 otherwise.

3. Use the circuit construction algorithm just described to implement the NOR operation shown in Figure 4.18(a). Remember that the truth table for the NOR operation is:

a	b	(a NOR b)
0	0	1
0	1	0
1	0	0
1	1	0

4. Use the circuit construction algorithm to implement the NXOR, the Not of the Exclusive OR operation, whose truth table is the following:

a	b	(a NXOR b)
0	0	1
0	1	0
1	0	0
1	1	1

Laboratory Experience 8

In the second Laboratory Experience of this chapter, you again use the circuit simulator software package. This time, you construct circuits using the sum-of-products algorithm discussed in this section and shown in Figure 4.21. Using the simulator to design, build, and test actual circuits will give you a deeper understanding of how to use the sum-of-products algorithm to create circuits that solve specific problems.

Dr. William Shockley (1910–1989)

Dr. William Shockley was the inventor (along with John Bardeen and Walter Brattain) of the transistor. His discovery has probably done as much to shape our modern world as any scientific advancement of the twentieth century. He received the 1956 Nobel Prize in Physics and, at his death, was a distinguished professor at Stanford University.

Shockley and his team developed the transistor in 1947 while working at Bell Laboratories. He left there in 1954 to set up the Shockley Semiconductor Laboratory in California—a company that was instrumental in the birth of the high-technology region called Silicon Valley. The employees of this company eventually went on to develop other fundamental advances in computing, such as the integrated circuit and the microprocessor.

Although Shockley's work has been compared with that of Pasteur, Salk, and Einstein in importance, his reputation and place in history have been forever tarnished by his outrageous and controversial racial theories. His education and training were in physics and electrical engineering, but Shockley spent the last years of his life trying to convince people of the genetic inferiority of blacks. He became obsessed with these ideas, even though he was ridiculed and shunned by colleagues who abandoned all contact with him. Although his work on the design of the transistor was of seminal importance, Shockley himself felt that his genetic theory on race and intelligence would ultimately be viewed as his most important contribution to science. By the time of his death in 1989, his intense racial bigotry prevented him from receiving the recognition that would otherwise have been his for monumental contributions in physics, engineering, and computer science.

This computation emphasizes the importance of the continuing research into the miniaturization of electrical components. (See the Special Interest Box on Moore's law earlier in this chapter.) If vacuum tubes were used instead of transistors, as was done in computers from about 1940 to 1955, the adder circuit shown in Figure 4.27 would be extraordinarily bulky; 2,208 vacuum tubes would occupy a space about the size of a large refrigerator. It would also generate huge amounts of heat, necessitating sophisticated cooling systems, and it would be very difficult to maintain. (Imagine the time it would take to locate a single burned-out vacuum tube from a cluster of 2,000.) Using something on the scale of the magnetic core technology described in Section 4.2.4 and shown in Figure 4.4, the adder circuit would fit into an area a few inches square. However, modern circuit technology can now achieve transistor densities greater than 1 billion transistors/cm². At this level, the entire ADD circuit of Figure 4.27 would easily fit in an area much, much smaller than the size of the period at the end of this sentence. That is why it is now possible to put powerful computer processing facilities not only in a room or on a desk but also inside a watch, a thermostat, or even inside the human body.

4.5 Control Circuits

The previous section described the design of circuits for implementing arithmetic and logical operations. However, there are other, quite different, types of circuits that are also essential to the proper functioning of a computer system. This section briefly describes one of these important circuit types, control circuits, which are used not to implement arithmetic operations but to determine the order in which operations are carried out and to select the correct data values to be processed. In a sense, they are the sequencing and decision-making circuits inside a computer. These circuits are essential to the proper function of a computer because, as we noted in Chapter 1, algorithms and programs must be well ordered and must always know which operation to do next. The two major types of control circuits are called multiplexors and decoders, and, like everything else described in this chapter, they can be completely described in terms of gates and the rules of logic.

A multiplexor is a circuit that has 2^N *input lines* and 1 *output line*. Its function is to select exactly one of its 2^N input lines and copy the binary value on that input line onto its single output line. A multiplexor chooses one specific input by using an additional set of N lines called *selector lines*. (Thus the total number of inputs to the multiplexor circuit is $2^N + N$.) The 2^N input lines of a multiplexor are numbered 0, 1, 2, 3, ... , $2^N - 1$. Each of the N selector lines can be set to either a 0 or a 1, so we can use the N selector lines to represent all binary values from 000 ... 0 (N zeros) to 111 ... 1 (N ones), which represent all integer values from 0 to $2^N - 1$. These numbers correspond exactly to the numbers of the input lines. Thus the binary number that appears on the selector lines can be interpreted as the identification number of the input line that is to be selected. Pictorially, a multiplexor looks like this:

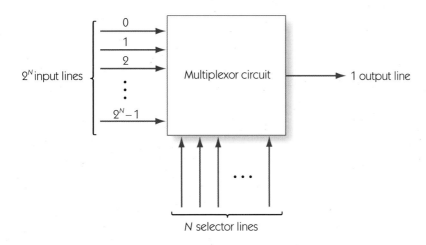

For example, if we had four (2^2) input lines (i.e., $N = 2$) coming into our multiplexor, numbered 0, 1, 2, and 3, then we would need two selector lines. The four binary combinations that can appear on this pair of selector lines are 00, 01, 10, and 11, which correspond to the decimal values 0, 1, 2, and 3, respectively (refer to Figure 4.2). The multiplexor selects the one input line whose identification number corresponds to the value appearing on the selector lines and copies the value on that input line to the output line. If, for example, the two selector lines were set to 1 and 0, then a multiplexor circuit would pick input line 2 because 10 in binary is 2 in decimal notation.

Implementing a multiplexor using logic gates is not difficult. Figure 4.28 shows a simple multiplexor circuit with $N = 1$. This is a multiplexor with two (2^1) input lines and a single selector line.

In Figure 4.28 if the value on the selector line is 0, then the bottom input line to AND gate 2 is always 0, so its output is always 0. Looking at

FIGURE 4.28

A two-input multiplexor circuit

AND gate 1, we see that the NOT gate changes its bottom input value to a 1. Because (1 AND a) is always a, the output of the top AND gate is equal to the value of a, which is the value of the input from line 0. Thus the two inputs to the OR gate are 0 and a. Because the value of the expression (0 OR a) is identical to a, by setting the selector line to 0 we have, in effect, selected as our output the value that appears on line 0. You should confirm that if the selector line has the value 1, then the output of the circuit in Figure 4.28 is b, the value appearing on line 1. We can design multiplexors with more than two inputs in a similar fashion, although they rapidly become more complex.

The second type of control circuit is called a **decoder** and it operates in the opposite way from a multiplexor. A decoder has N input lines numbered 0, 1, 2, ... , $N - 1$ and 2^N output lines numbered 0, 1, 2, 3, ... , $2^N - 1$.

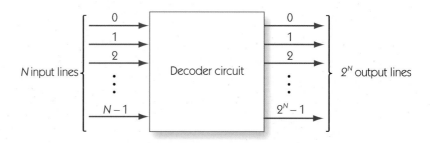

Each of the N input lines of the decoder can be set to either a 0 or a 1, and when these N values are interpreted as a single binary number, they can represent all integer values from 0 to $2^N - 1$. It is the job of the decoder to determine the value represented on its N input lines and then send a signal (i.e., a 1) on the single output line that has that identification number. All other output lines are set to 0.

For example, if our decoder has three input lines, it has eight (2^3) output lines numbered 0 to 7. These three input lines can represent all binary values from 000 to 111, which is from 0 to 7 in decimal notation. If, for example, the binary values on the three input lines are 101, which is a 5, then a signal (a binary 1) would be sent out by the decoder on output line 5. All other output lines would contain a 0.

Figure 4.29 shows the design of a 2-to-4 decoder circuit with two input lines and four (2^2) output lines. These four output lines are labeled 0, 1, 2, and 3, and the only output line that carries a signal value of 1 is the line whose identification number is identical to the value appearing on the two input lines. For example, if the two inputs are 11, then line 3 should be set to a 1 (11 in binary is 3 in decimal). This is, in fact, what happens because the AND gate connected to line 3 is the only one whose two inputs are equal to a 1. You should confirm that this circuit behaves properly when it receives the inputs 00, 01, and 10 as well.

FIGURE 4.29

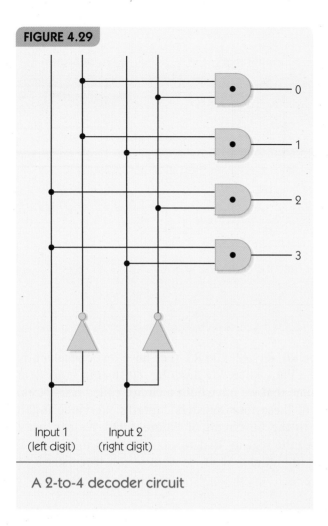

Input 1
(left digit)

Input 2
(right digit)

A 2-to-4 decoder circuit

Together, decoder and multiplexor circuits enable us to build computer systems that execute the correct instructions using the correct data values. For example, assume we have a computer that can carry out four different types of arithmetic operations—add, subtract, multiply, and divide. Furthermore, assume that these four instructions have code numbers 0, 1, 2, and 3, respectively. We could use a decoder circuit to ensure that the computer performs the correct instruction. We need a decoder circuit with two input lines. It receives as input the two-digit code number (in binary) of the instruction that we want to perform: 00 (add), 01 (subtract), 10 (multiply), or 11 (divide). The decoder interprets this value and sends out a signal on the correct output line. This signal is used to select the proper arithmetic circuit and cause it to perform the desired operation. This behavior is diagrammed in Figure 4.30.

Whereas a decoder circuit can be used to select the correct instruction, a multiplexor can help ensure that the computer executes this instruction using the correct data. For example, suppose our computer has four special

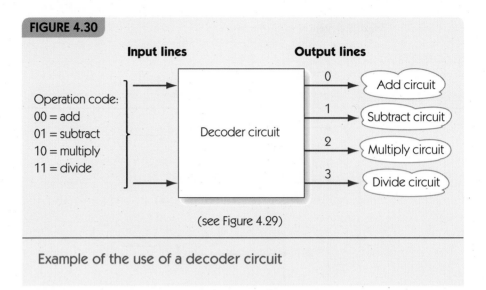

FIGURE 4.30

Example of the use of a decoder circuit

registers called R0, R1, R2, and R3. (For now, just consider a register to be a place to store a data value. We describe registers in more detail in the next chapter.) Assume that we have built a circuit called *test-if-zero* that can test whether any of these four registers contains the value 0. (This is actually quite similar to the CE circuit of Figure 4.23.) We can use a multiplexor circuit to select the register that we want to send to the test-if-zero circuit. This is shown in Figure 4.31. If we want to test if register R2 in Figure 4.31

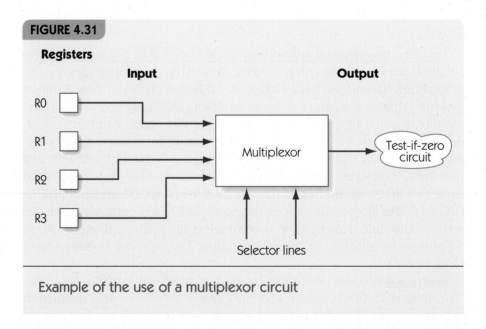

FIGURE 4.31

Example of the use of a multiplexor circuit

is 0, we simply put the binary value 10 (2 in decimal notation) on the two selector lines. This selects register R2, and only its value passes through the multiplexor and is sent to the test circuit.

There are many more examples of the use of control circuits in Chapter 5, which examines the execution of programs and the overall organization of a computer system.

4.6 Conclusion

We began our discussion on the representation of information and the design of computer circuits with the most elementary component, bistable electronic devices such as transistors. We showed how they can be used to construct logic gates that in turn can be used to implement circuits to carry out useful functions. Our purpose here was not to make you an expert in specifying and designing computer circuits but to demonstrate how it is possible to implement high-level arithmetic operations using only low-level electronic components such as transistors. We also demonstrated how it is possible to reorient our viewpoint and raise our level of abstraction. We changed the level of discussion from electricity to arithmetic, from hardware devices to mathematical behavior, from form to function. This is one of the first steps up the hierarchy of abstractions introduced in Figure 1.9.

Chapter 5 continues this "upward climb" to yet higher levels of abstraction. It shows how arithmetic circuits, such as compare-for-equality and addition (Section 4.4.3), and control circuits, such as multiplexors and decoders (Section 4.5), can be used to construct entire computer systems.

After reading this chapter, you might have the feeling that although you understand the individual concepts that are covered, you still don't understand, in the grand sense, what computers are or how they work. You might feel that you can follow the details but can't see the "big picture." One possible reason is that this chapter looks at computers from a very elementary viewpoint, by studying different types of specialized circuits. This is analogous to studying the human body as a collection of millions of cells of different types—blood cells, brain cells, skin cells, and so on. Cytology is certainly an important part of the field of biology, but understanding only the cellular structure of the human body provides no intuitive understanding of what people are and how we do such characteristic things as walk, eat, and breathe. Understanding these complex actions derives not from a study of molecules, genes, or cells, but from a study of higher-level organs and their interactions, such as the lungs, heart, and muscles.

That is exactly what happens in Chapter 5, in which we examine higher-level computer components such as processors, memory, and instructions and begin our study of the topic of computer organization.

EXERCISES

1. Given our discussion of positional numbering systems in Section 4.2.1, see whether you can determine the decimal value of the following numbers:

   a. 133 (base 4)

   b. 367 (base 8, also called *octal*)

   c. 1BA (base 16, also called *hexadecimal*. B is the digit that represents 11; A is the digit that represents 10.)

2. In Exercise 1c, we use the letters A and B as digits of the base-16 number. Explain why that is necessary.

3. Determine the decimal value of the following unsigned binary numbers:

   a. 11000

   b. 110001

   c. 1111111

   d. 1000000000

4. Using 8 bits, what is the unsigned binary representation of each of the following values:

   a. 23

   b. 55

   c. 275

   Did anything unusual happen when determining the correct answer to Part c?

5. Assume that the following 10-bit numbers represent signed integers using sign/magnitude notation. The sign is the leftmost bit and the remaining 9 bits represent the magnitude. What is the decimal value of each?

   a. 1000110001

   b. 0110011000

   c. 1000000001

   d. 1000000000

6. Give the 8-bit sign/magnitude representation of each of the following decimal values:

   a. +71

   b. −1

   c. −81

7. Assume that you tried to store the signed integer value −200 using an 8-bit sign/magnitude representation. What happened? What type of error does this represent?

8. Assume that we use 10 bits to represent signed integers, using sign/magnitude notation. What are the largest (in absolute value) positive and negative numbers that can be represented on our system?

9. Show the step-by-step addition of the following two 10-bit unsigned binary values, including showing the carry bit to each successive column:

   ```
     0011100011
   + 0001101110
   ```

10. Assume that our computer stores decimal numbers using 16 bits—10 bits for a sign/magnitude mantissa and 6 bits for a sign/magnitude base-2 exponent. (This is exactly the same representation shown on page 160.) Show the internal representation of the following decimal quantities.

    a. +7.5

    b. −20.25

    c. −1/64

11. Using the same decimal representation scheme described in Exercise 10, give the decimal value of each of the following 16-bit binary strings:

    a. 0111000000000111

    b. 1010001000100001 (*Note:* Is there something unusual about this representation? If so, what is it?)

12. In Exercises 10 and 11, we used 16 bits to represent decimal numbers, allocating 10 bits for the mantissa and 6 bits for the exponent. What would be the impact on our representation if we still used 16 bits for each number but instead allocated 12 bits for the mantissa and 4 bits for the exponent?

13. Using the ASCII code set given in Figure 4.3, show the internal binary representation for the following character strings:

    a. AbC

    b. Mike

    c. $25.00

    d. (a+b)

14. How many binary digits would it take to represent the following phrase in ASCII code? In Unicode? (Do not include the " " marks.)

    "Invitation to Computer Science"

15. a. How many bits does it take to store a 3-minute song using an audio encoding method that samples at the rate of 40,000 bits/second, has a bit depth of 16, and does not use compression? What if it uses a compression scheme with a compression ratio of 5:1?

    b. How many bits does it take to store an uncompressed 1,200 × 800 RGB color image? If we found out that the image actually takes only 2.4 Mbits, what is the compression ratio?

16. Show how run-length encoding can be used to compress the following text stream:

    xxxyyyyyyyzzzzAAxxxx

    What is the compression ratio? (Assume each digit and letter requires 8 bits.)

17. Using the variable-length code shown in Figure 4.8, give the internal coding of the following Hawaiian words along with the amount of savings over the standard fixed-length 4-bit representation:

    a. KAI

    b. MAUI

    c. MOLOKAI

    Explain the problem that occurred with Part c.

18. The primary advantage of using the binary numbering system rather than the decimal system to represent data is reliability, as noted in Section 4.2.3. Describe two disadvantages of using binary rather than decimal notation for the internal representation of information.

19. Assume that $a = 1$, $b = 2$, and $c = 2$. What is the value of each of the following Boolean expressions?

    a. $(a > 1)$ OR $(b = c)$

    b. $[(a + b) > c]$ AND $(b \leq c)$

    c. NOT $(a = 1)$

    d. NOT $[(a = b)$ OR $(b = c)]$

    e. $(a = 1)$ AND $(b = 1)$ AND $(c = 2)$

20. Assume that $a = 5$, $b = 2$, and $c = 3$. What problem do you encounter when attempting to evaluate the following Boolean expression?

    $(a = 1)$ AND $(b = 2)$ OR $(c = 3)$

    How can this problem be solved?

21. The truth table for a Boolean expression with two variables has four rows. The truth table for a Boolean expression with three variables has eight rows. How many rows would there be in a truth table with five variables?

22. Using the circuit construction algorithm of Section 4.4.2, design a circuit using only AND, OR, and NOT gates to implement the following truth table:

a	b	Output
0	0	1
0	1	1
1	0	1
1	1	0

    This operation is termed *NAND*, for *Not AND*, and it can be constructed as a single gate, as shown in Figure 4.17(a). Assume that you do not have access to a NAND gate and must construct it from AND, OR, and NOT.

23. Using the circuit construction algorithm of Section 4.4.2, design a circuit using only AND, OR, and NOT gates to implement the following truth table.

a	b	Output
0	0	1
0	1	1
1	0	0
1	1	1

    This operation is termed *logical implication*, and it is an important operator in symbolic logic.

24. Build a *majority-rules circuit*. This is a circuit that has three inputs and one output. The value of its output is 1 if and only if two or more of its inputs are 1; otherwise, the output of the circuit is 0. For example, if the three inputs are 0, 1, 1, your circuit should output a 1. If its three inputs are 0, 1, 0, it should output a 0. This circuit is frequently used in **fault-tolerant computing**—environments where a computer must keep working correctly no matter what, for example as on a deep-space vehicle where making repairs is impossible. In these conditions, we might choose to put three computers on board and have all three do every computation; if two or more of the systems produce the same answer, we accept it. Thus, one of the machines could fail and the system would still work properly.

25. Design an *odd-parity circuit*. This is a circuit that has three inputs and one output. The circuit outputs a 1 if and only if an even number (0 or 2) of its inputs are a 1. Otherwise, the circuit outputs a 0. Thus the sum of the number of 1 bits in the input and the output is always an odd number. (This circuit is used in error checking. By adding up the number of 1 bits, we can determine whether any single input bit was accidentally changed. If it was, the total number of 1s is an even number when we know it should be an odd value.)

26. Design a *1-bit subtraction circuit*. This circuit takes three inputs—two binary digits *a* and *b* and a borrow digit from the previous column. The circuit has two outputs—the difference (*a* − *b*), including the borrow, and a new borrow digit that propagates to the next column. Create the truth table and build the circuit. This circuit can be used to build *N*-bit subtraction circuits.

27. How many selector lines would be needed on a four-input multiplexor? On an eight-input multiplexor?

28. Design a *four-input multiplexor circuit*. Use the design of the two-input multiplexor shown in Figure 4.28 as a guide.

29. Design a *3-to-8 decoder circuit*. Use the design of the 2-to-4 decoder circuit shown in Figure 4.29 as a guide.

CHALLENGE WORK

1. Circuit optimization is a very important area of hardware design. As we mentioned earlier in the chapter, each gate in the circuit represents a real hardware device that takes up space on the chip, generates heat that must be dissipated, and increases costs. Therefore, the elimination of unneeded gates can represent a real savings. Circuit optimization investigates techniques to construct a new circuit that behaves identically to the original one but with fewer gates. The basis for circuit optimization is the transformation rules of symbolic logic. These rules allow you to transform one Boolean expression into an equivalent one that entails fewer operations. For example, the *distributive law* of logic says that $(a \cdot b) + (a \cdot c) = a \cdot (b + c)$. The expressions on either side of the = sign are functionally identical, but the one on the right determines its value using one less gate (one AND gate and one OR gate instead of two AND gates and one OR gate).

   Read about the transformation rules of binary logic and techniques of circuit optimization. Using these rules, improve the full adder circuit of Figure 4.27 so that it requires fewer than 2,208 transistors. Explain your improvements and determine exactly how many fewer transistors are required for your "new-and-improved" full adder circuit.

2. This chapter briefly described an alternative signed integer representation technique called two's complement representation. This popular method is based on the concepts of *modular arithmetic*, and it does not suffer from the problem of two different representations for the quantity 0. Read more about two's complement and write a report describing how this method works, as well as algorithms for

adding and subtracting numbers represented in two's complement notation. In your report, give the 16-bit, two's complement representation for the signed integer values +45, −68, −1, and 0. Then show how to carry out the arithmetic operations 45 + 45, 45 + (−68), and 45 − (−1).

3. In Section 4.2.2, we describe lossless compression schemes, such as run-length encoding and variable-length codes. However, most compression schemes in use today are lossy and only achieve extremely high rates of compression at the expense of losing some of the detail contained in the sound or image. Often they base their compression techniques on specific knowledge of the characteristics of the human ear or eye. For example, it is well known that the eye is much more sensitive to changes in brightness (luminance) than to changes in color (chrominance). The JPEG compression algorithm exploits this fact when it is compressing a photographic image.

Read about the JPEG image compression algorithm to learn how it is able to achieve compression ratios of 10:1 or even 20:1. A good place to start would be the JPEG home page, located at *www.jpeg.org*.

ADDITIONAL RESOURCES

CourseMate **For additional print and/or online resources relevant to this chapter, visit the Computer Science CourseMate at login.cengagebrain.com.**

Computer Systems Organization

5.1 Introduction

Chapter 4 introduced the elementary building blocks of computer systems—transistors, gates, and logic circuits. Though this information is essential to understanding computer hardware—just as knowledge of atoms and molecules is necessary for any serious study of chemistry—it produces a very low-level view of computer systems. Even students who have mastered the material may still ask, "OK, but how do computers *really* work?" Gates and circuits operate on the most elemental of data items, binary 0s and 1s, whereas people reason and work with more complex units of information, such as decimal numbers, character strings, variables, and instructions. To understand how computers process this kind of information, we must look at higher-level components than gates and circuits. We must study computers as collections of functional units or subsystems that perform tasks such as instruction processing, information storage, computation, and data transfer. The branch of computer science that studies computers in terms of their major functional units is computer organization, and that is the subject of this chapter. This higher-level viewpoint will give us a much better understanding of how a computer really works.

All of the functional units introduced in this chapter are built from the gates and circuits of Chapter 4. However, those elementary components will no longer be visible because we will adopt a different viewpoint, a different perspective, a different level of abstraction. This is an extremely important point; as we have said, the concept of abstraction is used throughout computer science. Without it, it would be virtually impossible to study computer design or any other large, complex system.

For example, suppose that system S is composed of a large number of elementary components a_1, a_2, a_3, ... interconnected in very intricate ways, as shown in Figure 5.1(a). This is equivalent to viewing a computer system as thousands or millions of individual gates. For some purposes, it might be necessary to view system S at this level of detail, but for other applications, the amount of detail could become overwhelming. To deal with this problem, we can redefine the primitives of system S by grouping the elementary components a_1, a_2, a_3, ..., as shown in Figure 5.1(b), and calling these larger units (A, B, C) the basic building blocks of system S. A, B, and C are treated as nondecomposable elements whose internal construction is hidden from

FIGURE 5.1

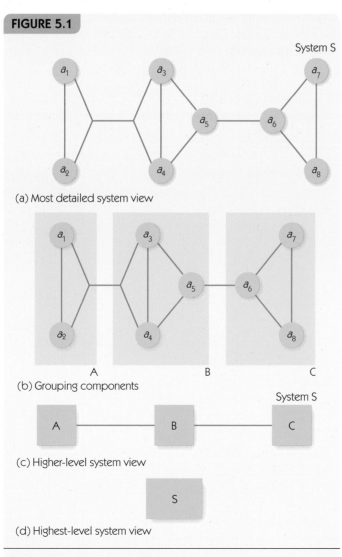

System S

(a) Most detailed system view

A   B   C

(b) Grouping components

System S

A ———— B ———— C

(c) Higher-level system view

S

(d) Highest-level system view

The concept of abstraction

view. We care only about what functions these components perform and how they interact. This leads to the higher-level system view shown in Figure 5.1(c), which is certainly a great deal simpler than the one shown in Figure 5.1(a), and this is how this chapter approaches the topic of computer hardware. Our primitives are much larger components, similar to A, B, and C, but internally they are still made up of the gates and circuits of Chapter 4.

This "abstracting away" of unnecessary detail can be done more than once. For example, at a later point in the study of system S, we might no longer care about the behavior of individual components A, B, and C. Instead, we might want to treat the entire system as a single primitive, nondecomposable entity whose inner workings are no longer important. This leads to the extremely simple system view shown in Figure 5.1(d), a view that we will adopt in later chapters.

Figures 5.1(a), (c), and (d) form what is called a hierarchy of abstractions. A hierarchy of abstractions of computer science forms the central theme of this text, and it was initially diagrammed in Figure 1.9. We have already seen this idea in action in Chapter 4, where transistors are grouped into gates and gates into circuits:

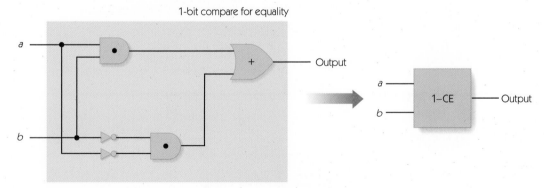

This process continues into Chapter 5, where we use the addition and comparison circuits of Section 4.4.3 to build an arithmetic unit and use the multiplexor and decoder circuits of Section 4.5 to construct a processor. These higher-level components become our building blocks in all future discussions.

5.2 The Components of a Computer System

There are a huge number of computer systems on the market, manufactured by dozens of different vendors. There are $50 million supercomputers, $1 million mainframes, midsized systems, workstations, laptops, tablets, and smartphones that cost less than a hundred dollars. In addition to size and cost, computers also differ in speed, memory capacity, input/output capabilities, and available software. The hardware marketplace is diverse, multifaceted, and ever changing.

However, in spite of all these differences, virtually every computer in use today is based on a single design. Although a $1 million mainframe, a $1,000 laptop, and a $100 smartphone might not seem to have much in common, they are all based on the same fundamental principles.

The same thing is true of automotive technology. Although a pickup truck, family sedan, and Ferrari racing car do not seem very similar, "under the hood" they are all constructed from the same basic technology: a gasoline-powered internal combustion engine turning an axle that turns the wheels. Differences among various models of trucks and cars are not basic theoretical differences but simply variations on a theme, such as a bigger engine, a larger carrying capacity, or a more luxurious interior.

The structure and organization of virtually all modern computers are based on a single theoretical model of computer design called the **Von Neumann architecture**, named after the brilliant mathematician John Von Neumann who proposed it in 1946. (You read about Von Neumann and his enormous contributions to computer science in the historical overview in Section 1.4.)

The Von Neumann architecture is based on the following three characteristics:

- Four major subsystems called **memory, input/output**, the **arithmetic/logic unit (ALU)**, and the **control unit**. These four subsystems are diagrammed in Figure 5.2. The ALU and the control unit are often bundled together in what is called the Central Processing Unit or CPU.

- The **stored program concept**, in which the instructions to be executed by the computer are represented as binary values and stored in memory.

- The **sequential execution of instructions**, in which one instruction at a time is fetched from memory and passed to the control unit, where it is decoded and executed.

This section looks individually at each of the four subsystems that make up the Von Neumann architecture and describes their design and operation. In the following section, we put all these pieces together to show the operation of the overall Von Neumann model.

FIGURE 5.2

Components of the Von Neumann architecture

5.2.1 Memory and Cache

Memory is the functional unit of a computer that stores and retrieves the instructions and the data being executed. All information stored in memory is represented internally using the binary numbering system described in Section 4.2.

Computer memory uses an access technique called *random access,* and the memory unit is frequently referred to as random access memory (RAM). RAM has the following three characteristics:

- Memory is divided into fixed-size units called cells, and each cell is associated with a unique identifier called an address. These addresses are the unsigned integers 0, 1, 2, ..., MAX.

- All accesses to memory are to a specified address, and we must always fetch or store a complete cell—that is, all the bits in that cell. The cell is the minimum unit of access.

- The time it takes to fetch or store the contents of a cell is the same for all the cells in memory.

A model of a random access memory unit is shown in Figure 5.3. (*Note:* Read-only memory (ROM) is random access memory into which

FIGURE 5.3

Structure of random access memory

information has been prerecorded during manufacture. This information cannot be modified or removed, only fetched. ROM is used to hold important system instructions and data in a place where a user cannot accidentally or intentionally overwrite them.)

As shown in Figure 5.3, the memory unit is made up of cells that contain a fixed number of binary digits. The number of bits per cell is called the cell size or the memory width, and it is usually denoted as W.

Earlier generations of computers had no standardized value for cell size, and computers were built with values of $W = 6, 8, 12, 16, 24, 30, 32, 36, 48,$ and 60 bits. However, computer manufacturers now use a standard cell size of 8 bits, and this 8-bit unit is universally called a *byte*. Thus, the generic term *cell* has become relatively obsolete, and it is more common now to refer to memory bytes as the basic unit. However, keep in mind that this is not a generic term but rather refers to a memory cell that contains exactly 8 binary digits.

With a cell size of 8 bits, the largest unsigned integer value that can be stored in a single cell is 11111111, which equals 255—not a very large number. Therefore, computers with a cell size of $W = 8$ often use multiple memory cells to store a single data value. For example, many computers use 2 or 4 bytes (16 or 32 bits) to store one integer, and either 4 or 8 bytes (32 or 64 bits) to store a single real number. This gives the range needed, but at a price. It may take several trips to memory, rather than one, to fetch a single data item.

Each memory cell in RAM is identified by a unique unsigned integer address 0, 1, 2, 3, ... If there are N bits available to represent the address of a cell, then the smallest address is 0 and the largest address is a string of N 1s:

$$\underbrace{1111\ldots11}_{N \text{ digits}}$$

which is equal to the value $2^N - 1$. Thus the range of addresses available on a computer is $[0 .. (2^N - 1)]$, where N is the number of binary digits used to represent an address. This is a total of 2^N memory cells. The value 2^N is called the maximum memory size or the address space of the computer. Typical values of N in the 1960s and 1970s were 16, 20, 22, and 24. Today all computers have at least 32 address bits allowing for up to 2^{32}, or about 4 billion, memory cells. However, 2^N represents the *maximum theoretical* memory size; a computer with N address bits does not necessarily come equipped with 2^N memory cells. It simply means that its memory can be expanded to 2^N. Figure 5.4 gives the value of 2^N for a number of values of N.

Because numbers like 65,536 (2^{16}) and 1,048,576 (2^{20}) are hard to remember, computer scientists use a convenient shorthand to refer to memory sizes (and other values that are powers of 2). It is based on the fact that the values $2^{10}, 2^{20}, 2^{30}, 2^{40},$ and 2^{50} are quite close in magnitude to one thousand, one million, one billion, one trillion, and one quadrillion, respectively. Therefore, the letters K (kilo, or thousand), M (mega, or million), G (giga, or billion), T (tera, or trillion), and P (peta, or quadrillion) are used to refer to these units.

FIGURE 5.4

N	Maximum Memory Size (2^N)
16	65,536
20	1,048,576
22	4,194,304
24	16,777,216
32	4,294,967,296
40	1,099,511,627,776
50	1,125,899,906,842,624

Maximum memory sizes

$2^{10} = 1K \,(= 1,024)$ 1 KB = 1 *kilobyte*

$2^{20} = 1M \,(= 1,048,576)$ 1 MB = 1 *megabyte*

$2^{30} = 1G \,(= 1,073,741,824)$ 1 GB = 1 *gigabyte*

$2^{40} = 1T \,(= 1,099,511,627,776)$ 1 TB = 1 *terabyte*

$2^{50} = 1P \,(= 1,125,899,906,842,624)$ 1 PB = 1 *petabyte*

Thus, a computer with a 16-bit address and $2^{16} = 65,536$ bytes of storage would have 64 KB of memory, because $2^{16} = 2^6 \times 2^{10} = 64 \times 2^{10} = 64$ KB. This was a popular size for computers of the 1960s and early 1970s. The 32-bit address, common in the 1980s, 1990s, and 2000s, and which supports an address space of $2^{32} = 4$ GB, has reached its limits. Therefore, most processors today provide 36-, 40-, 48-, or even 64-bit addresses. A 64-bit memory address would allow, at least theoretically, an address space of 2^{64} bytes, or 17 billion gigabytes!

When dealing with memory, it is important to keep in mind the distinction between an *address* and the *contents* of that address.

Address   *Contents*

42 | 1 |

The address of this memory cell is 42. The content of cell 42 is the integer value 1. As you will soon see, some instructions operate on addresses, whereas others operate on the contents of an address. A failure to distinguish between these two values can cause confusion about how some instructions behave.

The two basic memory operations are *fetching* and *storing*, and they can be described formally as follows:

- *value = Fetch(address)*

  Meaning: Fetch a copy of the contents of the memory cell with the specified *address* and return those contents as the result of the operation. The original contents of the memory cell that was accessed are unchanged.

This is termed a **nondestructive fetch**. Given the preceding diagram, the operation Fetch(42) returns the number 1. The value 1 remains in address 42.

- *Store(address, value)*

  Meaning: Store the specified *value* into the memory cell specified by *address*. The previous contents of the cell are lost. This is termed a **destructive store**. The operation Store(42, 2) stores the value 2 into cell 42, overwriting the previous value 1.

One of the characteristics of random access memory is that the time to carry out either a fetch or a store operation is the same for all 2^N addresses. At current levels of technology, this time, called the **memory access time**, is typically about 5–10 nsec (**nanosecond** = 1 nsec = 10^{-9} sec = 1 billionth of a second). Also note that fetching and storing are allowed only to an

Powers of 10

When we talk about volumes of information such as megabytes, gigabytes, and terabytes, it is hard to fathom exactly what those massive numbers mean. Here are some rough approximations (say, to within an order of magnitude) of how much textual information corresponds to each of the storage quantities just introduced, as well as the next few on the scale.

Quantity in Bytes	Base-10 Value	Amount of Textual Information
1 byte	10^0	One character
1 kilobyte	10^3	One typed page
1 megabyte	10^6	Two or three novels
1 gigabyte	10^9	A departmental library or a large personal library
1 terabyte	10^{12}	The library of a major academic research university
1 petabyte	10^{15}	All printed material in all libraries in North America
1 exabyte	10^{18}	All words ever printed throughout human history
1 zettabyte	10^{21}	—
1 yottabyte	10^{24}	—

entire cell. If we want, for example, to modify a single bit of memory, we first need to fetch the entire cell containing that bit, change the one bit, and then store the entire cell. The cell is the minimum accessible unit of memory.

There is one component of the memory unit shown in Figure 5.3 that we have not yet discussed, the *memory registers*. These two registers are used to implement the fetch and store operations. Both operations require two operands: the *address* of the cell being accessed and the *value*, either the value stored by the store operation or the value returned by the fetch operation.

The memory unit contains two special registers whose purpose is to hold these two operands. The Memory Address Register (MAR) holds the address of the cell to be accessed. Because the MAR must be capable of holding any address, it must be at least N bits wide, where 2^N is the address space of the computer.

The Memory Data Register (MDR) contains the data value being fetched or stored. We might be tempted to say that the MDR should be W bits wide, where W is the cell size. However, as mentioned earlier, on most computers the cell size is only 8 bits, and most data values occupy multiple cells. Thus the size of the MDR is usually a multiple of 8. Typical values of MDR width are 32 and 64 bits, which would allow us to fetch, in a single step, either an integer or a real value, respectively.

Given these two registers, we can describe a little more formally what happens during the fetch and store operations in a random access memory.

- Fetch(address)
  1. Load the address into the MAR.
  2. Decode the address in the MAR.
  3. Copy the contents of that memory location into the MDR.

- Store(address, value)
  1. Load the address into the MAR.
  2. Load the value into the MDR.
  3. Decode the address in the MAR.
  4. Store the contents of the MDR into that memory location.

For example, to retrieve the contents of cell 123, we would load the value 123 (in binary, of course) into the MAR and perform a fetch operation. When the operation is done, a copy of the contents of cell 123 would be in the MDR. To store the value 98 into cell 4, we load a 4 into the MAR and a 98 into the MDR and perform a store. When the operation is completed, the contents of cell 4 will have been set to 98, discarding whatever was there previously.

The operation "Decode the address in the MAR" means that the memory unit must translate the N-bit binary address stored in the MAR into the set of signals needed to access that one specific memory cell. That is, the memory unit must be able to convert the integer value 7, for example, in the MAR into the electronic signals needed to access *only* address 7 from all 2^N addresses in the memory unit. This might seem like magic, but it is actually a relatively easy task that applies ideas presented in the previous chapter. We can decode the address in the MAR using a decoder circuit of the type described in Section 4.5 and shown in Figure 4.29. (Remember that a decoder circuit has N inputs and 2^N outputs numbered 0, 1, 2, ... , $2^N - 1$. The circuit puts the signal 1 on the output line whose number equals the numeric value on the N input lines.) We simply copy the N bits in the MAR to the N input lines of a decoder circuit. Exactly one of its 2^N output lines is ON, and this line's identification number corresponds to the address value in the MAR.

For example, if $N = 4$ (the MAR contains 4 bits), then we have 16 addressable cells in our memory, numbered 0000 to 1111 (that is, 0 to 15). We could use a 4-to-16 decoder whose inputs are the 4 bits of the MAR. Each of the 16 output lines is associated with the one memory cell whose address is in the MAR and enables us to fetch or store its contents. This situation is shown in Figure 5.5.

If the MAR contains the 4-bit address 0010 (decimal 2), then only the output line labeled 0010 in Figure 5.5 is ON (that is, carries a value of 1). All

FIGURE 5.5

Organization of memory and the decoding logic

others are OFF. The output line 0010 is associated with the unique memory cell that has memory address 2, and the appearance of an ON signal on this line causes the memory hardware to copy the contents of location 2 to the MDR if it is doing a fetch, or to load the contents of the MDR into location 2 if it is doing a store.

The only problem with the memory organization shown in Figure 5.5 is that it does not scale very well. That is, it cannot be used to build a large memory unit. In modern computers, a typical value for N, the number of bits used to represent an address, is 32. A decoder circuit with 32 input lines would have 2^{32}, or more than 4 billion, output lines.

To solve this problem, memories are physically organized into a two-dimensional rather than a one-dimensional organization. In this structure, the 16-byte memory of Figure 5.5 would be organized into a two-dimensional 4×4 structure, rather than the one-dimensional 16×1 organization shown earlier. This two-dimensional layout is shown in Figure 5.6.

The memory locations are stored in *row major* order, with bytes 0–3 in row 0, bytes 4–7 in row 1 (01 in binary), bytes 8–11 in row 2 (10 in binary), and bytes 12–15 in row 3 (11 in binary). Each memory cell is connected to two selection lines, one called the *row selection line* and the other called the *column selection line*. When we send a signal down a single row selection

FIGURE 5.6

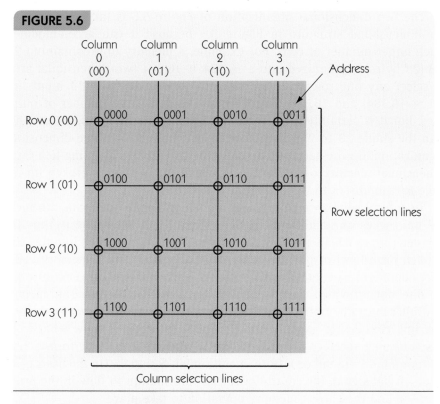

Two-dimensional memory organization

line and a single column selection line, only the memory cell located at the *intersection* of these two selection lines carries out a memory fetch or a memory store operation.

How do we choose the correct row and column selection lines to access the proper memory cell? Instead of using one decoder circuit, we use two. The first two binary digits of the addresses in Figure 5.6 are identical to the row number. Similarly, the last two binary digits of the addresses are identical to the column number. Thus, we should no longer view the MAR as being composed of a single 4-bit address, but as a 4-bit address made up of two distinct parts—the leftmost 2 bits, which specify the number of the row containing this cell, and the rightmost 2 bits, which specify the number of the column containing this cell. Each of these 2-bit fields is input to a separate decoder circuit that pulses the correct row and column lines to access the desired memory cell.

For example, if the MAR contains the 4-bit value 1101 (a decimal 13), then the two high-order (leftmost) bits 11 are sent to the row decoder, whereas the two low-order (rightmost) bits 01 are sent to the column decoder. The row decoder sends a signal on the line labeled 11 (row 3), and the column decoder sends a signal on the line labeled 01 (column 1). Only the single memory cell in row 3, column 1 becomes active and performs the fetch or store operation. Figure 5.6 shows that the memory cell in row 3, column 1 is the correct one—the cell with memory address 1101.

The two-dimensional organization of Figure 5.6 is far superior to the one-dimensional structure in Figure 5.5 because it can accommodate a much larger number of cells. For example, a memory unit containing 256 MB (2^{28} bytes) is organized into a 16,384 $\times$ 16,384 two-dimensional array. To select any one row or column requires a decoder with 14 input lines ($2^{14} = 16,384$) and 16,384 output lines. This is a large number of output lines, but it is certainly more feasible to build two 14-to-16,384 decoders than the single 28-to-256 million decoder required for a one-dimensional organization. If necessary, we can continue this process by going to a three-dimensional memory organization, in which the address is broken up into three parts and sent to three separate decoders.

To control whether memory does a fetch or a store operation, our memory unit needs one additional device called a fetch/store controller. This unit determines whether we put the contents of a memory cell into the MDR (a fetch operation) or put the contents of the MDR into a memory cell (a store operation). The fetch/store controller is like a traffic officer controlling the direction in which traffic can flow on a two-way street. This memory controller must determine in which direction information flows on the two-way link connecting memory and the MDR. In order to know what to do, this controller receives a signal telling it whether it is to perform a fetch operation (an F signal) or a store operation (an S signal). On the basis of the value of that signal, the controller causes information to flow in the proper direction and the correct memory operation to take place.

A complete model of the organization of a typical random access memory in a Von Neumann architecture is shown in Figure 5.7.

Let's complete this discussion by considering how complex it would be to study the memory unit of Figure 5.7, not at the abstraction level presented in that diagram, but at the gate and circuit level presented in Chapter 4. Let's assume that our memory unit contains 2^{30} cells (1 GB), each byte containing 8 bits. There is a total of about 8 billion bits of storage in this memory unit.

FIGURE 5.7

Overall RAM organization

A typical memory circuit used to store a single bit generally requires about 3 gates (1 AND, 1 OR, and 1 NOT) containing 7 transistors (3 per AND, 3 per OR, and 1 per NOT). Thus, our 1 GB memory unit (which is actually quite modest by today's standards) would contain roughly 24 billion gates and 56 billion transistors, and this does not even include the circuitry required to construct the decoder circuits, the controller, and the MAR and MDR registers! These numbers should help you appreciate the power and advantages of abstraction. Without it, studying a memory unit like the one in Figure 5.7 would be a much more formidable task.

Cache Memory. When Von Neumann created his idealized model of a computer, he described only a single type of memory. Whenever the computer needed an instruction or a piece of data, Von Neumann simply assumed it would get it from RAM using the fetch operation just described. However, as computers became faster, designers noticed that, more and more, the processor was sitting idle waiting for data or instructions to arrive. Processors were executing instructions so quickly that memory access was becoming a bottleneck. (It is hard to believe that a memory unit that can fetch a piece of data in a few billionths of a second can slow anything down, but it does.) As the following graph shows, during the period from 1980 to 2000, processors increased in performance by a factor of about 3,000, whereas memories became faster by a factor of only about 10.[1] This led to a huge imbalance between the capabilities of the processor and the capabilities of memory.

To solve this problem, designers needed to decrease memory access time to make it comparable with the time needed to carry out an instruction. It is possible to build extremely fast memory, but it is also quite expensive, and providing a few billion bytes or so of ultra–high-speed memory would make a computer prohibitively expensive.

However, computer designers discovered that it is not necessary to construct *all* of the memory from expensive, high-speed cells to obtain a

[1]From Hennessy, J., & Patterson, D. (2006). *Computer architecture: A quantitative approach* (4th ed.). Burlington, MA: Morgan Kaufmann.

significant increase in speed. They observed that when a program fetches a piece of data or an instruction, there is a high likelihood that

1. It will access that same instruction or piece of data in the very near future.
2. It will soon access the instructions or data that are located near that piece of data, where "near" means an address whose numerical value is close to this one.

Simply stated, this observation, called the principle of locality, says that when the computer uses something, it will probably use it again very soon, and it will probably use the "neighbors" of this item very soon. (Think about a loop in an algorithm that keeps repeating the same instruction sequence over and over.) To exploit this observation, the first time that the computer references a piece of data, it should copy that data from regular RAM memory to a special, high-speed memory unit called cache memory (pronounced "cash," from the French word *cacher*, meaning "to hide"). It should also copy the contents of memory cells located near this item into the cache. A cache is typically 5 to 10 times faster than RAM but much smaller—on the order of a few megabytes rather than a few gigabytes. This limited size is not a problem because the computer does not keep all of the data there, just those items that were accessed most recently and that, presumably, will be needed again immediately. The organization of the "two-level memory hierarchy" is as follows:

When the computer needs a piece of information, it does not immediately do the memory fetch operation described earlier. Instead, it carries out the following three steps:

1. Look first in cache memory to see whether the information is there. If it is, then the computer can access it at the higher speed of the cache.
2. If the desired information is not in the cache, then access it from RAM at the slower speed, using the fetch operation described earlier.
3. Copy the data just fetched into the cache along with the k immediately following memory locations. If the cache is full, then discard some of the older items that have not recently been accessed. (The assumption is that we will not need them again for a while.)

This algorithm significantly reduces the average time to access information. For example, assume that the average access time of our RAM is 10 nsec, whereas the average access time of the cache is 2 nsec. Furthermore, assume that the information we need is in the cache 70% of the time, a value called the **cache hit rate**. In this situation, 70% of the time we get what we need in 2 nsec, and 30% of the time we have wasted that 2 nsec because the information is not in the cache and must be obtained from RAM, which will take 10 nsec. Our overall average access time will now be

$$\text{Average access time} = (0.70 \times 2) + 0.30 \times (2 + 10) = 5.0 \text{ nsec}$$

which is a 50% reduction in access time from the original value of 10 nsec. A higher cache hit rate can lead to even greater savings.

A good analogy to cache memory is a home refrigerator. Without one we would have to go to the grocery store every time we needed an item; this corresponds to slow, regular memory access. Instead, when we go to the store we buy not only what we need now but also what we think we will need in the near future, and we put those items into our refrigerator. Now, when we need something, we first check the refrigerator. If it is there, we can get it at a much higher rate of speed. We only need to go to the store when the food item we want is not there.

Caches are found on every modern computer system, and they are a significant contributor to the higher computational speeds achieved by new machines. Even though the formal Von Neumann model contained only a

Practice Problems

Assume that our memory unit is organized as a 1,024 × 1,024 two-dimensional array of 8-bit bytes.

1. How big does the MAR register have to be?

2. How many bits of the MAR must be sent to the row decoder? To the column decoder?

3. Why is it unlikely that the size of the MDR register would be 8 bits?

4. If the average access time of this memory is 25 nsec and the average access time for cache memory is 10 nsec, what is the overall average access time if our cache hit rate is 80%?

5. What would happen to the overall average access time from Practice Problem 4 if we could somehow increase the cache hit rate to 90%?

6. In the previous problem, what would the cache hit rate have to be to reduce the average access time to 12.0 nsec?

7. Do you think that human memory is or is not a random access memory? Give an argument why or why not.

single memory unit, most computers built today have a multilevel hierarchy of random access memory.

5.2.2 Input/Output and Mass Storage

The input/output (I/O) units are the devices that allow a computer system to communicate and interact with the outside world as well as store information. The random access memory described in the previous section is volatile memory—the information disappears when the power is turned off. Without some type of long-term, nonvolatile memory, information could not be saved between shutdowns of the machine. Nonvolatile storage is the role of mass storage systems such as disks and tapes.

Of all the components of a Von Neumann machine, the I/O and mass storage subsystems are the most ad hoc and the most variable. Unlike the memory unit, I/O does not adhere to a single well-defined theoretical model. On the contrary, there are dozens of different I/O and mass storage devices manufactured by dozens of different companies and exhibiting many alternative organizations, making generalizations difficult. However, two important principles transcend the device-specific characteristics of particular vendors—*I/O access methods* and *I/O controllers*.

Input/output devices come in two basic types: those that represent information in *human-readable* form for human consumption and those that store information in *machine-readable* form for access by a computer system. The former includes such well-known I/O devices as keyboards, screens, and printers. The latter group of devices includes flash memory, hard drives, CDs, DVDs, and streaming tapes. Mass storage devices themselves come in two distinct forms: direct access storage devices (DASDs) and sequential access storage devices (SASDs).

Our discussion on random access memory in Section 5.2.1 described the fundamental characteristics of random access:

1. Every memory cell has a unique address.
2. It takes the same amount of time to access every cell.

A *direct access storage device* is one in which requirement number 2, equal access time, has been eliminated. That is, in a direct access storage device, every unit of information still has a unique address, but the time needed to access that information depends on its physical location and the current state of the device.

The best examples of DASDs are the types of disks listed earlier: hard drives, CDs, DVDs, and so on. A disk stores information in units called sectors, each of which contains an address and a data block containing a fixed number of bytes:

Sector

A fixed number of these sectors are placed in a concentric circle on the surface of the disk, called a track:

Individual sector

Track

Finally, the surface of the disk contains many tracks, and there is a single *read/write head* that can be moved in or out to be positioned over any track on the disk surface. The entire disk rotates at high speed under the read/write head. The overall organization of a typical disk is shown in Figure 5.8.

FIGURE 5.8

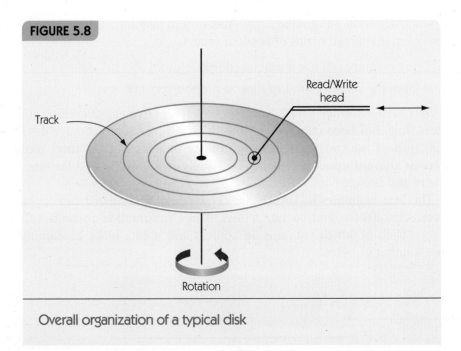

Read/Write head

Track

Rotation

Overall organization of a typical disk

The access time to any individual sector of the disk is made up of three components: seek time, latency, and transfer time. Seek time is the time needed to position the read/write head over the correct track; latency is the time for the beginning of the desired sector to rotate under the read/write head; and transfer time is the time for the entire sector to pass under the read/write head and have its contents read into or written from memory. These values depend on the specific sector being accessed and the current position of the read/write head. Let's assume a disk drive with the following physical characteristics:

Rotation speed = 7,200 rev/min = 120 rev/sec = 8.33 msec/rev
   (1 msec = 0.001 sec)

Arm movement time = 0.02 msec to move to an adjacent track
   (i.e., moving from track i to either track $i + 1$ or $i - 1$)

Number of tracks/surface = 1,000 (numbered 0 to 999)

Number of sectors/track = 64

Number of bytes/sector = 1,024

The access time for this disk can be determined as follows.

1. Seek Time

Best case = 0 msec (no arm movement)

Worst case = 999 × 0.02 = 19.98 msec (move from track 0 to track 999)

Average case = 300 × 0.02 = 6 msec (assume that on average, the read/write head must move about 300 tracks)

2. Latency

Best case = 0 msec (sector is just about to come under the read/write head)

Worst case = 8.33 msec (we just missed the first bit of the sector and must wait one full revolution)

Average case = 4.17 msec (one-half a revolution)

3. Transfer

1/64 × 8.33 msec = 0.13 msec (the time for one sector, or 1/64th of a track, to pass under the read/write head; this time will be the same for all sectors)

The following table summarizes these access time computations (all values are in milliseconds).

	Best	**Worst**	**Average**
Seek Time	0	19.98	6
Latency	0	8.33	4.17
Transfer	0.13	0.13	0.13
Total	0.13	28.44	10.3

The best-case time and the worst-case time to fetch or store a sector on the disk differ by a factor of more than 200, that is, 0.13 msec versus 28.44 msec. The average access time is about 10 msec, a typical value for current hard drive technology. This table clearly demonstrates the fundamental characteristic of all direct access storage devices, not just disks: They enable us to specify the address of the desired unit of data and go directly to that data item, but they cannot provide a uniform access time. Today, there is an enormous range of direct access storage devices in the marketplace, from small flash memory sticks that hold a few gigabytes, to hard drives, CDs, and DVDs that can store hundreds of gigabytes, to massive online storage devices that are capable of recording and accessing terabytes or even petabytes of data. (See the "Powers of Ten" Special Interest Box in this chapter for a definition of the metric prefix *peta-*.)

The second type of mass storage device uses the old access technique called *sequential access*. A sequential access storage device (SASD) does not require that all units of data be identifiable via unique addresses. To find any given data item, we must search all data sequentially, repeatedly asking the question, "Is this what I'm looking for?" If not, we move on to the next unit of data and ask the question again. Eventually we find what we are looking for or come to the end of the data.

A sequential access storage device behaves just like the old audio cassette tapes of the 1980s and 1990s. To locate a specific song, we run the tape for a while and then stop and listen. This process is repeated until we find the desired song or come to the end of the tape. In contrast, a direct access storage device behaves like a CD or DVD that numbers all the songs and allows you to select any one. (The song number is the address.) Direct access storage devices are generally much faster at accessing individual pieces of information, and that is why they are much more widely used for mass storage. However, sequential access storage devices can be useful in specific situations, such as sequentially copying the entire contents of memory or of a disk drive. This backup operation fits the SASD model well, and *streaming tape backup units* are common storage devices on computer systems.

One of the fundamental characteristics of many (though not all) I/O devices is that they are very, very *slow* when compared with other components of a computer. For example, a typical memory access time is about 10 nsec. The time to complete the I/O operation "locate and read one disk sector" was shown in the previous example to be about 10 msec.

Units such as nsec (billionths of a second), μsec (millionths of a second), and msec (thousandths of a second) are so small compared with human time scales that it is sometimes difficult to appreciate the immense difference between values like 10 nsec and 10 msec. The difference between these two quantities is a factor of 1,000,000, that is, 6 orders of magnitude. Consider that this is the same order of magnitude difference as between 1 mile and 40 complete revolutions of the Earth's equator, or between 1 day and 30 centuries!

It is not uncommon for I/O operations such as displaying an image on a monitor or printing a page on a printer to be 3, 4, 5, or even 6 orders of magnitude slower than any other aspect of computer operation. If there isn't something in the design of a computer to account for this difference, components that operate on totally incompatible time scales will be trying to talk to each other, which will produce enormous inefficiencies. The high-speed components will sit idle for long stretches of time while they wait for the slow I/O unit to accept or deliver the desired character. It would be like talking at the normal human rate of 240 words/min (4 words/sec) to someone who could respond only at the rate of 1 word every 8 hours—a difference of 5 orders of magnitude. You wouldn't get much useful work done!

The solution to this problem is to use a device called an I/O controller. An I/O controller is like a special-purpose computer whose responsibility is to handle the details of input/output and to compensate for any speed differences between I/O devices and other parts of the computer. It has a small amount of memory, called an *I/O buffer*, and enough *I/O control and logic* processing capability to handle the mechanical functions of the I/O device, such as the read/write head, paper feed mechanism, and screen display. It is also able to transmit to the processor a special hardware signal, called an interrupt signal, when an I/O operation is done. The organization of a typical I/O controller is shown in Figure 5.9.

Let's assume that we want to display one line (80 characters) of text on a screen. First, the 80 characters are transferred from their current location in memory to the I/O buffer storage within the I/O controller. This operation takes place at the high-speed data transfer rates of most computer components—hundreds of millions of characters per second. Once this information is in the I/O buffer, the processor can instruct the I/O controller to begin the output operation. The control logic of the I/O controller handles the actual transfer and display of these 80 characters to the screen. This

FIGURE 5.9

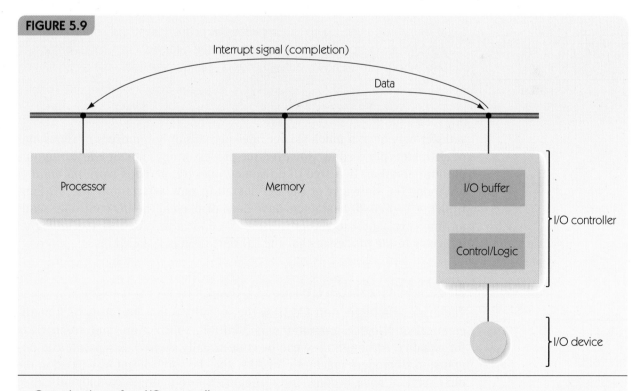

Organization of an I/O controller

Practice Problems

Assume a disk with the following characteristics:
- Number of sectors per track = 20
- Number of tracks per surface = 50
- Number of surfaces = 2 (called a *double-sided* disk)
- Number of characters per sector = 1,024
- Arm movement time = 0.4 msec to move 1 track in any direction
- Rotation speed = 2,400 rev/min

1. How many characters can be stored on this disk?

2. What are the best-case, worst-case, and average-case access times for this disk? (Assume that the average seek operation must move 20 tracks.)

3. What would be the average-case access time if we could increase the rotation speed from 2,400 rev/min to 7,200 rev/min?

4. What would be the average-case access time of the disk of the previous problem if we could reduce the arm movement time to 0.2 msec to move 1 track in any direction? (Again, assume that the average seek operation must move 20 tracks.)

5. *Defragmenting* a disk means to reorganize files on the disk so that as many pieces of the file as possible are stored in sectors on the same track, regardless of the surface it is on. Explain why defragmentation can be beneficial.

transfer may be at a much slower rate—perhaps only hundreds or thousands of characters per second. However, the processor does not sit idle during this output operation. It is free to do something else, perhaps work on another program. The slowness of the I/O operation now affects *only* the I/O controller. When all 80 characters have been displayed, the I/O controller sends an interrupt signal to the processor. The appearance of this special signal indicates to the processor that the I/O operation is finished.

5.2.3 The Arithmetic/Logic Unit

The arithmetic/logic unit (ALU) is the subsystem that performs such mathematical and logical operations as addition, subtraction, and comparison for equality. Although they can be conceptually viewed as separate components, in all modern machines the ALU and the control unit (discussed in the next section) have become fully integrated into a single component called the processor (the CPU). However, for reasons of clarity and convenience, we will describe the functions of the ALU and the control unit separately.

The ALU is made up of three parts: the registers, the interconnections between components, and the ALU circuitry. Together these components are called the data path.

A register is a storage cell that holds the operands of an arithmetic operation and that, when the operation is complete, holds its result. Registers are quite similar to the random access memory cells described in the previous section, with the following minor differences:

- They do not have a numeric memory address but are accessed by a special *register designator* such as A, X, or R0.

- They can be accessed much more quickly than regular memory cells. Because there are few registers (typically, a few dozen up to a hundred), it is reasonable to utilize the expensive circuitry needed to make the fetch and store operations 5 to 10 times faster than regular memory cells, of which there will be billions.

- They are not used for general-purpose storage but for specific purposes such as holding the operands for an upcoming arithmetic computation.

For example, an ALU might have three special registers called A, B, and C. Registers A and B hold the two input operands, and register C holds the result. This organization is diagrammed in Figure 5.10.

In most cases, however, three registers are not nearly enough to hold all the values that we might need. A typical ALU has 16, 32, or 64 registers. To see why this many ALU registers are needed, let's take a look at what

FIGURE 5.10

Three-register ALU organization

happens during the evaluation of the expression $(a \ / \ b) \times (c - d)$. After we compute the expression $(a \ / \ b)$, it would be nice to keep this result temporarily in a high-speed ALU register while evaluating the second expression $(c - d)$. Of course, we could always store the result of $(a \ / \ b)$ in a memory cell, but keeping it in a register allows the computer to fetch it more quickly when it is ready to complete the computation. In general, the more registers available in the ALU, the faster programs run.

A more typical ALU organization is illustrated in Figure 5.11, which shows an ALU data path containing 16 registers designated R0 to R15. Any of the 16 ALU registers in Figure 5.11 could be used to hold the operands of the computation, and any register could be used to store the result.

To perform an arithmetic operation with the ALU of Figure 5.11, we first move the operands from memory to the ALU registers. Then we specify

FIGURE 5.11

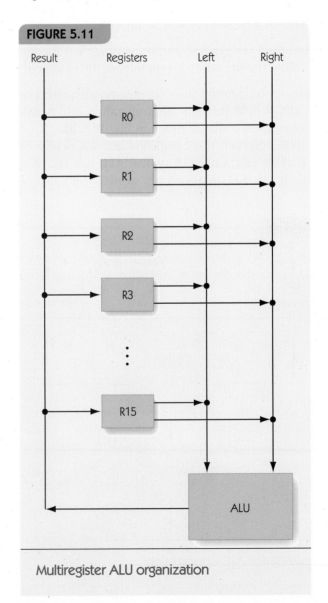

Multiregister ALU organization

which register holds the left operand by connecting that register to the communication path called "Left." In computer science terminology, a path for electrical signals (think of this as a wire) is termed a **bus**. We then specify which register to use for the right operand by connecting it to the bus labeled "Right." (Like RAM, registers also use nondestructive fetch so that when it is needed, the value is only copied to the ALU. It is still in the register.) The ALU is enabled to perform the desired operation, and the answer is sent to any of the 16 registers along the bus labeled "Result." (The destructive store principle says that the previous contents of the destination register will be lost.) If desired, the result can be moved from an ALU register back into memory for longer-term storage.

The final component of the ALU is the ALU circuitry itself. These are the circuits that carry out such operations as

$a + b$ (Figure 4.27)

$a = b$ (Figure 4.23)

$a - b$

$a \times b$

a / b

$a < b$

$a > b$

a AND b

Chapter 4 showed how circuits for these operations can be constructed from the three basic logic gates AND, OR, and NOT, and it showed the construction of logic circuits to perform the operations $a + b$ and $a = b$. The primary issue now is how to select the desired operation from among all the possibilities for a given ALU. For example, how do we tell an ALU that can perform the preceding eight operations that we want only the results of one operation, say $a - b$?

One possibility is to use the *multiplexor* control circuit introduced in Chapter 4 and shown in Figure 4.28. Remember that a multiplexor is a circuit with 2^N input lines numbered 0 to $2^N - 1$, N selector lines, and one output line. The selector lines are interpreted as a single binary number from 0 to $2^N - 1$, and the input line corresponding to this number has its value placed on the single output line.

Let's imagine for simplicity that we have an ALU that can perform four functions instead of eight. The four functions are $a + b$, $a - b$, $a = b$, and a AND b, and these operations are numbered 0, 1, 2, and 3, respectively (00, 01, 10, and 11 in binary). Finally, let's assume that every time the ALU is enabled and given values for a and b, it automatically performs all four possible operations rather than just the desired one. These four outputs can be input to a multiplexor circuit, as shown in Figure 5.12.

Now place on the selector lines the identification number of the operation whose output we want to keep. The result of the desired operation appears on the output line, and the other three answers are discarded. For example, to select the output of the subtraction operation, we input the

FIGURE 5.12

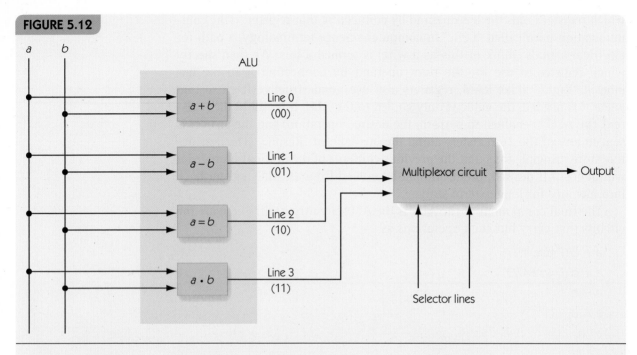

Using a multiplexor circuit to select the proper ALU result

binary value 01 (decimal 1) on the selector lines. This places the output of the subtraction circuit on the output line of the multiplexor. The outputs of the addition, comparison, and AND circuits are discarded.

Thus, the design philosophy behind an ALU is not to have it perform only the correct operation. Instead, it is to have *every* ALU circuit "do its thing" but then keep only the one desired answer.

Putting Figures 5.11 and 5.12 together produces the overall organization of the ALU of the Von Neumann architecture. This model is shown in Figure 5.13.

5.2.4 The Control Unit

The most fundamental characteristic of the Von Neumann architecture is the stored program—a sequence of machine language instructions stored as binary values in memory. It is the task of the control unit to (1) *fetch* from memory the next instruction to be executed, (2) *decode* it—that is, determine what is to be done, and (3) *execute* it by issuing the appropriate command to the ALU, memory, or I/O controllers. These three steps are repeated over and over until we reach the last instruction in the program, typically something called HALT, STOP, or QUIT.

To understand the behavior of the control unit, we must first investigate the characteristics of machine language instructions.

FIGURE 5.13

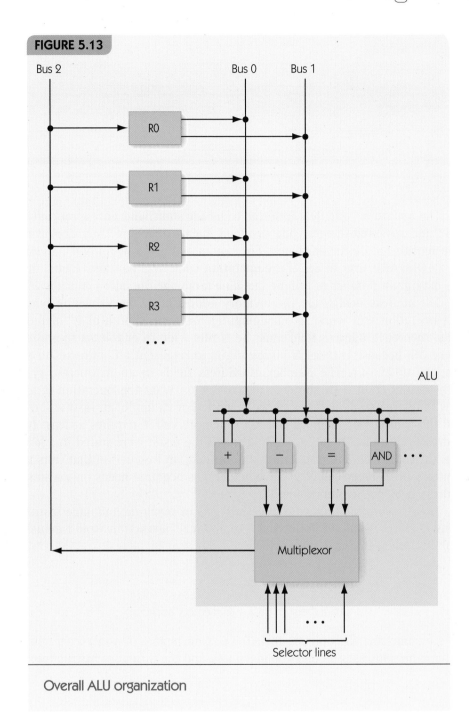

Overall ALU organization

Machine Language Instructions. The instructions that can be decoded and executed by the control unit of a computer are represented in machine language. Instructions in this language are expressed in binary, and a typical format is shown in Figure 5.14.

FIGURE 5.14

| Operation code | Address field 1 | Address field 2 | ... |

Typical machine language instruction format

The *operation code* field (referred to by the shorthand phrase *op code*) is a unique unsigned integer code assigned to each machine language operation recognized by the hardware. For example, 0 could be an ADD, 1 could be a COMPARE, and so on. If the operation code field contains k bits, then the maximum number of unique machine language operation codes is 2^k.

The *address field(s)* are the memory addresses of the values on which this operation will work. If our computer has a maximum of 2^N memory cells, then each address field must be N bits wide to enable us to address every cell because it takes N binary digits to represent all addresses in the range 0 to $2^N - 1$. The number of address fields in an instruction typically ranges from 0 to about 3, depending on what the operation is and how many operands it needs to do its work. For example, an instruction to add the contents of memory cell X to memory cell Y requires at least two addresses, X and Y. It could require three if the result were stored in a location different from either operand. In contrast, an instruction that tests the contents of memory cell X to see whether it is negative needs only a single address field, the location of cell X.

To see what this might produce in terms of machine language instructions, let's see what the following hypothetical instruction would actually look like when stored in memory.

Operation	Meaning
ADD X, Y	Add contents of memory addresses X and Y and put the sum back into memory address Y.

Let's assume that the op code for ADD is a decimal 9, X and Y correspond to memory addresses 99 and 100 (decimal), and the format of instructions is

op code	address 1	address 2
8	16	16

bits →

A decimal 9, in 8-bit binary, is 00001001. Address 99, when converted to an unsigned 16-bit binary value, is 0000000001100011. Address 100 is 1 greater: 0000000001100100. Putting these values together produces the instruction ADD X, Y as it would appear in memory:

00001001   0000000001100011   0000000001100100

op code   *address 1*   *address 2*

This is somewhat cryptic to a person, but is easily understood by a control unit.

The set of all operations that can be executed by a processor is called its instruction set, and the choice of exactly what operations to include or exclude from the instruction set is one of the most important and difficult decisions in the design of a new computer. There is no universal agreement on this issue, and the instruction sets of processors from different vendors may be completely different. This is one reason why a computer that uses an AMD Athlon 64 processor cannot directly execute programs written for a system that contains an Intel Core Duo. The operation codes and address fields that these two processors recognize are different and completely incompatible.

The machine language operations on most machines are quite elementary, and each operation typically performs a very simple task. The power of a processor comes not from the sophistication of the operations in its instruction set, but from the fact that it can execute each instruction very quickly, typically in a few billionths of a second.

One approach to designing instruction sets is to make them as small and as simple as possible, with perhaps as few as 30–50 instructions. Machines with this sort of instruction set are called *reduced instruction set computers* or RISC machines. This approach minimizes the amount of hardware circuitry (gates and transistors) needed to build a processor. The extra space on the chip can be used to optimize the speed of the instructions and allow them to execute very quickly. A RISC processor may require more instructions to solve a problem (because the instructions are so simple), but this is compensated for by the fact that each instruction runs much faster so the overall running time is less. The opposite philosophy is to include a much larger number, say 300–500, of very powerful instructions in the instruction set. These types of processors are called *complex instruction set computers*, or CISC machines, and they are designed to directly provide a wide range of powerful features so that finished programs for these processors are shorter. Of course, CISC machines are more complex, more expensive, and more difficult to build. As is often the case in life, it turns out that compromise is the best path—most modern processors use a mix of the two design philosophies.

A little later in this chapter, we will present an instruction set for a hypothetical computer to examine how machine language instructions are executed by a control unit. For clarity, we will not show these instructions in binary, as we did earlier. Instead, we will write out the operation code in English (for example, ADD, COMPARE, MOVE); use the capital letters X, Y, and Z to symbolically represent binary memory addresses; and use the letter R to represent an ALU register. Remember, however, that this notation is just for convenience. All machine language instructions are stored internally using binary representation.

Machine language instructions can be grouped into four basic classes called data transfer, arithmetic, compare, and branch.

1. *Data Transfer* These operations move information between or within the different components of the computer—for example:

> Memory cell → ALU register
>
> ALU register → memory cell
>
> One memory cell → another memory cell
>
> One ALU register → another ALU register

All data transfer instructions follow the nondestructive fetch/destructive store principle described earlier. That is, the contents of the *source cell* (where it is now) are never destroyed, only copied. The contents of the *destination cell* (where it is going) are overwritten, and its previous contents are lost.

Examples of data transfer operations include

Operation	Meaning
LOAD X	Load register R with the contents of memory cell X.
STORE X	Store the contents of register R into memory cell X.
MOVE X,Y	Copy the contents of memory cell X into memory cell Y.

2. *Arithmetic* These operations cause the arithmetic/logic unit to perform a computation. Typically, they include arithmetic operations like $+$, $-$, $\times$, and $/$, as well as logical operations such as AND, OR, and NOT. Depending on the instruction set, the operands may reside in memory or they may be in an ALU register.

Possible formats for arithmetic operations include the following examples. (*Note:* The notation CON(X) means the contents of memory address X.)

Operation	Meaning
ADD X,Y, Z	Add the contents of memory cell X to the contents of memory cell Y and put the result into memory cell Z. This is called a *three-address instruction*, and it performs the operation CON(Z) = CON(X) + CON(Y).
ADD X,Y	Add the contents of memory cell X to the contents of memory cell Y. Put the result back into memory cell Y. This is called a *two-address instruction*, and it performs the operation CON(Y) = CON(X) + CON(Y).
ADD X	Add the contents of memory cell X to the contents of register R. Put the result back into register R. This is called a *one-address instruction*, and it performs the operation R = CON(X) + R. (Of course, R must be loaded with the proper value before executing the instruction.)

Other arithmetic operations such as SUBTRACT, MULTIPLY, DIVIDE, AND, and OR would be structured in a similar fashion.

3. *Compare* These operations compare two values and set an indicator on the basis of the results of the compare. Most Von Neumann machines have a special set of bits inside the processor called *condition codes* (or a special register called a *status register* or *condition register*); these bits are set by the compare operations. For example, assume there are three 1-bit condition codes called GT, EQ, and LT that stand for greater than, equal to, and less than, respectively. The operation

Operation	Meaning
COMPARE X,Y	Compare the contents of memory cell X to the contents of memory cell Y and set the condition codes accordingly.

would set these three condition codes in the following way:

Condition	How the Condition Codes Are Set
CON (X) > CON (Y)	GT = 1 EQ = 0 LT = 0
CON (X) = CON (Y)	GT = 0 EQ = 1 LT = 0
CON (X) < CON (Y)	GT = 0 EQ = 0 LT = 1

4. *Branch* These operations alter the normal sequential flow of control. The normal mode of operation of a Von Neumann machine is *sequential*. After completing the instruction in address i, the control unit executes the instruction in address $i + 1$. (*Note:* If each instruction occupies k memory cells rather than 1, then after finishing the instruction starting in address i, the control unit executes the instruction starting in address $i + k$. In the following discussions, we assume for simplicity that each instruction occupies one memory cell.) The *branch instructions* disrupt this sequential mode.

Typically, determining whether to branch is based on the current settings of the condition codes. Thus, a branch instruction is almost always preceded by either a compare instruction or some other instruction that sets the condition codes. Typical branch instructions include

Operation	Meaning
JUMP X	Take the next instruction unconditionally from memory cell X.
JUMPGT X	If the GT indicator is a 1, take the next instruction from memory cell X. Otherwise, take the next instruction from the next sequential location.

(JUMPEQ and JUMPLT would work similarly on the other two condition codes.)

JUMPGE X	If *either* the GT or the EQ indicator is a 1, take the next instruction from memory location X. Otherwise, take the next instruction from the next sequential location.

(JUMPLE and JUMPNEQ would work in a similar fashion.)

HALT	Stop program execution. Don't go on to the next instruction.

These are some of the typical instructions that a Von Neumann computer can decode and execute. Challenge Work problem 2 at the end of this chapter asks you to investigate the instruction set of a real processor found inside a modern computer and compare it with what we have described here.

The instructions presented here are quite simple and easy to understand. The power of a Von Neumann computer comes not from having thousands of built-in, high-level instructions but from the ability to combine a great number of simple instructions into large, complex programs that can be executed extremely quickly. Figure 5.15 shows examples of how these simple machine language instructions can be combined to carry out some of the

FIGURE 5.15

Address	Contents
100	Value of a
101	Value of b
102	Value of c

Algorithmic notation		Machine Language Instruction Sequences	
	Address	Contents	(Commentary)
		⋮	
1. Set a to the value $b + c$	50	LOAD 101	Put the value of b into register R.
	51	ADD 102	Add c to register R. It now holds $b + c$.
	52	STORE 100	Store the contents of register R into a.
2. If $a > b$ then	50	COMPARE 100, 101	Compare a and b and set condition codes.
set c to the value a	51	JUMPGT 54	Go to location 54 if $a > b$.
Else	52	MOVE 101, 102	Get here if $a \leq b$, so move b into c
set c to the value b	53	JUMP 55	and skip the next instruction.
	54	MOVE 100, 102	Move a into c.
	55	· · ·	Next statement begins here.

Examples of simple machine language instruction sequences

high-level algorithmic operations first introduced in Level 1 and shown in Figure 2.9. (The examples assume that the variables a, b, and c are stored in memory locations 100, 101, and 102, respectively, and that the instructions occupy one cell each and are located in memory locations 50, 51, 52, ...)

Don't worry if these "miniprograms" are a little confusing. We treat the topic of machine language programming in more detail in the next chapter. For now, we simply want you to know what machine language instructions look like so that we can see how to build a control unit to carry out their functions.

Control Unit Registers and Circuits. It is the task of the control unit to fetch and execute instructions of the type shown in Figures 5.14 and 5.15. To accomplish this task, the control unit relies on two special registers called the program counter (PC) and the instruction register (IR) and on an *instruction decoder circuit*. The organization of these three components is shown in Figure 5.16.

Practice Problems

Assume that the variables a, b, c, and d are stored in memory locations 100, 101, 102, and 103, respectively, and that the constant value $+1$ is stored in memory location 104. Using any of the sample machine language instructions given in this section, translate the following pseudocode operations into machine language instruction sequences. Have your instruction sequences begin in memory location 50.

1. Set a to the value $b + c + d$

2. Set a to the value $(b \times d) - (c / d)$

3. Set a to the value $(a - 1)$

4. If $(a = b)$ then set c to the value of d

5. If $(a \leq b)$ then

    Set c to the value of d

    Else

    Set c to the value of $2d$ (that is, $d + d$)

6. Initialize a to the value d

    While $a \leq c$

    Set a to the value $(a + b)$

    End of the loop

FIGURE 5.16

Organization of the control unit registers and circuits

The program counter holds the address of the *next* instruction to be executed. It is like a "pointer" specifying which address in memory the control unit must go to in order to get the next instruction. To get that instruction, the control unit sends the contents of the PC to the MAR in memory and executes the Fetch(address) operation described in Section 5.2.1. For example, if the PC holds the value 73 (in binary, of course), then when the current instruction is finished, the control unit sends the value 73 to the MAR and fetches the instruction contained in cell 73. The PC gets incremented by 1 after each fetch because the normal mode of execution in a Von Neumann machine is sequential. (Again, we are assuming that each instruction occupies one cell. If an instruction occupied k cells, then the PC would be incremented by k.) Therefore, the PC frequently has its own incrementor ($+1$) circuit to allow this operation to be done quickly and efficiently.

The instruction register (IR) holds a copy of the instruction fetched from memory. The IR holds both the op code portion of the instruction, abbreviated IR_{op}, and the address(es), abbreviated IR_{addr}.

To determine what instruction is in the IR, the op code portion of the IR must be decoded using an *instruction decoder*. This is the same type of decoder circuit discussed in Section 4.5 and used in the construction of the memory unit (Figure 5.7). The k bits of the op code field of the IR are sent to the instruction decoder, which interprets them as a numerical value between 0 and $2^k - 1$. Exactly one of the 2^k output lines of the decoder is set to a 1—specifically, the output line whose identification number matches the operation code of this instruction.

Figure 5.17 shows a decoder that accepts a 3-bit op code field and has $2^3 = 8$ output lines, one for each of the eight possible machine language operations. The 3 bits of the IR_{op} are fed into the instruction decoder, and

FIGURE 5.17

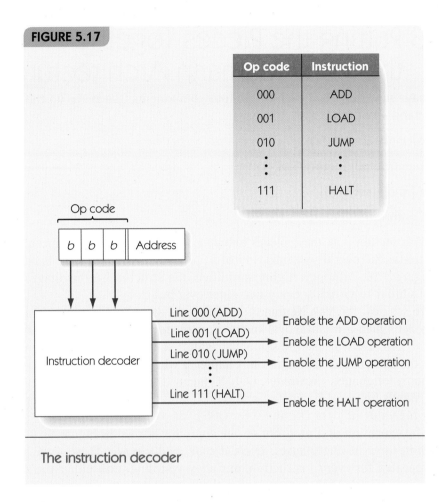

Op code	Instruction
000	ADD
001	LOAD
010	JUMP
⋮	⋮
111	HALT

The instruction decoder

they are interpreted as a value from 000 (0) to 111 (7). If the bits are, for example, 000, then line 000 in Figure 5.17 is set to a 1. This line enables the ADD operation because the operation code for ADD is 000. When a 1 appears on this line, the ADD operation: (1) fetches the two operands of the add and sends them to the ALU, (2) has the ALU perform all of its possible operations, (3) selects the output of the adder circuit, discarding all others, and (4) moves the result of the add to the correct location.

If the op code bits are 001 instead, then line 001 in Figure 5.17 is set to a 1. This time the LOAD operation is enabled because the operation code for LOAD is the binary value 001. Instead of performing the previous four steps, the hardware carries out the LOAD operation by: (1) sending the value of IR_{addr} to the MAR in the memory unit, (2) fetching the contents of that address and putting them in the MDR, and (3) copying the contents of the MDR into ALU register R.

For every one of the 2^k machine language operations in our instruction set, there exists the circuitry needed to carry out, step-by-step, the function of that operation. The instruction decoder has 2^k output lines, and each output line enables the circuitry that performs the desired operation.

5.3 Putting the Pieces Together— the Von Neumann Architecture

We have now described each of the four components that make up the Von Neumann architecture:

- Memory (Figure 5.7)

- Input/output (Figure 5.9)

- ALU (Figure 5.13)

- Control unit (Figures 5.16, 5.17)

This section puts these pieces together and shows how the entire model functions. The overall organization of a Von Neumann computer is shown in Figure 5.18. Although highly simplified, the structure in this diagram is quite similar to virtually every computer ever built!

To see how the Von Neumann machine of Figure 5.18 executes instructions, let's pick a hypothetical instruction set for our system, as shown in Figure 5.19. We will use the same instruction set in the Laboratory Experience for this chapter and again in Chapter 6 when we introduce and study assembly languages. (*Reminder:* CON(X) means the contents of memory cell X; R stands for an ALU register; and GT, EQ, and LT are condition codes that have the value of 1 for ON and 0 for OFF.)

The execution of a program on the computer shown in Figure 5.18 proceeds in three distinct phases: *fetch*, *decode*, and *execute*. These three steps are repeated for every instruction, and they continue until either the computer executes a HALT instruction or there is a fatal error that prevents it from continuing (such as an illegal op code, a nonexistent memory address, or division by zero). Algorithmically, the process can be described as follows:

> While we do not have a HALT instruction or a fatal error
>
> > Fetch phase
> >
> > Decode phase
> >
> > Execute phase
>
> End of the loop

This repetition of the fetch/decode/execute phase is called the *Von Neumann cycle*. To describe the behavior of our computer during each of these three phases, we will use the following notational conventions:

CON(A)	The *contents* of memory cell A. We assume that an instruction occupies 1 cell.
A → B	Send the value stored in register A to register B. The following abbreviations refer to the special registers and functional units of the Von Neumann architecture introduced in this chapter:
	PC The program counter
	MAR The memory address register

MDR	The memory data register
IR	The instruction register, which is further divided into IR_{op} and IR_{addr}
ALU	The arithmetic/logic unit
R	Any ALU register
GT, EQ, LT	The condition codes of the ALU
+1	A special increment unit attached to the PC
FETCH	Initiate a memory fetch operation (that is, send an F signal on the F/S control line of Figure 5.18).

FIGURE 5.18

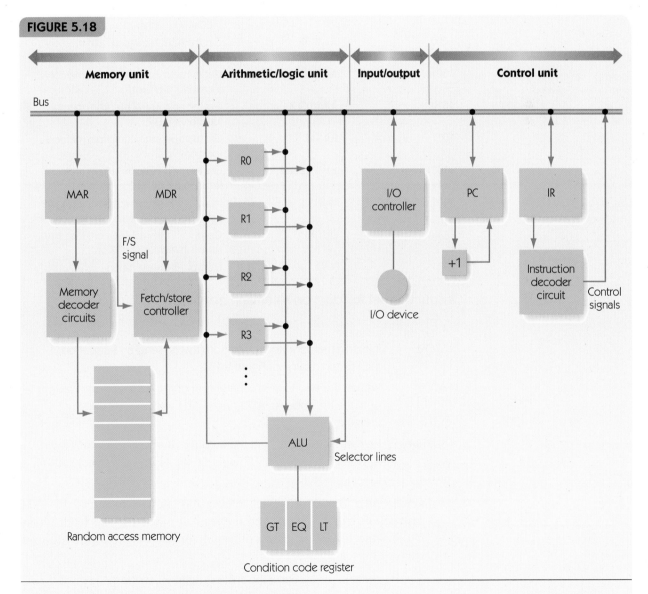

The organization of a Von Neumann computer

FIGURE 5.19

Binary Op Code	Operation	Meaning
0000	LOAD X	CON(X) → R
0001	STORE X	R → CON(X)
0010	CLEAR X	0 → CON(X)
0011	ADD X	R + CON(X) → R
0100	INCREMENT X	CON(X) + 1 → CON(X)
0101	SUBTRACT X	R – CON(X) → R
0110	DECREMENT X	CON(X) – 1 → CON(X)
0111	COMPARE X	if CON(X) > R then GT = 1 else 0
		if CON(X) = R then EQ = 1 else 0
		if CON(X) < R then LT = 1 else 0
1000	JUMP X	Get the next instruction from memory location X.
1001	JUMPGT X	Get the next instruction from memory location X if GT = 1.
1010	JUMPEQ X	Get the next instruction from memory location X if EQ = 1.
1011	JUMPLT X	Get the next instruction from memory location X if LT = 1.
1100	JUMPNEQ X	Get the next instruction from memory location X if EQ = 0.
1101	IN X	Input an integer value from the standard input device and store into memory cell X.
1110	OUT X	Output, in decimal notation, the value stored in memory cell X.
1111	HALT	Stop program execution.

Instruction set for our Von Neumann machine

STORE   Initiate a memory store operation (that is, send an S signal on the F/S control line of Figure 5.18).

ADD   Instruct the ALU to select the output of the adder circuit (that is, place the code for ADD on the ALU selector lines shown in Figure 5.18).

SUBTRACT   Instruct the ALU to select the output of the subtract circuit (that is, place the code for SUBTRACT on the ALU selector lines shown in Figure 5.18).

A. *Fetch phase* During the fetch phase, the control unit gets the next instruction from memory and moves it into the IR. The fetch phase is the same for every instruction and consists of the following four steps.

    1.   PC → MAR   Send the address in the PC to the MAR register.

    2.   FETCH   Initiate a fetch operation using the address in the MAR. The contents of that cell are placed in the MDR.

3.   MDR → IR   Move the instruction in the MDR to the instruction register so that we are ready to decode it during the next phase.

4.   PC + 1 → PC   Send the contents of the PC to the incrementor and put it back. This points the PC to the next instruction.

The control unit now has the current instruction in the IR and has updated the program counter so that it will correctly fetch the next instruction when the execution of this instruction is completed. It is ready to begin decoding and executing the current instruction.

B.   *Decode phase* Decoding the instruction is simple because all that needs to be done is to send the op code portion of the IR to the instruction decoder, which determines its type. The op code is the 4-bit binary value in the first column of Figure 5.19.

1. IR_{op} → instruction decoder

The instruction decoder generates the proper control signals to activate the circuitry to carry out the instruction.

C.   *Execution phase* The specific actions that occur during the execution phase are different for each instruction. Therefore, there will be a unique set of circuitry for each of the 2^k distinct instructions in the instruction set. The control unit circuitry generates the necessary sequence of control signals and data transfer signals to the other units (ALU, memory, and I/O) to carry out the intent of this instruction. The following examples show what signals and transfers take place during the execution phase of some of the instructions in Figure 5.19 using the Von Neumann model of Figure 5.18.

a) LOAD X   Meaning: Load register R with the current contents of memory cell X.

1. IR_{addr} → MAR   Send address X (currently in IR_{addr}) to the MAR.

2. FETCH   Fetch contents of cell X and place that value in the MDR.

3. MDR → R   Copy the contents of the MDR into register R.

b) STORE X   Meaning: Store the current contents of register R into memory cell X.

1. IR_{addr} → MAR   Send address X (currently in IR_{addr}) to the MAR.

2. R → MDR   Send the contents of register R to the MDR.

3. STORE   Store the value in the MDR into memory cell X.

c) ADD X   Meaning: Add the contents of cell X to the
                        contents of register R and put the result back
                        into register R.

   1. $IR_{addr} \rightarrow MAR$ Send address X (currently in IR_{addr}) to the MAR.

   2. FETCH   Fetch the contents of cell X and place it in the MDR.

   3. MDR $\rightarrow$ ALU   Send the two operands of the ADD to the ALU.

   4. R $\rightarrow$ ALU

   5. ADD   Activate the ALU and select the output of the ADD
                        circuit as the desired result.

   6. ALU $\rightarrow$ R   Copy the selected result into the R register.

d) JUMP X   Meaning: Jump to the instruction located in memory
                        location X.

   1. $IR_{addr} \rightarrow PC$ Send address X to the PC so the instruction stored
                        there is fetched during the next fetch phase.

e) COMPARE X   Meaning: Determine whether CON(X) < R, CON(X)
                        = R, or CON(X) > R, and set the condition codes
                        GT, EQ, and LT to appropriate values. (Assume all
                        codes are initially 0.)

   1. $IR_{addr} \rightarrow MAR$ Send address X to the MAR.

   2. FETCH   Fetch the contents of cell X and place it in the MDR.

   3. MDR $\rightarrow$ ALU   Send the contents of address X and register R to
                        the ALU.

   4. R $\rightarrow$ ALU

   5. SUBTRACT   Evaluate CON(X) – R. The result is not saved, and
                        is used only to set the condition codes. If CON(X)
                        – R > 0, then CON(X) > R and set GT to 1. If CON(X)
                        – R = 0, then they are equal and set EQ to 1. If
                        CON(X) – R < 0, then CON(X) < R and set LT to 1.

f) JUMPGT X   Meaning: If GT condition code is 1, jump to the
                        instruction in location X. We do this by loading the
                        address field of the IR, which is the address of
                        location X, into the PC. Otherwise, continue to the
                        next instruction.

   1. IF GT = 1 THEN $IR_{addr} \rightarrow PC$

These are six examples of the sequence of signals and transfers that occur during the execution phase of the fetch/decode/execute cycle. There is a unique sequence of actions for each of the 16 instructions in the sample instruction set of Figure 5.19 and for the 50–300 instructions in the instruction set of a typical

Von Neumann computer. When the execution of one instruction is done, the control unit fetches the next instruction, starting the cycle all over again. That is the fundamental sequential behavior of the Von Neumann architecture.

These six examples clearly illustrate the concept of abstraction at work. In Chapter 4, we built complex arithmetic/logic circuits to do operations like addition and comparison. Using these circuits, this chapter describes a computer that can execute machine language instructions such as ADD X and COMPARE X,Y. A machine language instruction such as ADD X is a complicated concept, but it is quite a bit easier to understand than the enormously detailed full adder circuit shown in Figure 4.27, which contains 800 gates and more than 2,000 transistors.

Abstraction has allowed us to replace a complex sequence of gate-level manipulations with the single machine language command ADD, which does addition without our having to know how—the very essence of abstraction. Well, why should we stop here? Machine language commands, though better than hardware, are hardly user friendly. (Some might even call them "user intimidating.") Programming in binary and writing sequences of instructions such as

01011010000011111010100001

is cumbersome, confusing, and very error-prone. Why not take these machine language instructions and make them more user oriented and user friendly? Why not give them features that allow us to write correct, reliable, and efficient programs more easily? Why not develop *user-oriented programming languages* designed for people, not machines? This is the next level of abstraction in our hierarchy, and we introduce that important concept in Level 3 of the text.

An Alphabet Soup of Speed Measures: MHz, GHz, MIPS, and GFLOPS

It is easy to identify the fastest car, plane, or train—just compare their top speeds in miles/hour (or km/hr) and pick the greatest. However, in the computer arena things are not so simple, and there are many different measures of speed.

The unit you might be most familiar with is *clock speed*, measured in either millions of cycles per second, called megahertz (MHz) or billions of cycles per second, called gigahertz (GHz). The actions of every computer are controlled by a central clock, and the "tick" rate of this clock is one possible speed measure. Processors today have clock rates of about 3–5 GHz. However, clock speed can be misleading because a machine's capability depends not only on the tick rate but also on how much work it can do during each tick. If machine A has a clock rate twice as fast as machine B, but each instruction on machine A takes twice as many clock cycles as machine B to complete, then there is no discernible speed difference.

(Continued)

Therefore, a more accurate measure of machine speed is *instruction rate,* measured in MIPS, an acronym for *millions of instructions per second.* The instruction rate measures how many machine language instructions of the type listed in Figure 5.19 (e.g., LOAD, STORE, COMPARE, ADD) can be fetched, decoded, and executed in one second. If a computer completes one instruction for every clock cycle, then the instruction rate is identical to the clock rate. However, many instructions require multiple clock ticks, whereas parallel computers can often complete multiple instructions in a single tick. Thus, MIPS is a better measure of performance because it tells you how much work is actually being done, in terms of completed instructions, in a given amount of time.

Finally, some people are only interested in how fast a computer executes the subset of instructions most important to their applications. For example, scientific programs do an enormous amount of floating-point (i.e., decimal) arithmetic, so the computers that execute these programs must be able to execute arithmetic instructions as fast as possible. For these machines, a better measure of speed might be the *floating-point instruction rate,* measured in GFLOPS—for billions of floating-point operations per second. This is like MIPS, except the instructions we focus most closely on are those for adding, subtracting, multiplying, and dividing real numbers. Modern processors can perform at a rate of about 5 GFLOPS with some of the more sophisticated ones running at speeds up to 50 GFLOPS.

There is no universal measure of computer speed, and that is what allows different computer vendors all to stand up and claim, "My machine is the fastest!"

Laboratory Experience 9

This Laboratory Experience introduces a software package that simulates the behavior of a Von Neumann computer. It will give you a chance to work with and observe the behavior of a Von Neumann machine quite similar to the one shown in Figure 5.18. Our simulated computer contains the same functional units introduced in this section, including memory, registers, arithmetic/logic unit, and control unit, and it uses the instruction set shown in Figure 5.19. The simulator allows you to observe the step-by-step execution of machine language instructions and watch the flow of information that occurs during the fetch, decode, and execute phases. It also allows you to write and execute your own machine language programs.

5.4 Non–Von Neumann Architectures

The Von Neumann architecture, which is the central theme of this chapter, has served the field well for over 60 years, but some computer scientists believe it may be reaching the end of its useful life.

The problems that computers are being asked to solve have grown significantly in size and complexity since the appearance of the first-generation machines in the late 1940s and early 1950s. Designers have been able to keep up with these larger and larger problems by building faster and faster Von Neumann machines. Through advances in hardware design, manufacturing methods, and circuit technology, computer designers have been able to take the basic sequential architecture described by Von Neumann in 1946 and improve its performance by 4 or 5 orders of magnitude. First-generation machines were able to execute about 10,000 machine language instructions per second. By the second generation, that had grown to about 1 million instructions per second. Today, even a small desktop PC can perform about 1 billion instructions per second, whereas larger and more powerful workstations can execute instructions at the rate of 5 billion instructions per second. Figure 5.20 shows the changes in computer speeds from the mid-1940s to the present.

(*Note:* The graph shown in Figure 5.20 is logarithmic. Each unit on the vertical axis is 10 times the previous one.) The period from about 1945 to about 1970 is characterized by exponential increases in computation speed. However, as Figure 5.20 shows, even though computer speeds are still increasing, the rate of improvement appears to be slowing down.

This slowdown is due to many things. One important limit on increased processor speed is the inability to place gates any closer together on a chip. (See the Special Interest Box "Moore's Law and the Limits of Chip Design" in Chapter 4.) Today's high-density chips contain billions of transistors separated by distances of only 50–100 nanometers (10^{-9} meters), and it is becoming exceedingly difficult (not to mention expensive) to accurately place individual components closer together. However, the time it takes to send signals between two parts of a computer separated by a given distance is limited by the fact that electronic signals cannot travel faster than the speed of light—299,792,458 meters per second. That is, when we carry out an operation such as:

PC → MAR

the signals traveling between these two registers cannot exceed 300 million meters/sec. If, for example, these two components were separated by 1 meter, it would take signals leaving the PC about 3 nanoseconds to reach the MAR, and nothing in this universe can reduce that value except a reduction of the distance separating them.

Even while the rate of increase in the performance of newer machines is slowing down, the problems that researchers are attempting to solve are growing ever larger and more complex. New applications in such areas as

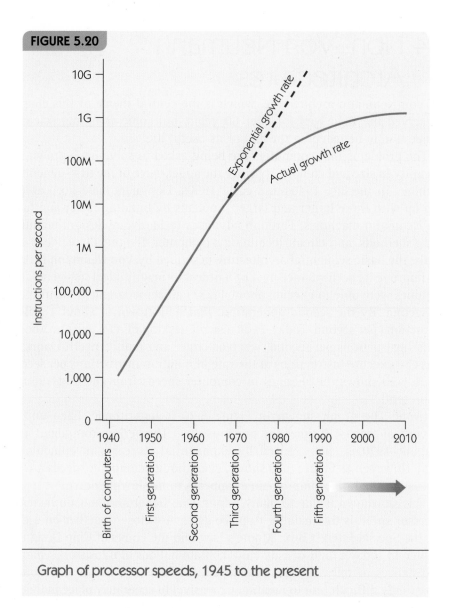

FIGURE 5.20

Graph of processor speeds, 1945 to the present

computational modeling, real-time graphics, and bioinformatics are rapidly increasing the demands placed on new computer systems. (We will look at some of these applications in Level 5, Chapters 13–16.) For example, to have a computer generate and display animated images without flicker it must generate 30 new frames each second. Each frame may contain as many as 3,000 × 3,000 separate picture elements (pixels) whose position, color, and intensity must be individually recomputed. This means that 30 × 3,000 × 3,000 = 270,000,000 pixel computations need to be completed every second. Each of those computations may require the execution of many instructions. (Where does this point move to in the next frame? How bright is it? Is it visible or hidden behind something else?) If we assume that it requires about 1,000 instructions per pixel to answer these questions (a reasonable approximation), then real-time computer animation requires a computer capable of executing 270,000,000 × 1,000 = 270 billion instructions per second. This is beyond the abilities of current processors, which are limited to about 5–10 billion instructions per second. The inability of the sequential one-instruction-at-a-time Von Neumann model to handle today's large-scale problems is called the Von Neumann bottleneck, and it is a major problem in computer organization.

To solve this problem, computer engineers are rethinking many of the fundamental ideas presented in this chapter, and they are studying nontraditional approaches to computer organization called non–Von Neumann architectures. They are asking the question, "Is there a different way to design and build computers that can solve problems 10 or 100 or 1,000 times larger than what can be handled by today's computers?" Fortunately, the answer to this question is a resounding, Yes!

One of the most important areas of research in these non–Von Neumann architectures is based on the following fairly obvious principle:

If you cannot build something to work twice as fast, build it to do two things at once. The results will be identical.

From this truism comes the principle of parallel processing–building computers not with one processor, as shown in Figure 5.18, but with tens, hundreds, or even thousands. If we can keep each processor occupied with meaningful work, then it should be possible to speed up the solution to large problems by 1, 2, or 3 orders of magnitude and overcome the Von Neumann bottleneck. For example, in the graphical animation example discussed earlier, we determined that we needed a machine that can execute 270 billion instructions/second, but today's processors are limited to about 5 billion instructions/second. However, let's say that we could have 54 processors all working together on this one problem; then we should (in theory!) have a sufficiently powerful system to solve our problem because 5 billion ops/sec per processor x 54 processors = 270 billion ops/sec. This is the idea behind the *dual-core* and *quad-core* processors that have two or four separate processors on a single chip.

The approach of placing multiple processors on a single chip is fine for a small number of processors, say two, four, or eight. However, we need a completely different approach to build large-scale parallel systems that contain hundreds or even thousands of processors.

There are two fundamentally distinct approaches to designing these massively parallel systems. The first technique is termed SIMD parallel processing. (SIMD stands for *single instruction stream/multiple data stream.*) It is diagrammed in Figure 5.21.

In the SIMD model, there is a single program whose instructions are fetched/decoded/executed in a sequential manner by one control unit, exactly as described earlier. However, the ALU (circuits and registers) is replicated many times, and each ALU has its own local memory where it may keep private data. When the control unit fetches an instruction (such as a LOAD, ADD, or STORE), it *broadcasts* that instruction to every ALU, which executes it in parallel on its own local data. Thus, if we have 100 replicated

FIGURE 5.21

A SIMD parallel processing system

ALUs, we can perform 100 parallel additions by having every ALU simultaneously execute the instruction

Operation	Meaning
ADD X	Add memory cell X to the contents of register R.

on its own local value of X, using its own personal copy of register R.

A good analogy to SIMD parallel processing is the game of Bingo. There is one caller (control unit) calling out a single number (the instruction) to the entire room. In the room listening are many people (ALUs) who simultaneously cover that number on their own private Bingo cards (local memories).

This style of parallelism is especially useful in operations on mathematical structures called **vectors**. A vector V is simply an ordered collection of values. For example, here is a six-element vector V, whose elements are termed $v_1, v_2, \ldots, v_6$.

	v_1	v_2	v_3	v_4	v_5	v_6
V	1	8	−13	70	9	0

Many operations on vectors work quite well under the SIMD parallel model. For example, to add the constant value $+1$ to a vector, you add it to every individual element in the vector; that is, you simultaneously compute $v_1 + 1, v_2 + 1, \ldots$. Thus the operation $V + 1$, when applied to the previous vector, produces the new vector 2, 9, −12, 71, 10, 1. On a SIMD machine, this vector addition operation can be implemented in a single step by distributing one element of the vector to each separate ALU. Then in parallel, each arithmetic unit executes the following instruction:

Operation	Meaning
INC v	v is an element of the vector V. This instruction increments the contents of that location by +1.

In one time unit, we can update all six elements of the vector *V*. In the traditional Von Neumann machine, we would have to increment each element separately in a sequential fashion, using six instructions:

INC *v*1

INC *v*2

⋮

INC *v*6

Our parallel vector addition operator runs six times as fast. Similar speedups are possible with other vector and array manipulations.

SIMD parallelism was the first type of parallel processing put into widespread commercial use. It was the technique used to achieve breakthroughs in computational speeds on the first supercomputers of the early 1980s.

A much more interesting and much more widely used form of parallelism is called MIMD parallel processing (*m*ultiple *i*nstruction stream/*m*ultiple *d*ata stream), also called cluster computing. In MIMD parallelism, we replicate entire processors rather than just the ALU, and every processor is capable of executing its own separate program in its own private memory at its own rate. This model of parallel processing is diagrammed in Figure 5.22.

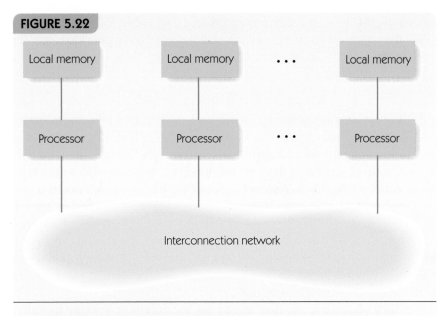

FIGURE 5.22

Local memory   Local memory   ● ● ●   Local memory

Processor   Processor   ● ● ●   Processor

Interconnection network

Model of MIMD parallel processing

Speed to Burn

The first computer to achieve a speed of 1 million floating-point operations per second, 1 *megaflop*, was the Control Data 6600 in the mid-1960s. The first machine to achieve 1 billion floating-point operations per second, 1 *gigaflop*, was the Cray X-MP in the early 1980s. Today almost all machines, even inexpensive laptops, can achieve gigaflop speeds. In 1996, the Intel Corporation announced that its ULTRA computer had successfully become the world's first *teraflop* machine. This $55 million computer contained 9,072 Pentium Pro processors, and on December 16, 1996, it achieved a sustained computational speed of 1 trillion operations per second.

However, on June 9, 2008, a major milestone in computer performance was reached. The Roadrunner massively parallel computer, constructed jointly by Los Alamos National Laboratories and IBM, achieved a sustained computational speed of 1,026 trillion floating-point operations per second, or 1 *petaflop*. To get an idea of how fast that is, consider that if all 6 billion people in the world worked together on a single problem, each person would have to perform 170,000 computations/second to equal the speed of this one machine. The system, which contains 18,000 processors and 98 terabytes of memory, cost about $100 million to design and build. It is used for basic research in astronomy, energy, and human genome science.

As of mid-2011, the fastest computer in the world is the Japanese K computer built by Fujitsu at the RIKEN Advanced Institute for Computational Science in Kobe, Japan. It contains 68,544 SPARC64 8-core processors for a total of 548,352 cores. On June 20, 2011 the system achieved a peak computational rate of 8.16 petaflops (see "The Tortoise and the Hare" Special Interest Box in Chapter 3).

Each processor/memory pair in Figure 5.22 is a Von Neumann machine of the type described in this chapter. For example, it could be a processor board of the type shown in Figure 5.18. Alternately, it could be a complete computer system, such as a desktop machine in a computer lab or the laptop in your dorm room. Each system is executing its own program in its own local memory at its own rate. However, rather than each having to solve the entire problem by itself, the problem is solved in a parallel fashion by all processors simultaneously. Each of the processors tackles a small part of the overall problem and then communicates its result to the other processors via the *interconnection network*, a communications system that allows processors to exchange messages and data.

A MIMD parallel processor would be an excellent system to help us speed up the New York City telephone directory lookup problem discussed in

Chapter 2. In the sequential approach that we described, the single processor doing the work must search all 20,000,000 entries from beginning to end (or until the desired name is found). The analysis in Chapter 3 showed that using sequential search and a computer that can examine 50,000 names per second takes an average of almost 3.5 minutes to find a particular name—much too long for the typical person to wait.

If we use 100 processors instead of one, however, the problem is easily solved. We just divide the 20,000,000 names into 100 equal-sized pieces and assign each piece to a different processor. Now each processor searches *in parallel* to see whether the desired name is in its own section. If it finds the name, it broadcasts that information on the interconnection network to the other 99 processors so that they can stop searching. Each processor needs only to look through a list of 200,000 names, which is 1/100 the amount of work it had to do previously. Instead of an average of 3.5 minutes, we now get our answer in 1/100 the time—about 2 seconds. Parallel processing has elegantly solved our problem.

MIMD parallelism is also a scalable architecture. *Scalability* means that, at least theoretically, it is possible to match the number of processors to the size of the problem. If 100 processors are not enough to solve the telephone book lookup problem, then 200 or 500 can be used instead, assuming the interconnection network can provide the necessary communications. (Communications can become a serious bottleneck in a parallel system.) In short, the resources applied to a problem can be in direct proportion to the amount of work that needs to be done. Massively parallel MIMD machines containing tens of thousands of independent processors have achieved solutions to large problems thousands of times faster than is possible using a single processor. (For an up-to-date listing of the fastest parallel computers, check the home page of *Top500*, a listing of the 500 most powerful computers in the world. Its URL is *www.top500.org*.)

The multiple processors within a MIMD cluster do not have to be identical or belong to a single administrative organization. Computer scientists realized that it is possible to address and solve massive problems by utilizing the resources of idle computers located around the world, regardless of whom they belonged to. This realization led to an exciting new form of MIMD parallelism called grid computing.

Grid computing enables researchers to easily and transparently access computer facilities without regard for their location. One of the most well-known grid computing applications is the SETI@home project (*Search for Extraterrestrial Intelligence*), which analyzes radio telescope data from distant stars to look for intelligent life in the universe. Users sign up to allow their personal computer, when idle, to participate in this massive search project. About 5.5 million people have signed up to be part of the SETI grid, and on any given day about 1,000–2,000 home computers, from Alabama to Wyoming, from Albania to Zimbabwe, contribute computational resources to this one task. You can read about the SETI@home project on its home page at *http://setiathome. ssl.berkeley.edu.*

The real key to using massively parallel processors is to design solution methods that effectively utilize the large number of available processors. It does no good to have 1,000 processors available if only 1 or 2 are doing useful work while 998 or 999 are sitting idle. That would be like having a large construction crew at a building site, where the roofers, painters, and plumbers sit around waiting for one person to put up the walls. The field of parallel algorithms, the study of techniques that makes efficient use of parallel architectures, is an important branch of research in computer science. Advances in this area will go a long way toward speeding the development

Quantum Computing

The parallel machines described in this section can overcome the "Von Neumann bottleneck" by performing multiple computations in parallel, rather than one at a time in strict sequential fashion. However, these systems are not a fundamental change in the underlying design of computers. Each machine in the MIMD cluster of Figure 5.22 is typically a traditional Von Neumann computer. The only difference is that we are using multiple machines to solve a problem rather than one.

However, computer scientists are also researching totally new designs unrelated to the Von Neumann architecture. One of the most unusual, most revolutionary, and most exciting is called **quantum computing**, in which computers are designed according to the principles of quantum mechanics, which describe the behavior of matter at the atomic and subatomic level. A quantum computer encodes information using some aspect of quantum-mechanical state, such as electron spin or photon polarization. However, unlike "traditional" data bits, which at any instant of time must be either a 0 or a 1 but not both, quantum theory says that a quantum bit, or *qubit,* can be either a 0 or a 1 or both a 0 and a 1 *at the same time.* In theory, a quantum computer could do multiple computations on different numbers at the same time. In fact, with just 500 qubits of quantum memory, each of which could be viewed as being both a 0 and a 1, we could theoretically perform 2^{500} simultaneous computations—a number larger than the total number of atoms in the universe. Now that is real parallel processing!

There are still a lot of obstacles to overcome before quantum computers become a reality, but a great deal of progress has been made in the last few years. There is much debate about whether a workable quantum computer will take 10 years, 25 years, or perhaps another century to design and construct. However, the underlying theory of quantum computing is sound, and a quantum computer will likely be a reality, even if we are not sure exactly when.

and use of large-scale parallel systems of the type shown in Figures 5.21 and 5.22. (Challenge Work problem 1 asks you to design a parallel addition algorithm.)

To solve the complex problems of the twenty-first century, the computers of the twenty-first century will probably be organized much more like the massively parallel processing systems of Figures 5.21 and 5.22 than like the 65-year-old Von Neumann model of Figure 5.18.

5.5 Summary of Level 2

In Chapter 4, we looked at the basic building blocks of computers: binary codes, transistors, gates, and circuits. This chapter examined the standard model for computer design, called the Von Neumann architecture. It also discussed some of the shortcomings of this sequential model of computation and described briefly how these might be overcome by the use of parallel computers.

At this point in our hierarchy of abstractions, we have created a fully functional computer system capable of executing an algorithm encoded as sequences of machine language instructions. The only problem is that the machine we have created is enormously difficult to use and about as unfriendly and unforgiving as it could be. It has been designed and engineered from a machine's perspective, not a person's. Sequences of binary encoded machine language instructions such as

    1011010000001011
    1001101100010111
    0000101101011001

give a computer no difficulty, but they cause people to throw up their hands in despair. We need to create a friendlier environment—to make the computer and its hardware resources more accessible. Such an environment would be more conducive to developing correct solutions to problems and satisfying a user's computational needs.

The component that creates this kind of friendly, problem-solving environment is called *system software*. It is an intermediary between the user and the hardware components of the Von Neumann machine. Without it, a Von Neumann machine would be virtually unusable by anyone but the most technically knowledgeable computer experts. We examine system software in the next level of our investigation of computer science.

EXERCISES

1. What are the advantages and disadvantages of using a very large memory cell size, say, $W = 64$ instead of the standard size $W = 8$? If each integer occupies *one* 64-bit memory cell and is stored using sign/magnitude notation, what are the largest (in terms of absolute value) positive and negative integers that can be stored? What if *two* cells are used to store integers?

2. At a minimum, how many bits are needed in the MAR with each of the following memory sizes?

   a. 1 million bytes

   b. 10 million bytes

   c. 100 million bytes

   d. 1 billion bytes

3. A memory unit that is said to be 640 KB would actually contain how many memory cells? What about a memory of 512 MB? What about a memory of 2 GB?

4. Explain what use read-only memory (ROM) serves in the design of a computer system. What type of information is kept in ROM, and how does that information originally get into the memory?

5. Assuming the square two-dimensional memory organization shown in Figure 5.6, what are the dimensions of a memory containing 1 MB (2^{20}) bytes of storage? How large would the MAR be? How many bits are sent to the row and column decoders? How many output lines would these decoders have?

6. Assume a 24-bit MAR that is organized as follows:

   row select lines   **column select lines**
       12 bits   12 bits

   What is the maximum size of the memory unit on this machine? What are the dimensions of the memory, assuming a square two-dimensional organization?

7. Assume that our MAR contains 20 bits, enabling us to access up to 2^{20} memory cells, which is 1 MB, but our computer has 4 MB of memory. Explain how it might be possible to address all 4 MB memory cells using a MAR that contains only 20 bits.

8. Assume that our MDR register is 16 bits wide while our machine language instructions are 32 bits wide. How might the fetch phase of the Von Neumann cycle have to be changed from what was described in the text?

9. Assume that a 1 gigaflop machine is connected to a printer that can print 780 characters per second. In the time it takes to print 1 page (65 lines of 60 characters per line), how many floating-point operations can the machine perform?

10. Assume that we have an arithmetic/logic unit that can carry out 20 distinct operations. Describe exactly what kind of multiplexor circuit would be needed to select exactly one of those 20 operations.

11. A CISC-style instruction set has a large number of high-level instructions that perform highly complex operations in a single step. What would be the major advantages of such a design? What would be some of the primary disadvantages?

12. Assume that a hard disk has the following characteristics:

   Rotation speed = 7,200 rev/min
   Arm movement time = 0.5 msec fixed startup time + 0.05 msec for each track crossed. (The startup time is a constant no matter how far the arm moves.) Assume on average the disk arm must move 150 tracks.
   Number of surfaces = 2 (This is a *double-sided* disk. A single read/write arm holds both read/write heads.)
   Number of tracks per surface = 500

Number of sectors per track = 20

Number of characters per sector = 1,024

a. How many characters can be stored on this disk?

b. What are the best-case, worst-case, and average-case access times for this disk?

13. What are the best-case, worst-case, and average-case access times for the disk described in Exercise 12 if we increase the rotational speed to 9,600 rpm?

14. In general, information is stored on a disk not at random but in specific locations that help to minimize the time it takes to retrieve that information. Using the specifications given in Exercise 12, where would you store the information in a 50 KB file on the disk to speed up subsequent access to that information?

15. Assume that our disk unit has one read/write head per *track* instead of only one per surface. (A *head-per-track disk* is sometimes referred to as a *drum*.) Using the specifications given in Exercise 12, what are the best-case, worst-case, and average-case access times? How much have the additional read/write heads helped reduce access times?

16. Using the specifications given in Exercise 12, what is the worst-case time required to read the entire contents of the disk; that is, to read every single sector on the disk? Assume the read arm is initially positioned at the beginning of the first sector of the first track, and that every track must be read from the very beginning, that is, from the very first sector on that track. This is actually a quite common operation and is used for things like making copies and backing up a disk.

17. Discuss some situations wherein a sequential access storage device such as a tape could be a useful form of mass storage.

18. Assume that we are receiving a message across a network using a modem with a rate of 56,000 bits/second. Furthermore, assume that we are working on a workstation with an instruction rate of 500 MIPS. How many instructions can the processor execute between the receipt of each individual bit of the message?

19. Consider the following structure of the instruction register.

op code	address-1	address-2
6 bits	18 bits	18 bits

a. What is the maximum number of distinct operation codes that can be recognized and executed by the processor on this machine?

b. What is the maximum memory size on this machine?

c. How many bytes are required for each operation?

20. If the size of the op code field in Exercise 19 were increased from 6 bits to 8 bits, what would now be the theoretical maximum size of the instruction set?

21. Assume that the variables v, w, x, y, and z are stored in memory locations 200, 201, 202, 203, and 204, respectively. Also assume that the code sequence you are writing begins in memory location 50. Using any of the machine language instructions shown in Section 5.2.4, translate the following algorithmic operations into their machine language equivalents.

a. Set v to the value of $x - y + z$ (Assume the existence of the machine language command SUBTRACT X, Y, Z that computes CON(Z) = CON(X) − CON(Y).)

b. Set v to the value $(w + x) - (y + z)$

c. If $(v \geq w)$ then

Set x to y

Else

Set x to z

d. While $y < z$ do

Set y to the value $(y + w + z)$

Set z to the value $(z + v)$

End of the loop

22. Assume that the variables a and b are stored in memory locations 300 and 301, respectively. Also assume that the three integer values +1, −1, and 0 are stored in memory locations 400, 401, and 402, respectively. Finally, assume that the code sequence

you are writing begins in memory location 50. Using any of the machine language instructions shown in Section 5.2.4, translate the following algorithmic operations into their machine language equivalents.

a. Set *a* to the value of *a* + *b* − 1

b. if *a* > 0

    Set *b* to the value +1

23. A student was asked to translate the following algorithmic operation into machine language, where *x* and *y* were stored in locations 500 and 501, respectively:

    Set *x* to the value of *y* + 19

Here is what was produced:

        LOAD 501

        ADD 19

        STORE 500

Is this translation correct? If not, describe the error and explain how to correct it.

24. Describe the sequence of operations that might go on inside the computer during the execution phase of the following machine language instructions. Use the notation shown in Section 5.3. Assume that the IR is divided into three separate parts that contain the op code, and the first and second address fields.

    a. MOVE X, Y   Move the contents of memory cell X to memory cell Y.

    b. ADD X, Y   Add the contents of memory cells X and Y. Put the result back into memory cell Y.

25. Describe the sequence of operations that might go on inside the computer during the execution phase of the following machine language instruction. Use the notation shown in Section 5.3. Assume that the IR is now divided into four separate parts (instead of three) that contain the op code, and the first, second, and third address fields.

    ADD X, v, Y   Add the contents of memory cell X and the integer value *v*. Put the result into memory cell Y.

So, for example, the operation ADD X, 1, Y would compute Y = X + 1.

CHALLENGE WORK

1. It is easy to write a sequential algorithm that sums up a 100-element vector:

$$Sum = a_1 + a_2 + a_3 + \ldots + a_{100}$$

It would look something like

    Set *i* to 1

    Set Sum to 0

    While *i* < 101 do the following

        Sum = Sum + a_i

        i = *i* + 1

    End of the loop

    Write out the value of Sum

    Stop

It is pretty obvious that this algorithm will take about 100 units of time, where a unit of time is equivalent to the time needed to execute one iteration of the loop. However, it is less easy to see how we might exploit the existence of *multiple* processors to speed up the solution to this problem.

Assume that instead of having only a single processor, you have 100. Design a parallel algorithm that utilizes these additional resources to speed up the solution to the previous computation. Exactly how much faster would your *parallel summation algorithm* execute than the sequential one? Did you need all 100 processors? Could you have used more than 100?

2. In this chapter, we described the Von Neumann architecture in broad, general terms. However, "real" Von Neumann processors, such as an Intel Dual-Core and the AMD Athlon XP, are much more

complex than the simple model shown in Figure 5.18. Pick one of these processors (perhaps the processor inside the computer you are using for this class) and take an in-depth look at its design. Specifically, examine such issues as

- Its instruction set and how it compares with the instruction set shown in Figure 5.19

- The collection of available registers

- The existence of cache memory

- Its computing speed in MIPS and MFLOPS or GFLOPS

- How much primary memory it has and how memory is addressed in the instructions

- Memory access time

- In what size "chunks" memory can be accessed

Write a report describing the real-world characteristics of the processor you selected.

ADDITIONAL RESOURCES

CourseMate **For additional print and/or online resources relevant to this chapter, visit the Computer Science CourseMate at login.cengagebrain.com.**

Chapter
17   Social Issues

Chapters
13, 14, 15, 16   Applications

Chapters
9, 10, 11, 12   The Software World

Chapters
6, 7, 8   The Virtual Machine

Chapters
4, 5   The Hardware World

Chapters
2, 3   The Algorithmic Foundations
                      of Computer Science

It has been said that computer science is "the science of building pretend worlds," meaning that the underlying hardware structure of a computer can be so difficult to work with that we must create more friendly and more usable "virtual worlds" in which to work and solve problems. Without that layer of abstraction between us and the machine, we would have to solve problems by applying only the ideas and capabilities presented in Level 2—binary numbers, digital circuits, absolute memory addresses, and machine language instructions.

In Level 3 (Chapters 6, 7, and 8), you will learn how these user-friendly "microworlds" are created to produce an environment in which efficient, safe, and productive problem solving is possible.

6.1 Introduction

Chapters 4 and 5 described a computer model, the *Von Neumann architecture*, that is capable of executing programs written in machine language. This computer has all the hardware needed to solve important real-world problems, but it has no "support tools" to make that problem-solving task easy. The computer described in Chapter 5 is informally known as a naked machine: hardware bereft of any helpful user-oriented features.

Imagine what it would be like to work on a naked machine. To solve a problem, you would have to create hundreds or thousands of cryptic machine language instructions that look like this:

> 1011010011010001110011110001000

and you would have to do that without making a single mistake because, to execute properly, a program must be completely error free. Imagine the likelihood of writing a perfectly correct program containing thousands of instructions like the one shown above. Even worse, imagine trying to locate an error buried deep inside that incomprehensible mass of 0s and 1s!

On a naked machine, the data as well as the instructions must be represented in binary. For example, a program cannot refer to the decimal integer +9 directly but must express it as

> 0000000000001001   (the binary representation of +9 using 16 bits)

You cannot use the symbol *A* to refer to the first letter of the alphabet but must represent it using its 8-bit ASCII code value, which is decimal 65:

> 01000001   (the 8-bit ASCII code for A; see Figure 4.3)

As you can imagine, writing programs for a naked machine is very difficult.

Even if you write the program correctly, your work is still not done. A program for a Von Neumann computer must be stored in memory prior to execution. Therefore, you must now take the program and store its instructions into sequential cells in memory. On a naked machine, the programmer must perform this task, one instruction at a time. Assuming that each instruction occupies one memory cell, the programmer loads the first instruction into address 0, the second instruction into address 1, the third instruction into address 2, and so on, until all have been stored.

Finally, what starts the program running? A naked machine does not do this automatically. (As you are probably coming to realize, a naked machine does not do *anything* automatically, except fetch, decode, and execute machine language instructions.) The programmer must initiate execution by storing a 0, the address of the first instruction of the program, in the program counter (PC) and pressing the START button. This begins the fetch/decode/execute cycle described in Chapter 5. The control unit fetches from memory the contents of the address in the PC, currently 0, and executes that instruction. The program continues sequentially from that point while the user prays that everything works because he or she cannot bear to face a naked machine again!

As this portrayal demonstrates, working directly with the underlying hardware is practically impossible for a human being. The functional units described in Chapter 5 are built according to what is easy for hardware to do, not what is easy for people to do.

To make a Von Neumann computer usable, we must create an *interface* between the user and the hardware. This interface does the following things:

- Hides from the user the messy details of the underlying hardware

- Presents information about what is happening in a way that does not require in-depth knowledge of the internal structure of the system

- Allows easy user access to the resources available on this computer

- Prevents accidental or intentional damage to hardware, programs, and data

By way of analogy, let's look at how people use another common tool—an automobile. The internal combustion engine is a complex piece of technology. For most of us, the functions of fuel-injection systems, distributors, and camshafts are a total mystery. However, most people find driving a car quite easy. This is because the driver does not have to lift the hood and interact directly with the hardware; that is, he or she does not have to drive a "naked automobile." Instead, there is an interface, the *dashboard*, which simplifies things considerably. The dashboard hides the details of engine operation that a driver does not need to know. The important things—such as oil pressure, fuel level, and vehicle speed—*are* presented in a simple, "people-oriented" way: oil indicator warning light, fuel gauge, and speed in miles or kilometers per hour. Access to the engine and transmission is achieved by a few simple operations: a key to start and stop, pedals to speed up or slow down, and a shift lever to go forward or backward.

We need a similar interface for our Von Neumann machine. This "computer dashboard" would eliminate most of the hassles of working on a naked machine and let us view the hardware resources of Chapter 5 in a much friendlier way. Such an interface does exist, and it is called system software.

6.2 System Software

6.2.1 The Virtual Machine

System software is a collection of computer programs that manages the resources of a computer and facilitates access to those resources. It is important to remember that we are describing software, not hardware. There are no black boxes wired to a computer labeled "system software." Software consists of sequences of instructions—namely, programs—that solve a problem. However, instead of solving *user* problems, such as looking up names in a telephone book, system software solves the problem of making a computer and its many resources easier to access and use.

System software acts as an *intermediary* between the users and the hardware, as shown in Figure 6.1. System software presents the user with a set of services and resources across the interface labeled A in Figure 6.1. These resources may actually exist, or they may be simulated by the software to give the user the illusion that they exist. The set of services and resources created by the software and seen by the user is called a **virtual machine** or a **virtual environment**. The system software, not the user, interacts with the actual hardware (that is, the naked machine) across the interface labeled B in Figure 6.1.

The system software has the following responsibilities, analogous to those of the automobile dashboard:

- Hides the complex and unimportant (to the user) details of the internal structure of the Von Neumann architecture

- Presents important information to the user in a way that is easy to understand

- Allows the user to access machine resources in a simple and efficient way

- Provides a secure and safe environment in which to operate

FIGURE 6.1

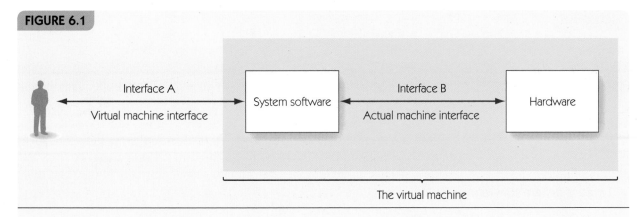

The role of system software

For example, to add two numbers, it is much easier to use simple notation such as $a = b + c$ than to worry about (1) loading ALU registers from memory cells b and c, (2) activating the ALU, (3) selecting the output of the addition circuit, and (4) sending the result to memory cell a. The programmer should not have to know about registers, addition circuits, and memory addresses but instead should see a virtual machine that "understands" the mathematical symbols $+$ and $=$.

After the program has been written, it should automatically be loaded into memory without the programmer having to specify where it should be placed or having to set the program counter. Instead, he or she should be able to issue one simple command (or one set of mouse clicks) to the virtual machine that says, "Run my program." Finally, when the program is running and generating results, the programmer should be able to instruct the virtual machine to send the program's output to the printer in Room 105, without reference to the details related to I/O controllers, interrupt signals, and code sets.

All the useful services just described are provided by the system software available on any modern computer system. The following sections show how this friendly, user-oriented environment is created.

6.2.2 Types of System Software

System software is not a single monolithic entity but a collection of many different programs. The types found on a typical computer are shown in Figure 6.2.

The program that controls the overall operation of the computer is the operating system, and it is the single most important piece of system software on a computer. It is the operating system that communicates with users, determines what they want, and activates other system programs, applications packages, or user programs to carry out their requests. The software packages that handle these requests include the following:

- *User interface*—All modern operating systems provide a powerful graphical user interface (GUI) that gives the user an intuitive visual

Types of system software

overview as well as graphical control of the capabilities and services of the computer.

- *Language services*—These programs, called *assemblers*, *compilers*, and *interpreters*, allow you to write programs in a high-level, user-oriented language rather than the machine language of Chapter 5 and to execute these programs easily and efficiently. They often include components such as text editors and debuggers.

- *Memory managers*—These programs allocate memory space for programs and data and retrieve this memory space when it is no longer needed.

- *Information managers*—These programs handle the organization, storage, and retrieval of information on mass storage devices such as the hard drives, CDs, DVDs, flash drives, and tapes described in Section 5.2.2. They allow you to organize your information in an efficient hierarchical manner, using directories, folders, and files.

- *I/O systems*—These software packages allow you to easily and efficiently use the many different types of input and output devices that exist on a modern computer system.

- *Scheduler*—This system program keeps a list of programs ready to run on the processor, and it selects the one that will execute next. The scheduler allows you to have a number of different programs active at a single time, for instance, surfing the Web while you are waiting for a file to finish printing.

- *Utilities*—These collections of library routines provide a wide range of useful services either to a user or to other system routines. Text editors, online help routines, image and sound applications, and control panels are examples of utility routines. Sometimes these utilities are organized into collections called program libraries.

These system routines are used during every phase of problem solving on a computer, and it would be virtually impossible to get anything done without them. Let's go back to the problem described at the beginning of this chapter—the job of writing a program, loading it into memory, running it, and printing the results. On a naked machine, this job would be formidable. On the virtual machine created by system software, it is much simpler:

Step	Task
1	Use a text editor to create program P written in a high-level, English-like notation rather than binary.
2	Use the file system to store program P on the hard drive in your home directory.
3	Use a language translator to translate program P from a high-level language into an equivalent machine language program M.
4	Use a scheduler to load, schedule, and run program M. The scheduler itself uses the memory manager to obtain memory space for program M.
5	Use the I/O system to print the output of your program on printer R.
6	If the program did not complete successfully, use a debugger to help you locate the error. Use a text editor to correct the program and the file system to store the newly modified program.

Furthermore, most of these operations are easily invoked via mouse clicks and the graphical interface provided by the operating system.

On a virtual machine, the low-level details of machine operation are no longer visible, and a user can concentrate on higher-level issues: writing the program, executing the program, and saving and analyzing results.

There are many types of system software, and it is impossible to cover them all in this section of the text. Instead, we will investigate two types of system software, and use these as representatives of the entire group. Section 6.3 examines assemblers, and Section 6.4 looks at the design and construction of operating systems. These two packages create a friendly and usable virtual machine. In Chapter 7, we will extend that virtual environment from a single computer to a collection of computers by looking at the system software required to create one of the most important and widely used virtual environments—a computer network. Finally, in Chapter 8 we will investigate one of the most important services provided by the operating system—system security.

6.3 Assemblers and Assembly Language

6.3.1 Assembly Language

One of the first places where we need a more friendly virtual environment is in our choice of programming language. Machine language, which is designed from a machine's point of view, not a person's, is complicated and virtually impossible to understand. What specifically are the problems with machine language?

- It uses binary. There are no natural language words, mathematical symbols, or other convenient mnemonics to make the language more readable.

- It allows only numeric memory addresses (in binary). A programmer cannot name an instruction or a piece of data and refer to it by name.

- It is difficult to change. If we insert or delete an instruction, all memory addresses following that instruction will change. For example, if we place a new instruction into memory location 503, then the instruction previously in location 503 is now in 504. All references to address 503 must be updated to point to 504. There may be hundreds of such references.

- It is difficult to create data. If a user wants to store a piece of data in memory, he or she must compute the internal binary representation for that data item. These conversion algorithms are complicated and time consuming.

Programmers working on early first-generation computers quickly realized the shortcomings of machine language. They developed a new language, called assembly language, designed for people as well as computers. Assembly languages created a more productive, user-oriented environment, and assemblers were one of the first pieces of system software to be widely used. When assembly languages first appeared in the early 1950s, they were one of the most important new developments in programming—so important, in fact, that they were considered an entirely new generation of language, analogous to the new generations of hardware described in Section 1.4.3. Assembly languages were termed *second-generation languages* to distinguish them from machine languages, which were viewed as *first-generation languages*.

Today, assembly languages are more properly called low-level programming languages, which means they are closely related to the machine language of Chapter 5. Each symbolic assembly language instruction is translated into exactly *one* binary machine language instruction.

This contrasts with languages like C++, Java, and Python, which are high-level programming languages. High-level languages are more user oriented, they are not machine specific, and they use both natural language and mathematical notation in their design. A single high-level language instruction is typically translated into *many* machine language instructions, and the virtual environment created by a high-level language is much more powerful than the one produced by an assembly language. We will discuss high-level languages in detail in Chapters 9 and 10.

Figure 6.3 shows a "continuum of languages," from the lowest level (closest to the hardware) to the highest level (most abstract, farthest from the hardware).

The machine language of Chapter 5 is the most primitive; it is the language of the hardware itself. Assembly language, the topic of this section, represents the first step along the continuum from machine language.

FIGURE 6.3

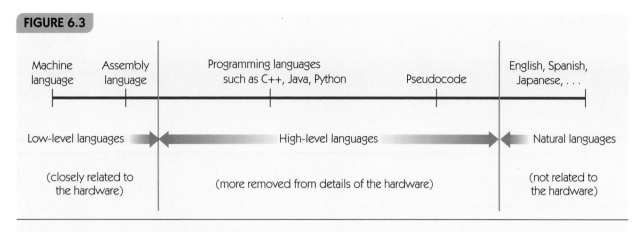

The continuum of programming languages

High-level programming languages like C++, Java, and Python are closer in style and structure to natural languages and are quite distinct from assembly language. Natural languages, such as English, Spanish, and Japanese, are the highest level; they are totally unrelated to hardware design.

A program written in assembly language is called the source program; it uses the features and services provided by the language. However, the processor does not "understand" assembly language instructions, in the sense of being able to fetch, decode, and execute them as described in Chapter 5. The source program must be translated into a corresponding machine language program, called the object program. This translation is carried out by a piece of system software called an assembler. (Translators for high-level languages are called compilers. They are discussed in Chapter 11.) Once the object program has been produced, its instructions can be loaded into memory and executed by the processor exactly as described in Section 5.3. The complete translation/loading/execution process is diagrammed in Figure 6.4.

There are three major advantages to writing programs in assembly language rather than machine language:

- Use of symbolic operation codes rather than numeric (binary) ones

- Use of symbolic memory addresses rather than numeric (binary) ones

- Pseudo-operations that provide useful user-oriented services such as data generation

This section describes a simple, but realistic, assembly language that demonstrates these three advantages.

Our hypothetical assembly language is composed of instructions in the following format:

    label: op code mnemonic   address field   --comment

The *comment field*, preceded in our notation by a double dash (--), is not really part of the instruction. It is a helpful explanation added to the

FIGURE 6.4

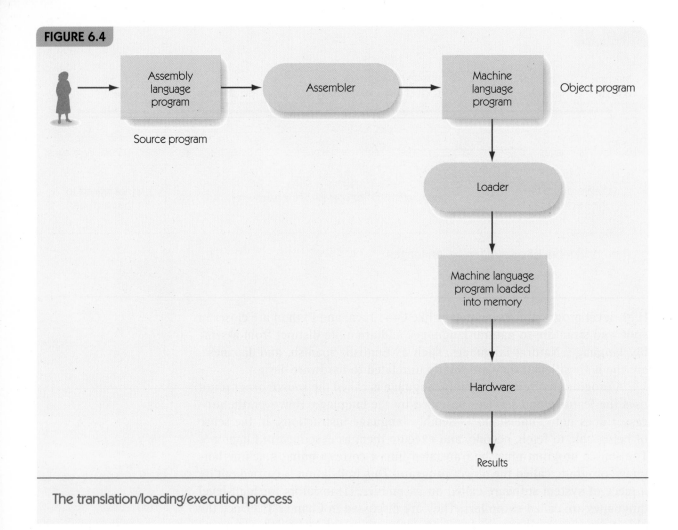

The translation/loading/execution process

instruction by a programmer and intended for readers of the program. It is ignored during translation and execution.

Assembly languages allow the programmer to refer to op codes using a symbolic name, called the *op code mnemonic*, rather than by a number. We can write op codes using meaningful words like LOAD, ADD, and STORE rather than obscure binary codes like 0000, 0011, and 0001. Figure 6.5 shows an assembly language instruction set for a Von Neumann machine that has a single ALU register R and three condition codes GT, EQ, and LT. Each numeric op code, its assembly language mnemonic, and its meaning are listed. This table is identical to Figure 5.19, which summarizes the language used in Chapter 5 to introduce the Von Neumann architecture and explains how instructions are executed. (However, Chapter 5 describes binary machine language and uses symbolic names only for convenience. In this chapter, we are describing assembly language, where symbolic names such as LOAD and ADD are actually part of the language.)

FIGURE 6.5

Binary Op Code	Operation	Meaning
0000	LOAD X	CON(X) → R
0001	STORE X	R → CON(X)
0010	CLEAR X	0 → CON(X)
0011	ADD X	R + CON(X) → R
0100	INCREMENT X	CON(X) + 1 → CON(X)
0101	SUBTRACT X	R − CON(X) → R
0110	DECREMENT X	CON(X) − 1 → CON(X)
0111	COMPARE X	if CON(X) > R then GT = 1 else 0
		if CON(X) = R then EQ = 1 else 0
		if CON(X) < R then LT = 1 else 0
1000	JUMP X	Get the next instruction from memory location X.
1001	JUMPGT X	Get the next instruction from memory location X if GT = 1.
1010	JUMPEQ X	Get the next instruction from memory location X if EQ = 1.
1011	JUMPLT X	Get the next instruction from memory location X if LT = 1.
1100	JUMPNEQ X	Get the next instruction from memory location X if EQ = 0.
1101	IN X	Input an integer value from the standard input device and store into memory cell X.
1110	OUT X	Output, in decimal notation, the value stored in memory cell X.
1111	HALT	Stop program execution.

Typical assembly language instruction set

Another advantage of assembly language is that it lets programmers use *symbolic addresses* instead of numeric addresses. In machine language, to jump to the instruction stored in memory location 17, you must refer directly to address 17; that is, you must write JUMP 17 (in binary, of course). This is cumbersome, because if a new instruction is inserted anywhere within the first 17 lines of the program, the jump location changes to 18. The old reference to 17 is incorrect, and the address field must be changed. This makes modifying programs very difficult, and even small changes become big efforts. It is not unlike identifying yourself in a waiting line by position—as, say, the 10th person in line. As soon as someone in front of you leaves (or someone cuts in line ahead of you), that number changes. It is far better to identify yourself using a characteristic that does not change as people enter or exit the line. For example, you are the person wearing the green suit with the orange and pink shirt. Those characteristics won't change (though maybe they should).

In assembly language, we can attach a *symbolic label* to any instruction or piece of data in the program. The label then becomes a permanent identification for this instruction or data, regardless of where it appears in the program or where it may be moved in memory. A label is a name (followed by a colon to identify it as a label) placed at the beginning of an instruction.

```
LOOPSTART:        LOAD X
```

The label LOOPSTART has been attached to the instruction LOAD X. This means that the name LOOPSTART is *equivalent to* the address of the memory cell that holds the instruction LOAD X. If, for example, the LOAD X instruction is stored in memory cell 62, then the name LOOPSTART is equivalent to address 62. Any use of the name LOOPSTART in the address field of an instruction is treated as though the user had written the numeric address 62. For example, to jump to the load instruction shown above, we do not need to know that it is stored in location 62. Instead, we need only write the instruction

```
JUMP   LOOPSTART
```

Symbolic labels have two advantages over numeric addresses. The first is *program clarity*. As with the use of mnemonics for op codes, the use of meaningful symbolic names can make a program much more readable. Names like LOOPSTART, COUNT, and ERROR carry a good deal of meaning and help people to understand what the code is doing. Memory addresses such as 73, 147, and 2001 do not. A second advantage of symbolic labels is *maintainability*. When we refer to an instruction via a symbolic label rather than an address, we no longer need to modify the address field when instructions are added to or removed from the program. Consider the following example:

```
        JUMP      LOOP
          ⋮          ← point A

LOOP:   LOAD     X
```

Say a new instruction is added to the program at point A. When the modified program is translated by the assembler into machine language, all instructions following point A are placed in a memory cell whose address is 1 higher than it was before (assuming that each instruction occupies one memory cell). However, the JUMP refers to the LOAD instruction only by the name LOOP, not by the address where it is stored. Therefore, neither the JUMP nor the LOAD instruction needs to be changed. We need only retranslate the modified program. The assembler determines the new address of the LOAD X instruction, makes the label LOOP equivalent to this new address, and places this new address into the address field of the JUMP LOOP instruction. The assembler does the messy bookkeeping previously done by the machine language programmer.

The final advantage of assembly language programming is *data generation*. In Section 4.2.1 we showed how to represent data types such as unsigned and signed integers, floating-point values, and characters in binary. When writing in machine language, the programmer must do these conversions. In assembly language, however, the programmer can ask the assembler to do them by using a special type of assembly language op code called a pseudo-op.

A pseudo-op (preceded in our notation by a period to indicate its type) does not generate a machine language instruction like other operation codes. Instead, it invokes a service of the assembler. One of these services is generating data in the proper binary representation for this system. There are typically assembly language pseudo-ops to generate integer, character, and (if the hardware supports it) real data values. In our sample language, we will limit ourselves to one data generation pseudo-op called .DATA that builds signed integers. This pseudo-op converts the signed decimal integer in the address field to the proper binary representation. For example, the pseudo-op

```
FIVE:       .DATA       +5
```

tells the assembler to generate the binary representation for the integer +5, put it into memory, and make the label "FIVE" equivalent to the address of that cell. If a memory cell contains 16 bits, and the next available memory cell is address 53, then this pseudo-op produces

address	contents
53	0000000000000101

and the name FIVE is equivalent to memory address 53. Similarly, the pseudo-op

```
NEGSEVEN: .DATA     −7
```

might produce the following 16-bit quantity, assuming sign/magnitude representation:

address	contents
54	1000000000000111

and the symbol NEGSEVEN is equivalent to memory address 54.

We can now refer to these data items by their attached label. For example, to load the value +5 into register R, we can say

```
LOAD        FIVE
```

This is equivalent to writing LOAD 53, which loads register R with the contents of memory cell 53—that is, the integer +5. Note that if we had incorrectly said

```
LOAD        5
```

the *contents* of memory cell 5 would be loaded into register R. This is not what we intended, and the program would be wrong. This is a good example of why it is so important to distinguish between the address of a cell and its contents.

To add the value –7 to the current contents of register R, we write

```
ADD        NEGSEVEN
```

The contents of R (currently +5) and the contents of address NEGSEVEN (address 54, whose contents are –7) are added together, producing –2. This becomes the new contents of register R.

When generating data values, we must be careful not to place them in memory locations where they can be misinterpreted as instructions. In Chapter 4, we said that the only way a computer can tell that the binary value 01000001 represents the letter *A* rather than the decimal value 65 is by the context in which it appears. The same is true for instructions and data. They are indistinguishable from each other, and the only way a Von Neumann machine can determine whether a sequence of 0s and 1s is an instruction or a piece of data is by how we use it. If we attempt to execute a value stored in memory, then that value *becomes* an instruction whether we meant it to be or not.

For example, if we incorrectly include the following sequence in our program:

```
LOAD       X
.DATA      +1
```

then, during the execution phase, after executing the LOAD X command, the processor will come to the memory location where the .DATA pseudo-op has stored the value +1. The processor will fetch, decode, and attempt to execute the data value +1 as if it were an "instruction." This might sound meaningless, but to a processor, it is not. The representation of +1, using 16 bits, is

```
0000000000000001
```

Because this value is being used as an instruction, some of the bits will be interpreted as the op code and some as the address field. If we assume a 16-bit, one-address instruction format, with the first 4 bits being the op code and the last 12 bits being the address field, then these 16 bits will be interpreted as follows:

```
0000                000000000001
op code             address
```

The "op code" is 0, which is a LOAD on our hypothetical machine (see Figure 6.5), and the "address field" contains a 1. Thus, the data value +1 has accidentally turned into the following instruction:

```
LOAD      1        --Load the contents of memory cell 1 into register R
```

This is obviously incorrect, but how is the problem solved? The easiest way is to remember to place all data created by the program using the .DATA pseudo-op in locations where they cannot possibly be executed.

Practice Problems

1. Assume that register R and memory cells 80 and 81 contain the following values:

   R: 20   memory cell 80: 43   memory cell 81: 97

   Using the instruction set shown in Figure 6.5, determine what value ends up in register R and memory cells 80 and 81 after each of the following instructions is executed. Assume that each question begins with the values shown above.

   a. LOAD 80
   b. STORE 81
   c. COMPARE 80
   d. ADD 81
   e. IN 80
   f. OUT 81

2. Assume that memory cell 50 contains a 4 and label L is equivalent to memory location 50. What value does each of the following LOAD instructions load into register R?

   a. LOAD 50
   b. LOAD 4
   c. LOAD L
   d. LOAD L+1 (Assume that this is legal.)

3. Explain why both the HALT operation code described in Figure 6.5 and the .END pseudo-op mentioned at the end of this section are needed in an assembly language program and what might happen if one or both were omitted.

4. Explain exactly what would occur if a processor tried to execute the following pair of instructions:

   ```
           LOAD    L
   L:      .DATA   1
   ```

One convenient place that meets this criterion is after a HALT instruction because the HALT prevents any further execution. The data values can be referenced, but they cannot be executed.

A second service provided by pseudo-ops is *program construction*. Pseudo-ops that mark the beginning (.BEGIN) and end (.END) of the assembly language program specify where to start and stop the translation process, and they do not generate any instructions or data. Remember that it is the HALT instruction, not the .END pseudo-op, that terminates execution of the program. The .END pseudo-op ends the translation process. Figure 6.6, which shows the organization of a typical assembly language program, helps explain this distinction.

FIGURE 6.6

.BEGIN	--This must be the first line of the program
⋮	--Assembly language instructions like those in Figure 6.5
HALT	--This instruction terminates execution of the program
⋮	--Data generation pseudo-ops such as
	--.DATA are placed here, after the HALT
.END	--This must be the last line of the program

Structure of a typical assembly language program

6.3.2 Examples of Assembly Language Code

This section describes how to use assembly language to translate algorithms into programs that can be executed on a Von Neumann computer. Today, software development is rarely performed in assembly language except for very special-purpose tasks; most programmers use higher-level languages such as those mentioned in Figure 6.3 and described in Chapters 9 and 10. Our purpose in offering these examples is to demonstrate how system software, in this case an assembler, can create a user-oriented virtual environment that supports effective and productive problem solving.

One of the most common operations in any algorithm is the evaluation of arithmetic expressions. For example, the sequential search algorithm of Figure 2.13 contains the following arithmetic operations:

Set the value of i to 1 (Line 2).
⋮

Add 1 to the value of i (Line 7).

These algorithmic operations can be translated quite easily into assembly language as follows:

```
          LOAD        ONE    --Put a 1 into register R
          STORE       I      --Store the constant 1 into i
          ⋮
          INCREMENT   I      --Add 1 to memory location i
          ⋮                  --This data should be placed after the HALT
   I:     .DATA       0      --The index value, initially 0
   ONE:   .DATA       1      --The integer constant 1
```

Note how readable this code is, compared with machine language, because of such op code mnemonics as LOAD and STORE and the use of descriptive labels such as I and ONE.

Another example is the following assembly language translation of the arithmetic expression $A = B + C - 7$. (Assume that B and C have already been assigned values.)

```
        LOAD       B         --Put the value B into register R
        ADD        C         --R now holds the sum (B + C)
        SUBTRACT   SEVEN     --R now holds (B + C – 7)
        STORE      A         --Store the result into A
        ⋮                    --This data should be placed after the HALT
A:      .DATA      0
B:      .DATA      0
C:      .DATA      0
SEVEN:  .DATA      7         --The integer constant 7
```

Another important algorithmic operation involves testing and comparing values. The comparison of values and the subsequent use of the outcome to decide what to do next are termed a *conditional* operation, which we first saw in Section 2.2.3. Here is a conditional that outputs the larger of two values x and y. Algorithmically, it is expressed as follows:

Input the value of x
Input the value of y
If $x \geq y$ then
    Output the value of x
Else
    Output the value of y

In assembly language, this conditional operation can be translated as follows:

```
        IN         X         --Read the first data value
        IN         Y         --and now the second
        LOAD       Y         --Load the value of Y into register R
        COMPARE    X         --Compare X to Y and set the condition codes
        JUMPLT     PRINTY    --If X is less than Y, jump to PRINTY
        OUT        X         --We get here only if X ≥ Y, so print X
        JUMP       DONE      --Skip over the next instruction and continue
PRINTY: OUT        Y         --We get here if X < Y, so print Y
DONE:   ⋮                   --The program continues here

                            --The following data go after the HALT
X:      .DATA      0         --Space for the two data values
Y:      .DATA      0
        ⋮
```

Another important algorithmic primitive is *looping*, which was also introduced in Section 2.2.3. The following algorithmic example contains a while loop that executes 10,000 times.

Step	Operation	Explanation
1	Set *i* to 0	Start the loop counter at 0
2	While the value of $i < 10,000$ do	Lines 3 through 9
3–8	⋮	Here is the loop body that is to be done 10,000 times
9	Add 1 to the value of *i*	Increment the loop counter
10	End of the loop	
11	Stop	

This looping construct is easily translated into assembly language.

```
             LOAD       ZERO       --Initialize the loop counter to 0
             STORE      I          --This is Step 1 of the algorithm
LOOP:        LOAD       MAXVALUE   --Put 10,000 into register R
             COMPARE    I          --Compare I against 10,000
             JUMPEQ     DONE       --If I = 10,000 we are done (Step 2)
               ⋮                   --Here is the loop body (Steps 3–8)
             INCREMENT  I          --Add 1 to I (Step 9)
             JUMP       LOOP       --End of the loop body (Step 10)
DONE:        HALT                  --Stop execution (Step 11)
ZERO:        .DATA      0          --This is the constant 0
I:           .DATA      0          --The loop counter; it goes from
                                   --0 to 10,000
MAXVALUE:    .DATA      10000      --Maximum number of executions
               ⋮
```

As a final example, we will show a complete assembly language program (including all necessary pseudo-ops) to solve the following problem:

> Read in a sequence of nonnegative numbers, one number at a time, and compute a running sum. When you encounter a negative number, print out the sum of the nonnegative values and stop.

Thus, if the input is

```
8
31
7
5
−1
```

then the program should output the value 51, which is the sum $(8 + 31 + 7 + 5)$. An algorithm to solve this problem is shown in Figure 6.7, using the pseudocode notation of Chapter 2.

Our next task is to convert the algorithmic primitives of Figure 6.7 into assembly language instructions. A program that does this is shown in Figure 6.8.

FIGURE 6.7

Step	Operation
1	Set the value of *Sum* to 0
2	Input the first number *N*
3	While *N* is not negative do
4	Add the value of *N* to *Sum*
5	Input the next data value *N*
6	End of the loop
7	Print out *Sum*
8	Stop

Algorithm to compute the sum of nonnegative numbers

FIGURE 6.8

```
            .BEGIN                      --This marks the start of the program
            CLEAR       SUM             --Set the running sum to 0 (line 1)
            IN          N               --Input the first number N (line 2)
--The next three instructions test whether N is a negative number (line 3)
AGAIN:      LOAD        ZERO            --Put 0 into register R
            COMPARE     N               --Compare N and 0
            JUMPLT      NEG             --Go to NEG if N < 0
--We get here if N ≥ 0. We add N to the running sum (line 4)
            LOAD        SUM             --Put SUM into R
            ADD         N               --Add N. R now holds (N + SUM)
            STORE       SUM             --Put the result back into SUM
--Get the next input value (line 5)
            IN          N
--Now go back and repeat the loop (line 6)
            JUMP        AGAIN
--We get to this section of the program only when we encounter a negative value
NEG:        OUT         SUM             --Print the sum (line 7)
            HALT                        --and stop (line 8)
--Here are the data generation pseudo-ops
SUM:        .DATA       0               --The running sum goes here
N:          .DATA       0               --The input data are placed here
ZERO:       .DATA       0               --The constant 0
--Now we mark the end of the entire program
            .END
```

Assembly language program to compute the sum of nonnegative numbers

Of all the examples in this chapter, the program in Figure 6.8 demonstrates best what is meant by the phrase *user-oriented virtual environment*. Although it is not as clear as natural language or the pseudocode of Figure 6.7, this program can be read and understood by humans as well as computers. Tasks such as modifying the program and locating an error are significantly easier on the code of Figure 6.8 than on its machine language equivalent.

The program in Figure 6.8 is an important milestone in that it represents a culmination of the algorithmic problem-solving process. Earlier chapters introduced algorithms and problem solving (Chapters 1, 2, 3), discussed how to build computers to execute algorithms (Chapters 4, 5), and introduced

Practice Problems

1. Using the instruction set in Figure 6.5, translate the following algorithmic operations into assembly code. Show all necessary .DATA pseudo-ops.

   a.   Add 1 to the value of x
   b.   Add 50 to the value of x
   c.   Set x to the value $y + z - 2$
   d.   If $x > 50$ then output the value of x, otherwise input a new value of x
   e.   sum = 0
        I = 0
        While I < 50 do
             sum = sum + I;
             I = I + 1;
        End of the loop

2. Using the instruction set in Figure 6.5, write a complete assembly language program (including all necessary pseudo-ops) that reads in numbers and counts how many inputs it reads until it encounters the first negative value. The program then prints out that count and stops. For example, if the input data is 42, 108, 99, 60, 1, 42, 3, –27, then your program outputs the value 7 because there are seven nonnegative values before the appearance of the negative value –27.

3. Now modify your program from Practice Problem 2 so that if you have not encountered a negative value after 100 inputs, your program stops and outputs the value 100.

4. Discuss how the modifications you had to make in Practice Problem 3 were made easier by the use of assembly language in place of binary machine language.

Laboratory Experience 10

This section of Chapter 6 introduced assembly language instructions and programming techniques. However, as mentioned before, you do not learn programming and problem solving by reading and watching but rather by doing and trying. In this Laboratory Experience, you will program in an assembly language that is virtually identical to the one shown in Figure 6.5. You will be able to design and write programs like the one shown in Figure 6.8 and execute them on a simulated Von Neumann computer. You will observe the effect of individual instructions on the functional units of this machine and produce results.

This experience should give you a much deeper understanding of the concepts of assembly language programming and the Von Neumann architecture. It will also tie together the hardware concepts of Level 2 (Chapters 4 and 5) and the virtual machine system software concepts of Level 3. This lab shows how an assembly language program is written, translated, and loaded into a Von Neumann machine and executed by that machine using the ideas presented in the previous chapters.

system software that enables us to code algorithms into a language that computers can translate and execute (Chapter 6). The program in Figure 6.8 is the end product of this discussion: It can be input to an assembler, translated into machine language, loaded into a Von Neumann computer, and executed to produce answers to our problem. This algorithmic problem-solving cycle is one of the central themes of computer science.

6.3.3 Translation and Loading

What must happen in order for the assembly language program in Figure 6.8 to be executed on a processor? Figure 6.4 shows that before our source program can be run, we must invoke two system software packages—an *assembler* and a *loader*.

An assembler translates a symbolic assembly language program, such as the one in Figure 6.8, into machine language. We usually think of translation as an extremely difficult task. In fact, if two languages differ greatly in vocabulary, grammar, and syntax, it can be quite formidable. (This is why a translator for a high-level programming language is a very complex piece of software.) However, machine language and assembly language are very similar, and therefore an assembler is a relatively simple piece of system software.

An assembler must perform the following four tasks, none of which is particularly difficult.

1. Convert symbolic op codes to binary.

2. Convert symbolic addresses to binary.

3. Perform the assembler services requested by the pseudo-ops.

4. Put the translated instructions into a file for future use.

Let's see how these operations are carried out using the hypothetical assembly language of Figure 6.5.

The conversion of symbolic op codes such as LOAD, ADD, and SUBTRACT to binary makes use of a structure called the *op code table*. This is an alphabetized list of all legal assembly language op codes and their binary equivalents. Part of an op code table for the instruction set of Figure 6.5 is shown in Figure 6.9. (The table assumes that the op code field is 4 bits wide.)

The assembler finds the operation code mnemonic in column 1 of the table and replaces the characters with the 4-bit binary value in column 2. (If the mnemonic is not found, then the user has written an illegal op code, which results in an error message.) Thus, for example, if we use the mnemonic SUBTRACT in our program, the assembler converts it to the binary value 0101.

To look up the code in the op code table, we could use the sequential search algorithm introduced in Chapter 2 and shown in Figure 2.13. However, using this algorithm may significantly slow down the translation of our program. The analysis of the sequential search algorithm in Chapter 3 showed that locating a single item in a list of N items takes, on the average, $N/2$ comparisons if the item is in the table and N comparisons if it is not. In Chapter 5, we stated that modern computers may have as many as 500 machine language instructions in their instruction set, so the size of the op code table of Figure 6.9 could be as large as $N = 500$. This means that using

---

FIGURE 6.9

Operation	Binary Value
ADD	0011
CLEAR	0010
COMPARE	0111
DECREMENT	0110
HALT	1111
⋮	
STORE	0001
SUBTRACT	0101

Structure of the op code table

sequential search, we perform an average of $N/2$, about 250, comparisons for every op code in our program. If our assembly language program contains 10,000 instructions (not an unreasonably large number), the op code translation task requires a total of 10,000 instructions × 250 comparisons/ instruction = 2.5 million comparisons. That is a lot of searching, even for a computer.

Because the op code table of Figure 6.9 is sorted alphabetically, we can instead use the more efficient binary search algorithm discussed in Section 3.4.2 and shown in Figure 3.18. On the average, the number of comparisons needed to find an element using binary search is not $N/2$ but (lg N), the logarithm of N to the base 2. [*Note:* (lg N) is the value k such that $2^k = N$.] For a table of size $N = 500$, $N/2$ is 250, whereas (lg N) is approximately 9 ($2^9 = 512$). This says that on the average, we find an op code in the table, assuming it is there, in about 9 comparisons rather than 250. If our assembly language program contains 10,000 instructions, then the op code translation task requires only about 10,000 × 9 = 90,000 comparisons rather than 2.5 million, a reduction of 2,410,000. By selecting a better algorithm, we achieve an increase in speed of about 96%—quite a significant improvement!

This example demonstrates why algorithm analysis, introduced in Chapter 3, is such a critically important part of the design and implementation of software. Replacing a slow algorithm with a faster one can turn an insoluble problem into a solvable one and a worthless solution into a highly worthwhile one. Remember that, in computer science, we are looking not just for correct solutions but for efficient ones as well.

After the op code has been converted into binary, the assembler must perform a similar task on the address field. It must convert the address from a symbolic value, such as X or LOOP, into the correct binary address. This task is a bit more difficult than converting the op code because the assembler itself must determine the correct numeric value of all symbols used in the label field. There is no "built-in" address conversion table equivalent to the op code table of Figure 6.9.

In assembly language, a symbol is defined when it appears in the label field of an instruction or data pseudo-op. Specifically, the symbol is given the value of the address of the instruction to which it is attached. Assemblers usually make two passes over the source code, where a **pass** is defined as the process of examining and processing every assembly language instruction in the program, one instruction at a time. During the *first pass* over the source code, the assembler looks at every instruction, keeping track of the memory address where this instruction will be stored when it is translated and loaded into memory. It does this by knowing where the program begins in memory and knowing how many memory cells are required to store each machine language instruction or piece of data. It also determines whether there is a symbol in the label field of the instruction. If there is, it enters the symbol and the address of this instruction into a special table that it is building called a **symbol table**.

We can see this process more clearly in Figure 6.10. The figure assumes that each instruction and data value occupies one memory cell and that the first instruction of the program will be placed into address 0.

The assembler looks at the first instruction in the program, IN X, and determines that when this instruction is loaded into memory, it will go into memory cell 0. Because the label LOOP is attached to that instruction, the name LOOP is made equivalent to address 0. The assembler enters the (name, value) pair (LOOP, 0) into the symbol table. This process of associating a symbolic name with a physical memory address is called **binding**, and the two primary purposes of the first pass of an assembler are (1) to bind all symbolic names to address values and (2) to enter those bindings into the symbol table. Now, any time the programmer uses the name LOOP in the address field, the assembler can look up that symbol in column 1 of the symbol table and replace it with the address value in column 2, in this case address 0. (If it is not found, the programmer has used an undefined symbol, which produces an error message.)

The next six instructions of Figure 6.10(a), from IN Y to JUMP LOOP, do not contain labels, so they do not add new entries to the symbol table. However, the assembler must still update the counter it is using to determine the address where each instruction will ultimately be stored. The variable used to determine the address of a given instruction or piece of data is called the *location counter*. The location counter values are shown in the third column of Figure 6.10(a). Using the location counter, the assembler can determine that the address values of the labels DONE,

---

FIGURE 6.10

Label	Code		Location Counter	Symbol Table	
				Symbol	Address Value
LOOP:	IN	X	0	LOOP	0
	IN	Y	1	DONE	7
	LOAD	X	2	X	9
	COMPARE	Y	3	Y	10
	JUMPGT	DONE	4		
	OUT	X	5		
	JUMP	LOOP	6		
DONE:	OUT	Y	7		
	HALT		8		
X:	.DATA	0	9		
Y:	.DATA	0	10		

(a)   (b)

Generation of the symbol table

X, and Y are 7, 9, and 10, respectively. It binds these symbolic names and addresses and enters them in the symbol table, as shown in Figure 6.10(b). When the first pass is done, the assembler has constructed a symbol table that it can use during pass 2. The algorithm for pass 1 of a typical assembler is shown (using an alternative form of algorithmic notation called a *flowchart*) in Figure 6.11.

FIGURE 6.11

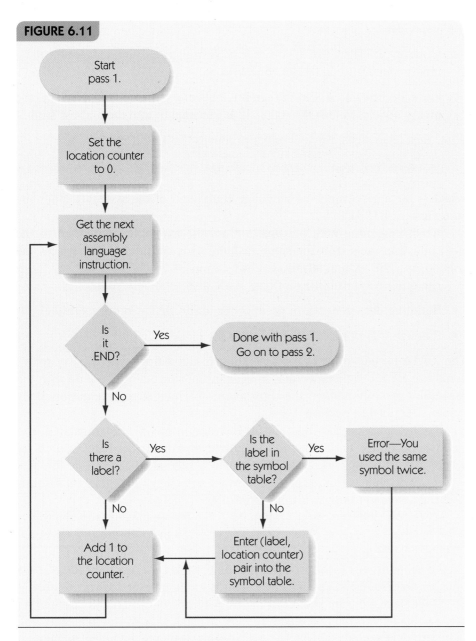

Outline of pass 1 of the assembler

During the *second pass*, the assembler translates the source program into machine language. It has the op code table to translate mnemonic op codes to binary, and it has the symbol table to translate symbolic addresses to binary. Therefore, the second pass is relatively simple, involving two table lookups and the generation of two binary fields. For example, if we assume that our instruction format is a 4-bit op code followed by a single 12-bit address, then given the instruction

SUBTRACT   X

the assembler

1. looks up SUBTRACT in the op code table of Figure 6.9 and places the 4-bit binary value 0101 in the op code field

2. looks up the symbol X in the symbol table of Figure 6.10(b) and places the binary address value 0000 0000 1001 (decimal 9) into the address field

After these two steps, the assembler produces the 16-bit instruction

0101 0000 0000 1001

which is the correct machine language equivalent of the assembly language statement SUBTRACT X.

When it is done with one instruction, the assembler moves on to the next and translates it in the same fashion. This continues until it sees the pseudo-op .END, which terminates translation.

The other responsibilities of pass 2 are also relatively simple:

- Handling data generation pseudo-ops (only .DATA in our example)

- Producing the object file needed by the loader

The .DATA pseudo-op asks the assembler to build the proper binary representation for the signed decimal integer in the address field. To do this, the assembler must implement the sign/magnitude integer representation algorithms described in Section 4.2.

Finally, after all the fields of an instruction have been translated into binary, the newly built machine language instruction and the address of where it is to be loaded are written out to a file called the object file. (On Windows machines, this is referred to as an .exe file.) The algorithm for pass 2 of the assembler is shown in Figure 6.12.

After completion of pass 1 and pass 2, the object file contains the translated machine language object program, referred to in Figure 6.4. One possible object program for the assembly language program of Figure 6.10(a) is shown in Figure 6.13. (Note that a real object file contains only the address and instruction fields. The meaning field is included here for clarity only.)

The object program shown in Figure 6.13 becomes input to yet another piece of system software called a loader. It is the task of the loader to read instructions from the object file and store them into memory for execution. To do this, it reads an address value—column 1 of Figure 6.13—and

FIGURE 6.12

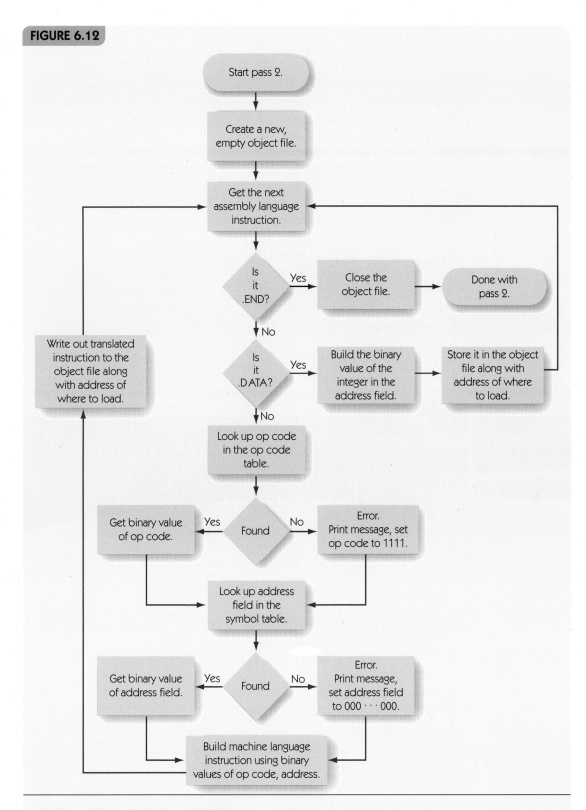

Outline of pass 2 of the assembler

FIGURE 6.13

Instruction Format:		Op Code	Address
		4 bits	12 bits

Object Program:

Address	Machine Language Instruction	Meaning	
0000	1101 000000001001	IN	X
0001	1101 000000001010	IN	Y
0010	0000 000000001001	LOAD	X
0011	0111 000000001010	COMPARE	Y
0100	1001 000000000111	JUMPGT DONE	
0101	1110 000000001001	OUT	X
0110	1000 000000000000	JUMP LOOP	
0111	1110 000000001010	OUT	Y
1000	1111 000000000000	HALT	
1001	0000 000000000000	The constant 0	
1010	0000 000000000000	The constant 0	

Example of an object program

Practice Problems

1. Translate the following algorithm into assembly language using the instructions in Figure 6.5.

Step	Operation
1	Set *Negative Count* to 0
2	Set *i* to 1
3	While *i* ≤ 50 do Lines 4 through 6
4	Input a number *N*
5	If *N* < 0 then increment *Negative Count* by 1
6	Increment *i* by 1
7	End of the loop
8	Output the value of *Negative Count*
9	Stop

2. What is the machine language representation of each of the following instructions? Assume the symbol table values are as shown in Figure 6.10(b) and the instruction format is that of Figure 6.13.

    a. COMPARE   Y
    b. JUMPNEQ   DONE
    c. DECREMENT   LOOP

3. What is wrong or inconsistent with the instruction that is shown in Practice Problem 2c?

4. Take the assembly language program that you developed in Practice Problem 1 and determine the physical memory address associated with each label in the symbol table. (Assume the first instruction is loaded into address 0 and that each instruction occupies one cell.)

5. Is the following assembly language pseudo-op illegal? Explain why or why not.

TWO: .DATA 1

a machine language instruction—column 2 of Figure 6.13—and stores that instruction into the specified memory address. This operation is repeated for every instruction in the object file. When loading is complete, the loader places the address of the first instruction (0 in this example) into the program counter (PC) to initiate execution. The hardware, as we learned in Chapter 5, then begins the fetch, decode, and execute cycle starting with the instruction whose address is located in the PC, namely the beginning of this program.

6.4 Operating Systems

To carry out the services just described (translate a program, load a program, and run a program), a user must issue **system commands**. These commands may be lines of text typed at a terminal, such as

>assemble MyProg	(Invoke the assembler to translate a program called MyProg.)
>run MyProg	(Load the translated MyProg and start execution.)

or, more commonly, they may be represented by icons displayed on the screen and selected with a mouse, button, or finger tap, using a technique called *point-and-click*.

Regardless of how the process is initiated, the important question is: What program examines these commands? What piece of system software waits for requests and activates other system programs like a translator or loader to service these requests? The answer is the operating system, and, as shown in Figure 6.2, it is the "top-level" system software component on a computer.

Some of the more well-known operating systems in widespread use today include Windows (7, Vista, XP), Mac OS X, Linux, Google Android for mobile devices, and Apple iOS for the iPhone and iPad.

6.4.1 Functions of an Operating System

An operating system is an enormously large and complex piece of software that has many responsibilities within a computer system. This section examines five of the most important tasks that it performs.

The User Interface. The operating system is executing whenever no other piece of user or system software is using the processor. Its most important task is to wait for a user command delivered via the keyboard, mouse, finger tap, or other input device. If the command is legal, the operating system activates and schedules the appropriate software package to process the request. In this sense, the operating system acts like the computer's *receptionist* and *dispatcher.*

Operating system commands usually request access to hardware resources (processor, printer, communication lines, camera), software services (translator, loader, Web browser, application program), or information (data files, contact lists). Examples of typical operating system commands are shown in Figure 6.14. Modern operating systems can execute dozens or even hundreds of different commands.

After a user enters a command, the operating system determines which software package needs to be loaded and put on the schedule for execution. When that package completes execution, control returns to the operating system, which waits for a user to enter the next command. This user interface algorithm is diagrammed in Figure 6.15.

The user interfaces on the operating systems of the 1950s, 1960s, and 1970s were text oriented. The system displayed a *prompt character* on the screen to indicate that it was waiting for input, and then it waited for something to happen. The user entered commands in a special, and sometimes quite complicated, command language. For example, on the UNIX operating

FIGURE 6.14

- Translate a program
- Run a program
- Save information in a file
- Retrieve a file previously stored
- List all the files for this user
- Print a file on a specified device
- Delete or rename a file
- Copy a file from one I/O device to another
- Let the user set or change a password
- Establish a network connection
- Tell me the current time and date

Some typical operating system commands

FIGURE 6.15

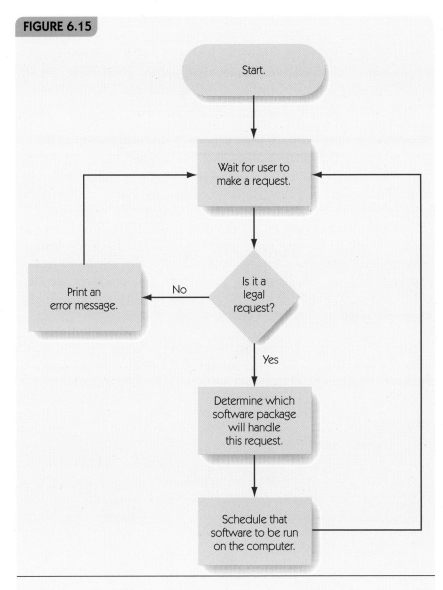

User interface responsibility of the operating system

system, widely used on personal computers and workstations, the following command asks the system to list the names and access privileges of the files contained in the home directory of a user called mike:

> ls -al /usr/mike/home   (">" is the prompt character)

As you can see, commands were not always easy to understand, and learning the command language of the operating system was a major stumbling block for new users. Unfortunately, without first learning some basic commands, no useful work could be done.

Because users found text-oriented command languages very cumbersome, virtually all modern operating systems utilize a graphical user interface, or *GUI*. To communicate with a user, a GUI supports visual aids and point-and-click operations, rather than textual commands. The interface uses *icons, pull-down menus, scrolling* and *resizable windows*, and other visual elements and graphical metaphors that make it much easier for a user to formulate requests.

For example, Figure 6.16 shows a window listing the contents of the folder called BookImage. One of these items is a folder called Home. To display all the files contained in this folder, a user simply points to it and clicks, and the list of its files appears in a new window. Compare the clarity of that operation with the preceding UNIX command that does virtually the same thing.

Graphical interfaces are an excellent example of the high-level virtual machine created by the operating system. A GUI hides a great deal of the underlying hardware and software, and it makes the computer or device appear very easy to use. In reality, the device that produces the elegant interface shown in Figure 6.16 is identical to the "naked" Von Neumann machine described in Chapters 4 and 5.

System Security and Protection. In addition to being a receptionist, the operating system also has the responsibilities of a *security guard*—controlling access to the computer and its resources. It must prevent unauthorized users

FIGURE 6.16

Example of a graphical user interface

from accessing the system and prevent authorized users from doing unauthorized things.

At a minimum, the operating system must not allow people to access the computer if they have not been granted permission. In the "olden days" of computing (the 1950s and 1960s), security was implemented by physical means—walls and locked doors around the computer and security guards at the door to prevent unauthorized access. However, when telecommunications networks appeared on the scene in the late 1960s and 1970s (we will discuss them in detail in Chapter 7), access to computers over networks became possible from virtually anywhere in the world, and responsibility for

A Machine for the Rest of Us

In January 1984, Apple Computer launched its new line of Macintosh computers with a great deal of showmanship: a TV commercial at the 1984 NFL Super Bowl. The company described the Macintosh as a computer that anyone could understand and use—"a machine for the rest of us." People who saw and used it quickly agreed, and in the early days, its major selling point was that "a Macintosh is much easier to use than an IBM PC." However, the Macintosh and IBM PC were extremely similar in terms of hardware, and they both used something like the architecture of Figure 5.18. Both systems used Von Neumann–type processors, and these processors executed similar sets of machine language instructions exactly as described in Chapter 5. In fact, in 2006 Apple began using the same type of Intel processors as in the IBM PC and its clones. It certainly was not the underlying hardware that created these huge differences in ease of use.

What made the Macintosh easier to use was its radically new graphical user interface, created by two system software packages called the Finder and System. They produced a sophisticated visual environment that most users found much easier to understand than the text-oriented interface of MS-DOS, the most popular PC-based operating system of the 1980s and early 1990s. IBM users quickly realized the importance of having a powerful user interface, and in the early- and mid-1990s began to switch to Microsoft Windows, which provided a windowing environment similar to the Macintosh. Newer versions of these systems, such as Mac OS X, Windows Vista, and Windows 7, all represent attempts at creating an even more powerful and easy-to-use virtual environment.

We can see now that it was wrong for Apple to say that "a Macintosh is easier to use than a PC." What it should have said is that "the virtual machine environment created by the Macintosh operating system is easier to use than the virtual machine environment created by the Windows operating system." However, maybe that was just a little too wordy!

access control migrated from the guard at the door to the operating system inside the machine.

In most operating systems, access control means requiring a user to enter a legal *username* and *password* before any other requests are accepted. If an incorrect username or password is entered, the operating system does not allow access to the computer. (See the Special Interest Box "Password Pointers" in Chapter 8.)

It is also the operating system's responsibility to safeguard the *password file* that stores all valid username/password combinations. It must prevent this file from being accessed by any unauthorized users because that would compromise the security of the entire system. This is analogous to putting a lock on your door but also making sure that you don't lose the key. (Of course, some privileged users, called superusers—usually computer center employees or system administrators—must be able to access and maintain this file.) To provide this security, the operating system may choose to encrypt the password file using an encoding algorithm that is extremely difficult to crack. A thief must steal not only the encrypted text but also the algorithm to change the encrypted text back to the original clear text. Without this information, the stolen password file is useless. Operating systems use encryption algorithms whenever they must provide a high degree of security for sensitive information. We will learn more about these encryption algorithms in Chapter 8.

Even when valid users gain access to the system, there are things they should not be allowed to do. The most obvious is that they should be able to access only their own personal information. They should not be able to look at the files or records of other users. Therefore, when the operating system gets a request such as

> *> open filename (Open a file and allow this user to access it.)*
>
> *(Or click Open in the File menu.)*

it must determine who is the owner of the file—that is, who created it. If the individual accessing the file is not the owner, then it usually rejects the request. However, most operating systems allow the owner of a file to provide a list of additional authorized users or a general class of authorized users, such as all students or all faculty. Like the password file, these *authorization lists* are highly sensitive files, and operating systems generally store them in an encrypted format.

Most modern operating systems not only determine whether you are allowed to access a file, they also check what operations you are permitted to perform on that file. The following hierarchically ordered list shows the different types of operations that users may be permitted to do on a file:

- Read the information in the file but not change it
- Append new information to the end of the file but not change existing information
- Change existing information in the file
- Delete the file from the system

FIGURE 6.17

File: GRADES

Name	Permitted Operations
Smith	R (R = Read only)
Jones	RA (A = Append)
Adams	RAC (C = Change)
Doe	RACD (D = Delete)

Authorization list for the file GRADES

For example, the grade file GRADES of a student named Smith could have the authorization list shown in Figure 6.17.

This authorization list says that Smith, the student whose grades are in the file, has the right to access his or her own file, but only to read the information.

Jones, a clerk in the administration center, can read the file and can append new grades to the end of the file at the completion of the term. Adams, the school's registrar, can read and append information and is also allowed to change the student's grades if an error was made. Doe, the director of the computer center, can do all of these operations as well as delete the file and all its information.

Permission to look at information can be given to a number of people. However, changing information in a file is a sensitive operation (think about changing a payroll file), and permission to make changes must be limited. Deleting information is the most powerful and potentially damaging operation of all, and its use must be restricted to people at the highest level. It is the operating system's responsibility to help ensure that individuals are authorized to carry out the operation they request.

Computers today play such a critical role in the storage and management of military, medical, economic, and personal data that this security responsibility has taken on an increasingly important role. We will investigate this topic in detail in Chapter 8.

Efficient Allocation of Resources. Section 5.2.2 described the enormous difference in speed between a processor and an I/O unit: up to 5 orders of magnitude. A hardware device called an I/O controller (Figure 5.9) frees the processor to do useful work while the I/O operation is being completed. What useful work can a processor do in this free time? What ensures that this valuable resource is used efficiently? Again, it is the operating system's responsibility to see that the resources of a computer system are used efficiently as well as correctly.

To ensure that a processor does not sit idle if there is useful work to do, the operating system keeps a *queue* (a waiting line) of programs that are ready to run. Whenever the processor is idle, the operating system picks one of these jobs and assigns it to the processor. This guarantees that the processor always has something to do.

To see how this algorithm might work, let's define the following three classes of programs:

Running   The one program currently executing on the processor (assume only a single processor on the computer)

Ready   Programs that are loaded in memory and ready to run but are not yet executing

Waiting   Programs that cannot run because they are waiting for an I/O operation (or some other time-consuming event) to finish

Here is how these three lists might look at some instant in time:

Waiting	Ready	Running
	B	A
	C	
	D	

There are four programs, called A, B, C, and D, in memory. Program A is executing on the processor; B, C, and D are ready to run and are in line waiting their turn. Assume that program A performs the I/O operation "read a sector from the disk." (Maybe it is a word processor, and it needs to get another piece of the document on which you are working.) We saw in Section 5.2.2 that, relative to processing speeds, this operation takes a long time, about 10 msec or so. While it is waiting for this disk I/O operation to finish, the processor has nothing to do, and system efficiency plummets.

To solve this problem, the operating system can do some shuffling. It first moves program A to the waiting list because it must wait for its I/O operation to finish before it can continue. It then selects one of the ready programs (say B) and assigns it to the processor, which starts executing it. This leads to the following situation:

Waiting	Ready	Running
A	C	B
	D	

Instead of sitting idle while A waits for I/O, the processor works on program B and gets something useful done. This is equivalent to working on another project while waiting for your secretary to fetch a document, instead of waiting and doing nothing.

Perhaps B also does an I/O operation. If so, then the operating system repeats the same steps. It moves B to the waiting list, picks any ready program (say C) and starts executing it, producing the following situation:

Waiting	Ready	Running
A	D	C
B		

As long as there is at least one program that is ready to run, the processor always has something useful to do.

At some point, the I/O operation that A started finishes, and the "I/O completed interrupt signal" described in Section 5.2.2 is generated. The appearance of that signal indicates that program A is now ready to run, but it cannot do so immediately because the processor is currently assigned to C. Instead, the operating system moves A to the ready list, producing the following situation:

Waiting	*Ready*	*Running*
B	D	C
	A	

Programs cycle from running to waiting to ready and back to running, each one using only a portion of the resources of the processor.

In Chapter 5, we stated that the execution of a program is an unbroken repetition of the fetch/decode/execute cycle from the first instruction of the program to the HALT. Now we see that this view may not be completely accurate. For reasons of efficiency, the running history of a program may be a sequence of starts and stops—a cycle of execution, waits for I/O operations, waits for the processor, followed again by execution. By having many programs loaded in memory and sharing the processor, the operating system can use the processor to its fullest capability and run the overall system more efficiently.

The Safe Use of Resources. Not only must resources be used *efficiently*, they must also be used *safely*. That doesn't mean an operating system must prevent users from sticking their fingers in the power supply and getting electrocuted! The job of the operating system is to prevent programs or users from attempting operations that cause the computer system to enter a state where it is incapable of doing any further work—a "frozen" state where all useful work comes to a grinding halt.

Practice Problems

1. Assume that programs spend about 25% of their time waiting for I/O operations to complete. If there are two programs loaded into memory, what is the likelihood that both programs will be blocked waiting for I/O and there will be nothing for the processor to do? What percentage of time will the processor be busy? (This value is called *processor utilization*.) By how much does processor utilization improve if we have four programs in memory instead of two?

2. Why are passwords extremely vulnerable to security breaches? Suggest ways to improve their use and reduce the risk associated with them.

To see how this can happen, imagine a computer system that has one laser printer, one data file called D, and two programs A and B. Program A wants to load data file D and print it on the laser printer. Program B wants to do the same thing. Each of them makes the following requests to the operating system:

Program A	Program B
Get data file D.	Get the laser printer.
Get the laser printer.	Get data file D.
Print the file.	Print the file.

If the operating system satisfies the first request of each program, then A "owns" data file D and B has the laser printer. When A requests ownership of the laser printer, it is told that the printer is being used by B. Similarly, B is told that it must wait for the data file until A is finished with it. Each program is waiting for a resource to become available that will never become free. This situation is called a **deadlock**. Programs A and B are in a permanent waiting state, and if there is no other program ready to run, all useful work on the system ceases.

More formally, deadlock means that there is a set of programs, each of which is waiting for an event to occur before it may proceed, but that event can be caused only by another waiting program in the set. Another example is a telecommunications system in which program A sends messages to program B, which acknowledges their correct receipt. Program A cannot send another message to B until it knows that the last one has been correctly received.

Program A	Program B
Message →	
	← Acknowledge
Message →	
	← Acknowledge
Message →	

Suppose B now sends an acknowledgment, but it gets lost. (Perhaps there was static on the line, or a lightning bolt jumbled the signal.) What happens? Program A stops and waits for receipt of an acknowledgment from B. Program B stops and waits for the next message from A. Deadlock! Neither side can proceed, and unless something is done, all communication between the two will cease.

How does an operating system handle deadlock conditions? There are two basic approaches, called *deadlock prevention* and *deadlock recovery*. In deadlock prevention, the operating system uses resource allocation algorithms that prevent deadlock from occurring in the first place. In the example of the two programs simultaneously requesting the laser printer and the data file, the problem is caused by the fact that each program has a portion of the resources needed to solve its problem, but neither has all that it requested. To prevent this, the operating system can use the following algorithm:

> If a program cannot get all the resources that it needs, it must give up all the resources it currently owns and issue a completely new request.

Essentially, this resource allocation algorithm says, "If you cannot get everything you need, then you get nothing." If we had used this algorithm, then after program A acquired the laser printer but not the data file, it would have had to relinquish ownership of the printer. Now B could get everything it needed to execute, and no deadlock would occur. (It could also work in the reverse direction, with B relinquishing ownership of the data file and A getting the needed resources. Which scenario unfolds depends on the exact order in which requests are made.)

In the telecommunications example, one deadlock prevention algorithm is to require that messages and acknowledgments never get garbled or lost. Unfortunately, that is impossible. Real-world communication systems (telephone, microwave, satellite) do make errors, so we are powerless to guarantee that deadlock conditions can never occur. Instead we must detect them and recover from them when they do occur. This is typical of the class of methods called *deadlock recovery algorithms*.

For example, here is a possible algorithmic solution to our telecommunications problem:

> *Sender:* Number your messages with the nonnegative integers 0, 1, 2, … and send them in numerical order. If you send message number i and have not received an acknowledgment for 30 seconds, send message i again.

> *Receiver:* When you send an acknowledgment, include the number of the message you received. If you get a duplicate copy of message i, send another acknowledgment and discard the duplicate.

Using this algorithm, here is what might happen:

Program A	Program B
Message (1) →	
	← Acknowledge (1)
Message (2) →	
	← Acknowledge (2)
	(Assume this acknowledgment is lost.)

At this point, we have exactly the same deadlock condition described earlier. However, this time we are able to recover in a relatively short period. For 30 seconds nothing happens. However, after 30 seconds A sends message (2) a second time. B acknowledges it and discards it (because it already has a copy), and communication continues:

Program A	Program B
(Wait 30 seconds.)	
Message (2) →	(Discard this duplicate copy but acknowledge it.)
	← Acknowledge (2)
Message (3) →	

We have successfully recovered from the error, and the system is again up and running.

Regardless of whether we prevent deadlocks from occurring or recover from those that do occur, it is the responsibility of the operating system to create a virtual machine in which the user never sees deadlocks and does not worry about them. The operating system should create the illusion of a smoothly functioning, highly efficient, error-free environment—even if, as we know from our glimpse behind the scenes, that is not always the case. (We all know how frustrating it can be when the computer freezes up, and we must reboot. A well-designed operating system will make this an extremely rare event.)

Summary. In this section, we have highlighted some of the major responsibilities of the critically important software package called the operating system:

- User interface management (a receptionist)

- Control of access to the system and to data files (a security guard)

- Program scheduling and activation (a dispatcher)

- Efficient resource allocation (an efficiency expert)

- Deadlock detection and error detection (a traffic officer)

These are by no means the operating system's only responsibilities, which can also include such areas as input/output processing, allocating priorities to programs, swapping programs in and out of memory, recovering from power failures, managing the system clock, and dozens of other tasks, large and small, essential to keeping the computer system running smoothly.

As you can imagine, given all these responsibilities, an operating system is an extraordinarily complex piece of software. An operating system for a large network of computers can require millions of lines of code, take thousands of person-years to develop, and cost more to develop than the hardware on which it runs. Even operating systems for personal computers and workstations (such as Windows, Linux, and Mac OS X) are huge programs (see the Special Interest Box in this chapter, "Now That's Big!") developed over periods of years by teams of dozens of computer scientists. Designing and creating a high-level virtual environment is a difficult job, but without it, computers would not be so widely used nor anywhere near as important as they are today.

6.4.2 Historical Overview of Operating Systems Development

Like the hardware on which it runs, system software has gone through a number of changes since the earliest days of computing. The functions and capabilities of a modern operating system described in the previous section did not appear all at once but evolved over many years.

The Open Source Movement

The design and development of an operating system like Windows 7 or Mac OS X is an enormous undertaking that can take thousands of person-years to complete. Furthermore, the likelihood of getting everything correct is quite small. (We have all had the experience of being frustrated by the freezes, errors, and crashes of our operating system.) One of the ways that people are attempting to address this issue is via the *open source movement*. This is a worldwide movement of people who feel that the best way to develop efficient and bug-free software is to enlist the cooperation of interested, skilled, and altruistic programmers who are willing to work for free. They are inspired simply by the goals of producing high-quality software and of working cooperatively with like-minded individuals. The software is distributed to anyone who wants to use it, and it can be modified, improved, and changed by any user. This is quite different from the proprietary approach to software development within a corporation such as IBM or Microsoft, in which the development process is kept secret, and the source code is not shared with anyone else.

Essentially, the open source movement encourages contributions to the development process from anyone in the world, in the belief that the more open the process and the more eyes examining the code, the more likely it is that errors or invalid assumptions will be located and corrected. Both the Linux operating system and the Apache Web server package were developed using the open source model.

During the *first generation* of system software (roughly 1945–1955), there really were no operating systems and there was very little software support of any kind—typically just the assemblers and loaders described in Section 6.3. All machine operation was "hands-on." Programmers would sign up for a block of time and, at the appointed time, show up in the machine room carrying their programs on punched cards or tapes. They had the entire computer to themselves, and they were responsible for all machine operation. They loaded their assembly language programs into memory along with the assembler and, by punching some buttons on the console, started the translation process. Then they loaded their program into memory and started it running. Working with first-generation software was a lot like working on the naked machine described at the beginning of the chapter. It was attempted only by highly trained professionals intimately familiar with the computer and its operation.

System administrators quickly realized that this was a horribly inefficient way to use an expensive piece of equipment. (Remember that these early computers cost millions of dollars.) A programmer would sign up for an hour of computer time, but the majority of that time was spent analyzing results and trying to figure out what to do next. During this "thinking time," the system was idle and doing nothing of value. Eventually, the need to keep machines busy led to the development of a *second generation* of system software called batch operating systems (1955–1965).

In second-generation batch operating systems, rather than operate the machine directly, a programmer handed the program (typically entered on punched cards) to a trained computer operator, who grouped it into a "batch"—hence the name. After a few dozen programs were collected, the operator carried this batch of cards to a small I/O computer that put these programs on tape. This tape was carried into the machine room and loaded onto the "big" computer that actually ran the users' programs, one at a time, writing the results to yet another tape. During the last stage, this output tape was carried back to the I/O computer to be printed and handed to the programmer. The entire cycle is diagrammed in Figure 6.18.

This cycle might seem cumbersome and, from the programmer's point of view, it was. (Every programmer who worked in the late 1950s or early 1960s has horror stories about waiting many hours—even days—for a program to be returned, only to discover that there was a missing comma.) From the computer's point of view, however, this new batch system worked wonderfully, and system utilization increased dramatically. No longer were there delays while a programmer was setting up to perform an operation. There were no long periods of idleness while someone was mulling over

Now That's Big!

The most widely used measure of program size is *source lines of code* (abbreviated SLOC). This is a count of the total number of nonblank, noncomment lines in a piece of software. According to Wikipedia (*www.wikipedia.org*), the estimated size of Mac OS X 10.4, one of the most widely used operating systems in the world, is 86 million SLOC. If you were to print out the entire program, at 60 lines per printed page, you would generate about 1,433,000 pages of output, or roughly the number of pages in 4,000 full-length novels. If you were to store that output on a bookshelf, it would stretch more than the length of an American football field.

It is estimated that the average programmer can produce about 40 lines of correct code per day. If that number is correct, then the Mac OS X operating system represents 2,150,000 person-days, or (at 240 working days per year) about 9,000 person-years of effort.

FIGURE 6.18

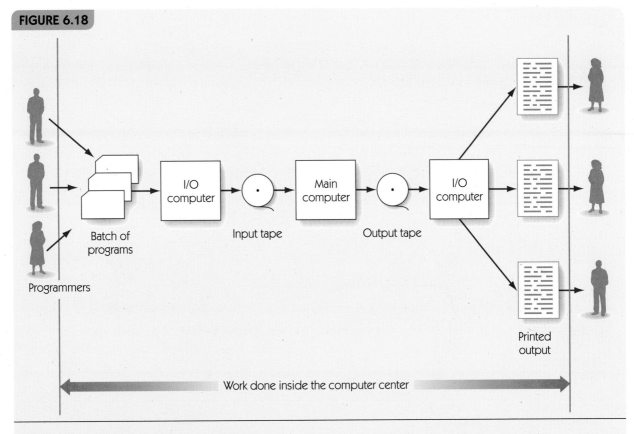

Operation of a batch computer system

what to do next. As soon as one job was either completed normally or halted because of an error, the computer went to the input tape, loaded the next job, and started execution. As long as there was work to be done, the computer was kept busy.

Because programmers no longer operated the machine, they needed a way to communicate to the operating system what had to be done, and these early batch operating systems were the first to include a *command language*, also called a *job control language*. This was a special-purpose language in which users wrote commands specifying to the operating system (or the human operator) what operations to perform on their programs. These commands were interpreted by the operating system, which initiated the proper action. The "receptionist/dispatcher" responsibility of the operating system had been born. A typical batch job was a mix of programs, data, and commands, as shown in Figure 6.19.

By the mid-1960s, the use of integrated circuits and other new technologies had boosted computational speeds enormously. The batch operating system just described kept only a single program in memory at any one time. If that job paused for a few milliseconds to complete an I/O operation (such as read a disk sector or print a file on the printer), the processor simply waited.

FIGURE 6.19

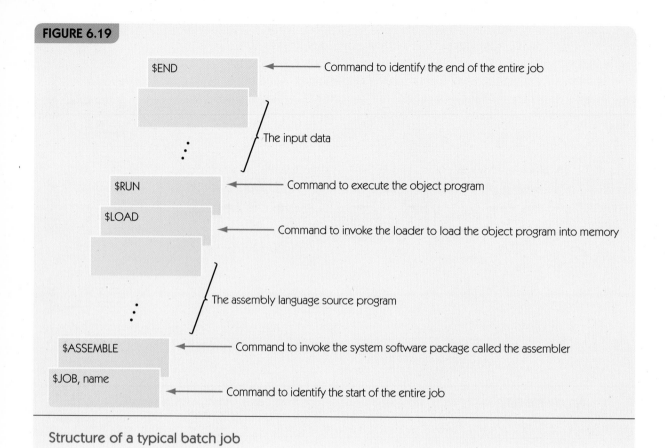

$END ⟵——————— Command to identify the end of the entire job

The input data

$RUN ⟵——————— Command to execute the object program

$LOAD

⟵——————— Command to invoke the loader to load the object program into memory

The assembly language source program

$ASSEMBLE ⟵——————— Command to invoke the system software package called the assembler

$JOB, name

⟵——————— Command to identify the start of the entire job

Structure of a typical batch job

As computers became faster, designers began to look for ways to use those idle milliseconds. The answer they came up with led to a *third generation* of operating systems called **multiprogrammed operating systems** (1965–1985).

In a multiprogrammed operating system, many user programs are simultaneously loaded into memory, rather than just one:

Memory

| Operating System |
| Program 1 |
| Program 2 |
| Program 3 |

If the currently executing program pauses for I/O, one of the other ready jobs is selected for execution so that no time is wasted. As we described earlier, this cycle of running/waiting/ready states led to significantly higher processor utilization.

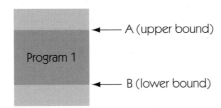

To make this all work properly, the operating system had to protect user programs (and itself) from damage by other programs. When there was a single program in memory, the only user program that could be damaged was your own. Now, with many programs in memory, an erroneous instruction in one user's program could wreak havoc on any of the others. For example, the seemingly harmless instruction

> STORE 1000   --Store the contents of register R into memory cell 1000

should not be executed if the physical address 1000 is not located within this user's program. It could wipe out an instruction or piece of data in someone else's program, causing unexpected behavior and (probably) incorrect results.

These third-generation operating systems kept track of the upper and lower address bounds of each program in memory

and ensured that no program ever attempted a memory reference outside this range. If it did, then the system ceased execution of that program, produced an error message, removed that program from memory, and began work on another ready program.

Similarly, the operating system could no longer permit any program to execute a HALT instruction because that would shut down the processor and prevent it from finishing any other program currently in memory. These third-generation systems developed the concept of *user operation codes* that could be included in any user program and *privileged operation codes* whose use was restricted to the operating system or other system software. The HALT instruction became a privileged op code that could be executed only by a system program, not by a user program.

These multiprogrammed operating systems were the first to have extensive protection and error-detection capabilities, and the "traffic officer" responsibility began to take on much greater importance than in earlier systems.

During the 1960s and 1970s, computer networks and telecommunications systems (which are discussed in detail in Chapter 7) developed and grew rapidly. Another form of third-generation operating system evolved to take advantage of this new technology. It is called a time-sharing system, and it is a variation of the multiprogrammed operating system just described.

In a time-sharing system, many programs can be stored in memory rather than just one. However, instead of requiring the programmer to load all system commands, programs, and data in advance, a time-sharing system allows them to be entered online—that is, entered dynamically by users

FIGURE 6.20

Configuration of a time-shared computing system

sitting at terminals and communicating interactively with the operating system. This configuration is shown in Figure 6.20.

The terminals are connected to the central computer via communication links and can be located anywhere. This new system design freed users from the "tyranny of geography." No longer did they have to go to the computer to hand in their deck of cards; the services of the computer were delivered directly to them via their terminal. However, now that the walls and doors of the computer center no longer provided security and access control, the "security guard/watchman" responsibility became an extremely important part of operating system design. (We will discuss the topic of computer security at length in Chapter 8.)

In a time-sharing system, a user would sit down at a terminal, log in, and initiate a program or make a request by entering a command:

>run   MyJob

In this example, the program called MyJob would be loaded into memory and would compete for the processor with all other ready programs. When the program was finished running, the system would again display a prompt (">") and wait for the next command. The user could examine the results of the last program, think for a while, and decide what to do next, rather than having to determine the entire sequence of operations in advance. For example, say there is a mistake in the program and we want to correct it using a text editor. We can enter the command

>edit   MyJob

which loads the text editor into memory, schedules it for execution, and causes the file system to load the file called MyJob.

However, one minor change was needed to make this new system work efficiently. In a "true" multiprogrammed environment, the only event, other than termination, that causes a program to be *suspended* (taken off the processor) is the execution of a slow I/O operation. What if the program currently executing is heavily *compute-bound*? That is, it does mostly computation and little or no I/O (for example, computing the value of π to a million decimal places). It could run for minutes or even hours before it is suspended and the processor is given to another program. During that time, all other programs would have to sit in the ready queue, waiting their turn. This is analogous to being in line at a bank behind someone depositing thousands of checks.

In a noninteractive environment, this situation may be acceptable because no one is sitting at a terminal waiting for output. In fact, it may even be desirable because a compute-bound job keeps the processor heavily utilized. In a time-sharing system, however, this waiting would be disastrous. There *are* users sitting at terminals communicating directly with the system and expecting an immediate response. If they do not get some type of response soon after entering a command, they may start banging on the keyboard and, eventually, give up. (Isn't that what you would do if the party at the other end of a telephone did not respond for several minutes?)

Therefore, to design a time-sharing system, we must make the following change to the multiprogrammed operating system described earlier. A program can keep the processor until *either* of the following two events occurs:

- It initiates an I/O operation.

- It has run for a maximum length of time, called a *time slice.*

Typically, this time slice is on the order of about a tenth of a second. This might seem like a minuscule amount of time, but it isn't. As we saw in Chapter 5, a typical time to fetch and execute a machine language instruction is about 1 nsec. Thus, in the 0.1-second time slice allocated to a program, a modern processor could execute roughly 100 million machine language instructions.

The basic idea in a time-sharing system is to service many users in a circular, round-robin fashion, giving each user a small amount of time and then moving on to the next. If there are not too many users on the system, the processor can get back to a user before he or she even notices any delay. For example, if there are five users on a system and each one gets a time slice of 0.1 second, a user will wait no more than 0.5 second for a response to a command. This delay would hardly be noticed. However, if 40 or 50 users were actively working on the system, they might begin to notice a 4- or 5-second delay and become irritated. (This is an example of the "virtual environment" created by the operating system *not* being helpful and supportive!) The number of simultaneous users that can be serviced by a time-sharing system depends on (1) the speed of the processor, (2) the time slice given to each user, and (3) the type of operation each user is doing (i.e., how many use the full time slice, and how many stop before that).

Time sharing was the dominant form of operating system during the 1970s and 1980s, and time-sharing terminals appeared throughout government offices, businesses, and campuses.

The early 1980s saw the appearance of the first personal computers, and in many business and academic environments the "dumb" terminal began to be replaced by these newer PCs. Initially, the PC was viewed as simply another type of terminal, and during its early days it was used primarily to access a central time-sharing system. However, as PCs became faster and more powerful, people soon realized that much of the computing being done on the centralized machine could be done much more conveniently and cheaply by the microcomputers sitting on their desktops.

During the late 1980s and the 1990s, computing rapidly changed from the centralized environment typical of batch, multiprogramming, and time-sharing systems to a *distributed environment* in which much of the computing was done remotely in the office, laboratory, classroom, and factory. Computing moved from the computer center out to where the real work was being done. The operating systems available for early personal computers were simple *single-user operating systems* that gave one user total access to the entire system. Because personal computers were so cheap, there was really no need for many users to share their resources, and the time-sharing and multiprogramming designs of the third generation became less important.

Although personal computers were relatively cheap (and were becoming cheaper all the time), many of the peripherals and supporting gear—laser printers, large disk drives, tape backup units, and specialized software packages—were not. In addition, e-mail was growing in importance, and stand-alone PCs were unable to communicate easily with other users and partake in this important new application. The personal computer era required a new approach to operating system design. It needed a virtual environment that supported both *local computation* and *remote access* to other users and shared resources.

This led to the development of a *fourth-generation* operating system called a network operating system (1985–present). A network operating system manages not only the resources of a single computer, but also the capabilities of a telecommunications system called a *local area network*, or *LAN* for short. (We will take a much closer look at these types of networks in Chapter 7.) A LAN is a network that is located in a geographically contiguous area such as a room, a building, or a campus. It is composed of personal computers (workstations), and special shared resources called *servers*, all interconnected via a high-speed link made of coaxial or fiber-optic cable. A typical LAN configuration is shown in Figure 6.21.

The users of the individual computers in Figure 6.21, called *clients*, can perform local computations without regard to the network. In this mode, the operating system provides exactly the same services described earlier: loading and executing programs and managing the resources of this one machine.

FIGURE 6.21

A local area network

However, a user can also access any one of the shared network resources just as though it were local. These resources are provided by a computer called a *server* and can include a special high-quality laser printer, a shared file system, or access to an international computer network. The system software does all the work needed to access those resources, hiding the details of communication and competition with other nodes for this shared resource.

Network operating systems create a virtual machine that extends beyond the boundaries of the local system on which the user is working. They let us access a huge pool of resources—computers, servers, and other users—exactly as though they were connected to our own computers. This fourth-generation virtual environment, exemplified by operating systems such as Windows 7, Windows Vista, Mac OS X, and Linux, is diagrammed in Figure 6.22.

One important variation of the network operating system is called a real-time operating system. During the 1980s and 1990s, computers got smaller and smaller, and it became common to place them inside other pieces of equipment to control their operation. These types of computers are called embedded systems; examples include computers placed inside automobile engines, microwave ovens, thermostats, assembly lines, airplanes, and watches.

For example, the Boeing 787 Dreamliner jet contains hundreds of embedded computer systems inside its engines, braking system, wings, landing gear, and cabin. The central computer controlling the overall operation of the airplane is connected by a LAN to these embedded computers that monitor system functions and send status information.

In all the operating systems described thus far, we have implied that the system satisfies requests for services and resources in the order received.

FIGURE 6.22

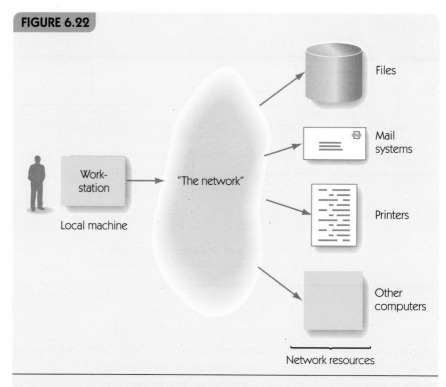

The virtual environment created by a network operating system

In some systems, however, certain requests are much more important than others, and when these important requests arrive, we must drop everything else to service them. Imagine that the central computer on our Boeing 787 receives two requests. The first request is from a cabin monitoring sensor that wants the central system to raise the cabin temperature a little for passenger comfort. The second message comes from the onboard collision detection system and says that another plane is approaching on the same flight path, and there is about to be a midair collision. It would like the central computer to take evasive action. Which request should be serviced next? Of course, the collision detection message, even though it arrived second.

A real-time operating system manages the resources of embedded computers that are controlling ongoing physical processes and that have requests that must be serviced within fixed time constraints. This type of operating system guarantees that it can service these important requests within that fixed amount of time. For example, it may guarantee that, regardless of what else it is currently doing, if a collision detection message arrives, the software implementing collision avoidance will be activated and executed within 50 milliseconds. Typically, the way that this guarantee is implemented is that all requests to a real-time operating system are *prioritized*. Instead of being handled in first-come, first-served order, they are handled in priority sequence, from most important to least important, where "importance" is defined in terms of the time-critical nature of the request. A real-time operating system lets passengers be uncomfortably cool for a few more seconds while it handles the problem of avoiding a midair collision.

6.4.3 The Future

The discussions in this chapter demonstrate that, just as there have been huge changes in hardware over the last 50 years, there have been equally huge changes in system software. We have progressed from a first-generation environment in which a user personally managed the computing hardware, using a complicated text-oriented command language, to current fourth-generation systems in which users can request services from anywhere in a network, using enormously powerful and easy-to-use graphical user interfaces.

And just as hardware capabilities continue to improve, there is a good deal of computer science research directed at further improving the high-level virtual environment created by a modern fourth-generation operating system. A fifth-generation operating system is certainly not far off.

These next-generation systems will have even more powerful user interfaces that incorporate not only text, touch, and graphics but photography, speech, fax, video, and TV. These *multimedia user interfaces* will interact with users and solicit requests in a variety of ways. Instead of point-and-click, a fifth-generation system will allow you to speak the command, "Please display my meeting schedule for May 6." The visual display may include separate windows for a verbal reminder about an important event, a map of how to reach the meeting site, and a digital photograph of the person with whom you are meeting. Just as text-only systems are now viewed as outmoded, today's text and graphics system may be viewed as too limiting for high-quality user/system interaction.

A fifth-generation operating system will typically be a massively **parallel processing system** that can efficiently manage computer systems containing hundreds or even thousands of processors (today's multicore machines typically contain only two, four, or six processors per chip). Such an operating system will need to recognize opportunities for parallel execution, send the separate tasks to the appropriate processor, and coordinate their concurrent execution, all in a way that is transparent to the user. On this virtual machine, a user will be unaware that multiple processors even exist except that programs run 10, 100, or 1,000 times faster. Without this type of software support, a massively parallel system would be a "naked parallel processor" just as difficult to work with as the "naked machine" discussed at the beginning of this chapter.

Finally, new fifth-generation operating systems will create a truly **distributed computing environment** in which users do not need to know the location of a given resource within the network. In current network operating systems, the details of how the communication is done are hidden, but the existence of separate nodes in the network are not (see Figure 6.22). The user is aware that a network exists and must specify the network node where the work is to be done. In a typical modern network operating system, a user issues the following types of commands:

- Retrieve file F on file server S.

- Run program P on machine M.

- Save file F on file server T.

- Print file F on print server Q.

Compare these commands with the instructions the manager of a business gives to an assistant: "Get this job done. I don't care how or where. Just do it, and when you are done, give me the results." The details of how and where to get the job done are left to the underling. The manager is concerned only with results.

In a truly distributed operating system, the user is the manager and the operating system the assistant, and the user does not care where or how the system satisfies a request as long as it gets done correctly. The users of a distributed system do not see a network of distinct sites or "local" and "remote" nodes. Instead, they see a single logical system that provides resources and services. The individual nodes and the boundaries between them are no longer visible to the user, who thinks only in terms of *what* must be done, not *where* it will be done or *which* node will do it. This situation is diagrammed in Figure 6.23. The concept of a single large collection of accessible resources whose location is not known to the user is often referred to as **cloud computing** after the model of the computational cloud shown in Figure 6.23.

In a distributed operating system, the commands shown earlier might be expressed as follows:

- Access file F wherever it is located.

- Run program P on any machine currently available.

- Save file F wherever there is sufficient room.

- Print file F on any laser printer that is not currently in use.

FIGURE 6.23

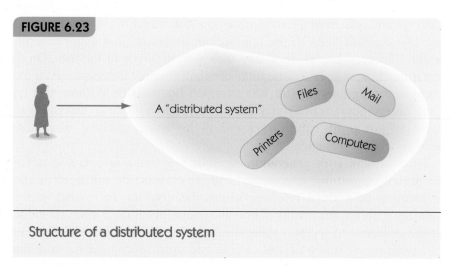

Structure of a distributed system

This is certainly the most powerful virtual environment we have yet described, and an operating system that creates such an environment would significantly enhance the productivity of all its users. These "fifth-generation dashboards" will make using the most powerful and most complex computer system as easy as driving a car—perhaps even easier. Surfing the Web or using smartphone apps gives us a good indication of what it will be like to work on a distributed system. When we click on a link, we have no idea at all where that information is located and, moreover, we don't care. We simply want that page or application to appear on our screen. To us, the Web behaves like one giant logical system even though it is spread out across hundreds of countries and hundreds of millions of computers.

Figure 6.24 summarizes the historical evolution of operating systems, much as Figure 1.8 summarized the historical development of computer hardware.

FIGURE 6.24

Generation	Approximate Dates	Major Advances
First	1945–1955	No operating system available Programmers operated the machine themselves
Second	1955–1965	Batch operating systems Improved system utilization Development of the first command language
Third	1965–1985	Multiprogrammed operating systems Time-sharing operating systems Increasing concern for protecting programs from damage by other programs Creation of privileged instructions and user instructions Interactive use of computers Increasing concern for security and access control First personal computer operating systems
Fourth	1985–present	Network operating systems Client-server computing Remote access to resources Graphical user interfaces Real-time operating systems Embedded systems
Fifth	??	Multimedia user interfaces Massively parallel operating systems Distributed computing environments

Some of the major advances in operating systems development

EXERCISES

1. Describe the user interface in other high-technology devices commonly found in the home or office, such as a DVD player, audio system, television, copier, or microwave oven. Pick one specific device and discuss how well its interface is designed and how easy it is to use. Does the device use the same techniques as computer system interfaces, such as menus and icons?

2. Can you think of situations where you might *want* to see the underlying hardware of the computer system? That is, you want to interact with the actual machine, not the virtual machine. How could you accomplish this? (Essentially, how could you bypass the operating system?)

3. Assume that you write a letter in English and have a friend translate it into Spanish. In this scenario, what is equivalent to the source program of Figure 6.4? The object program? The assembler?

4. Assume that memory cells 60 and 61 and register R currently have the following values:

   Register R: 13

   60: 472

   61: –1

   Using the instruction set in Figure 6.5, what is in register R and memory cells 60 and 61 after completion of each of the following operations? Assume that each instruction starts from the above conditions.

   a. LOAD 60
   b. STORE 60
   c. ADD 60
   d. COMPARE 61
   e. IN 61 (Assume that the user enters 50.)
   f. OUT 61

5. Assume that memory cell 79 contains the value +6. In addition, the symbol Z is equivalent to memory location 79. What is placed in register R by each of the following load commands?

   a. LOAD 79
   b. LOAD 6
   c. LOAD Z
   d. LOAD Z + 1 (Assume that this is allowed.)

6. Say we accidentally execute the following piece of data:

   .DATA 16387

   Describe exactly what happens. Assume that the format of machine language instructions on this system is the same format shown in Figure 6.13.

7. What is the assembly language equivalent of each of the following binary machine language instructions? Assume the format described in Figure 6.13 and the numeric op code values shown in Figure 6.5.

   a. 0101001100001100

   b. 0011000000000111

8. Is the following data generation pseudo-op legal or illegal? Why?

   THREE: .DATA 2

9. Using the instruction set shown in Figure 6.5, translate the following algorithmic primitives into assembly language code. Show all necessary .DATA pseudo-ops.

   a. Add 3 to the value of K
   b. Set K to the value $(L + 1) - (M + N)$
   c. If $K > 10$ then output the value of K
   d. If $(K > L)$ then output the value of K and increment K by 1

      otherwise output the value of L and increment L by 1
   e. Set K to 1

      Repeat the next two lines until $K > 100$

      Output the value of K

      Increment K by 1

      End of the loop

10. What, if anything, is the difference between the following two sequences of instructions for adding the value 2 to the variable *X*?

    LOAD X   INCREMENT X
    ADD TWO   INCREMENT X
    .
    .
    .
    TWO: .DATA 2

11. Look at the assembly language program in Figure 6.8. Is the statement CLEAR SUM on Line 2 necessary? Why or why not? Is the statement LOAD ZERO on Line 4 necessary? Why or why not?

12. Modify the program in Figure 6.8 so that it separately computes and prints the sum of all positive numbers and all negative numbers and stops when it sees the value 0. For example, given the input

    12, −2, 14, 1, −7, 0

    your program should output the two values 27 (the sum of the three positive values 12, 14, and 1) and −9 (the sum of the two negative numbers −2 and −7) and then halt.

13. Write a complete assembly language program (including all necessary pseudo-ops) that reads in a series of integers, one at a time, and outputs the largest and smallest values. The input will consist of a list of integer values containing exactly 100 numbers.

14. Assume that we are using the 16 distinct op codes in Figure 6.5. If we write an assembly language program that contains 100 instructions and our processor can do about 50,000 comparisons per second, what is the maximum time spent doing operation code translation using:

    a. Sequential search (Figure 2.9)
    b. Binary search (Figure 3.19)

    Which one of these two algorithms would you recommend using? Would your conclusions be significantly different if we were programming in an assembly language with 300 op codes rather than 16? If our program contained 50,000 instructions rather than 100?

15. What value is entered in the symbol table for the symbols AGAIN, ANS, X, and ONE in the following program? (Assume that the program is loaded beginning with memory location 0.)

	.BEGIN	
	--Here is the program	
	IN	X
	LOAD	X
AGAIN:	ADD	ANS
	SUBTRACT	ONE
	STORE	ANS
	OUT	ANS
	JUMP	AGAIN
	--Here are the data	
ANS:	.DATA	0
X:	.DATA	0
ONE:	.DATA	1
	.END	

16. Look at the assembly language program in Figure 6.8. Determine the physical memory address associated with every label in the symbol table. (Assume that the program is loaded beginning with memory location 0.)

17. Is the following pair of statements legal or illegal? Explain why.

    LABEL: .DATA   3
    LABEL: .DATA   4

    If it is illegal, will the error be detected during pass 1 or pass 2 of the assembly process?

18. What are some drawbacks in using passwords to limit access to a computer system? Describe some other possible ways that an operating system could limit access. In what type of application might these alternative safeguards be appropriate?

19. Why are authorization lists so sensitive that they must be encrypted and protected from unauthorized change? What kind of damage can occur if these files are modified in unexpected or unplanned ways?

20. Assume that any individual program spends about 50% of its time waiting for I/O operations to be completed. What percentage of time is the processor doing useful work (called *processor utilization*) if there are three programs loaded into memory? How many programs should we keep in memory if we want processor utilization to be at least 95%?

21. Here is an algorithm for calling a friend on the telephone:

Step	Operation
1.	Dial the phone and wait for either an answer or a busy signal
2.	If the line is not busy then do Steps 3 and 4
3.	Talk as long as you want
4.	Hang up the phone, you are done
5.	Otherwise (the line is busy)
6.	Wait exactly 1 minute
7.	Go back to Step 1 and try again

During execution, this algorithm could get into a situation where, as in the deadlock problem, no useful work can ever get done. Describe the problem, explain why it occurs, and suggest how it could be solved.

22. Explain why a batch operating system would be totally inadequate to handle such modern applications as airline reservations and automated teller machines.

23. In a time-sharing operating system, why is system performance so sensitive to the value that is selected for the time slice? Explain what type of system behavior would occur if the value selected for the time slice were too large. What if it were too small?

24. As hardware (processor/memory) costs became significantly cheaper during the 1980s and 1990s, time-sharing became a much less attractive design for operating systems. Explain why this is the case.

25. Determine whether the computer system on which you are working is part of a local area network. If it is, determine what servers are available and how they are used. Is there a significant difference between the ways you access local resources and remote resources?

26. The following four requests could come in to an operating system as it is running on a computer system:

- The clock in the computer has just "ticked," and we need to update a seconds counter.

- The program running on processor 2 is trying to perform an illegal operation code.

- Someone pulled the plug on the power supply, and the system will run out of power in 50 msec.

- The disk has just read the character that passed under the read/write head, and it wants to store it in memory before the next one arrives.

In what order should the operating system handle these requests?

Challenge Work

1. In Chapter 2, we wrote a number of algorithms that worked on a list of values rather than a single value. That is, our algorithm contained statements such as

   Get values for $A_1, A_2, \ldots, A_N$, the list to be searched

   In statements like this, we are dealing with individual data items such as A_1 and A_2, but they are also part of a collection of items, the list called A. A collection of related data items is called a *data structure*. High-level programming languages like C++, Java, and Python provide users with a rich collection of data structures that go by such names as arrays, sets, and lists. We can program with these structures just as though they were an inherent part of the hardware of the computer. However, the discussions in the previous two chapters have shown that data structures such as lists of numbers do *not* exist directly in hardware. There are no machine language instructions that can carry out the type of algorithmic command shown in the pseudocode statement just given. When you write an instruction that uses a structure such as a list, the language translator (that is, the assembler or compiler) must map it into what is available on the hardware—the machine language instruction set shown in Figure 5.19 and the sequential addresses in our memory. (This is another good example of the virtual environment created by a piece of system software.)

Write an assembly language program to sum up a list of 50 numbers that are read in and stored in memory. Here is the algorithm you are to translate:

Read in 50 numbers $A_1, A_2, \ldots, A_{50}$

Set *Sum* to 0

Set *i* to 1

While the value of *i* is less than or equal to 50

    $Sum = Sum + A_i$

    $i = i + 1$

End of the loop

Write out the value of Sum

Stop

To implement this algorithm, you must simulate the concept of a list of numbers using the assembly language resources that are available. (*Hint:* Remember that in the Von Neumann architecture there is no distinction between an instruction and a piece of data. Therefore, an assembly language instruction such as LOAD A can be treated as data and modified by other instructions.)

ADDITIONAL RESOURCES

CourseMate **For additional print and/or online resources relevant to this chapter, visit the Computer Science CourseMate at login.cengagebrain.com.**

Computer Networks, the Internet, and the World Wide Web

7.1 Introduction

Every once in a while there occurs a technological innovation of such importance that it forever changes society and the way its people live, work, and communicate. The invention of the printing press by Johannes Gutenberg in the mid-fifteenth century was one such development. The books and manuscripts it produced helped fuel the renewed interest in science, art, and literature that came to be called the Renaissance, an era that influenced Western civilization for more than 500 years. The Industrial Revolution of the eighteenth and early nineteenth centuries made consumer goods such as clothing, furniture, and cooking utensils affordable to the middle class, and changed European and American societies from rural to urban and from agricultural to industrial. More recently, we are certainly aware of the massive social changes, both good and bad, wrought by inventions like the telephone, automobile, television, and computer.

Many people feel that we are witnessing yet another breakthrough, one with the potential to make as great a change in our lives as those just mentioned. This innovation is the *computer network*—computers connected together for the purpose of exchanging personal messages, resources, and information. During the early stages of network development, the only information exchanged was text such as e-mail, database records, and technical papers. However, the material sent across a network today can be just about anything—television and radio shows, videos, music, photographs, and movies, to name just a few. If information can be represented in the 0s and 1s of binary (as described in Section 4.2), it can be transmitted across a network.

The possibilities created by this free flow of data are enormous. Networks can equalize access to information and eliminate the concept of "information haves" and "information have-nots." Students in a poorly funded rural school would no longer be handicapped by an out-of-date library collection. A physician practicing in an emerging economy would be able to transmit medical records, test results, and X-ray images to specialists anywhere in the world and have immediate access to the databases and reference works of major medical centers. Small-business owners could use the network to locate suppliers and customers on an international scale. Researchers would have the same ability to communicate with experts in their discipline whether they were in New York, New Delhi, or New Guinea.

Networking can also foster the growth of democracy and global understanding by providing unrestricted access to newspapers, magazines, radio, and television, as well as supporting the unfettered exchange of diverse and competing thoughts, ideas, and opinions. Because we live in an increasingly information-oriented society, network technology contains the seeds of massive social and economic change, as was seen in Tunisia, Egypt, Libya, and Bahrain in early 2011, in what some journalists are calling a "Twitter Revolution." It is no surprise that during civil uprisings, political leaders who want to prevent the dissemination of opposing ideas often move quickly to restrict both Internet and Web access.

In Chapter 6, we saw how system software can create a user-friendly "virtual machine" on top of the raw hardware of a single computer. In today's world, computers are seldom used as isolated, stand-alone devices, and the modern view of a virtual machine has expanded into a worldwide collection of interconnected systems and resources. In this chapter, we take a detailed look at the underlying technology of computer networks—what they are, how they work, and the benefits they can bring. We also examine the most widely used network, the Internet, and its most important application, the World Wide Web.

7.2 Basic Networking Concepts

A computer network is a set of independent computer systems connected by telecommunication links for the purpose of sharing information and resources. The individual computers on a network are referred to as nodes or *hosts*, and they can range in size from smartphones, tablets, and tiny laptops to massively parallel supercomputers. In this section, we describe some of the basic technical characteristics of a computer network.

7.2.1 Communication Links

The communication links used to build a network vary widely in physical characteristics, error rate, and transmission speed. In the approximately 45 years that networks have existed, telecommunications facilities have undergone enormous changes.

In the early days of networking, the most common way to transmit data was via switched, dial-up telephone lines. The term *switched, dial-up* means that when you dial a telephone number, a circuit (i.e., a path) is temporarily established between the caller and callee. This circuit lasts for the duration of the call, and when you hang up it is terminated.

The voice-oriented dial-up telephone network was originally a totally *analog* medium. As we first explained in Chapter 4, this means that the

Blogs

One of the most important Web applications is the *blog*, a contraction of the term *Web log*. A **blog** is a Web-based publication consisting of virtually any periodic articles that its writer(s) want to share with the general public. Sometimes it contains nothing more than a daily journal—"what I did today." More commonly, the articles are political, social, or cultural essays that reflect the opinions and biases of the blog author(s). Whereas some blogs are produced by a community of like-minded people sharing responsibility for writing and posting articles, the majority are simply the thoughts and feelings of individuals with a computer and the necessary "blogware"— software for editing, organizing, and publishing on the Web. (According to Technorati, a blog rating and tracking Web site, as of mid-2010 there were about 126 million blogs worldwide with about 175,000 new sites coming online daily!)

Our history is filled with stories of individual crusaders who published fiery newsletters supporting or decrying some governmental or social policy. For example, the *Federalist Papers* by Alexander Hamilton and James Madison were written in support of the proposed U.S. Constitution. The *Liberator* was a fervent antislavery newsletter published in Boston by William Lloyd Garrison, a Quaker abolitionist. However, there was a limit to the audience that these early crusaders could reach, set by the cost of printing and the time required to distribute these newsletters to readers. (At the peak of its influence, the *Liberator* had a circulation of fewer than 3,000.) The Web has changed all that. It costs virtually nothing to write and post your thoughts on a Web page, and if your ideas become widely discussed (perhaps by being mentioned on TV, radio, newspapers, or shared via Facebook or Twitter), a blog might be read each day by millions of readers.

physical quantity used to represent information, usually voltage level, is continuous and can take on any value. An example of this is shown in Figure 7.1(a). Although analog is fine for transmitting the human voice, which varies continuously in pitch and volume, a computer produces *digital* information—specifically, a sequence of 0s and 1s, as shown in Figure 7.1(b).

For the binary signals of Figure 7.1(b) to be transmitted via a switched, dial-up telephone line, the signal must be restructured into the analog representation of Figure 7.1(a). The device that accomplishes this is a modem, which modulates, or alters, a standard analog signal called a *carrier wave* so that it encodes binary information. The modem modifies the physical characteristics of the carrier wave, such as amplitude or frequency, so that it is in one of two distinct states, one state representing 0 and the other state representing 1. Figure 7.2 shows how a modem can modulate the amplitude (height) of a carrier wave to encode the binary signal 1010.

At the other end of the transmission line, a modem performs the inverse operation, which is called *demodulation*. (Modem is a contraction of the two terms *mo*dulation and *dem*odulation.) It takes the received waveform, separates the carrier from the encoded digital signal, and passes the digital data on to the computer.

FIGURE 7.1

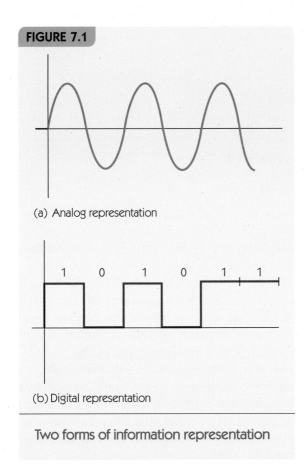

(a) Analog representation

(b) Digital representation

Two forms of information representation

FIGURE 7.2

Modulation of a carrier to encode binary information

Initially, these analog encoding and decoding operations could not be done very quickly because of the high error rate and low capacity, or **bandwidth**, of a switched telephone line. In the early days of telecommunications—the 1970s and 1980s—the rate at which information could be sent and received via a phone line was limited to about 1,200–9,600 bits per second (bps). Advances in dial-up modem design produced devices that can transmit at 56,000 bps, or 56 Kbps, an order-of-magnitude increase. However, this is still much too slow to handle the transmission of multimedia-based documents such as Web pages, MP3 files, and streaming video.

The dial-up telephone system is still used occasionally for remote access to networks, and some computers still come equipped with a built-in 56 Kbps modem. However, their limited speed makes dial-up links inconvenient for applications where speed is vital or you are sending large volumes of data, and the role of analog telephone lines in data communications is rapidly diminishing.

A technology called broadband is rapidly replacing modems and analog phone lines for data communications to and from our homes, schools, and offices. The term *broadband* generally refers to any communication link with a transmission rate exceeding 256,000 bps. In the case of home users, there are currently two widely available broadband options—digital subscriber line (DSL) and cable modem.

A digital subscriber line (DSL) uses the same wires that carry regular telephone signals into your home, and therefore is provided by either your local telephone company or someone certified to act as its intermediary. Although it uses the same wires, a DSL signal uses a different set of frequencies, and it transmits digital rather than analog signals. Therefore, the voice traffic generated by talking with a friend on the phone does not interfere with a Web page being simultaneously downloaded by someone else in the family. Furthermore, unlike the modem which requires that you explicitly establish a connection (dial a number) and end a connection (hang up), a DSL is a permanent "always-on" link, which eliminates the aggravating delay of dialing and waiting for the circuit to be established.

A digital subscriber line is often *asymmetric*. This means it does not have the same transmission speed in the download direction (from the network to your computer) as in the upload direction (from your computer to the network). That is because most users consume much more data than they generate. For example, to obtain a Web page, your computer sends a request message to the machine with that page. (It does this by sending the address of that page, such as *www.macalester.edu*.) This request message is small and contains only a few dozen characters. However, the Web page you receive—complete with applets, graphics, and plug-ins—could contain millions of bits. To handle this imbalance, a DSL provides greater bandwidth coming in to your computer than going out. Typical DSL speeds are 5–15 million bits per second (Mbps) for downloads and 1–2 Mbps for uploads—still much more than is available from a dial-up modem.

The second option for broadband communications is a cable modem. This technology makes use of the links that deliver cable TV signals into your home, so it is offered by cable TV providers. Some of the link capacity previously allocated for TV signals is now used for data communications. Like a DSL, a cable modem also provides an always-on link and offers speeds slightly higher than those available from DSL—about 10–20 Mbps for downloads and 1–3 Mbps for uploads.

In the commercial and office environment, the most widely used broadband technology is Ethernet. Ethernet was developed in the mid-1970s by computer scientists at the Xerox PARC research center in Palo Alto, California. It was originally designed to operate at 10 Mbps using coaxial cable. However, 10 Mbps is too slow for many applications, so in the early 1990s researchers developed a "new and improved" version, called Fast Ethernet, which transmits at 100 Mbps across coaxial cable, fiber-optic cable, or regular twisted-pair copper wire.

Because even 100 Mbps may not be fast enough for multimedia applications, computer science researchers began investigating the concept of gigabit networking—transmission lines that support speeds of 1 billion bits per second (Gbps). In the early 1990s, the U.S. government funded a long-term research project called NREN, the *National Research and Education Network*. One of its goals was to investigate the design and implementation of wide area gigabit data networks. The project was successful, and in 1998 the first international gigabit Ethernet standard was adopted by the IEEE (Institute of Electrical and Electronics Engineers), an international professional society responsible for, among other things, developing industrial standards in the area of telecommunications. The standard supports communication on an Ethernet cable at 1,000 Mbps (1 Gbps), 100 times faster than the original 10 Mbps standard. Most classrooms and office buildings today are wired to support 10 Mbps, 100 Mbps, and 1,000 Mbps—18,000 times faster than a 56K modem! In addition, virtually every PC sold today comes with a built-in Ethernet interface, and new homes and dorm rooms are often equipped with Ethernet links.

However, not willing to rest on their laurels (and realizing that even faster networks will be needed to support future research and development), work immediately began on a new *10-gigabit Ethernet* standard, a version of Ethernet with a data rate of 10 billion bits per second. That standard was adopted by the IEEE in 2003. To get an idea of how fast that is, in a single second a 10 Gbps Ethernet network could transmit the entire contents of 1,700 books, each 300 pages long. In June 2010, the IEEE ratified the *100-gigabit Ethernet* standard defining a local area network that can transmit data at the almost unimaginable rate of 100 billion bits per second!

Do applications truly need to transmit information at billions of bits per second? To answer that question, let's determine how long it takes to transmit a high-resolution color image, such as a CAT scan, a satellite image, or a single movie frame, at different transmission speeds. As described in Section 4.2, a high-resolution color image contains at least 5 million picture elements (pixels), and each pixel is encoded using 8–24 bits. If we assume 16 bits per pixel, then a single uncompressed image would contain at least 80,000,000 bits of data. If the image is compressed before it is sent, and the compression ratio is 10:1 (see Section 4.2 for a definition of compression ratio), then we must transmit a total of 8 million bits to send this single image. Figure 7.3 shows the time needed to send this amount of information at the speeds discussed in this chapter.

Figure 7.3 clearly demonstrates the need for high-speed communications to support applications such as video-on-demand and medical imaging. Receiving an 8 Mb image using a 56 Kbps modem takes 2.4 minutes, an agonizingly long time. (You have probably had the experience of waiting for what seemed like forever as a Web page s-l-o-w-l-y appeared on your screen.) That same 8 Mb image can be received in 4 seconds using a DSL or cable modem with a download speed of 2 Mbps, 0.8 second using a 10 Mbps Ethernet, and a blazing 0.08 second with 100 Mbps Ethernet.

FIGURE 7.3

Line Type	Speed	Time to Transmit 8 Million Bits (One Compressed Image)	
Dial-up phone line	56 Kbps	2.4	minutes
DSL line, cable modem	2 Mbps	4	seconds
Ethernet	10 Mbps	0.8	second
Fast Ethernet	100 Mbps	0.08	second
Gigabit Ethernet	1 Gbps	0.008	second
10-gigabit Ethernet	10 Gbps	0.0008	second
100-gigabit Ethernet	100 Gbps	0.00008	second

Transmission time of an image at different transmission speeds

However, even 0.08 second might not be fast enough if an application requires the rapid transmission of either multiple images or a huge amount of data in a short period of time. For example, to watch a real-time video image without flicker or delay, you need to stream at least 24 frames per second. Any less and the human eye notices the time delay between frames. If each frame contains 8 Mb, you need a bandwidth of 8,000,000 $\times$ 24 = 192 Mbps. This is beyond the speed of modems, DSL, cable modems, and even 100 Mbps Ethernet, but it is achievable using gigabit networks. These high-speed networks are widely used in such data-intensive applications as exchanging 3D medical images, transmitting weather satellite data, and supporting collaboration among researchers sharing astronomical star images.

An extremely important development in the field of telecommunications is the rapid growth of wireless data communication using radio, microwave, and infrared signals. In the wireless world, users no longer need to be physically connected to a wired network to access data, just as mobile phones liberated telephone users. Using wireless, you can be sipping coffee in your favorite café, riding in a car, lounging at the beach, or working on the factory floor and still send and receive e-mail, access online databases, or surf the Web. The ability to deliver data to users regardless of their location is called mobile computing.

There are two forms of wireless data communications. In a wireless local area network (WLAN), a user transmits from his or her computer to a local wireless *base station*, often referred to as a *wireless router*, that is no more than a few hundred feet away. This base station is then connected to a traditional wired network, such as a DSL or cable modem, to provide full Internet access. This is the type of wireless configuration typically found in a home, library, office, or coffee shop because it is cheap, simple, low powered, and easy to install. A typical local wireless configuration is shown in the diagram on the next page.

One of the most widely used standards for wireless local access is called Wi-Fi, short for Wireless Fidelity. It is also referred to by its official name, the IEEE 802.11 wireless network standards. Wi-Fi is used to connect a computer to the Internet when it is within range (typically 150–300 feet or 45–90 meters) of a wireless base station, often advertised in stores and shops as a Wi-Fi hot spot (a router). Wi-Fi systems generally use the 2.4 GHz radio band for communications and support download transmission speeds of about 10–50 Mbps. Researchers are investigating the use of higher radio frequencies to support high-speed gigabit Wi-Fi communication.

A relatively new development in wireless networking is metropolitan Wi-Fi service. A number of cities in the United States, Europe, and Asia have installed Wi-Fi routers every few blocks throughout the city, often on top of telephone poles or building roofs. These routers provide convenient, low-cost wireless Internet access to all residents.

Another popular wireless standard is Bluetooth. It is a low-power wireless standard used to communicate between devices located quite close to each other, typically no more than 30–50 feet (10–15 meters). Bluetooth is often used to support communication between wireless computer peripherals, such as printers, mice, and keyboards and a laptop or desktop system close by. Bluetooth also supports information exchange between digital devices such as mobile phones, cameras, and video game consoles.

Although Wi-Fi is great for communicating with a nearby router, its transmission limitations mean it cannot provide mobile Internet access from a car or outdoor site far from any base station. To handle this type of wireless communications, we need a different type of network called a wireless wide area network (WWAN). In this type of network, the computer (often a tablet or smartphone) transmits messages to a remote base station provided by a telecommunications company, which may be located many miles away. The base station is usually a large cellular antenna placed on top of a tower or building, providing both long-distance voice and data communication services to any system within sight of the tower. One of the most popular wide area wireless technologies is called 4G. It offers voice services as well as data communication at rates of 5 to 20 Mbps, comparable to DSL or cable modem. Other popular WWAN technologies include WiMAX and LTE.

Although wireless data communication is an exciting development in computer networking, it is not without problems that must be studied and solved. For example, some forms of wireless, such as microwaves, are line of sight, traveling only in a straight line. Because of the curvature of the Earth, transmitters must be placed on top of hills or tall buildings, and they cannot be more than about 10–50 miles (15–80 kilometers) apart, depending on height. Other types of wireless media suffer from environmental problems; they are strongly affected by rain and fog, cannot pass through obstacles such as buildings or large trees, and have higher error rates than wired communication. Although a few random "clicks" and "pops" do not disrupt voice communications over a mobile phone, it can be disastrous in data communications. For example, if you are transmitting data at 10 million bits per second (Mbps), a breakup on the line that lasts only one-tenth of a second could potentially cause the loss of one million bits of data. Wireless is often slower than wired communication (a few Mbps rather than hundreds of Mbps or Gbps), which may make it inappropriate for the transfer of large amounts of data. Finally, there is the issue of security. Currently, it is not difficult to intercept wireless transmissions and gain unauthorized access to user messages. All of these are ongoing concerns being investigated by the computer science and telecommunications research community. However, the rapid increase in the number of mobile devices along with the ease and convenience of remote access guarantees the continuing growth and popularity of wireless data communications.

7.2.2 Local Area Networks

There are two types of computer networks. A local area network (LAN) connects hardware devices such as computers, printers, and storage devices that are all in close proximity. (A diagram of a LAN was provided in Figure 6.21.) Examples of LANs include the interconnection of machines in one

Practice Problems

1. Show how the 4-bit digital value 0110 is converted to an analog signal by a modem that modulates the *frequency* of a carrier wave, rather than its amplitude.

2. Consider an uncompressed 1,200 × 780 image, with each pixel stored using an 8-bit gray scale representation. If we want to transmit the entire image in under 1 second, what is the minimum acceptable transmission speed?

3. How long would it take to transmit that 1,200 × 780 image from Practice Problem 2 using a 1-gigabit Ethernet network?

Ubiquitous Computing

The rapid growth of wireless communications, along with the availability of extremely cheap microprocessors, has led to an exciting new area of computer science research called **ubiquitous computing**, also called *pervasive computing*. In the early days of computing, a single large mainframe served many users. In the PC era, a single desktop machine served a single user. In the ubiquitous computing model, many computers work together to serve a single user, and rather than being perched on a desktop, they become nearly invisible. The idea is that computers will become so commonplace that they will blend into the background and disappear from our consciousness, much as electricity has today. The goal is to create a system that is embedded in the environment, providing its service in a seamless, efficient manner.

Computers will be located inside our appliances, furnaces, lights, clocks, and even clothing to provide useful services in a transparent fashion. For example, your car could automatically inform the heating and electrical system in your home that you will be arriving shortly so please turn up the heat and activate the entrance lights. All of this could be done without requiring any user intervention.

Topics of research in this area include such things as *wearable computing, intelligent appliances,* and *smart homes.* As described by Mark Weiser of Xerox, "Ubiquitous computing is invisible, *everywhere* computing that does not sit on the desktop but lies deep inside the woodwork."

room, in the same office building, or on a single campus. An important characteristic of a LAN is that the owner of the computers is also the owner of the means of communications. Because a LAN is located entirely on private property, the owner can install telecommunications facilities without having to purchase services from a third-party provider such as a phone or cable company, although a third-party provider is needed to connect the LAN to the outside world.

The previous section described how a wireless local network is set up using Wi-Fi and a router connected to a wired network. Here we take a look at the properties of that wired network. Wired LANs can be constructed using a number of different interconnection strategies, as seen in Figure 7.4. In the bus topology, Figure 7.4(a), all nodes are connected to a single, shared communication line. If two or more nodes use the link at the same time, the messages collide and are unreadable, and, therefore, nodes must take turns using the line. The cable modem technology described in Section 7.2.1 is

FIGURE 7.4

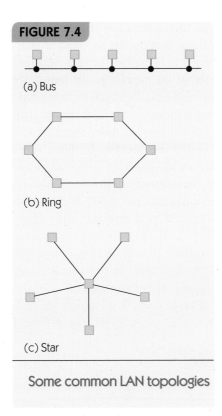

(a) Bus

(b) Ring

(c) Star

Some common LAN topologies

based on a bus topology. A number of homes are all connected to the same shared coaxial cable. If two users want to download a Web page at the exact same time, then the effective transmission rate is lower than expected because one of them must wait.

The **ring** topology of Figure 7.4(b) connects the network nodes in a circular fashion, with messages circulating around the ring in either a clockwise or counterclockwise direction until they reach their destination. Finally, the **star** network, Figure 7.4(c), has a single central node that is connected to all other sites. This central node can route information directly to any other node in the LAN. Messages are first sent to the central site, which then forwards them to the correct location.

There are many different LAN technologies available in the marketplace, but the most widely used is Ethernet, which you learned about in the previous section. It is the model that we will use to describe the general behavior of all LANs.

Ethernet uses the bus topology of Figure 7.4(a). To send a message, a node places the message, including the destination address, on the cable. Because the line is shared, the message is received by every other node (assuming no one else sent at the exact same time and garbled our data). Each node looks at the destination address to see if it is the intended recipient. If so, it accepts the message; if not, it discards it.

There are two ways to construct an Ethernet LAN. In the first method, called the shared cable, a wire (such as twisted-pair copper wire, coaxial cable, or fiber-optic cable) is literally strung around and through a building. Users tap into the cable at its nearest point using a device called a *transceiver*, as shown in Figure 7.5(a). Because of technical constraints, an Ethernet cable has a maximum allowable length. For a large building or campus, it may be necessary to install two or more separate cables and connect them via hardware devices called repeaters or bridges.

A repeater is a device that simply amplifies and forwards a signal. In Figure 7.5(b), if the device connecting the two LANs is a repeater, then every message on LAN1 is forwarded to LAN2, and vice versa. Thus, when two Ethernet LANs are connected by a repeater, they function exactly as if they were a single network.

A bridge is a "smarter" device that has knowledge about the nodes located on each separate network. It examines every message to see if it should be forwarded from one network to another. For example, if node A is sending a message to node B, both of which are on LAN1, then the bridge

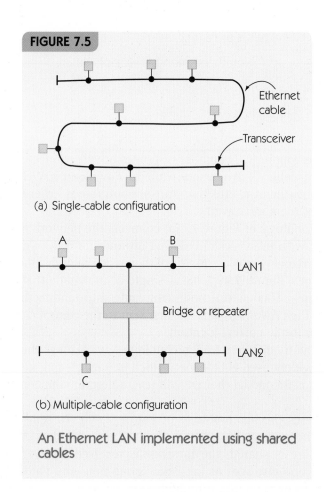

FIGURE 7.5

(a) Single-cable configuration

(b) Multiple-cable configuration

An Ethernet LAN implemented using shared cables

does nothing with the message. However, if node A on LAN1 is sending a message to node C on LAN2, then the bridge copies the message from LAN1 onto LAN2 so node C is able to see it and read it.

In the second approach to constructing an Ethernet LAN, there is no shared cable strung throughout the building. Instead, there is a box called a switch located in a room called a *wiring closet*. The switch contains a number of *ports*, with a wire leading from each port to an Ethernet interface in the wall of a room in the building, or to a wireless router somewhere in the building. To connect to the network, we first activate that port, typically by flipping an on/off button, and then plug our machine into the wall socket. This approach is shown in Room 101 of Figure 7.6. Alternately, we could use Wi-Fi to transmit from our computer to a wireless router located somewhere in the building. This router would then connect to one of the Ethernet ports in the switch. This approach is shown in Room 103 of Figure 7.6. In either case, it is no longer necessary to climb into the ceiling or crawl through ductwork looking for the cable because the shared cable is located inside the switch instead of inside the building walls. That is why switches are the most widely used technique for constructing LANs.

FIGURE 7.6

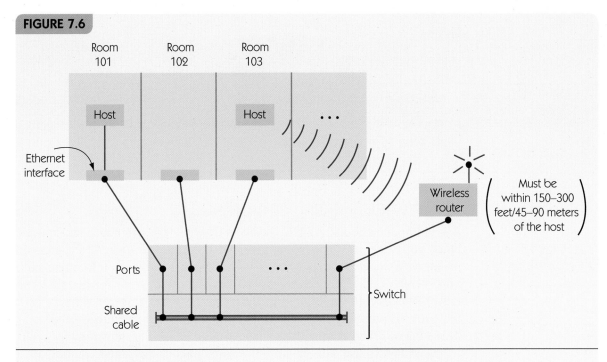

An Ethernet LAN implemented using a switch

Practice Problems

1. Explain why message collisions would or would not occur on local area networks that used the ring topology of Figure 7.4(b) or the star topology of Figure 7.4(c).

2. What changes, if any, must be made to our description of the Ethernet protocol to allow a message to be sent by node A on a local area network to *every other* node on that same LAN? This operation is called **broadcasting**.

3. Assume you are given the following configuration of three local area networks, called LAN1, LAN2, and LAN3, connected by bridges B1 and B2.

   Explain exactly how node A on LAN1 sends a message to node B on LAN3.

4. What security issues could arise from the use of an Ethernet-like bus topology to implement a local area network?

7.2.3 Wide Area Networks

A **wide area network (WAN)** connects devices that are not in close proximity but rather are across town, across the country, or across the ocean. Because WANs cross public property, users must purchase telecommunications services, like those described in Section 7.2.1, from an external provider. Typically, these are **dedicated point-to-point lines** or wireless links that directly connect two machines, not the shared channels found on a LAN such as Ethernet. The typical structure of a WAN is shown in Figure 7.7.

Most WANs use a **store-and-forward, packet-switched** technology to deliver messages. Unlike a LAN, in which a message is broadcast on a shared channel and is received by all nodes, a WAN message must "hop" from one node to another to make its way from source to destination. The unit of transmission in a WAN is a **packet**—an information block with a fixed

FIGURE 7.7

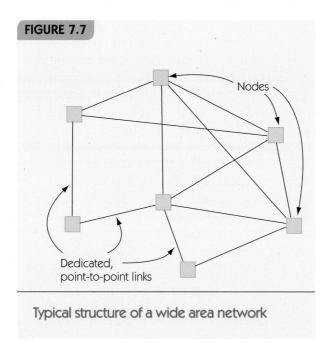

Typical structure of a wide area network

maximum size that is transmitted through the network as a single unit. If you send a short message, then it can usually be transmitted as a single packet. However, if you send a long message, the source node may "chop" it into N separate packets (such as the first 1,000 characters, the next 1,000 characters, and so on) and send each packet independently through the network. When the destination node has received all N packets, it reassembles them into a single message.

For example, assume the following six-node WAN:

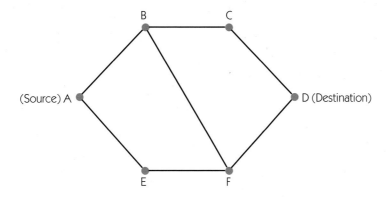

To send a message from source node A to destination node D, the message could go from A → B → C → D. Alternately, the message may travel from A → B → F → D or A → E → F → D. The exact route is determined by the network, not the user, based on which path can deliver the message most quickly. If the message is large, it may be broken up into multiple packets, and each one may take a different route.

One of the nicest features of a store-and-forward network is that the failure of a single line or a single node does not necessarily bring down the entire network. For example, assume the line connecting node B to node C in the previous diagram crashes. Nodes B and C can still communicate via the route B → F → D → C. Similarly, if node F fails completely, nodes E and D, located on either side of F, can still exchange messages. However, instead of talking via node F, they now use the route E → A → B → C → D.

Reliability and fault tolerance were the reasons that WANs were first studied in the late 1960s and early 1970s. The U.S. military was interested in communication systems that could survive and function even if some of their components were destroyed, as might happen in time of war or civil unrest. Their research ultimately led to the creation of the Internet. (We will have much more to say about the history of networking and the Internet later in this chapter.)

7.2.4 Overall Structure of the Internet

We have defined two classes of networks, LANs and WANs, but all real-world networks, including the Internet, are a complex mix of both network types.

For example, a company or a college would typically have one or more LANs connecting its local computers—a Computer Science department LAN, a humanities building LAN, an administration building LAN, and so forth. These individual LANs might then be interconnected into a wide area "company network" that allows users to send e-mail to other employees in the company and access the resources of other departments. These individual networks are interconnected via a device called a router. Like the bridge in Figure 7.5(b), a router transmits messages between two distinct networks. However, unlike a bridge, which connects two identical types of networks, routers can transmit information between networks that use totally different communication techniques—much as an interpreter functions between two people who speak different languages. For example, a router, not a bridge, is used to send messages from a wireless Wi-Fi network to a wired Ethernet LAN (as discussed in the previous section), or from an Ethernet LAN to a packet-switched, store-and-forward WAN. We can see this type of interconnection structure in Figure 7.8.

The configuration in Figure 7.8 allows the employees of a company or the students of a college to communicate with each other, or to access local resources. But how do these people reach users outside their institution, or access remote resources such as Web pages that are not part of their own network? Furthermore, how does an individual home user who is not part of any company or college network access the larger community? The answer is that a user's individual computer or a company's private network is connected to the world through an Internet service provider (ISP). An ISP is a business whose purpose is to provide access from a private network (such as a corporate or university network) to the Internet or from an individual's computer to the Internet. This access occurs through a WAN owned by the ISP, as shown in Figure 7.9. An ISP typically provides many ways for a user to connect to this

FIGURE 7.8

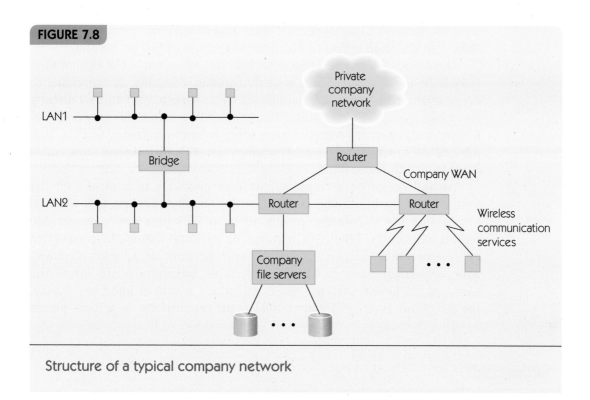

Structure of a typical company network

FIGURE 7.9

Structure of a network using an ISP

network, from 56 Kbps modems to dedicated broadband telecommunication links with speeds in excess of hundreds of millions of bits per second.

The scope of networking worldwide is so vast, a single ISP cannot possibly hope to directly connect a single campus, company, or individual to every other computer in the world, just as a single airport cannot directly serve every possible destination. Therefore, ISPs (that is, ISP networks) are hierarchical, interconnecting to each other in multiple layers, or tiers, that provide ever-expanding geographic coverage. This hierarchical structure is diagrammed in Figure 7.10.

An individual or a company network connects to a *local ISP*, the first level in the hierarchy. This local ISP typically connects to a *regional* or *national ISP* that interconnects all local ISPs in a single geographic region or country. Finally, a regional or national ISP might connect to an *international ISP*, also called a *tier-1 network* or an *Internet backbone*, which provides global coverage. This hierarchy is similar to the standard telephone system. When you place a call to another country, the telephone line from your home or office connects to a local phone

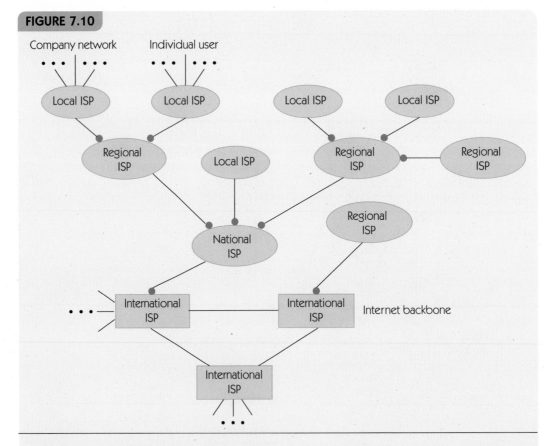

FIGURE 7.10

Hierarchy of Internet service providers

switching center, which establishes a connection to a regional switching center, which establishes a connection to a national switching center. This national center has high-speed connections to similar national switching centers in other countries, which are connected, in turn, to regional and then local switches to establish a connection to the phone you are calling. The diagram in Figure 7.10 is a pictorial representation of that enormously complex telecommunications entity we call the Internet. The Internet is not a single computer network; instead, it is a huge interconnected "network of networks" that includes nodes, LANs, WANs, bridges, routers, and multiple levels of ISPs.

Firewalls

In April 2011, Sony informed its 77 million PlayStation users that their credit card data, billing addresses, and personal data could have been stolen by thieves who hacked into the company's private network. Sadly, this type of information-based crime is becoming all too common.

For hundreds of years, the term *firewall* meant a physical barrier installed in a building or vehicle to prevent the spread of fire and smoke. That meaning has expanded in the past few years with the growth of computer networks and the increasingly important role they play in such areas as national security, medicine, banking, and e-commerce. Because of networks, it is no longer possible to prevent the theft of information by stationing guards at the front door of your business, as the perpetrators may be thousands of miles away sitting at a keyboard. This has led to a good deal of research into the concept of computer **firewalls**, devices placed at the entry points to a company's private network to protect it from unauthorized access. These firewalls implement the security guidelines set up by the company, guidelines such as *address filtering*, specifying which Internet addresses to allow in and which to keep out, and *service filtering*, listing exactly which applications on your system should or should not be accessed over the network.

However, like a determined spammer who is constantly outwitting the latest spam filter, the determined hacker is committed to learning about and breaching whatever new firewall algorithm has been developed for the marketplace. It is an ongoing game of cat and mouse and, so far, it appears that the criminal community's mouse is keeping one step ahead of the IT developers' cat.

We'll have more to say about security issues in Chapter 8.

FIGURE 7.11

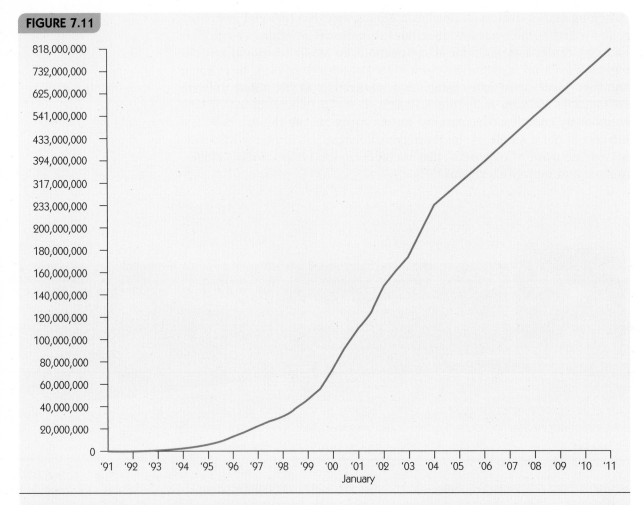

Internet domain survey host count graph

Source: Internet systems consortium (*www.isc.org*)

As of early 2011, there were about 818 million nodes (hosts) and hundreds of thousands of separate networks located in more than 230 countries. A graph of the number of host computers on the Internet over the last 20 years is shown in Figure 7.11. (This figure is really an undercount because there are numerous computers located behind protective firewalls that will not respond to any external attempts to be counted.)

How does something as massive as the Internet actually work? How is it possible to get 818 million machines around the world to function efficiently as a single system? We answer that important question in the next section.

7.3 Communication Protocols

When you talk on the telephone, there is an accepted set of procedures that you should follow. For example, when you answer the phone, you should say "Hello," and then wait for the individual on the other end to respond. The conversation continues until someone says "Goodbye," at which time both parties hang up. You might call this "telephone etiquette"—the conventions that allow orderly exchanges to take place. Imagine what would happen if someone were unaware of them. Such a person might pick up the phone but not say anything. Hearing silence, the caller would be totally confused, think the call did not get through, and hang up.

Similar etiquette applies to computer networks. To have meaningful communications, we need a set of procedures that specifies how the exchanges will take place. This "network etiquette" is achieved by means of network protocols.

In networking, a protocol is a mutually agreed-upon set of rules, conventions, and agreements for the efficient and orderly exchange of information. Even though the Internet has hundreds of millions of machines made by dozens of manufacturers and located in hundreds of countries, they can all exchange messages correctly and efficiently for one simple reason: They have all agreed to use the same protocols to govern that exchange.

You might think that something as massive and global as the Internet would be managed by either the governments of the major industrialized nations or an international agency like the United Nations. In fact, the Internet is operated by the Internet Society, a nonprofit, nongovernmental, professional society composed of more than 100 worldwide organizations (e.g., foundations, governmental agencies, educational institutions, companies) in 180 countries united by the common goal of maintaining the viability and health of the Internet. This group, along with its subcommittees, the Internet Architecture Board (IAB) and the Internet Engineering Task Force (IETF), establishes and enforces network protocol standards. (Perhaps the fact that the Internet developed outside the scope of governmental bureaucracies and their "red tape" is exactly what has allowed it to become so enormously successful!) To learn more about the Internet Society and its activities, check out its home page at *www.isoc.org.*

The protocols that govern the operation of the Internet are set up as a multilayered hierarchy, with each layer addressing one aspect of the overall communications task. They are structured in this way because of the volatility of telecommunications and networking. By dividing the protocols into separate, independent layers, a change to the operation of any one layer will not necessarily cause a change to other layers, making maintenance of the Internet much easier.

The Internet protocol hierarchy, also called a protocol stack, has five layers, and their names and some examples are listed in Figure 7.12. This hierarchy is also referred to as TCP/IP, after the names of two of its most important protocols.

FIGURE 7.12

Layer	Name	Examples
5	Application	HTTP, SMTP, FTP
4	Transport	TCP, UDP
3	Network	IP
2b	Logical Link Control	PPP, Ethernet ⎫
2a	Medium Access Control	Ethernet ⎬ Data Link layer
1	Physical	Modem, DSL, Cable modem, Wi-Fi, 4G

The five-layer TCP/IP protocol hierarchy

In the following sections, we briefly describe the responsibilities of each of the five layers in the hierarchy shown in Figure 7.12.

7.3.1 Physical Layer

The **Physical layer protocols** govern the exchange of binary digits (bits) across a physical communication channel, such as a fiber-optic cable, copper wire, or wireless radio channel. These protocols specify such things as:

- How we know when a bit is present on the line
- How much time the bit will remain on the line
- Whether the bit is in the form of a digital or an analog signal
- What physical quantities are used to represent a binary 0 and a binary 1
- The shape of the connector between the computer and the transmission line

The goal of the Physical layer is to create a "bit pipe" between two computers, such that bits put into the pipe at one end can be read and understood by the computer located at the other end, as shown in Figure 7.13.

Once you select a Physical layer protocol by purchasing a modem, getting a digital subscriber line, or using a mobile phone with wireless data capabilities, you can transmit binary signals across a physical channel. From this point on in the protocol stack, you no longer need to be concerned

FIGURE 7.13

The concept of a bit pipe

about such engineering issues as voltage levels, wavelengths, or radio frequencies. These details are hidden inside the Physical layer, which provides all of the necessary bit transmission services. From now on, all you need to know about the communication channel is that when you ask the Physical layer to send a bit, it does so, and when you ask the Physical layer to get a bit, it retrieves a 0 or a 1.

7.3.2 Data Link Layer

The Physical layer protocols create a bit pipe between two machines connected by a communication link. However, this link is not an error-free channel, and due to interference or weather or any number of other factors, it can introduce errors into the transmitted bit stream. The bits that come out might not be an exact copy of the bits that went in. This creates what is called the error detection and correction problem—how do we detect when errors occur, and how do we correct them?

Also, because we want to receive complete messages, and not raw streams of bits, we need to know which bits in the incoming stream belong together; that is, we need to identify the start and the end of a message. This is called the framing problem. It is the job of the Data Link protocols to address and solve these two issues—error handling and framing. This process is done in two stages called Layer 2a, *Medium Access Control*, and Layer 2b, *Logical Link Control*. Together these two services form the Layer 2 protocol called the Data Link layer.

In Section 7.2.1, we described how local area networks communicate by having multiple machines connected to a single, shared communication line (Figures 7.5 and 7.6). However, although shared by many machines, at any single point in time, this line is capable of sending and receiving only a single message. Attempting to send two or more messages at the same time results in all messages being garbled and none getting through. In this environment, a necessary first step in transmitting a message is determining how to allocate this shared line among the competing machines. The Medium Access Control protocols determine how to arbitrate ownership of a shared communication line when multiple nodes want to send messages at the same time.

This could be done in a *centralized* manner by creating a single master control node responsible for determining who gets ownership of the line at any instant in time. Although easy to do, centralized control is rarely used. One reason is that it can be slow. Each node sends its request to the master, who must decide which node gets the line, and then inform every other node of its decision. This takes a good deal of time, making the network highly inefficient. Another problem is that centralized control is not fault tolerant. If the master node fails, the entire network is inoperable.

Most Medium Access Control protocols, including Ethernet, use a *contention-based* approach in which there is no central authority and all nodes compete equally for ownership of the line. When a node wants to send a message, it first listens to the line to see whether or not it is currently in use. If the line is idle, then the node transmits immediately. If the line is busy, the node wanting to send monitors the status of the line and, as soon as it becomes idle, it transmits. This situation is diagrammed in Figure 7.14(a), in which node B wants to send but notices that A is using the line. B listens and waits until A is finished, and as soon as that occurs, B is free to send.

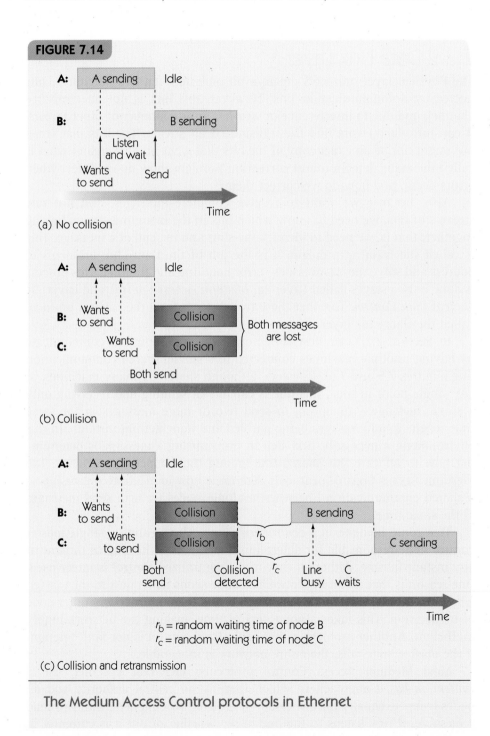

FIGURE 7.14

(a) No collision

(b) Collision

r_b = random waiting time of node B
r_c = random waiting time of node C

(c) Collision and retransmission

The Medium Access Control protocols in Ethernet

However, there is still a problem. If two or more users want to send a message while the line is in use, then both are monitoring its status. As soon as the line is idle, both transmit at exactly the same time. This is called a collision, and it is a common occurrence in contention-based networks like Ethernet. When a collision occurs, all information is lost. This scenario is shown in Figure 7.14(b). According to the Ethernet protocols, when a collision occurs, the colliding nodes immediately stop sending, wait a random amount of time, and then attempt to resend. Because it is unlikely that both nodes will select the exact same random waiting period, one of them should be able to acquire the line and transmit while the other node waits a little longer. This situation is diagrammed in Figure 7.14(c).

One reason the Ethernet protocol is so popular is that control is *distributed*. Responsibility for network operation is shared by all nodes in the network rather than centralized in a single master controller. Each node makes its own decisions about when to listen, when to send, and when to wait. That means that the failure of one node does not affect the operation of any other node in the network.

If our network uses point-to-point links like those in Figure 7.7, rather than shared lines, we do not need the Medium Access Control protocols just described because any two machines along the path are connected by a dedicated line. Therefore, regardless of whether we are using a shared channel or a point-to-point link, we now have a sender and a receiver, who want to exchange a single message, and these two nodes are directly connected by a channel. It is the job of the Layer 2b Logical Link Control protocols to solve the error detection and correction problem and ensure that the message traveling across this channel from source to destination arrives correctly.

How is it possible to turn an inherently error-prone bit pipe like the one in Figure 7.13 into an error-free channel? In fact, we cannot eliminate errors, but we can detect that an error has occurred and retransmit a new and unblemished copy of the original message. The ARQ algorithm, for *a*utomatic *r*epeat re*q*uest, is the basis for all Data Link Control protocols in current use.

Remember that at this point, nodes A and B are directly connected by a physical link. When A wants to send a message to B, it first adds some additional information to form a packet. It inserts a sequence number (1, 2, 3, ...) uniquely identifying this packet, and it adds some error-checking bits that allow B to determine if the packet was corrupted during transmission. Finally, it adds a start of packet (SOP) and end of packet (EOP) delimiter to allow node B to determine exactly where the packet begins and ends.

Thus, the packet M sent from A to B looks like Figure 7.15. This packet is sent across the communication channel, bit by bit, using the services of the Physical layer protocols described in the previous section. When B receives the packet, it examines the error-check field to determine if the packet was transmitted correctly.

What makes the ARQ algorithm work is that node A maintains a *copy* of the packet after it has been sent. If B correctly receives the packet, it returns to A a special acknowledgment message, abbreviated ACK, containing the

FIGURE 7.15

A message packet sent by the Data Link protocols

sequence number of the correctly received packet. Node A now knows that this packet was correctly received and can discard its local copy. It is now free to send the next message:

A	B	
M(1) →		Send the first packet from A to B
	← ACK(1)	B says to A, "I got it," A can discard it
M(2) →		Send the second packet from A to B
	← ACK(2)	B says to A, "I got it," A can discard it
⋮		

If B does not correctly receive the packet (or the packet is lost entirely), then A will not receive the ACK message from B. After waiting a reasonable amount of time, A resends the message to B using the copy stored in its memory:

A	B	
M(1) →		Send the first packet from A to B
	← ACK(1)	B says to A, "I got it," A can discard it
M(2) →		Send the second packet from A to B
		No response; wait for a while
M(2) →		and resend the second packet from A to B
	← ACK(2)	B says to A, "I got it," A can discard it
⋮		

The ACK for a correctly received packet is itself a message and can be lost or damaged during transmission. If an ACK is lost, then A incorrectly assumes that the original packet was lost and retransmits it. However, B knows this is a duplicate because it has the same sequence number as the packet received earlier. It simply acknowledges the duplicate and discards it. This ARQ algorithm guarantees that every message sent (eventually) arrives at the destination.

Thus, we can think of the Data Link layer protocols as creating an error-free "message pipe," in which messages go in one end and always come out the other end correct and in the proper sequence.

• • • M(3) M(2) M(1) ⟶   ⟶ • • • M(3) M(2) M(1)

Message pipe

Practice Problems

Node A and node B are exchanging messages using the ARQ algorithm described in this section. State what action node B should take in each of the following situations:

Node A	Node B
1. M(3) →	
	← ACK(3)
M(3) →	
	?
2. M(3) →	
	← ACK(3)
M(4) →	
	?
3. M(3) →	
	← ACK(3)
M(5) →	
	?

7.3.3 Network Layer

The first two layers of the protocol stack enable us to transmit messages from node A to node B, but only if these two nodes are directly connected by a physical link. If we look back at the model of a wide area network shown in Figure 7.7, we see that the great majority of nodes are *not* directly connected. It is the job of the end-to-end Network layer protocols to deliver a message from the site where it was created to its ultimate destination. To accomplish this delivery task, every node must agree to use the same addressing scheme so that everyone is able to identify that ultimate destination. Thus, the two critical responsibilities of the Network layer are:

- Creating a universal addressing scheme for all network nodes
- Delivering messages between any two nodes in the network

Every node in the network must run the identical Network layer protocol, and it is one of the most important parts of the protocol stack. It is often said that the Network layer is the "glue" that holds the entire network together. The Network layer in the Internet is called IP, for Internet Protocol.

You have almost certainly been exposed to the host naming scheme used by the Internet, as you use it in all your e-mail and Web applications. For example, the machines of the two authors of this book have the following names:

macalester.edu

iupui.edu.

However, these host names are not the actual names that nodes use to identify each other in IP. Instead, nodes identify each other using a 32-bit IP address, often written as four 8-bit numeric quantities in the range 0–255, each grouping separated by a dot. For example, the machine referred to as macalester.edu has the 32-bit IP address 141.140.1.5. In binary, it appears as follows:

```
10001101  10001100  00000001  00000101
   141       140        1         5
```

and this is the actual destination address placed inside a message as it makes its way through the Internet. Looking at the numeric address shown above,

I Can't Believe We've Run Out

When the Internet was started in the early 1970s, its designers selected a 32-bit addressing scheme believing, quite reasonably, that the 2^{32} = 4 billion+ addresses would be more than enough for a long, long time. Well, that long, long time unexpectedly arrived on February 4, 2011 when the Internet Corporation for Assigned Names and Numbers (ICANN) announced that it had just handed out the very last unused block of network addresses. It had completely run out!

Fortunately, this is not yet a catastrophic situation because the recovery and reallocation of addresses previously given out but which were never actually assigned will allow the current addressing scheme to continue functioning for another few years. However, as ICANN likes to say, "four billion addresses is simply not enough for seven billion people." For that reason, Internet engineers have proposed a "next generation" set of protocols, called IPv6.

The transition to IPv6, which has a 128-bit address field, will certainly solve the "lack of addresses" problem, although there is no firm agreement on exactly when this new standard will ultimately be implemented. The new Internet protocol provides for 2^{128} = 300 undecillion unique addresses—that's a 3 followed by 38 zeros. The designers were determined never to run out of addresses again!

it is easy to understand why people prefer symbolic names. Whereas it is easy for humans to remember mnemonic character strings, imagine having to remember a sequence of 32 binary digits. (This is reminiscent of the benefits of assembly language over machine language.)

It is the task of a special Internet application called the Domain Name System (DNS) to convert from a symbolic host name such as macalester.edu to its equivalent 32-bit IP address 141.140.1.5. The DNS is a massive database, distributed over literally thousands of machines that, in total, contain the host name-to-IP address mappings for the 818 million or so host computers on the Internet. When you use a symbolic host name, such as mySchool.edu, this character string is forwarded to a computer called a *local name server* that checks to see if it has a data record containing the IP address for this symbolic name. If so, it returns the corresponding 32-bit value. If not, the local name server forwards it on to a remote name server (and possibly another, and another, ...) until it locates the name server that knows the correct IP address.

Let's use the diagram shown earlier to see how the Network layer operates:

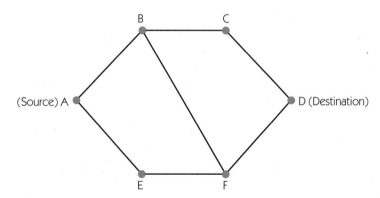

Assume A wants to send a message to D. First, node A uses the DNS to obtain the 32-bit IP address of node D, which it inserts into its message. Because there is no direct path from A to D, the message is sent along a multi-hop path reaching from A to D. (Each of these direct machine-to-machine hops uses the Data Link layer protocols described in the previous section.) In this example, there are four possibilities—ABCD, AEFD, ABFD, and AEFBCD—and the process of selecting one specific path is called routing.

Routing algorithms are highly complex because of the massive volume of data that must be maintained and the enormous amount of processing required to determine the optimal route, called the *shortest path*. The shortest path between two nodes is not necessarily the shortest path in length, but the path via which the message can travel the fastest. To determine the shortest path between every pair of nodes, we need to know the time delay between every connected pair of nodes in the network. In the previous example, this is the time to get from A to B, from B to C, from A to E, and so on. For small networks, it is feasible to have all this data, but for networks like the Internet, with hundreds of millions of nodes and links, this is an unimaginably huge amount of data to obtain and keep current.

Even if we were somehow able to collect all this data, we are still not finished. Now we must determine exactly which path to select. One possible algorithm is to determine the time required to send a message along *every* path from a source to a destination and then pick the one with the smallest delay. For example, to determine the optimal path from A to D, we could start out by summing the individual delays from A to B, B to C, and C to D, which would give us the time to get from A to D using the route A → B → C → D. We now repeat this process for every other path from A to D and pick the smallest.

However, in Section 3.5, we showed that, as the number of network nodes increases, the solution time for these "brute force" algorithms grows exponentially. Therefore, this method is infeasible for any but the tiniest networks. Fortunately, there are much better algorithms that can solve this problem in $\Theta(N^2)$ time, where N is the number of nodes in the network. (The Internet uses a method called *Dijkstra's shortest path algorithm*.) For large networks, where $N = 10^8$ or 10^9, an $\Theta(N^2)$ algorithm might require on the order of 10^{16} or 10^{18} calculations to determine the best route from any node to another—still an enormous amount of work.

There are additional problems that make routing difficult. One complication is *topological change*. The Internet is highly dynamic, with new links and new nodes added on an almost daily basis. Therefore, a route that is optimal now may not be optimal in a couple of days or even a couple of hours. For example, the optimal route from A to D in our diagram may currently be A → B → C → D. However, if a new high-speed line is added connecting nodes E and D, this might change the shortest path to A → E → D. Because of frequent changes, routing tables must be recomputed often.

There is also the question of *network failures*. It may be that when everything is working properly, the optimal route from A to D is A → B → C → D. But what if node B fails? Rather than have all communications between A and D suspended, it would be preferable for the network to switch to an alternative route that does not pass through node B, such as A → E → F → D. This ability to dynamically reroute messages allows a WAN to continue operating even in the presence of node and link failures.

The Network layer has many other responsibilities not mentioned here, including network management, broadcasting, and locating mobile nodes that move around the network. The Network layer is truly a complex piece of software.

With the addition of the Network layer to our protocol stack, we no longer have just a bit pipe or a message pipe, but a true "network delivery service" in which messages are delivered between any two nodes in the network, regardless of their location:

Practice Problems

Given the following six-node wide area network for which the numbers attached to the links are a measure of the "delay" in using that link (e.g., some lines could be more heavily used than others and therefore have a longer wait time), answer the following questions:

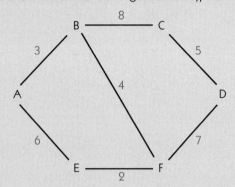

1. What is the shortest path from node A to node D, where shortest path is defined as the path with the smallest sum of the delays on each individual link? Explain exactly how you went about finding that path.

2. Do you think the algorithm you used in Practice Problem 1 works if we redraw the graph so it has 26 nodes rather than 6 and about 50 links rather than 10? Why or why not?

3. What if the link connecting node F to node D fails? What is now the shortest path from node A to node D? Could the failure of any single link in this network prevent nodes A and D from communicating?

4. What if the delay from node A to node E were reduced from six units to four? Would that change the shortest path from A to D?

7.3.4 Transport Layer

Imagine that 123 Main St. is a large, multistory office building with thousands of tenants. When you address a letter to an employee who works in this building, it is not enough to write:

Joe Smith

123 Main St.

My Town, Minnesota

This identifies the correct building, but how do the people in the central mailroom locate "Joe Smith" from among the thousands of people who work there? We need to provide a more descriptive address, one that not only identifies the correct building but also exactly where inside this building Mr. Smith works:

Joe Smith

Acme Services Inc., Suite 2701

123 Main St.

My Town, Minnesota

The same situation exists on the Internet. Every host computer has an IP address that uniquely identifies it. However, there may be many application programs running on that one machine, each one "doing its own thing." When a message comes in, how do we know which application program it is for and where to deliver it?

We need a second level of address that identifies not only a specific machine but also a specific program running on that machine. This "program identifier," usually just a small integer value, is called a port number, and it serves the same role as the address line "Acme Services Inc., Suite 2701." Assigning port numbers to programs and remembering which program goes with which port is a part of the Transport layer protocols. Although each host computer has one IP address, it may at any instant in time have many active ports.

The relationship between these two address types is shown in Figure 7.16. This diagram shows two hosts: Host A whose IP address is 101.102.103.104 and Host B with IP address 105.106.107.108. Host A is currently running two programs called W and X (perhaps a Web browser and an e-mail client), with port numbers 12 and 567, respectively, while Host B is executing two programs named Y and Z, with port numbers 44 and 709, respectively.

The Transport layer protocols create a "program-to-program" delivery service, in which we don't simply move messages from one host to another, but from a specific program at the source to a specific program at the destination.

FIGURE 7.16

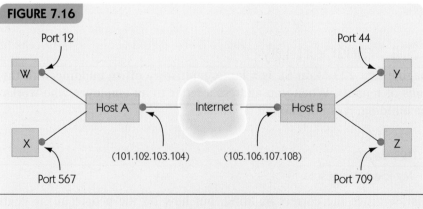

Relationship between IP addresses and port numbers

In the example in Figure 7.16, it is the job of the Network layer protocol to deliver the message from the host with IP address 101.102.103.104 to the host with IP address 105.106.107.108, at which point its responsibilities are over. The Transport protocol at the destination node examines the newly arrived message to determine which program should get it, based on the port number field inside the message. For example, if the port number field is 709, then the information in the message is forwarded to application program Z. (What program Z does with this information and exactly what that message means are not part of the Transport protocols but rather the Application protocols discussed in the following section.)

How does a program (such as W or X) learn the port number of another program (such as Y or Z) running on a remote machine somewhere out in the network? The answer is that all important applications on the Internet use *well-known port numbers*. Just as it is widely known in the United States that directory assistance is found at 555-1212 and police and fire emergencies are reported to 911, fixed integer values are assigned to certain applications, and those values are made known to every machine on the Internet. For example, the HTTP protocol, which allows us to access remote Web pages (and which we discuss in the following section), always uses port 80. If you want to get a Web page from another machine, you simply need to talk to the program that is listening for messages on port 80.

Figure 7.18 later in the chapter lists the port numbers of some common Internet applications. A list of all well-known port assignments is contained in the report titled *Assigned Numbers on the Internet* (RFC 1700) available over the Internet.[1] The only time you need to get a new port number is when you are developing a new application.

The other primary responsibility of the Transport layer has to do with errors and reliability. When we introduced the Data Link layer in Section 7.3.2, we said that one of its tasks is to take the inherently unreliable physical channel underneath it and turn it into an efficient and error-free channel. That same type of relationship exists between the Transport layer and the layer underneath it, namely the Network layer.

The Network layer of the Internet, IP, is an inherently unreliable communication channel. IP uses what is called a *good faith* transmission model. That means that it tries very hard to deliver a message from source to destination, but it does not guarantee delivery. In this sense, IP is like the post office. The post office does a very good job of delivering mail, and the overwhelming majority of letters do get through. However, it does not guarantee that absolutely every letter you send will arrive, and it does not guarantee that letters will arrive either within a specific time period or in exactly the same order that they were originally posted. If you need these features, you have to use some type of "special handling" service such as Registered Mail or Express Mail.

---

[1]RFCs, as we mention in the Challenge Work section, are technical documents that describe virtually all aspects of Internet behavior. They are all available online at *www.faqs.org/rfcs*.

In a sense, the Transport layer represents just this type of "special handling" service. Its job is to create a high-quality, error-free, order-preserving, end-to-end delivery service on top of the unreliable delivery services provided by IP. On the Internet, the primary transport protocol is TCP (Transport Control Protocol). (There is another transport protocol called *UDP* for *U*ser *D*atagram *P*rotocol. We will not be discussing it here.)

TCP requires that the two programs at the source and destination node initially establish a connection. That is, they must first inform each other of the impending message exchange, and they must describe the "quality of service" they want to receive. This connection does not exist in a hardware sense—there is no "wire" stretched between the two nodes. Instead, it is a logical connection that exists only as entries in tables. However, TCP can make this logical connection behave exactly as if there were a real connection between these two programs. This logical view of a TCP connection is shown in Figure 7.17.

Once this connection has been established, messages can be transmitted from the source program to the destination program. Programs P1 and P2 appear to have a direct, error-free link between them. In reality, however, their communications go from P1 to A, B, C, D, and finally to P2, using the services of the Data Link protocol for each link along the way.

TCP uses the same ARQ algorithm described in our discussion of the Data Link level. The receiving program must acknowledge every message correctly received. If a message is lost in the network and does not arrive, the sending program does not receive an acknowledgment and eventually resends it. Every message is ultimately delivered to the application program waiting for it and, therefore, this TCP connection does function like an error-free channel.

Every message sent on this TCP connection contains a sequence number—1, 2, 3, ... If messages are received out of order (say message 3

FIGURE 7.17

Logical view of a TCP connection

comes in before message 2 because of errors along the route), then TCP simply holds the later message (message 3) until the earlier message (message 2) correctly arrives. At that time, it can deliver both messages to the application program in the proper order. From the destination's point of view, this TCP connection always delivers messages in the proper order.

With these four protocol layers in place, we now have a complete end-to-end delivery service. The network can transmit a message from a program anywhere in the network to another program anywhere in the network—and can do it both correctly and efficiently. The only thing left to specify is the *content* of those messages; that is, what does a program want to say to another program? Essentially we are asking the question: "What types of applications do we want to give to our network users and exactly how do we implement them?" We answer that fundamental question as we look at the very top layer of our protocol stack—the Application layer.

7.3.5 Application Layer

The Application layer protocols are the rules for implementing the end-user services provided by a network, and they are built on top of the four protocol layers described in previous sections. These services are the reason that networks exist in the first place, and the appearance of exciting new and critically important applications (often called *killer apps*) has fueled the rapid growth of networking and the Internet—e-mail in the 1970s, chat rooms in the 1980s, the Web and e-commerce in the 1990s, and social networking in the twenty-first century. Figure 7.18 lists a few of the important application protocols on the Internet upon which these killer apps are built.

It is not possible in this one section to discuss all the protocols listed in Figure 7.18. Instead, we will use the HTTP protocol, which is used by the World Wide Web to access and deliver Web pages, to serve as a general

FIGURE 7.18

Acronym	Name	Application	Well-Known Port
HTTP	Hypertext Transfer Protocol	Accessing Web pages	80
SMTP	Simple Mail Transfer Protocol	Sending electronic mail	25
POP3	Post Office Protocol	Receiving electronic mail	110
IMAP	Internet Message Access Protocol	Receiving electronic mail	143
FTP	File Transfer Protocol	Accessing remote files	21
TELNET	Terminal Emulation Protocol	Accessing remote terminals	23
DNS	Domain Name System	Translating symbolic host names to 32-bit IP addresses	42

Some popular application protocols on the Internet

model for how Application layer services are typically built on top of the TCP/IP protocol stack.

A single Web page is identified by a symbolic string called a Uniform Resource Locator, abbreviated URL. URLs have three parts, and they look like this:

protocol://host address/page

The first part, *protocol*, indicates the type of information contained in this page. The most common format is hypertext, and we access it using the Hypertext Transfer Protocol (HTTP). (The Web is designed to accept and transfer other types of information as well. Thus, we could use the protocol identifier "news" to obtain information from bulletin boards and news groups, or "mailto," which allows us to send and receive e-mail documents via the Web.) The second part of the URL is the *host address* of the machine where the page is stored. This is the symbolic host name first discussed in Section 7.3.3. The third and last part of the URL is the *page* identification, which is usually a file stored on the specified machine. Thus, a typical URL might look like the following:

http://www.macalester.edu/about

This identifies a hypertext ("http") document stored in a file called *about* located on a host computer whose symbolic name is *www.macalester.edu*. (*Note:* "http" is the default protocol. Thus, the previous URL can also be written as simply *www.macalester.edu/about*.)

Before we can use HTTP to transfer a Web page, we must first establish a connection between the http client program (the Web browser being run by the user) and port 80, the port number of the HTTP Web server located at the node where the Web page resides, namely *www.macalester.edu*. The network uses the TCP protocol described in Section 7.3.4 to establish this connection. Thus, we can clearly see how the HTTP application protocol is built on top of the TCP/IP protocol stack just described.

Once we establish this connection, we use the HTTP application protocol to access the desired Web page. An HTTP *request message* is sent on the TCP connection from the client to the server, specifying the name of a Web page. A second HTTP message type, called a *response message*, is returned from the server to the client along the same TCP connection. The response contains a status code specifying whether or not the request was successful and, if it was, it includes the requested page.[2]

Let's illustrate how these pieces work together using a simple example. Imagine that you are using a Web browser and have just clicked on the following URL:

http://www.macalester.edu/about

---

[2]We have probably all had the experience of seeing return code 404: Page Not Found, which means the requested document does not exist on this server.

The following sequence of events takes place:

1. Your browser scans the URL and extracts the host name of the machine to which it must connect—*www.macalester.edu*. (Let's disregard the issue of how this symbolic name is converted to its corresponding 32-bit IP address.)

2. Your browser asks TCP to establish a connection between itself and port 80 (the Web server) of the machine called *www.macalester.edu*.

3. When the TCP connection between your browser and the Web server is established, the browser scans the URL to identify the page you want to access. In this case, it is */about*. The browser constructs an HTTP 'GET' message, which requests the contents of that Web page. This GET message looks something like the following:

   GET /about HTTP /1.1
   Host: www.macalester.edu
   Accept-language: English

   This message says that we want a copy of the English language page */about* located at *www.macalester.edu*, and it should be accessed using the http protocol, version 1.1. (An actual GET message is a bit more complex and includes a number of additional fields not shown here.)

4. The GET message in Step 3 is transmitted across the Internet from the client's Web browser program at the source node to the Web server at the destination node using the services of TCP/IP as well as the Data Link and Physical layer protocols.

5. When the GET message arrives, it is delivered to the Web server program (which is listening on port 80). The Web server locates the file named in the GET message and creates a response message containing a copy of the contents of that file. This response message looks something like the following:

   HTTP/1.1 200 OK
   Connection: close
   Date: Thursday, 29 Mar 2012
   Content Length: 53908
   Content Type: text/html
   . . . (the contents of the Web page go here) . . .

   This response message says that the server successfully found the file (code 200), and it contains 53,908 bytes of text. It also says that after the Web page has been sent, the TCP connection between the browser and the server will be closed. Finally, there is a copy of the entire Web page. (Again, some fields in the response message have been omitted for clarity.)

6. This HTTP response message in Step 5 is transmitted across the Internet from the Web server back to the port of the client's Web browser using the services of TCP/IP as well as the Data Link and Physical layer protocols.

7. The message is delivered to your browser, and the page is displayed on the screen. The TCP connection between the two programs is terminated.

Something similar to this occurs every time we click on a new URL. This sequence of events is diagrammed in Figure 7.19.

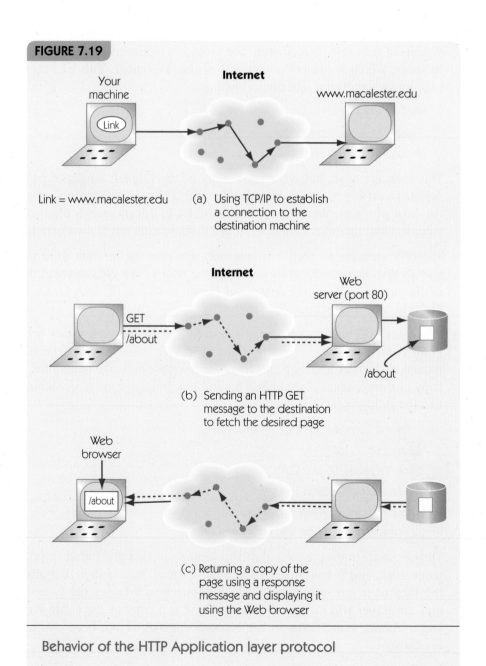

FIGURE 7.19

Your machine

Internet

www.macalester.edu

Link

Link = www.macalester.edu

(a) Using TCP/IP to establish a connection to the destination machine

Internet

Web server (port 80)

GET /about

/about

(b) Sending an HTTP GET message to the destination to fetch the desired page

Web browser

/about

(c) Returning a copy of the page using a response message and displaying it using the Web browser

Behavior of the HTTP Application layer protocol

Laboratory Experience 11

We have just completed a rather long and complex discussion of how a computer network functions. The chapter presented a good deal of technical material that for some can be fairly difficult to grasp. To help clarify these ideas, this Laboratory Experience illustrates network behavior using a software package called a network simulator. This simulator allows you to observe and control many of the technical concepts introduced in this section, concepts such as packets, messages, error detection, error correction, and routing.

7.4 Network Services and Benefits

At the beginning of this chapter, we said that networks have the potential to create enormous social change. Now that we have looked at how they are designed and built, let's briefly examine the services they can offer and their impact on society.

7.4.1 Interpersonal Communications

Electronic mail (e-mail) has been the single most popular application of networks for the last 35 years. It is estimated that about 250 billion e-mail messages are transmitted across the Internet *every day*! When the Internet was first developed, its designers thought that it would be an ideal way to access advanced, high-performance hardware and software. Instead, they found that it was a wonderfully effective way to support interpersonal communication, and e-mail rapidly became the dominant application.

E-mail is *convenient*. You can send a message whenever you want, and it waits for the recipient to log on and read it at his or her convenience. E-mail is *fast*. A message from the United States typically arrives anywhere in the world in less than a minute, even though it may have to pass through 15 or 20 nodes along the way (using the packet-switched protocols described in the previous section). E-mail supports *multimedia*. The contents of your electronic messages are not limited to characters but can also include a wide range of *attachments*, including photographs, text, graphics, and sound. Finally, e-mail is a *broadcast medium*. A computer can send a letter to a thousand recipients as easily as it can send it to one (which may, in fact, be a detriment rather than an advantage as we see in the Special Interest Box titled "Spam").

An interesting application related to e-mail that flourished during the 1980s and 1990s was the bulletin board system, usually abbreviated as BBS.

A bulletin board is a shared public file where anyone can post messages and everyone is free to read the postings of others. It is an electronic version of the bulletin boards commonly seen in grocery stores, cafés, and public libraries. Most BBSs are associated with a particular topic or special area of interest. These specialized bulletin boards, called *newsgroups,* were a wonderful way to create a community of individuals who share a common interest and want to exchange ideas and opinions. Today BBSs have evolved into Internet forums and chat rooms that support the real-time exchange of messages. In addition to simply posting a message that can be read at a later time, they also support interactive messaging—what the sender types appears immediately on the screen of one or more individuals, allowing for the direct exchange of ideas. Two other popular forms of message exchange are texting and *instant messaging (IM),* the rapid exchange of messages, often using wireless technology.

The enormous popularity of using digital technology to keep in touch with other people (e-mail, BBS, chat, text, IM) eventually led to the development of social networks—systems that create communities of users who share common interests and activities and that provide multiple methods

Spam

Spam is electronic "junk mail"—unsolicited e-mail sent to thousands, even millions, of network users without their permission or knowledge. It is not certain where the term *spam* came from, but the best guess is from the famous Monty Python comedy routine in which the word *spam* is repeated over and over, making it a synonym for the seemingly endless repetition of silly or worthless words.

Junk mail in the form of advertising flyers and political brochures has been a staple of surface mail for many years. But there is a natural cap on its volume—the sender has to pay the post office to deliver it. So, if a mailing is not likely to produce a profitable return or have a worthwhile purpose, it will not be sent.

However, e-mail does not have that built-in cap, and it is beginning to clutter our electronic mail boxes and consume enormous amounts of bandwidth. Approximately 80% of the e-mail sent across the Internet is spam, about 72 trillion worthless messages per year. Because the Internet is a public facility, there is little that can be done to regulate spam. A number of companies have developed *spam filters* that attempt to determine which e-mails are useful and which are spam. Unfortunately, as soon as a filter is developed and released, the "spammers" quickly figure out a way to beat it and get their e-mail through to your machine. Probably the best filter developed so far (and for the near future) is the Delete button on your keyboard!

of online interaction. (See the Special Interest Box titled "Social Networking" later in this chapter.) Social networks like Facebook and Twitter are becoming the killer apps of the twenty-first century. They have become a way to not only keep in touch with friends and family, but also to influence social development and impact social change on a national and international scale. We will discuss some of the ethical and legal issues related to social networking in Chapter 17.

7.4.2 Resource Sharing

Another important network service is resource sharing, the ability to share *physical resources*, such as a printer or storage device, as well as *logical resources*, such as software and data.

The prices of computers and peripherals have been dropping for many years, so it is tempting to think that everyone should buy their own I/O units or mass storage devices. However, that is not a cost-effective way to configure computer systems. For example, a high-quality color printer may be used rather infrequently. Buying everyone in the office his or her own printer would leave most of them idle for long periods of time. It is far more efficient to have a few shared printers, called print servers, which can be accessed whenever needed. Similarly, if a group of users requires access to a data file or a piece of software, it makes sense to keep a single copy on a shared network disk, called a file server. A network file server can be a cost-effective way to provide shared backup services to multiple sites as well as make it easier to access information from multiple devices such as your desktop computer at work, your tablet computer at home, and your smartphone on the road.

The style of computing wherein some nodes provide services while the remaining nodes are users (or clients) of those services is called, naturally enough, client/server computing. We have seen two examples—print servers and file servers—but there are many others, such as mail servers, name servers, compute servers, and Web servers. The philosophy behind the client/server model is that we use a network to share resources that are too widespread, too expensive, or used too infrequently to warrant replication at every node. A diagram of the client/server model of computing is shown in Figure 7.20.

Information sharing is another important service, and a network is an excellent way to access scientific, medical, legal, and commercial data files stored on systems all over the world. (In fact, it was the need to share information efficiently among hundreds of physicists that led to the development of the World Wide Web in the early 1990s.) For example, information can be distributed among the geographically dispersed sites of a multinational corporation and shared as needed, using a distributed database. Web pages can be exchanged between remote systems. Files can be transmitted anywhere in the world using FTP, which is mentioned in Figure 7.18, and online databases can be accessed by authorized users regardless of location.

FIGURE 7.20

The client/server model of computing

Many network sites now provide a special service called a data warehouse. These nodes contain massive amounts of information that can be electronically searched for specific facts or documents. Frequently, such sites contain highly specialized information, such as geopolitical data, current stock prices, real estate records, or information on case law and legal precedents. Today, it is more common for students, scientists, businesspeople, and politicians to search for information online than in the stacks of a library.

Another important resource-sharing service is the ability to support collaborative group efforts in producing a shared document such as a user's manual, grant application, or design specification. Workers on a project can communicate via the network; hold virtual conferences; check electronic calendars and schedule meetings automatically; and share, discuss, and edit documents in progress online. A rapidly growing network application is *collaborative software*, also known as groupware or a wiki (the Hawaiian word for fast or quick). This is software that facilitates the efforts of individuals connected by a network and working on a single, shared project. One of the most successful examples of this sharing is *Wikipedia*, an online encyclopedia written, reviewed, and maintained by hundreds of thousands of volunteers working independently. Wikipedia currently includes over 3.7 million English-language articles as well as 14 million entries in 281 languages from Polish to Portuguese, French to Finnish, Tajik to Tagalog. (By comparison, the *Encyclopedia Britannica* has about 0.5 million articles.) Currently, Wikipedia is used by over 400 million people per year.

7.4.3 Electronic Commerce

Electronic commerce (or just e-commerce) is a general term applied to any use of computers and networking to support the paperless exchange of goods, information, and services in the commercial sector. The idea of using computers and networks to do business has been around for some time; the early applications of e-commerce include (1) the automatic deposit of paychecks, (2) automatic teller machines (ATMs) for handling financial transactions from remote sites, and (3) the use of scanning devices at checkout counters to capture sales and inventory information in machine-readable form.

More recently, the focus has been on the use of the Internet and the World Wide Web to advertise and sell goods and services. Initially, the Internet was used mostly by scientists and engineers. However, the business world soon came to appreciate the potential of a communications medium that could cheaply and reliably reach millions of people around the world. In the last 10–15 years, traffic on the Internet has changed from primarily academic and professional to heavily commercial. For example, as of early 2011, there were about 151,000,000 host computers in the .com (U.S. commercial) domain, while fewer than 12,000,000 were in the .edu domain (U.S. educational institutions).

Today, about 5% of total retail sales in the United States are online, about $175 billion annually. This is up from less than 1% in 2001. Worldwide, online retail sales are expected to top $1 trillion by 2013. Furthermore, using sites such as eBay and craigslist, individuals, not just corporations, can reach a national or even international audience to buy and sell their products.

We will have much more to say about electronic commerce and commercial uses of the Internet in Chapter 14.

7.5 A Brief History of the Internet and the World Wide Web

In the preceding sections, we discussed the technical characteristics and services of networks in general. However, to most people, the phrase *computer network* isn't a generalized term but a very specific one—the global Internet and its most popular component, the World Wide Web.

In this section, we highlight the history, development, and growth of the Internet and the World Wide Web. Much of the information in the following pages is taken from the original 1997 article "A Brief History of the Internet," written by its original designers and available on the World Wide Web.[3]

In the words of its designers, "The Internet has revolutionized the computer and communications world like nothing before. It is at once a worldwide broadcasting capability, a mechanism for information dissemination, and a medium for collaboration and interaction between individuals and their computers without regard for geographic location."

---

[3]Leitner, B., Cerf, V., Kahn, R., Kleinrock, L., Lynch, D., Postel, J., Roberts, L., and Wolff, S. (December 10, 2003). *A Brief History of the Internet.* See *http://www.isoc.org/internet/history/brief.shtml*

7.5.1 The Internet

The Internet is not a recent development but an idea that has been around for more than 45 years. The concept first took shape during the early and mid-1960s and was based on the work of computer scientists at MIT and the RAND Corporation in the United States and the NPL Research Laboratory in Great Britain. The first proposal for building a computer network was made by J. C. R. Licklider of MIT in August 1962. He wrote his colleagues a memo titled (somewhat dramatically) "The Galactic Network," in which he described a globally interconnected set of computers through which everyone could access data and software. He convinced other researchers at MIT, including Larry Roberts and Leonard Kleinrock, of the validity of his ideas. From 1962 to 1967, they and others investigated the theoretical foundations of wide area networking, especially such fundamental technical concepts as protocols, packet switching, and routing.

In 1966, Roberts moved to the Advanced Research Projects Agency (ARPA), a small research office of the Department of Defense charged with developing technology that could be of use to the U.S. military. ARPA was interested in packet-switched networking because it seemed to be a more secure form of communications during wartime. (Traditional dial-up telephones were considered too vulnerable because the failure of the central phone switch would completely cut all voice communications. As we described earlier, a WAN can automatically route around a failed line or node in order to maintain communications.)

ARPA funded a number of network-related research projects, and in 1967 Roberts presented the first research paper describing ARPA's plans to build a wide area packet-switched computer network. For the next two years, work proceeded on the design of the network hardware and software. The first two nodes of this new network, called the ARPANET, were constructed at UCLA and the Stanford Research Institute (SRI), and in October 1969, the first computer-to-computer network message was sent. Later that same year two more nodes were added (the University of California–Santa Barbara and the University of Utah), and by the end of 1969, the budding four-node network was off the ground.

The ARPANET grew quickly during the early 1970s, and it was formally demonstrated to the scientific community at an international conference in 1972. It was also in late 1972 that the first killer app was developed—electronic mail. It was an immediate success and caused an explosion of growth in people-to-people traffic rather than the people-to-machine or machine-to-machine traffic that dominated usage in the first few years. (It is interesting to note that by 2009 the e-mail volume in the United States was about 90 trillion messages per year. Now that is a killer app!)

The success of the ARPANET in the 1970s led other researchers to develop similar types of computer networks to support information exchange within their own specific scientific area: HEPNet (High Energy Physics Network), CSNET (Computer Science Network), and MFENet (Magnetic Fusion Energy Network). Furthermore, corporations started to notice the success of the

ARPANET and began developing proprietary networks to market to their customers: SNA (Systems Network Architecture) at IBM and DECNet from Digital Equipment Corporation. The 1970s were a time of rapid expansion of networks in both the academic and commercial communities.

Farsighted researchers at ARPA, in particular Robert Kahn, realized that this rapid and unplanned proliferation of independent networks would lead to incompatibilities and prevent users on different networks from communicating with each other, a situation that brings to mind the problems that national railway systems have sharing railcars because of their use of a different gauge track. Kahn knew that to obtain maximum benefits from this new technology, all networks would need to communicate in a standardized fashion. He developed the concept of internetworking, which stated that any WAN is free to do whatever it wants *internally*. However, at the point where two networks meet, both must use a common addressing scheme and identical protocols—that is, they must speak the same language.

This is the same concept that governs the international telephone system. Every country is free to build its own internal phone system in whatever way it wants, but all must agree to use a standardized worldwide numbering system (country code, city code), and each must agree to send and receive telephone calls outside its borders in the format standardized by the worldwide telephone regulatory agency.

Figure 7.21 is a diagram of a "network of networks." It shows four WANs called A, B, C, and D interconnected by a device called a gateway that makes the internetwork connections and provides routing between different WANs.

To allow the four WANs of Figure 7.21 to communicate, Kahn and his colleagues needed to create (1) a standardized way for a node in one WAN to identify a node located in a different WAN and (2) a universally recognized message format for exchanging information across WAN boundaries. Kahn,

FIGURE 7.21

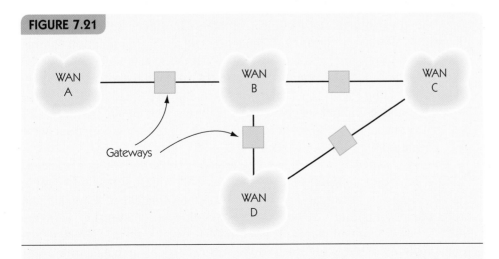

A network of networks

along with Dr. Vinton Cerf of Stanford, began working on these problems in 1973, and together they designed the solutions that became the framework for the Internet. Specifically, they created both the hierarchical host naming scheme that we use today and the TCP/IP protocols that are the "common language" spoken by networks around the world. (These protocols were discussed in Sections 7.3.3 and 7.3.4.)

During the late 1970s and early 1980s, work proceeded on implementing and installing TCP/IP on not only mainframe computers but also on the PCs and desktop machines that were just starting to appear in the marketplace. It is a tribute to the power and flexibility of the TCP/IP protocols that they were able to adapt to a computing environment quite different from the one that existed when they were first created. Originally designed to work with the large mainframe computers of the 1970s, they were successfully implemented in the modern computing environment—desktop PCs connected by LANs.

By the early 1980s, TCP/IP was being used all around the world. Even networks that internally used other communication protocols implemented TCP/IP to exchange information with nodes outside their own community. At the same time, exciting new applications appeared that were designed to meet the growing needs of the networking community. (Many of these application protocols were introduced in Section 7.3.5.) For example, *Telnet* is a software package that allows users to log on remotely to another computer and use it as though it were their own local machine. *FTP (File Transfer Protocol)* provides a way to move files around the network quickly and easily. Along with e-mail (still wildly popular), these and other new applications added more fuel to the superheated growth of computer networks.

With TCP/IP becoming a *de facto* networking standard, a global addressing scheme, and a growing set of important applications, the infrastructure was in place for the creation of a truly international network. The Internet, in its modern form, had slowly begun to emerge.

Although many of the technical problems had been solved, networking had yet to make a significant impact on the general population for one very important reason: In order to use the ARPANET, you needed a research grant from the U.S. Department of Defense (DOD). By the early 1980s, many people were using the Internet, but they were almost exclusively physicists, engineers, and computer scientists at a select set of secure military and research centers. For example, in 1982, 13 years after its creation, there were only 235 computers connected to the ARPANET.

One last step was needed, and it was taken by the National Science Foundation (NSF) in 1984. In that year, the NSF initiated a project whose goal was to bring the advantages of the Internet to the *entire* academic and professional community, regardless of discipline or relationship with the DOD. The NSF planned and built a national network called *NSFNet*, which used TCP/IP technology identical to the ARPANET. This new network interconnected six NSF supercomputer centers with dozens of new regional networks set up by the NSF. These new regional networks included thousands of users at places like universities, government agencies, libraries, museums, medical centers, and even high schools. Thus, by the mid-1980s, this emerging "network of networks" had grown to include many new sites and, even more important, a huge group of first-time users, such as students, faculty, librarians, museum staff, politicians, civil servants, and urban planners, to name just a few.

At about the same time, other countries began developing wide area TCP/IP backbone networks like NSFNet to interconnect their own medical centers, schools, research centers, and government agencies. As these national networks were created, they were also linked into this expanding network, and the user population continued to expand. For the first time since the development of networking, the technology had begun to have an impact on the wider community. A diagram of the state of internetworking in the late 1980s is shown in Figure 7.22.

FIGURE 7.22

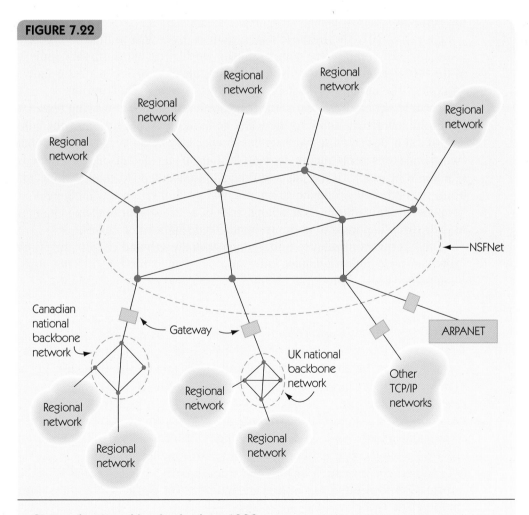

State of networking in the late 1980s

Some time in the late 1980s, the term ARPANET ceased to be used because, as Figure 7.22 shows, the ARPANET was now only one of many networks belonging to a much larger collection. (By 1990, it had grown to 300,000 computers on 3,000 separate networks.) People began referring to this entire collection of interconnected networks as "the Internet," though this name was not officially accepted by the U.S. government until October 24, 1995.

Once the public had easy access, the Internet became an immediate success and grew rapidly. By the middle of 1993, it included 1.8 million host computers and roughly 5 to 10 million active users, and its size was doubling every year. In fact, it had become so successful that the NSF decided it was time to get out of the "networking business." The goal of the NSF is to fund basic research, not to operate an ongoing commercial enterprise. In April 1995, NSFNet closed up shop. The exit of the U.S. government from the networking arena created business opportunities for new firms called Internet service providers that offered the Internet access once provided by the ARPANET and NSFNet.

By early 2011, the Internet had grown to over 800 million computers located in just about every country in the world. The extraordinary growth of the Internet continues to this very day. Figure 7.11 in Section 7.2.4 shows a graph of the number of host computers connected to the Internet.

The Internet has been one of the biggest success stories in moving research out of the laboratory and into the wider community. What began as the wild idea of a few dedicated researchers has grown, in only 45 years, into a global communications infrastructure moving trillions of bits of data among hundreds of millions of people. It has adapted time and time again—to changes in usage (from research and academic to commercial and entertainment), changes in hardware (from mainframes to laptops, tablets, and smartphones), and changes in scale (from hundreds of nodes to hundreds of millions of nodes).

The Internet continues to undergo massive growth and change, this time from the most important new killer app developed for the Internet since e-mail—the World Wide Web.

7.5.2 The World Wide Web

Tim Berners-Lee, a researcher at CERN, the European High Energy Physics Laboratory in Geneva, Switzerland, first developed the idea for a hypertext-based information distribution system in 1989. Because physics research is often done by teams of people from many different universities, he wanted to create a way for scientists throughout Europe and North America to easily and quickly exchange information such as research articles, journals, and experimental data. Although they could use existing Internet services such as FTP and e-mail, Berners-Lee wanted to make information sharing easier and more intuitive for people unfamiliar with computer networks.

Beginning in 1990, Berners-Lee designed and built a system using the concept of hypertext, a collection of documents interconnected by pointers,

Geography Lesson

The Internet is a truly "global phenomenon," affecting the way people work, shop, and communicate throughout the world. Consider that, whereas the United Nations has 192 member states, the Domain Name System (DNS) of the Internet includes entries for 239 countries, territories, and possessions. The DNS includes standardized domain names for such places as (you may want to get out your atlas) Comoros (.km), Nauru (.nr), Bouvet Island (.bv), Kiribati (.ki), Svalbard and Jan Mayen Islands (.sj), and St. Pierre and Miquelon (.pm). The smallest nonempty DNS domain is .yt–Mayotte, a French territory located off the coast of Madagascar. It contains exactly one host computer!

called *links*, as shown in Figure 7.23. Traditional documents are meant to be read linearly from beginning to end, but users of hypertext documents (called *pages* in Web parlance) are free to navigate the collection in whatever order they want, using the links to move freely from page to page. Berners-Lee reasoned that the idea of hypertext matched up very well with the concept of networking and the Internet. Hypertext documents could be stored on the machines of the Internet, and a link would be the name of a page along with the IP address of the machine where that page is stored. He called his hypertext link a URL, an acronym for Uniform Resource Locator, and it is the worldwide identification of a Web page located on a specific host computer on the Internet.

FIGURE 7.23

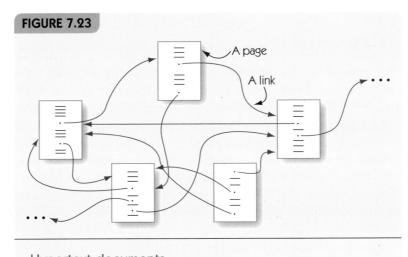

Hypertext documents

Berners-Lee named his new information system the World Wide Web, and it was completed and made available to all researchers at CERN in May 1991, the date that marks the birth of the Web. It became an instant success, and traffic on the CERN Web server increased by 1,000% in its first two years of use. In April 1993, the directors of CERN, realizing the beneficial impact that the Web could have on research throughout the world, announced that, effective immediately, all Web technology developed at CERN would be freely available to everyone without fees or royalties. For many people, this important announcement really marks the emergence of the World Wide Web on a global scale.

A powerful graphical Web browser, called Mosaic, was developed in late 1993 and made available to the general public so that they could begin to use this new service. With the appearance of Mosaic, the World Wide Web began to "take off." It was a network application that offered users exactly what they needed most—access to massive amounts of helpful information whenever they wanted it. Other browsers soon appeared in the marketplace, including Netscape Navigator (1994), Microsoft Internet Explorer (1995), Apple's Safari (2003), Mozilla Firefox (2004), and Google Chrome (2008).

In late 1995, the NSF conducted a study of the different types of traffic on the Internet as a percentage of all information sent. At that time, the World Wide Web represented 23.9% of the total volume of Internet traffic, even though it had been in existence for only four years!

Since that time, the Web has continued to grow exponentially, containing roughly 300 million distinct Web sites by early 2011. It is by far the fastest growing component of the Internet. The Web's colorful graphics and simple point-and-click method of accessing information has made it the Internet killer app of the twenty-first century. It has become the vehicle for bringing the capabilities of networking to everyone—from toddlers to senior citizens and kindergarten students to Ph.D.s. For many people, the World Wide Web *is* the Internet.

7.6 Conclusion

Computer networking has changed enormously in the 45 or so years that it has been around. From a specialized communication system devoted to academic research, it has blossomed into a worldwide information system. What was once the esoteric domain of a few thousand scientists is now used by billions of people, the vast majority of whom have no formal training in computer science. From providing access to technical databases and research journals, it has become a way for the average citizen to shop, chat, stay informed, and be entertained. There is every reason to believe that the Internet will continue to grow and evolve as much in the coming years as it has in the past.

The most pressing issue facing the Internet today is not technology and new applications. Those issues have been and will continue to be addressed and solved by the computer science community. The biggest concern today

Social Networking

Computer networks were originally created to provide scientists and engineers with easy access to important software packages and data files stored on remote computers. However, the first Internet killer app was rather unexpected and something quite different—e-mail—and while many of those early e-mail messages did contain technical content, even more were of the "Wanna meet for lunch today?" variety.

Linking people together for purposes of social interaction has been a popular use of computer networks since their earliest days. Following the enormous success of e-mail in the early 1970s, there were many other attempts to foster online communities. The first bulletin board system (BBS) appeared in 1978. It allowed users to dial a central site using a time-sharing terminal, read and post notices, chat, play online games, and exchange messages. In 1980, a system called *Usenet* was developed. It was similar to a BBS with the added feature of having *newsgroups*—users with a mutual interest in one particular topic, such as spaceflight, Chinese cooking, or Minnesota Vikings football. BBSs were popular from the late 1970s until the mid-1990s when they began to be replaced by Web-based applications. One of the earliest examples of this was the *wiki*, a collaborative shared document built and maintained by a community of online users. The most well-known and widely used wiki is the online encyclopedia Wikipedia.

The use of Web-based social networking sites has grown to the point where they are some of the most well-known and widely used applications on the Internet, and there is hardly a person today who is not thoroughly familiar with them and, more likely, a registered member. *Facebook*, developed in 2004 by Mark Zuckerberg while a student at Harvard, has 600 million active users worldwide (almost 10% of the Earth's population), and it receives over 1 billion visits per month. *LinkedIn*, a career-oriented social network, also started in 2003, has 100 million registered users, and receives about 50 million visits per month.

Twitter, another popular social networking tool created in 2006 by Jack Dorsey, allows users to keep up with those in their circle of friends with "tweets," short (140 character) text-based posts that appear on the users' and friends' pages. Twitter, with 200 million users and 65 million tweets per day, is the second largest social network after Facebook.

is how the growth and direction of networking will be managed and controlled. In its early days, the Internet was run by a core group of specialists without a financial stake in its future, and its management was relatively simple. Currently, the Internet is managed by the *Internet Society*, the nonprofit agency first introduced in Section 7.3. Now that it is a global phenomenon that affects millions of people and generates hundreds of billions of dollars in revenue, the Internet is being pulled and tugged by many new constituencies and stakeholders, such as corporations, politicians, lawyers, advertisers, government agencies, and manufacturers. The question now is who will speak for the Internet in the future and who will help shape its destiny. As the designers of the Internet warned at the end of their paper (see footnote 3 on page 375) on the history of networking:

If the Internet stumbles, it will not be because we lack for technology, vision, or motivation. It will be because we cannot set a direction and march collectively into the future.

EXERCISES

1. Show how a modem would encode the 5-bit binary sequence 11001 onto an analog carrier by

   a. Modifying its amplitude (the height of the carrier wave)

   b. Modifying its frequency (the number of waves per second)

2. A modem can also modify the *phase* of a carrier wave to encode binary data. Find out what the phase of a signal is and determine how it can be modified so that it can encode the same 5-bit signal 11001 used in Exercise 1.

3. Explain why noise and interference have a more serious impact on an analog transmission line (like a telephone link) than on a digital transmission line.

4. Determine the total time it takes to transmit an uncompressed grayscale image (with 8 bits/pixel) from a screen with a resolution of 1,280 × 840 pixels using each of the following media:

   a. A 56 Kbps modem

   b. A 1.5 Mbps DSL line

   c. A 100 Mbps Ethernet link

5. Assume that we need to transmit a 1,440 × 900 uncompressed color image (using 16 bits per color pixel) over a computer network in less than 0.01 second. What is the minimal necessary line speed to meet this goal?

6. a. Assume there are one million books in your campus library. Approximate (to the nearest order of magnitude) how many bytes of data there are if all these books were stored online and accessible across a computer network.

   b. How long does it take to transfer the entire collection of books if the data rate of the transmission medium is 10 Mbps, the speed of the original Ethernet? How long does it take if we have a line with a speed of 1 Gbps? (This value represents the time needed to download your entire campus library.)

7. Why is an address field needed in the Ethernet LAN protocol? Can you think of a useful situation where you might want either to omit the address field entirely or to use some "special" address value in the address field?

8. After reviewing the description of the Ethernet protocol in Section 7.3.2, how do you think this

protocol behaves in a very heavily loaded network—that is, a network environment where there are lots of nodes attempting to send messages? Explain what behavior you expect to see and why.

9. The Ethernet is a distributed LAN protocol, which means that there is no centralized control node and that the failure of a single node can never bring down the entire network. However, can you think of any advantage to the creation of a centralized LAN in which one node is in charge of the entire network and makes all decisions about who can send a message and who must wait? Explain.

10. Agree or disagree with the following assertion and state why:

> In an Ethernet network, even though there are collisions, every message is guaranteed to be delivered in some maximum amount of time T.

11. a. Assume there is a wide area network with N nodes, where $N \geq 2$. What is the *smallest* number of point-to-point communication links such that *every* node in the network is able to talk to every other node? (*Note:* A network in which some nodes are unable to exchange messages with other nodes because there is no path between them is called *disconnected*.)

    b. If you are worried about having a disconnected network, what type of interconnection structure should you use when configuring your network?

12. In Exercise 11, you determined the minimum number of links needed to ensure that *every* one of the N nodes in a network can communicate with every other node. However, most networks have far more than this minimum. What are the advantages of having these "extra" nodes in the network?

13. What happens to the store-and-forward protocol of Figure 7.8 if a packet M is repeatedly sent from node A to node B but never correctly arrives at B? (Perhaps the link from A to B is broken.) What modifications can we make to this protocol to handle this situation?

14. The ARQ algorithm described in Section 7.3.2 is quite inefficient because the sending node must stop sending until it receives an explicit ACK from the receiving node. Can you design a modification to the ARQ protocol that makes it more efficient by not requiring the sender to stop and wait each time it sends a message? Describe your revised protocol in detail.

15. How could we *broadcast* a message using an ARQ algorithm? That is, how do we send the same message to 100 different nodes on a WAN?

16. Given the following diagram, where the numbers represent the time delays across a link:

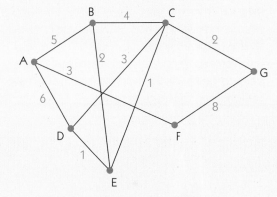

    a. How many simple paths (those that do not repeat a node) are there from node A to G?

    b. What is the *shortest path* from node A to node G? What is the overall delay?

    c. If node E fails, does that change the shortest path? If so, what is the new shortest path?

17. Here is a simple heuristic (approximation algorithm) for routing a message from node A to node B in a reasonable amount of time. The algorithm assumes that *every* node in the network has at least two outgoing links.

> Assume A has n outgoing links, $n \geq 2$, with delays to the node on the other side of $a_1, a_2, \ldots, a_n$. Select the link with the shortest delay and send the message on that line. If the message arrives at node B, you are done. Otherwise, repeat this process until the message does arrive at its intended destination, but do *not* send the

message directly back to the node from where it just came. That is, if the message was sent from A to C, then C should not return the message to A. In this case, choose the second-lowest delay value for the outgoing line.

Will this heuristic always deliver the message from node A to node B? If not, explain why.

18. What are some of the specific responsibilities performed by the device called a gateway (diagrammed in Figure 7.21) that is placed between two different types of networks to allow them to communicate?

19. In Section 7.3.4, we said that the Transport layer turns the inherently unreliable Network layer into an error-free delivery service. However, the Network layer uses the services of the Data Link layer, which is guaranteed to correctly deliver messages on a point-to-point link. For example, assume we have the following four-node network:

If the Network layer is sending a message from A to D via B, it can be sure that a message sent by the Data Link layer from A to B will always correctly get to B, and a message sent from B to D will always correctly get to D. How then is it possible for the Network layer to be unable to correctly deliver a message from A to D?

20. What are the advantages of breaking up a single logical message into a number of fixed-sized packets and then sending each one of those packets independently through the network?

21. Look at the home page of the Internet Society (*www.isoc.org*) and read about one of the designers of the original ARPANET—Larry Roberts, Leonard Kleinrock, Vinton Cerf, Robert Kahn, John Postel, or others. Learn about the early days of networking and the contributions that these individuals made to the ultimate development of the Internet. The home page of the Internet Society has links to many other places that provide a wealth of fascinating information about networks in general and the Internet and the Web in particular.

CHALLENGE WORK

The TCP/IP protocols are the heart and soul of the Internet, and they describe the fundamental rules that govern all communications in the network. Read more about the TCP/IP protocols and write a report describing their basic characteristics and giving a simple overview of the way that they work.

One of the best places to go for this information is a set of documents called RFCs (Request for Comments). These are a series of documents produced by the Internet Engineering Task Force (IETF) that describe virtually all aspects of the Internet's behavior, including its protocols. Some RFCs contain enormously detailed technical specifications of the workings of the Internet, while others are more informational or tutorial (even humorous) in nature. A good place to start is RFC 1180, "A TCP/IP Tutorial." A complete set of all the Internet RFCs is located at *www.faqs.org/rfcs*, and it can be searched using the searchable database located at that Web site.

ADDITIONAL RESOURCES

 For additional print and/or online resources relevant to this chapter, visit the Computer Science CourseMate at login.cengagebrain.com.

Information Security

8.1 Introduction

Information security means, of course, keeping information secure—that is, protected from those who should not have access to it. Information security could cover information locked in your filing cabinet, stuffed somewhere in your purse or wallet, or lying around on your desk. But today it usually means electronic information, data stored on your computer's hard disk or your cell phone, or data being transmitted across wired or wireless network connections.

In the early days of computing, when big mainframes were the only option, physical security was enforced by securing the rooms housing these machines. Only authorized persons had access. Now that there is a machine on virtually every desktop, a laptop in many briefcases, and a cell phone in every pocket, that kind of physical security is harder to obtain, but you can take some obvious steps: Don't leave your laptop lying around; never leave your workstation running when you are not in the room; do not share your password with anyone; and don't lose your cell phone!

However, the danger of someone nearby swiping your laptop or cell phone pales in comparison with the risks the Internet and the World Wide Web (discussed in the previous chapter) have brought. As our virtual environment expands, we celebrate the ability to reach out from our desktop, laptop, or handheld device to the rest of the world, receiving information, entertainment, and communications from thousands of sources. But we may be less aware of the potential for thousands of sources around the world to reach into our machines to do harm or steal information.

Security can be breached at many different points in the "virtual machine" we have presented in the last few chapters. Flaws in assembly language programming can be exploited, operating system protections can be circumvented, and computer networks (wired or wireless) present all kinds of opportunities for viewing, manipulating, or destroying data. Consequences can range from annoyance to identity theft to major economic losses or threats to national security. Because there are so many ways in which security can be compromised, and the consequences can be so serious, information security is an important topic of both research and practice.

8.2 Threats and Defenses

You are no doubt aware of the possible threats to the security of your personal property, such as your car or the contents of your home or apartment. That's why you probably carry auto and home or renter's insurance. Aside from fire, flood, or other accidents, someone can steal your property, causing you financial harm and emotional distress. Everyone wants a secure environment. Your defenses against theft are to employ locks and possibly an alarm system. The alarm system only comes into play in an active manner if security has already been breached, but the announcement that a property is alarmed can be a deterrent to break-ins. While it's true that an experienced thief can quickly pick a lock, it's easier to break into an unlocked house. Be it thieves or computer hackers, either will attack the most vulnerable spots.

This section discusses the threat of individual computers being accessed by the wrong people, and also the threats to which a computer is exposed through network connections; in addition, it describes various defenses against these threats.

8.2.1 Authentication and Authorization

The first line of defense against illicit use of, or threats to, computer resources and sensitive information is a strong authentication and authorization process.

Authentication. You want to start up your computer. You want to retrieve your e-mail. You want to access your online bank account to transfer money or pay a bill. What's the first thing you have to do in all these cases? Generally, it is to log on to your machine or to the appropriate Web page by giving your user ID and password. (You may also be asked to

How Hackers Became Crackers

Every new technology develops its own set of "undesirables"—those who see a new technology in terms not of potential benefits but of increased opportunities for misuse, just as automobiles brought wonderful benefits but also car thieves and drunk drivers. In computer science, our abusive subculture goes by the name **hackers**.

Originally, the word *hacker* did not have a negative connotation. It was a mildly complimentary term for people who knew how to get things done on a computer—those somewhat strange and quirky individuals who seemed to know all the incomprehensible details about how computers worked, in essence, computer enthusiasts. They were the "tinkerers" and "fixers" who could enter some weird sequence of commands that miraculously cured whatever was wrong with your system.

As computers became more and more important to the functioning of society, and as computer networks increased the number of machines that could be accessed by individuals, the term *hacker* began to take on a different meaning. Some hackers turned their talents to figuring out how to override security measures to gain unauthorized access to other computers. Why? Perhaps for fun, or just because they could—the computer equivalent of joyriding in a stolen automobile. The results at first were relatively harmless. But soon these explorations turned to exploitations—ways to attack computer systems and cause destruction. Sometimes the word **cracker** is used to denote those who break in to someone else's computer (like "cracking" a safe) as opposed to the more innocent "hacker" of the original use of the word. The general usage, however, is "hacker" for both types of intent. Computer code (scripts) or even downloadable programs for hacking can be found on the Internet. So it's possible to be an amateur hacker with little or no understanding of the technical aspects involved. "Professional" hackers view with disdain those *script kiddies* who resort to such tactics. Be aware, though, that any type of hacking is illegal and punishable under the law by fines or imprisonment. Just as vandalism is not considered a harmless prank, the misuse of information technology is no longer viewed as the harmless intellectual play of "computer jockeys." It is seen for what it is—a serious crime with serious consequences and very severe penalties.

Hacking is no longer the province solely of individuals. Just as there are organized "professional" auto theft rings that operate on a national or even international scale, there are organized hacking groups. Computer hacking on a large scale costs governments and businesses billions of dollars per year in terms of lost business, stolen information, and, more intangibly, loss of trust. Computer attacks from one country on the computing resources of another country with intent to damage or destroy computer systems or steal sensitive information are no longer mere "hacking" but cross over into **cyberwarfare**.

answer a special "security question.") This authentication process on your computer is managed by your machine's operating system, as we learned in Chapter 6. On the Web page, it is managed by the operating system of the Web server computer. Authentication is the process of verifying that you really are the person who has the right to access this computer, whether it is your local machine or the Web server. The operating system maintains a file of user IDs and corresponding passwords. When a user attempts to log on to the machine, the operating system reads the user ID and checks that the password matches the password for that user in the password file. Hackers breaking into a computer system look for a file of user IDs and passwords as the "Open, Sesame" for all locked doors.

If the user ID/password list were just in the form of

```
Tijara     popsicle
Murphy   badboy2
Jaylynn   mom
   ...
```

then the entire system would be compromised if this password file were stolen (copied). Instead, the operating system *encrypts* the password for a given user—converts it into a representation that cannot be understood without the appropriate decryption algorithm. The encryption process that is used is called a hash function; this form of encryption is easy to apply but hard to undo. The hash function takes the password the user originally chooses, chops it up, and stirs it around according to a given formula. As a very simple example, suppose the hash function process is the following:

1. Take each letter in the password and replace it with a number representing its place in the alphabet (a → 1, b → 2, etc.). Leave each digit in the password alone. In the preceding case, "badboy2" would become

   2 1 4 2 15 25 2

2. Add up these digits to get a single integer. In this example

   $2 + 1 + 4 + 2 + 15 + 25 + 2 = 51$

3. Divide the integer from Step 2 by 7 and find the remainder. In this example, dividing 51 by 7 gives a remainder of 2 (51 equals 7×7 with 2 left over).

4. Add 1 to the result from Step 3, then multiply the new number by 9. In this example, the result equals $(2 + 1) \times 9 = 27$.

5. Reverse the digits in the integer from Step 4 and then replace each digit with the corresponding letter of the alphabet. The result for this example is 72, which becomes gb.

The encrypted password file would contain an entry of

```
Murphy  gb
```

and the original password is discarded.

Now when Tom Murphy attempts to log on, he gives "Murphy" as the user ID and enters a password. The operating system applies the hash function to that password and compares the encrypted result to the encrypted value "gb" stored in the password file for that user ID. If there is a match, Tom is recognized as an authorized user and allowed access to the computer.

You may have forgotten a password to some online account at, let's say, Ninth Street Bank, and asked for help. The people in charge of Ninth Street Bank's Web server will e-mail you a temporary password that will allow you to log on and then require you to reset your password to something you choose (which will change your entry in the password file). You might find this annoying and wonder why they didn't just send you your original password. As we've just seen, the system at online Ninth Street Bank doesn't actually know your original password, only its encrypted form and—as we are about to see—this isn't enough information to regenerate the original password.

If you managed to steal the encrypted password file, you would not be able to recover the original password, even if you knew the steps of the algorithm. In our simple example, you could reverse Steps 5 and 4, but not Step 3. For example,

chjbup5

also hashes to gb, so clearly the process is not reversible. In fact, algorithms for hashing seem to be well known for each operating system, but, as we have seen here, knowledge of the hashing algorithm does not give you (or the system administrator) certain knowledge of the original password, even if you have the encrypted password file.

But this appears to raise another problem. What if Fred and Alice have two different passwords that hash to the same encrypted value? What if Fred and Alice chose the same original password? In general, this is not a problem—both Fred and Alice can log in using their respective passwords. But if Fred stole the password file and saw that his password and Alice's password hashed to the same value, he would have a better than random chance of guessing Alice's password; he would certainly try his own password with Alice's user ID, and he would be successful if indeed the passwords were the same.

To solve this problem, some operating systems keep a third entry for each user in the password file, namely the exact time at which the user created the password. This *timestamp* gets appended to the original password, and the result is then run through the encryption algorithm. That way, two identical passwords do not hash to the same value because the probability that they were created at the exact same instant in time is infinitesimally small. This also solves the problem of two nonidentical passwords that otherwise would hash to the same value. When someone attempting to log on gives his or her password, the operating system consults the password file, appends the timestamp for that user ID to the password just entered, encrypts the result, and compares it with the encrypted password entry for that user ID in the password file.

Nonetheless, there are ways in which the operating system's authentication process is vulnerable. Consider Ravi, who has not stolen the password file but nevertheless knows Alice's user ID and wants to hack into Alice's account. Because Ravi knows Alice personally, he might try to guess her password. He might try her nickname, the name of her pet poodle, the title of her favorite band. Of course he could also try "alice", "123456", or—a perennial favorite—"password". Many systems set "password" as the default value, and if Alice hasn't changed (or been required to change) her password, this will get Ravi into Alice's account. Failing at these attempts, Ravi might use a brute force attack by trying all possible passwords. Suppose there are n possible characters that can be used in a password (at least uppercase and lowercase letters and the 10 digits are possibilities). To try all possible passwords of length k or less would require

$$n^1 + n^2 + \ldots + n^k = \frac{n(n^k - 1)}{n - 1}$$

attempts. On the average, Ravi might be successful after about

$$(n^1 + n^2 + \ldots + n^k)/2$$

attempts. But this will be very time consuming (see Exercise 3 at the end of this chapter). In addition, most systems have a lockout after some number of failed tries, which would foil this approach.

For someone who has stolen the password file, a better way to find a password is by using password-cracking software. For a given user ID (which our villain knows because the user ID is not encoded), password-cracking software will first try all words in its built-in dictionary, encrypting each with the well-known hash function and comparing the result with the password file. Such software is amazingly fast and can try a million or more potential passwords per second. If this fails, it will then go on to more sophisticated techniques such as word list substitutions for common phrases. With knowledge of the hash algorithm, the software might use a *rainbow table*, a precomputed list of passwords and their hash values, so checking for a particular hash value just requires a search of the hash values in the table. A brute force attack is a last resort.

Surprisingly, the easiest way to obtain someone's password is not to steal the password file (hard to do) or to guess that person's password (time consuming), but to use social engineering. Social engineering is the process of using people to get the information you want. If Ravi wants Alice's password, he might just ask her! In a business setting, he might get a chance to snoop around her office and find the yellow sticky note containing her password attached to her monitor or stuck beneath her keyboard. He might violate "password etiquette" and watch over her shoulder while she logs on. Or he could try an indirect approach; he could call Alice's (gullible) secretary and, posing as an IT technician, explain that Alice has called the IT service group about some computer problems she is experiencing and that to fix them, he needs Alice's password. Most companies try to educate their employees about the dangers of social engineering.

Your best defense against someone guessing your password is to be smart about how you choose and use your password.

Password Pointers

Choosing passwords

- Use long passwords (at least eight characters)
- Use a mixture of uppercase and lowercase letters, digits, and special symbols (if allowed on your system)
- Consider using the first letters of some long phrase that is meaningful to you, mixed with some digits or special symbols; for example, the password "Timptlwswa" could be an acronym for "This is my password that I won't share with anyone"
- Avoid personal information such as your name, user ID, pet's name, or birthdate
- Avoid common dictionary words
- Avoid such obvious choices as "abcde", "123456", or "Hello"

Using passwords

- Change your password often (many systems require this) and do not reuse old passwords
- Use different passwords for different applications
- Don't tell anyone your password
- Don't write your password down
- Be wary when your browser offers to remember a password for you
- Be very careful about entering a password over an unencrypted wireless network

Managing passwords may be a bit of a hassle, but security measures are always a balancing act between user convenience and user protection.

Although user IDs and passwords are the most common authentication mechanism, there are other options. Many systems ask you to preselect answers to a list of questions about personal information that you will know but others may not (the first name of your maternal grandmother, the city in which you went to high school, etc.). Then when you present your user ID, you must respond with the correct answer to one of these questions before you are even asked for your password. Some laptops now use *biometric information*, that is, fingerprint scanning. Some company networks use a *one-time password* scheme that works as follows: The legitimate user enters his or her user ID and partial password. Each user has a small device that then generates the (random) last half of the password, which is good only for a few seconds. The system knows both the first half and last half and checks for a match after the user enters the last half. In this way, the password is quite secure because it is only valid for a very short time.

Practice Problem

Using the hash function described in this section, verify that the password "chjbup5" also hashes to "gb".

Don't forget the most basic physical security principles—maintain control of your laptop and handheld devices, including your cell phone; be sure no one peers over your shoulder in your office or on the airplane; lock your office door when you leave; and so on. In a secure business or government environment, video surveillance cameras can enhance security, and visitors to a secure server site are checked against an access list and logged in to and out of the room.

Authorization. Authorization governs what an authenticated user is allowed to do. Enforcing authorization rules is also one of the jobs of the operating system, as discussed in Chapter 6. On your own machine, you may have administrative privileges and be able to see everything on the machine. On your banking Web site, you can only see your own account information. The operating system maintains access control lists. Depending on who the users are, they have various privileges, such as

- Read access (can read a particular file)
- Write access (can modify a particular file)
- Execute access (can run a particular program file)
- Delete access (can delete a particular file)

As a student in a class, you have read/write/delete access to your own files. You have execute access and read access to programs and files the instructor has placed in a common folder. The instructor probably has access to the files of all students in the class. The system administrator or superuser has access to everything, and is the person who sets up the authorization privileges for all other users. A careful operating system will check every access every time by every user.

8.2.2 Threats from the Network

Once your handheld device, your personal computer, a business computer, or a Web server computer is connected to the Internet, there are many more possibilities for harm. Attacks can come from anonymous sources anywhere in the world via many intermediate nodes that maintain varying levels of security. Recall the complexity of the Internet, the fact that it is not specifically governed by any one entity, and the idea that the whole point is to share information, and it is clear what a difficult task "Internet security" can be.

Most of these threats come in the form of malware (*mal*icious soft*ware*) that can attack an individual computer. The most common attacks to individual computers are by viruses, worms, Trojan horses, and denial of service.

Virus. A virus is a computer program that, like a biological virus, infects a host computer and then spreads. It embeds itself within another program or file. When that program or file is activated, the virus copies itself and attacks other files on the system. The results may be as simple as taunting pop-up messages, but could also include erratic behavior or drastic slowdown of the computer, corrupted or deleted files, loss of data, or system crashes. The virus is spread from one machine to another by passing on the infected file, perhaps on a flash drive. By far the most common mechanism for spreading a virus, however, is through e-mail attachments. An infected file is attached to an e-mail message and sent out to 100 people, for example. Anyone who downloads and opens the attachment causes the virus to replicate the infected file and perhaps send it out as an e-mail attachment to the first 100 people in that person's personal address book. In this way, a virus can potentially spread like wildfire across the Internet.

Worm. A worm is very similar to a virus, but it can send copies of itself to other nodes on a computer network without having to be carried by an infected host file. It is a self-replicating piece of software that can travel from node to node without any human intervention. In its most benign form, a worm can clog the Internet so that legitimate traffic is slowed or shut out completely. In addition, the worm might also subvert the host systems it passes through so that, at a later time, those systems can be controlled by the worm's author and used to send spam (junk) e-mail, deface Web pages, or perform other mischief.

Trojan Horse. A Trojan horse (in the software world) is a computer program that does some harmless little job but also, unbeknownst to the user, contains code to perform the same kinds of malicious attacks as viruses and worms—corrupt or delete files, slow down the computer, and the like. It might also upload or download files, capture the user's address book to send out spam e-mail, hide a keystroke logger that captures the user's passwords and credit card numbers (and sends them to someone else), or even put the computer under someone else's remote control at some point in the future. A computer can become infected by a Trojan horse when the user downloads infected software from a malicious Web site. In fact even visiting an infected Web site can, behind the scenes, download a Trojan horse (an attack called a drive-by exploit or drive-by download).

Denial of Service. A denial-of-service (DOS) attack is typically directed at a business or government Web site. The attack automatically directs browsers, usually on many machines, to a single URL at roughly the same time. The result causes so much network traffic to the targeted site that it is effectively shut down to legitimate users. (Spam e-mail can accomplish a similar, but less targeted effect, by flooding the Internet with e-mail messages that consume available bandwidth and clog mail servers.) If many machines are perpetrating this mischief, it's called a *distributed denial-of-service attack,* or *DDOS.* A DDOS may use thousands of machines, enabling much heavier attack traffic and at the same time making it harder to track down and disable all of the attacking machines. Many times, these machines are personal computers that were infected at some point by a Trojan horse. Then at a later time, the Trojan horse is activated in all these machines, putting them under the command of a single controller. This collection of machines is sometimes called a zombie army or botnet (short for "ro*bot net*work" because the machines act like robots under someone else's control).

Beware the Trojan Horse

The "Trojan horse" usually refers to a wooden horse in Greek mythology that the Greeks left as a "gift" for their enemies, the Trojans, during the Trojan War. When the Trojans pulled the horse into the city, the Greek soldiers hiding inside sneaked out under cover of nightfall, opened the gates of Troy to the Greek army, and Troy was defeated.

In the same way, Trojan horse software works by hiding destructive code within some seemingly legitimate program where it waits until it can sneak out and spring into action. A Trojan horse known as Coreflood or AF Core Trojan has some dangerous capabilities. It can infect the computing capability of an entire network. If a system administrator logs on to an infected machine, say for routine maintenance, the Trojan horse infects the system administrator's machine and thereafter any machine the system administrator logs on to. The current variation of Coreflood captures banking or brokerage account user IDs, passwords, and balance information. In 2008, a security company was able to find a host computer where the Coreflood perpetrators maintained a database of over 50 GB of data they had stolen from over 378,000 computers during the previous 16 months, including 14,000 machines within a global hotel chain network. Widespread attacks also occurred at financial institutions, hospitals, and even a law enforcement agency. At the time of this writing, the authors of the Coreflood attack have not been identified. However, in 2011 the FBI and the U.S. Department of Justice seized several Coreflood command-and-control servers. Now, when a botnet (zombie) machine attempts to contact a Coreflood server, it reaches a substitute server that orders Coreflood to uninstall itself from the botnet machine. In addition, Coreflood now cannot further update itself, which will allow antivirus software to detect and remove Coreflood from infected machines. Eventually the botnet should be dismantled entirely.

Don't Mess with Amazon

On December 10, 2010, a DDOS attack was launched against Amazon.com by a hacker group called Anonymous. The attack came as a reprisal when Amazon's Web hosting service refused to continue to host Wikileaks pages (Wikileaks had previously released many U.S. State Department secret documents) yet sold an e-book purportedly containing some of the same leaked information. The attack lasted less than an hour, however, because Anonymous realized it was having little effect. Its botnet (about 2,000 machines) was not big enough to bring down the Amazon servers. The reason is that Amazon is geared to withstand peak traffic by pushing work off to a network of servers that has huge spare capacity. And as this attack occurred in the time frame of Amazon's busy holiday season, it just looked like a little extra blip.

The cybersecurity firm Damballa estimated an increase in the total number of PC botnet slaves of over 600% in 2010 compared with 2009.[1] This is due at least in part to a growing number of "do-it-yourself" botnet construction kits that are commercially available through underground channels. To appreciate the scale of the botnet problem, consider that in March 2010, Spanish authorities arrested the controllers of one of the largest botnets in history, the Mariposa, estimated to involve 12 million computers. Used to steal information from companies, governments, and educational institutions in over 190 countries, the subnets of the system were also available for lease to other cybercriminals.

Phishing. Phishing is not a direct attack on a computer. Instead, **phishing** is a practice used to illegally obtain sensitive information such as credit card numbers, account numbers, and passwords. An e-mail is sent claiming to be from a legitimate organization such as a bank, credit card company, or online retailer asking the recipient to click on a link to update or verify his or her account information. Often the message contains a warning that your account will be suspended or canceled if you fail to provide this information (although this personal information is already on file with the legitimate organization if indeed you do have an account there). The link takes the unwary user to a fake Web site that appears to be legitimate and captures the information the user enters. Despite the fact that no legitimate bank or other financial organization ever operates this way, many people fall for this scheme and become victims of identity theft, suffering financial losses that in total cost consumers hundreds of millions of dollars.

[1]www.damballa.com/downloads/r_pubs/Damballa_2010_Top_10_Botnets_Report.pdf

The term *phishing* came about because perpetrators cast out bait, in the form of e-mail messages, to a large number of potential victims in the hope that one or two will "bite" and fall for this scam. The cost to mount a phishing attack is minimal, so even a tiny number of "bites" brings a profit. The success rate is actually quite low; statistical data shows that only about 12 of every 1,000,000 bank customers will receive a phishing e-mail and follow a link to a fake Web site, and only half of those will actually enter personal data. But there were over 67,000 distinct phishing attacks worldwide in the last half of 2010, and each such attack can target millions of individuals.

Never follow the link in such a message or reply to the message; instead, delete the message immediately. If you want to check an account's status, open a separate browser window and access your account information as you normally would.

In March 2011, 342 institutions were the targets of phishing attacks, meaning that e-mail was sent supposedly from these institutions. The Anti-Phishing Working Group (APWG) is an industry and law enforcement association

Gone Phishin'

In 2011, a major security breach occurred at a marketing services company called Epsilon. This company is an e-mail service provider, sending out e-mail on behalf of its 2,500 corporate clients. Epsilon retains e-mail addresses for the customers of these clients, and the address lists for customers of about 50 of those businesses were stolen, probably millions of individual e-mail addresses. Hence, many individuals who may have read a small article about this and thought, "I've never heard of Epsilon, I surely don't have an account with them, so this can't affect me," woke up a day or two later to e-mail messages from companies such as Target, J. P. Morgan Chase, Best Buy, and Citigroup, with whom they do have an account. These messages assured customers (acting on information supplied by Epsilon) that no financial or sensitive data such as account numbers, credit card numbers, login information, or balances was stolen, only names and e-mail addresses. The messages went on to warn against the possibility of fraudulent e-mails as a result and in most cases provided advice not to give out personal or financial information in response to e-mail requests, not to open e-mail from unknown senders, and so forth.

Even though no financial data was obtained, experts warn that this security breach could lead to waves of *spear phishing*—phishing sent to targeted audiences. In other words, if information is known about companies with whom you do business on a regular basis, an e-mail message can be crafted to align with your probable interests and known business relationships so as to create more convincing "bait" on which you are more likely to "nibble."

Defense Against the Dark Arts

You may feel at this point that you should just unplug your computer from the Internet or disable your wireless capability. The good news is you can protect yourself.

- Be sure your computer has up-to-date **antivirus software** from a reputable company. Such software can detect worms, viruses, and Trojan horses by distinctive "signatures" those programs carry. It cleans your machine of infected files. Most antivirus software comes with a feature for automatic updates; this is necessary because the "good guys" have to keep up with the new ideas from the "bad guys."
- Be sure your computer has up-to-date **firewall software** from a reputable company. Firewall software guards the access points to your computer, blocking communications to or from sites you don't permit.
- Be sure your computer has up-to-date **antispyware** from a reputable company. Antispyware routinely scans your computer for any "spyware" programs that may have infected your machine—programs that capture information on what Web sites you have visited and what passwords and credit card numbers you have used.
- Be sure to install the latest **security patches** or updates to your operating system, whatever operating system you use. All operating systems are vulnerable.
- Don't open e-mail attachments from unknown sources, especially files with .exe or .zip extensions.
- Don't download software except from reputable sources.
- Don't send personal or financial information in response to any e-mail ("My wealthy Nigerian uncle left me a fortune that I am willing to share with you but I need your account number . . .").

Practice Problem

Do some research on the Morris worm, the first major computer worm. Who wrote it, when was it released, how did it spread, what are the estimates of how much damage it caused (in dollar amounts), and what happened to the originator of the worm?

focusing on helping eliminate identity theft resulting from phishing (*www. antiphishing.org/index.html*). It provides discussion forums, maintains statistics, and tests promising technology solutions. The average phishing site is left online for about three days, making it difficult to catch those responsible.

8.3 Encryption

Much of the thrust of information security, as we have talked about it so far, is to devise defenses so that the "bad guys" can't steal our information. If, despite these precautions, files on a computer hard disk or packets passing along a network connection are illegally accessed and fall into the wrong hands, we can still protect their contents through encryption. Essentially, this makes the information meaningless to the bad guys even if they do manage to steal it. We've already discussed encryption of the password file by the operating system as a security measure, in case the password file is stolen. In this section, we discuss various other encryption mechanisms, which apply both to data stored and data sent.

8.3.1 Encryption Overview

Cryptography is the science of "secret writing." A message (*plaintext*) is encoded (encrypted) before it is sent, for the purpose of keeping its content secret if it is intercepted by the wrong parties. The encrypted message is called *ciphertext*. The ciphertext is decoded (decrypted) back to plaintext when it is received, in order to retrieve the original information. More formally, **encryption** is the process of using an algorithm to convert information into a representation that cannot be understood or utilized by anyone without the appropriate decryption algorithm; **decryption** is the reverse of encryption, using an algorithm that converts the ciphertext back into plaintext. Encryption and decryption date back thousands of years. The most famous instances of cryptography occur in military history, beginning with Julius Caesar of the Roman Empire, who developed the Caesar cipher, discussed in the next section. In more modern times, the military importance of cryptography was illustrated by the German Enigma code cracked by the Allies during World War II.[2]

Encryption and decryption are inverse operations because decryption must "undo" the encryption and reproduce the original text. (An exception is hash function encoding, used for password encryption, which is a one-way code and does not involve decryption.) There are many encryption/decryption algorithms, and of course both the sender and receiver must use the same system. A **symmetric encryption algorithm** requires the use of a secret key known to both the sender and receiver. The sender encrypts the plaintext using the key. The receiver, knowing the key, is easily able to reverse the

---

[2]In May 2011, the British National Museum of Computing reconstructed one of the early British decryption machines, using circuits from old telephone exchanges. See *www.bbc.co.uk/ news/technology-13566878*.

process and decrypt the message. One of the difficulties with a symmetric encryption algorithm is how to securely transmit the secret key so that both the sender and the receiver know what it is; in fact, this approach seems to simply move the security problem to a slightly different level, from transmitting a message to transmitting a key. In an asymmetric encryption algorithm, also called a public key encryption algorithm, the key for encryption and the key for decryption are quite different, although related. Person A can make an encryption key public, and anyone can encrypt a message using A's public key and send it to A. Only A has the decryption key, however, so only A can decrypt the message. This approach avoids the difficulty of secret key transmission, but it introduces a new problem: The relationship between the decryption key and the encryption key must be sufficiently complex that it is not possible to derive the decryption key from the public encryption key.

8.3.2 Simple Encryption Algorithms

Caesar Cipher. A Caesar cipher, also called a *shift cipher*, involves shifting each character in the message to another character some fixed distance farther along in the alphabet. Specifically, let *s* be some integer between 1 and 25 that represents the amount of shift. Each letter in the message is encoded as the letter that is *s* units farther along in the alphabet, with the last *s* letters of the alphabet shifted in a cycle to the first *s* letters. For example, if $s = 3$, then *A* is encoded as *D, B* is encoded as *E, X* is encoded as *A*, and *Z* is encoded as *C*. The integer *s* is the secret key. Decoding a message, given knowledge of *s*, simply means reversing the shift. For example, if $s = 3$, then the code word DUPB is decoded as ARMY.

The Caesar cipher is an example of a stream cipher; that is, it encodes one character at a time. This makes it easy to encode just by scanning the plaintext and doing the appropriate substitution at each character. On the other hand, there are only 25 possible keys, so a ciphertext message could be decoded by brute force, that is, by simply trying all possible keys.

In addition, the Caesar cipher is a *substitution cipher*, whereby a single letter of plaintext generates a single letter of ciphertext. We can replace the simple shift mechanism of the Caesar cipher with a more complex substitution mechanism, for example:

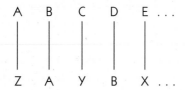

(Can you guess the substitution algorithm being used?) However, in any simple substitution cipher, the structure of the plaintext is maintained in the ciphertext—letter frequency, occurrence of double letters, frequently occurring letter combinations, and so forth. With a sufficiently long message, an experienced *cryptanalyst* (code breaker) can use these clues to recover the plaintext.

Block Cipher. In a block cipher, a group or block of plaintext letters gets encoded into a block of ciphertext, but not by substituting one character at a time for each letter. Each plaintext character in the block contributes to more than one ciphertext character, and each ciphertext character is the result of more than one plaintext letter. It is as if each plaintext character in a block gets chopped into little pieces, and these pieces are scattered among the ciphertext characters in the corresponding block. This tends to destroy the structure of the plaintext and make decryption more difficult.

As a simple example, we'll use a block size of 2 and an encoding key that is a 2 × 2 arrangement of numbers called a *matrix*. Here A and B

$$A = \begin{bmatrix} 1 & 2 \\ 3 & 4 \end{bmatrix} \qquad B = \begin{bmatrix} 5 & 1 \\ 2 & 1 \end{bmatrix}$$

are matrices. We can define an operation of matrix multiplication as follows. The product $A \times B$ will also be a 2 × 2 matrix, where the element in row i, column j of $A \times B$ is obtained by multiplying each element in row i of A by its corresponding element in column j of B and adding the results. So to obtain the element in row 1, column 1 of the result, we multiply the row 1 elements of A by the corresponding column 1 elements of B and add the results:

$$\begin{bmatrix} 1 & 2 \\ 3 & 4 \end{bmatrix} \times \begin{bmatrix} 5 & 1 \\ 2 & 1 \end{bmatrix} = \begin{bmatrix} 9 & \\ & \end{bmatrix}$$
$$1*5 + 2*2 = 5 + 4 = 9$$

To obtain the element in row 1, column 2 of the result, we multiply the row 1 elements of A by the corresponding column 2 elements of B and add the results:

$$\begin{bmatrix} 1 & 2 \\ 3 & 4 \end{bmatrix} \times \begin{bmatrix} 5 & 1 \\ 2 & 1 \end{bmatrix} = \begin{bmatrix} 9 & 3 \\ & \end{bmatrix}$$

The completed product A × B is $\begin{bmatrix} 9 & 3 \\ 23 & 7 \end{bmatrix}$.

However, for encryption purposes, we are going to modify this definition. When we add up the terms for each element, whenever we exceed 25, we will start over again, counting from 0. In this scheme, $26 \rightarrow 0$, $27 \rightarrow 1$, $28 \rightarrow 2, \ldots, 52 \rightarrow 0$, and so on.

Not every 2 × 2 matrix can serve as an encryption key; we need an *invertible matrix*. This is a matrix M for which there is another matrix M' such that

$$M' \times M = \begin{bmatrix} 1 & 0 \\ 0 & 1 \end{bmatrix}$$

For example, $\begin{bmatrix} 3 & 5 \\ 2 & 3 \end{bmatrix}$ is invertible because for $M' = \begin{bmatrix} 23 & 5 \\ 2 & 23 \end{bmatrix}$

$$M' \times M = \begin{bmatrix} 23 & 5 \\ 2 & 23 \end{bmatrix} \times \begin{bmatrix} 3 & 5 \\ 2 & 3 \end{bmatrix} = \begin{bmatrix} 79 & 130 \\ 52 & 79 \end{bmatrix}$$

$$\rightarrow \begin{bmatrix} 1 & 0 \\ 0 & 1 \end{bmatrix} \quad \text{(remember that any value > 25}$$
$$\text{gets wrapped around to 0).}[3]$$

---

[3]The mathematical function modulo 26 is being applied.

This property is what allows M' to reverse the effect of M. Also, part of our encryption algorithm is a simple substitution (mapping) S that maps letters into numbers; we'll let S be really simple here: $S(A) = 1$, $S(B) = 2$, ... , $S(Z) = 26$. Obviously S is reversible, and we'll call the reverse mapping S': $S'(1) = A$, $S'(2) = B$, ... , $S'(26) = Z$.

To encode our message, we break it up into two-character blocks. Suppose the first two characters form the block $(D\ E)$. We apply the S mapping to this block to get $(4\ 5)$. Now we multiply $(4\ 5) \times M$ by treating $(4\ 5)$ as the row of some matrix (and remember to wrap around if the result exceeds 25):

$$(4\ 5) \times \begin{bmatrix} 3 & 5 \\ 2 & 3 \end{bmatrix} = (4*3 + 5*2 \quad 4*5 + 5*3)$$
$$= (22\ 35) \rightarrow (22\ 9)$$

Finally, apply the S' mapping to get from digits back to characters: $S'(22\ 9) = (V\ I)$. This completes the encoding, and $(V\ I)$ is the ciphertext for the message block $(D\ E)$. Notice that the digit 4 (i.e., the plaintext letter D) contributed to both the 22 (V) and the 9 (I), as did the digit 5 (i.e., the plaintext letter E). This *diffusion* (scattering) of the plaintext within the ciphertext is the advantage of a block cipher.

For decoding, we reverse the previous steps. Starting with the ciphertext $(V\ I)$, we first apply S to get $(22\ 9)$. We then multiply $(22\ 9)$ by M', the inverse of the encoding key (remembering to wrap around if the result exceeds 25):

$$(22\ 9) \times \begin{bmatrix} 23 & 5 \\ 2 & 23 \end{bmatrix} = (22*23 + 9*2 \quad 22*5 + 9*23)$$
$$= (524\ 317) \rightarrow (4\ 5)$$

Finally, we apply S' to get back—voilà!—the plaintext $(D\ E)$.

Figure 8.1 summarizes the steps. Again, the matrix M is the secret encryption key, from which the decryption key M' can be derived.

FIGURE 8.1

Encoding
1. Apply S mapping to plaintext block.
2. Multiply result times M, applying wraparound.
3. Apply S' to the result.

Decoding
1. Apply S mapping to ciphertext block.
2. Multiply result times M', applying wraparound.
3. Apply S' to the result.

Steps in encoding and decoding for a block cipher

Practice Problems

1. Using a Caesar cipher with $s = 5$, encrypt the message NOW IS THE HOUR.

2. A messenger tells you that the secret key for today for the Caesar cipher is $s = 26$. Should you trust the messenger? Why, or why not?

Laboratory Experience 12

The software for this Laboratory Experience uses a block cipher of block size 2. You will be able to encrypt and decrypt messages. The encryption key is again a matrix, but the encryption algorithm is quite different from that of the block cipher discussed in this section.

8.3.3 DES

Both of the previous encryption algorithms—the Caesar cipher and an elementary block cipher—are too simplistic to provide much real security. DES (Data Encryption Standard) is an encryption algorithm developed by IBM in the 1970s for the U.S. National Bureau of Standards (now called the U.S. National Institute of Standards and Technology, or NIST), and is certified as an international standard by the International Organization for Standardization, or ISO (the same organization that certifies the MP3 digital audio format, as discussed in Chapter 4). One might expect this internationally standard algorithm to rest upon some extremely complex and obscure operations, but the DES algorithm actually uses very simple operations—however, it uses them over and over.

DES was designed to protect electronic information, so the plaintext is a binary string of 0s and 1s, just as it is stored in a computer. As we learned in Chapter 4, this means that ordinary text has already undergone an encoding using ASCII or Unicode to convert characters to bit strings. This encoding,

Hiding in Plain Sight

Steganography is the practice of hiding the very existence of a message. It's an old idea; an ancient Greek ruler was said to have sent a (not very urgent) message by tattooing the message on the shaved head of one of his slaves and then sending the slave off after his hair had grown back. The message was revealed on the other end by once more shaving the messenger's head.

These days, steganography has again come into favor in the form of hidden text within images posted on the Web. As we learned in Chapter 4, a colored digital image is composed of individual pixels; in the usual RGB format, 8 bits are allocated for each of the red, green, and blue color components. This allows for $2^8 = 256$ variations of intensity for each color. Let's say the red component in a pixel has the following 8-bit value:

11010010

The least significant bit (the rightmost 0) contributes the least to the color intensity. If this bit is changed from 0 to 1, the red component becomes

11010011

This tiny change (1/256th of the original red color) will not be detectable to the human eye viewing the image.

A text file can be hidden in an image file by changing (if needed) the least significant bit of each byte of the image file to match the binary form of the characters in the text. For example, if the first letter of the text file to be hidden is "A", with ASCII code 01000001, then the first 8 bytes of the image file would be modified (if needed) so that the least significant bits are 0, 1, 0, 0, 0, 0, 0, and 1. To the naked eye, the image appears unaltered.

In the following set of images, the image on the left is the original. The image on the right uses steganography to hide 668 KB of text, over 140 double-spaced pages. Can you see any difference?

however, is not for the purposes of secrecy, and has nothing to do with the cryptographic encoding we are talking about in this chapter.

DES is a block cipher, and the blocks are 64 bits long, meaning that 64 plaintext bits at a time are processed into 64 ciphertext bits. The key is a 64-bit binary key, although only 56 bits are actually used. The algorithm begins by sending the plaintext 64-bit string through an initial *permutation* (rearrangement). The algorithm then cycles through 16 "rounds." Each round i performs the following steps:

1. The incoming 64-bit block is split into a left half L_i and a right half R_i. The right half R_i gets passed through unchanged to become the left half of the next round, L_{i+1}.

2. In addition, the 32 bits in the right half get permuted according to a fixed formula and then expanded to 48 bits by duplicating some of the bits. Meanwhile, the 56-bit key is also permuted (the result is passed on as the key to the next round) and then reduced to 48 bits by omitting some of the bits. These two 48-bit strings are matched bit by bit, using an XOR (exclusive OR) gate for each bit. Figure 8.2 shows the standard symbol for an XOR gate, along with its truth table.

3. The resulting 48-bit string undergoes a substitution and reduction to emerge as a 32-bit string. This string is permuted one more time, and the resulting 32-bit string is matched bit by bit, using XOR gates, with the left half L_i of the input. The result is passed to the next round as the new right half R_{i+1}.

After all 16 rounds are complete, the final left and right halves are recombined into a 64-bit string that is permuted one more time, and the resulting 64-bit string is the ciphertext. Figure 8.3 outlines the steps involved in the DES algorithm.

Two important points about the DES algorithm: The first is that every substitution, reduction, expansion, and permutation is determined by a well-known set of tables. So, given the same plaintext and the same key,

FIGURE 8.2

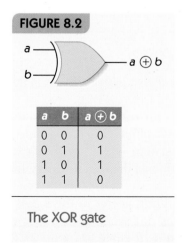

a	b	$a \oplus b$
0	0	0
0	1	1
1	0	1
1	1	0

The XOR gate

FIGURE 8.3

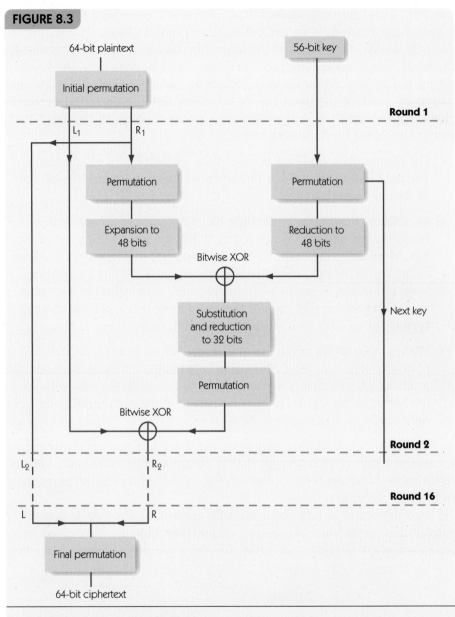

The DES encryption algorithm

everyone using DES ends up with the same ciphertext. The "secret" part is the initial key. The second point is that the same algorithm serves as the decryption algorithm—just start with the ciphertext and apply the sequence of keys in reverse order, that is, the round-16 key first and the original secret key last.

With increased computing power in the hands of those trying to break a code, a 56-bit key does not seem as formidable as when DES was first introduced. It might even be feasible to try all 2^{56} (72,057,594,037,927,936) possible keys. *Triple DES* improves the security of DES; it requires two 56-bit keys (which can be thought of as a 112-bit key length), and runs the DES algorithm three times: Encode using key 1, decode the result using key 2, encode the result using key 1 again.

Concerns about the eventual breakdown of DES in the face of ever-increasing computing power prompted NIST in 1997 to request proposals for a successor encryption scheme. The result was AES (Advanced Encryption Standard), which was adopted for use by the U.S. government in 2001. AES is based on the Rijndael (pronounced Rin-dahl) algorithm, named for the two Belgian cryptographers who designed it, Vincent Rijmen and Joan Daemen. Like DES, AES uses successive rounds of computations that mix up the data and the key. The key length can be 128, 192, or even 256 bits, and the algorithm appears to be very efficient.

Cracking DES

In 1997, the Electronic Frontier Foundation, a nonprofit civil-liberties organization, began to build the DES Cracker, a PC connected to a large array of custom chips. The entire configuration cost less than $250,000 to build (a very reasonable price at the time for big computing power). This machine was intended to apply brute force techniques (trying all possible 56-bit keys) to crack ciphertext encoded using DES. In 1998, the machine was used to respond to a challenge in the form of a ciphertext message posed by RSA Laboratories, the research component of RSA Security, a leading electronic security company. The DES Cracker could test 88 billion keys per second, and it found the correct 56-bit key in less than three days.

This result had political and economic overtones because the U.S. government at the time had strict controls on the export of cryptographic software, most of which was limited to encryption algorithms using a 40-bit key or less. This hampered overseas sales of software products with strong encryption. The government also pressured industry within the United States to limit the use of cryptography to DES, claiming that DES codes were highly secure and nearly impossible to crack, a claim clearly refuted by this challenge. The designer of the DES Cracker machine noted that searching for a 40-bit key (the export limit at the time) using the DES Cracker would take 3–12 seconds.

Some people suspected that the government wanted to keep weak encoding in use in order to be able to access information, perhaps infringing on personal privacy. The U.S. export policy was made less restrictive in 1998, although not as a result of the DES Cracker.

8.3.4 Public Key Systems

The encryption algorithms we have discussed so far have all been symmetric encryption algorithms, requiring that both the sender and receiver have knowledge of the key. Our final algorithm is an asymmetric, or public key, encryption algorithm. Remember that the main difficulty with a symmetric algorithm is how to securely transmit the secret key. In a public key system, the encryption key for messages to go to a particular receiver is broadcast to everyone, but the decryption key cannot be derived from it and is known only by the receiver.

The most common public key encryption algorithm is RSA, named for its developers, Ron Rivest, Adi Shamir, and Len Adleman at MIT (founders of RSA Security—see the Special Interest Box, "Cracking DES"). This algorithm, developed in 1977, is based on results from the field of mathematics known as *number theory*.

A *prime number* is an integer greater than 1 that can only be written as the product of itself and 1. For example, 2, 3, 5, 7, 11, ... are prime numbers; you can only write 7, for example, as $7 = 1 \times 7$, the product of 1 and 7. The numbers 4, 6, 8, 10, and 12, for example, are not prime because they can be factored in a nontrivial way:

$$4 = 2 \times 2 \qquad 6 = 2 \times 3 \qquad 8 = 2 \times 2 \times 2$$
$$10 = 2 \times 5 \qquad 12 = 2 \times 2 \times 3$$

Any positive integer is either a prime number or a number that can be written in a unique way as a product of prime factors. For example, $12 = 2 \times 2 \times 3$ is the product of three prime factors. The success of RSA encryption depends on the fact that it is extremely difficult to find the prime factors for n if n is a large number. So although information encrypted using RSA is technically not secure, it is secure in practice because of the large amount of computation necessary to find the prime factors of the encoding key.

Here's how RSA works. Two large prime numbers p and q are chosen at random, and their product $n = p \times q$ is computed. The product $m = (p - 1) \times (q - 1)$ is also computed. Next, a large random number e is chosen in such a way that e and m have no common factors other than 1. This step guarantees the existence of a unique integer d between 0 and m, such that when we compute $e \times d$ using the same sort of wraparound arithmetic we used in the block encoding scheme—that is, whenever we reach m, we start over again counting from 0—the result is 1. There are computationally efficient ways to produce p, q, e, and d.

For example, suppose we pick $p = 3$ and $q = 7$ (a trivially small case). Then,

1. $n = p \times q = 3 \times 7 = 21$

2. $m = (p - 1) \times (q - 1) = 2 \times 6 = 12$

3. Choose $e = 5$ ($e = 5$ and $m = 12$ have no common factors)

4. Then $d = 5$ because $e \times d = 5 \times 5 = 25 = 2 \times 12 + 1$, so when we compute $e \times d$ using wraparound arithmetic with respect to 12, we get 1.

Now the number pair $(n,\ e)$ becomes the public encryption key, and d is the decryption key. Let's suppose that the plaintext message has been converted into an integer P, using some sort of mapping from characters to numbers. The encryption process is to compute P^e using wraparound arithmetic with respect to n (when you reach n, make that 0). Continuing with our example, suppose $P = 3$. Then the ciphertext is computed as

5. $3^5 = 243 = 11 \times 21 + 12 \rightarrow 12$

(Note that the sender uses both parts of the public key, e and n, to compute the ciphertext.) The receiver decodes the ciphertext C by computing C^d using wraparound arithmetic with respect to n. In our example,

6. $12^5 = 248832 = 11849 \times 21 + 3 \rightarrow 3$

Of course, our example has a major problem in that d is the same as e. Obviously, in a real case, you want e and d to be different. The whole point is that even though n and e are known, the attacker must determine d, which involves finding the prime factors p and q of n. There is no known computationally efficient algorithm for this task.

Your Secret Is Safe with Me

What if one could encrypt data and then send it off to some application software where it could be analyzed, manipulated, and used without ever needing to be decrypted? For example, you send your encrypted tax data off to tax application software somewhere in "the cloud," and that software can prepare your tax forms without ever needing to read the real data, just the encrypted data. Now that would be security! This seemingly magical idea was in fact proposed by Ron Rivest, Len Adleman—of RSA fame—and Michael Dertouzos in 1978, but how to actually do this remained unsolved until 2009 when a young IBM researcher named Craig Gentry found a solution, but a computationally inefficient solution. In April 2011, DARPA (Defense Advanced Research Projects Agency) announced that it is funding $20 million worth of research to find a more efficient solution.

Practice Problem

You receive a message "17" that was sent using the RSA public encryption key (21, 5) of the example in this section. Decode this to find the original numeric message. (You might want to use a spreadsheet to help with this computation.)

8.4 Web Transmission Security

One area where the public is very security conscious is in making online purchases, which require the purchaser to send out across the network his or her name, address, and—most worrisome of all—credit card number. One method for achieving secure transfer of information on the Web is SSL (Secure Sockets Layer). This is a series of protocols developed by Netscape Communications (Netscape was an early Web browser) in the mid-1990s. The TLS (Transport Layer Security) protocol, first defined in 1999, is based on SSL and is nearly identical to SSL. TLS has a few technical security improvements over SSL, but the major difference is that TSL is nonproprietary and is a standard supported by the Internet Engineering Task Force (IETF). The IETF is an open organization of individuals concerned with "the evolution of the Internet architecture and the smooth operation of the Internet."[4]

Both TLS and SSL are in use and are supported by all Web browsers. Technically, TSL/SSL fits between the Transport layer, with its TCP protocols, and the Application layer, with its HTTP protocols (both discussed in the previous chapter). When you see a closed lock icon at the top or bottom of your Web browser page, or when the URL displayed begins with HTTPS (instead of HTTP), then you can be assured that the communication between your browser and the Web server (the vendor's Web computer) is secure and protected by TLS or SSL. TLS/SSL allows a client (the purchaser's Web browser) and a Web server to agree on the encryption methods to be used, exchange the necessary security keys, and authenticate the identity of each party to the other. (Here we are again with *encryption* and *authentication*, the two pillars of security we've seen before.)

Now that we know a bit more about encryption, we might ask what encryption algorithm TLS/SSL uses; is it DES encryption or the newer, stronger RSA encryption? Surprisingly, it is both. One of the problems with the RSA algorithm is the computational overload for encryption/decryption. What often happens is that RSA is used in the initial stage of communication between client and server. For example, in response to a client request,

---

[4]*www.ietf.org/overview.html*

FIGURE 8.4

Initiate TLS/SSL, request RSA/DES encryption

Authentication certificate, acknowledge
RSA/DES, server public key

Client

DES key, encrypted with server's public key

Web server

Acknowledgment encrypted with DES key

Secure data exchange

A TLS/SSL session

the server may send the client its public key along with an authentication certificate. This is a certificate issued by a trusted third-party certificate authority; it's like a letter of introduction that attests that the server belongs to the organization the browser thinks it is talking to.

The client, using RSA and the public key of the server, encodes a short message containing the keys for a symmetric encryption algorithm. Because only keys are being encrypted, the message is short and the encryption can be done quickly with little RSA overhead. The server receives and decodes this message and responds to the client with a message encoded using the symmetric key. The client and server have now established a secure exchange of keys (one of the issues with a symmetric encryption algorithm) and can complete the transaction using, for example, DES. Figure 8.4 illustrates the major steps in this process, although the technical details may require a few additional transmissions between the client and the server. The exchange of setup information between the client and server, preparatory to exchanging real data, is known as a *handshake*.

8.5 Think Small, Think Big

Up to now, we have treated security as if it were always a matter between your personal computer and the rest of the world. But there are many other places where computing devices interact with the rest of the world.

Embedded computers are computational devices such as chips, processors, or computers that are embedded within another system. Unlike a general-purpose computer that can be programmed to do many different things, embedded computers usually perform just one or two tasks as part of the system in which they occur. Frequently this means they are small devices that you never see, and the ability to package more and more transistors on a single chip has contributed to the growth of embedded computers. Where are they found?

- In your car
- In your home thermostat
- In your home alarm system
- In your cell phone
- In your digital clock or watch
- In your iPod or MP3 player
- In your video game console
- In your TV remote controller
- In your digital camera
- In your credit card
- In your microwave
- In your car's navigation system
- In your car's emergency and vehicle diagnostics system (i.e., General Motors OnStar)
- In a plane's flight control system
- In a bank ATM
- In a hospital patient monitoring system

Well, you get the idea—embedded computers are everywhere! It is estimated that 98% of all new CPUs (Central Processing Units) are used in embedded systems.

Embedded computers differ from conventional computers in other ways as well. Input and output are usually not via keyboard and screen, respectively; instead, input may be data sent from sensors within the surrounding system, and output may be commands to control devices within the system. The embedded computer has very limited memory and processing capacity. And its response time is often in the "real-time" category (a plane's flight control system has to respond instantly, so does the patient monitoring system, and you hope your antilock brakes do that as well). For these same safety-critical systems, reliability is a key requirement.

But reliability is not the same as security. Security comes into the picture when these embedded systems become networked or even Internet-enabled. Your car's navigation system gets updates from the Web, the home alarm system connects over a network to the alarm company, the electric company may connect with your thermostat to raise the temperature slightly during peak air-conditioning load times, and sensors that monitor manufacturing processes communicate to streamline the production flow. The challenge is how to build security into network-enabled embedded computers that have little extra memory, often have energy constraints, and have no system administrator at hand to deal with security updates or breaches.

On the other end of the spectrum, computer systems control much of the world's vital infrastructure such as utility plants, electric grid systems, transportation, telecommunications, and financial markets, to say nothing of defense and military installations. It is not hard to imagine terrorist groups and perhaps hostile foreign powers contemplating attacks on one of these systems. President Obama gave a "policy review" speech on cybersecurity in May of 2009, but it was not until May of 2011 that the president outlined a plan for cybersecurity. In terms of infrastructure security, the plan calls for the president to designate critical industries, which would then draw up their own plans and standards for cybersecurity. The Department of Homeland Security would be able to scrutinize these plans, add additional standards, and publicly criticize those it found inadequate, but would have no authority to impose fines.

Safeguarding vital infrastructure is a complex but extremely important issue, and much work remains to be done. This is not just a United States issue, but a concern of every industrialized nation.

First Your Car, Then Your Water Supply

Researchers at the University of California, San Diego, and the University of Washington have proven that it is possible to undermine the security of the embedded cellular and Bluetooth systems used by a car's emergency and vehicle diagnostics system. Researchers were able to insert malicious software that in turn led to remote control of the car's electronic control units and thus the ability to override the car's vehicle controls. In theory, someone could remotely unlock your car, start the engine, then walk up and drive it away. Even more serious, someone could possibly disable your antilock brake system, shut down the steering, and crash your car while it's running.*

A Southern California water company hired a security firm to check its computer networks for vulnerabilities. The team, in just one day, got control of the computers that add chemical treatments to drinking water.**

---

* *New York Times*, March 9, 2011, *www.nytimes.com/2011/03/10/business/10hack.html*
** *Los Angeles Times*, March 28, 2011, *http://articles.latimes.com/2011/mar/28/nation/la-na-cyber-war-20110328*

8.6 Conclusion

In this chapter, we've looked at components of information security, both on an isolated local computer and on a machine exposed to the network. Whether it's an individual's personal data, corporate information, sensitive government data, or infrastructure installations, all are under threat. Still, a bit of caution and common sense can go a long way. As the well-worn watchword says, "Security: It's Everybody's Business."

8.7 Summary of Level 3

We have seen that the hardware described in Chapters 4 and 5 is, by itself, nearly unusable. Working directly with the hardware components of a Von Neumann machine—processors, memory, ALU—is impossible for any but the most technically knowledgeable users. To make the system accessible, the system software must create a people-oriented *virtual machine* or *virtual environment* that is easy to understand and use. In addition to ease of use, this virtual environment provides a number of other services, including resource management, security, access control, and efficient resource use. A great deal of work has been done to try to identify and create an optimal virtual environment.

Operating systems—a critical component of the virtual environment—have evolved from early batch systems through multiprogramming and time-sharing to the current network and real-time operating systems. Most modern operating systems allow us to use a large collection of machines, called a computer network, almost as easily as if it were a single logical system. Network technology has expanded our virtual environment to encompass a worldwide grid of interconnected computers. More and more, the computer user on a networked system can deal only with *what* operations need to be done, not with where or how they can be done. Perhaps they are being done "in the cloud." The future of computer systems definitely lies in the direction of more abstract and more powerful virtual environments.

As our virtual environment has expanded, our most important asset—our data—is increasingly at risk for theft or destruction by clever outsiders with malicious intent. Constant vigilance is required to maintain information security so that our virtual environment is not only user-friendly but also safe.

Now that we have created a vastly more usable environment in which to work, what do we want to do with it? Well, we probably want to write programs that solve important problems. In the next level of the text, we will begin our study of the software world.

EXERCISES

1. The following are three possible logon scenarios. Explain why answer (c) below is preferable in terms of system security.

    a. Welcome to XYZ computing
       Enter username: jones
       Invalid username
       Enter username:

    b. Welcome to XYZ computing
       Enter username: smith
       Enter password: password
       Invalid access
       Enter username:

    c. Enter username: smith

       Enter password: password
       Invalid access
       Enter username: smith
       Enter password: FpQr56
       Welcome to XYZ computing

2. Using the hash function described in Section 8.2.1, find the encrypted forms of the following passwords:

    a. fido
    b. blank
    c. ti34pper

3. Password characters on a certain system are limited to 26 uppercase letters [A ... Z], 26 lowercase letters [a ... z], 10 digits [0 ... 9], and 3 special symbols [#, $, %]. Suppose a password-cracking tool can generate and test 10,000,000 character strings (potential passwords) per second. Could all possible passwords of length 10 or less be generated and tested in under 1 week's time? (Use a spreadsheet to help find the answer.)

4. *Merriam-Webster's Collegiate Dictionary*, 11th ed. (Merriam-Webster, Inc., 2003), contains over 225,000 entries. Using a password-cracking tool that can process 1.7 million words per second,

   how long would it take to test each word in the dictionary as a possible password?

5. A virus attacks a single user's computer and within one hour embeds itself in 50 e-mail attachment files sent out to other users. By the end of the hour, 10% of these have been opened and have infected their host machines. If this process continues, how many machines will be infected at the end of 5 hours? Can you find a formula for the number of machines infected after *n* hours?

6. A certain individual has a Hilton account, a Ritz-Carlton account, and a Marriott International account (all these companies were corporate victims of the Epsilon data theft). The following e-mail message is sent to this individual. Point out clues that should alert this individual that he/she is the victim of a phishing attack.

   > We here at Marriott appreciate your loyalty as a customer. We want to make things more easy for you when you travel, so we have partnered with Hilton and Ritz-Carlton to create a unified rewards program. Now when you stay at any of these fine brand hotels, you will earn award points that can apply to a future stay at any of the three hotels. For you we will quick set this up, just click on the link below to get started:
   >
   > *www.Mariott.com*

7. Read about one of the following. Decide whether there seems to be enough evidence to put it in the category of cyberwarfare:

    a. Stuxnet
    b. 2007 – Estonia
    c. Byzantine Hades

8. *Risk analysis* is one way to monitor security in an organization. Risk analysis can be a time-consuming process; it involves a number of steps, some of which require "educated guessing." Nevertheless, the process alone raises awareness of security

issues even if no immediate actions are taken as a result. The steps are:

i.   Identify assets (infrastructure, people, hardware, software, reputation, etc.).

For the rest of this list, we'll concentrate on a single asset.

ii. Determine vulnerability (what event or events might happen to the asset. For example, the building could catch fire, the Web site could be hacked, etc.).

For the rest of this list, we'll concentrate on a single asset vulnerable to a single event.

iii. Estimate the probability per year of this event (based on past data, expert estimates, etc.). Take current security measures into account.

iv. Estimate the expected cost if this event occurs (cost to repair or replace, cost of lost business, etc.).

v.   Compute risk exposure = cost estimate * probability estimate.

vi. Identify any additional security measure X that would help protect against this event, what it would cost, and do a calculation of the risk exposure with the additional security measure X in place.

vii. Do a cost-benefit analysis:
(Risk exposure without X – Risk exposure with X) – Cost of X

You have a small Web-based business that uses a single server to manage your Web page and your customer information. Over the past four years, your Web site has been hacked and taken down twice. You estimate that the cost of this event is $600 to clean the server and reload the Web page and $12,000 in lost business while the server is down.

a.   You could purchase a backup server for a cost of $3,000, which you estimate would reduce the probability per year of losing your Web site to 0.2. Would this be a cost-effective security measure?

b.   What if you reevaluate the probability per year with the backup server to be 0.3. Does this change your answer?

9.   Using a Caesar cipher with $s = 5$, decode the received message RTAJ TZY FY IFBS.

10. The centurion who was supposed to inform you of s was killed en route, but you have received the message MXX SMGX UE PUHUPQP in a Caesar cipher. Find the value of s and decode the message.

11. You receive a message that was encoded using a block encoding scheme with the encoding matrix

$$M = \begin{bmatrix} 3 & 2 \\ 7 & 5 \end{bmatrix}$$

a.   Verify by computing $M' \times M$ that $M' = \begin{bmatrix} 5 & 24 \\ 19 & 3 \end{bmatrix}$
(Remember to wrap around if a value is > 25.)

b.   Decode the ciphertext message MXOSHI.

12. The DES algorithm combines two bit strings by applying the XOR operator on each pair of corresponding bits. Compute the 6-bit string that results from $100111 \oplus 110101$.

13. To decode a message encrypted using DES requires finding the key from among the 2^{56} possible 56-bit binary keys. Although you might find the key early on, the worst case is that you have to test all 2^{56} possible DES keys.

a.   How long would this take using the six-core desktop described in the Special Interest Box, "The Tortoise and the Hare" in Chapter 3? Assume that a single key can be tested in one floating-point operation.

b.   How long would this take using the Japanese "K" supercomputer described in the Special Interest Box, "The Tortoise and the Hare" in Chapter 3? Assume that a single key can be tested in one floating-point operation.

14. Using the RSA encryption algorithm, pick $p = 11$ and $q = 7$. Find a set of encryption/decryption keys e and d.

15. Using the RSA encryption algorithm, let $p = 3$ and $q = 5$. Then $n = 15$ and $m = 8$. Let $e = 11$.

a.   Compute d.

b.   Find the code for 3.

c.   Decode your answer to part (b) to retrieve the 3.

16. If a message is encrypted using AES with a key length of 256 bits, the brute force approach to decryption involves generating each of the 2^{256} possible keys in turn until one is found that decodes the encrypted message. Quantum computing was discussed in Chapter 5. Using a quantum computer, how many qubits are required to represent all 2^{256} possible keys simultaneously?

CHALLENGE WORK

1. In this chapter, we discussed hash functions (hash algorithms) as a means to protect passwords. Another application is *message integrity*: A hash algorithm is applied to a message and the resulting hash is appended to the original message when it is transmitted. Upon receipt, the message is rehashed to produce a new hash that is compared with the original. If the two hashes match, it is deemed that the message has not been altered in transmission. This is based on the assumption that any change in the message would produce a change in the hash. The standard hash algorithm for message integrity has been SHA-1 (Secure Hash Algorithm-1).

   a. Read about how the basic assumption was challenged in 2005 by a Chinese cryptographer named Xiaoyun Wang, who found a shorter way to produce two different messages that hash to the same value under SHA-1.

   b. Read about the competition launched by NIST (National Institute of Standards and Technology) in 2007 to produce a new and more secure hash algorithm that will be known as SHA-3. Has the winning algorithm been selected yet?

2. Find information about a well-known computer virus or worm. Answer as many of the following questions as you can, and be sure to list your sources.

   a. What is the name of the virus or worm?
   b. When did it first appear?
   c. Who wrote it?
   d. How was it spread?
   e. What systems did it attack?
   f. What were its observable effects?
   g. What are the technical details on how it worked?
   h. What was the "cure"?
   i. Did it spawn "copycat" attacks?
   j. What was its economic impact?
   k. Was the perpetrator found, arrested, convicted?

3. The Vigenère cipher was first proposed in the sixteenth century. At its heart is the Vigenère table (shown below), where each row represents a Caesar cipher of the letters of the alphabet shown in the row of column headers. The shift for row A is $s = 0$, for row B it is $s = 1$, for row C it is $s = 2$, etc. Thus in row C, the column header A is shifted 2 characters to become C, B becomes D, and so forth. The key to the Vigenère cipher is a secret word or phrase known only to the sender and receiver. Each letter in the key is used to encode a letter in the plaintext by finding in the table the row of the key letter and the column of the plaintext letter; their intersection is the ciphertext letter for that plaintext letter. When every letter in the key has been used, the key is repeated.

For example, suppose the key is

   SONG

and the plaintext message is

   MEETATNOON

Because the key is shorter than the plaintext, it will have to be used several times:

   SONGSONGSO

   MEETATNOON

The first character of the ciphertext is found at the intersection of row S and column M; it is E. The second character of the ciphertext is found at the intersection of row O and column E; it is S. The complete ciphertext is

    ESRZSHAUGB

To decode a received message, you reverse this process. Again matching the key characters to the ciphertext characters,

    SONGSONGSO
    ESRZSHAUGB

find the ciphertext character in the key character's row; the plaintext character is the corresponding column heading. Thus in row S, the E occurs in column M, so M is the corresponding plaintext.

You receive the following ciphertext message that you know was encoded using the Vigenère cipher with a secret key of PEANUTS:

    DREVZUQAENQ

Decode the ciphertext to find the plaintext.

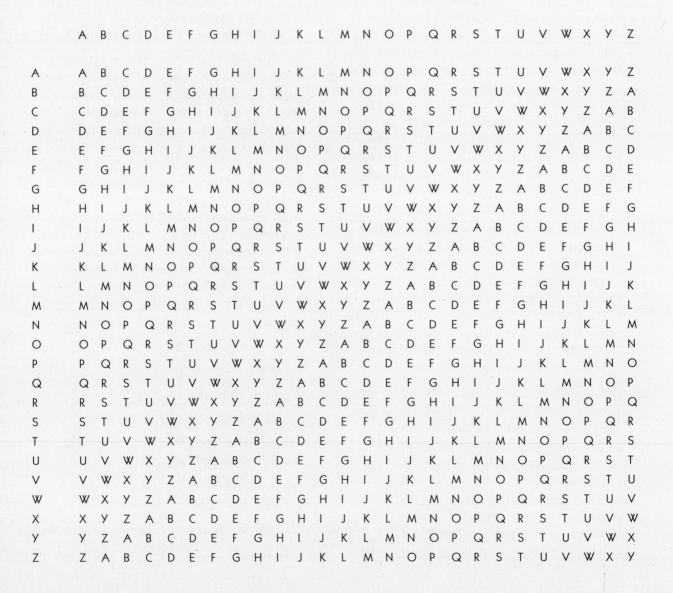

ADDITIONAL RESOURCES

CourseMate For additional print and/or online resources relevant to this chapter, visit the Computer Science CourseMate at login.cengagebrain.com.

Chapter
17
Social Issues

Chapters
13, 14, 15, 16
Applications

Chapters
9, 10, 11, 12
The Software World

Chapters
6, 7, 8
The Virtual Machine

Chapters
4, 5
The Hardware World

Chapters
2, 3
The Algorithmic Foundations
of Computer Science

In Level 4, we return to our original focus on algorithms as the heart of computer science. Algorithms are devised to solve problems. Computer programs express these algorithms in the form of a programming language, harnessing the power of the hardware and the system software to bring algorithms to life.

Chapter 9 presents a framework for comparing several popular programming languages: Ada, C++ (pronounced C plus plus), C# (pronounced C sharp), Java, and Python. A more detailed introduction to any of these languages can be found in one of the five separate online chapters. Go to **www.cengagebrain.com**. At the CengageBrain home page, search for the ISBN of this book (found above the bar code on the back cover) using the search box at the top of the page. At the Invitation page, click "Access now"; this will take you to the page where these free online chapters can be found. The chapters are also available on the CourseMate for this text.

Other programming languages and different language design philosophies are introduced in Chapter 10. Chapter 11 explains how high-level programming language statements are translated into low-level machine language statements that can be executed by the hardware. Chapter 12 demonstrates that, in spite of all the power of modern hardware and software, and no matter how clever we may be in designing algorithms, problems exist that have no algorithmic solution.

Introduction to High-Level Language Programming

9.1 The Language Progression

As of the end of Chapter 8, we have a complete and workable computer system. We have a virtual environment in which we can pretend that we are communicating directly with the computer, even though we are using a language (assembly language) more suited to human communication than is (binary) machine language. We know about the system software needed to support this virtual environment, including the assembler that translates assembly language programs into machine language, as well as the operating system that actually accepts requests to load and execute a program, and coordinates and manages the other software tools needed to accomplish this task. Our system also includes the network technologies and protocols that extend the virtual world across our campus, throughout our office building, and around the world, and we are aware of the need for protection against the security threats to which we are exposed as our virtual world widens.

But this puts us somewhat ahead of our story. In Chapter 6, we talked about the progression from machine language to assembly language, but today, using computers to solve problems often involves writing programs in a high-level programming language. This section continues the progression of programming languages from assembly language (where we left off in our language story) to high-level languages.

9.1.1 Where Do We Stand and What Do We Want?

At the end of Chapter 6, we were back in the "early days" of computing—the 1950s—when assembly language had just come into existence. As a step up from machine language, it was considered a reasonable programming environment because the people writing computer programs were for the most part technically oriented. Many had backgrounds in engineering or (as it would later be called) computer science. They were familiar with the inner workings of a computer and were accustomed to dealing with difficult problems steeped in mathematical notation, so the tedious precision of assembly language programming did not deter them. Also, because assembly language is so closely tied to machine language, assembly language programmers could see the kinds of processor activity that the assembly language instructions would generate. By being sufficiently clever in their choice of instructions, they could often shave a small amount off the execution time or amount of memory that their programs required. For example, the following sequence of assembly language instructions:

```
        LOAD    X
        ADD     ONE
        STORE   X

          .       .
          .       .
          .       .

ONE:    .DATA   1
```

could be replaced by the single instruction

```
        INCREMENT X
```

This is not the sort of performance improvement obtained by changing from a sequential search algorithm to a binary search algorithm. Instead, it is a fine-tuning improvement that may save a few millionths of a second, or even a few seconds if these instructions occur inside a loop that is executed many times. But remember that in this era, people did not have powerful personal computers at their disposal. Programmers were competing for the resources of a mainframe computer, and although these computers were physically large, they did not have the processing speed or memory capacity of today's systems. Conserving machine resources, even in tiny amounts, was important.

Over the next few decades, however, computer usage became widespread, permeating society to a degree that would probably not have been believed in the 1950s. "Nontechie" types needed to write programs too, and they demanded a more user-friendly programming environment. This was provided through the use of high-level programming languages (which we talk about in this chapter and the next) and also through evolving operating systems and other system software (which were discussed in Chapter 6). In turn, these high-level languages opened the door for new programmers. Also during this period, incredible technological strides made machines so powerful that conserving resources was no longer the issue it once was, and the overhead of execution time occasioned by the use of high-level programming languages became acceptable.

Let's review some of the aspects of assembly language programming that made people look for better alternatives. Suppose our task is to add two integers. In the assembly language of Chapter 6, the following instructions would have to be included (assume that B and C have already been assigned values).

```
        LOAD        B
        ADD         C
        STORE       A
         .           .
         .           .
         .           .
A:      .DATA        0
B:      .DATA        0
C:      .DATA        0
```

The three .DATA statements request storage for signed integers, generate the binary representation of the integer value 0 to occupy that storage initially, and ensure that the labels A, B, and C are bound to those memory locations. The LOAD statement copies the current contents of the memory location labeled B into the ALU register R, the ADD statement adds the current contents of the memory location labeled C to what is currently in register R, and the STORE instruction copies the contents of R (which is now $B + C$) into the memory location labeled A.

To perform a simple arithmetic task, we had to manage all the data movement of the numbers to be combined as well as the resulting answer. This is a microscopic view of a task—we'd like to be able to say something like "add B and C, and call the result A," or better yet, something like "$A = B + C$." But each assembly language statement corresponds to at most one machine language statement (you may recall from Chapter 6 that the pseudo-op .DATA statements do not generate any machine language instructions). Therefore, individual assembly language statements, though easier to read, can be no more powerful than the operations of the underlying instruction set. For the same reason, assembly language programs are machine specific. An assembly language statement that runs on machine X is nothing but a slightly "humanized" machine language statement for X, and it will not execute on a machine Y that has a different instruction set. Indeed, machine Y's assembler won't know what to do with such a statement.

Finally, assembly language instructions are rather stilted. STORE A does not sound much like the sort of language we customarily speak, though STORE is certainly more expressive than its binary machine language counterpart.

To summarize, assembly language has the following disadvantages:

- The programmer must "manually" manage the movement of data items between and among memory locations and registers (although such data items can be assigned mnemonic names).

- The programmer must take a microscopic view of a task, breaking it down into tiny subtasks at the level of what is going on in individual memory locations.

- An assembly language program is machine specific.

- Statements are not natural-language-like (although operations are given mnemonic code words as an improvement over a string of bits).

We would like to overcome these deficiencies, and *high-level programming languages* were created to do just that. Thus, we have the following expectations of a program written in a high-level language:

- The programmer need not manage the details of the movement of data items within memory or pay any attention to exactly where those items are stored.

- The programmer can take a macroscopic view of tasks, thinking at a higher level of problem solving (add *B* and *C*, and call the result *A*). The "primitive operations" used as building blocks in algorithm construction (see Chapter 1) can be larger.

- Programs are portable rather than machine specific.

- Programming statements are closer to natural language and use standard mathematical notation.

High-level programming languages are often called third-generation languages, reflecting the progression from machine language (first generation) to assembly language (second generation) to high-level language. They are another step along the continuum shown in Chapter 6, Figure 6.3. This also suggests what by now you have suspected: We've reached another layer of abstraction, another virtual environment designed to further distance us from the low-level electronic components of the machine.

9.1.2 Getting Back to Binary

There is a price to pay for this higher level of abstraction. When we moved from machine language to assembly language, we needed a piece of system software—an assembler—to translate assembly language instructions into machine language (object code). This was necessary because the computer itself—that is, the collection of electronic devices—can respond only to binary machine language instructions. Now that we have moved up another layer in the language in which we communicate with the computer, we need another translator to convert our high-level language instructions into machine language instructions. Such a piece of system software is called a *compiler*. Rather than doing the whole translation job clear down to object code, the compiler often translates high-level language instructions (source code) only into low-level code rather close to machine language (the hard part of the translation) and then turns the final (simple) translation job over to a second translator. Compilers for some high-level languages generate low-level code that is machine-specific assembly language, and the second translator is an assembler for that machine's assembly language. Compilers for other high-level languages generate low-level code that—while still machine independent—is nonetheless very easy to convert to the final object code for any particular machine language.

Some tasks (e.g., sorting or searching) need to be performed often, as part of solving other problems. The code for such a useful task can be written as a group of high-level language instructions and thoroughly tested to be sure it is correct. Then the object code for the task can be stored in a code library. A program can just request that a copy of this object code be included along with its own object code. A piece of system software called a linker inserts requested object code from code libraries into the object code for the requesting program. The resulting object code is often called an executable module. Thus, a high-level program might go through the transitions shown in Figure 9.1. Compare this with Figure 6.4.

The work of the compiler is discussed in more detail in Chapter 11. Let us note here, however, that the compiler has a much tougher job than the assembler. An assembler has a one-for-one translation task because each assembly language instruction corresponds to (must be translated into) at most one machine language instruction. A single high-level programming

FIGURE 9.1

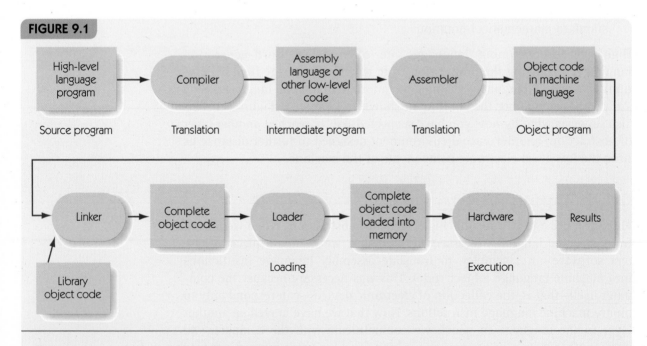

Transitions of a high-level language program

language instruction, on the other hand—precisely because a high-level language is more expressive than assembly language—can "explode" into many assembly language instructions.

9.2 A Family of Languages

Most of today's popular high-level programming languages fall into the same philosophical family; they are procedural languages (also called imperative languages). A program written in a procedural language consists of sequences of statements that manipulate data items. The programmer's task is to devise the appropriate step-by-step sequence of "imperative commands"—instructions in the programming language—that, when carried out by the computer, accomplish the desired task.

Procedural languages follow directly from the Von Neumann computer architecture described in Chapter 5, an architecture characterized by sequential fetch-decode-execute cycles. A random access memory stores and fetches values to and from memory cells. Thus it makes sense to design a language whose most fundamental operations are storing and retrieving data values. For example,

```
a = 1;          //store value 1 in location a
c = a + b;      //retrieve a and b, add, store result in
                //location c
```

Even though a high-level programming language allows the programmer to think of memory locations in abstract rather than physical terms, the programmer is still directing, via program instructions, every change in the value of a memory location.

Ada, C++, C#, Java, and Python Online Chapters

To explore programming through the lens of a particular programming language, and to get a sense of what programming in a high-level language is like, try one or more of the online chapters found on the CourseMate for this text and online at **www.cengagebrain.com**. At the CengageBrain home page, search for the ISBN of this book (found above the bar code on the back cover). At the Invitation page, click "Access now". These PDF documents can be read online, downloaded to your computer, or printed out and read on paper. Each chapter includes language-specific exercises and practice problems.

The languages we have chosen to discuss from this procedural language family are Ada, C++, C#, Java, and Python. These languages differ in the rules (the *syntax*) for exactly how statements must be written and in the meaning (*semantics*) of correctly written statements. Rather than fill up pages and pages of this book with the details of each of these languages, we've created online chapters for you to investigate the language(s) of your choice (or your instructor's choice) in much more detail than you will see here. See the Special Interest Box on the previous page for information on accessing the online chapters.

9.3 Two Examples in Five-Part Harmony

At this point you might (or might not) have studied one or more of the online chapters for Ada, C++, C#, Java, or Python. In either case, you might be interested to see how these languages are similar and how they differ. In this section, we'll look at two sample problems and their solutions in each of the five languages. Don't be overly concerned about the details; just try to get the "big picture" in each of these solutions.

9.3.1 Favorite Number

Our first problem is trivially simple. Nonetheless, it will allow you to observe some of the significant syntactic differences in these five languages. A pseudocode version is shown in Figure 9.2.

Next, we show this same algorithm implemented in Ada (Figure 9.3), C++ (Figure 9.4), C# (Figure 9.5), Java (Figure 9.6), and Python (Figure 9.7). The program code in each figure is easily recognizable as a formalized version of the pseudocode—it uses some mechanism to get the user's favorite number, then sets the value of *n* to *n* + 1, and finally writes the output. The syntax, however, varies with the language. In particular, each language has its own way of reading input (from the keyboard), performing a computation, and writing output (to the screen). There's also a variation in the amount of "startup" required just to get to the actual algorithm implementation part. Each language has a notation (--, //, or #) that denotes a program comment, and each language has its own set of special "punctuation marks." For example, four of the five languages (Python being the exception) require a semicolon to terminate an executable program statement.

FIGURE 9.2

1. Get value for the user's favorite number, *n*
2. Increase *n* by 1
3. Print a message and the new value of *n*

Pseudocode algorithm for favorite number

FIGURE 9.3

```
--Ada program for the
--favorite number algorithm

WITH TEXT_IO;

PROCEDURE FavoriteNumber IS
  PACKAGE INT_IO IS NEW TEXT_IO.INTEGER_IO(INTEGER);

      n : INTEGER;                --user's favorite number

BEGIN
  --Get the user's favorite number
  TEXT_IO.PUT("What is your favorite number? ");
  INT_IO.GET(n);

  --Compute the next number
  n := n + 1;

  --Write the output
  TEXT_IO.NEW_LINE;
  TEXT_IO.PUT("My favorite number is 1 more than that, ");
  INT_IO.PUT(n, 4);
  TEXT_IO.NEW_LINE;
  TEXT_IO.NEW_LINE;
END FavoriteNumber;
```

Ada program for favorite number

FIGURE 9.4

```
//C++ program for the
//favorite number algorithm

#include <iostream>
using namespace std;

void main()
{
    int n;     //user's favorite number

    //get the user's favorite number
    cout << "What is your favorite number? ";
    cin  >> n;
```

C++ program for favorite number *(continues)*

FIGURE 9.4 (CONTINUED)

```
    //compute the next number
    n = n + 1;

    //write the output
    cout << endl;
    cout << "My favorite number is 1 more than that, "
        << n << endl;
    cout << endl << endl;
}
```

C++ program for favorite number

FIGURE 9.5

```
//C# program for the
//favorite number algorithm

using System;

namespace InvitationCSharp

{
    class FavoriteNumber
    {
        static void Main(string[] args)
        {
            int n;   //user's favorite number

            //get the user's favorite number
            Console.Write("What is your favorite number? ");
            n = Convert.ToInt32(Console.ReadLine());

            //compute the next number
            n = n + 1;

            //write the output
            Console.WriteLine();
            Console.Write("My favorite number is ");
            Console.WriteLine("1 more than that, " + n);
            Console.WriteLine();
            Console.WriteLine();
        }
    }
}
```

C# program for favorite number

FIGURE 9.6

```java
//Java program for the
//favorite number algorithm

import java.util.*;
public class FavoriteNumber
{
    public static void main(String[] args)
    {
        int n;          //user's favorite number
        Scanner inp = new Scanner(System.in);    //to read input

        //get the user's favorite number
        System.out.print("What is your favorite number? ");
        n = inp.nextInt();

        //compute the next number
        n = n + 1;

        //write the output
        System.out.println();
        System.out.println("My favorite number is 1 more "
            + "than that, " + n);
        System.out.println();
        System.out.println();
    }
}
```

Java program for favorite number

FIGURE 9.7

```python
#Python program for the
#favorite number algorithm

#get the user's favorite number
n = int(input("What is your favorite number? "))

#compute the next number
n = n + 1

#write the output
print()
print("My favorite number is 1 more than that,", n)

#finish up
input("\n\nPress the Enter key to exit");
```

Python program for favorite number

9.3.2 Data Cleanup (Again)

Now that you've seen a bare-bones sample for each language, let's implement a solution to a considerably more interesting problem. In Chapter 3, we discussed several algorithms to solve the data cleanup problem. In this problem, the input is a set of integer data values (answers to a particular question on a survey, for example) that may contain 0s, although 0s are considered to be invalid data. The output is to be a clean data set where the 0s have been eliminated. Figure 9.8 is a copy of Figure 3.16. It shows the pseudocode for the converging-pointers data cleanup algorithm, the most time- and space-efficient of the three data cleanup algorithms from Chapter 3.

Our pseudocode does not specify the details of how to "get values." In the favorite number example, the single input value was entered at the keyboard. The survey data, however, is probably already stored in an electronic file. It might have been collected via an online survey that captured the responses or via paper forms that have been scanned to capture the data in digital form. Designing our programs to read input data from a file, however, is a bit more than we want to get into, so we'll again assume the input data is typed in at the keyboard.

The pseudocode algorithm of Figure 9.8 is implemented in Ada (Figure 9.9), C++ (Figure 9.10), C# (Figure 9.11), Java (Figure 9.12), and Python (Figure 9.13).

As with the previous, simpler example, you can see that each program follows the outline of the pseudocode algorithm. Each language supports if statements and while loops. The extent of the while loop is denoted by curly braces { } in three of the languages, by *loop ... end loop* in Ada, and (although this is less evident) by a colon and indentation in Python.

FIGURE 9.8

1. Get values for *n* and the *n* data items
2. Set the value of *legit* to *n*
3. Set the value of *left* to 1
4. Set the value of *right* to *n*
5. While *left* is less than *right* do Steps 6 through 10
6.   If the item at position *left* is not 0 then increase *left* by 1
7.   Else (the item at position *left* is 0) do Steps 8 through 10
8.   Reduce *legit* by 1
9.   Copy the item at position *right* into position *left*
10.   Reduce *right* by 1
11. If the item at position *left* is 0, then reduce *legit* by 1
12. Stop

The converging-pointers algorithm for data cleanup

FIGURE 9.9

```
--Ada program for the converging-pointers
--data cleanup algorithm

WITH TEXT_IO;

PROCEDURE DataCleanup IS
  PACKAGE INT_IO IS NEW TEXT_IO.INTEGER_IO(INTEGER);

    maxList : constant := 50;   --maximum list size
    n : INTEGER;                --max number of data elements
                                --in list
    data : array(0..maxList - 1) of INTEGER; --create the empty
                                                   --list
    i : INTEGER;                --index variable
    left : INTEGER;             --algorithm left pointer into
                                --the list
    right: INTEGER;             --algorithm right pointer
                                --into the list
    legit: INTEGER;             --counts number of legitimate
                                --(nonzero) data values

BEGIN
  --Get the values for n and the n data items
  TEXT_IO.PUT("How many numbers are in the list? (maximum is ");
  INT_IO.PUT(maxList,2);
  TEXT_IO.PUT(") ");
  INT_IO.GET(n);

  i := 0;
  TEXT_IO.PUT("Enter the first number: ");
  INT_IO.GET(data(i));

  while i < n - 1
   loop
    i := i + 1;
    TEXT_IO.PUT("Enter next number: ");
    INT_IO.GET(data(i));
   end loop;

  --Set the value of legit, left, and right
  legit := n - 1;
  left := 0;
  right := n - 1;

  TEXT_IO.NEW_LINE;
  TEXT_IO.PUT("The original list is: ");
```

Ada converging-pointers algorithm *(continues)*

FIGURE 9.9 (CONTINUED)

```ada
   i := 0;
   while i <= legit
    loop
     INT_IO.PUT(data(i), 4);
     i := i + 1;
    end loop;
   TEXT_IO.NEW_LINE;
   TEXT_IO.NEW_LINE;

   --move the pointers together,
   --swapping value at right for 0 at left

   while left < right
    loop
     if data(left)/= 0
      then
       left := left + 1;
      else
       legit := legit - 1;
       data(left) := data(right);
       right := right - 1;
     end if;
    end loop;
   if data(left) = 0
    then
     legit := legit - 1;
   end if;

   --final output
   TEXT_IO.PUT("The cleaned list is: ");

   i := 0;
   while i <= legit
    loop
     INT_IO.PUT(data(i), 4);
     i := i + 1;
    end loop;
   TEXT_IO.NEW_LINE;

END DataCleanup;
```

Ada converging-pointers algorithm

There are several different ways of creating the memory space to hold the list of data values. And, as we saw before, each language does I/O (from keyboard to screen) using different syntax, and requires different "start-up" code. But the output of each version looks like Figure 9.14, where boldface indicates user input.

FIGURE 9.10

```cpp
//C++ program for the converging-pointers
//data cleanup algorithm

#include <iostream>
using namespace std;

void main()
{
    const int MAXLIST = 50;          //maximum list size
    int n;                //max number of data elements in list
    int data[MAXLIST]; //create the empty list
    int i;                //index variable
    int left, right;     //algorithm pointers into the list
    int legit;            //counts number of legitimate (nonzero)
                          //data values

    //Get the values for n and the n data items
    cout << "How many numbers are in the list? ";
    cout << "(maximum is " << MAXLIST << ") ";
    cin >> n;

    i = 0;
    cout << "Enter the first number: ";
    cin >> data[i];

    while (i < n - 1)
    {
        i = i + 1;
        cout << "Enter next number: ";
        cin >> data[i];
    }

    //Set the value of legit, left, and right
    legit = n - 1;
    left = 0;
    right = n - 1;

    cout << endl;
    cout << "The original list is" << endl;

    i = 0;
    while (i <= legit)
    {
        cout << data[i] << " ";
        i = i + 1;
    }
    cout << endl << endl;

    //move the pointers together,
    //swapping value at right for 0 at left
```

C++ converging-pointers algorithm *(continues)*

FIGURE 9.10 (CONTINUED)

```
    while (left < right)
     {
         if (data[left] != 0)
             left = left + 1;
         else
         {
             legit = legit - 1;
             data[left] = data[right];
             right = right - 1;
         }
     }
     if (data[left] == 0)
             legit = legit - 1;

     //final output
     cout << "The cleaned list is" << endl;
     i = 0;
     while (i <= legit)
     {
         cout << data[i] << " ";
         i = i + 1;
     }
     cout << endl << endl;

}
```

C++ converging-pointers algorithm

FIGURE 9.11

```
//C# program for the converging-pointers
//data cleanup algorithm

using System;

namespace InvitationCSharp
{
    class DataCleanup
    {
        static void Main(string[] args)
        {
            const int maxList = 50;        //maximum list size
            int n;                         //max number of data
                                           //elements in list
            int[] data = new int[maxList]; //create the empty
                                           //list
            int i;                         //index variable
```

C# converging-pointers algorithm *(continues)*

FIGURE 9.11 (CONTINUED)

```
            int left, right;              //algorithm pointers
                                          //into the list
            int legit;                    //counts number of
                                          //legitimate
                                          //(nonzero) data
                                          //values

            //Get the values for n and the n data items
            Console.Write("How many numbers are in the list? ");
            Console.Write("(maximum is " + maxList + ") ");
            n = Convert.ToInt32(Console.ReadLine());

            i = 0;
            Console.Write("Enter the first number: ");
            data[i] = Convert.ToInt32(Console.ReadLine());

            while (i < n - 1)
            {
                i = i + 1;
                Console.Write("Enter next number: ");
                data[i] = Convert.ToInt32(Console.ReadLine());
            }

            //Set the value of legit, left, and right
            legit = n - 1;
            left = 0;
            right = n - 1;

            Console.WriteLine();
            Console.WriteLine("The original list is");

            i = 0;
            while (i <= legit)
            {
                Console.Write(data[i] + " ");
                i = i + 1;
            }
            Console.WriteLine();
            Console.WriteLine();

            //move the pointers together,
            //swapping value at right for 0 at left

            while (left < right)
            {
                if (data[left] != 0)
                    left = left + 1;
                else
```

C# converging-pointers algorithm *(continues)*

FIGURE 9.11 (CONTINUED)

```
                {
                    legit = legit - 1;
                    data[left] = data[right];
                    right = right - 1;
                }
            }
            if (data[left] == 0)
                legit = legit - 1;

            //final output
            Console.WriteLine("The cleaned list is");
            i = 0;
            while (i <= legit)
            {
                Console.Write(data[i] + " ");
                i = i + 1;
            }
            Console.WriteLine();
            Console.WriteLine();
        }
    }
}
```

C# converging-pointers algorithm

FIGURE 9.12

```
//Java program for the converging-pointers
//data cleanup algorithm

import java.util.*;
public class DataCleanup
{
    public static void main(String[] args)
    {
        final int MAXLIST = 50;          //maximum list size
        int n;                           //max number of data
                                         //elements
                                         //in the list
        int[] data = new int[MAXLIST];   //create the empty list
        int i;                           //index variable
        int left, right;                 //algorithm pointers
                                         //into the list
        int legit;                       //counts number of
                                         //legitimate (nonzero)
                                         //data values
```

Java converging-pointers algorithm *(continues)*

FIGURE 9.12 (CONTINUED)

```java
    Scanner inp = new Scanner(System.in);   //to read input


    //Get the values for n and the n data items
    System.out.print("How many numbers are in the list? ");
    System.out.print(" (maximum is " + MAXLIST + ") ");
    n = inp.nextInt();

    i = 0;
    System.out.print("Enter the first number: ");
    data[i] = inp.nextInt();

    while (i < n - 1)
    {
        i = i + 1;
        System.out.print("Enter next number: ");
        data[i] = inp.nextInt();
    }

    //Set the value of legit, left, and right
    legit = n - 1;
    left = 0;
    right = n - 1;

    System.out.println();
    System.out.println("The original list is");

    i = 0;
    while (i <= legit)
    {
        System.out.print(data[i] + " ");
        i = i + 1;
    }
    System.out.println();
    System.out.println();

    //move the pointers together,
    //swapping value at right for 0 at left

    while (left < right)
    {
        if (data[left] != 0)
            left = left + 1;
        else
        {
            legit = legit - 1;
            data[left] = data[right];
            right = right - 1;
        }
    }
```

Java converging-pointers algorithm *(continues)*

FIGURE 9.12 (CONTINUED)

```java
        if (data[left] == 0)
            legit = legit - 1;

        //final output
        System.out.println("The cleaned list is");
            i = 0;
        while (i <= legit)
        {
            System.out.print(data[i] + " ");
            i = i + 1;
        }

        System.out.println();
    }
}
```

Java converging-pointers algorithm

FIGURE 9.13

```python
#Python program for the converging-pointers
#data cleanup algorithm

#Get the values for n and the n data items
n = int(input("How many numbers are in the list: "))
data = []   #create an empty list

i = 0
number = int(input("Enter first number: "))
data.append(number)   #append a value to the data list
while i < n - 1:
    i = i + 1
    number = int(input("Enter next number: "))
    data.append(number)

#Set the value of legit, left, and right
legit = n - 1
left = 0
right = n - 1

print()
print("The original list is")
i = 0
while i <= legit:
    print(data[i],end=" ")
    i = i + 1
print()
```

Python converging-pointers algorithm *(continues)*

FIGURE 9.13 (CONTINUED)

```
print()

#move the pointers together,
#swapping value at right for 0 at left

while left < right:
    if data[left] != 0:
        left = left + 1
    else:
        legit = legit - 1
        data[left] = data[right]
        right = right - 1
if data[left] == 0:
    legit = legit - 1

#final output
print("The cleaned list is")
i = 0
while i <= legit:
    print(data[i], end=" ")
    i = i + 1

#finish up
input("\n\nPress the Enter key to exit");
```

Python converging-pointers algorithm

FIGURE 9.14

```
How many numbers are in the list? (maximum is 50) 10
Enter the first number: 0
Enter next number: 24
Enter next number: 16
Enter next number: 0
Enter next number: 36
Enter next number: 42
Enter next number: 23
Enter next number: 21
Enter next number: 0
Enter next number: 27

The original list is
0 24 16 0 36 42 23 21 0 27

The cleaned list is
27 24 16 21 36 42 23
```

Output from the various data cleanup implementations

Each of the five languages supports many more programming features than are shown in our examples. Consult the online language chapters for more in-depth programming concepts (including functions, parameter-passing, object-oriented programming, and graphical programming) supported by each of these languages.

9.4 Feature Analysis

If you have studied one (or more) of the online chapters for Ada, C++, C#, Java, or Python, then the "features" of that programming language will be familiar to you. You can compare them with the features of the other languages by scanning Figure 9.15 starting on page 446. If you haven't studied any of these languages in detail, the figure will still give you a brief reference on each of them. Figure 9.15 compares only the features that are included in the online chapter for each language, so it should not be viewed as a comprehensive list of features for any of these languages.[1]

9.5 Meeting Expectations

At the beginning of this chapter, we gave four expectations for programs written in a high-level programming language. Now that we have been introduced to the essentials of writing programs in such a language, it is time to see how well these expectations have been met.

1. *The programmer need not manage the details of the movement of data items within memory or pay any attention to exactly where those items are stored.* The programmer's only responsibilities are to declare (or in the case of Python, create) all constants and variables the program will use. This involves selecting identifiers to represent the various data items and indicating the data type of each, either in the declaration statement or, in the case of Python, in an assignment statement. The identifiers can be descriptive names that meaningfully relate the data to the problem being solved. Data values are moved as necessary within memory by program instructions that simply reference these identifiers, without the programmer knowing which specific memory locations contain which values, or what value currently exists in an ALU register. The concepts of memory address and movement between memory and the ALU, along with the effort of generating constant data values, have disappeared.

2. *The programmer can take a macroscopic view of tasks, thinking at a higher level of problem solving.* Instead of moving data values here and there and carefully orchestrating the limited operations available

---

[1]For example, each of these languages supports a for-loop (counting loop), but this was not discussed in the online chapters and is not included in Figure 9.15.

at the machine language or assembly language level, the programmer can, for example, write the formula to compute the circumference of a circle given its radius. The details of how the instruction is carried out—how the data values are moved about and exactly how the multiplication of real number values is done—are handled elsewhere. Compare the power of conditional and looping instructions—which are tools for algorithmic problem solving and resemble the operations with which we constructed algorithms in pseudocode—with the assembly language instructions LOAD, STORE, JUMP, and so on, which are tools for data and memory management.

3. *Programs written in a high-level language will be portable rather than machine specific.* Program developers use a variety of approaches to make their programs portable to different platforms. For programs written in most high-level languages, the program developer runs through the complete translation process to produce an executable module (as shown in Figure 9.1), and it is the executable module that is sold to the user, who runs it on his or her own machine. The program developer doesn't usually give the user the source code to the program, for a multitude of reasons. First, the program developer does not want to give away the secrets of how the program works by revealing the code to someone who could make a tiny modification and then sell this "new" program. Second, the program developer wants to prevent the user from being able to change the code, rendering a perfectly good program useless, and then complaining that the software is defective. And finally, if the program developer distributes the source code, then all users must have their own translators to get the executable module needed to run on their own machines.

The developer can compile the program on any kind of machine as long as there is a compiler on that machine for the language in which the program is written. However, there must be a compiler for each (high-level language, machine-type) pair. If the program is written in C++, for example, and the program developer wants to sell his or her program to be used on a variety of computers, he or she needs to compile the same program on a PC using a C++ compiler for the PC, on a Mac using a C++ compiler for the Mac, and so on, to produce all the various object code versions. The program itself is independent of the details of each particular computer's machine language because each compiler takes care of the translation. This is the "portability" we seek from high-level language programs.

Even the availability of the appropriate compiler may not guarantee that a program developed on one type of machine can be compiled on a different type of machine. Each programming language has a certain core of instructions that are considered standard. Any respectable compiler for that language must support that core. In fact, national and international standards groups such as ANSI (American National Standards Institute) and ISO (International Organization for

FIGURE 9.15

Feature	Ada	C++	C#
Comment	--	//	//
Include object code from code libraries	WITH WITH TEXT_IO;	#include <> #include <iostream> using namespace std;	using using System;
Statement terminator	;	;	;
Statement continuation character	N/A	N/A	N/A
Block delimiter	keyword pairs BEGIN ... END loop ... end_loop then ... else ... endif	{...}	{...}
Free format	yes	yes	yes
Case sensitive	no	yes	yes
Reserved words	yes (BEGIN, INTEGER, FLOAT, ...)	yes (void, double, ...)	yes (void, double, ...)
Identifiers	letters, digits, or underscore; must begin with a letter; cannot be a reserved word	letters, digits, or underscore; cannot begin with a digit; cannot be a reserved word	letters, digits, or underscore; cannot begin with a digit; cannot be a reserved word
Named constants	yes	yes	yes
Declarations	before use, in declarative portion of procedure or function speed : INTEGER;	before use, generally at the top of a function int speed;	before use, generally at the top of a function int speed;
Strong typing	yes	yes	yes
Implicit (automatic) typecasting	no	yes—int to double in input, assignment, arithmetic expressions	yes—int to double in input, assignment, arithmetic expressions
Explicit typecasting	yes FLOAT(number)	yes double(number)	yes Convert.To Double(number)
Primitive data types			
Integer	INTEGER	int	int
Decimal	FLOAT	double	double
Character	CHARACTER	char	char
String			

Feature analysis of five high-level languages (examples in blue) *(continues)*

FIGURE 9.15 (CONTINUED)

Java	Python
//	#
import import java.util.*;	import import math
;	end of line unless followed by statement continuation character
N/A	\
{...}	: followed by indentation
yes	no, due to indentation signifying blocks of code
yes	yes
yes (class, public, ...)	yes (if, while, ...)
letters, digits, or underscore; cannot begin with a digit; cannot be a reserved word	letters, digits, or underscore; cannot begin with a digit; cannot be a reserved word
yes	no
before use, generally at the top of a method int speed;	no—variable is created when a value is assigned to it
yes	no—variable assumes data type of value assigned to it
yes—int to double in input, assignment, arithmetic expressions	yes—assignment statement sets data type of variable; int to float in arithmetic expressions
yes (double)number	yes float(number)
int	int
double	float
char	
	string

Feature analysis of five high-level languages (examples in blue) *(continues)*

FIGURE 9.15 (CONTINUED)

Feature	Ada	C++	C#
Composite data type	array	array	array
Literal string	yes—enclose in " "	yes—enclose in " "	yes—enclose in " "
String concatenation	&		+
Input from keyboard	INT_IO.GET(...); requires I/O package for integers FLO_IO.GET (...); requires I/O package for floating-point numbers TEXT_IO.GET(...)	cin >> cin >> number;	Console.ReadLine() returns a string; typecast to numeric data type if needed
Output to screen	INT_IO.PUT(...); requires I/O package for integers FLO_IO.PUT(...); requires I/O package for floating-point numbers TEXT_IO.PUT(...);	cout << cout << number;	Console.Write(string); or Console.WriteLine(string);
Output formatting	yes FLO_IO.PUT(time, 5, 2, 0);	yes cout.setf(ios::fixed); cout.precision(2);	yes time.ToString("#.##")
Assignment operator	:=	=	=
Arithmetic operators	+, -, *, /, mod, **	+, -, *, /, %	+, -, *, /, %
Comparison operators	=, <, <= , >, >=, /=	==, <, <=, >, >=, !=	==, <, <=, >, >=, !=
Boolean operators	and, or, not	&&, ||, !	&&, ||, !
Control structures			
Conditional	if ... or if ... then then ... ... else endif; ... end if;	if ( ) or if ( ) {...} {...} else {...}	if ( ) or if ( ) {...} {...} else {...}
Looping	while ... or loop loop ... ... exit when ... ; end loop; end loop;	while ( ) or do {...} {...} while( );	while ( ) or do {...} {...} while( );

Feature analysis of five high-level languages (examples in blue) (continues)

FIGURE 9.15 (CONTINUED)

Java	Python
array	list
yes—enclose in " "	yes—enclose in " "
+	+
use the Scanner class method Scanner inp = new Scanner(System.in); number = inp.nextInt();	input ("prompt") returns a string; typecast to numeric data type if needed
System.out.print(string); or System.out.println(string);	print(string)
yes import java.text.*; DecimalFormat p = new DecimalFormat("0.00"); System.out.println(p.format(time));	yes print("%5.2f" % time)
=	=
+, -, *, /, %	+, -, *, /, //, %
==, <, <=, >, >=, !=	==, <, <=, >, >=, !=
&&, ||, !	and, or, not

if ( ) or if ( )
{...}   {...}
else
{...}
	if ... : or if ... :
	  ... ...
	else:
	  ...
	(colon and indentation required)

while ( ) or do
{...}   {...}
         while ( );
	while ... : or while True:
	  ... ...
	        if ... :
	           break
	(colon and indentation required)

Feature analysis of five high-level languages (examples in blue) *(continues)*

FIGURE 9.15 (CONTINUED)

Feature	Ada	C++	C#
Modularity	via functions and procedures, which are nested within other functions or procedures	via functions	via functions
Local scope	yes—variables declared within functions or procedures are known only there	yes—variables declared within functions are known only there	yes—variables declared within functions are known only there
Arguments/Parameters	yes—must match in number, order, data type	yes—must match in number, order, data type	yes—must match in number, order, data type
Parameter passing	default: pass by value (or use *in* in parameter list) Use *out* or *in out* in parameter list for pass by reference	default: pass by value Use & in parameter list for pass by reference	default: pass by value Use *ref* in both parameter list and argument list for pass by reference
Math-like module (computes and returns a single value)	keyword FUNCTION in header, give returned data type in function header, return statement with computed expression in function body	give returned data type in function header, return statement with computed expression in function body	give returned data type in function header, return statement with computed expression in function body
Procedure-like module	keyword PROCEDURE in header	use *void* in function header	use *void* in function header
Object-oriented programming	supported via tagged record type	supported	required—everything is part of a class
Class terminology	object properties; primitive operations	member variables, member functions	member variables, member functions
Scope	object properties are private, primitive operations are public	public—known everywhere private—known only within class protected—known within class and subclass	public—known everywhere private—known only within class protected—known within class and subclass
Module invocation	module-identifier(object-identifier, argument list)	object-identifier.function-identifier(argument list)	object-identifier.function-identifier(argument list); static function can be invoked without an object
Inheritance	yes	yes	yes
Separate compilation	yes	yes	yes

Feature analysis of five high-level languages (examples in blue) *(continues)*

FIGURE 9.15 (CONTINUED)

Java	Python
via methods	via functions
yes—variables declared within methods are known only there	yes—variables declared within functions are known only there
yes—must match in number, order, data type	yes—must match in number and order; parameters will pick up passed data type
pass by value	the effect of pass by value is achieved if the function invocation is a stand-alone statement (changing the parameter value by an assignment statement creates a new local variable and does not change the original argument value); the effect of pass by reference is to invoke the function on the right side of an assignment statement and send the changed value(s) back via a return statement
give returned data type in method header, return statement with computed expression in method body	return statement with computed expression in function body
use *void* in method header; no values returned to invoking module	use no return statement or use return statement with multiple values where function invocation is on the right side of assignment statement
required—everything is part of a class	supported
instance variables, instance methods	attributes, methods
public static instance method—known everywhere public instance method—known everywhere private instance variable or instance method—known only within class	class methods are public class attributes are public by default; they are "semi-private" if declared with __ before the identifier, but still can be referenced anywhere if class name is used, as in swimmingPool_Circle__radius
for public static: class-identifier.method-identifier(argument list) for public: object-identifier.method-identifier(argument list)	object-identifier.method-identifier(argument list); "self" must be first parameter in method parameter list
yes	yes
required—must have separate file for each class	yes

Feature analysis of five high-level languages (examples in blue)

Standardization), which develop standards for an incredible number of things, also develop standards for programming languages. Compilers are thus built to support "ANSI-standard language X." However, there are often useful features or types of instructions that are not considered a standard part of the language and that some compilers support and some do not. If a program is written to take advantage of some of these extra features that are available on a particular compiler—often referred to as extensions, or "bells and whistles"—the program may not work with a different compiler. The price for using nonstandard features is the risk of sacrificing portability.

The standardization process (for anything, including a programming language) is necessarily a slow one because it seeks to satisfy the interests of a number of groups, such as consumers, industry, and government. If official standardization comes too late, it must bow to what may have become a de facto standard by common usage. If standardization is imposed too early, it may thwart the development of new ideas or technology.

Newer languages such as Java and C# were developed specifically to run on a variety of hardware platforms without the need for a separate compiler for each type of machine. A compiler for Java or C# translates the source code program into very low-level code (called *bytecode* in Java and *Microsoft Intermediate Language* in C#). The resulting programs are not machine-language code for any real machine, but they can easily be translated into any specific machine language. The program developer only needs to do one compilation to produce low-level code and then can distribute the resulting program to the various users. The final translation/execution of the low-level code into the machine language of a particular user's machine is done by a small piece of software on the user's machine (a Java bytecode interpreter for Java or a Just In Time compiler for C#).

The Python language takes a still different approach to portability. A Python program is *interpreted* rather than compiled, which means that it is translated from source code into object code every time it is executed. As a consequence, each user's machine has to have a Python interpreter, but such an interpreter is available for virtually every operating system, and is small, quick, and free. In the spirit of open source code development, Python developers are happy to send their source code to users.

4. *Programming statements in a high-level language will be closer to natural language and will use standard mathematical notation.* High-level languages provide us with statements that give natural implementations of pseudocode instructions such as "while condition do something ..." or "if condition do something ...." While pseudocode is still somewhat stilted, it is nonetheless close to natural language. We can also use standard mathematical notation such as $A + B$ and $A > B$.

9.6 The Big Picture: Software Engineering

Because any high-level language program ultimately must be translated by a compiler or interpreter, there are very stringent syntax rules about punctuation, use of keywords, and so on for each program statement. If something about a program statement cannot be understood by the compiler, then the compiler cannot translate the program; if the compiler cannot translate a program, then its instructions cannot be executed. This obstacle leads beginning programming students to conclude that the bulk of the effort in the software development process should be devoted to implementation— that is, restating an algorithm in computer code and ridding that code of syntax errors to the point where it finally executes.

In fact, implementation represents a relatively small part of the software development life cycle—the overall sequence of steps needed to complete a large-scale software project. Studies have shown that on big projects (system software such as operating systems or compilers, for example, or large applications such as writing a program to manage an investment company's portfolio), the initial implementation of the program may occupy only 10%–20% of the total time spent by programmers and designers. About 25%–40% of their time is spent on problem specification and program design—important planning steps that must be completed prior to implementation. Another 40%–65% is spent on tasks that follow implementation—reviewing, modifying, fixing, and improving the original code and writing finished documentation. Although there is no universal agreement on the exact sequence of steps in the software development life cycle, Figure 9.16 summarizes one possible breakdown. We'll discuss each of these steps shortly.

Beginning programming students might not see or appreciate the entire software development life cycle because the programming assignments usually solved in introductory classes are extremely and unrealistically small. This can create a skewed and misleading view of the software development process. It is somewhat akin to a civil engineering student building a matchstick bridge that is 5 inches long; a multitude of new problems must be addressed when that task is scaled up to a full-sized, real-life bridge.

9.6.1 Scaling Up

The programs that students write in an introductory course may have 50–100 lines of code. Even by the end of the course, programs are usually not longer than a few hundred lines. Real-world programs are often orders of magnitude larger. Compilers or some operating systems contain many thousands of lines. Truly large software systems, such as the NASA Space Shuttle ground control system and the data management system of the U.S. Census Bureau, may require the development of millions of lines of code. To give you an idea of how very large that is, a printed listing of a one-million-line program would be 17,000 pages long—about the size of 50 books. (Also

FIGURE 9.16

1. Before Implementation
    a. Feasibility study
    b. Problem specification
    c. Program design
    d. Algorithm selection or development, and analysis
2. Implementation
    a. Coding
    b. Debugging
3. After Implementation
    a. Testing, verification, and benchmarking
    b. Documentation
    c. Maintenance

Steps in the software development life cycle

see the Special Interest Box "Now That's Big!" in Chapter 6.) The difference in complexity between a million-line software package and a hundred-line homework assignment is equivalent to the difference in scale between a 300-page novel and a single sentence!

Figure 9.17 categorizes software products in terms of size, the number of programmers needed for development, and the duration of the development effort. These numbers are very rough approximations, but they give you an idea of the size of some widely used software packages. Analogous building construction projects are also listed.

Virtually all software products developed for the marketplace are neither trivial nor small. Most fall instead into either the Medium or the Large category of Figure 9.17. The Very Large and Extremely Large categories are enormous intellectual enterprises. It would be impossible to develop correct and maintainable software systems of that size without extensive planning and design, just as it is impossible to build a 50-story skyscraper without paying a great deal of attention to project planning and project management. Neither endeavor can be carried out by a single individual; a team development effort is essential in building software, just as in constructing buildings. Such projects also entail estimation of costs and budgets, personnel management, and scheduling issues, which are typical concerns for large engineering projects, and therefore the term software engineering is often applied to these large-scale software development projects.

9.6.2 The Software Development Life Cycle

Each step in the software development life cycle, as shown in Figure 9.16 and described in the following paragraphs, has its own purpose and activities. Each should also result in a written document that reflects past decisions

FIGURE 9.17

Category	Typical Number of People	Typical Duration	Product Size in Lines of Code	Examples	Building Analogy
Trivial	1	1–2 weeks	< 500	Student homework assignments	Small home improvement
Small	1–3	A few weeks or months	500–2,000	Student team projects, advanced course assignments	Adding on a room
Medium	2–5	A few months to 1 year	2,000–10,000	Research projects, simple production software such as assemblers, editors, recreational and educational software	Single-family house
Large	5–25	1–3 years	10,000–100,000	Most current applications— word processors, spreadsheets, operating systems for small computers, compilers	Small shopping mall
Very Large	25–100	3–5 years	100,000–1 M	Airline reservations systems, inventory control systems for multinational companies	Large office building
Extremely Large	> 100	> 5 years	> 1 M	Large-scale real-time operating systems, advanced military work, international telecommunications networks	Massive skyscraper

Size categories of software products

and guides future actions. Keep in mind that every major software project is developed as a team effort, and these documents help keep various members of the team informed and working toward a common goal.

1. *The feasibility study*—The feasibility study evaluates a proposed project and compares the costs and benefits of various solutions. One choice might be to buy a new computer system for this project. Even though the cost of computer hardware has dropped dramatically, computers are still significant purchases. In addition to the costs of the machine itself, there may be costs for peripherals such as laser printers

and telecommunications links. The costs of software (purchased or produced in-house); equipment maintenance; salary for developers or consultants, technical support people, and data entry clerks—these must all be factored in, as well as the costs incurred in training new users on the system. The overall cost of using a computer to solve a problem can be much higher than expected, and it *can* be more than the value of the information produced. Other options should also be considered. Thus, the feasibility study should address the following question:

What are the relative costs and benefits of the following choices?

- Buying a new computer system and writing or buying software
- Writing new software for an existing computer system
- Using the resources of "cloud computing" (see Chapter 6)
- Outsourcing the work to a contractor
- Revising the current manual process for solving this problem
- Cutting back the scope of the project to better align it with existing resources
- Other solutions ...

At the end of the feasibility study, a *feasibility document* expresses the resulting recommendations. The creation of this document can be a very complex process involving considerations that are the provinces of business, law, management, economics, psychology, and accounting as well as computer science. The purpose of the feasibility study is to make all project stakeholders aware of the costs, risks, and benefits of various development paths as a guide to deciding on the approach to use.

2. *Problem specification*—If it is determined that the project is feasible and will benefit from a computer solution, and that the software development is to go forward, we move on to the problem specification phase. Problem specification involves developing a clear, concise, and unambiguous statement of the exact problem the software is to solve. Because the original problem statement used in the feasibility study is written in a natural language, such as English, it may be unclear, incomplete, or even internally contradictory. This rough initial problem statement must be transformed into a complete problem specification. During the problem specification phase, the software developers and their "customers"—those who are commissioning the software and will be its eventual users—must resolve each and every inconsistency, ambiguity, and gap. It is much easier and cheaper to make changes at this stage than to make changes in software months down the road. Consider how much more practical it is to change your mind when looking at the blueprints of your new home than after the foundation has been dug and the walls have started to go up.

The *problem specification document* expresses the final and complete problem specification and guides the software developers in all subsequent decisions. The specification document describes exactly how a program behaves in all circumstances—not only in the majority of cases, but even under the most unusual conditions. It includes a description of the data expected to be input to the program, as well as what results should be computed and how these results are to be displayed as output. It may also include limitations on the time allotted to produce those computations or on the amount of memory the program requires.

Vital Statistics for Real Code

The Windows operating system was created by Microsoft Corporation. Development of this system (which was originally called the Interface Manager) began in 1981. Subsequently renamed Microsoft Windows, the system was not released until November 1985, after 55 person-years of effort. Since then, there have been a number of evolutions, such as Windows NT, Windows 2000, Windows XP, Windows Vista, and Windows 7.

The Windows NT development project began with a team of 10 or 12 people and expanded to include more than 200 in both technical and support staff roles. Over the four-year development effort for the first version, which was released in 1993, this translated into hundreds of person-years of labor merely to get the system out the door, to say nothing of maintenance work required to support this version and the efforts to upgrade it to new versions. The final system contained several hundred thousand lines of code. This is a Very Large project by the standard of Figure 9.17. Windows 95, released in August 1995, required about 8 million lines of code, which clearly puts it into the "massive skyscraper" (i.e., Extremely Large) category of Figure 9.17.

The Windows XP operating system was released in 2001. It has more than 40 million lines of code, which even presses the envelope of our Extremely Large category. Windows Vista was released in 2007 after more than five years of development. Its 50 million lines of code probably made it the single largest software development project ever at the time it was released. Windows 7 was released in October 2009. Windows 7 is based on Vista but with additional capabilities, so we can imagine that it goes well beyond 50 million lines of code.

The fifth major release of the Mac OS X operating system, Mac OS X Tiger, released in 2005, had 86 million lines of code.

The complexity of software projects of this magnitude is breathtaking. Not only technical capabilities, but also planning, teamwork, communication, and management skills are vital to successful completion.

Once agreed to by the developer and the customer, this document becomes essentially a legal contract describing what the developer promises to provide and what the customer agrees to accept. Like a contract, it usually includes a delivery schedule and a price, and it is signed by both the customer and the developer.

3. *Program design*—Now that it is clear *what* is to be done, the program design phase is the time to plan *how* it is to be done. In a traditional programming approach, the divide-and-conquer strategy (also called top-down decomposition) comes into play. Tasks are broken down into subtasks, which are broken down into sub-subtasks, and so on, until each piece is small enough to code comfortably. These pieces work together to accomplish the total job. In an *object-oriented approach*, the appropriate objects are identified, together with their data and the subtasks they must perform. This allows classes to be designed with variables to store the data, and functions (also called *methods*) to carry out these subtasks. Objects from these classes cooperate to accomplish the total job.

The larger the project, the more crucial it is to think of it in terms of smaller building blocks, or helpful classes, that are created separately and then properly assembled to solve the problem at hand. Although small programs of 50–100 lines can be thought of in one piece, 100,000-line programs cannot. However, it is possible to treat a 100,000 line program as a collection of about 1,000–2,000 smaller pieces, each containing about 50–100 lines.

The *program design document* breaks the problem down into subtasks and sub-subtasks, or into various classes. Some of this design may be documented graphically, through structure charts or through class diagrams that give the properties and functions of each class. Modules that carry out subtasks in a traditional design, or that carry out some service that the objects of a class provide, are ultimately translated into separate sections of code. There must also be a complete specification of each module: what it is to do, what information it needs to know in order to do it, and what the rest of the program needs to get from it when it is done. This information must be sufficiently detailed that a programmer can use the description as a guide to writing code for the module in the language of choice.

Program design is one of the truly creative and interesting parts of the software development life cycle. It is related to coding in roughly the same way that designing an airplane is related to riveting a wing.

4. *Algorithm selection or development, and analysis*—Once the various subtasks have been identified, algorithms must be found to carry them out. For example, one subtask may be to search a list of numbers for some particular value. In Chapters 2 and 3, we examined two different algorithms for searching—sequential search and binary search. If there is a choice of algorithms, it must be determined which is more suitable for this particular task, and perhaps which is more efficient. It may also be

that an algorithm has to be developed from scratch. This, too, is a very creative process. Documentation of this phase includes a description of the algorithms chosen or developed, perhaps in pseudocode, an analysis of their efficiency (as we did in Chapter 3), and a rationale for their use.

5. *Coding*—Coding is the process of translating the detailed designs into computer code. If the design has been carefully developed, this should be a relatively routine job. Perhaps reusable code can be pulled from a program library, or a useful class can be employed. Coding is the step that usually comes to mind when people think of software development. However, as we have shown, a great deal of important preparatory work precedes the actual production of code. Inexperienced programmers may think that they will save time by skipping the earlier phases and getting right to the coding. The opposite is usually true. In all but the most trivial of programs, tackling coding without first doing problem specification, program design, and algorithm selection or development ultimately leads to more time being spent and a poorer outcome. The coding phase also results in a written document, namely the listing of the program code itself.

6. *Debugging*—Debugging is the process of locating and correcting program errors, and it can be a slow and expensive operation that requires as much effort as writing the program in the first place. Errors can occur because a program statement fails to follow the correct rules of syntax, which makes the statement unrecognizable by the compiler and results in an error. Though irritating, these syntax errors are accompanied by messages from the compiler that help to pinpoint the problem. Other errors, called runtime errors, occur only when the program is run using certain sets of data that result in some illegal operation, such as dividing by zero. The system software also provides messages to help detect the cause of runtime errors. The third, and most subtle, class of errors is logic errors. These are errors in the algorithm used to solve the problem. Some incorrect steps that result in wrong answers are performed, but there are no error messages to help pinpoint the problem. Indeed, the first step in debugging a logic error is to notice that the answers are wrong. For example, if our algorithm calls for us to add 317 to the value of A, but we accidently translate this as:

```
A = A + 371;
```

our mistake will not produce an error message as the statement is syntactically correct and semantically meaningful. The only way we know there is an error is to notice the incorrect result in A.

Debugging has always been one of the most frustrating, agonizing, and time-consuming steps in the programming process. Extensive time spent on debugging usually means that insufficient time was spent on carefully specifying, organizing, and structuring the solution. If the design is poor, then the resulting program is often a structural mess, with convoluted, hard-to-understand logic. On the other hand, devoting careful attention to the design phases can help reduce the amount of debugging that must be done.

Careful documentation of the debugging process includes notes on the problems found and on how the code was changed to solve them. This may prevent later changes from reintroducing old errors.

7. *Testing, verification, and benchmarking*—Even though a program produces correct answers for 1, 5, or even 1,000 data sets, how can we be sure that it is 100% correct and will work on all data? One approach, called empirical testing, is to design a special set of test cases, called a *test suite*, and run the program using this special test data. Test data that are carefully chosen to exercise all the different logic paths through a program can help uncover errors. In a conditional statement, for example, one set of data should make the Boolean expression true, so that one block of code is executed. Another set of data should make the same Boolean expression false, so that the other block of code is executed. The quantity of the test data does not matter; what matters is that the data cover all the various cases. The goal of empirical testing is to make sure that every statement in the software has been executed at least once. Having said that, we should note that in all but the most trivial programs, it is not possible to "cover all the cases." The best that can be said is that the more thorough the testing, the higher the level of our confidence that the program is correct.

It's not a good plan to wait until the complete program is "finished" before testing takes place. In a program of any size, that's too late to identify where an error occurs. Unit testing takes place on each module (subtask code) as it is completed. As these tested modules are combined to work together, integration testing is done to see that the modules communicate the necessary data between and among themselves and that all modules work together smoothly. And if anything is changed on an already-tested module, regression testing is done to be sure that this change hasn't introduced a new error into code that was previously correct.

A second, and totally different, approach to confirming a program's correctness is to use mathematical logic. Program verification can be used to prove that if the input data to a program satisfies certain conditions, then, after the program has been run on these data, the output data satisfies certain other conditions. This is not a magic wand that gives us blanket assurance that the program will absolutely behave as we want. Furthermore, the program verification process can be difficult and time consuming. That's why program testing is used much more than formal program verification to reduce the risk of program errors.

In addition to correctness, the problem specification may require certain performance characteristics such as the amount of time to compute the results. Benchmarking the program means running it on many data sets to be sure its performance falls within those required limits. At the completion of testing (or verification) and benchmarking, we should have a correct and efficient program that is ready for delivery. Of course, all of the testing, verification, and benchmarking results are committed to paper as evidence that the program meets its specifications.

8. *Documentation*—Program documentation is all of the written material that makes a program understandable. This includes internal documentation, which is part of the program code itself. Good internal documentation consists of choosing meaningful names for program identifiers, using plenty of comments to explain the code, and separating the program into short modules, each of which does one specific subtask. External documentation consists of any materials assembled to clarify the program's design and implementation. Although we have put this step rather late in the software development process, note that each preceding step produces some form of documentation. Program documentation goes on throughout the software development life cycle. The final, finished program documentation is written in two forms. Technical documentation enables programmers who later have to modify the program to understand the code. Such information as structure charts or class diagrams, descriptions of algorithms, and program listings fall in this category. User documentation helps users run the program. Such documentation includes online tutorials, answers to frequently-asked questions (FAQs), help systems that the user can bring up while the program is running, and (less often) written user's manuals.

9. *Maintenance*—Programs are not static entities that, once completed, never change. Because of the time and expense involved in developing software, successful programs are used for a very long time. It is not unusual for a program to still be in use 15 or 20 years after it was written. (Microsoft Word was first developed and released in 1983!) In fact, the typical life cycle for a medium- to large-sized software package is 1–3 years in development and 5–15 years in the marketplace. During this long period of use, errors may be uncovered, new hardware or system software may be purchased on which the program has to run, user needs may change, and the whims of the marketplace may fluctuate. The original program must be modified and brought out in new versions to meet these changing needs. Program maintenance, the process of adapting an existing software product, may consume as much as 65% of the total software development life cycle budget. If the program has been well planned, carefully designed, well coded, thoroughly tested, and well documented, then program maintenance is a much easier task. Indeed, it is with an eye to program maintenance (and to reducing its cost) that we stress the importance of these earlier steps.

Maintenance should not really be viewed as a separate step in the software development life cycle. Rather, it involves repetition of some or all of the steps previously described, from a feasibility study through implementation, testing, and updated documentation. Maintenance reflects the fact that the software development life cycle is truly a *cycle*, during which it is necessary to redo earlier phases of development as our software changes, grows, and matures.

9.6.3 Modern Environments

Modern software development environments have had a great impact on the software development life cycle process. Most programming languages are now presented within an **integrated development environment**, or **IDE**. The IDE lets the programmer perform a number of tasks within the shell of a single application program, rather than having to use a separate program for each task. Consider some of the system software tasks described in Section 6.2: Use a *text editor* to create a program; use a *file system* to store the program; use a *language translator* to translate the program to machine language; and if the program does not work correctly, use a *debugger* to help locate the errors.

A modern programming IDE provides a text editor, a file manager, a compiler, a linker and loader, and tools for debugging, all within this one piece of software. This can significantly speed up program development.

Many IDEs enable programmers to create sample graphical user interfaces (GUIs), called **prototypes**, that can be shown to prospective users in the initial stages of software development. These prototypes do not have any functionality, but they can give users a good idea of what the final software package will look like—much like seeing a small-scale mock-up of a proposed new building before it is actually built. This *rapid prototyping process* allows any misunderstandings or miscommunications between user and programmer to be identified and corrected early in the development process.

Finally, there are software packages that track requirements from the initial specification through the design process to final code, to make sure that nothing gets lost along the way. These packages may also support graphical design of the various program elements, such as classes, and facilitate their translation into code.

9.6.4 Agile Software Development

The software development process described in Section 9.6.2 is also known as the **waterfall model** of software development. Think of a series of waterfalls moving a river down and down through various plateaus. In the software development process, these plateaus would be the feasibility study, problem specification, program design, etc.—all the steps we outlined in Section 9.6.2. This imagery suggests that software development is a completely sequential process, that is, one step must be completed before moving on to the next, and that previous steps are never revisited. The waterfall model was originally developed to describe manufacturing processes, where a step such as "cut sheet metal" definitely had to be completed (and never revisited) before "weld the seams."

Software development is much more fluid, and in fact there is wiggle room in the waterfall model. The program design phase may bring out issues that require revisiting the problem specification, the debugging phase obviously requires some amount of recoding, and testing and documentation are done throughout the process. Thus, the "pure" waterfall model of software development is seldom used in favor of a more flexible approach that is instead guided by the waterfall model.

Around 2001, a new software development model known as agile software development started to be used. The dictionary definition of the word *agile* is: "marked by ready ability to move with quick easy grace; having a quick, resourceful and adaptable character." This suggests flexibility, nimbleness, and the ability to adjust to changes. Let's revisit a phrase or two from our discussion of the waterfall model: "The problem specification document expresses the final and complete problem specification and guides the software developers in all subsequent decisions. ... Once agreed to by the developer and the customer, this document becomes essentially a legal contract describing what the developer promises to provide and what the customer agrees to accept." Sounds like a done deal.

The whole agile software development philosophy is a recognition that the problem specification is never a "done deal," that there are bound to be changes, that the development team must be "agile" in its response to these changes, and that the customer should be involved in working with the development team throughout the process. Agile software development is actually a whole suite of methods and processes that help to promote this flexible and ready response to meet a shifting and ever-changing target.

One of the ideas of agile software development, pair programming, has even made its way into some college computer science classes. Pair programming involves two programmers (students) at a single workstation. At any given point in time, one is writing code and the other is actively observing. The observer watches each line of code for possible errors, but also is thinking about the overall approach, what problems may lie ahead, possibly spotting improvements that could be made. The roles of the two individuals are switched frequently. The emphasis is on cooperation, not competition. Pair programming, if done well, actually produces better code more quickly than a single programmer, but of course there is the added cost of two people working together. So for any particular project, the relative costs and benefits of pair programming need to be weighed.

9.7 Conclusion

In this chapter, we have seen how the use of a high-level language overcomes many of the disadvantages of assembly language programming, creating a more comfortable and useful environment for the programmer. In a high-level language, the programmer need not manage the storage or movement of data values in memory. The programmer can think about the problem at a higher level, can use program instructions that are both more powerful and more natural-language-like, and can write a program that is much more portable among various hardware platforms. The online language chapters (on Ada, C++, C#, Java, and Python) spell out the mechanisms used by each language to give the programmer these more powerful problem-solving abilities. In this chapter, we've seen two small sample programs in each language plus a brief comparison of some of the features of these languages.

We also discussed the entire software development life cycle, noting that for large, real-world programs, software development must be a managed discipline. Coding is but a small part of the software development process.

The high-level languages we have investigated so far all belong to the procedural language family. In the next chapter, we'll look briefly at several more procedural languages as well as other languages that take quite a different approach to problem solving.

EXERCISES

Each online language chapter has its own set of exercises. See the Special Interest Box on page 429 for instructions on accessing the online chapters.

CHALLENGE WORK

1. Write a program in the language of your choice to implement the sequential search algorithm of Chapter 3, Figure 3.1, except that instead of searching a list of names for a particular name, have the program search a list of integers for a particular integer. Use the same input mechanism as in the data cleanup programs of Section 9.3.2 to get the list of integers to be searched. Then get the target number to be searched for. The program should output "Successful search, the value is in the list" or "Unsuccessful search, the value is not in the list." Be sure to test your program for both outcomes.

2. In Chapter 8, we learned about a simple encryption algorithm called a Caesar cipher. Write a program in the language of your choice to implement the Caesar cipher algorithm.

   a. Write a main function (method, procedure) that collects a message from the user and writes it out again. Assume for simplicity that the message contains no more than 10 characters and that only the 26 uppercase letters of the alphabet are used. Use an array of 10 elements to store the message. Ask the user to enter no more than 10 characters, one per line, and to terminate the message by entering some special character such as "%." Use a variable to keep track of the number of array elements actually used (which could be fewer than 10 if the message is short) so that you do not write out meaningless characters stored at the end of the array.

   b. Because you will be writing out the contents of the message array several times, write a helper function (method, procedure) *WriteMessage* to do this task. Now rewrite your main function

so that it uses *WriteMessage* to write out the message array.

   c. Write a function (method, procedure) to modify the array to represent the encoded form of the message using a Caesar cipher. Have the main function ask for the shift amount. Pass this information, along with the message array and the number of array elements actually used, to the encoding function. To get from one character to the character *s* units along in the alphabet, you can simply add *s* to the original character. This works for everything except the end of the alphabet; here you will have to be a bit more clever to cycle back to the beginning of the alphabet once the shift is applied. Have the main function invoke the encoding function and then invoke *WriteMessage* to write out the encoded form of the message.

   d. Write a function (method, procedure) to modify the array containing the encoded message back to its original form. This function also needs as arguments the number of array elements used and the value of the shift amount, as well as the array itself. The body of the function should accomplish the reverse of the encoding function. Have the main function invoke the decoding function and then write out the decoded form of the message, which should agree with the original message.

   e. Test your program with different values for *s* and different word lengths.

3. In Chapter 7, we learned about the *routing problem* in computer networks, which consists of finding the optimal path from a source node

to a destination node. Each hop along a path represents a communication channel between two nodes that has an associated "cost"; the cost might actually be a monetary cost to use a leased line, but it could also be a cost in terms of the volume of traffic the line typically carries. In either case, the "shortest path" is the one with the lowest cost. As mentioned in Chapter 7, the Internet uses Dijkstra's shortest path algorithm to solve this problem. If node x is the source node and receives a message for node y, then x only needs to know the shortest path from itself to node y. But an alternative is to have a centralized site periodically compute the "all-pairs shortest path" from any node to any other node, and then broadcast that information to all nodes in the network. The algorithm for the all-pairs shortest path, called *Floyd's algorithm*, is simpler to implement than Dijkstra's algorithm.

A two-dimensional array (table) is used to represent the nodes in the network. If there are n nodes in the network, the array is $n \times n$ in size. The entry in position i, j of the array is the length (cost) of the line from i to j. For example, the following network has five nodes, numbered 0 through 4.

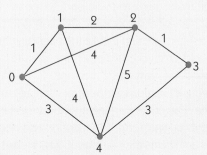

It is represented by the 5×5 array shown here.

	0	1	2	3	4
0	0	1	4	∞	3
1	1	0	2	∞	4
2	4	2	0	1	5
3	∞	∞	1	0	3
4	3	4	5	3	0

The entry in row 1, column 4 is 4 because the length of the line between node 1 and node

4 is 4. The entry in row 0, column 3 is ∞ because there is no direct line between nodes 0 and 3. All the entries on the "main diagonal" (positions [0,0], [1,1], [2,2], [3,3], and [4,4]) are 0 because there is a 0-length link from a node to itself.

Floyd's algorithm operates on the array A of the graph. A pseudocode description of the algorithm is:

```
set the value of k to 0
while (k <= n − 1) do
    set the value of i to 0
    while (i <= n − 1) do
        set the value of j to 0
        while (j <= n − 1) do
            if A [i, k] + A [k, j] < A [i, j]
                A [i, j] = A [i, k] + A [k, j]
            end of the j-loop
        end of the i-loop
end of the k-loop
```

When this algorithm terminates, the entry in position [i, j] of the array represents the length of the shortest path between nodes i and j, although this algorithm does not say what the intermediate nodes on the shortest path are.

Write a program in the language of your choice to solve the all-pairs shortest path problem for a graph with five nodes. The program gets the values for each row of the array from the user, runs Floyd's algorithm, and writes out the resulting array. Use 500 for "infinity," which assumes all legitimate line lengths are less than 500.

Try your program for the graph shown here. From the output of your program, what is the length of the shortest path from node 2 to node 4? By looking at the graph, what are the nodes on this path?

4. Exercise 1 asks you to write a program to search a list of integers for a particular value. Your program asks the user to enter the list at the keyboard, the same mechanism we have used for collecting data in the examples of this chapter. It is more

realistic to read the list from a preexisting data file stored on the computer's hard drive. Ask your instructor how to read a file in the language of your choice, then create a data file and write the sequential search program again, this time using file input data. Output can be to the screen, as before.

5. Again create a data file of random integers. Then write a program in the language of your choice to implement the selection sort algorithm of Figure 3.6 using file input data. Write a separate function (method, procedure) to find the location of the largest number in the unsorted section of the list (see Figure 2.14) and have your main function call that as needed. Write your sorted list to another data file.

6. Read more about software engineering and write a short paper on one or more of the following topics:

   - Black-box and white-box testing
   - CASE tools
   - Code refactoring
   - Code review
   - Configuration management
   - Data dictionary
   - Extreme programming (XP)
   - JAD (Joint Application Development) sessions
   - Quality assurance
   - Rapid prototyping
   - Requirements tracing
   - Software metrics
   - Stubs and drivers
   - Version control

ADDITIONAL RESOURCES

CourseMate **For additional print and/or online resources relevant to this chapter, visit the Computer Science CourseMate at login.cengagebrain.com.**

10.1 Why Babel?

The biblical story of the Tower of Babel takes place at a time when "the whole earth had one language and few words." The people began to build a city with a mighty tower when, suddenly, everyone began speaking in different tongues and could no longer communicate. They became confused, abandoned the tower, and scattered "over the face of all the earth." A shared enterprise was impossible to pursue without the mutual understanding fostered by a common language, and (the message this story was intended to convey) the power of what people could do was thus forever limited. In modern times, it has been argued that if all peoples of the earth spoke a common language, the chances of war would be greatly reduced.

Similarly, it might seem that having all computer programs written in the same programming language would have an appealing simplicity. Chapter 9 gave a brief comparison of five general-purpose programming languages: Ada, C++, C#, Java, and Python. By now, you may have also studied one or more of these languages in some depth through the online language chapters. But again, why aren't all programs written in the best one of these languages? Or does each of these languages have some things it can't do that some of the other languages can do? If so, then why aren't all programs written in some "superlanguage" that overcomes these deficiencies?

There are multiple programming languages not so much because there are tasks that one language cannot do but because each language was designed to meet specific needs. Consequently, one language might be better suited than others for writing certain kinds of programs. The situation is somewhat analogous to the automobile market. The basic automotive needs of the country probably could be served by a single car model and a single truck model. So why do we have seemingly endless models from which to choose? The answer lies partly in competition: Automotive companies are all trying to claim a share of the market. More than that, though, the answer lies in the variety of ways we use our automobiles. Although a luxury car could be used for off-roading, it is not designed for that use; a four-wheel-drive vehicle does the job better, more safely, and more efficiently. Although a sports car could be used to haul Little Leaguers home from the ball game, it is not designed for that use; an SUV or minivan serves this purpose better. The diversity of tasks for which we use our automobiles has promoted a variety of automotive models, each designed to handle a particular range of tasks.

The same thing applies to programming languages. For example, we *could* use C++ to write programs for solving engineering problems (and it has indeed been so used). However, C++ was not designed with engineering applications in mind. Although C++ supports the basic arithmetic operations of addition, subtraction, multiplication, and division by providing simple operators (+, –, *, /) to do these tasks, there is no operator for exponentiation— that is, raising a value to a power. Computing $2.84^{1.8}$ in a C++ program, for example, can certainly be done but it requires some effort.[1] Calculations involving exponents are performed hundreds of times in many engineering and other numerical-based applications, so why not use a language that provides an operator for exponentiation, a language designed with such tasks in mind? Ada has such an exponentiation operator, as does FORTRAN, which we'll discuss in the next section.

Similarly, suppose our program writes complicated sales reports with columns of figures and blocks of information strategically located on the page. Specifying the exact placement of output on the page is rather tedious in C++ or Java. Why not use a language that allows detailed output formatting because it was designed with such a purpose in mind? Again, we'll briefly discuss such a language—COBOL—in the next section.

What if we want a program to interact with a database, to manipulate graphics, or to act as a hyperlinked Web page? Any of these specialized tasks is probably best done with a language designed for just that purpose.

A major reason, then, for the proliferation of programming languages is the proliferation of programming tasks. Another reason is that different philosophies have developed about how people should think when they are writing programs. This has resulted in several families of programming

---

[1]The C++ expression for $2.84^{1.8}$ is exp(1.8*log(2.84)), or, somewhat shorter, pow(2.84, 1.8), using functions available in the math library that are linked in with a #include <cmath> directive.

languages that take quite different approaches from the ones we've looked at so far, and we'll see some of these approaches in Section 10.4.

10.2 Procedural Languages

As mentioned earlier, all the languages of Chapter 9 (Ada, C++, C#, Java, and Python) are *procedural languages*. Programs written in such languages differ in the way the statements must be arranged on a line and in how variables can be named. They differ in the details of assigning a new value to a variable, in the mechanisms the language provides for directing the flow of control through conditional and looping statements, and in the statement forms that control input and output. They also differ in the way programs can be broken down into modules to handle separate tasks, and in how those modules share information. We noted some of these syntactical differences in the Feature Analysis table (Figure 9.15) of Chapter 9. But all procedural language programs tell the computer in a step-by-step fashion how to manipulate the contents of memory locations. In a general sense, then, the languages are quite similar, just as French, Spanish, and Italian are all members of the family of Romance languages. In this section, we concentrate, not on syntactical differences, but on the history and "intent" of some of the most important procedural languages—important in that, of the many programming languages that have come and gone over the years, these became widely used. The languages of Chapter 9 are included here, but there are additional languages as well.

10.2.1 Plankalkül

What??? OK, this language never became widely used. In fact, it was never even implemented. It's a programming language designed by Konrad Zuse who, you may recall from Chapter 1, built a computer in Germany during World War II. The manuscript describing this programming language was completed in 1945 but was not published until 1972. The manuscript contained a number of complex algorithms written in Plankalkül (the name means "formal system for planning"). The language itself, although burdened with obscure notation, contained a number of sophisticated concepts that, had they been known earlier, might have changed the development of programming languages. As the very first attempt to design a high-level programming language for computers, Zuse's proposal was a very important milestone in the field of computing, although it never received the attention it deserved.

10.2.2 FORTRAN

The name FORTRAN derives from *FOR*mula *TRAN*slation. The very name indicates its affiliation with "formulas" or engineering-type applications. Developed in the mid-1950s by a group at IBM headed by John Backus, in conjunction with some IBM computer users, the first commercial version of FORTRAN was released in 1957. This makes FORTRAN the first high-level programming language that was actually implemented. Early computer users were often engineers who were solving problems with a heavy mathematics or computational flavor. FORTRAN has some features ideally suited to these applications, such as the exponentiation operator we mentioned earlier, the ability to carry out extended-precision arithmetic with many decimal places of accuracy, and the ability to work with the complex number system. Updated versions of FORTRAN (FORTRAN II, FORTRAN IV, FORTRAN 77, Fortran 90, Fortran 2003, Fortran 2008, and High Performance Fortran) have been introduced over the years, incorporating new data types and new statements to direct the flow of control. Fortran 2003 and Fortran 2008 support object-oriented programming.

Early versions of FORTRAN did not allow the use of mathematical symbols such as < to compare two quantities; the keypunches that were used to create the punched cards on which early FORTRAN programs were submitted to the computer had no such symbols. Thus the condition

```
number < 0
```

would have been expressed in early FORTRAN as

```
NUMBER .LT. 0
```

(Before Fortran 90, variable identifiers had to be uppercase.) Early versions of FORTRAN also had no while loop mechanism. The effect of a while loop was obtained by using an IF statement together with GO TO statements. The pseudocode

```
input number
while (number >= 0)
{
    .
    .
    .
    input number
}
```

would have been accomplished by

```
      READ(*,*) NUMBER
10    IF (NUMBER .LT. 0) GO TO 20
          .
          .
          .
      READ(*,*) NUMBER
      GO TO 10
20    ...
```

READ is the FORTRAN implementation of "input," so the first line inputs a value for *NUMBER*. If *NUMBER* is less than 0, the GO TO statement transfers control to statement 20. If *NUMBER* is greater than or equal to 0, something is done and then another value for *NUMBER* is obtained. Control is then redirected by the second GO TO statement back to statement 10 where the new value is tested.

Directing the flow of control by GO TO statements is similar to using the various JUMP statements in the assembly language of Chapter 6, and it reflects the fact that FORTRAN's developers were, after all, working from assembly language. In the absence of an equivalent to the while statement, there is no choice but to use GO TO statements to implement looping, as shown previously. Excessive and careless use of GO TOs, however, can make a program very difficult to read. (Imagine reading a novel where in the middle of page 49 you are told to stop reading this page and to begin reading at the top of page 215. Then, when you reach page 218, you are told to stop, go back, and start reading page 125. You might wonder whether you were really following the plot.) Code filled with GO TO statements that send the flow of control all over the place can be a nightmare. Such "spaghetti code" tangled across hundreds of lines can be very difficult to unravel. Given that a GO TO statement is available, it is up to the programmer's individual discipline to avoid abusing it. The potential for such abuse prompted the well-known computer scientist E. W. Dijkstra to write a letter headed "Go To Statement Considered Harmful," which appeared in the *Communications of the ACM* (Association for Computing Machinery) in 1968. This sparked the "GO TO controversy," which debated the merits of replacing the GO TO statement with more controlled programming language constructs such as the while loop. From our perspective many years later, when almost every language has a looping construct, this controversy seems rather quaint, but it provoked lively discussion at the time.

FORTRAN was designed to support numerical computations. This led to concise mathematical notation (aside from the early < dilemma just mentioned) and to the availability of a number of mathematical functions within the language. Another design goal was to optimize the resulting object code, that is, to produce object code that took as little space and executed as efficiently as possible. (Remember that when FORTRAN was developed, machine resources were scarce and precious.) FORTRAN allows external libraries of well-written, efficient, and thoroughly tested code modules that are separately compiled and then drawn on by any program that wants to use their capabilities. Because of FORTRAN's extensive use as a programming language over the years, a large and well-tested FORTRAN library collection exists, so in many cases programmers can use existing code instead of having to write all code from scratch. This feature is sometimes highly touted for newer languages, but FORTRAN designers got there first. FORTRAN was an extremely successful language; millions of lines of FORTRAN code are still in use, and thanks to its evolution over time, FORTRAN has remained an effective language for engineering applications and heavy-duty "number crunching" for such tasks as climate modeling, computational fluid dynamics, and computational economics.

Old Dog, New Tricks #1

FORTRAN was first introduced in 1957. In the history of computing, this is roughly the Jurassic Age. But FORTRAN is no extinct dinosaur. Instead, it is a chameleon, changing with the times. Thanks to ever-increasing hardware capability, FORTRAN runs on PCs while still providing the power to help supercomputers tackle some of the most compute-intensive problems ever. However, programmers can now use an environment with a graphical user interface to develop code, and that code can present a graphical user interface to the ultimate user of the program.

As further proof of FORTRAN's continued usefulness, a standard for HPF (High Performance Fortran) has been developed. This version of FORTRAN is designed to run on massively parallel processors that can bring huge amounts of computer horsepower to bear. Parallelism is especially useful for speeding up the kinds of calculations on large arrays that often occur in scientific and engineering problems, FORTRAN's traditional domain. Problems with real-time response requirements in the areas of signal processing and image processing are also appropriate for HPF parallelism.

FORTRAN can "talk with" many other modern programming languages, which allows the creation of mixed-language programs that capture the best features of each language for the application at hand. Given these adaptations, FORTRAN, in one form or another, is likely to live on for quite some time.

Practice Problems

1. Write a FORTRAN condition to test whether the value of *ITIME* is less than or equal to 7. Use early FORTRAN syntax.

2. Using the if/then/else construct introduced in Chapter 2, rewrite the following FORTRAN code fragment so that it does not require any GO TO statements:

```
        IF (X .LT. 3) GO TO 10
        A = 1
        GO TO 20
   10   A = 2
        GO TO 30
   20   B = 3
   30           . . .
```

10.2.3 COBOL

The name COBOL derives from *CO*mmon *B*usiness-*O*riented *L*anguage. COBOL was developed in 1959 and 1960 by a group headed by Admiral Grace Murray Hopper of the U.S. Navy. FORTRAN and COBOL were the dominant high-level languages of the 1960s and 1970s. COBOL was designed to serve business needs such as managing inventories and payrolls. In such applications, summary reports are important output products. Much of the processing in the business world concerns updating "master files" with changes from "transaction files." For example, a master inventory file contains names, manufacturers, and quantities available for various items in inventory; a transaction file contains names and quantities of items sold out of inventory or delivered to inventory over some period of time. The master file is updated from the transaction file on a daily or weekly basis to reflect the new quantities available, and a summary report is printed. The user doesn't interact directly with the COBOL program; rather, the user prepares the master file (once) and the transaction file (regularly). As is consistent with this intended usage, COBOL is far more adept at handling file input than keyboard input.

In the design of COBOL, particular attention was paid to input formatting for data being read from files and to output formatting both for writing data to a file and for generating business reports with information precisely located on the page. Therefore, much of a COBOL program may be concerned with formatting, described by "PICTURE clauses" in the program.

COBOL was also designed such that programs describe what they are doing in natural language phrases. As a result, COBOL programs are rather verbose. Instead of a succinct and mathematical statement

```
sum = a + b;
```

COBOL says

```
ADD A TO B GIVING SUM.
```

This compromise actually sacrifices one of the goals of high-level languages that we enumerated in the previous chapter, to use standard mathematical notation, but this deliberate decision on the part of the COBOL language designers allows COBOL programs to be written by people who are less "formula-oriented."

COBOL programs are highly portable across many different COBOL compilers, are quite easy to read, and are very well suited to manipulating large data files. Because COBOL has been around for a long time, there are many existing COBOL applications. COBOL probably provides as much as 60% of the existing code base (between 180 billion and 200 billion lines of COBOL code), making it, even today, the most widely used language in the world.

Nonetheless, the continuing importance of COBOL as a commercial programming language had perhaps been overlooked by those outside the business world until the "Year 2000 problem" came along. The Y2K problem (K stands for *kilo,* or "thousand") dealt with a lurking time bomb in legacy code (i.e., old, but still-running programs), primarily COBOL code. When these programs were written, their authors never imagined their longevity. In addition, computer memory was at a premium, so efficiency was the order of the day. Why store four digits of a date (1967, say) when two digits (67)—the "19" prefix was to be assumed—would be sufficient and would take less space? Furthermore, code was entered on punched paper cards, and no one wanted an instruction to have to be continued on to a second card because of four-digit dates instead of two. In the new millennium, "02" should mean "2002," but in these programs it would be interpreted as "1902."

Making code Y2K-compliant was technically simple: Just change every date reference to four digits instead of two. It was the magnitude of the task that was staggering because it was necessary to locate each line of code where a date entry needed to be changed. Huge sums of government and corporate money were spent to address the problem and, despite dire predictions on the potential consequences of Y2K, it proved to be a "nonevent"—probably because of the massive effort made to address the problem.

So, does post-Y2K mark the death of COBOL? No—all this money was not spent on code that businesses planned to throw away. On the contrary, the majority of business transactions, billions of them per day, are still done on COBOL code that has now been updated and is likely to continue to run for the foreseeable future. What are these business transactions? Retail point-of-sale systems, banking, insurance, payroll, ATMs, hospital systems, government systems—just imagine the load on such systems in even one day! COBOL has stood the test of time, even though, after the Y2K crisis, it has slipped back into relative anonymity. New applications in other languages have to integrate with these existing COBOL programs. It is estimated that around 5 billion lines of new COBOL code are added to still-in-use systems every year. Doesn't sound like a dying language, does it? The current international standard for COBOL was approved in September 2002. The standards working group for COBOL posted its draft recommendations for a new international standard in June 2008 and a final version was expected to be approved by 2010, but, as of this writing, is still under

Practice Problems

1. Write statements in your choice of language from Chapter 9 that are equivalent to the following COBOL statements:

   ```
   MOVE INPUT-NUMBER TO OUTPUT-NUMBER.
   ADD INPUT-NUMBER TO SUM-OF-VALUES.
   ```

2. How might the following algorithmic construct be rendered in COBOL?

   Set diameter = 2 * radius

discussion. COBOL, like FORTRAN, changes and improves over time. Meanwhile, however, the pool of trained COBOL programmers is being depleted by retirements and deaths and is not being replenished by new graduates, many of whom have never been exposed to COBOL.

10.2.4 C/C++

C was developed in the early 1970s by Dennis Ritchie at AT&T Labs. It was originally designed for systems programming, in particular for writing the operating system UNIX. UNIX had been developed at Bell Labs a short time before and was originally written primarily in assembly language. Ritchie sought a high-level language in which to rewrite the operating system in order to gain all the advantages of high-level languages: ease of programming, portability, and so on.

Since that time, C has become a popular general-purpose language for two major reasons. One is the close relationship between C and UNIX. UNIX has been implemented on many different computers (and is the basis for the Mac OS X operating system). UNIX provides many "tools" that support C programming. A second reason for C's popularity is its efficiency—that is, the speed with which its operations can be executed. This efficiency derives from the fact that C programs can make use of low-level information such as knowledge of where data are stored in memory. In this respect, C is closer to assembly language than are other high-level languages, yet it still has the powerful statements and portability to many machines that high-level languages offer. You can imagine C humming along as a high-level language but then, every once in a while when efficiency is really important, slipping into a low-level, machine-dependent configuration. One of the goals of a high-level language is to provide a level of abstraction that shields the programmer from any knowledge of the actual hardware/memory cells used during program execution, as depicted in Figure 10.1(a). C provides this outlook, unless the programmer wants to make use of the low-level constructs available in C that give him or her a direct view of the actual hardware, which Figure 10.1(b) depicts.

For example, suppose *number* is a variable in a C program with the value 234. The value of *number* is stored in some specific memory location with address, say, 1000 (Figure 10.2). Then *&number* in that same program refers to the memory address where the value of *number* is stored, in this case, 1000. Note the distinction between the content of a memory cell and the address of that cell. Here *number* refers to the value 234, but *&number* refers to the address 1000. It is possible to write a C program statement that passes *&number* as an argument to an output function so that the program actually writes out the memory address value (1000). The ability to print an actual memory address is not available in most other high-level languages.

C not only provides a way to see the actual memory address where a variable is stored, it also gives the programmer some control over the address where information is stored. C includes a data type called *pointer*. Variables

FIGURE 10.1

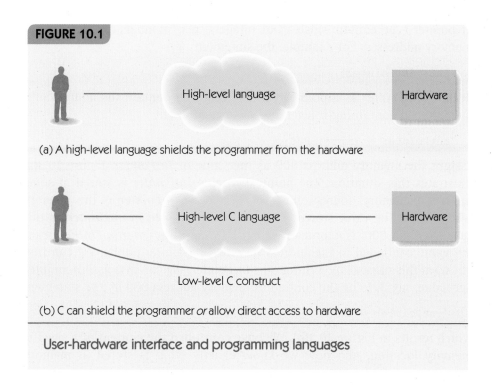

(a) A high-level language shields the programmer from the hardware

Low-level C construct

(b) C can shield the programmer *or* allow direct access to hardware

User-hardware interface and programming languages

FIGURE 10.2

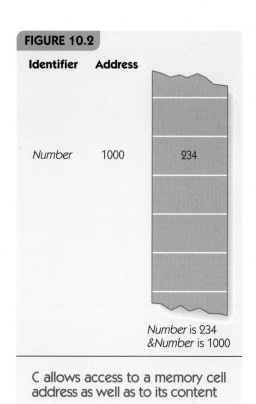

Number is 234
&Number is 1000

C allows access to a memory cell address as well as to its content of pointer type contain—instead of integers, real numbers, or characters—memory addresses. For example, the statement

```
int* intPointer;
```

declares *intPointer* as a pointer variable that will contain the address of a memory cell containing integer data. The assignment

```
intPointer = (int*) 800;
```

assigns the memory address 800 as the value of *intPointer*. Figure 10.3(a) illustrates this situation: The pointer variable *intPointer* is stored at some unknown memory address, but the content of *intPointer* is the memory address 800. The value stored at the address contained in *intPointer*, in this case stored at 800, is denoted by **intPointer*. In other words, **intPointer* is the value contained in the address to which *intPointer* points. We can find out what this value is by writing out **intPointer*. We can also assign an integer value, say 3, to be the content of memory address 800 by the statement

```
*intPointer = 3;
```

which results in Figure 10.3(b). We have controlled the content of a specific memory location, and now we know exactly what is stored in memory

FIGURE 10.3

(a) The value 800 is assigned to *intPointer*

(b) The value 3 is assigned to **intPointer*

Storing a value in a specific memory location using C

location 800. Similarly, if *number* is an integer variable that has been stored somewhere in memory, then the statement

```
*intPointer = number;
```

results in the value of *number* being stored in memory cell 800.

This capability for low-level memory manipulation resembles the assembly language programming of Chapter 6. It is fraught with the problems we sought to avoid by going to high-level languages in the first place; specifically, the programmer is assuming responsibility for what is stored where. For example, what if memory cell 800 in our example is not a memory cell allocated to this program? Perhaps something needed by another program, or even by the operating system, has been overwritten. However, the fact that it enables the programmer to reach down into the machine level is precisely why C is useful for writing system software such as operating systems, assemblers, compilers, programs that allow the computer to interact with input/output devices, and so on.

A program to interact with an I/O device is called a device driver. Consider, for example, the problem of writing a device driver for the mouse on a PC. The USB port of the computer, to which the mouse is connected, reads changes in the mouse position by changes in voltage levels. It stores the voltage levels in fixed locations in memory, as allocated by the operating system. The job of the mouse driver is to translate voltage levels to specific locations on the screen so that any application software that uses the mouse, such as a word processor, does not have to interact with low-level hardware information (abstraction again!). The mouse driver program would have to access the specific memory locations where voltage information is stored. A language like C provides such a capability.

C is the most widely used language for writing system software because of the versatility its design philosophy bestowed on it. It combines the power of a high-level language with the ability to circumvent that level of abstraction and work at the assembly-language-like level. But C is also used for a great deal of general-purpose computing.

The C++ language was developed in the early 1980s by Bjarne Stroustrup, also at AT&T Labs. C++ is in fact a "superset" of C, meaning that all of the C language is part of C++. Everything that can be done in C—including the ability to change the contents of specific memory locations—can be done in C++. But C++ adds many new features to C, giving it more sophistication and cleaner ways to do certain tasks. The most significant extension of C that C++ provides is the ability to do object-oriented programming.

C++ was first commercially released by AT&T in 1985. Like many other languages, C++ has evolved over time. The standardization process for the language took more than 10 years, in part because of this evolution. In November 1997, the combined C++ subcommittees of ANSI and ISO submitted their C++ standards draft, part of a document of some 800 pages, for final ISO approval. The standards were finally approved in 1998. Standardization, object orientation, and a strong collection of library code have helped to

Practice Problems

1. Suppose a C/C++ program uses a variable called *Rate*. Explain the distinction in the program between *Rate* and *&Rate*.

2. Suppose that *Rate* is an integer variable in a C/C++ program with the value 10 and that *intPointer* is a pointer variable for integer data. *Rate* is stored at memory address 500. After the statement

   ```
   intPointer = &Rate;
   ```

   is executed, what is the value of **intPointer*?

make C++ one of the most popular of the modern "industrial-strength" languages. A new international standard was approved in 2011.

10.2.5 Ada

Probably more than any other language we have mentioned, Ada has a long and interesting development history. It began in the mid-1970s when the various branches of the U.S. armed services set about trying to develop a common high-level programming language for use by defense contractors. They began by specifying the requirements that the language would have to meet, including such characteristics as efficiency, reliability, readability, and maintainability.

The original set of requirements, first circulated for discussion in 1975, was known as "Strawman." Successively tighter and more thorough requirements bore the names "Woodenman" and "Tinman." The Tinman requirements were approved in 1976, and a large number of existing programming languages were evaluated in the light of these requirements. All were found wanting, and it became clear that a new language would have to be developed. The "Ironman" specification, issued in 1977, became the standard against which to measure a new language. A design competition was held, and the requirements were further specified in "Steelman."

The eventual language design winner was chosen in 1979, and the new language was christened Ada, after Ada Augusta Byron Lovelace, daughter of the poet Lord Byron and later the wife of Lord Lovelace. Ada was trained in mathematics and science at the wish of her mother, who sought to steer Ada away from the mental instability and moral lapses she despised in Lord Byron. Lady Ada Lovelace is regarded as the world's first programmer on the basis of her correspondence with Charles Babbage and her published notes on his work with the Analytic Engine (see the Special Interest Box on Charles Babbage and Ada Augusta Byron in Chapter 1).

An updated requirements document, less imaginatively named the Ada 9X Requirements and issued in December 1990, became the basis for the Ada 95 Reference Manual, an international standard. The current Ada 2005 standard is an amended version of the Ada 95 standard, and a new international standard may be ready in 2012.

Ada, like C++, is a large language, and it was accepted not only in the defense industry, where its use was mandated by the U.S. Department of Defense, but also for other technological applications and as a general-purpose language as well. Ada is known for its multiprocessing capability—the ability to allow multiple tasks to execute independently and then synchronize and communicate when directed. It is also known as a strongly object-oriented language.

The Department of Defense "Ada mandate" was terminated in 1997, but by then Ada was well established as a programming language supporting good software engineering practice, safety, and reliability. Today, Ada is still strong in the transportation industry (aircraft, helicopters, subway systems, European high-speed train control systems) and in safety monitoring systems at nuclear reactors, as well as in financial and communication systems. Its proponents tout Ada as "the language designed for building systems that really matter."

10.2.6 Java

Unlike FORTRAN, COBOL, C, C++, and Ada, which were carefully developed as programming languages, Java, a modern, object-oriented language, was almost an accident. In early 1991, Sun Microsystems Inc. created a team of top-notch software developers and gave them free rein to do whatever

Practice Problem

What do you think is accomplished by the following Ada program?

```
with ada_io; use ada_io;
procedure simple is
begin
   for i in 1..10 loop
      put(i);
      put(' ');
   end loop;
   new_line;
end;
```

creative thing they wanted. The somewhat secret "Green Team" isolated itself and set to work mapping out a strategy. Its focus was on the consumer electronics market. Televisions, VCRs, stereo systems, laser disc players, and video game machines all operated on different CPUs. Over the next 18 months, the team worked to develop the graphical user interface (GUI), a programming language, an operating system, and a hardware architecture for a handheld, remote-control device called the *7 that would allow various electronic devices to communicate over a network. In contrast to the high-end workstations that were a Sun hallmark, the *7 was designed to be small, inexpensive, easy to use, reliable, and equipped with software that could function over the multiple hardware platforms the consumer electronics market represented.

Armed with this technology, Sun went looking for a business market but found none. In 1993, Mosaic, the first graphical Internet browser, was created at the National Center for Supercomputing Applications, and the World Wide Web began to emerge. This development sent the Sun group in a new direction, where their capabilities with platform-independence, reliability, security, and GUI paid off: They wrote a Web browser.

The programming language component of the *7 was named Oak, for a tree outside language developer James Gosling's window. Later renamed Java, the language was used for the Web browser. The Web browser was released in 1995, and the first version of the Java programming language itself was released in 1996. After that, Java gained market share among programming languages at quite a phenomenal rate.

Java programs come in two flavors: applications and applets. Applications are complete stand-alone programs that reside and run on a self-contained computer; these are the kinds of programs we illustrated in Chapter 9. But Java's development went hand in hand with the development of Web browsers. Applets (small applications) are programs designed to run from Web pages. Applets are embedded in Web pages on central servers; when the user views a Web page with a Java-enabled browser, the applet's code is temporarily transferred to the user's system (whatever that system may be) and interpreted/executed by the browser itself. Today's common Web browsers, such as Microsoft Internet Explorer and Mozilla Firefox, are Java-enabled. Java applets bring audio, video, and real-time user interaction to Web pages, making them "come alive" and become much more than static hyperlinked text. For example, a Java applet might display an animated analog clock face on the screen that shows your computer system's time, or a streaming ticker tape of stock market quotes, or a form that allows you to book an airline reservation online. Java applets held much of the original appeal of the Java language, but big, serious programs are also written using Java applications.

Java is an object-oriented language based on C++, but it avoids some of the features that can make C/C++ programs error-prone. For example, in C++ we could declare an array of 12 integers by

```
int hits[12];
```

The equivalent statement in Java is

```
int hits[] = new int[12];
```

Both Java and C++ number individual array locations beginning with 0, so there is no *hits[12]* in either case. In C++, you can write an assignment statement such as

```
hits[12] = 5;
```

that destroys the contents of some memory location outside the array, and the program will go merrily on its way. Such an assignment in Java would cause a runtime error.

One of the main features of Java is its portability; recall that platform independence was one of the goals of the original Sun "Green Team." In most languages, source code gets compiled into the object code for a particular machine, which means that the developer who wants to distribute executable code needs to compile the source code on each target platform, using the appropriate compiler. The Java programmer, however, compiles source code just once, into low-level code called Java bytecode, which is then distributed to the various users. Bytecode is not itself the language of any real machine, but it can be easily translated into any specific machine language. This final translation/execution of bytecode is done by software called a Java bytecode interpreter, which must be present on each user machine. This approach is workable because the Java bytecode interpreter is a small piece of software; even your Web browser contains one.

10.2.7 Python

The Python language was originally created in the early 1990s by Guido van Rossum at Stichting Mathematisch Centrum in the Netherlands. Its development is now overseen by the Python Software Foundation, but Van Rossum still has the final stamp of approval on "official" features of the language. However, unlike other languages we have mentioned here, Python is an open source

Practice Problem

Output in Java is handled by requesting the predefined Java System.out object to invoke a println() function. Also, the + operator stands for string concatenation. What is the output after execution of the following Java statement if *number* has the value 7?

```
System.out.println("The answer is" + number);
```

language. (See the Special Interest Box "The Open Source Movement" in Chapter 6.) The source code is freely available and can be used, distributed, or modified by anyone. Python's advocates claim that having a community of people interested in using and improving the language has led to a better language than would have resulted from standardized or proprietary code.

Python is an interpreted language, meaning it is translated from source to object code at every execution. Python was originally used for system administration tasks and as a Web interface language. But with the development of an extensive library of supporting code, Python has become a powerful language for more general use.

Python's main distinguishing feature among the procedural family of languages is its ease of use. The syntax rules for Python are relaxed and intuitive, making it easy to develop programs rapidly. However, this lack of rigidity can put the responsibility for careful usage on the programmer rather than on the compiler/interpreter.

10.2.8 C# and .NET

In June 2000, Microsoft introduced the C# language. This language is a successor in spirit to C++, but it is a totally new language. Therefore, it has no backward-compatibility issues, as C++ had with C. C# is designed to make some improvements over C++ in safe usage, and it shares many features with Java. As an example of potentially unsafe usage, a C++ program can

Practice Problem

The following are some sample programming statements (from Ada, C++, C#, Java, and Python) to output the programmer's typical first message of Hello World:

a. `System.out.print("Hello World");`
b. `WITH TEXT_IO;`
    `TEXT_IO.PUT("Hello World");`
c. `print("Hello World")`
d. `using System;`
    `Console.Write("Hello World");`
e. `#include <iostream>`
    `using namespace std;`
    `cout << "Hello World";`

Given our claims about the simplicity of Python syntax, which of these would you judge to be the Python output statement?

The "Popularity" Contest

There is a Web site that keeps track, on a monthly basis, of the most "popular" programming languages. According to this site, "popularity" is not about the best language or the one with the most lines of code that have been written. It is based mainly on data gleaned from Web searches about the number of practicing programmers, courses taught, and third-party vendors. Nonetheless, it is an interesting site. Visit

www.tiobe.com/index.php/content/paperinfo/tpci/index.html

to see how your favorite language rates at the moment. For May 2011, the top four were, in order, Java, C, C++, and C#. Python was #7. But Python won the award for the highest rise of ratings for the year for both 2007 and 2010.

dynamically grab additional memory for its use during program execution, but the programmer is responsible for releasing that memory when the program no longer needs it to reduce the possibility of running out of memory. In C#, however, this process of garbage collection—reclaiming memory no longer needed by the program—is handled automatically.

It is impossible to discuss C# without discussing the Microsoft .NET Framework that supports C# and other programming languages. The .NET Framework is essentially a giant collection of tools for software development. It was designed so that traditional text-based applications, GUI applications, and Web-based programs can all be built with equal ease. For example, the .NET Framework provides a whole library of classes for building GUIs with menus, buttons, text boxes, and so forth. And it is the .NET Framework (actually a part of the .NET Framework called the *Common Language Runtime* or *CLR*) that handles garbage collection for a C# program or for any other language that uses the .NET platform. All .NET programs—in whatever language—are compiled into Microsoft Intermediate Language (MSIL) code. Like Java bytecode, MSIL is not tied to any particular platform. The final step of compiling MSIL code into object code is done by a just-in-time (JIT) compiler (part of the CLR) on the user's machine. So, like Java, the developer achieves portability across multiple platforms because source code is compiled only once, into the MSIL.

There is one notable difference between the Java approach and the .NET approach. The Java bytecode translator is an interpreter, meaning that a program is translated into object code and executed statement by statement. At the end of program execution, no object code is retained and the next time the program executes, the interpreter must repeat this task. The just-in-time compiler, on the other hand, senses when a particular module of MSIL code is being called, translates that module into object code, and then executes it. At the end of program execution, the object code for that module is still there, and if the program executes again with no changes, it can be run directly without invoking the JIT compiler. This difference between interpreted and compiled code leads to more efficient program execution.

Over 60 programming languages have been adapted to fit into the .NET Framework—for example, Ada, FORTRAN, COBOL, C++, C# (of course), and Visual Basic .NET (see the "Old Dog, New Tricks #2" Special Interest Box). That means applications written in any of these languages have access to the tools provided within the .NET Framework and, because all of these languages compile to MSIL, applications can be written that mix and match modules in various languages. Thus, the choice of which language to use becomes less an issue of language capability and more a matter of personal preference and familiarity.

Old Dog, New Tricks #2

BASIC (*Beginner's All-purpose Symbolic Instruction Code*) is a programming language that was developed by John Kemeny at Dartmouth College in 1963–1964. As the name suggests, it was intended to be a general language. It was also designed to be easy to learn and use. During the 1960s, programming was a rather difficult task relegated to technical professionals or, in the academic world, to advanced undergraduate engineering, math, and physics majors. BASIC was Kemeny's attempt to design a programming language easy enough for anyone to learn, including high school and elementary school students. This effort was very successful. BASIC was supplied with most microcomputers throughout the 1980s, and as such it introduced many people, in and out of school, to simple programming ideas.

BASIC got a new lease on life and a whole new look when Microsoft released Visual Basic in 1991. Visual Basic supplied tools to create a sophisticated GUI application by simply dragging components such as buttons and text boxes from a Toolbox onto a form, and then writing BASIC code to allow those components to respond to events, such as the click of a button. This programming ease made Visual Basic a very popular language for rapid prototyping of Windows applications, and the number of VB programmers outstripped the total of C, C++, and Java programmers. Subsequent versions of Visual Basic produced an ever-more-powerful language. Now Visual Basic .NET is a fully object-oriented language that, like the other .NET languages, can take advantage of all the built-in .NET Framework tools. Old languages that can evolve with the times need never die!

Practice Problem

A running Visual Basic program produces the following GUI:

The user types a name in the text box called *txtName,* then clicks the button called *btnShowName.* This "click event" is handled by the following Visual Basic module. Explain what you think happens when this module is executed.

```
Private Sub btnShowName_Click(ByVal sender As System.Object,
                ByVal e As System.EventArgs)
        lblDisplay.Text = txtName.Text
End Sub
```

In April 2003, only three years after the first release of C# and .NET, C# and the CLI (Common Language Infrastructure—a significant subset of the .NET tools) were adopted as ISO standards. C# continues to grow in popularity as a programming language.

10.3 Special-Purpose Languages

Although each of the procedural languages we have mentioned has its own strong points, all are more or less general-purpose languages. In this section, we visit three languages that were each designed for one specialized task. These three are merely representative; many other specialized languages exist.

10.3.1 SQL

Our first specialized language is *SQL,* which stands for *S*tructured *Q*uery *L*anguage. SQL is designed to be used with databases, which are collections of related facts and information. We'll do some work with databases in Chapter 14, but here is the general idea. A database stores data; the user of the database must be able to add new data and to retrieve data already stored. For example, a database contains information on vendors with which a retail store does business. For each vendor, it contains the name, address, and phone number of the vendor, the name of the product line the vendor sells, and the amount of stock purchased from that vendor during the previous business quarter. The database user should be able to add information on a new vendor and retrieve information on a vendor already in the database.

But if this is all that a database can do, it simply acts as an electronic filing cabinet. Databases can also be queried—that is, the user can pose questions to the database. Queries can furnish information that is more than the sum of its parts because they combine the individual data items in various ways. For example, the vendor database can be queried to obtain the names of all vendors with whom the store has done more than $40,000 worth of business in the past quarter or all vendors from a certain zip code. Such queries might be framed in SQL as

```
SELECT NAME
FROM VENDOR
WHERE PURCHASE > 40000;

SELECT NAME
FROM VENDOR
WHERE ZIP = 95082;
```

SQL is the language used to frame database queries. SQL was developed by IBM, and in 1986, it was adopted by the American National Standards Institute (ANSI) as the standard query language in the United States; it has since been adopted by the International Organization for Standardization (ISO) as an international standard. Even database systems that provide users with easier—even graphical—ways to frame queries are simply using a front end that eventually translates the query into an equivalent SQL statement.

An SQL query does not give specific directions as to how to retrieve the desired result. Instead, it merely describes the desired result. This makes SQL similar in flavor to a logic programming language, which we'll see in a later section.

10.3.2 HTML

HTML stands for *H*yper*T*ext *M*arkup *L*anguage. It is used to create HTML documents that, when viewed with Web browser software, become Web pages. An HTML document consists of the text to be displayed on the Web page, together with a number of special characters called tags that achieve formatting, special effects, and references to other HTML documents. Although we speak of "HTML programming," that's a bit of a stretch. The program is just giving the Web browser instructions on how to display text; there's no computation or processing going on as we think of with programming in general.

HTML tags are enclosed in angle brackets (< >) and often come in pairs. The end tag, the second tag in the pair, looks like the begin tag, the first tag in the pair, but with an additional / in front.

The overall format for an HTML document is

```
<html>
  <head>
    <title> stuff to go in the title bar </title>
  </head>
  <body>
     stuff to go on the page
  </body>
</html>
```

Here we see the paired tags for the document as a whole (<html>, </html>), the head (<head>, </head>), the title (<title>, </title>)—framing what appears in the title bar of the page window—and the body (<body>, </body>)—framing what is on the page itself.

Of course, other material needs to go between the beginning and ending "body" tags, or the page will be blank. Figure 10.4 shows an HTML document,

FIGURE 10.4

```
<html>
  <head>
    <title>First Page</title>
  </head>

  <body>
    <h1>This is an H1 heading</h1>
    <p>This text is <b>BOLD</b> and this text is
        <i>italic</i> </p>
    <p>Below is a bulleted list:</p>
    <ul>
        <li>First item</li>
        <li>Second item</li>
    </ul>
    <p>Here is a link to another Web page,
        <a href="http://PBS.org">PBS</a></p>
    <p>And here is an image:</p>
    <img src="flower1.jpg"
        alt="Sunflowers in a field">
  </body>
</html>
```

HTML code for a Web page

FIGURE 10.5

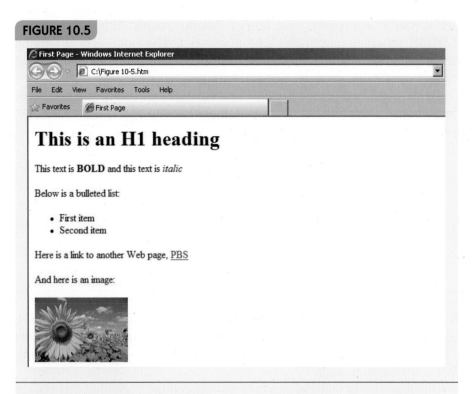

Body of the Web page generated by the HTML code in Figure 10.4

FIGURE 10.6

HTML Tag	Purpose
h1	Create H1 heading (bold with largest font size)
p	New paragraph
b	Bold
i	Italic
ul	Unordered list (bulleted list)
li	List item
a href = "..."	Provides hyperlink address
img src = "..."	Gives the source (location) for the image file

Some HTML tags

and Figure 10.5 shows how the Web page actually looks when viewed with a Web browser. By comparing the two, you can probably understand the meaning of the tags used, as explained in Figure 10.6. Technically, *href* is an attribute of the "a" tag that indicates a link to another document, in this case the home page of the well-known PBS Web site. Similarly, *src* is an attribute of the "img" tag that gives the "source" for the image. In Figure 10.4,

Laboratory Experience 13

This Laboratory Experience will give you practice in HTML programming. Due to powerful Web editor software, you don't have to know HTML in order to create a Web page, but HTML is what lies "under the hood" of all Web pages—even Facebook!—so this will give you an insight into the basics of Web page creation. You will also learn how to use your Web browser to perform simple file transfers from special computers called FTP servers. This will enable you to access a wealth of software and data files in the public domain.

the source is just the image filename, meaning that the image file is in the same folder as the HTML code file; if the image file were elsewhere, the source would have to show the pathname where the image file can be found. The second attribute of the img tag, the *alt* attribute, is displayed if the image file cannot be located. The text in the *alt* attribute is also used by assistive technologies for the blind, who would otherwise be unable to "see" the image.

Early word processors required the user to type in various codes manually to mark text for boldface, italic, and so forth. Later, more sophisticated word processors with GUI interfaces reduced these tasks to point and click. The same has come to pass with HTML code. HTML documents themselves are simply text files that can be created using any text editor by typing the appropriate tags. But Web editor software makes it possible to create HTML code by, for example, highlighting text and clicking a button to insert the tags for making the text boldface.

10.3.3 JavaScript

A scripting language is a "lightweight" language that is interpreted (translated, then executed, statement by statement). Scripting language code fragments can be embedded in Web pages to make those pages active rather than static. JavaScript is such a language; keep in mind that JavaScript is not the same as the full-blown Java programming language.

Consider the HTML page from the previous section. When this page is displayed by the Web browser, the user has no interaction with the page except possibly to click on the hypertext link to go to another page. In particular, the image on the page is fixed. The Web page can be made a little more interesting if the image changes when the user hovers the mouse over the current image. In fact, let's switch back and forth between the

Beyond HTML

The tags in HTML are, as we have seen, specified. The tag pair <b> </b>, for example, is used to display the enclosed text as boldface. The writer of the HTML document cannot invent new tags. *XML (eXtensible Markup Language)* is a newer markup language. It is a "metalanguage," that is, a markup language for markup languages. Using XML, the writer can create his or her own tags; an XML document is not about displaying information but about how to structure and interpret information to be displayed. An XML document usually also contains or refers to a *schema* that describes the data, and the body of the XML document can then be checked against the schema to be sure that it is a well-formed document. All modern browsers support mechanisms that translate XML documents into HTML documents for display. XML allows for flexible document interchange across the Web; for example, in May 2003, the National Library of Medicine announced a "Tagset" for journal articles to provide a single format in which journal articles that originate from many different publishers and societies can be archived. As another example, LegalXML is a collection of XML standards for sharing and transmitting legal documents of various kinds, such as documents between courts and attorneys, court transcripts, electronic contracts, and so on. More commonly, XML-based file formats now form the basis for office productivity tools, such as Microsoft Office, OpenOffice, and Apple iWork.

original image and a second image as the user moves the mouse into and out of the image area of the page. To accomplish this, we'll use a JavaScript function called *imageSwitch()*. The JavaScript code will be placed within <script></script> tags to alert the browser that these statements are to be interpreted as JavaScript commands.

The *imageSwitch()* function has to accomplish two tasks. One is to reset the *src* attribute of the "img" tag. But we have to say what image tag we are modifying, so in the original image tag we'll add an *id* attribute. Basically, we are giving the image a name; we'll call it *mainImage*. This name is not the name of an actual visual image (a picture); it's the name of the image element on the page that holds a picture as determined by its *src* attribute. In the original image tag, we'll also add two additional attributes that are event handlers, that is, they respond to the events of the user moving the mouse over the image element (a MouseOver event) or moving the mouse away from the image element (a MouseOut event). For either of those two events, we want to call the *imageSwitch()* function. Figure 10.7 shows the new image tag for the page.

FIGURE 10.7

```
<img src="flower1.jpg" id="mainImage"
        alt="Sunflowers in a field"
        onMouseOut="imageSwitch()"
        onMouseOver="imageSwitch()">
```

The new HTML <img> (image) tag

The *imageSwitch()* function itself uses a variable called *nextPicName* that contains the image filename for the new picture, the one being switched to. The image element *src* attribute will be set to the value of this variable. The code is

```
document.getElementById("mainImage")
        .src=nextPicName;
```

This statement locates the appropriate image element by its id (even though in this case there is only one image element on the page) and assigns *nextPicName* to its *src* attribute.

The second task of the *imageSwitch()* function is to make sure that *nextPicName* is updated to the appropriate value in preparation for the next image switch. This is accomplished by an if/then/else statement, one of the basic algorithmic constructs we introduced in Chapter 2. The code is straightforward: If we just changed to the flower2.jpg image, then we should be ready next time to change to the flower1.jpg image, and vice versa.

```
if(nextPicName=="flower2.jpg")
{
        nextPicName = "flower1.jpg";
}
else
{
        nextPicName = "flower2.jpg";
}
```

We are just about done. The only remaining thing is to initialize the *nextPicName* variable. We'll use another JavaScript function called *startValue()* to do that task. Because the page loads with the *flower1.jpg* image showing, the *nextPicName* value (the new image value) should be *flower2.jpg*. In the HTML body, we'll use the "onload" event handler to invoke the *startValue()* function to get things started.

Figure 10.8 shows the complete HTML page with the embedded JavaScript.

FIGURE 10.8

```html
<html>
  <head>
    <title>First Page</title>

    <script language = "JavaScript">

    function startValue()
    {
      nextPicName = "flower2.jpg";
    }

    function imageSwitch()
    {
      //switch photo to nextPicName
      document.getElementById("mainImage")
          .src=nextPicName;

      //set up for the next switch
      if(nextPicName=="flower2.jpg")
      {
            nextPicName = "flower1.jpg";
      }
      else
      {
            nextPicName = "flower2.jpg";
      }
    }
    </script>

  </head>

  <body onload="startValue()">
    <h1>This is an H1 heading</h1>
    <p>This text is <b>BOLD</b> and this text is
        <i>italic</i> </p>
    <p>Below is a bulleted list:</p>
    <ul>
        <li>First item</li>
        <li>Second item</li>
    </ul>
    <p>Here is a link to another Web page,
        <a href="http://PBS.org">PBS</a></p>
    <p>And here is an image:</p>
    <img src="flower1.jpg" id="mainImage"
        alt="Sunflowers in a field"
        onMouseOut="imageSwitch()"
        onMouseOver="imageSwitch()">
  </body>
</html>
```

JavaScript embedded in an HTML page

PHP

Web pages that are designed using HTML are generally static Web pages, that is, their content looks the same each time the page is opened in your browser. However, when you visit your favorite online store, the content is different with each visit, reflecting, for example, items on sale or the newest products. These are dynamic Web pages (their content changes) that are stored on the Web server of the online merchant. Dynamic pages are often tied to a behind-the-scenes product database. If a new product becomes available or a price changes because of a sale, the change is made in one place in the underlying database. Whenever any dynamic page tied to the database is requested from the server, the latest database information is loaded into the page before it is sent back to your Web browser, and your browser then displays it. The HTML for the various pages does not have to be constantly rewritten to incorporate the new data.

PHP (which originally stood for Personal Home Pages but now stands for PHP: Hypertext Preprocessor) is a *server-side scripting language*. Like JavaScript, PHP is embedded within HTML code in Web pages hosted on a server. PHP is particularly adept at making database connections for dynamic Web pages. The PHP code, when executed, sets up a connection to the database and formats HTML code on the page to include the new data values. In December 2010, a survey of 6.7 million domains showed that 59% were using PHP (*phpadvent.org/2010/usage-statistics-by-ilia-alshanetsky*).

Practice Problems

1. Describe the result of executing the following SQL query on the vendor database.

```
SELECT NAME
FROM VENDOR
WHERE CITY = 'CHICAGO';
```

2. Given the following HTML statement, what does the corresponding line of text on the Web page look like?

```
<p>These are the <i>times</i> that try
   <b>men's souls</b></p>
```

(Continued)

3. Type the HTML code of Figure 10.4 into a text editor such as Notepad. Save the file with an .html extension. Find a small .jpg image (it need not be sunflowers!) and store it in the same folder as the .html file. Then double-click on the .html file to bring it up in your browser. Does it look like Figure 10.5?

10.4 Alternative Programming Paradigms

Computer scientists are fond of the word *paradigm*. A paradigm is a model or mental framework for representing or thinking about something. The paradigm of procedural programming languages says that a sequence of detailed instructions is provided to the computer. Each instruction accesses or modifies the contents of a memory location. If the computer carries out these instructions one at a time, then the final result of all the memory cell manipulations is the solution to the problem at hand. This sounds suspiciously like our definition of an algorithm in Chapter 1 ("a well-ordered collection of unambiguous and effectively computable operations that when executed produces a result..."). In fact, programming in a procedural language consists of

- Planning the algorithm

- Capturing the "unambiguous and effectively computable operations" as program instructions

In a procedural programming language, then, we must pay attention to the details of exactly how the computer is going to accomplish the desired task in a step-by-step fashion. In object-oriented programming, the procedural paradigm still holds, but the step-by-step instructions may be split into multiple small sets that are encapsulated within classes.

In this section, we look at programming languages that use alternatives to the procedural approach—languages based on other paradigms. It is as though we have studied French, Spanish, and Italian (different but related languages) and are now about to embark on a study of Arabic, Japanese, or sign language—languages totally different in form, structure, and alphabet. Alternative paradigms for programming languages include viewing a program's actions as

- A combination of various transformations on items (functional programming)

- A series of logical deductions from known facts (logic programming)

- Multiple copies of the same subtask or multiple subtasks of the same problem being performed simultaneously by different processors (parallel programming)

We'll look briefly at each of these alternative programming paradigms, focusing on the different conceptual views rather than on the details of language syntax. In short, this chapter won't make you an expert programmer, or even a novice programmer, in any of these languages, but you'll have a sense of some of the different approaches to programming languages that have been developed. Both LISP, mentioned in the next section, and Prolog, discussed in Section 10.4.2, are often used in artificial intelligence work; for more information on artificial intelligence, see Chapter 15.

10.4.1 Functional Programming

Functional programming had its start with the design of the LISP (*LISt Processing*) programming language by John McCarthy at MIT in 1958. This makes LISP second only to FORTRAN in longevity. John Backus (who, you will recall, led the development of FORTRAN) argued for functional programming as opposed to "conventional Von Neumann languages" and introduced the language FP (for *Functional Programming*) in 1977. Other functional programming languages or dialects of LISP have been developed. We look at examples using Scheme—a functional programming language that was derived from LISP in the late 1970s.

A **functional programming language** views every task in terms of (surprise!) functions. Unlike the more general usage of the word function in some procedural programming languages, *function* in this context means something like a mathematical function—a recipe for taking an argument (or possibly several arguments) and doing something with them to compute a single value. More formally, when the arguments are given values, the function transforms those values, according to some specified rule, into a corresponding resulting value. Different values for the arguments can produce different resulting values. The doubling function $f(x) = 2x$ transforms the argument 3 into 6 because $f(3) = 2*3 = 6$, and it transforms the argument 6 into 12 because $f(6) = 2*6 = 12$. In the grand sense, we can think of a program as a function acting on input data (the arguments) and transforming them into the desired output.

In a functional programming language, certain functions, called *primitive functions* or just *primitives*, are defined as part of the language. Other functions can be defined and named by the programmer. To define the doubling function using Scheme, we could say

```
(define (double x)
      (* 2 x))
```

The keyword *define* indicates that we are defining a new function. The function name and its list of arguments follow in parentheses. The function name is *double*, and *x* is its single argument. The definition says that when this function is invoked, it is to multiply the argument value by 2. Having defined the function, we can now invoke it in a program by giving the function name, followed by a list of values for the arguments of the function. (For the *double* function, there is only one number in the list of argument values because there is only one argument.) Scheme responds immediately to a function invocation by displaying the result, so the following interaction occurs as the user invokes the *double* function with various argument values (boldface indicates what the user types).

(double 4)
8
(double 8)
16

Here's the definition of another function:

```
(define (square x)
    (* x x))
```

which says that the function named *square*, when invoked, is to multiply the single argument value by itself. Thus a dialog with Scheme could be

(square 3)
9

Functions, once defined, can be used in the definition of other functions. This can lead to nested tasks that must be performed. The function *polynomial*, defined by

```
(define (polynomial x)
    (double (square x)))
```

is the function that we write mathematically as $g(x) = 2x^2$. Using this function, the dialog could be

(polynomial 3)
18

When the *polynomial* function is invoked with the argument 3, Scheme consults the function definition and sees that this is really

```
(double (square 3))
```

Thus, the polynomial function must invoke the *double* function, and it is to invoke that function with an argument value of (square 3). Therefore, the first thing to do is to invoke the *square* function with an argument value of 3. The result is $3^2 = 9$. This 9 gets used as the argument value for the double function, resulting in 18. The total computation is equivalent to $g(3) = 2(3)^2 = 2(9) = 18$.

Here we've defined one function (*polynomial*) in terms of another function (*double*) acting on the result of applying a third function (*square*). In functional programming languages, we can build complex combinations of functions that use the results of applying other functions, which use the results of applying still other functions, and so on. In fact, functional programming languages are sometimes called **applicative languages** because of this property of repeatedly applying functions.

As the name LISP suggests, LISP processes lists of things and so does Scheme. The arguments to functions, then, are often lists. As a trivial case, "nothing" can be thought of as an empty list, which is called *nil*. We will use four primitive list-processing functions available in Scheme. The first function is called *list*. This function can have any number of arguments, and its action is to create a list out of those arguments. Therefore,

(list 3 4 5)

evaluates to the list 3, 4, 5, which we write as

(3 4 5)

Two other list-processing functions are called *car* (pronounced as when it means an automobile) and *cdr* (pronounced "could-er"). (The names have historical significance from the distant past. Car stands for "Contents of Address Register," and cdr stands for "Contents of Decrement Register." These registers were part of the architecture of the IBM 704 computer on which LISP was originally implemented.) The *car* function takes a nonempty list as its argument and produces as a result the first element in that list. Therefore, a dialog with Scheme could consist of

(car (list 3 4 5))
3

The *cdr* function takes a nonempty list as its argument and produces as a result the list that remains after the first element has been removed. Therefore,

(cdr (list 3 4 5))

evaluates to the list

(4 5)

As a special case, when the *cdr* function is applied to an argument consisting of a one-element list, the empty list is produced as the result. Thus,

(cdr (list 5))

evaluates to the list *nil*. Note that the *car* function applied to a list evaluates to a list element, whereas the *cdr* function applied to a list evaluates to another, shorter list.

One final primitive list-processing function is *null?*, which has a single list as its argument and evaluates to true if the list is *nil* (empty) and to false if the list is nonempty. Armed with these primitives, we can at last write a little Scheme program (Figure 10.9) to add some nonnegative integers.

Dialog with the program in Figure 10.9 could result in

(adder (list 3 4 5))
12

Let's see how this works. Our function *adder* was defined to have one argument, symbolically denoted in the definition by *input-list*. Now we're

FIGURE 10.9

```
(define (adder input-list)
  (cond ((null? input-list) 0)
    (else (+ (car input-list)
      (adder (cdr input-list))))))
```

Scheme program to add nonnegative integers

invoking this function where the argument has the value of (*list* 3 4 5); that is to say, the function is to operate on (3 4 5). The *cond* function (short for "conditional") is acting like an if-else statement: It is equivalent to

```
if (null? input-list)
   total = 0;
else
   total = (car input-list) + (adder(cdr input-list));
```

The condition "null? input-list" is evaluated and found to be false because *input-list* at this point is (*list* 3 4 5). The else clause is executed, and it says to add two quantities. The first of these two quantities is (*car input-list*), which is (*car* (*list* 3 4 5)), or 3. Thus, 3 is to be added to the second quantity. The second quantity is the result of invoking the *adder* function on the argument (*cdr input-list*), which is (*cdr* (*list* 3 4 5)), or (4 5). The value, as constructed so far, is therefore

$$3 + (adder (list 4 5))$$

Now the program invokes the *adder* function again, this time with an argument of (*list* 4 5) instead of (*list* 3 4 5). Once again we test whether this list is *nil* (it isn't), so we add together

$$(car (list 4 5)) + (adder (cdr (list 4 5)))$$

or

$$4 + (adder (list 5))$$

The *adder* function is invoked again with an argument of (*list* 5). The list still is not *nil*, so we add together

$$(car (list 5)) + (adder (cdr (list 5)))$$

or

$$5 + (adder nil)$$

A final invocation of the *adder* function, this time with the *nil* list as its argument, takes the other branch of the *cond* statement, which results in 0. Altogether, then, we've done

(adder (*list* 3 4 5))

or

(adder (3 4 5)) =
      3 + (*adder* (4 5)) =
      3 + 4 + (*adder* (5)) =
      3 + 4 + 5 + (*adder nil*) =
      3 + 4 + 5 + 0 = 12

The definition of the *adder* function involves the *adder* function again, this time acting on a shorter list. Note in our example how we invoke the *adder* function repeatedly—first on (3 4 5), then on (4 5), next on (5), and finally on *nil*. Something that is defined in terms of "smaller versions" of itself is said to be **recursive**, so the *adder* function is a recursive function.

Recursion is one of the features of functional languages that makes possible short and elegant solutions to many problems. Although recursion is a dominant mode of operation in functional languages, many procedural languages also support recursion, so that's not the major argument for using a functional language. Then what is the benefit of going to a functional language?

A functional language allows for clarity of thought; data values are transformed by flowing, as it were, through a stream of mathematical functions. The programmer has no concern about where intermediate values are stored, nor indeed about how a "list" could occupy many memory cells. Another layer of abstraction has been offered to the programmer—the rarefied layer of pure mathematics. Because functions are described in a mathematical way by what they do to an item of data rather than by how they modify memory cells in the process of doing it, the possibility of side effects is eliminated. A **side effect** occurs when a function, in the course of acting on its argument values to produce a result value, also changes other values that it has no business changing. Implementing a function in a procedural language, where the major mode of operation is modification of memory cells, opens the door to potential side effects.

It's All in How You Look At It

We used recursion to define the function to add a list, as follows: Add the first list element to the result of adding the rest of the list elements together. The recursive way of thinking takes a bit of getting used to. For example,

- Reading a book can be defined as reading the first page followed by reading the rest of the book.

(Continued)

- Climbing a ladder can be defined as climbing the first rung followed by climbing the rest of the ladder.
- Eating a six-course meal can be defined as eating the first course followed by eating the rest of the meal.

Having learned to program in a procedural language, some people are initially uncomfortable with the recursive style of functional languages. It might seem as if mysterious things are going on in the background and suddenly there's a result.

Consider the following scenario. You are standing in a long line at the grocery store, and you'd like to know exactly how many people are ahead of you.

Solution #1: You step out of line to get a better view and count the number of people. Your algorithm is something like:

> count = 0
> while there is an uncounted person
>   pick the next uncounted person
>   increment count
> stop

This is an iterative (looping) solution.

Solution #2: You ask the person in line ahead of you how many people are in line ahead of him. When he responds, you add 1 to his count, and that's the number of people ahead of you. You have to have faith that all the people in line ahead of you know how to do the same process, and that when the person ahead of you finally responds, he'll be giving you the correct answer for how many people are ahead of him. This is a recursive solution. Here's how it works in more detail.

You   Jose   Anna   Tom

You ask Jose how many people are ahead of him. He tells you to wait, and he asks Anna, "How many people are ahead of you?" Anna asks Jose to wait, and she asks Tom, "How many people are ahead of you?" Tom can answer this question, so he tells Anna, "There are 0 people ahead of me." Anna adds 1 (to account for Tom), then tells Jose, "There is 1 person ahead of me." Jose adds 1 to this count (to account for Anna), then tells you, "There are 2 people ahead of me." Finally receiving this news from Jose, you add one (to account for Jose), and then you know there are 3 people ahead of you. You just ask the correct question, wait for a bit, and then there's your answer (unless you are the special *base case* of Tom, who actually has to provide the first answer).

Many people argue for using a functional language like Scheme as a *first* programming language because of its simplicity, clarity, and elegance.

Practice Problems

1. To what does each of the following evaluate?
   a. **(cdr (list 1 2 3 4))**
   b. **(car (cdr (list 4 5 6)))**

2. Define a function in Scheme that adds 3 to a number.

Laboratory Experience 14

This Laboratory Experience will guide you through some functional programming exercises. You'll see that a higher level of problem solving is possible than in procedural languages, where you have to write step-by-step instructions to manipulate data values by way of specific memory locations. You will need your own LISP or Scheme interpreter; a free Scheme interpreter is available to download at *www.gnu.org/software/mit-scheme/*.

10.4.2 Logic Programming

Functional programming gets away from explicitly instructing the computer about the details of each step to be performed; instead, it specifies various transformations of data and then allows combinations of transformations to be performed. Logic programming languages go a step further toward not specifying exactly how a task is to be done. In logic programming, various facts are asserted to be true, and on the basis of these facts, a logic program can infer or deduce other facts. When a *query* (a question) is posed to the program, it begins with the storehouse of facts and attempts to apply logical deductions, in as efficient a manner as possible, to answer the query. Logic programming languages are sometimes called declarative languages (as opposed to procedural languages) because their programs, instead of issuing step-by-step commands, make declarations or assertions that various facts are true.

A logic program relates to a domain of interest in which the declarations make sense (such as medicine, literature, or chemistry), and the queries are related to that domain. Logic programming has been used to write *expert systems*. In an expert system about a particular domain, a human "expert" in that domain contributes facts based on his or her knowledge and experience. A logic program using these facts as its declarations can then make inferences that are close to those the human expert would make.

The best-known logic programming language is Prolog, which was developed in France at the University of Marseilles in 1972 by a group headed by A. Colmerauer. Prolog stands for *PRO*gramming in *LOG*ic; the language was originally intended as a tool for natural language processing. Prolog received a great boost when the Japanese announced their Fifth Generation Project in 1981. The goal of this effort, which proved to be too ambitious, was to transform society through computers that make logical inferences and interact with human beings in a "natural" way through both spoken and written language.

Prolog programs consist of *facts* and *rules*. A *fact* expresses a property about a single object or a relationship among several objects. For example, let's write a Prolog program in the domain of American history. We are interested in which U.S. presidents were in office when certain events occurred and in the chronology of those presidents' terms in office. Here is a short list of facts (declarations):

```
president(lincoln, gettysburg_address).
president(lincoln, civil_war).
president(nixon, first_moon_landing).
president(jefferson, lewis_and_clark).
president(kennedy, cuban_missile_crisis).
president(fdr, world_war_II).
before(jefferson, lincoln).
before(lincoln, fdr).
before(fdr, kennedy).
before(kennedy, nixon).
```

The interpretation of these facts is fairly obvious. For example, the declaration

```
president(jefferson, lewis_and_clark).
```

asserts or declares that Jefferson was the U.S. president during the Lewis and Clark expedition. And

```
before(kennedy, nixon).
```

asserts that Kennedy was president before Nixon. (There are a number of versions of Prolog available; the version we use requires that identifiers for specific items begin with lowercase letters and have no internal blanks.)

This list of facts constitutes a Prolog program. We interact with the program by posing queries; this is the way Prolog programs are executed.

For example, the user could make the following query (boldface indicates what the user types):

?-before(lincoln, fdr).

Prolog responds

```
Yes.
```

because "before(lincoln, fdr)" is a fact in the program. After every response, Prolog also asks

```
More? (Y/N):
```

because there may be multiple responses to the query. If we want to see further responses, we answer Yes. If we answer yes when there are no further responses, as in this case, Prolog simply responds

```
No.
```

Here's some further dialogue with Prolog using this same program. (We won't write the "More? (Y/N):" that appears after each Prolog response.)

?-president(lincoln, civil_war).
```
Yes.
```
?-president(bush, iraq).
```
No.
```

The first query corresponds to a declaration in the program, and the second does not. The "No" response does not signify that the statement is false, only that its truth value is unknown because it is not part of the collection of facts in the program.

More complicated queries can be phrased. A query of the form A, B is asking Prolog whether fact A and fact B are both in the program. Thus, a query such as

?-president(lincoln, civil_war), before(lincoln, fdr).

produces a Yes response because both facts are in the program. The interpretation is that Lincoln was president during the Civil War and that Lincoln was president before FDR.

So far, Prolog appears to be little more than some sort of retrieval system that does lookups on a table of facts. But Prolog can do much more. Variables can be used within queries, and this is what gives Prolog its power. Variables must begin with uppercase letters. The query

?-president(lincoln, X).

is asking for a match against facts in the program of the form

```
president(lincoln,"something")
```

In other words, X can stand for anything that is in the "president relation" with Lincoln. The responses are

```
X = gettysburg_address
X = civil_war
```

because both

```
president(lincoln, gettysburg_address).
president(lincoln, civil_war).
```

are facts in the program. (Remember that in order to see more than one response, we have to keep answering Yes when asked "More? (Y/N):".)

Let's describe what it means for one president to precede another in office. It may appear that the *before* relation already takes care of this. Certainly if "before(X, Y)" is true, then President X precedes President Y. However, in our sample program,

```
before(lincoln, fdr).
before(fdr, kennedy).
```

are both true, but that does not tell us that Lincoln precedes Kennedy (which is also true). Of course, we could add another *before* fact to cover this case, but that is an *ad hoc* patch. Instead, let's add further declarations to the program to define the *precedes* relation. We already know that two presidents in the *before* relation should also be in a *precedes* relation. Furthermore, from the previous example, it would appear that if X is before Z and Z is before Y, then "precedes(X, Y)" should also be true. But we can say more than that: if X is before Z and Z precedes Y, then "precedes(X, Y)" should be true. This extension means that Jefferson precedes Kennedy because

	before(fdr, kennedy)
implies	precedes(fdr, kennedy)

	before(lincoln, fdr)
	precedes(fdr, kennedy)
implies	precedes(lincoln, kennedy)

and

	before(jefferson, lincoln)
	precedes(lincoln, kennedy)
implies	precedes(jefferson, kennedy)

Using this reasoning, we have derived three new "precedes" facts that were not in the original list of facts.

Thus, we want to say that there are two ways in which X can precede Y:

precedes(X,Y) if before(X,Y)
precedes(X,Y) if before(X,Z) and precedes(Z,Y)

We can make declarations in our Prolog program that express the *precedes* relation, but this time the declarations are stated as rules rather than as facts. A Prolog *rule* is a declaration of an "if A then B" form, which means that if A is true (A is a fact), then B is also true (B is a fact). The actual Prolog declarations follow; think of the notation B :– A as meaning "if A then B."

```
precedes(X,Y) :- before(X,Y).
precedes(X,Y) :- before(X,Z), precedes(Z,Y).
```

The rule for *precedes* includes *precedes* as part of its definition; it is therefore a recursive rule.

Our Prolog program now consists of the facts and rules shown in Figure 10.10. Here's some further dialogue, using the new program. Be sure you understand why each query receives the response or responses it does.

?-precedes(fdr, kennedy).

```
Yes.
```

?-precedes(lincoln, nixon).

```
Yes.
```

?-precedes(lincoln, X).

```
X = fdr
X = kennedy
X = nixon
```

Let's add one final declaration to the program—a declaration that says that event X occurred earlier than event Y if X took place during President R's term in office, Y took place during President S's term in office, and President R precedes President S. (Do you agree with this definition of the *earlier* relation?) Here's the rule:

```
earlier(X,Y) :- president(R,X), president(S,Y),
                precedes(R,S).
```

Then a final query of

?-earlier(world_war_II, X).

produces the responses

```
X = first_moon_landing
X = cuban_missile_crisis
```

FIGURE 10.10

```
president(lincoln, gettysburg_address).
president(lincoln, civil_war).
president(nixon, first_moon_landing).
president(jefferson, lewis_and_clark).
president(kennedy, cuban_missile_crisis).
president(fdr, world_war_II).

before(jefferson, lincoln).
before(lincoln, fdr).
before(fdr, kennedy).
before(kennedy, nixon).

precedes(X,Y) :- before(X,Y).
precedes(X,Y) :- before(X,Z), precedes(Z,Y).
```

A Prolog program

In this simple example, it is easy to check that the responses to our queries are correct, and it is also not difficult to do the necessary comparisons with the program declarations to see how Prolog was able to arrive at its responses. The interesting thing to note, however, is that the program consists solely of declaratives (facts and rules), not instructions about what steps to take in order to produce the answers. The program provides the raw material, and in the logic programming paradigm, this raw material is inspected more or less out of our sight, and without our detailed instructions, to deduce the answers to a query.

Figure 10.11 illustrates the situation. The programmer builds a **knowledge base** of facts and rules about a certain domain of interest; this knowledge base constitutes the program. Interaction with the program takes place by posing queries—sometimes rather complex queries—to an **inference engine** (also called a *query interpreter*). The inference engine is a piece of software that is supplied as part of the language itself; that is, it is part of the compiler or interpreter, not something the programmer has to write. The inference engine can access the knowledge base, and it contains its own rules of deductive reasoning based on symbolic logic. For example, a Prolog inference engine processing the program in Figure 10.10 would conclude that

        precedes(fdr, kennedy)

is true from the rule of the form

        if before(X, Y) then precedes(X, Y)

together with the fact

        before(fdr, kennedy).

because it is a rule of deductive reasoning (known as **modus ponens**) that "if A then B" together with "A" must result in "B." The programmer need not supply this rule or instruct the inference engine when it should be applied. Thus,

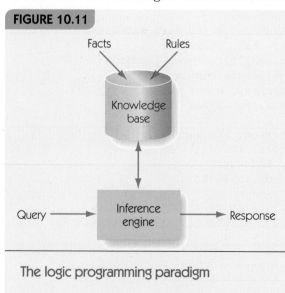

FIGURE 10.11

The logic programming paradigm

Practice Problems

Using the Prolog program of Figure 10.10, what is the result of each of the following queries?

1. ?-before(jefferson, kennedy).
2. ?-president(X, lewis_and_clark).
3. ?-precedes(jefferson, X).

the inference engine can be thought of as providing still another layer of abstraction between the programmer and the machine. The programmer supplies the fundamental facts and rules about the domain but does not direct the computer's step-by-step processing of those facts and rules to answer a query.

This is a somewhat idealistic view of logic programming; in actuality, the idiosyncrasies of Prolog compilers mean that programmers do need to understand something about the order in which rules of logic will be applied. Yet, Prolog still gives us a good sense of the logic programming paradigm, where the intent is to concentrate on the "what" [is true] rather than on the "how" [to find it] that is the hallmark of procedural programming. You can experiment with Prolog at the following Web site: *www.csse. monash.edu.au/~lloyd/tildeLogic/Prolog.toy.*

10.4.3 Parallel Programming

Chapter 5 described how the complex scientific problems of the twenty-first century—climate modeling, genomic research, artificial intelligence—are testing the limits of the Von Neumann model of sequential processing. Figure 10.12 lists some of the "grand challenges" identified by the government-sponsored High Performance Computing and Communications Initiative for the 1990s.

FIGURE 10.12

- 72-hour weather prediction
- Modeling oil reservoirs
- Chemical dynamics
- Vehicle dynamics
- Fluid turbulence
- Human genome project
- Ocean circulation model

"Grand Challenge" computing problems of the 1990s

For the most part, these remain significant challenges today, along with a host of new research questions that have arisen in the intervening years. Parallel processing offers the promise of providing the computational speed required to solve these important large-scale problems.

Parallel processing is really a catchall term for a variety of approaches to computing architectures and algorithm design. Let's review the two models of parallel architectures introduced in Chapter 5:

- *SIMD (single instruction stream/multiple data stream)*—A single control unit broadcasts a single program instruction to multiple ALUs, all of which carry out that instruction in unison, using globally shared data as well as private data stored in local memory.

- *MIMD (multiple instruction stream/multiple data stream)*—Interconnected processors independently execute their own program on their own data, communicating as needed with other processors. The MIMD model includes a number of different structures, such as multicore computing, in which two or more processors are packaged together on a single integrated circuit, and *cluster computing*, in which independent systems such as mainframes, desktops, or laptops are interconnected by a local area network (LAN) like the Ethernet or a wide area network (WAN) such as the Internet.

The algorithms with which we are most familiar, like those introduced in Chapters 2 and 3, operate sequentially because they were originally designed for Von Neumann–type execution. To reap the full benefit of a parallel architecture, we need to develop totally new algorithms that exploit this collection of processing resources. After all, it does not do any good to have 100 people available to help with a project if only one is doing any useful work, while the other 99 sit idle. (In contrast to other sections of this chapter, this one does not describe a specific parallel programming language. Instead, we introduce and discuss some general principles of parallel languages and algorithms.)

An example of SIMD parallel processing, first presented in Chapter 5, involves adding a constant value K to each element of a six-element vector V. Assume that we have six ALUs with unique ID numbers from 1 to 6. Each ALU has its own local or "private" data consisting of one of the six vector components; that is, the ALU with ID 1 has a private copy of element $V[1]$ in its local memory. The ALU with ID 2 has a private copy of element $V[2]$ in its local memory, and so forth. Because all ALUs need access to the constant value K, it is stored in shared global memory that is accessible to everyone. This allocation of processing units, memory units, and data values is diagrammed in Figure 10.13.

A language designed to support SIMD parallel processing would allow you to declare a data value "public," which places it into global shared memory. The language would also allow you to declare a vector "private," which means the individual elements of the vector are distributed into the private memory unit of each ALU. Finally, a SIMD-style language allows you to write something like the following:

FIGURE 10.13

Model of SIMD processing

```
PARALLEL [I..J]
      statements
END PARALLEL
```

The meaning of this statement is that every ALU with an ID number from I to J inclusive will, in unison, execute the block of statements enclosed within the PARALLEL block, using data stored in global memory and its own private memory.

With these statements available to us, our vector addition problem could be solved in a SIMD parallel fashion as follows:

```
K : public
V : private
      . . .
PARALLEL [1..6]
    V = V + K
END PARALLEL
```

In this SIMD algorithm, every processing element executes in unison the exact same instruction, namely the vector addition operation $V = V + K$. However, each one uses the element of V stored in its private memory. The result is that the six elements of vector V are updated concurrently. Rather than taking six units of time to be solved, as is the case with a sequential solution, the problem is now solved in one unit of time, a speedup factor of six.

The first MIMD example we look at is the problem initially presented in Chapter 5—locating a single name among all the names in the New York City telephone book. However, let's now assume that we have 101 independent processors to assist with this task. To take advantage of these resources, let's designate one processor, say ID number 101, to handle input/output while the remaining ones, those with ID numbers 1 to 100, are assigned to the search task. The job of the input/output processor is to input the 20,000,000-element phone book, partition it into 100 separate chunks of

FIGURE 10.14

Model of MIMD processing

size 200,000, and send these chunks to the 100 search processors along with the NAME we are looking for. After distributing this data, the input/output processor waits for one of the search processors to find the correct phone number and send it back. It then prints this result (or, more likely, speaks it) and terminates. This MIMD data allocation strategy is diagrammed in Figure 10.14.

Now, in parallel, the 100 search processors execute the sequential search algorithm on their chunk of data, called YOURLIST, to see if NAME is contained in this segment. However, they do not have to do this in instruction-by-instruction lockstep; instead, each processor executes independently. Here is the outline of the program distributed to each of the 100 search processors:

```
// this is the program run by processors numbered 1
// to 100.
// These are the ones carrying out the search task.
YOURLIST = LIST[1..200000]  // the sublist of
                            // names to be searched
NAME                        // the one name we
                            // are searching for
. . .
RECEIVE YOURLIST, NAME FROM PROCESSOR 101
. . .
// Each processor now executes the following
// instructions at its own rate
FOUND EQUALS FALSE
SEQSEARCH (YOURLIST, NAME, FOUND, PHONENUM)
IF FOUND
    SEND PHONENUM TO PROCESSOR 101
ELSE
    DO NOTHING
END
HALT
```

Each search processor initially waits for a message from the input/output processor containing its segment, *YOURLIST*, of the overall list, and *NAME*. This is achieved via a RECEIVE instruction. When that message arrives, the processor executes the sequential search algorithm, called SEQSEARCH, to determine if *NAME* is located within its 200,000-element sublist. If *NAME* is located within that list, then SEQSEARCH will exit with *FOUND* set to true, and that processor will SEND the correct phone number to processor 101. If *NAME* is not found, the variable *FOUND* will remain false, and that processor will "Do nothing" and halt. The SEND/RECEIVE commands used to exchange information are called *message-passing primitives*, and they are a very important part of MIMD programming languages.

To complete this solution, we need a second program, the one executed by the input/output processor. Its job is easy to describe—distribute data to all 100 processors and wait for a result to arrive from whatever processor finds the answer. This program might look like the following:

```
// this is the program run by processor 101
SET P TO 1
SET N TO THE NAME FOR WHICH WE ARE SEARCHING
// distribute the data to all 100 search processors
REPEAT 100 TIMES
     SET LIST TO THE NEXT 200,000 NAMES IN THE
       PHONE BOOK
     SEND LIST, NAME TO PROCESSOR P
     ADD 1 TO P
END LOOP
RECEIVE PHONE NUMBER FROM ANY PROCESSOR
OUTPUT THE PHONE NUMBER
HALT
```

Note the differences between this example and the previous SIMD code. There is no need to specifically indicate parallelism using a PARALLEL statement. Instead, the parallelism is implemented automatically by having multiple processors executing their programs concurrently. Note that every processor does not use the same program. In this case, there are two programs, one for the search processors and one for the input/output processor. Furthermore, even though 100 processors are executing the same program, they are not all executing the same sequence of instructions. For example, if *NAME* occurs exactly one time in the phone book, then 99 processors will execute the ELSE clause and "do nothing." The one processor that does find *NAME* will SEND the correct phone number to processor 101. Finally, note the difference in how we handle the concept of global data. In the SIMD example, every processor needed access to the variable K, so it was placed in global shared memory. In the MIMD example, every processor needed access to *NAME*, but in this case there is no global shared memory. Instead, we explicitly SEND this value to every processor, using message-passing primitives.

This phone book search is a rather simplified example of MIMD parallelism for two reasons. First, there were only two distinct programs, and 100 of the 101 processors were executing the same one. In many MIMD algorithms, there are many more distinct programs. The situation here is equivalent to having 101 people building a house and having 100 of those 101 doing the exact same task. In most cases, there will be carpenters, roofers, plumbers, masons, and so forth, all performing their own specific tasks. The second reason why this is a simplified example is that there is little communication between processors. In this algorithm, processors receive data at the start of the program and (possibly) send a result at the end. There is no communication during the computation itself. However, in most MIMD algorithms, there is message passing going on throughout the computation for such purposes as sharing intermediate computations, exchanging temporary data, and providing status information. For example, in the home-building analogy mentioned previously, the people putting up the walls must communicate their status (progress) to the roofers, who are waiting for wall construction to finish before they can begin. (This example is simple for a third reason—it does not deal with the possibility that *NAME* is not in the phone book. If that occurs, all 100 search processors will execute the ELSE clause and "Do nothing." The input/output processor will be sitting and waiting to RECEIVE a result that never will be SENT.)

A better example of MIMD parallel processing occurs when a **divide-and-conquer model** is used to solve a task. In this approach, the problem is successively partitioned into smaller and smaller parts and sent off to other processors, until each one has only a trivial job to perform. Each processor then completes that trivial operation and returns its result to the processor that sent it the task. These processors in turn do a little work and give the results back to the processors that gave them the tasks, and so on, all the way back to the originating processor. In this model, there is far more communication between processors.

For example, the task of finding the largest number in a list can be solved in a MIMD parallel fashion using the divide-and-conquer model. (The sequential version of this algorithm was presented in Chapter 2.) The original list of numbers is assigned to the top-level processor, which partitions the list into two parts and sends each half to a different processor. Each of these two processors divides its list in half and hands it off to yet two other processors, and so on, creating the pyramid effect shown in Figure 10.15.

At the bottom of the pyramid is a collection of processors that only have to find the largest number in a one-element list, a trivial task. They each pass this result up to their "parent" processor, which selects the larger of the two numbers it receives and passes that value up to its parent. All the way up the pyramid, each processor has only to select the larger of the two numbers it receives from its "children." When the processor at the top of the pyramid completes this task, the problem of finding the overall largest number has been solved.

Using a single processor, finding the largest of N numbers takes $\Theta(N)$ time because each of the N numbers in the list must be examined exactly once. (This order of complexity was introduced and discussed in Chapter 3.) However, the

FIGURE 10.15

The divide-and-conquer approach using multiple processors

parallel approach diagrammed in Figure 10.15 traverses the pyramid from top to bottom and then back to the top. Because the N numbers are divided into two halves at each step, until the lists are of length one, this down-and-up-the-pyramid process requires $(2 * \ln_2(N))$ steps, and a parallel solution to the "Find Largest" algorithm is $\Theta(\ln_2(N))$. (Logarithmic efficiency was discussed in Section 3.4.2.) This can lead to enormous speedup in the solution time because the function $\ln_2(N)$ grows at a much slower rate than N. For example, if $N = 1,000,000$, then using a sequential approach to finding the largest number takes on the order of 1,000,000 steps, whereas our parallel solution needs only on the order of $2 * \ln_2(1,000,000) = 40$ steps, a potential speedup of 25,000!

We would expect the use of parallelism to reduce processing time because subtasks are being executed concurrently. However, one potential roadblock to achieving these higher levels of speedup is the amount of communication traffic between processors, both to distribute code and data and to share status and results. At some point, an increase in the number of processors can become more of a hindrance than a help, due to the extra data communication required. This is analogous to having too many people serve on a committee. The work involved in keeping everyone informed can slow down rather than speed up the work. In that case, it could actually be more efficient to have fewer people working on the task. One of the most important areas of research in parallel processing is the design and development of efficient parallel algorithms that keep processors busy, minimize communications, and significantly speed up the overall execution time.

A final form of parallelism, a type we will discuss again in Chapter 15, is the *neural network*. Patterned after the human brain, neural networks can involve massive interconnections of many extremely simple devices. They are one of the most interesting areas of artificial intelligence.

Let Me Do That for You

Section 9.1 described the evolution of sequential programming languages from machine language to assembly language to high-level languages like C++, Java, and Python. A similar evolution is happening with parallel programming languages. Most of the parallel languages in current use, such as OpenMP, MPI, Cilk, and X10, require programmers to personally manage all aspects of parallelism—allocating data to global and local memory units, distributing programs, and sending and receiving messages. That is not unlike low-level assembly languages that required programmers to format data and manage memory, tasks that humans do not do very well.

However, just as assembly languages evolved into high-level languages in which compilers perform these mundane tasks, the field of parallel programming languages is also evolving. Today, *automatic parallelization* is an active area of computer science research. The goal of automatic parallelization is to design and build parallel compilers that accept sequential code and automatically "discover" opportunities for parallel execution. The compiler then converts this sequential code into parallel code that runs efficiently on SIMD or MIMD machines. The ultimate goal is to relieve programmers of the error-prone task of manually coding the complex details of parallel algorithms, something that humans, again, do not do very well.

In spite of many years of research, as yet there has been limited success in achieving this goal. Today only a few parallel compilers can generate parallel code that is anywhere close to the efficiency of what can be produced by good human programmers. With the increasing number of ever-more-powerful multicore supercomputers, it's important for software solutions to advance just as rapidly.

Practice Problems

1. Explain how parallel processing can be used to evaluate the expression

   $A + B + C + D$

   If each addition operation takes one "time slot," what savings can be achieved by using parallel processing instead of sequential processing?

2. Explain how you could get the parallel telephone book lookup problem to work correctly even if the desired NAME were not contained within the book.

Parallel Computing with Titanium

A programming language called Titanium is a parallel version of Java. It was developed at the University of California, Berkeley, and is specifically designed to support high-performance scientific computing on massively parallel machines. Using Titanium, mathematicians from the University of New York and computer scientists from the University of California, Berkeley, have developed software to model the fluid dynamics (blood flow, blood coagulation) of the human heart.

10.5 New Languages Keep Coming

After our discussion of many programming languages that fall into several programming language categories, you might think that surely all programming needs have been met with existing languages. But new languages and new paradigms continue to be developed, perhaps in the hope of finding the "silver bullet" of an easy-to-use, efficient, general-purpose computing language that enforces good programming practices to allow quick production of error-free code on all computing platforms.... .

Here are two more relatively new programming languages. It remains to be seen whether they will stand the test of time and become widely used "standard" languages.

10.5.1 Go

Go is a programming language developed at Google. One of the people involved in its development was Ken Thompson, a recipient, along with Dennis Ritchie, of the 1983 Turing Award (see Chapter 12) for the development of UNIX. When Go was released in 2009, there was some controversy over the name because there was a logic programming language named Go! (with exclamation point) already in existence. Nonetheless, the name has been retained.

What prompted the development of yet another programming language? Here is a quote from the FAQ (Frequently Asked Questions) page at *http://golang.org*:

> Go was born out of frustration with existing languages and environments for systems programming. Programming had become too difficult and the choice of languages was partly to blame. One had to choose either efficient compilation, efficient execution, or ease of programming; all three were not available in the same mainstream

language. Programmers who could were choosing ease over safety and efficiency by moving to dynamically typed languages such as Python and JavaScript rather than C++ or, to a lesser extent, Java.

Go is an attempt to combine the ease of programming of an interpreted, dynamically typed language with the efficiency and safety of a statically typed, compiled language. It also aims to be modern, with support for networked and multicore computing. Finally, it is intended to be *fast*: it should take at most a few seconds to build a large executable on a single computer. To meet these goals required addressing a number of linguistic issues...a new language was called for.

Go is an open source language (see "The Open Source Movement" Special Interest Box in Chapter 6). The source code is available for anyone to examine and use, and changes or additions can be proposed. As noted in the quote, two of the target areas for Go applications are systems programming and programming for multicore machines. Go is in use to support several Google internal projects.

10.5.2 F#

F# is a new Microsoft language. Developed in 2005, it is now included as a language in the Microsoft development environment Visual Studio 2010. In contrast to the open source Go language, F# is a proprietary language, that is, it is intellectual property belonging to Microsoft Corporation. F# is primarily a functional language, although it has some object-oriented characteristics and some parallel programming characteristics. Because it is supported by the Microsoft .NET Framework, it has access to all the common libraries of .NET.

Let's look at how some of the simple function operations we looked at in Scheme can be done in F#. Instead of the keyword *define* indicating that we are about to define a function, F# uses *let*. So we can write the following F# code:

```
let double x = 2 * x
let square x = x * x
let polynomial x = double(square x)
```

And the result of

polynomial 3

is again 18.

F# also has list-processing capabilities. Instead of taking a list and extracting the first element (the *car* operation in Scheme) or the rest of the list minus the first element (the *cdr* operation in Scheme), F# builds up a list by pushing an element onto the front of the list. This operation is denoted by ::, so that the result of

```
let newlist = 1 :: [2; 3]
```

is the list [1; 2; 3].

The *adder* function in Scheme (Figure 10.9) is a recursive function that repeatedly strips off the front element of the list and adds it to the sum of the remaining list. An equivalent function in F# does the same thing, but in a slightly different way. Figure 10.16 shows the F# function. Given a list x, it "matches" this list to see whether it is the empty list [ ], for which the value of the sum of the elements, 0, can be returned immediately, or whether it is of the form y::z, that is, the element y pushed on the front of a list z, in which case the value returned by the function is y plus the sum of the values in list z.

So let's see how this works if we ask for

SumList [3; 4; 5]

The list [3; 4; 5] is not empty, but it does have the form 3::[4; 5], so the value, as constructed so far, is

3 + *SumList* [4; 5]

Invoking the *SumList* function on the list [4; 5], this list is not the empty list, but it does have the form 4::[5], so the value, as constructed so far, is

3 + 4 + *SumList* [5]

Once again, the *SumList* function is invoked, this time on the list [5]. Again, this is not the empty list, but it does have the form 5:: [ ], so the value, as constructed so far, is

3 + 4 + 5 + *SumList* [ ]

On the final invocation of *SumList*, using the empty list [ ], the result of 0 is returned. Thus the final result is

3 + 4 + 5 + 0 = 12

F# has found its way into many applications:

- The Microsoft Xbox Live TrueSkill rating system

- Mathematical models to analyze investment portfolios

- A program to balance the power generation schedule for a number of power stations

- An expert system to help make decisions about offshore oil exploration

FIGURE 10.16

```
let rec SumList x =
    match x with
    | []     -> 0
    | y::z   -> y + SumList z
```

F# program to add nonnegative integers

As these last two example languages clearly demonstrate, even though the field of programming language design is now well over 50 years old, it is still a fertile area of creative research.

10.6 Conclusion

There is an entire spectrum of programming languages, each with its own features that make it more suitable for some types of applications than for others. A number of well-known languages (FORTRAN, COBOL, C, C++, Ada, Java, C#, Python) fall into the traditional, procedural paradigm. Procedural languages can be object oriented, leading to a different program design perspective and the promise of software reuse. Some languages (such as SQL, HTML, and JavaScript) are designed as special-purpose tools. Still others rely on combinations of function evaluations (a functional language–Scheme), logical deductions from specified facts (a logic programming language–Prolog), or a parallel programming approach. And new languages continue to be developed. Figure 10.17 lists the languages we have discussed, along with some of the other major languages. A few words about this figure are in order. It is hard to pinpoint a date for a programming language. Should it be when the language was developed, when it was first commercially used, or when it became standardized? It is also sometimes hard to pigeonhole a language as to paradigm. Although we've tried to make clear distinctions in this chapter, some languages combine features drawn from several approaches. Finally, your favorite language may have been omitted. (By all means, add it to the table.) At any rate, it is certain that the programming language world has been and continues to be a "Tower of Babel."

FIGURE 10.17

Name	Date	Type
FORTRAN	1955–57	Procedural
ALGOL 60	1958–60	Procedural
COBOL	1959–60	Procedural
BASIC	1963–64	Procedural
PL/1	1964	Procedural
ALGOL-68	1968	Procedural
Pascal	1971	Procedural
C	1974	Procedural
Modula-2	1977	Procedural

Programming languages at a glance *(continues)*

FIGURE 10.17 (CONTINUED)

Name	Date	Type
Ada	1979	Procedural/Parallel
Oberon	1988	Procedural/Parallel
Go	2009	Procedural/Parallel
Smalltalk	1971–1980	Object oriented
Flavors	1979	Object oriented
C++	1983	Object oriented
Eiffel	1987	Object oriented
Visual Basic	1988	Object oriented
Python	1990	Object oriented
Java	1995	Object oriented
Alice	1995	Object oriented
C#	2000	Object oriented
SQL	1986	Database queries
Perl	1987	Text extraction/reporting
HTML	1994	Hypertext authoring
LISP	1958	Functional
APL	1960	Functional
Scheme	1975	Functional
FP	1977	Functional
ML	1978	Functional
Haskell	1992	Functional
F#	2005	Functional
Prolog	1972	Logic
Datalog	1977	Logic
Occam II	1987	Parallel
Linda	1989	Parallel
High Performance Fortran	1993	Parallel
Titanium	1999	Parallel
Chapel	2010	Parallel
Lua	1993	Scripting language
Ruby	1995	Scripting language/object oriented
JavaScript	1996	Scripting language
VBScript	1996	Scripting language
PHP	1997	Server-side scripting language
ASP	1997	Server-side scripting language
JSP	1999	Server-side scripting language

Programming languages at a glance

The trend in programming language design is to develop still higher levels of abstraction. This allows the human programmer to think in bigger pieces and in more novel or conceptual ways about solving the problem at hand. We would like eventually to be able to write programs that contain only the instruction "Solve the problem." Yet, we must remember that code written in any high-level programming language is still of no use to the computer trying to execute that code. No matter how abstract and powerful the language for front-end communication with the computer, the machine itself is still toiling away at the level of binary digits, absolute memory addresses, and machine language instructions. The services of an appropriate translator must be employed to take the code down into the machine language of that computer. The workings of a translator will be discussed in Chapter 11.

EXERCISES

1. What is the output from the following section of FORTRAN code?

```
    ISUM = 0
    I = 1
20 IF (I .GT. 4) GO TO 30
    ISUM = ISUM + I
    I = I + 1
    GO TO 20
30 WRITE(*,*) ISUM
```

2. Translate the following assembly language program into (early) FORTRAN.

```
          IN        NUMBER
AGAIN:    LOAD      NUMBER
          COMPARE   ZERO
          JUMPGT    OUTPUT
          LOAD      ISUM
          ADD       NUMBER
          STORE     ISUM
          IN        NUMBER
          JUMP      AGAIN
OUTPUT:   OUT       ISUM
          HALT
NUMBER:   .DATA     0
ISUM:     .DATA     0
ZERO:     .DATA     0
```

3. Exponentiation is expressed in FORTRAN by **; that is, 3**2 means 3^2. If *I* has the value 7 and *J* has the value 3, what is the value of the following FORTRAN expression?

```
((I - J)**2)/2
```

4. What is the value of *RESULT* after execution of the following COBOL code? Assume that *INITIAL* has the value 100.

```
MOVE INITIAL TO INDEX.
ADD 1 TO INDEX.
ADD INITIAL TO INDEX.
ADD INITIAL TO INDEX GIVING
   RESULT.
```

5. What is true after the following statements in a C program have been executed?

```
int* intPointer;
intPointer = (int*) 500;
*intPointer = 10;
```

6. Write a section of C code that stores in memory location 1000 the integer value currently in *SAM*.

7. The following section of Ada code conveys the services that a "teller" object can perform. What are these services?

```
task type teller is
  -- Entries to do simple
  -- transactions and return status
     entry deposit ( id : cust_id;
       val : in money; stat : out
       status );
     entry withdraw ( id : cust_id;
       val : in money; stat : out
       status );
     entry balance ( id : cust_id;
       val : out money; stat :
       out status );
end teller;
```

8. In the following two Java output statements,

```
System.out.println("Hello. Welcome
  to this program.");
System.out.print("Tell me your
  favorite number: ");
```

Why do you think the first uses *println* and the second uses *print*?

9. In Python, indentation is used to indicate the extent of a block of code. What is the output of the following Python code?

```
first = 3
second = 5
if first < second:
    print ("second is bigger")
else:
    print ("but this time ")
print ("first is bigger")
```

10. In C#, *&&* is the symbol for the Boolean AND operation, and || is the symbol for the Boolean OR operation. What is the truth value of the following Boolean expressions?

    a. $(3 <= 3)$ *&&* $(7 > 5)$
    b. $(3 < 3) || (7 > 5)$
    c. $(4 < 1)$ *&&* $(3 > 2)$

11. Which procedural language might be most appropriate for a program to do each of the following applications and why?

    a. Compute trajectories for a satellite launcher.
    b. Monitor an input device feeding data from an experiment to the computer.
    c. Process the day's transactions at an ATM (automated teller machine).

12. In the vendor database described in Section 10.3.1, the user wants to know all of the cities where there are vendors from whom the store bought more than $10,000 worth of stock the previous business quarter. Write an SQL query for this information.

13. Describe the text on a Web page that results from the HTML statement:

```
<p><center> <font size = 12 color
  = "green"> How Now Brown Cow
  </center></p>
```

14. Using a text editor (such as Notepad) and two image files of your own, create the HTML page shown in Figure 10.8. Save the file with an .html extension, then double-click to open it in your Web browser. Does it behave as you expect?

15. What is the result of the following Scheme expression?

```
(car (cdr (cdr (list 16 19 21))))
```

16. Write a Scheme function that returns a list consisting of the first two values in the input list but in the opposite order.

17. Consider the following Scheme function:

```
(define (mystery input-list)
  (cond ((null? input-list) 0)
    (else ( + 1 (mystery (cdr
      input-list))))))
```

What is the result of invoking the function as follows?

(mystery (list 3 4 5))

Explain what this function does in general.

18. Consider the following Scheme function:

```
(define (unknown n)
  (cond ((= n 1) 1)
    (else (* n (unknown (- n 1))))))
```

The condition (= n 1) means "If $n = 1 \ldots$ ". What is the result of the following function invocation?

(unknown 4)

19. After the rule

earlier(X,Y) :- president(R,X),
   president(S,Y), precedes(R,S).

is added to the Prolog program of Figure 10.10, what is the result of each of the following queries?

a. **?-earlier(lewis_and_clark, civil_war).**

b. **?-earlier(world_war_II, first_moon_landing).**

c. **?-earlier(X, world_war_II).**

20. Here is the beginning of a Prolog program about a family. The facts are

```
male(eli)
male(bill)
male(joe)
female(mary)
female(betty)
female(sarah)
parent-of(eli, bill)
parent-of(mary, bill)
parent-of(bill, joe)
parent-of(bill, betty)
parent-of(bill, sarah)
```

The declaration

```
male(eli)
```

asserts that Eli is male, and

```
parent-of(eli, bill)
```

asserts that Eli is Bill's parent. Draw a "family tree" based on these facts.

21. Add to the Prolog program of Exercise 20 a rule to define "father-of".

22. Add to the Prolog program of Exercise 20 a rule to define "daughter-of".

23. a. Add to the Prolog program of Exercise 20 a rule to define "ancestor-of".

   b. After this rule is added, determine the result of the query

   ?-ancestor-of(X, sarah).

24. Go to the "toy" Prolog Web site at *www.csse. monash.edu.au/~lloyd/tildeLogic/Prolog.toy*

   Pay attention to the syntax of the program that is already there. In particular, notice that in this version, each statement ends with a period and the :- symbol is now <=. Load the Prolog program of Figure 10.10 and run it, making some of the queries used in Section 10.4.2.

25. Suppose the symbolic arrangement of Figure 10.15 is used in a divide-and-conquer algorithm to compute the largest element in a list of eight elements. Assume that the time to partition a list in half and pass it to subprocessors is $0.003n$ msec, where n is the size of the list to be partitioned. Assume that the time to compare two values and find the larger of the two is 1 μsec. Assume that the time to pass the larger value back to a parent processor is 0.001 μsec. Compute the time required to do this task compared with doing it on a sequential processor that uses the Find Largest algorithm of Chapter 2, which also involves a series of comparisons of two values and finding the larger of the two.

26. In the telephone number lookup example of parallel processing, the input/output processor may wait forever if NAME appears nowhere in the telephone directory. Assume that the code for processors

1–100 remains the same, and modify the code for processor 101 to output a message and then stop execution if NAME is not in the telephone directory. (*Hint*: Assume that you have the ability to run a countdown timer in processor 101.)

27. What is the result of the F# statement

```
myFunction([3; 7])
if
myFunction x = 2::x
```

CHALLENGE WORK

1. Visual Basic .NET (see the "Old Dog, New Tricks #2" Special Interest Box) supplies a "toolbox" that makes creation of a graphical user interface a simple matter of dragging and dropping the objects you want (e.g., buttons, labels, and text boxes) onto a form object. The resulting Windows-based programs operate in an *event-driven mode*. Instead of proceeding from beginning to end under the control of the program instructions, an event-driven program starts up and then waits for some "event" to occur. An event is generally caused by some user action such as clicking on a button. Each of the form objects can have a code module to respond to such events.

    The following shows a simple Visual Basic .NET form that contains two text boxes, a label, and a button. The user types his or her first name and last name into the two text boxes. When the user clicks the button, the name is displayed in the label as

    Lastname, Firstname

    If you have Visual Basic .NET (available in Microsoft Visual Studio), open a new Visual Basic Windows Application. Drag objects from the Toolbox to create a form that looks like the one shown on the next page. Give each of these objects a meaningful name by changing its Name property in the Properties window. Use the Text property of each object to set what that object displays (the text boxes and label should initially be blank and the button should say "Name Writer").

    The only code required is a response to the button's Click event. Double-click the button and then write a code statement that concatenates—in the correct order—the Text properties of the two text boxes, together with a comma, and assigns the result to the Text property of the label. Run your program (press the function key F5 on the keyboard) to test it. (*Hints*: Visual Basic uses & as the concatenation operator. A form object's property is referenced by giving the name of the object, followed by a dot, followed by the property name, as in lblOutput.Text.)

2. Find information on one of the Grand Challenge problems of Figure 10.12. Write a report on the following:

    • What the problem involves

    • The benefits to be obtained from solving it

    • Why it is computationally challenging

    • Why parallel processing may be able to, or has been able to, help solve it

    • The current state of progress toward a solution

3. Using a text editor (such as Notepad) and three image files of your own, create the HTML page shown in Figure 10.8. Save the file with an .html extension and be sure it runs properly in your browser. Change the Javascript so that the image cycles through picture 1 to picture 2 to picture 3 to picture 1, and so forth, as the user moves the mouse into and out of the image area. (*Hint:* check the Web for the Javascript if...else if...else statement.)

4. There are small examples online of programs written in Go. Go (no pun intended!) to *http://golang.org* and in the Examples drop-down box below the code window, select Fibonacci Closure. Click Pop Out to get a bigger window to see the code. The Fibonacci sequence is a famous sequence of numbers invented by Leonardo Fibonacci in the year 1202 to model the population growth of rabbits. The first two numbers in the sequence are 1, 1. Successive numbers in the sequence are obtained by adding the two previous numbers. For example, the third Fibonacci number is the sum of the first two Fibonacci numbers, $1 + 1 = 2$.

a. Write the first six numbers in the Fibonacci sequence.

b. Compile and run the Fibonacci Closure Go program. What is the output?

c. Some of the Go syntax is similar to C/C++. How does Go indicate comments?

d. One bit of C/C++ syntax is missing from Go. On the FAQ page, what does it say about ending statements with semicolons?

e. Can you guess the semantics (meaning) of the following statement?

```
a, b := 0, 1
```
What about the next statement?

```
a, b = b, a+b
```
(*Note:* You can modify and recompile/rerun the code to test possible equivalent statements.)

ADDITIONAL RESOURCES

For additional print and/or online resources relevant to this chapter, visit the Computer Science CourseMate at login.cengagebrain.com.

Compilers and Language Translation

11.1 Introduction

Although the high-level languages you learned about in the previous two chapters vary greatly in structure and behavior, they all share one feature: No computer in the world can understand them. There are no "Java computers" or "C++ processors" that can directly execute programs written in the high-level languages of Chapters 9 and 10. In Chapter 6, you learned that assembly language must be translated into machine language prior to execution. High-level languages must also be translated into machine language prior to execution—in this case by a special piece of system software called a *compiler*. Compilers for languages like those discussed in Chapters 9 and 10 are very complex programs. They contain tens of thousands of lines of code and may require dozens or hundreds of person-years to complete. Unlike the assemblers of Chapter 6, these translators are not easy to design or implement.

There is a simple explanation for the vast difference in complexity between assemblers and compilers. Assembly language and machine language are related *one to one*; that is, one assembly language instruction produces exactly one machine language instruction. Therefore, translation is really a replacement process in which the assembler looks up a symbolic value in a table (either the op code table or the symbol table) and replaces it by its numeric equivalent:

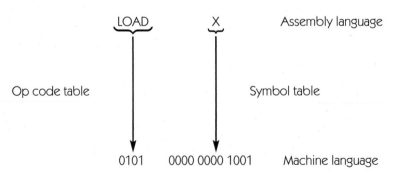

This is equivalent to translating English into Spanish by looking up each individual English word in an English/Spanish dictionary and replacing it with exactly one Spanish word:

This is a simple way to do translation, and this approach does work for assemblers. Unfortunately, it does not work for most English sentences. Often, a single English word must be translated into a multiword Spanish phrase or vice versa. This same problem exists in the translation of high-level programming languages like Java, C++, or Python.

The relationship between a high-level language and machine language is not one to one but *one to many*. That is, one high-level language statement, such as an assignment or conditional statement, usually produces *many* machine language or assembly language instructions. For example,

Java   **Assembly Language**

a = b + c – d;   →   LOAD B

                                ADD C

                                SUBTRACT D

                                STORE A

To determine which machine language instructions must be generated, a compiler cannot simply look up a name in a table. Instead, it must do a thorough linguistic analysis of the structure (syntax) and meaning (semantics) of each high-level language statement. This is far more difficult than table lookup. In fact, building a compiler for a modern high-level programming language can be one of the most difficult system software projects.

When performing a translation, a compiler has two distinct goals. The first is *correctness*. The machine language code produced by the compiler must do exactly what the high-level language statement describes, and nothing else. For example, here is a typical Java assignment statement:

```
A = (B + C) - (D + E);
```

Assume that a compiler translates this statement into the following assembly language code:

```
-- Compute the term (B + C)
LOAD B        -- Register R holds the value of B
ADD C         -- Now it holds the result (B + C)
STORE B       -- Let's store the result temporarily in B (see comments below)
-- Next compute the term (D + E)
LOAD D        -- Register R holds the value of D
ADD E         -- Now it holds the result (D + E)
STORE D       -- Let's store the result temporarily in D (see comments below)
-- Finally, subtract the two terms and store the result in A
LOAD B        -- This loads (B + C)
SUBTRACT D    -- This is (B + C) – (D + E)
STORE A       -- Put the result in A. We are done translating the statement
```

This translation is *wrong.* Although the code does evaluate (B + C) – (D + E) and stores the result into A, it does two things it should not do. The translated program destroys the original contents of the variables B and D when it does the first two STORE operations. This is *not* what the Java assignment operator is supposed to do, and this compiler has produced an incorrect machine language translation of the original high-level language statement.

In addition to correctness, a compiler has a second goal. The code it produces should be reasonably *efficient and concise.* Even though memory costs have come down and processors are much faster, programmers will not accept gross inefficiencies in either execution speed or size of the compiled program. They might not care whether a compiler eliminates every wasted nanosecond or every unnecessary memory cell, but they do want it to produce reasonably fast and efficient machine language code. For example, to compute the sum $2x_0 + 2x_1 + 2x_2 + ... + 2x_{50000}$, an inexperienced programmer might write something like the following:

```
sum = 0.0;
i = 0;
while (i <= 50000)        {
        sum = sum + (2.0 * x[i]);
        i = i + 1;
}
```

This loop includes the time-consuming multiplication operation (2.0 * $x[i]$). By the rules of arithmetic, this operation can be moved outside the loop and done just once. A "smart" compiler should recognize this and translate the previous fragment as though it had been written as follows:

```
sum = 0.0;
i = 0;
while (i <= 50000)    {
       sum = sum + x[i];
       i = i + 1;
};
sum = sum * 2.0;
```

By restructuring the loop, a smart compiler saves 49,999 unnecessary multiplications.

As you can see, we have our work cut out for us in this chapter. We want to describe how to construct a compiler that can read and interpret high-level language statements, understand what they are trying to do, correctly translate their intentions into machine language without errors or unexpected side effects, and do all of this efficiently. Building a compiler is a major undertaking.

The remainder of this chapter gives an overview of the steps involved in building a compiler for a procedural, Java-like, or C++-like language. No single chapter could investigate the subtleties and complexities of this huge subject. We can, however, give you an appreciation for some of the issues and concepts involved in designing and implementing this important piece of system software.

11.2 The Compilation Process

The general structure of a compiler is shown in Figure 11.1. Because there is a good deal of variability in the design and organization of a compiler, this diagram should be viewed as a model rather than as an exact description of how all compilers are structured.

FIGURE 11.1

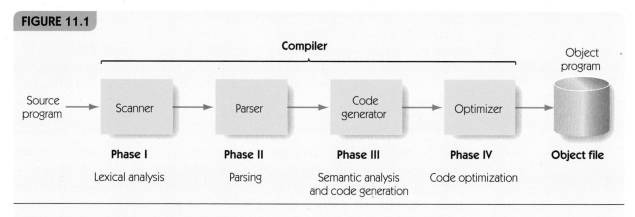

General structure of a compiler

The four phases of compilation listed in Figure 11.1 are:

- *Phase I: Lexical analysis*—The compiler examines the individual characters in the source program and groups them into syntactical units, called tokens, that will be analyzed in succeeding stages. This operation is analogous to grouping letters into words prior to analyzing text.

- *Phase II: Parsing*—The sequence of tokens formed by the scanner is checked to see whether it is syntactically correct according to the rules of the programming language. This phase is roughly equivalent to checking whether the words in the text form grammatically correct sentences.

- *Phase III: Semantic analysis and code generation*—If the high-level language statement is structurally correct, then the compiler analyzes its meaning and generates the proper sequence of machine language instructions to carry out these actions.

- *Phase IV: Code optimization*—The compiler takes the generated code and sees whether it can be made more efficient, either by making it run faster or having it occupy less memory.

When these four phases are complete, we have a correct and efficient machine language translation of the original high-level language *source program*. In the final step, this machine language code, called the *object program*, is written to an *object file*. We have reached the stage labeled "Machine language program" from Chapter 6, Figure 6.4, and the resulting object program can be handled in exactly the fashion shown there. That is, it can be loaded into memory and executed by the processor to produce the desired results.

The overall sequence of operations performed on a high-level language program is summarized in Figure 11.2. The following sections take a closer look at each of the four phases of the compilation process.

11.2.1 Phase I: Lexical Analysis

The program that performs lexical analysis is called a lexical analyzer, or more commonly a scanner. Its job is to group input characters into units called tokens—syntactical units that are treated as single, indivisible entities for the purposes of translation. For example, take a look at the following assignment statement:

```
a = b + 319 - delta;
```

You probably see an assignment statement containing some symbols (*a*, *b*, *delta*), a number (319), and some operators (=, +, −, ;). However, your eyes and your brain actually do a great deal of processing to create these objects, just as they do a great deal of processing to create words, sentences, and paragraphs from the individual characters on this page. In the assignment statement shown previously, high-level linguistic objects

FIGURE 11.2

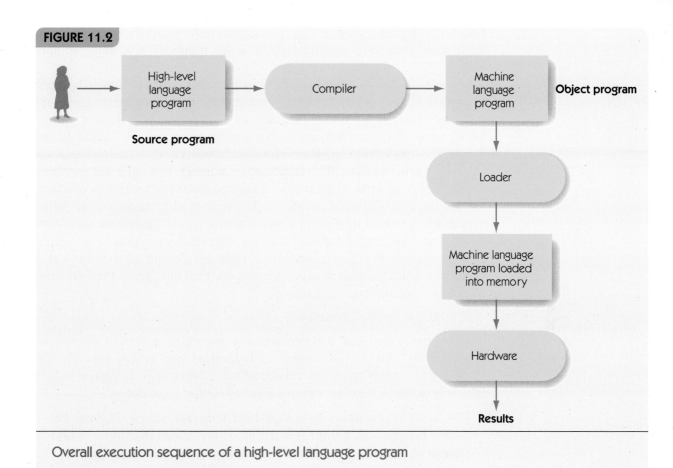

Overall execution sequence of a high-level language program

such as symbols and numbers do not yet exist. Initially, there are only the following 21 characters:

tab, a, blank, =, blank, b, blank, +, blank, 3, 1, 9, blank, –,
blank, d, e, l, t, a, ;

It is the task of the scanner to discard nonessential characters, such as blanks and tabs, and then group the remaining characters into high-level syntactical units such as symbols, numbers, and operators. A scanner would construct from the preceding example the following eight tokens:

a
=
b
+
319
–
delta
;

Now our compiler no longer has to deal with individual characters. Instead, it can work at the level of symbols (*a*, *b*, *delta*), numbers (319), and operators (=, +, −, ;).

In addition to building tokens, a scanner must classify tokens by their type—that is, is it a symbol, is it a number, or is it an assignment operator? Whereas a modern high-level language like C++, Java, or Python may have 50 or more different token types, our simple examples are limited to the 11 classifications listed in Figure 11.3.

The scanner assigns the classification number 1 to all legal symbols, such as *a*, *b*, and *delta*. Similarly, all unsigned numbers, regardless of value, are assigned classification number 2. The reason all symbols and all numbers can be grouped into single classifications is that the grammatical correctness of a statement depends only on whether a legal symbol or a legal number appears in a given location. It does not depend on exactly which symbol or which number is actually used. For example, given the following model of an assignment statement:

"*symbol*" = "*symbol*" + "*number*";

it is possible to state that it is syntactically correct, regardless of which specific "symbol" and "number" are actually used (as long as they are all legal).

Using the token types and classification values shown in Figure 11.3, it is now possible to describe exactly what a scanner must do:

The input to a scanner is a high-level language statement from the source program. Its output is a list of all the tokens contained in that statement, as well as the classification number of each token found.

FIGURE 11.3

Token Type	Classification Number
symbol	1
number	2
=	3
+	4
−	5
;	6
==	7
if	8
else	9
(	10
)	11

Typical token classifications

Here are some examples (using the classification values shown in Figure 11.3):

Input: `a = b + 319 - delta;`

Output:

Token	**Classification**
a	1
=	3
b	1
+	4
319	2
–	5
delta	1
;	6

Input: `if (a == b) xx = 13; else xx = 2;`

Output:

Token	**Classification**
if	8
(	10
a	1
==	7
b	1
)	11
xx	1
=	3
13	2
;	6
else	9
xx	1
=	3
2	2
;	6

Regardless of which programming language is being analyzed, every scanner performs virtually the same set of operations: (1) It discards blanks and other nonessential characters and looks for the beginning of a token; (2) when it finds the beginning, it puts characters together until (3) it detects the end of the token, at which point it classifies the token and begins looking for the next one. This algorithm works properly regardless of what the tokens look like.

We can see this process more clearly by looking at an algorithm for grouping natural language characters into words:

This is English.
Este es Espanol.
Kore wa Nihongo desu.

Even though these three sentences are written in very different languages—English, Spanish, and Japanese—the algorithm for constructing words

Practice Problems

1. Using the token types and classification numbers given in Figure 11.3, determine the output of a scanner given the following input statements:
   a. `x = x + 1;`
   b. `if (a + b42 == 0) a = zz - 12;`

2. Do you think a scanner would classify the following sequence of symbols as a single token or as multiple tokens? Give a reason for your choice.
   a. abc−def
   b. abc_def
   c. abc def

3. The following character sequence is illegal in virtually all programming languages:
   `X = ; ( 14 hello`
   What would you expect a scanner to do if it encounters such a sequence?

is identical: (1) Discard blanks until you find a nonblank character; (2) group characters together until (3) you encounter either a blank or the character ".". You have now built a word. Go back to Step 1 and repeat the entire sequence to locate the next word. This is essentially the same algorithm that is used to build a lexical scanner for high-level programming languages.

11.2.2 Phase II: Parsing

During the parsing phase, a compiler determines whether the tokens recognized by the scanner during Phase I fit together in a grammatically meaningful way. That is, it determines whether they are a syntactically legal statement of the programming language. This step is analogous to diagramming a sentence. For example, to prove that the sequence of words

The man bit the dog

is a correctly formed sentence, we must show that the individual words can be grouped together structurally to form a proper English language sentence:

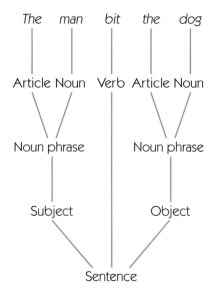

If we are unable to diagram the sentence, then it is not correctly formed. For example, when we try to analyze the sequence, "The man bit the", here is what happens:

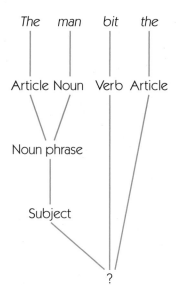

At this point in the analysis, we are stuck because there is no object for the verb "bit." We cannot diagram the sentence and must conclude that it is not properly formed.

The same thing happens with statements in a programming language, which are roughly analogous to sentences in a natural language. If a compiler is able to "diagram" a statement such as $a = b + c$, it concludes that the statement is structurally correct:

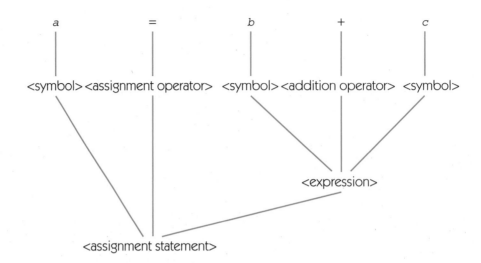

The structure shown above is called a **parse tree**. It starts from the individual tokens in the statement, a, $=$, b, $+$, and c, and shows how these tokens can be grouped into predefined grammatical categories such as <symbol>, <assignment operator>, and <expression> until the desired goal is reached— in this case, <assignment statement>. (We will explain shortly why we are writing the names of these grammatical categories inside the angle brackets "<" and ">".) The successful construction of a parse tree is proof that this statement is correctly formed according to the rules of the language. If a parser cannot produce such a parse tree, then the statement is not correctly formed.

In the field of compiler design, the process of diagramming a high-level language statement is called **parsing**, and it is done by a program called a **parser**. The output of a parser is either a complete parse tree or an error message if one cannot be constructed.

Grammars, Languages, and BNF. How does a parser know how to construct the parse tree? What tells it how the pieces of a language fit together? For example, in the statement shown previously, you might wonder how the parser knows that the format of an assignment statement in our language is

<symbol> = <expression>

The answer is that it does not know; we must tell it. The parser must be given a formal description of the **syntax**—the grammatical structure—of the language that it is going to analyze. The most widely used notation for representing the syntax of a programming language is called **BNF**, an acronym for **Backus-Naur Form**, named after its designers John Backus and Peter Naur.

In BNF, the syntax of a language is specified as a set of rules, also called productions. The entire collection of rules is called a grammar. Each individual BNF rule looks like this:

left-hand side ::= "definition"

The *left-hand side* of a BNF rule is the name of a single grammatical category, such as <symbol>, <expression>, or <assignment statement>. The BNF operator ::= means "is defined as," and "definition," which is also called the *right-hand side*, specifies the grammatical structure of the symbol appearing on the left-hand side of the rule. The definition may contain any number of objects. For example, here is a BNF rule that defines how an <assignment statement> is formed:

<assignment statement> ::= <symbol> = <expression>

This rule says that the syntactical construct called <assignment statement> is defined as a <symbol> followed by the token = followed by the syntactical construct called <expression>. To have a structurally correct assignment statement, these three objects must all be present in exactly that order.

A BNF rule that gives one possible definition for the English language construct called <sentence> follows.

<sentence> ::= <subject> <verb> <object>

This rule says that a <sentence> is defined as a <subject> followed by a <verb> followed by an <object>. It is this rule that allowed us to parse "The man bit the dog."

Finally, the simple BNF rule

<addition operator> ::= +

says that the grammatical construct <addition operator> is defined as the single character +.

If a parser is analyzing a statement in a language and it sees exactly the same sequence of objects that appears on the right-hand side of a BNF rule, it is allowed to replace them with the one grammatical object on the left-hand side of that rule. For example, given our BNF rule for <assignment statement>:

<assignment statement> ::= <symbol> = <expression>

if a parser encounters the three objects <symbol>, =, and <expression> next to each other in the input, it can replace them with the object appearing on the left-hand side of the rule—in this case, <assignment statement>. In a sense, the parser is constructing one branch of the parse tree, which looks like this:

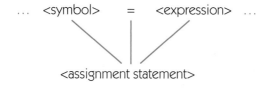

We say that the three objects, <symbol>, =, and <expression>, *produce* the grammatical category called <assignment statement>, and that is why a BNF rule is also called a production.

BNF rules use two different types of objects, called terminals and nonterminals, on the right-hand side of a production. Terminals are the actual tokens of the language recognized and returned by a scanner. The terminals of our language are the 11 tokens listed in Figure 11.3:

<symbol>	==
<number>	if
=	else
+	(
−	)
;	

The important characteristic of terminals is that they are not defined any further by other rules of the grammar. That is, there is no rule in the grammar that explains the "meaning" of such objects as <symbol>, =, +, and *if*. They are simply elements of the language, much like the words *man*, *bit*, and *dog* in our earlier example.

The second type of object used in a BNF rule is a nonterminal. A nonterminal is not an actual element of the language but an intermediate grammatical category used to help explain and organize the language. For example, in the analysis of the English sentence, "The man bit the dog," we used grammatical categories called article, noun, verb, noun phrase, subject, and object. These categories help us understand the structure of the sentence and show that it is correctly formed, but they are not actual words of the sentence being studied.

In every grammar, there is one special nonterminal called the goal symbol. This is the final nonterminal, and it is the nonterminal object that the parser is trying to produce as it builds the parse tree. When the parser has produced the goal symbol using all the elements of the sentence or statement, it has proved the syntactical correctness of the sentence or statement being analyzed. In our English language example, the goal symbol is <sentence>. In our assignment statement example, it is, naturally, <assignment statement>. When this nonterminal goal symbol has been produced, the parser has finished building the tree, and the statement has been successfully parsed. The collection of all statements that can be successfully parsed is called the *language* defined by a grammar.

All nonterminals are written inside angle brackets; examples include <expression> and <assignment statement>. Some terminals are also written in angle brackets when they do not represent actual characters of the language but rather groups of characters constructed by the scanner, such as <symbol> or <number>. However, it is easy to tell the difference between the two. A terminal such as <symbol> is not defined by any other rule of the language. That is, there is no rule anywhere in the grammar that looks like this:

<symbol> ::= "definition of a symbol"

Terminal symbols are like the words and punctuation marks of a language, and a parser does not have to know anything more about their syntactical structure to analyze a sentence.

However, nonterminals are constructed by the parser from more elementary syntactical units. Therefore, nonterminals such as <expression> and <assignment statement> must be further defined by one or more rules that specify exactly how this nonterminal is constructed. For example, there must exist at least one rule in our grammar that has the nonterminal <expression> as the left-hand side. This rule tells the parser how to form expressions from other terminals and nonterminals:

> <expression> ::= "definition of expression"

Similarly, there must be at least one rule that specifies the structure of an assignment statement:

> <assignment statement> ::= "definition of assignment statement"

We can summarize the difference between terminals and nonterminals by saying that terminals never appear on the left-hand side of a BNF rule, whereas nonterminals must appear on the left-hand side of one or more rules.

The three symbols <, >, and ::= used as part of BNF rules are termed **metasymbols**. This means that they are symbols of one language (BNF) that are being used to describe the characteristics of another language. In addition to these three, there are two other metasymbols used in BNF definitions. The vertical bar, |, means OR, and it is used to separate two alternative definitions of a nonterminal. This could be done without the vertical bar by just writing two separate rules:

> <nonterminal> ::= "definition 1"

> <nonterminal> ::= "definition 2"

However, it is sometimes more convenient to use the | character and write a single rule:

> <nonterminal> ::= "definition 1" | "definition 2"

For example, the rule

> <arithmetic operator> ::= + | − | * | /

says that an arithmetic operator is defined as either a +, or a −, or an *, or a /. Without the | operator, we would need to write four separate rules, which would make the grammar much larger. Here is a rule that defines the nonterminal <digit>:

> <digit> ::= 0 | 1 | 2 | 3 | 4 | 5 | 6 | 7 | 8 | 9

We will see many more examples of the use of the OR operator.

The final metasymbol used in BNF definitions is the Greek character lambda, Λ, which represents the **null string**—nothing at all. It is possible that a nonterminal can be "empty," and the symbol Λ is used to indicate this. For example, the nonterminal <signed integer> can be defined as an

Practice Problems

1. Write a single BNF rule that defines the nonterminal
   <Boolean operator>. (Assume that the three possible Boolean operators are
   AND, OR, and NOT.)

2. Create a BNF grammar that describes all one- or two-character identifiers that begin
   with the letter *i* or *j*. The second character, if present, can be any letter or digit.
   What is the goal symbol of your grammar?

3. Write a BNF grammar that describes Boolean expressions of the form

   (var op var)

   where *var* can be one of the symbols *x*, *y*, and *z*, and *op* can be one of the three
   relational operators ==, >, and <. The parentheses are part of the expression.

4. Using the grammar created in Practice Problem 3, show the parse tree for the
   expression (*x* > *y*).

5. Using the grammar created in Practice Problem 3, show what happens when you
   try to parse the illegal expression (*x* ==).

6. Modify your grammar from Practice Problem 3 so that the enclosing parentheses
   are optional. That is, Boolean expressions can be written as either (var op var) or
   var op var.

optional sign preceding an integer value, such as +7 or −5 or 8. To define
the idea of an optional sign in BNF, we could say:

> <signed integer> ::= <sign> <number>
> <sign> ::= + | − | Λ

which says that <sign> may be either a + or a −, or it may be omitted
entirely.

Parsing Concepts and Techniques. Given this brief introduction to
grammars, languages, and BNF, we can now explain how a parser works. A
parser receives as input the BNF description of a high-level language and
a sequence of tokens recognized by the scanner. The fundamental rule of
parsing follows.

*If, by repeated applications of the rules of the grammar, a parser can
convert the sequence of input tokens into the goal symbol, then that
sequence of tokens is a syntactically valid statement of the language. If
it cannot convert the input tokens into the goal symbol, then this is not
a syntactically valid statement of the language.*

To illustrate this idea, here is a three-rule grammar:

Number	Rule
1	<sentence> ::= <noun> <verb>.
2	<noun> ::= bees | dogs
3	<verb> ::= buzz | bite

The grammar contains five terminals: bees, dogs, buzz, bite, and the character "." (a period). It also contains three nonterminals: <sentence>, <noun>, and <verb>. The goal symbol is <sentence> because it is the one nonterminal that does not appear on the right-hand side of any other rule. In addition to the grammar, we also provide a sequence of tokens such as *dogs*, *bite*, and ".". The parser attempts to transform these tokens into the goal symbol <sentence> using the three BNF rules given above:

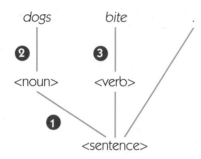

In this case, the parse was successful. (The numbers in the diagram indicate which rule is being applied.) Thus, "dogs bite." is a syntactically valid sentence of the language defined by this three-rule grammar. However, the following sequence of tokens:

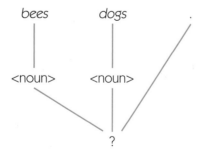

leads to a dead end. We have not yet produced the goal symbol <sentence>, but there is no rule in the grammar that can be applied to the sequence <noun> <noun> ".". That is, no sequence of terminals and nonterminals in the parse tree constructed so far matches the right-hand side of any rule. This means that "bees dogs." is not a valid sentence of this language.

Grammars for "real" high-level languages like C++, Python, or Java are very large, containing many hundreds of productions; therefore, it is not feasible to use these grammars as examples. Even a grammar describing individual statements can be quite complex. For example, the BNF description of an assignment statement, complete with variables, constants, operators, parentheses, and function calls, can easily require 20 or 30 rules. Therefore, the following examples all use highly simplified "toy" languages to keep the level of detail manageable and enable us to focus on important concepts.

Our first example is a grammar for a highly simplified assignment statement in which the only operator is +, numbers are not permitted, and the only allowable variable names are x, y, and z. A first attempt at designing a grammar for this simplified assignment statement is shown in Figure 11.4.

If the input statement is $x = y + z$, then the parser can determine that this statement is correctly formed because it can construct a parse tree (Figure 11.5). The parse tree of Figure 11.5 is the output of the parser, and it is the information that is passed on to the next stage in the compilation process.

FIGURE 11.4

Number	Rule
1	<assignment statement> ::= <variable> = <expression>
2	<expression> ::= <variable> | <variable> + <variable>
3	<variable> ::= x | y | z

First attempt at a grammar for a simplified assignment statement

FIGURE 11.5

Parse tree produced by the parser

Building a parse tree like the one in Figure 11.5 is not as easy as it may appear. Often two or more rules of a grammar may be applied to the current input string, and the parser is not sure which one to choose. For example, assume that our grammar includes the following two rules:

Number	Rule
1	<t1> ::= A B
2	<t2> ::= B C

and that the statement being parsed contains the three-character string … A B C …. We could apply either Rule 1:

or Rule 2:

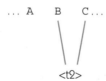

One of these choices might be correct, whereas the other might lead down a grammatical dead end, and the parser has no idea which is which.

You are probably not aware that a similar situation occurs in the example shown in Figure 11.5. Assume that the parser reaches this position in building the parse tree for the statement $x = y + z$:

In Figure 11.5, the parser next groups the three objects <variable>, +, and <variable> into an <expression> using Rule 2. However, at this point the parser has other options. For example, it could choose to parse the nonterminal <variable> generated from the symbol y to <expression> using Rule 2 and then parse the sequence <variable> = <expression> to <assignment statement> using Rule 1. This produces the parse tree shown on the next page.

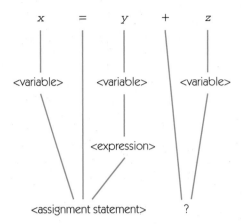

Unfortunately, this is the wrong choice. Although the parser does generate the goal symbol <assignment statement>, it does not use all of the tokens. An extra plus sign and <variable> are not used. (It accidentally parsed the assignment statement $x = y$ instead of $x = y + z$.) The parser has gone down the wrong path and reached a point where it is unable to continue. It must now go back to the point where it made the incorrect choice and try something else. For example, it might choose to parse the nonterminal <variable> generated from z to <expression> using Rule 2. Unfortunately, this is also a dead end; it produces the sequence <variable> + <expression>, which does not match the right-hand side of any rule.

The process of parsing is a complex sequence of applying rules, building grammatical constructs, seeing whether things are moving toward the correct answer (the goal symbol), and, if not, "undoing" the rule just applied and trying another. It is much like finding one's way through a maze. You try one path and if it works, fine. If not, you back up to where you made your last choice and try another, hoping that this time it will lead in the right direction.

This sounds like a haphazard and disorganized way to analyze statements, and in fact, it is. However, "real" parsing algorithms don't rely on a random selection of rules, as our previous discussion may have implied. Instead, they try to be a little more clever in their choices by looking ahead to see whether the rule they plan to apply will or will not help them to reach the goal. For example, assume we have the following input sequence:

A B C

and this grammar:

<goal> ::= <term> C
<term> ::= A B | B C

We have two choices on how to parse the input string. We can either group the two characters A B to form a <term>, or we can group B C instead. A random choice causes us to be wrong about half the time, but if a parser is clever and looks ahead, it can do a lot better. It is easy to see that grouping B C to produce the nonterminal <term> leads to trouble, because there is no rule telling us what to do with the sequence A <term>. We quickly come to a dead end:

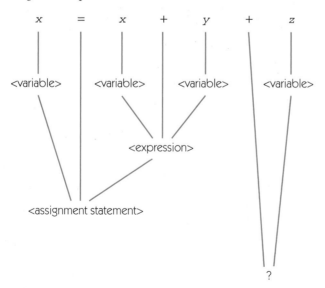

However, by choosing to group the tokens A B into <term> instead of B C, the parser quickly produces a correct parse tree:

There are many well-known look-ahead parsing algorithms that use the ideas just described. These algorithms "look down the road" a few tokens to see what would happen if a certain choice is made. This helps keep the parser moving in the right direction, and it significantly reduces the number of false starts and dead ends. These algorithms can do very efficient parsing, even for large languages with hundreds of rules.

There is another important issue in the design of grammars. Let's assume we attempt to parse the following assignment statement:

    x = x + y + z

using the grammar in Figure 11.4. No matter how hard we try to build a parse tree, it is just not possible:

All other attempts lead to a similar result.

The problem is that the grammar in Figure 11.4 does not correctly describe the desired language. We wanted a language that allowed expressions containing an *arbitrary number* of plus signs. However, the grammar of Figure 11.4 describes a language in which expressions may contain at most a single addition operator. More complicated expressions such as $x + y + z$ cannot be parsed, and they are erroneously excluded from our language.

One of the biggest problems in building a compiler for a programming language is designing a grammar that

- Includes every valid statement that we want to be in the language

- Excludes every invalid statement that we do not want to be in the language

In this case, a statement that should be a part of our language ($x = x + y + z$) was excluded. If this statement were contained in a program, the parser would not recognize it and the user would receive an error message for a statement that is not really in error. The grammar in Figure 11.4 is wrong in the sense that it does not define the language that we want.

Let's redo the grammar of Figure 11.4 so that it describes an assignment statement that allows expressions containing an arbitrary number of occurrences of the plus sign. That is, our language will include such statements as

```
x = x + y + z
x = x + y + x + y + x + z + z
```

This second attempt at a grammar is shown in Figure 11.6.

The grammar in Figure 11.6 does recognize and accept expressions with more than one plus sign. For example, here is a parse tree for the statement $x = x + y + z$:

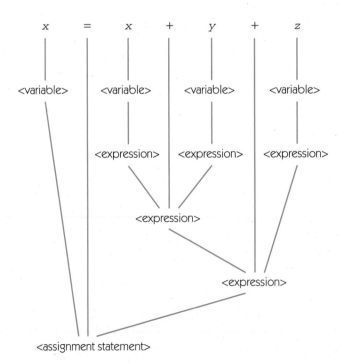

FIGURE 11.6

Number	Rule
1	<assignment statement> ::= <variable> = <expression>
2	<expression> ::= <variable> | <expression> + <expression>
3	<variable> ::= x | y | z

Second attempt at a grammar for assignment statements

Note that Rule 2 of Figure 11.6 uses the nonterminal <expression> on both the left-hand and the right-hand side of the same rule. In essence, the rule defines the nonterminal symbol <expression> in terms of itself. This is called a **recursive definition**, and its use is very common in BNF. It is recursion that allows us to describe an expression not just with one or two or three or ... plus signs but with an *arbitrary* and *unbounded* number, as shown here.

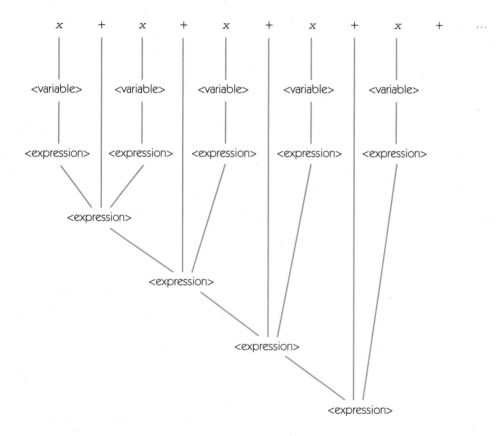

We have solved one problem: that of making sure our grammar defines a language that includes expressions with multiple addition operators. Unfortunately, though, one problem has disappeared, another has arisen, and the grammar of Figure 11.6 is still not quite correct. To demonstrate this new problem, let's take the same statement that we have been analyzing:

    x = x + y + z

and construct a second parse tree using the grammar of Figure 11.6. Both trees are shown in Figure 11.7.

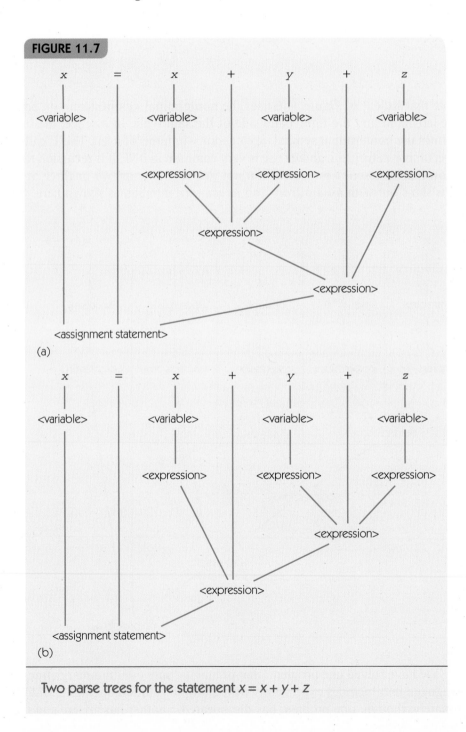

FIGURE 11.7

(a)

(b)

Two parse trees for the statement x = x + y + z

Using this assignment statement and the grammar in Figure 11.6, it is possible to construct *two* distinct parse trees. This might not seem to be a problem because the construction of a parse tree has been used only to demonstrate that a statement is correctly formed. Building two parse trees implies that the parser has demonstrated correctness in two different ways.

However, a parse tree not only serves to demonstrate that a statement is correct, it also assigns it a specific *meaning*, or *interpretation*. The next phase of compilation uses this parse tree to understand what a statement means, and it generates code on the basis of that meaning. The existence of two different parse trees implies two different interpretations of the same statement, which is disastrous. A grammar that allows the construction of two or more distinct parse trees for the same statement is said to be ambiguous.

This problem can occur in natural languages as well as programming languages. Consider the following ambiguous sentence:

I saw the man in the store with the dogs.

This sentence has two distinct meanings depending on how we choose to parse it:

Interpretation 1:	I saw the man in the *store* (with the dogs).
Meaning:	The man I viewed was in a pet store that sells dogs.
Interpretation 2:	I saw the *man* in the store (with the dogs).
Meaning:	The man I viewed was walking his dogs and was inside some type of store.

These two interpretations say very different things, so the sentence leaves us confused about what the speaker meant. In the areas of languages and grammars, ambiguity is decidedly not a desirable property.

The two parse trees shown in Figure 11.7 correspond to the following two interpretations of the assignment statement $x = x + y + z$.

$x = (x + y) + z$	(Do the operation $x + y$ first.)
$x = x + (y + z)$	(Do the operation $y + z$ first.)

Because addition is associative—that is, $(a + b) + c = a + (b + c)$—in this case the ambiguity does not cause a serious problem. However, if the statement were changed slightly to

$x = x - y - z$

then these two different interpretations lead to completely different results:

$x = (x - y) - z$	which evaluates to $x - y - z$
$x = x - (y - z)$	which evaluates to $x - y + z$

We now have a situation in which a statement could mean one thing using compiler C on machine M and something totally different using compiler C′ on machine M′, depending on which parse tree it happens to construct. This

FIGURE 11.8

FIGURE 11.8

Number	Rule
1	<assignment statement> ::= <variable> = <expression>
2	<expression> ::= <variable> | <expression> + <variable>
3	<variable> ::= x | y | z

Third attempt at a grammar for assignment statements

contradicts the spirit of machine independence, which is a basic characteristic of all high-level languages.

To solve the problem, the assignment statement grammar must be rewritten a third time so that it is no longer ambiguous. This new grammar is shown in Figure 11.8. To see that the grammar of Figure 11.8 is not ambiguous, try parsing the statement $x = x + y + z$ in the two ways shown in Figure 11.7. You will see that one of these two parse trees cannot be built.

Figure 11.9 shows the BNF grammar for a simplified version of an *if-else* statement that allows only a single assignment statement in the two separate clauses and allows the *else* clause to be omitted. The <Boolean expres­sion> can include at most a single use of the relational operators ==, <, and >. The nonterminal <assignment statement> is defined in the same way as in Figure 11.8. Figure 11.10 then shows the parse tree for the statement

```
if (x == y) x = z;   else x = y;
```

using the grammar of Figure 11.9.

Even though this *if-else* statement has been greatly simplified, its grammar still requires seven rules, and its parse trees can be quite "bushy." Grammars for real statements, not our toy ones, rapidly become large and complicated, and BNF grammars for programming languages like C++, Python, and Java contain many hundreds of productions.

FIGURE 11.9

Number	Rule
1	<if statement> ::= if (<Boolean expression>) <assignment statement> ; <else clause>
2	<Boolean expression> ::= <variable> | <variable> <relational> <variable>
3	<relational> ::= == | < | >
4	<variable> ::= x | y | z
5	<else clause> ::= else <assignment statement> ; | Λ
6	<assignment statement> ::= <variable> = <expression>
7	<expression> ::= <variable> | <expression> + <variable>

Grammar for a simplified version of an *if-else* statement

FIGURE 11.10

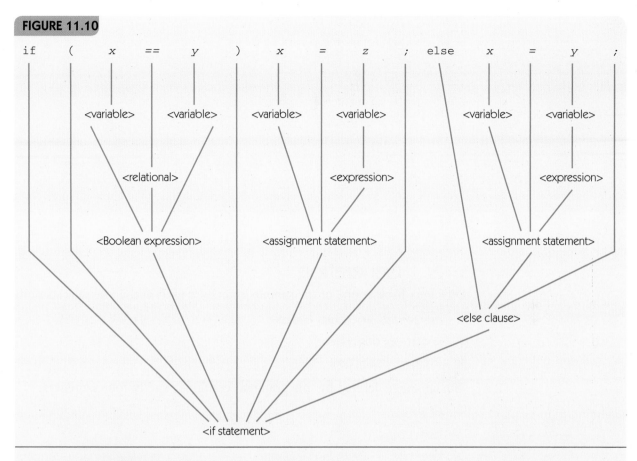

Parse tree for the statement if (x == y) x = z; else x = y;

Practice Problems

1. Using the grammar of Figure 11.8, show the parse tree for the assignment statement

   x = x + y

2. Using the grammar of Figure 11.8, show the parse tree for the assignment statement

   x = x + y + z

3. Using the grammar of Figure 11.9, show the parse tree for the statement

   if (x > y) x = y;

4. What language is described by the following pair of rules?

   <string> ::= <character> | <character> <string>
   <character> ::= a | b

   (Continued)

5. Write a BNF grammar that describes strings containing any number of repetitions of the character pair AB. That is, all of the following strings are part of the language: AB ABAB ABABAB ABABABABAB …

6. Is the following grammar ambiguous?

   <goal> ::= <left> <op> <right>

   <left> ::= a | b

   <op> ::= *

   <right> ::= c | d

11.2.3 Phase III: Semantics and Code Generation

Let's look back at one of the sample grammars used in the previous section:

   <sentence> ::= <noun> <verb> .

   <noun> ::= dogs | bees

   <verb> ::= bite | bark

The language defined by this grammar contains exactly four sentences:

   dogs bite.

   dogs bark.

   bees bite.

   bees bark.

For each of these four sentences, we can construct a parse tree showing that it is (structurally, at least) a valid sentence of the language:

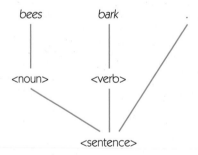

There is one problem, though. Although the sentence "bees bark." is structurally valid, it makes no sense whatsoever! During parsing, a compiler deals only with the *syntax* of a statement—that is, its grammatical structure. At that point, the only "correctness" that a compiler can determine is grammatical correctness with respect to the syntactical rules of the language. Another example of this limitation is the sentence, "The man bit the dog." This sentence is structurally correct, but its meaning is somewhat unusual!

The next phase of translation, during which a compiler examines the semantics of a programming language statement, deals with this issue. It analyzes the meaning of the tokens and tries to understand the *actions* they perform. If the statement is meaningless, as "bees bark." is, then it is semantically rejected, even though it is syntactically correct. If the statement is meaningful, then the compiler translates it into machine language.

It is easy to give examples of English-language sentences that are syntactically correct but semantically meaningless:

The orange artichoke flew through the elephant.

But what are semantically meaningless statements in high-level programming languages?

One possibility is the following assignment statement:

```
sum = a + b;
```

This is obviously correct syntactically, but what if the variables *sum*, *a*, and *b* are declared as follows:

```
char a;
double b;
int sum;
```

What does it mean to add a character to a real number? What would possibly be the result of adding the letter *Q* to 3.1416? In most cases, this operation has no meaning, and perhaps it should be rejected as semantically invalid.

To check for this semantic error, a compiler must look at the parse tree to see whether there is a branch that looks something like this:

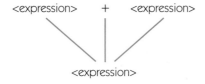

If there is such a branch, then the compiler must examine the data types of the two expressions to see whether they "make sense." That is, it must determine whether addition is defined for the data types of the two expressions.

The compiler does this by examining the semantic records associated with each nonterminal symbol in the grammar, such as <expression> and <variable>. A semantic record is a data structure that stores information about a nonterminal, such as the actual name of the object and its data type. For example, the nonterminal <variable> might have been constructed from the actual character variable named CH. This relationship is represented by a link between the nonterminal <variable> and a semantic record containing the name CH and its data type, char. Pictorially, we can represent this link as shown on the next page.

Semantic record

CH | char

Name   Data type

The initial semantic records in our parse tree are built by the compiler when it sees the declarations of new objects. Additional semantic records are constructed as the parse tree grows and new nonterminals are produced. Thus, a more realistic picture of the parse tree for the expression $a + b$ (assuming both are declared as integers) would look like this:

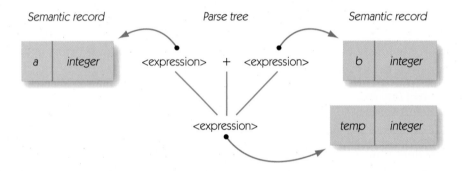

This parse tree says that we are adding two <expression>s that are integer variables named *a* and *b*. The result is an <expression> stored in the integer variable *temp*, a name picked by the compiler. Because addition is well defined for integers, this operation makes perfectly good sense, and the compiler can generate machine language instructions to carry out this addition. If, however, the parse tree and its associated semantic records looked like this:

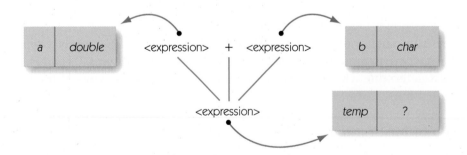

the compiler determines that this is not a meaningful operation because addition is not defined between a real number and a character. The compiler rejects this parse tree for semantic rather than syntactical reasons.

Thus, the first part of code generation involves a pass over the parse tree to determine whether all branches of the tree are semantically valid. If so, then the compiler can generate machine language instructions. If not, there is a semantic error, and generation of the machine language is suppressed because we do not want the processor to execute meaningless code. This step is called semantic analysis.

Following semantic analysis, the compiler makes a second pass over the parse tree, not to determine correctness but to produce the translated code. Each branch of the parse tree represents an action, a transformation of one or more grammatical objects into other grammatical objects. The compiler must determine how that transformation can be accomplished in machine language. This step is called code generation.

Let's work through the complete semantic analysis and code generation process using the parse tree for the assignment statement $x = y + z$, where x, y, and z are all integers. The example uses the instruction set shown in Chapter 6, Figure 6.5.

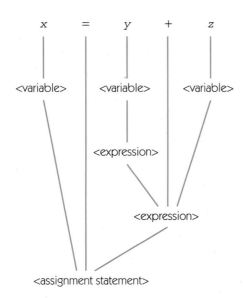

Typically, code generation begins at the productions in the tree that are nearest to the original input tokens. The compiler takes each production and, one branch at a time, translates that production into machine language operations or data generation pseudo-ops. For example, the following branch in the parse tree:

can be implemented by allocating space for the variable y using the .DATA pseudo-op

```
Y:     .DATA     0
```

In addition to generating this pseudo-op, the compiler must build the initial semantic record associated with the nonterminal <variable>. This semantic record contains, at a minimum, the name of this <variable>, which is *y*, and its data type, which is integer. (The data type information comes from the *int* declaration, which is not shown.) Here is what is produced after analyzing and translating the first branch of the parse tree:

Identical operations are done for the branches of the parse tree that produce the nonterminal <variable> from the symbols *x* and *z*, leading to the following situation:

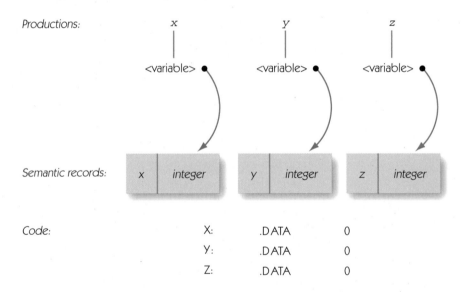

The production that transforms the nonterminal <variable> generated from *y* into the nonterminal <expression>

does not generate any machine language code. This branch of the tree is really just the renaming of a nonterminal to avoid the ambiguity problem discussed earlier. This demonstrates an important point: Although most branches of a parse tree produce code, some do not. Although no code is produced, the compiler must still create a semantic record for the new non-terminal <expression>. It is identical to the one built for the nonterminal <variable>.

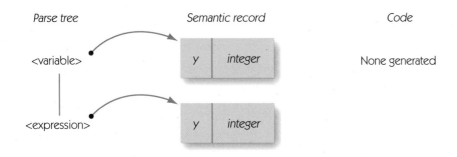

The branch of the parse tree that implements addition:

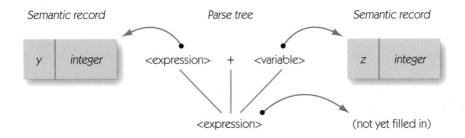

can be translated into machine language using the assembly language instruction set presented in Section 6.3.1. The compiler loads the value of <expression> into a register, adds the value of <variable>, and stores the resulting <expression> into a temporary memory location. This can be accomplished using the LOAD, ADD, and STORE operations in our instruction set. The names used in the address field of the instructions are determined by looking in the semantic records associated with the nonterminals <expression> and <variable>. The code generated by this branch of the parse tree is

```
LOAD      Y
ADD       Z
STORE     TEMP
```

TEMP is the name of a memory cell picked by the compiler to hold the result (Y + Z). Whenever the compiler creates one of these temporary variables, it must also remember to generate memory space for it using the DATA pseudo-op

```
TEMP:     .DATA     0
```

In addition, the compiler records the name (TEMP) and the data type (*integer*) of the result in the semantic record associated with this new nonterminal called <expression>. Here is what is produced by this branch of the parse tree:

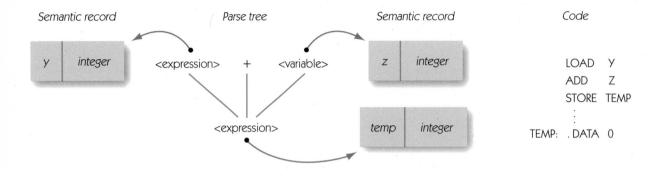

The final branch of the parse tree builds the nonterminal called <assignment statement>:

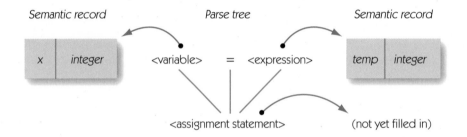

This production is translated into machine language by loading the value of the <expression> on the right-hand side of the assignment operator, using a LOAD instruction, and storing it, via a STORE operation, into the <variable> on the left-hand side of the assignment operator. Again, the names used in the address fields of the machine language instructions are obtained from the semantic records associated with <variable> and <expression>. The machine language code generated by this branch of the parse tree is

```
LOAD     TEMP
STORE    X
```

The compiler must also build the semantic record associated with the newly created nonterminal <assignment statement>. The name (*x*) and the data type (integer) of the variable on the left-hand side of the assignment operator are copied into that semantic record because the value stored in that variable is considered the value of the entire assignment statement.

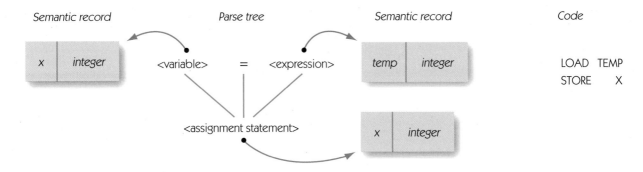

Our compiler has now analyzed every branch in the parse tree, and it has produced the following translation. (We have separated the pseudo-ops and executable instructions for clarity.)

```
        LOAD        Y
        ADD         Z
        STORE       TEMP
        LOAD        TEMP
        STORE       X

          .
          .
          .

X:      .DATA       0
Y:      .DATA       0
Z:      .DATA       0
TEMP:   .DATA       0
```

This is an exact translation of the assignment statement $x = y + z$.

Figure 11.11 shows the code generation process for the slightly more complex assignment statement $x = x + y + z$. The branches of the parse tree are labeled and referenced by comments in the code. (The parse tree was constructed using the grammar shown in Figure 11.8.)

The code of Figure 11.11 could represent the end of the compilation process because generating a correct machine language translation was our original goal. However, we are not quite finished. In the beginning of the chapter, we said that a compiler really has *two* goals: correctness and efficiency. The first goal has been achieved, but not necessarily the second. We have produced correct code, but not necessarily good code. Therefore, the next and final operation is *optimization*, where the compiler polishes and fine-tunes the translation so that it runs a little faster or occupies a little less memory.

FIGURE 11.11

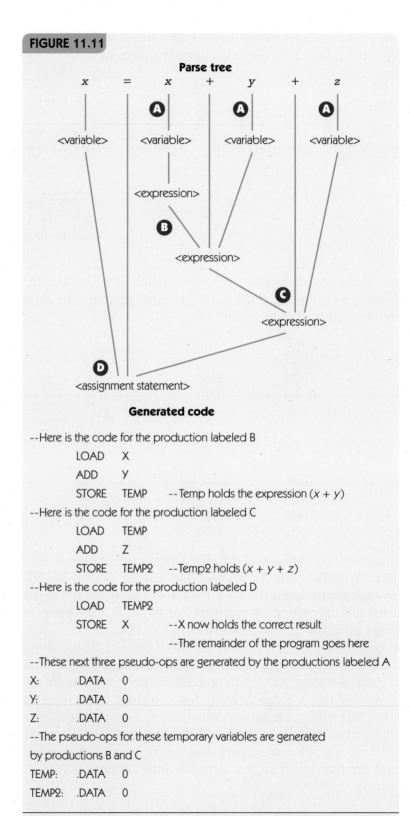

Parse tree

Generated code

```
--Here is the code for the production labeled B
        LOAD    X
        ADD     Y
        STORE   TEMP      --Temp holds the expression (x + y)
--Here is the code for the production labeled C
        LOAD    TEMP
        ADD     Z
        STORE   TEMP2     --Temp2 holds (x + y + z)
--Here is the code for the production labeled D
        LOAD    TEMP2
        STORE   X         --X now holds the correct result
                          --The remainder of the program goes here
--These next three pseudo-ops are generated by the productions labeled A
X:      .DATA   0
Y:      .DATA   0
Z:      .DATA   0
--The pseudo-ops for these temporary variables are generated
by productions B and C
TEMP:   .DATA   0
TEMP2:  .DATA   0
```

Code generation for the assignment statement $x = x + y + z$

Practice Problem

Go through the code generation process for the simple assignment statement $x = y$.
The parse tree for this statement is

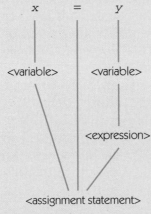

For each branch in the tree, show what semantic records are created and what code
is generated.

11.2.4 Phase IV: Code Optimization

As you learned in Chapter 10, the first high-level language and compiler was
FORTRAN, which appeared in 1957. (It was created by John Backus, the *B* of
*B*NF.) At that time, everyone programmed in assembly language because nothing else was available. Given all the shortcomings of assembly language, you
might think that programmers flocked to FORTRAN and thanked their lucky
stars that it was available. After all, it is certainly a lot easier to understand the
statement $a = b + c$ than the rather cryptic sequence LOAD B, ADD C, STORE A.

Laboratory Experience 15

In this Laboratory Experience, you will be able to observe how a compiler actually
translates a program written in the type of high-level statements you learned about in
Chapter 9. You will observe as a compiler carries out each of the phases of translation
described in the preceding sections. You can view the original source code, the
translated object code, and the symbol table produced by the compiler.

In fact, programmers did not accept this new language very quickly. The reason had nothing to do with the power and expressiveness of FORTRAN. Everyone admitted that it was far superior to assembly language in terms of clarity and ease of use. The problem had to do with *efficiency*—the ability to write highly optimized programs that contained no wasted microseconds or unnecessary memory cells.

In 1957 (early second-generation computing), computers were still enormously expensive; they typically cost millions of dollars. Therefore, programmers cared more about avoiding wasted computing resources than simplifying their job. The productivity of programmers earning $2.00/hour was unimportant compared with optimizing the use of a multimillion-dollar computer system. In 1957, the guiding principle was "Programmers are cheap, hardware is expensive!"

When programmers used assembly language, they were working on the actual machine, not the virtual machine created by the system software (and described in Chapters 6 and 7). They were free to choose the instructions that ran most quickly or used the least amount of memory. For example, if the INCREMENT, LOAD, and STORE instructions execute in 1 µsec, whereas an ADD takes 2 µsec, then translating the assignment statement $x = x + 3$ as

```
INCREMENT    X        -- x + 1   This takes 1 µsec
INCREMENT    X        -- x + 2   This takes 1 µsec
INCREMENT    X        -- x + 3   and this takes 1 µsec
```

requires 3 µsec to execute. This code runs 25% faster than if it had been translated as

```
LOAD      X        -- This takes 1 µsec
ADD       THREE    -- x + 3 This takes 2 µsec
STORE     X        -- and this takes 1 µsec
   .
   .
   .
THREE: .DATA    3
```

which takes 4 µsec to execute and requires an additional memory cell for the integer constant 3. When programmers wrote in assembly language, they were free to choose the first of these sequences rather than the second, knowing that it is faster and more compact. However, in a high-level language like FORTRAN, a programmer can only write $x = x + 3$ and hope that the compiler is "smart enough" to select the faster of the two implementations.

Because efficiency was so important to programmers of the 1950s and 1960s, these early first- and second-generation compilers spent a great deal of time doing code optimization. In fact, Backus himself did not regard language design as a difficult problem, but merely a prelude to the real problem: designing a compiler which could produce efficient programs. These compiler pioneers were quite successful in solving many of the problems of optimization, and early FORTRAN compilers produced object programs that ran nearly as fast as highly optimized assembly language code produced by top-notch programmers. After seeing these startling results, programmers of the 1950s and 1960s were eventually won over. They could gain the benefits of high-level languages—a powerful virtual environment—without loss of efficiency. The code optimization techniques developed by Backus and others were one of the most important reasons for the rapid acceptance of high-level programming languages during the early years of computer science.

However, conditions have changed dramatically since 1957. Because of impressive reductions in hardware costs, code optimization no longer plays the central role it did 50 or 60 years ago. Programmers rarely worry about saving a few memory cells when even an inexpensive laptop has 2–8 GB of memory. Similarly, as processor speeds increase to 1–10 Gflops (billions of floating-point instructions per second), removing a few instructions becomes much less important. For example, eliminating the execution of 1,000 unnecessary instructions saves only 0.000001 second on a 1 Gflop machine. Therefore, compilers are no longer judged solely on whether they produce highly optimized code.

Whereas hardware costs are dropping, programmer costs are rising dramatically. A powerful high-speed graphics workstation can be purchased for as little as $1,000, but the programmers developing software for that system may earn 75 to 150 times that in annual salary. The operational phrase of the twenty-first century is the exact opposite of what was true in the 1950s: "Hardware is cheap, people are expensive!" The goal in compiler design today is to provide a wide array of compiler tools that simplify the programmer's task and increase his or her productivity. This includes such tools as visual development environments that use graphics and video to let the programmer see what is happening, sophisticated online debuggers to help programmers locate and correct errors, and reusable *code libraries*, which contain a large collection of prewritten program units. When a compiler is embedded within a collection of supporting software development routines such as debuggers, editors, toolkits, and libraries, it is called an *integrated development environment (IDE)*. It is these types of programmer optimizations, rather than code optimizations, that have taken center stage in language and compiler design.

However, this does not mean that code optimization is no longer of any importance or that programmers will tolerate any level of code inefficiency. A little bit of effort by a compiler can often pay large dividends in reduced memory space and lower running time. Thus, optimization algorithms are still part of most compilers. Let's briefly survey what they do and how they help improve the finished product.

There are two types of optimization: local optimization and global optimization. The former is relatively easy and is included as part of most compilers. The latter is much more difficult, and it is usually omitted from all but the most sophisticated and expensive production-level *optimizing compilers*.

In local optimization, the compiler looks at a very small block of instructions, typically from one to five. It tries to determine how it can improve the efficiency of this local code block without regard for what instructions come before or after. It is as though the compiler has placed a tiny "window" over the code, and it optimizes only the instructions inside this optimization window:

```
        .
        .
        .
    instruction
   ┌─────────────┐
   │ instruction │
   │ instruction │    ←      The optimization window
   │ instruction │
   └─────────────┘
    instruction
        .
        .
        .
```

Here is a list of some possible local optimizations:

1. **Constant evaluation**—Arithmetic expressions are fully evaluated at compile time if possible, rather than at execution time.

   High-level statement: $x = 1 + 1;$

   Nonoptimized code: LOAD   ONE   *Optimized code:*   LOAD   TWO
                               ADD   ONE   STORE   X
                               STORE   X

2. **Strength reduction**—Slow arithmetic operations are replaced with faster ones. For example, on most computers increment is faster than addition, addition is faster than multiplication, which is faster than division. Whenever possible, the compiler replaces an operation with one that is equivalent but executes more quickly.

   High-level statement: $x = x * 2;$ // x times 2 is equivalent to $x + x$

   Nonoptimized code: LOAD   X   *Optimized code:*   LOAD   X
                             MULTIPLY TWO   ADD   X
                             STORE   X   STORE   X

3. **Eliminating unnecessary operations**—Instructions that are correct, but not necessary, are discarded. For example, because of the nondestructive read principle, when a value is stored from a register into memory, its value is still in the register, and it does not need to be reloaded. However, because the code generation phase translates each statement individually, there may be some unnecessary LOAD and STORE operations:

   High-level statement: $x = y;$
                              $z = x;$

   Nonoptimized code: LOAD Y   -- This is $x = y$ *Optimized code:*   LOAD   Y
                              STORE X   STORE   X
                              LOAD X   -- This is $z = x$ STORE   Z
                              STORE Z

The code in Figure 11.11 contains two opportunities for local optimizations:

- There are unnecessary LOAD and STORE operations. For example, the first four instructions in Figure 11.11 read

```
LOAD      X
ADD       Y
STORE     TEMP
LOAD      TEMP
```

The STORE and LOAD operations on Lines 3 and 4 are both unnecessary because the sum (X + Y) is still in register R.

- The code uses two memory cells called TEMP and TEMP2 to hold temporary values. Neither of these variables is needed.

Locally optimized code for the assignment statement $x = x + y + z$ is shown in Figure 11.12. It uses only 7 instructions and data generation pseudo-ops rather than the 13 of Figure 11.11, a savings of about 45%.

The second type of optimization is **global optimization**, and it is much more difficult. In global optimization, the compiler looks at large segments of the program, not just small pieces, to determine how to improve performance. The compiler examines large blocks of code such as *while* loops, *if* statements, and procedures to determine how to speed up execution. This is a much harder problem, both for a compiler and for a human programmer, but it can produce enormous savings in time and space. For example, earlier in the chapter we showed a loop that looked like this:

```
sum = 0.0;
i = 0;
while (i <= 50000) {
    sum = sum + (2.0 * x[i]);
    i = i + 1;
}
```

FIGURE 11.12

```
        LOAD      X
        ADD       Y
        ADD       Z
        STORE     X       --X now holds the correct result
          .
          .                 --The remainder of the program goes here
          .
X:      .DATA     0
Y:      .DATA     0
Z:      .DATA     0
```

Optimized code for the assignment statement $x = x + y + z$

"Now I Understand," Said the Machine

Chapter 6 showed that translating assembly language into machine language is relatively easy. This chapter demonstrated that translating high-level programming languages into machine language is more difficult, but it still can be done. What about the next step—the translation of natural languages such as English? If a computer could understand our spoken languages, then we could use them, rather than the formal languages studied in Chapters 9 and 10, to communicate.

Getting computers to understand and use natural language is a far more difficult problem than translating programming languages like Java and C++. In fact, for many years **natural language understanding** was viewed as the single most difficult research problem in computer science. Demonstrated success was always "just over the next hill," but for many years true natural language understanding remained an unattainable goal. This did not surprise researchers who were quick to point out that millions of years of evolution left virtually every animal except humans without sophisticated language capabilities. Many in computer science were pessimistic about the possibility of ever giving a computer true language understanding capabilities. However, that pessimism was shown to be unfounded when, in February 2011, a computer program called Watson, developed by artificial intelligence and natural language researchers at IBM, defeated two human players in a game of Jeopardy! The computer was presented with the exact same questions as the other contestants, Ken Jennings and Brad Rutter, the two most successful players in the game's history. Watson had to parse and understand natural language sentences that might include puns, similes, metaphors, and obscure pop culture references, then search its vast database to find the correct answer, and "buzz in" before either of the two human contestants. Watson won the game and the first place prize of $1 million. Following his loss at the hands of Watson, Ken Jennings said "Brad and I were the first knowledge-industry workers to be put out of work by this new generation of 'thinking' machine. 'Quiz show contestant' may be the first job made redundant by Watson, but I'm sure it won't be the last." IBM researchers continue to refine and improve the natural language and data access algorithms that were used on the TV show. The company sees a bright future in fields like medical diagnosis, business analytics, and tech support, which can be automated by question-answering software like Watson's.

By moving the multiplication operation outside the loop, it is possible to eliminate 49,999 unnecessary and time-consuming operations. A good optimizing compiler would analyze the entire loop and restructure it as follows:

```
sum = 0.0;
i = 0;
while (i <= 50000) {
    sum = sum + x[i];
    i  =  i + 1;
};
sum = sum * 2.0;
```

Such restructuring requires the ability to look at more than a few instructions at a time. The compiler cannot look at only a small "optimization window" but must be able to examine and analyze large segments of code. It requires a compiler that can see the "big picture," not just a small scene. Seeing this big picture is difficult, and many compilers are unable to do the type of global optimizations just discussed.

We close this section with one extremely important fact about code optimization: It *cannot* make an inefficient algorithm efficient. As we learned in Chapter 3, the efficiency of an algorithm is an inherent characteristic of its structure. It is not something programmed in by a programmer or optimized by a compiler. A sequential search program, written by a team of world-class programmers and optimized by the best compiler available, will not run as fast as a nonoptimized binary search program written by first-year computer science students. Code optimization should not be seen as a way to create fast, efficient programs. That goal is achieved when we decide which algorithm to use. Optimization is more like the "frosting on the cake," whereby we take a good algorithm and make it just a little bit better.

11.3 Conclusion

This chapter has touched on some of the many issues involved in compiler design. Topics such as syntax, grammars, parsing, semantics, and optimization are rich and complex, each worthy of an entire book rather than one brief chapter. In addition, there are topics not even mentioned here that play an important role in compiler design:

- Development environments and support tools
- Compilers for alternative languages, such as functional, object-oriented, or parallel languages
- Language standardization
- Top-down versus bottom-up parsing algorithms
- Error detection and recovery

The key point is that, unlike building the assemblers of Chapter 6, building a compiler is hard, and compilers for languages like C++, Python, and Java are large, complicated pieces of software. John Backus reported that the construction of the first FORTRAN compiler in 1957 required about 18 person-years of effort to design, code, and test. Even though we know much more today about how to build compilers, and numerous support tools are available to assist in this effort, it still requires a large team of programmers working months or years to build a correct and efficient compiler for a modern high-level programming language.

This chapter and the previous two chapters looked at the implementation phase of software development. They focused on the languages used to write programs and the methods used to translate programs into instructions that can be executed by the hardware. However, there are limits to computing. Chapter 12 will show that, no matter how powerful your hardware capabilities and no matter how sophisticated and expressive your programming language, there are some problems that simply cannot be solved algorithmically.

EXERCISES

1. Identify the tokens in each of the following statements. (You do not need to classify them; just identify them.)

   a. if (a == b1) a = x + y;
   b. delta = epsilon + 1.23 – sqrt(zz);
   c. print(Q);

2. Assume that we are working in a programming language that allows underscores (_) in variable names. When a scanner sees a character string such as AB_CD, is it more likely to classify this string as the single five-character token AB_CD or as three separate tokens: AB, _, CD? Explain your answer.

3. In some programming languages, a comment can be enclosed either in braces { } or in the symbols (* *). How do you think a scanner would group the four symbols {, }, (*, *) for purposes of classification? That is, would each symbol be given

   its own classification number or would some share classifications?

4. Using the token types and classification values given in Figure 11.3, show the output of a scanner when it is presented with each of the following statements:

   a. limit = begin + end
   b. a = b – 1;
   c. if (c == 50) x = 1; else y = x + 44;
   d. thenelse == error –

5. a. Write a BNF grammar that describes the structure of a nonterminal called <number>. Assume that <number> contains an optional + sign followed by exactly two decimal digits, the first of which cannot be a 0. Thus 23, +91, and +40 are legal, but 9, +01, and 123 are not.

   b. Using your grammar from Exercise 5a, show a parse tree for the value +90.

6. a. Write a BNF grammar that describes the structure of U.S. telephone numbers, which can be either (xxx)xxx-xxxx or xxx-xxxx, where x can be any digit from 0 to 9.

   b. Modify your grammar from Exercise 6a so that (1) the middle digit of an area code must be either a 0 or a 1, (2) the first digit of an area code cannot be a 0 or a 1, and (3) the first digit of the seven-digit phone number cannot be a 0 or a 1.

   c. Using your grammar from either Exercise 6a or 6b, show a parse tree for the phone number (612)555-1212.

7. a. Write a BNF grammar for identifiers that consist of an arbitrarily long string of letters and digits, the first one of which must be a letter.

   b. Using your grammar from Exercise 7a, show a parse tree for the identifier AB5C8.

8. Assume that we represent dollar amounts in the following way:

       $number.numberCR

   The dollar sign and the dollar value must be present. The cents part (including both the decimal point and the number) and the CR (which stands for CRedit and is how businesspeople represent negative numbers) are both optional, and *number* is a variable-length sequence of one or more decimal digits. Examples of legal dollar amounts include $995, $99CR, $199.95, and $500.000CR.

   a. Write a BNF grammar for the dollar amount just described.

   b. Modify your grammar so that the cents part is no longer an arbitrarily long sequence of digits but is exactly two digits, no more and no less.

   c. Using your grammar from either Exercise 8a or 8b, show a parse tree for $19.95CR.

9. Describe the language defined by the following grammar:

       <goal> ::= <letter> | <letter> <next>
       <next> ::= , <letter>
       <letter> ::= A

10. How does the language defined by the following grammar differ from the language defined by the grammar in Exercise 9?

        <goal> ::= <letter> | <letter> <next>
        <next> ::= , <letter> | <letter> <next>
        <letter> ::= A

11. a. Create a BNF grammar that describes simple Boolean expressions of the form

        var AND var
        var OR var

    where *var* is one of the symbols w, x, y, and z.

    b. Modify your grammar from Exercise 11a so that the Boolean expressions can be of the form

        expr AND expr
        expr OR expr

    where *expr* is either a simple variable (w, x, y, or z) or an expression of the form

        (var == var)   (var < var)   (var > var)

    c. Modify your grammar one more time to allow a Boolean expression to have an *arbitrary* number of terms connected by either AND or OR. That is, your expressions can be of the form

        expr AND expr OR expr OR expr AND expr....

12. Using the grammar of Figure 11.8, show a parse tree for the statement

        y = x + y + y + z

    Is your parse tree unique? If not, how many other parse trees exist for this statement? What does the existence of these different trees imply about the meaning of this assignment statement?

13. What is the language defined by the following pair of BNF rules?

        <number> ::= <digit> | <digit> <number>
        <digit> ::= 0 | 1

    Where have you seen this language before?

14. Write a BNF grammar that describes an arbitrarily long string of the characters a, b, and c. The string can contain any number of occurrences of these three letters (including none) in any order. The strings "empty", a, accaa, abcabccba, and bbbbb are all valid members of this language.

15. What are the different interpretations of the following English language sentence?

    I bought a shirt in the new store that was too large.

16. Write a BNF grammar to describe the following hypothetical input statement:

    ```
    input(var, var, … , var);
    ```

    The statement begins with the word *input*, followed by a left parenthesis, and then one or more variables, each variable separated from the one after it by a comma. The entire statement ends with a right parenthesis and a semicolon. Variable names are arbitrarily long strings of digits and letters, the first of which must be a letter.

17. Discuss what other information, in addition to name and data type, might be kept in a semantic record. From where would this other information come?

18. Referring to the parse tree in Figure 11.11, why is the production that appears to the left of the = sign in that figure not labeled with an A? Does this production generate any code?

19. Assume that our language specifically permits you to assign an integer value to a real variable. The compiler handles this *mixed mode* by generating code to perform data conversion from an integer to a real representation. Consider the following declarations:

    ```
    int x;
    double y;
    ```

    The assignment statement $y = x$ is legal in this language. Explain how a compiler handles the previous assignment statement. You do not have to show the exact code that would be generated; just describe how a compiler deals with the statement, and show at what point in the code generation process the compiler discovers that it needs to produce the data conversion instructions.

20. Explain how the concept of *algebraic identities* could be exploited during the code optimization phase of compilation. An algebraic identity is a relationship that is true for all values of the unknowns. For example,

    $$x + 0 = x \text{ for all values of } x.$$
    $$x * 0 = 0 \text{ for all values of } x.$$

    Describe other identities and explain how they could become part of the optimization phase. Is this considered local or global optimization?

21. Assume that we wrote the following pairs of assignment statements:

    $$\text{Delta} = 2.9 + (a + b + c * 3) / (x - 5.7);$$
    $$\text{Epsilon} = (a + b + c * 3) + \text{sqrt}(3.1 * y);$$

    How can a compiler optimize the execution of these two statements? Is this considered local or global optimization?

22. If we assume that all mathematical operations take 5 nsec (5 billionths of a second) to execute, how much time does your optimization from Exercise 21 actually save? What does this value say about the importance of compiler optimizations?

23. How do you think a compiler translates into machine language a branch in the parse tree that looks like the following?

Show the code that can be generated from this production and the semantic record created for the new nonterminal symbol <Boolean expression>.

CHALLENGE WORK

1. Our discussion on lexical analysis in Section 11.2.1 may lead you to believe that every lexical analyzer is unique and built "from scratch." In fact, it is quite rare to write a scanner when building a compiler for a new language because there exists a special program called a *scanner generator* that can, with the appropriate input, act as a "universal scanner" for any language. To use a scanner generator, we need to provide only a formal linguistic description of the tokens in our language and their classification. This description is input to the scanner generator, which then locates and classifies tokens according to the description provided. Thus, instead of writing a program called a scanner, you provide data to an already written program called a scanner generator.

One of the most widely used scanner generators is a program called *lex*, and it has been used to build dozens of compilers, assemblers, and other linguistic interfaces. Read about scanner generators in general and lex in particular. Find out how they work and the techniques for describing the structure and classification of tokens. Then show how you formally describe in lex the following token types:

a. Identifiers
b. Signed integers
c. Signed real numbers

If your installation has lex available, enter your formal descriptions and have lex locate tokens of each of these types.

2. The techniques described in Challenge Exercise 1 also work for the parsing phase of the compilation process. That is, instead of writing a parsing program, we can provide data to an already written program that will do the job for us. A special program called a *parser generator*, also called a *compiler-compiler*, can act as a universal parser for any language that can be described using BNF notation. To use a parser generator, you simply input the productions of the grammar of your language and the sequence of tokens to be parsed. The output of the parser generator is a parse tree if the sequence of tokens is legal according to your productions or an error message if it is not.

The most widely used parser generator is a program called *yacc*, an acronym for "Yet Another Compiler-Compiler." Yacc, like lex, has been used to build a great number of compilers. Read about parser generators and yacc, and write a report describing how yacc works and how you formally represent BNF productions. If you have yacc available at your installation, enter the BNF rules for <assignment statement> and let yacc parse the statement

```
x = y + z;
```

ADDITIONAL RESOURCES

 CourseMate **For additional print and/or online resources relevant to this chapter, visit the Computer Science CourseMate at login.cengagebrain.com.**

12.1 Introduction

The central topic of this book has been, in one way or another, algorithmic problem solving. We've discussed the concept of an algorithm, how to represent algorithms, the importance of their correctness and efficiency in solving problems, the hardware that executes algorithms, the various levels of abstraction in which a programmer deals with algorithms, and, finally, the system software that translates these abstractions back to the elementary hardware level. It might seem as though algorithms, and problems solvable by algorithms, represent the entire scope of the computer science universe.

However, *there are problems that do not have any algorithmic solution*! Be sure you understand why this is such a powerful statement. There are many problems for which no algorithmic solution has yet been found, but for which we might find one if we were only clever enough to discover it. Indeed, such new discoveries are being made all the time. But there are also problems for which no algorithmic solution exists; it does not matter how inventive we may be, how much time we spend looking, or how remarkable our hardware or software; *no algorithms will ever be found that solve these problems.*

We will prove this statement later in this chapter by actually finding such a problem. This is a rather difficult task because failing to find an algorithmic solution to a problem does not prove that one does not exist. It might only mean that we have not yet been able to figure out an algorithm. Instead, we must show that no one can ever find such an algorithm—that one does not exist.

Algorithms, as noted in Chapter 1, are carried out by computing agents (such as people, robots, computers). Throughout most of this book, we've assumed that the computing agent is a real computer. Ordinarily, we would choose to execute an algorithm on the most modern, high-speed computer available, with all the bells and whistles we could possibly find. But to show that something cannot be done by *any* computer, we want the bells and whistles to get out of the way so we can concentrate on the fundamental nature of "computerness." What we need is a simple, "ideal" computer—something easy to work with yet theoretically as powerful as the real thing. We need a *model* of a computer; indeed, to consider algorithms in general, we need a model of a computing agent.

12.2 What Is a Model?

Model cars, model trucks, model airplanes, and dolls (model people) are forever popular with children. Children use these toys to "play" at being grown up—at being drivers, pilots, and parents—because the toys capture the spirit of the objects they model. A model car looks like a car. The more expensive the model, the more realistic its features. But although the model captures the essence of a car, it is (usually) smaller in scale, omits many of the details of a real car, and does not have the full functionality of a real car.

Models are an important way of studying many physical and social phenomena. Weather systems, climate cycles, the spread of epidemics, population demographics, and chemical molecules—all are phenomena that have been studied via modeling. (In fact, we will look at some of these applications in Chapter 13.) Like a model car, a model of such a phenomenon

1. Captures the essence—the important properties—of the real thing

2. Probably differs in scale from the real thing

3. Omits some of the details of the real thing

4. Lacks the full functionality of the real thing

The model might be a physical model or a pencil-and-paper mathematical model. For example, a physical model of a chemical molecule might use Velcro®-covered balls stuck together in a certain way to represent the molecular structure. This model illustrates certain important properties: how many atoms of each element are present and where they are located in relation to one another. It is much larger than the real molecule, does not display the details of the chemical bonding, and is certainly not a real molecule. An alternative "physical" model—a computer visualization—is shown in Chapter 13, Figure 13.12.

A simple example of a mathematical model is the equation for the distance d that a moving vehicle travels as the product of rate r and time t:

$$d = r \times t$$

Although this equation can give approximate information, it ignores the variations in the speed of the vehicle by assuming that the rate is a constant. Because this is not a physical model, it does not have a size as such, but there is a difference in time scale from the actual moving vehicle. A calculation that a vehicle traveling at a constant rate of 60 miles per hour for 2 hours will cover a distance of 120 miles can be done in an instant by simply plugging values into the equation.

What can be gained by studying models if they do not behave in exactly the same way as the real thing? For one thing, they can enhance our understanding of the real system being modeled. By changing some aspect within the model, we can immediately see the effects of that change. These changes might be very costly, difficult, or dangerous to make in the real phenomena. The benefit is that models give us a safe and controlled environment to play with "what ifs"—what might be the effect if this or that factor in the real system were changed? The answers can be used to guide future decisions. Models can also provide environments for learning and practicing interactions with various phenomena. An aircraft flight simulator, for example, can give the trainee pilot realistic experience in a danger-free setting. Finally, not only can models give us information about existing phenomena, they can also be used as design tools. A model of a new design may reveal major flaws without the time, expense, and potential danger of building a prototype. (We will look more closely at these applications of models in Chapter 13.)

Whether a model is used to predict the behavior of an existing system or as a test bed for a proposed design, the information it provides is only as good as the assumptions made in building the model. If the model does not incorporate the major aspects of the system being studied, if relationships are represented incorrectly, or if so much detail has been omitted as to make the model a totally inaccurate representation, then little faith can be placed in the results it produces.

Practice Problems

1. Describe some situation (besides aircraft pilot training) in which a simulator would be useful as a training device.

2. What factors might a model of groundwater pollution need to include? What are the advantages of a good model? Are there potential disadvantages to using such a model?

12.3 A Model of a Computing Agent

12.3.1 Properties of a Computing Agent

To construct a good model of the "computing agent" entity—one that enables us to explore the capabilities and limitations of computation in the most general sense—we must make certain that we capture the fundamental properties of a computing agent while suppressing lower-level details. This means we must decide which features are central to a computing agent and which are relatively incidental and can be ignored. For example, a computing agent must be able to follow the instructions in an algorithm. The instructions must be presented in some form that makes sense to the computing agent, but it does not matter whether the instructions are presented in English or Japanese—or in words as opposed to pictures.

However the instructions are presented, the computing agent must be able to comprehend them. Likewise, the computing agent must be able to receive any data pertinent to the task. When we dealt with real computers, we described this as an input task, but the ability to accept input is central to any computing agent—whether a human being following instructions or a programmable DVR. The instructions and data must be stored somewhere during the execution of the algorithm. In addition, they must be retrievable, whether from a computer's memory, the DVR microprocessor's memory, a human being's memory, or a written sheet of paper to which the human being refers.

The computing agent must be able to act in accordance with algorithm instructions. These instructions may take into account the present situation or state of the computing agent, as well as the particular input item being processed. In a real computer, a conditional operation may say, "If condition A then do B else do C." Condition A may involve the value of some variable or variables that have already been read into memory; we may think of the contents of memory (i.e., how the various bits are set) as the present state of the computer. The DVR microprocessor may have an instruction that says, "If the time is 7:00 p.m. and I am programmed to record at 7:00 p.m., then turn on." Here the action of the DVR depends on both the input of the current time from its clock and the "state" of its programming, just as a human being carrying out the algorithm of ordering lunch from a menu reacts both to the "input" (what items are on the menu) and to his or her present state of hunger.

Finally, the computing agent is expected to produce output because the outcome of an algorithm must be an observable result. The computer displays results on a screen, prints them on a sheet of paper, or writes them to a file; the DVR records bits on a disc; the human being speaks or writes.

To summarize, we require that any computing agent be able to do all of the following:

1. Accept input.

2. Store information in and retrieve it from memory.

3. Take actions according to algorithm instructions; the choice of what action to take may depend on the present state of the computing agent, as well as on the input item presently being processed.

4. Produce output.

Of course, a real computer has all of these capabilities and is an example of a computing agent, as are a human being and a programmable DVR. The DVR, however, has a very limited set of primitive operations it can perform, so it can react only to a very limited algorithm. The computer, though it has a limited set of simple primitives, is a general-purpose computing agent because, as we have seen in the previous chapters, those primitives can be combined and organized to accomplish complex tasks. The "primitive operations" available to human beings haven't been fully explored, but in many ways they seem to exceed those of a computer, and we would certainly classify a human being as a general-purpose computing agent.

In the next section, we will discuss one particular model for a computing agent. It will have the four required properties just specified, and it will represent a general-purpose computing agent able to follow the instructions of many different algorithms.

12.3.2 The Turing Machine

We think of "computing" as a modern activity—something done by electronic computers. But interest in the theoretical nature of computation far predates the advent of modern computers. By the end of the nineteenth century, mathematicians were interested in formalizing the nature of proof, with two goals in mind. First, a formal basis for mathematical proofs would guarantee the correctness of a proof because the proof would contain no intuitive statements, such as "It is clear that ..." or "We can now see that ...". Second, a formal basis for proofs might allow for mechanical theorem-proving, where correct proofs could be generated simply by following a set of rules. In 1931, the Austrian logician Kurt Gödel looked at formal systems to describe the ordinary arithmetic of numbers. He demonstrated that in any reasonable system, there are true statements about arithmetic that cannot be proved using that system. This led to interest in finding a way to recognize which statements are indeed unprovable in a formal system—that is, in finding a computational procedure (what we have called an algorithm) to recognize such statements. This in turn led to an investigation of the nature of computation itself, and a number of mathematicians in the mid-1930s proposed various models of computational procedures, along with models of computing agents to carry out those procedures. We will look at the model proposed by Alan Turing.

A Turing machine includes a (conceptual) tape that extends infinitely in both directions. The tape is divided into cells, each of which contains one symbol. The symbols must come from a finite set of symbols called the tape alphabet. The alphabet for a given Turing machine always contains a

FIGURE 12.1

.	.	.	b	b	0	1	1	b	b	.	.	.

A Turing machine tape

special symbol *b* (for "blank"), usually both of the symbols 0 and 1 (zero and one), and sometimes a limited number of other symbols, let's say *X* and *Y*, used as placeholders or markers of some kind. At any point in time, only a finite number of the cells contain nonblank symbols. Figure 12.1 shows a typical tape configuration, with three nonblank cells containing the alphabet symbols 0, 1, 1, respectively.

The tape is used to hold the input to the Turing machine. We know that input must be presented to a computing agent in a form it can understand; for a Turing machine, this means that the input must be expressed as a finite string of nonblank symbols from the alphabet. The Turing machine writes its output on the tape, again using the same alphabet of symbols. The tape also serves as memory.

The rest of the Turing machine consists of a unit that reads one cell of the tape at a time and writes a symbol in that cell. There is a finite number *k* of "states" of the machine, labeled 1, 2, ... , *k*, and at any moment the unit is in one of these states. A state can be thought of as a certain condition; the Turing machine may reach this condition partly on the basis of its history of events, much as your "hungry state" is a condition reached because of the meals you have skipped recently.

Figure 12.2 shows a particular Turing machine configuration. Using the tape of Figure 12.1, the machine is currently in state 1 and is reading the cell containing the symbol 0, so the 0 is what the machine is seeing as the current input symbol.

FIGURE 12.2

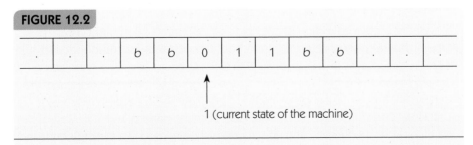

.	.	.	b	b	0	1	1	b	b	.	.	.

1 (current state of the machine)

A Turing machine configuration

Alan Turing, Brilliant Eccentric

The Turing machine was proposed as a model for a computing agent by the brilliant British mathematician Alan Turing in 1936. Turing began by thinking of how to generalize the typewriter as an "automatic device." But despite its name, the Turing machine is not a machine at all. It is a model of the pencil-and-paper type that captures the essential features of a computing agent.

Alan Turing (1912–1954) was a colorful individual and a brilliant thinker. Stories abound about his "absentminded professor" demeanor, his interest in running (through the streets of London with an alarm clock flopping about, tied to his belt by a piece of twine), and his fascination with a children's radio show whose characters he would discuss daily with his mother. Convicted of homosexual acts in 1952, he chose drug treatment over prison, primarily because he feared a prison term would impede his intellectual work. There was even a Broadway play (*Breaking the Code*) written about him, years after his death by suicide.

Turing made three distinct and remarkable contributions to computer science. First, he devised what is now known as the Turing machine, using it—as we will see in this chapter—to model computation and to discover that some problems have no general computable solution. Second, during World War II, his team at the British Foreign Office built the Colossus machine, which used cryptanalysis, the science of code breaking, to break the secret code used on the German Enigma machine. The details of this work, carried on in a Victorian country mansion called Bletchley Park, were kept secret until many years later. Breaking the code enabled the British to gain access to intelligence about German submarine movements, which contributed significantly toward winning the war. Third, after the war Turing investigated what it means for machines to "think." We'll discuss his early contribution to *artificial intelligence* in Chapter 15.

In November 2010, a collection of offprints of 15 of Turing's 18 published papers (including his first published paper, as well as his initial plans for computing and artificial intelligence) was put up for auction at the famous Christie's auction house. Bids failed to reach the minimum set price, which bought time for supporters of the Bletchley Park Trust to raise enough money to purchase the collection (aided by a gift of $100,000 from Google and a large grant from the National Heritage Memorial Fund of the United Kingdom). The documents will be housed in a climate-controlled, secure area at Bletchley Park and will be available for public display.

The Turing machine is designed to carry out only one type of primitive operation. Each time such an operation is done, three actions take place:

1. Write a symbol in the cell (replacing the symbol already there).

2. Go into a new state (it might be the same as the current state).

3. Move one cell left or right.

The details of the actions (what to write, what the new state is, and which direction to move) depend on the current state of the machine and on the contents of the tape cell currently being read (the input). Turing machine instructions describe these details. Each instruction tells what to do for a specific current state and current input symbol, as follows:

> if (you are in state *i*) and (you are reading symbol *j*) then
>> write symbol *k* onto the tape
>>
>> go into state *s*
>>
>> move in direction *d*

The Turing machine's single primitive operation is to check its current state and the current input symbol being read, look for an instruction that tells what to do under these circumstances, and then carry out the three actions specified by that instruction. For example, one Turing machine instruction might say

> if (you are in state 1) and (you are reading symbol 0) then
>> write symbol 1 onto the tape
>>
>> go into state 2
>>
>> move right

If a Turing machine is in the configuration shown in Figure 12.2 (where the current state is 1 and the current input symbol is 0), then this instruction applies. After the machine executes this instruction, its next configuration is shown in Figure 12.3, where the previous 0 symbol has been overwritten with a 1, the state has changed to state 2, and the "read head" has moved one cell to the right on the tape.

FIGURE 12.3

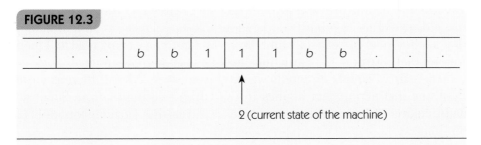

2 (current state of the machine)

The next Turing machine configuration after executing one instruction

Let's develop a shorthand notation for Turing machine instructions. There are five components:

- Current state
- Current symbol
- Next symbol
- Next state
- Direction of move

We'll give these five things in order and enclosed in parentheses.

(current state, current symbol, next symbol, next state, direction of move)

The instruction that we talked about earlier,

if (you are in state 1) and (you are reading symbol 0) then

write symbol 1 onto the tape

go into state 2

move right

is therefore represented by the 5-tuple:

(1,0,1,2,*R*)

Similarly, the Turing machine instruction

(2,1,1,2,*L*)

stands for

if (you are in state 2) and (you are reading symbol 1) then

write symbol 1 onto the tape

go into state 2

move left

In following this instruction, the machine writes in the current cell the same symbol (1) as was already there and remains in the same state (state 2) as before.

A Turing machine can execute a whole sequence of instructions. A clock governs the action of the machine. Whenever the clock ticks, the Turing machine performs its primitive operation; that is, it looks for an instruction that applies to its current state and the symbol currently being read and then follows that instruction. Instructions may be used more than once.

There are a couple of details we've glossed over. What if there is more than one instruction that applies to the current configuration? Suppose, as in Figure 12.2, that the current state is 1, that the current symbol is 0, and that

(1,0,1,2,*R*)

(1,0,0,3,*L*)

both appear in the same collection of instructions. These instructions are in conflict. Should the Turing machine write a 1, go to state 2, and move right, or should it write a 0, go to state 3, and move left? We'll avoid this ambiguity by requiring that a set of instructions for a Turing machine can never contain two different instructions of the form

$(i, j, -, -, -)$

$(i, j, -, - , -)$

On the other hand, what if there is no instruction that applies to the current state and current symbol for the machine? In this case, we specify that the machine halts, doing nothing further.

We impose two additional conventions on the Turing machine regarding its initial configuration when the clock begins. The start-up state is always state 1, and the machine is always reading the leftmost nonblank cell on the tape. This ensures that the Turing machine has a fixed and definite starting point.

Now let's do a sample Turing machine computation. Suppose the instructions available to a Turing machine are

1. $(1,0,1,2,R)$

2. $(1,1,1,2,R)$

3. $(2,0,1,2,R)$

4. $(2,1,0,2,R)$

5. $(2,b,b,3,L)$

Also suppose the Turing machine's initial configuration is again that of Figure 12.2, reprinted here:

This satisfies our convention about starting in state 1 at the leftmost nonblank cell on the tape. The Turing machine looks for an appropriate instruction for its current state, 1, and its current input symbol, 0, which means it looks for an instruction of the form $(1,0,-,-,-)$. Instruction 1 applies; this was our sample instruction earlier, and the resulting configuration agrees with Figure 12.3:

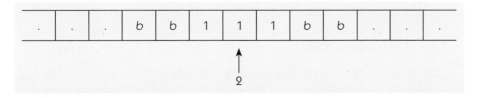

At the next clock tick, with current state 2 and current symbol 1, the Turing machine looks for an instruction of the form (2,1,–,–,–). Instruction 4 applies and, after the appropriate actions are performed, the resulting configuration is

Instruction 4 applies again and results in

Instruction 5 now applies, leading to

At this point, the machine is in state 3 reading the symbol 0. Because there are no instructions of the form (3,0,–,–,–), the machine halts. The Turing machine computation is complete.

Although we numbered this collection of instructions for reference, the Turing machine does not necessarily execute instructions in the order of this numbering. Some instructions may not be executed at all, and some more than once. The sequence of instructions used depends on the input written on the tape.

How does the Turing machine stack up against our list of required features for a computing agent?

1. *It can accept input*–The Turing machine can read symbols on its tape.

2. *It can store information in and retrieve it from memory*–The Turing machine can write symbols on its tape and, by moving around over the tape, can go back and read those symbols at a later time, so the tape has stored that information.

3. *It can take actions according to algorithm instructions, and the choice of action to take may depend on the present state of the computing agent*

and on the input item presently being processed—Certainly the Turing machine satisfies this requirement insofar as Turing machine instructions are concerned; the present state and present symbol being processed determine the appropriate instruction, and that instruction specifies the actions to be taken.

4. *It can produce output*—The Turing machine writes symbols on its tape in the course of its normal operation. If (when?) the Turing machine halts, what is written on the tape at that time can be considered output.

In the Turing machine computation that we just finished, the input was the string of symbols 011 (ignoring the surrounding blanks) and the output was the string of symbols 100. Starting with the same input tape but with a different set of instructions could result in different output. Given the benefit of hindsight, we could say that we wrote this particular set of instructions to carry out the task of transforming the string 011 into the string 100. Writing a set of Turing machine instructions to allow a Turing machine to carry out a certain task is similar to writing a computer program to allow a computer to carry out a certain task. We can call such a collection of instructions a Turing machine program.

Thus, a Turing machine does capture those properties we identified as essential for a computing agent, which qualifies it as a model of a computing agent. Furthermore, it represents a general computing agent in the sense that, like a real computer, it can follow many different sets of instructions (programs) and thus do many different things (unlike the one-job-only DVR). By its very simplicity of operation, it has eliminated many real-world details, such as exactly how symbols are read from or written to the tape, exactly how data are to be encoded into a string of symbols from the alphabet to be written on the tape, exactly how a string of symbols on the tape is to be interpreted as meaningful output, and exactly how the machine carries out the activities of "changing state." In fact, the Turing machine is such a simple concept that we may wonder how good a model it really is. Did we eliminate too many details? We'll answer the question of how good a model the Turing machine is later in the chapter.

A Turing machine is different in scale from any real computing agent in one respect. A Turing machine can, given the appropriate instructions, move right or left to the blank portion of the tape and write a nonblank symbol. When this happens, the machine has gobbled up an extra cell to use for information storage purposes—that is, as memory. Depending on the instructions, this could happen over and over, which means that there is *no limit* to the amount of memory available to the machine. Any real computing agent has a limit on the memory available to it. In particular, a real computer, though it has a certain amount of internal memory and has access to external memory in the form of disks or tapes on which data can be stored, still has such a limit. There are only so many disks or tapes in the world.

This difference in scale means that a Turing machine (elementary device though it may seem to be) actually has more capability in one respect than any real computer that exists or ever will exist. Therefore, we must be careful about the use of the Turing machine model and the conclusions we draw from it about "real" computing (i.e., computing on a real computer). If we find some task that a Turing machine can perform (because of its limitless memory), it *may* not be a task that a real computer could perform.

Practice Problems

1. Given the Turing machine instruction (2,b,1,3,L) and the configuration

.	.	b	1	1	b	b	.	.

↑
2

draw the next configuration.

2. A Turing machine has the following instructions:

(1,0,0,2,R)

(2,1,1,2,L)

(2,0,1,2,R)

(1,b,1,1,L)

For each of the following configurations of this Turing machine, draw the next configuration.

a.

.	.	b	1	0	1	b	.	.

↑
1

b.

.	.	b	1	1	1	b	.	.

↑
2

c.

.	.	b	1	0	1	b	.	.

↑
2

d.

.	.	b	0	1	1	b	.	.

↑
1

3. Consider a Turing machine that has the following two instructions:

   (1,1,0,2,R)

   (2,1,1,1,R)

   Determine its output when it is run on the following tape. (Remember that a Turing machine starts in state 1, reading the leftmost nonblank cell.)

12.4 A Model of an Algorithm

An algorithm is a collection of instructions intended for a computing agent to follow. If we accept the Turing machine as a model of a computing agent, then the instructions for a Turing machine should be a model of an algorithm. Remember from our definition in Chapter 1 that an algorithm must

1. Be a well-ordered collection

2. Consist of unambiguous and effectively computable operations

3. Halt in a finite amount of time

4. Produce a result

Let's consider an arbitrary collection of Turing machine instructions and see whether it exhibits these properties of an algorithm.

1. *Be a well-ordered collection*—The Turing machine must know which operation to carry out first and which to do next at any step. We have already specified the initial conditions for a Turing machine computation: that the Turing machine must begin in state 1, reading the leftmost nonblank cell on the tape. We have also insisted that in any collection of Turing machine instructions, there cannot be two different instructions that both begin with the same current state and current symbol. Given this requirement, there is never any confusion about which operation to do next. There is *at most* one instruction that matches the current state and current symbol of the Turing machine. If there is one instruction, the Turing machine executes the operation that instruction describes. If there is no instruction, the Turing machine halts.

2. *Consist of unambiguous and effectively computable operations*—Recall that this property is *relative to the computing agent*; that is, operations must be understandable and doable by the computing agent. Each individual Turing machine instruction describes an operation that (to the Turing machine) is unambiguous, requiring no additional explanation,

and any Turing machine is able to carry out the operation described. After all, Turing machine instructions were designed for Turing machines to be able to execute.

3. *Halt in a finite amount of time*—For a Turing machine to halt when executing a collection of instructions, it must reach a configuration where no appropriate instruction exists. This depends on the input given to the Turing machine—that is, the contents initially written on the tape. Consider the following set of Turing machine instructions:

$(1,0,0,1,R)$

$(1,b,b,1,R)$

and suppose the tape initially contains, as its nonblank portion, the single symbol 1. The initial configuration is

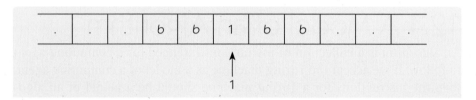

and the machine halts immediately because there is no applicable instruction. On the other hand, suppose the same set of instructions is used with a starting tape that contains the single symbol 0. The Turing machine computation is then

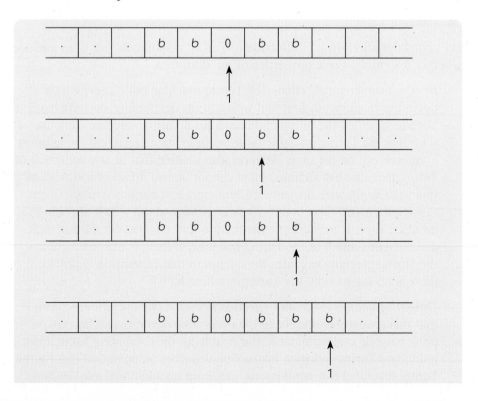

We can see that the second instruction applies indefinitely and that this Turing machine will never halt.

Typically, an algorithm is designed to carry out a certain type of task. Let us agree that *for input appropriate to that task*, the instructions must be such that the Turing machine does indeed eventually halt. If the Turing machine is run on a tape containing data that are not appropriate input for the task of interest, it need not halt.

This may seem to be a change in our definition of an algorithm, but it simply confirms that there is always a "universe of discourse" connected with the problem we are trying to solve. For example, we can use a simple algorithm for dividing one positive integer by another using repeated subtraction until the result is negative. Thus, $7 \div 3$ can be computed using this algorithm as follows:

$$7 - 3 = 4$$
$$4 - 3 = 1$$
$$1 - 3 < 0$$

The quotient is 2 because two subtractions could be done before the result became negative. However, if we attempt to use this same approach to compute $7 \div (-3)$, we get

$$7 - (-3) = 10$$
$$10 - (-3) = 13$$
$$13 - (-3) = 16$$
$$16 - (-3) = 19$$

and so on.

The process would never halt because the result would never become negative. Yet, this approach is still an algorithm *for the problem of dividing two positive numbers* because it does produce the correct result and then halt when given input suitable for this problem.

4. *Produce a result*—We have already imposed the requirement that the Turing machine instructions must lead to a halting configuration when executed on input appropriate to the problem being solved. Whatever is written on the tape when the machine halts is the result.

A collection of Turing machine instructions that obeys the restrictions we have specified satisfies the properties required of an algorithm. Yet, it is not a "real" algorithm because it is not designed to be executed by a "real" computing agent. It is a model of an algorithm, designed to be executed by the model computing agent called a Turing machine.

Most of the time, no distinction is made between a Turing machine as a computing agent and the instructions (algorithm) it carries out—a machine together with a set of instructions is called "a Turing machine" and is thought of as an algorithm. Thus, we say we are going to write a Turing machine to do a particular task, when we really mean that we are going to write a set of instructions—a Turing machine program, an algorithm—to do that task.

12.5 Turing Machine Examples

Because the Turing machine is such a simple device, it may seem nearly impossible to write a program for a Turing machine that carries out any interesting or significant task. In this section, we look at a few Turing machines that, though they do not accomplish anything earthshaking, should convince you that Turing machines can do some rather worthwhile things.

12.5.1 A Bit Inverter

Let's assume that the only nonblank portion of the input tape for a particular Turing machine consists of a string of bits (0s and 1s). Our first Turing machine moves along its tape inverting all of the bits—that is, changing 0s to 1s and 1s to 0s. (Recall that our sample Turing machine computation inverted the bits in the string 011, resulting in the string 100. Do you think that machine is a bit inverter? What if the leftmost nonblank symbol on the input tape is a 1?)

The Turing machine must begin in state 1 on the leftmost nonblank cell. Whatever the current symbol that is read, the machine must invert it by printing its opposite. Machine state 1 must, therefore, be a state in which 0s are changed to 1s and 1s are changed to 0s. This is exactly what we want to happen everywhere along the tape, so the machine never needs to go to another state; it can simply move right while remaining in state 1. When we come to the final blank, we want to halt. This can be accomplished by making sure that our program does not contain any instruction of the form

$$(1,b,-,-,-)$$

This describes the Turing machine algorithm in words, but let's represent it more precisely. In the past, we've used pseudocode to describe algorithms. Here we'll use an alternative form of representation that corresponds more closely to Turing machine instructions. A state diagram is a visual representation of a Turing machine algorithm, where circles represent states, and arrows represent transitions from one state to another. Along each transition arrow, we show three things: the input symbol that caused the transition, the corresponding output symbol to be printed, and the direction of movement. For the bit inverter Turing machine, we have only one state and hence one circle in the state diagram, shown in Figure 12.4.

FIGURE 12.4

State diagram for the bit inverter machine

The arrow originating in and returning to state 1 marked 1/0/R says that when in state 1 (the only state) reading an input symbol of 1, the machine should print the symbol 0, move right, and remain in state 1. The arrow marked 0/1/R says that when in state 1 reading an input symbol of 0, the machine should print the symbol 1, move right, and remain in state 1.

The complete Turing machine program for the bit inverter is

1. $(1,0,1,1,R)$ Change the symbol 0 to 1.

2. $(1,1,0,1,R)$ Change the symbol 1 to 0.

(We've added a comment to each instruction to explain its purpose.) Here's a sample computation using this machine, beginning with the string 1101 on the tape:

Using instruction 2,

Using instruction 2 again,

Using instruction 1,

Using instruction 2,

and the machine halts with the inverted string 0010 as output on the tape.

Bit inversion might seem like a trivial task, but recall that in Chapter 4 we introduced an electronic device called a NOT gate that is essentially a bit inverter and is one of the components of a real computer.

12.5.2 A Parity Bit Machine

An extra bit, called an *odd parity bit*, can be attached to the end of a string of bits. The odd parity bit is set such that the number of 1s in the whole string of bits, including the parity bit, is odd. Thus, if the string preceding the parity bit has an odd number of 1s, the parity bit is set to 0 so that there is still an odd number of 1s in the whole string. If the string preceding the parity bit has an even number of 1s, the parity bit is set to 1 so that the number of 1s in the whole string is odd. As an example, the following string of bits includes as its rightmost bit an odd parity bit:

    1100010101

The parity bit is set to 1 because there are four 1s (an even number) in the string before the parity bit; the total number of 1s is five (an odd number). Another example of odd parity is the string

    101100

Practice Problems

1. Is the Turing machine shown here equivalent to the one shown in Figure 12.4? Why or why not?

2. Explain exactly what would happen to the Turing machine of Practice Problem 1 if it were given a completely blank tape as input.

where the parity bit (the rightmost bit) is a 0 because three 1s (an odd number) appear in the preceding string. Our job here is to write a Turing machine that, given a string of bits on its input tape, attaches an odd parity bit at the right end.

We know from Chapter 4 that information in electronic form is represented as strings of bits. Parity bits are used to detect errors that occur as a result of electronic interference when transmitting such strings (see Exercise 25, Chapter 4). If a single bit (or any odd number of bits) is changed from a 1 to 0 or from a 0 to 1, then the parity bit is incorrect, and the error can be detected. A correct copy of the information can then be retransmitted. Again, we are devising a Turing machine for a significant real-world task.

Our Turing machine must somehow "remember" whether the number of 1s so far processed is even or odd. We can use two states of the machine to represent these two conditions. Because the Turing machine begins in state 1, having read zero 1s so far (zero is an even number), we can let state 1 represent the even parity state, where an even number of 1s has been read so far. We'll let state 2 represent the odd parity state, where an odd number of 1s has been read so far.

We can read the input string from left to right. Until we get to the end of the bit string, the symbol printed should always be the same as the symbol read because none of the bits in the input string should change. But every time a 1 bit is read, the parity should change, from even to odd or from odd to even. In other words, the state should change from 1 to 2 or from 2 to 1. Reading a 0 bit does not affect the parity and therefore should not change the state. Thus, if we are in state 1 reading a 1, we want to go to state 2; if we are in state 1 reading a 0, we want to stay in state 1. If we are in state 2 reading a 1, we want to go to state 1; if we are in state 2 reading a 0, we want to stay in state 2.

When we come to the end of the input string (when we first read a blank cell), we write the parity bit, which is 1 if the machine is in state 1 (the even parity state) or 0 if the machine is in state 2 (the odd parity state). Then we want to halt, which is accomplished by going into state 3, for which there are no instructions. The state diagram for our parity bit machine is given in Figure 12.5.

The Turing machine program is as follows:

1. $(1,1,1,2,R)$ Even parity state reading 1, change state.

2. $(1,0,0,1,R)$ Even parity state reading 0, don't change state.

3. $(2,1,1,1,R)$ Odd parity state reading 1, change state.

4. $(2,0,0,2,R)$ Odd parity state reading 0, don't change state.

5. $(1,b,1,3,R)$ End of string in even parity state, write 1 and go to state 3.

6. $(2,b,0,3,R)$ End of string in odd parity state, write 0 and go to state 3.

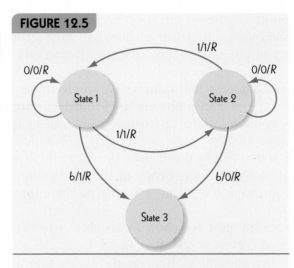

FIGURE 12.5

State diagram for the parity bit machine

Let's do an example. The initial string is 101, which contains an even number of 1s. Therefore, we want to add a parity bit of 1 and have the final output be the string 1011. Because this final string contains three 1 bits, it has the correct parity. Here's the initial configuration:

Using instruction 1,

Using instruction 4,

Using instruction 3,

and finally using instruction 5 to write the parity bit, we get

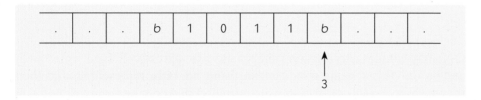

whereupon the machine halts.

12.5.3 Machines for Unary Incrementing

Turing machines can be written to accomplish arithmetic using the non-negative numbers 0, 1, 2, and so on. Working with these numbers poses a problem we did not face with the bit inverter or the parity bit machine. In those examples, we were manipulating only bits (i.e., 0s and 1s), already part of the Turing machine alphabet of symbols. We can't put numbers like 2, 6, or 754 in cells of the Turing machine tape because these symbols are

Practice Problem

1. a. What should the output be when the parity bit Turing machine is run on the following input?

   ... b11101b...

   b. Now run the parity bit Turing machine on this tape and see whether you get the answer you expected from Practice Problem 1a.

not part of the alphabet. Therefore, our first task is to find a way to encode such numbers using 0s and 1s. We could use binary representation, as a real computer does. Instead, let us agree on a simpler **unary representation** of numbers (*unary* means that we will use only *one* symbol, namely 1). In unary representation, any unsigned whole number n is encoded by a sequence of $n + 1$ 1s. Thus,

Number	Turing Machine Representation
0	1
1	11
2	111
3	1111
.	.
.	.
.	.

(You may wonder why we don't simply use 1 to represent 1, 11 to represent 2, and so on. This scheme would mean using no 1s to represent 0, and then the machine could not distinguish a single 0 on the tape from nothing—all blanks—on the tape.)

Using this unary representation of numbers, let's write Turing machines to accomplish some basic arithmetic operations. We can write a Turing machine to add 1 to any number; such a machine is often called an *incrementer*. Using the unary representation of numbers just described, we need only stay in state 1 and travel over the string of 1s to the right-hand end. When we encounter the first blank cell, we write a 1 in it and go to state 2, which has no instructions, in order to halt. Figure 12.6 shows the state diagram.

The Turing machine for the incrementer is

1. $(1,1,1,1,R)$ Pass to the right over 1s.

2. $(1,b,1,2,R)$ Add a single 1 at the right-hand end of the string.

FIGURE 12.6

1/1/R

State 1

State 2

b/1/R

State diagram for the incrementer

Here's a quick sample computation:

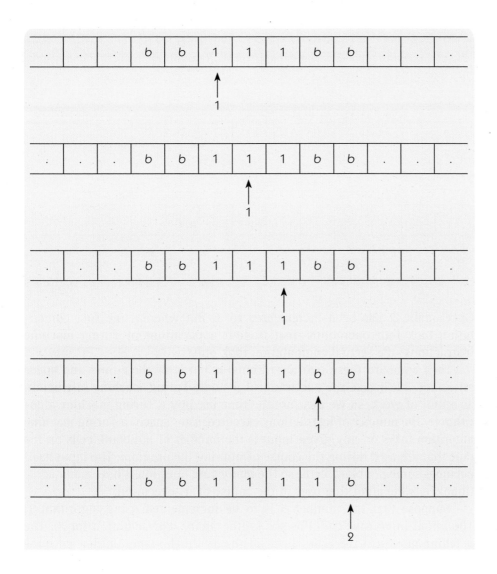

at which point the machine halts. The output on the tape is the representation of the number 3. The machine thus incremented the input, 2, to the output, 3.

Here is another algorithm to accomplish the same task. The preceding algorithm moved to the right-hand end of the string and added a 1. But the increment problem can also be solved by moving to the left-hand end of the string and adding a 1. The Turing machine program for this algorithm is

(1,1,1,1,L)   Pass to the left over 1s.

(1,b,1,2,L)   Add a single 1 at the left-hand end of the string.

If we apply this algorithm to the same input tape, the computation is

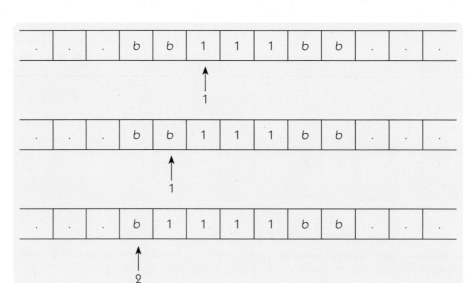

Once again, 2 has been incremented to 3. But whereas the first computation took four operations—that is, four applications of Turing machine instructions—the second computation took only two.

Let's compare these two algorithms in terms of their time and space efficiency. We'll take the execution of a single Turing machine instruction as a unit of work, so we measure the time used by a Turing machine algorithm by the number of instructions executed. The "space" a Turing machine algorithm takes on any given input is the number of nonblank cells on the tape that are used during the course of running the program. The input itself occupies some nonblank cells, so the interesting question is how many additional cells the algorithm uses in the course of its execution.

Suppose that the number 5 is to be incremented using algorithm 1. The initial input tape contains six 1s (the unary representation for 5). The machine moves to the right, over all the 1s on the tape, until it encounters the first blank cell. It writes a 1 into the blank cell and then halts. An instruction is executed for each move to the right. By the time the blank cell is reached, six instruction executions have been done; actually, the first instruction has been executed six times. One final execution, this time of the second instruction, completes the task. Altogether, seven steps are required, two more than the number 5 we are incrementing. One "extra" step comes because of the unary representation, with its additional 1, and a second "extra" step is used to write over the blank cell. Therefore, it is easy to see that if the problem is to increment the number n, then $n + 2$ steps would be required using algorithm 1. Algorithm 2 does a constant number of steps (two) no matter what the size of n. Both algorithms use $n + 2$ cells on the tape: $n + 1$ for the initial input and one more for incrementing. The algorithms are equivalent in space efficiency, but algorithm 2 is more time efficient.

FIGURE 12.7

The Number to Be Incremented, n	Number of Steps Required	
	Algorithm 1	Algorithm 2
10	12	2
100	102	2
1,000	1,002	2
10,000	10,002	2

Time efficiency for two Turing machine algorithms for incrementing

With an input such as 5, our example here, the difference in time effi-ciency between the two algorithms does not seem great. Figure 12.7 shows the steps required by algorithms 1 and 2 for larger problems. As the input gets larger, the difference in efficiency becomes more obvious. If our hypo-thetical Turing machine actually existed and could do, say, one step per second, then algorithm 1 would take 2 hours, 46 minutes, and 42 seconds to increment the number 10,000. Algorithm 2 could do the same job in 2 seconds! This significant difference gives a definite edge to algorithm 2 as the preferable solution method for this problem. Using the notation of Chap-ter 3, algorithm 1 is a linear time $\Theta(n)$ algorithm, whereas algorithm 2 is a constant time $\Theta(1)$ algorithm.

Although we can compare two Turing machine algorithms for the same task, we can't really compare the efficiency of a Turing machine algorithm with an algorithm that runs on a "real" computer. For one thing, the data representation is probably different (numbers aren't written in unary form). But more to the point, the basic unit of work is different. It takes many Turing machine operations to do a trivial task because the entire concept of a Turing machine is so simplistic. Turing machines, as we saw in our few examples, work by carefully moving, changing, and keep-ing track of individual 0s and 1s. Given such a limited range of activities, a Turing machine must exert a lot of effort to accomplish even mildly interesting tasks.

12.5.4 A Unary Addition Machine

A Turing machine can be written to add two numbers. Again using unary representation, let's agree to start with the two numbers on the tape sep-arated by a single blank cell. When the Turing machine halts, the tape should contain the unary representation of the sum of the two numbers. The separating blank should be gone. If we erase the leftmost 1 and then fill in the separating blank with a 1, this has the effect of sliding the entire first number one cell to the right on the tape. Also, both numbers are originally written on the tape using unary representation, which means that there is an extra 1 for each number. When we are finished, we want to have only one extra 1, for the unary representation of the sum. Therefore, a second 1 should be removed from the tape. Our plan is to erase the two leftmost 1s on the tape, proceed rightward to the separating blank, and replace the blank with a 1.

For example, suppose we want to add 2 + 3. The original tape representation (rather than drawing the individual cells, we'll just show the tape contents) is

$$\ldots bb\underset{2}{111}\,b\underset{3}{1111}\,bb\ldots$$

and the final representation—somewhere on the tape—should be the unary representation for the number 5,

$$\ldots bb\underset{5}{111111}\,bbbb\ldots$$

Our algorithm will accomplish this transformation in stages. First, we erase the leftmost 1:

$$\ldots bbb11\,b1111\,bb\ldots$$

We then erase a second 1 from the left end (see Exercise 26 at the end of this chapter for the case when there is no "second 1"):

$$\ldots bbbb1\,b1111\,bb\ldots$$

and then move to the right and fill in the blank with a 1:

$$\ldots bbbb\underset{5}{111111}\,b\ldots$$

The Turing machine begins in state 1, so we use that state to erase the leftmost 1 and move right, changing to state 2. The job of state 2 is to erase the second 1 and move right, changing to state 3. State 3 must move across any remaining 1s until it encounters the blank, which it changes to a 1 and then goes into a "halting state" with no instructions, state 4. A state diagram (Figure 12.8) illustrates the desired transitions to next states.

FIGURE 12.8

State diagram for the addition machine

Here is the Turing machine program:

1. $(1,1,b,2,R)$ Erase the leftmost 1 and move right.
2. $(2,1,b,3,R)$ Erase the second 1 and move right.
3. $(3,1,1,3,R)$ Pass over any 1s until a blank is found.
4. $(3,b,1,4,R)$ Write a 1 over the blank and halt.

Try "running" this machine on the preceding 2 + 3 problem.

Practice Problems

1. Set up the input and run the addition Turing machine to compute 3 + 4.
2. Write a Turing machine that, when run on the tape

    $\ldots b11110b\ldots$

produces an output tape of

    $\ldots b11101b\ldots$

Laboratory Experience 16

In this Laboratory Experience, you will run a Turing machine simulator. Using Turing machine algorithms that we have developed in the text, you can set up the input tape and then run the machine. You can watch as the Turing machine passes from state to state and see which instruction it is executing at each step. You can also see whether the input tape is modified at any step, and how (or whether) the machine reaches a halting configuration.

12.6 The Church–Turing Thesis

Just how good is the Turing machine as a model of the concept of an algorithm? We've already seen that any Turing machine exhibits the properties of an algorithm, and we've even produced Turing machine algorithms for a couple of important tasks. But perhaps we were judicious in our choice of tasks and happened to use those for which Turing machine instructions could be devised. We should ask whether there are other tasks that are "doable" by an algorithm but not "doable" by a Turing machine.

Of course, the answer to this question is yes. A Turing machine cannot program a DVR or shampoo hair, for example—tasks for which algorithms were given in Chapter 1. But suppose we limit the task to one for which the input and output can be represented symbolically, that is, using letters and numbers. Symbolic representation is, after all, how we traditionally record information such as names, addresses, telephone numbers, pay rates, yearly profits, temperatures, altitudes, times, Social Security numbers, grade point averages, growth rates, and so on. Taking a symbolic representation of information and manipulating it to produce a symbolic representation of other information covers a wide range of tasks, including everything done by "traditional" computing. Now let's ask a modified version of our previous question: Are there symbol manipulation tasks that are "doable" by an algorithm but not "doable" by a Turing machine?

The answer to this question is generally considered to be no, as stated by the **Church–Turing thesis**, named for Alan Turing and another famous mathematician, Alonzo Church.

The Church–Turing thesis makes quite an extraordinary claim. It says that any symbol manipulation task that has an algorithmic solution can also be carried out by a Turing machine executing some set of Turing machine instructions. Processing the annual Internal Revenue Service records, for example, or calculating positions for global navigation satellite systems such as GPS can be done (according to this claim) using Turing machines. The thought of writing a Turing machine program to process IRS records is mind-boggling, but our examples may have convinced you that it is possible. Although such a program can be written, one can hardly imagine how many centuries it would take to execute, even with a very rapid "system clock." But the Church–Turing thesis says nothing about how efficiently the task will be done, only that it *can* be done by some Turing machine.

There are really two parts to writing a Turing machine for a symbol manipulation task. One part involves encoding symbolic information as strings of 0s and 1s so that it can appear on Turing machine tapes. This is not difficult, and we know that real computers store all information, including graphical information, in binary. The other part is the heart of the challenge: Given that we get the input information encoded on a Turing machine tape, can we write the Turing machine instructions that produce

DEFINITION
Church–Turing Thesis: If there exists an algorithm to do a symbol manipulation task, then there exists a Turing machine to do that task.

The Turing Award

The most prestigious technical award given by the Association for Computing Machinery is the annual **Turing Award**, named in honor of Alan Turing. It is sometimes called the computer science Nobel Prize, and is given to an individual selected for "contributions of lasting and major technical importance to the computer field." Some of the individuals we've mentioned in this book have been recipients of the Turing Award, which was first given in 1966:

1971:   John McCarthy (Chapter 10)

1972:   E. W. Dijkstra (Chapter 10)

1977:   John Backus (Chapters 10 and 11)

1983:   Dennis Ritchie, Ken Thompson (Chapter 10)

2004:   Vinton Cerf and Robert Kahn (Chapter 7)

Other recipients of the award have made contributions in areas we have discussed or will discuss in later chapters:

1975:   Allen Newell as one of the founding fathers of artificial intelligence (AI), beginning his work in this area in 1954 (Chapter 15)

1981:   Edgar F. Codd for fundamental contributions to database management systems (Chapter 14)

1982:   Stephen A. Cook for exploring the class of problems that in Chapter 3 we called "suspected intractable"

1986:   John Hopcroft and Robert Tarjan for their work on analysis of algorithms (Chapter 3)

1990:   Fernando J. Corbato for pioneering work on general-purpose, time-shared mainframe operating systems (Chapter 6)

1992:   Butler Lampson for work in the 1970s and early 1980s on hardware and software that demonstrated solutions to problems of distributed computing done on personal workstations linked by a local area network (Chapter 7)

1999:   Frederick P. Brooks, Jr., for landmark contributions to computer architecture, operating systems, and software engineering (Chapters 5, 6, 9)

2001:   Ole-Johan Dahl and Kristen Nygaard for ideas fundamental to the emergence of object-oriented programming (Chapter 9)

2002:   R. Rivest, A. Shamir, and L. Adleman for seminal contributions to the theory and applications of cryptography (Chapter 8)

(Continues)

2005: Peter Naur for fundamental contributions to programming language design, to compiler design, and to the art and practice of computer programming (Chapters 10 and 11)

2008: Barbara Liskov for contributions to practical and theoretical foundations of programming language and system design (Chapters 6 and 9)

2010: Leslie Valiant for transformative contributions to the theory of computation ... and the theory of parallel and distributed computing (Chapters 10 and 12)

the encoded form of the correct output? Figure 12.9 illustrates the problem. The bottom arrow is the algorithmic solution to the symbol manipulation task we want to emulate. To perform this emulation, we must first encode the symbolic input into a bit string on a Turing machine tape (upward-pointing left arrow), write the Turing machine that solves the problem (top arrow), and, finally, decode the resulting bit string into symbolic output (downward-pointing right arrow). The Church–Turing thesis asserts that this process can always be done.

What exactly is a *thesis*? According to the dictionary, it is "a statement advanced for consideration and maintained by argument." That sounds less than convincing–hasn't the Church–Turing thesis been proved? No, and that's why it is called a thesis, not a theorem. Theorems are ideas that can be proved in a formal, mathematical way, such as "the sum of the interior angles of a triangle equals 180°." The Church–Turing thesis can never be proved because–despite all our talk about algorithms and their properties– the definition of an algorithm is still descriptive, not mathematical. It would be like trying to "prove" that an ideal day at the beach is sunny and 85°F.

FIGURE 12.9

Emulating an algorithm by a Turing machine

We might all agree on this, but we'll never be able to "prove" it. Well, then, the Church–Turing thesis makes a remarkable claim and can never be proved! Sounds pretty suspicious—what are the arguments on its behalf? There are two.

One argument is that early on, when the thesis was first put forward, whenever computer science researchers described algorithmic solutions for tasks, they also tried to find Turing machines for those tasks. They were always successful; no one was ever able to put forth an algorithm for a task for which a Turing machine was not eventually found. This does not mean that no such task exists, but it lends weight to a body of evidence in support of the thesis.

A second argument on behalf of the thesis is the fact that a number of other mathematicians attempted to find models for computing agents and algorithms. All of these proved to be equivalent to Turing machines and Turing machine programs in that whatever could be done by these other computing agents running their algorithms could also be done by a Turing machine running a Turing machine program, and vice versa. This suggests that the Turing machine captures all of these other ideas about "algorithms."

The Church–Turing thesis is now widely accepted by computer scientists. They no longer feel it necessary to write a Turing machine when they talk about an algorithmic computation. After describing an algorithm to carry out some task, they simply say, "Now let *T* be the Turing machine that does this task." You may make your own decision about the Church–Turing thesis, but in this book we will go along with convention and accept it as true. We therefore accept the Turing machine as an ultimate model of a computing agent and a Turing machine program as an ultimate model of an algorithm. We are saying that Turing machines define the limits of computability—that which can be done by symbol manipulation algorithms. What can be done by an algorithm is doable by a Turing machine, and what is not doable by a Turing machine cannot be done by an algorithm. In particular, if we find a symbol manipulation task that no Turing machine can perform (in its elementary way of moving around over a tape of 0s and 1s), then there is no algorithm for this task, and no real computer, no matter how sophisticated, will ever be able to do it either. That's why the Turing machine is so important. You can now see where this is all leading in terms of our search for a problem that has no algorithmic solution. Suppose we can find a (symbol manipulation) problem for which we can prove that no Turing machine exists to solve it. Then, because of the Church–Turing thesis, no algorithm exists to solve it either. The problem is an uncomputable or unsolvable problem.

If we pose a problem and try to construct a Turing machine to solve it but are not successful, that alone does not prove that no Turing machine exists. What we must do is actually prove that no one can ever find such a Turing machine—that it is not possible for a Turing machine to exist that solves this problem. It may appear that the introduction of Turing machines hasn't helped at all and that we are confronted by the same dilemma we faced at the beginning of this chapter. But Alan Turing, in the late 1930s, found such a problem and proved its unsolvability.

12.7 Unsolvable Problems

The problem Turing found is an ingenious one that itself involves Turing machine computations. A Turing machine that is executing an algorithm (a collection of Turing machine instructions) to solve some task must halt when begun on a tape containing input appropriate to that task. On other kinds of input, the Turing machine may not halt. It is easy enough for us to decide whether any specific configuration of a given Turing machine is a halting configuration. If a Turing machine program consists of the following four instructions:

$(1,0,1,2,R)$

$(1,1,0,2,R)$

$(2,0,0,2,R)$

$(2,b,b,2,L)$

then the configuration

is a halting configuration because there is no instruction of the form $(2,1,-,-,-)$. It is also easy to see that this configuration will arise if the Turing machine is begun on the tape

...b01bbb...

Similarly, we can see that if the Turing machine is begun on the tape

...b1bbb...

then it will never halt. Instead, after the first step (clock tick), the machine will cycle forever between the two configurations

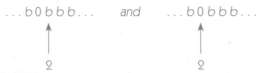

In a more complicated case, however, if we know the Turing machine program and we know the initial contents of the tape, then it may not be so easy to decide whether the Turing machine will eventually halt when begun on that tape. Of course, we can always simply execute the Turing machine—that is, carry out the instructions. We don't have all day to wait for the answer, so we'll set a time-out for our Turing machine system clock. Let's say we are willing to wait for 1,000 clock ticks. If we come to a halting configuration within the first 1,000 steps, then we know the answer: This Turing machine, running on this input tape, halts. But suppose we do not come to a halting configuration within the first 1,000 clock ticks. Can we say that the machine will never halt? Should we wait another 1,000 clock ticks? 10,000 clock ticks? Just running the Turing machine doesn't necessarily enable us to decide about halting. Here is the problem we propose to investigate:

> Decide, given any collection of Turing machine instructions together with any initial tape contents, whether that Turing machine will ever halt if started on that tape.

This is a clear and unambiguous problem known as the halting problem. Does it have a Turing machine solution? Can we find one Turing machine that will solve every instance of this problem—that is, one that will give us the answer "Yes, halts" or "No, never halts" for every (Turing machine, initial tape) pair?

This is an uncomputable problem; we will show that no Turing machine exists to solve this problem. Remember that we said it was not sufficient to look for such a machine and fail; we actually have to prove that no such machine can exist. The way to do this is to assume that such a Turing machine does exist and then show that this assumption leads to an impossible situation, so such a machine could not exist after all. This approach is called a proof by contradiction.

Assume, then, that P is a Turing machine that solves the halting problem. On the initial tape for P we have to put a description—using the binary digits 0 and 1—of a collection T of Turing machine instructions, as well as the initial tape content t on which those instructions run. This is the encoding part of Figure 12.9. Translating Turing machine instructions into binary form is tedious but not difficult. For example, we can use unary notation for machine states and tape symbols, designate the direction in which the read unit moves by 1 for R (right) and 11 for L (left), and separate the parts of a Turing machine instruction by 0s. Let's use T^* to symbolize the binary form of the collection T of Turing machine instructions. P is then run on a tape containing both T^* and t, so the initial tape for P looks like the following, where T^* and t may occupy many cells of the tape:

$$\ldots b b T^* b t b b \ldots$$

Our assumption is that P will always give us an answer ("Yes, halts" or "No, never halts"). P's yes/no answer would be its output—what is written on the tape when P halts; therefore, P itself must always halt. Again, because the output is written on P's tape, it also has to be in binary form, so let's say that a single 1 and all the rest blanks represents "yes," and a single 0 and all the rest blanks represents "no." This is the decoding part of Figure 12.9. To summarize:

> When begun on a tape containing T* and t
>> P halts with 1 on its tape exactly when T eventually halts when begun on t
>>
>> P halts with 0 on its tape exactly when T never halts when begun on t

FIGURE 12.10

Input

T^*bt

p

Output

Halts with
1 on tape
exactly when
T eventually
halts on *t*

Halts with
0 on tape
exactly when
T never
halts on *t*

Hypothetical Turing machine *P* running on *T**
and *t*

Figure 12.10 is a pictorial representation of the actions of *P* when started on a tape containing *T** and *t*.

When *P* halts with a single 1 on its tape, it does so because there are no instructions allowing *P* to proceed in its current state when reading 1. For example, *P* might be in state 9, and there is no instruction of the form

(9,1,–,–,–)

for machine *P*. Let's imagine adding more instructions to *P* to create a new machine *Q* that behaves just like *P* except that when it reaches this same configuration, it moves forever to the right on the tape instead of halting. To do this, pick some state not in *P*, say 52, and add the following two new instructions to *P*:

(9,1,1,52,*R*)
(52,*b*,*b*,52,*R*)

Figure 12.11 represents *Q*'s behavior when started on a tape containing *T** and *t*.

Finally, we'll create a new machine *S*. This machine first makes a copy of what appears on its input tape. (This is a doable, if tedious, task. The machine must "pick up" a 0 or 1 by going to a particular state, move to another part of the tape, and write a 0 or 1, depending on the state. It travels back and repeats the process; however, each time it picks up a 0 or 1, it must mark the tape with some marker symbol, say *X* for 0 and *Y* for 1, so that it doesn't try to pick it up again. At the end of the copying, the markers must be changed back to 0s and 1s.) After *S* is finished with its copying job, it uses the same instructions as machine *Q*.

FIGURE 12.11

Input $T^* bt$

Output

Never halts exactly when T eventually halts on t

Halts with 0 on tape exactly when T never halts on t

Q

Hypothetical Turing machine Q running on T^* and t

Now what happens when machine S is run on a tape that contains S^*, the binary representation of S's own instructions? S first makes a copy of S^* and then turns the computation over to Q, which is now running on a tape containing S^* and S^*. Figure 12.12 shows the result; this figure follows from Figure 12.11 where T^* and t are both S^*.

FIGURE 12.12

Input S^*

$S^* bS^*$

Output

Never halts exactly when S eventually halts on S^*

Halts with 0 on tape exactly when S never halts on S^*

S

Hypothetical Turing machine S running on S^*

Figure 12.12 represents the behavior of *S* running on input *S**. The final outcome is either (left output)

S running on input S* never halts

exactly when S halts running on S*—this is a contradiction

or (right output)

S running on input S* halts with 0 on the tape

exactly when S never halts running on S*—also a contradiction

(Perhaps you'll need to read this several times while looking at Figure 12.12 to convince yourself of what we have said.) We have backed ourselves into a corner here, but that's good. This is exactly the impossible situation we were hoping to find.

We assumed that there was a Turing machine that could solve the halting problem, and this assumption led to an impossible situation. The assumption is therefore incorrect, and no Turing machine can exist to solve the halting problem. Therefore, no algorithm can exist to solve this problem. The halting problem is an example of an unsolvable or uncomputable problem.

The halting problem seems rather abstract; perhaps we don't care whether it is unsolvable. However, real computer programs written in real programming languages to run on real computers are also symbol manipulation algorithms and, by the Church–Turing thesis, can be simulated by Turing machines. This means that the unsolvability of the halting problem has practical consequences. For example, we know that some C++, Java, or Python programs can get stuck in infinite loops. It would be nice to have a program that you could run ahead of time on any C++, Java, or Python program, together with its input, that would tell you, "Uh-oh, if you run this program on this input, it will get into an infinite loop," or "No problem, if you run this program on this input, it will eventually stop." The unsolvability of the halting problem says that no such program is possible. Other unsolvable problems, related to the halting problem, have the following practical consequences:

- No program can be written to decide whether any given program always stops eventually, no matter what the input.

- No program can be written to decide whether any two programs are equivalent (will produce the same output for all inputs).

- No program can be written to decide whether any given program run on any given input will ever produce some specific output.

This last case means it is impossible to write a general automatic program tester—one that for any program can check whether, given input *A*, it produces correct output *B*. That is why program testing plays such an important role in the software development life cycle described in Chapter 9.

It is important to note, however, that these problems are unsolvable because of their generality. We are asking for *one* program that will

Couldn't Do, Can't Do, Never Will Be Able to …

Unsolvable problems are not confined to problems about running programs (Java programs, C++ programs, Python programs, or Turing machines).

In Chapter 11, we talked about grammars that can be described in Backus-Naur Form (BNF) and about how a compiler parses a programming language statement by applying the rules of its grammar. We noted that ambiguous grammars are not suitable for programming languages because they can allow multiple interpretations of a statement. It would be nice to have a test (an algorithm) to decide whether any BNF grammar is ambiguous. This is an unsolvable problem—no such algorithm can exist. Deciding whether any two such grammars produce the same language is also unsolvable.

One of the earliest "decision problems" was posed by the British mathematician David Hilbert in 1900. Consider quadratic equations of the form

$$ax^2 + bx - c = 0$$

where a, b, and c are integers. We can easily decide whether any one such equation has integer solutions by applying the quadratic formula to solve the equation. But consider more general polynomial equations in several unknowns, such as

$$ax^4 + by^2 + cz^6 + dw^4 + e = 0$$

where the unknowns are x, y, z, and w and the coefficients (a, b, c, d, and e) are integers. Is there an algorithm to decide whether any such equation has integer solutions? In 1970, this problem was finally shown to be unsolvable.

Practice Problems

1. Explain how a proof by contradiction is done.

2. a. Write in your own words a description of the halting problem.

   b. Write a paragraph that describes the proof of the unsolvability of the halting problem.

Laboratory Experience 17

Using the same Turing machine simulator as before, you can now design and run your own Turing machine algorithms for simple problems. You will add states to an initially empty machine by describing the purpose of the new state and adding instructions for that state. You then run your machine on an appropriate input tape to see whether it behaves as intended.

decide something about *any* given program. It may be very easy to write a program *A* that can make a decision only about a specific program *B* by utilizing specialized properties of *B*. (*Analogy:* If I ask you to be ready to write "I love you" in English, you can do it; if I ask you to be ready to write "I love you" in any language I might later specify, you can't do it.)

12.8 Conclusion

We began this chapter by proposing that there exist problems for which no solution algorithm exists. To prove such a statement, we looked for appropriate models of "computing agent" and "algorithm" that would enable us to concentrate on the fundamental nature of computation. We discussed the nature of models in general and their importance in helping us understand real phenomena. After developing a list of properties inherent in any computing agent, we defined the Turing machine, noted that it incorporates these properties, and accepted it as a model of a computing agent. A Turing machine program incorporates the properties of an algorithm described in Chapter 1, so we accepted it as a model of an algorithm. Are these good models? Do they capture everything that is fundamental about computing and algorithms? After looking at a few Turing machines devised to do some simple tasks, we stated our position with a resounding *yes* in the form of the Church–Turing thesis: Not only is a Turing machine program an example of an algorithm, but every symbolic manipulation algorithm can be done by a Turing machine (we believe). This leap of faith—putting total confidence in Turing machine programs as models of algorithms—allows us to define the boundaries of computability. If it can't be done by a Turing machine, then it is not computable. Thus, the real value of Turing machines as models of computability is in exposing problems that are uncomputable—problems for which no algorithmic solution exists no matter how intelligent we are or how long we keep looking. As a practical matter, recognizing uncomputable problems certainly saves time; we are less likely to devote our lives to searching for algorithms that can never be. As a philosophical matter, it is important to know that computability has its limits, beyond which lies the great abyss of the uncomputable!

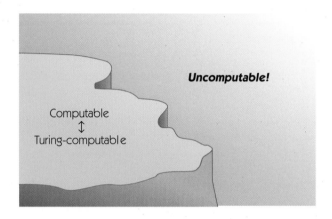

12.9 Summary of Level 4

In Level 4, we examined in some detail your choice of one procedural programming language as an example of a means for expressing algorithms at a high level of abstraction. Other high-level languages exist, including other procedural languages, special-purpose languages, and those that follow other philosophies, such as functional languages and logic-based languages. Because algorithms written in high-level languages ultimately run on low-level hardware, program translators must convert from one level of algorithmic expression to another. We've looked at the series of tasks that a language compiler must be able to perform to carry out this conversion. This final chapter of Level 4 proved that there are limits to computability—that there exist problems that can never be solved algorithmically.

With all of the hardware and software mechanisms in place to implement algorithmic problem solutions, we are ready to proceed to the next level—the level of applications—to see some of the ways in which computers (and algorithms) are being put to use.

The first application we examine relates very closely to what we have discussed in this chapter—building models. In this chapter, we constructed a formal model of an algorithm to prove the existence of unsolvable problems, but in Chapter 13, we will build simulation models that help us to solve important problems such as predicting the weather, creating new medicines, tracking our economy, and designing safe and efficient airplanes.

EXERCISES

In this set of exercises, when writing Turing machine algorithms, include comments for each instruction or related group of instructions. The comments should convey information in terms of the algorithm the Turing machine is accomplishing. Thus, the instruction

(1,0,0,1,*R*)

might have a comment such as, "Pass to the right over all the 0s," not a comment such as, "In state 1 looking at a 0, write a 0, stay in state 1, and move right," which provides no additional information.

1. Describe what factors might be included in a model for the spread of an epidemic.

2. Say an automobile manufacturer designs a new car using a sophisticated and detailed computer simulation, but no prototype vehicles, and the auto-mobile is later found to have a defect. Do you think the manufacturer is accountable? Is the manufacturer accountable if it builds prototypes that do not reveal the defect, but does not do a simulation?

3. Give an example of a potential use of computerized models in

   a. The pharmaceutical industry
   b. The food processing industry
   c. The insurance industry

4. Which of the following can be considered computing agents and why?

   a. A clock radio
   b. A thermostat
   c. A video camera
   d. A programmable calculator

5. Given the Turing machine instruction

   (1,1,0,2,*L*)

   and the configuration

   . . . *b* 1 0 *b* . . .

   1

   draw the next configuration.

6. A Turing machine contains only the following instructions:

   (1,1,1,1,*R*)

   (1,*b*,1,2,*R*)

   Can this machine ever reach the following configuration? Explain your answer.

   . . . *b* 0 1 *b* . . .

   ↑

   1

7. Is the following a legitimate Turing machine? Why or why not?

   (1,1,0,2,*R*)

   (1,0,0,3,*R*)

   (2,1,1,2,*R*)

   (3,0,0,3,*R*)

   (2,0,0,4,*L*)

   (3,0,1,4,*L*)

   (4,1,1,5,*R*)

   (4,0,0,5,*R*)

8. Find the output for the Turing machine

   (1,1,1,2,*R*)

   (1,0,0,2,*R*)

   (1,*b*,1,2,*R*)

   (2,0,0,2,*R*)

   (2,1,0,1,*R*)

   when run on the tape

   . . . *b* 1 0 0 1 *b* . . .

9. Find the output for the Turing machine

   (1,1,1,2,*L*)

   (2,*b*,0,3,*L*)

   (3,*b*,1,4,*R*)

   (4,0,1,4,*R*)

   when run on the tape

   . . . *b* 1 *b* . . .

10. Describe the behavior of the Turing machine

    (1,1,1,2,R)

    (2,0,0,1,L)

    when run on the tape

    ...b101b...

11. Describe the behavior of the Turing machine

    (1,1,1,1,R)

    (1,0,0,2,L)

    (2,1,0,2,L)

    (2,b,1,3,L)

    (3,b,b,1,R)

    when run on the tape

    ...b101b...

12. Describe the behavior of the following Turing machine on any input tape containing a binary string:

    (1,1,1,1,R)

    (1,0,0,1,R)

    (1,b,1,1,R)

13. Write a Turing machine that, when run on the tape

    ...b11111b...

    produces an output tape of

    ...b01111b...

    You can accomplish this using only one instruction.

14. Say a Turing machine is supposed to change any string of 1s to a string of 0s. For example,

    ...b111b...

    should become

    ...b000b...

    Will the following Turing machine do the job? Why or why not?

    (1,1,0,2,R)

    (2,1,0,3,R)

    (3,1,0,4,R)

15. a. Write a Turing machine that, when run on the tape

    ...b111111b...

    produces an output tape of

    ...b111110b...

    b. Write a Turing machine that, when run on any tape containing a unary string, changes the rightmost 1 to 0 and then halts. (If your solution to Exercise 15a was sufficiently general, you will not have to change it here.)

16. Write a Turing machine to perform a *unary decrement* (the opposite of an increment). Assume that $n > 0$.

17. Write a Turing machine to perform a unary decrement. Assume that n may be 0, in which case a single 0 should be output on the tape to signify that the operation results in a negative number.

18. Write a Turing machine that operates on any binary string and changes it to a string of the same length with all 1s. It should, for example, change the tape

    ...b0110010b...

    to

    ...b1111111b...

    However, you must write instructions that allow your Turing machine to work on *any* binary string, not just the one shown here.

19. Write a Turing machine that operates on any string of 1s and changes it to a string of alternating 1s and 0s.

20. The parity-bit Turing machine of Section 12.5.2 uses an odd parity bit scheme. Write a Turing machine that uses an even parity bit scheme.

21. Write a Turing machine that *efficiently* adds 3 to any unary number.

22. Write a Turing machine that begins on a tape containing a single 1 and never halts but successively displays the strings

    ... b 1 b ...
    ... b 0 1 0 b ...
    ... b 0 0 1 0 0 b ...
    and so on.

23. Write a Turing machine that operates on the unary representation of any number and decides whether the number is 0; your machine should produce an output tape containing the unary representation of 1 if the number was 0 and the unary representation of 2 if the number was not 0.

24. Write a Turing machine that takes any unary string of an *even* number of 1s and halts with the first half of the string changed to 0s. (*Hint:* You may need to use a "marker" symbol such as *X* or *Y* to replace temporarily any input symbols you have already processed and do not want to process again; at the end, your program must "clean up" any marker symbols.)

25. Write a Turing machine that takes as input the unary representation of any two different numbers, separated by a blank, and halts with the representation of the larger of the two numbers on the tape. (*Hint:* You may need to use a "marker" symbol such as *X* or *Y* to replace temporarily any input symbols you have already processed and do not want to process again; at the end, your program must "clean up" any marker symbols.)

26. The Turing machine described in Section 12.5.4 to add two unary numbers was designed to erase the two leftmost 1s on the tape, move to the right to the blank separating the two numbers, and replace the blank with a 1. If the first of the two numbers being added is 0, then there are not two 1s before the separating blank. Does the algorithm still work in this case?

27. Draw a state diagram for a Turing machine that takes any string of 1s and changes every third 1 to a 0. Thus, for example,

    ... b 1 1 1 1 1 1 b ...

    becomes

    ... b 1 1 0 1 1 0 b ...

28. Draw a state diagram for a Turing machine that increments a binary number. Thus, if the binary representation of 4 is initially on the tape,

    ... b 1 0 0 ...

    then the output is the binary representation of 5,

    ... b 1 0 1 ...

    or if the initial tape contains the binary representation of 7,

    ... b 1 1 1 b ...

    then the output is the binary representation of 8,

    ... b 1 0 0 0 b ...

29. Analyze the time and space efficiency of the following Turing machine operating on a unary string of length n.

    $(1,1,1,1,R)$

    $(1,b,b,2,L)$

    $(2,1,0,2,L)$

    $(2,b,b,3,R)$

    $(3,0,1,3,R)$

30. Suppose we already have Turing machine instructions to copy a unary string; we also know how to add two unary numbers. Describe (in words only) the design of a Turing machine to multiply two unary numbers.

31. Two other Turing machine unary addition algorithms follow.

    1. Fill in the separating blank with a 1, go to the far right end, and erase two 1s.

    2. Erase a 1 on the left end, fill in the separating blank with a 1, and erase a 1 on the right end.

    a. Do both of these algorithms work correctly?

    b. Write the Turing machine for each of these algorithms.

    c. Informally, which of the three addition algorithms (the one given in the chapter and these two) seems most time efficient?

    d. Suppose that the numbers to be added are n and m. The original tape contains the unary representation of n, followed by a blank, followed by the unary representation of m.

Write exact expressions in terms of n, m, or both for the time efficiency of each of the three algorithms. Does this confirm your answer from Exercise 31c?

e. Again assuming that the numbers to be added are n and m, write an exact expression for the space efficiency of each of the three algorithms.

We have considered Turing machines as computation devices, turning input to output according to some specific requirement. Turing machines can also be used as **recognizers**, deciding whether the string of characters initially on its tape matches a certain pattern. The following problem uses a Turing machine in this way.

32. A *palindrome* is a string of characters that reads the same forward and backward, such as radar or IUPUI. Write a Turing machine to decide whether any binary string is a palindrome by halting with a blank tape if the string is a palindrome and halting with a nonblank tape if the string is not a palindrome.

   Note: The world's longest single-word palindrome is the Finnish word for "lye dealer":

   Saippuakivikauppias

   Other palindromes include:

   Slap a ham on Omaha pals

   Do geese see god

   A man a plan a canal Panama

Recall from Chapter 11 that the job of the parser in a compiler is also to recognize strings that match patterns, where the patterns are given by means of a grammar expressed in BNF notation. Exercises 33–36 use BNF grammar notation.

33. The following BNF grammar defines a set of binary strings.

   <string> ::= <one> | <one><string>
   <one> ::= 1

   a. Describe the language defined by this grammar.

   b. Write a Turing machine to decide whether any binary string is a string in this language by halting with a blank tape if the string is in the language and halting with a nonblank tape if the string is not in the language.

34. The following BNF grammar defines a set of binary strings.

   <string> ::= <zero><zero><string> | <one>
   <zero> ::= 0
   <one> ::= 1

   a. Describe the language defined by this grammar.

   b. Write a Turing machine to decide whether any binary string is a string in this language by halting with a blank tape if the string is in the language and halting with a nonblank tape if the string is not in the language.

35. The following BNF grammar defines a set of binary strings.

   <string> ::= <zero><A><zero>
   <A> ::= <zero><B><zero>
   <B> ::= <one><B> | <one>
   <zero> ::= 0
   <one> ::= 1

   a. Describe the language defined by this grammar.

   b. Write a Turing machine to decide whether any binary string is a string in this language by halting with a blank tape if the string is in the language and halting with a nonblank tape if the string is not in the language.

36. The following BNF grammar defines a set of binary strings.

   <string> ::= <zero><one> | <zero><string><one>
   <zero> ::= 0
   <one> ::= 1

   a. Describe the language defined by this grammar.

   b. Write a Turing machine to decide whether any binary string is a string in this language by halting with a blank tape if the string is in the language and halting with a nonblank tape if the string is not in the language.

37. Your boss gives you a computer program and a set of input data and asks you to determine whether the program will get into an infinite loop running on these data. You report that you cannot do this job, citing the Church–Turing thesis. Should your boss fire you? Explain.

38. What is the significance of the unsolvability of the halting problem?

39. The *uniform halting problem* is to decide, given any collection of Turing machine instructions, whether that Turing machine will halt for every input tape. This is an unsolvable problem. Which of the three practical consequences of unsolvability problems described in

Section 12.7 follows from the uniform halting problem?

40. The *10-step halting problem* is to decide, given any collection of Turing machine instructions, together with any initial tape contents, whether that Turing machine will halt within 10 steps when started on that tape. Explain why the 10-step halting problem is computable.

CHALLENGE WORK

1. Several alternative definitions of Turing machines exist, all of which produce machines that are equivalent in computational ability to the Turing machine defined in this chapter. One of these alternative definitions is the *multitrack Turing machine*. In a multitrack Turing machine, there are multiple tapes. The machine reads a cell from each of the tapes and, on the basis of what it reads, it writes a symbol on each tape, changes state, and moves left or right. Diagram (a) shows a two-track Turing machine currently in state 1 reading a 1 on the first tape and a 0 on the second tape.

   An instruction for this Turing machine has the following form:

   > (current state, current first tape symbol, next first tape symbol, current second tape symbol, next second tape symbol, next state, direction of move)

   An instruction of the form $(1,1,0,0,0,2,R)$ applied to the machine configuration of Figure 12.13 results in the configuration shown in diagram (b).

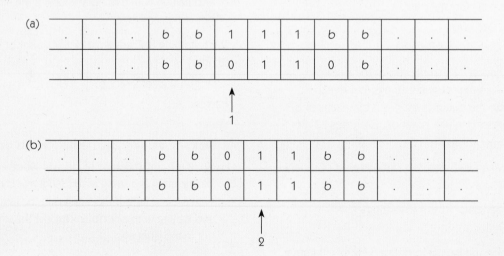

As in the original Turing machine definition, some conventions apply. Each tape can contain only a finite number of nonblank symbols, and the leftmost nonblank symbols must initially "line up" on the two tapes. The read head begins in this leftmost nonblank position in state 1. At any time, if no instruction applies to the current machine configuration, the machine halts.

a. Design a two-track Turing machine that compares two binary strings and decides whether they are equal. If the strings are equal, the machine halts in some fixed state; if they are not equal, the machine halts in some other fixed state.

b. Solve this same problem using the Turing machine defined in this chapter.

c. Prove the following statement: Any computation that can be carried out using a regular Turing machine can be done using a two-track Turing machine.

d. On the basis of Challenge Exercise 1a and 1b, make an argument for the following statement: Any computation that can be carried out using a two-track Turing machine can be done using a regular Turing machine.

2. Read some biographical information on Alan Turing and write a report on his life, concentrating particularly on his contributions in computability theory, cryptography, and artificial intelligence.

ADDITIONAL RESOURCES

CourseMate **For additional print and/or online resources relevant to this chapter, visit the Computer Science CourseMate at login.cengagebrain.com.**

Level 4 focused on programming languages and software development. In this section, titled *Applications*, we answer the question, What kind of programs do we want to write? Now that we have introduced the hardware (Level 2) and software (Levels 3, 4) tools that implement algorithms, we need to take a look at the specific types of problems we want to address using these tools.

Of course, there are far too many applications to survey them all; indeed, there is hardly an area of society that has not been significantly influenced and changed by the rapid growth of information technology. Therefore, rather than trying to briefly survey a large number of applications, we will, instead, examine a few important applications in depth. These applications exemplify the enormous effect that computing has on our work and on our daily lives.

CHAPTER 13

Simulation and Modeling

13.1 Introduction

The computational devices of the nineteenth and early twentieth centuries were used to solve important mathematical and scientific problems of the day. We saw this in the historical review of computing in Chapter 1: Charles Babbage's Difference Engine evaluated polynomial functions; Herman Hollerith's punched card machines carried out a statistical analysis of the 1890 census; ENIAC computed artillery ballistic tables; and Alan Turing's Colossus cranked away at Bletchley Park, breaking the "unbreakable" German Enigma code. The users of these early computing devices were primarily mathematicians, physicists, and engineers.

Today, there is hardly a field of study or aspect of our society—from art to zoology, business to entertainment—that has not been profoundly changed by information technology. Now we use computers in many "nonscientific" ways, such as playing games (a topic we will investigate in Chapter 16), surfing the Web, listening to music, and sharing videos.

However, the physical, mathematical, engineering, and economic sciences are still some of the largest users of computing and information technology. In this chapter, we investigate perhaps the single most important scientific use of computing—computational modeling. This application is having a major impact on many quantitative fields, including chemistry, biology, medicine, meteorology, ecology, geography, and economics.

13.2 Computational Modeling

13.2.1 Introduction to Systems and Models

The *scientific method* entails observing the behavior of a system and formulating a hypothesis that tries to understand and explain that behavior. We then design and carry out experiments to either prove or disprove the validity of our hypothesis. This is the fundamental way of obtaining new scientific knowledge and understanding.

Scientists often work with a model of a system rather than experimenting on the "real thing." Models were discussed in Chapter 12, where the Turing machine was presented as a model of a computing agent. A **model** is a representation of the system being studied, which we claim behaves much like the original. If that claim is true, then we can experiment on the model and use these results to understand the behavior of the actual system. For example, *physical models* (small-scale replicas) have been in use for many years, and we are all familiar with the idea of testing a model airplane in a wind tunnel to understand how the full-sized aircraft would behave.

In this chapter, we are not interested in physical models but in computational models, also called simulation models. In a computer simulation, a physical system is modeled as a set of mathematical equations and/or algorithmic procedures that capture the fundamental characteristics and behavior of a system. This computational model is then translated into a computer program written in one of the high-level languages of Chapters 9 and 10 and executed on the Von Neumann computer described in Chapters 4 and 5.

Why construct a simulation model? Why not simply study the system itself, or a physical replica of the system? There are many reasons:

- *Existence*—The system might not yet exist, so it is not possible to experiment directly on the actual system. In fact, we might be using a model to help us with the construction of the system.

- *Physical realization*—The system is not constructed from entities that can be represented by physical objects. For example, it may be a social system (e.g., welfare policies, labor practices) that can only be simulated on a computer.

- *Safety*—It might be too dangerous to experiment on the actual system or a physical replica. For example, you would not want to try out a new monetary policy that could economically devastate a population or build a nuclear reactor using a new and unproven technology.

- *Speed of construction*—It might take too much time to construct a physical model. Sometimes it is faster to design and build a computer simulation.

- *Time scale*—Some physical systems change too slowly or too quickly. For example, an elementary particle in a high-speed accelerator may decompose in 10^{-15} seconds. At the other end of the time scale, some ecosystems take thousands of years to react to a modification. A simulation can easily model fractions of a second or billions of years because time is simply a parameter in an equation.

- *Ethical behavior*—Some physical models have serious moral and ethical consequences, perhaps the best known being the use of animals in medical research. In this case, a computational model could eliminate a great deal of suffering.

- *Ease of modification*—If we are not happy with our original design, we would need to construct a brand-new physical model. In a simulation, we only need to change some numerical parameters and rerun the existing model.

This last advantage—ease of modification—makes computational modeling a particularly attractive tool for designing totally new systems. We initialize the system, observe its response, and if we are not satisfied, modify the parameters and run the model again. We repeat this process over and over, always trying to improve performance. Only when we think we have created the best design possible would we actually build it. This "interactive" approach to design, called computational steering, is usually infeasible using physical models, as it would take too much time. This interactive design methodology is diagrammed in Figure 13.1.

Computational models are therefore an excellent way to design new systems and to study and improve the behavior of existing systems. Virtually every branch of science and engineering makes use of models, and it is not unusual today to see chemists, biologists, physicists, ecologists, and physicians conducting fundamental research at their computer screens rather than in the laboratory.

Computational models often use advanced mathematical techniques far beyond the scope of this text (and solving them often requires the large-scale parallel computers described in Chapter 5). Therefore, in the following pages we often must rely on rather simple examples, far simpler than the models you will encounter in the real world. However, even these simple examples illustrate the enormous power and capabilities of computational modeling.

13.2.2 Computational Models, Accuracy, and Errors

Legend says that in the late sixteenth century, the famed scientist Galileo Galilei dropped two balls from the top of the Tower of Pisa—a massive iron cannonball and a lighter wooden one—to disprove the Aristotelian theory, which predicted that heavy objects would fall faster than light ones. When Galileo dropped the two balls, they hit the ground at the same time, exactly

FIGURE 13.1

Using a simulation in an interactive design environment

as he had hypothesized. Whether this event actually took place (and there is considerable debate), it is an excellent example of scientific experimentation using a physical system, in this case two balls of different weight, a high platform, and the Earth below.

Today, we do not need to climb the Tower of Pisa because there is a well-known mathematical model that describes the behavior of a falling mass acted upon only by the force of gravity:

$$d = v_{init}\, t + 1/2\; gt^2$$

This equation says that if a mass in free fall has an initial velocity v_{init} meters/sec at time 0, then at time t it will have fallen a distance of d meters. (Notice that the object's mass is not part of the equation. This is exactly what Galileo was trying to demonstrate.) The factor g is the acceleration due to gravity, which is assumed to be 9.8 meters/sec^2 everywhere along the Earth's surface.

Using this model, we can reproduce aspects of Galileo's sixteenth-century experiment without having to travel to Italy. For example, we can determine the time when the two balls Galileo dropped from the 54-meter-high Tower of Pisa would have hit the ground, assuming that their initial velocity was 0.0:

$$54 = (0 * t) + 1/2 * 9.8 * t^2$$
$$t^2 = 11.02$$
$$t = 3.32 \text{ seconds}$$

This simple example shows the beauty and simplicity of computational models. Such models can provide quick answers to questions without the cumbersome setup often required of physical experiments. This model is also easy to modify. For example, if we want to know how long it takes those same two balls to hit the ground when dropped from a height of 150 meters, rather than 54, we reset d to 150 and solve the same equation:

$$150 = (0 * t) + 1/2 * 9.8 * t^2$$
$$t^2 = 30.6$$
$$t = 5.53 \text{ seconds}$$

To use a physical model, Galileo would have had to scour the sixteenth-century world to find a 54-meter-high tower.

Unfortunately, modeling is not quite as simple as we have just described, and there are a number of issues that must be addressed and solved to make this technique workable.

The first issue is achieving the proper balance between *accuracy* and *complexity*. Our model must be an accurate representation of the physical system, but at the same time, it must be simple enough to implement as a program or set of equations and solve on a computer in a reasonable amount of time. Often this balance is not easy to achieve, as most real-world systems are acted upon by a large number of external factors. We need to decide which of those factors are important enough to be included in our model and which can safely be omitted without jeopardizing the validity of our conclusions.

For example, the model of a falling body given earlier is inaccurate because it does not account for the effects of air resistance. (It is only an appropriate model if the object is falling in a vacuum.) Whereas the effect of air resistance on a cannonball is minimal, imagine dropping a feather! The model would produce totally inaccurate results, and our conclusions about how the system behaves would be wrong. It is obvious that we need to incorporate the effects of air resistance into our model if we have any hope of producing worthwhile and useful results.[1]

Our model also assumes that the Earth is a perfect sphere and that the acceleration due to gravity is constant everywhere along its surface. That assumption is not quite true. The Earth is a "slightly squashed" sphere with a radius of 6,378 km at the equator and 6,357 km at the poles. This means that the acceleration due to gravity is a tiny bit greater at the North and South Poles than at the equator, because the poles are 21 km closer to the center of the Earth. Is this something for which we should account? Is this effect important when constructing a model of a freely falling body? In this case, probably not—because the miniscule error resulting from this approximation will almost certainly not affect our conclusions.

This is how computational models are built. We include the truly important factors that act upon our system so that our model is an accurate representation but omit the unimportant factors that would only make the model harder to build, understand, and solve. As you might imagine, identifying these factors and distinguishing the important from the unimportant can be a daunting task.

Another problem with building simulations is that we may not know, in a mathematical sense, exactly how to describe certain types of systems and behaviors. The gravitational model given earlier is an example of a continuous model. In a continuous model, we write out a set of explicit mathematical equations that describes the behavior of a system as a continuous function of time t. These equations are then solved on a computer system to produce the desired results. Unfortunately, there are many systems that cannot be modeled using precise mathematical equations because researchers have not discovered exactly what those equations should be. Simply put, science is not yet sufficiently knowledgeable about how some systems function to characterize their behavior using explicit mathematical formulae.

In some cases, what makes these systems difficult to model is that they contain stochastic components. This means there are parts of the system that display *random behavior*, much like the throw of the dice or the drawing of a playing card. In these cases, we cannot say with certainty what will happen to our system because it is the very essence of randomness that we can never know exactly which event will occur next. An example of this is a model of a business in which customers walk into the store at random times. In these cases, we need to build models that use *statistical approximations* rather than precise and exact equations. We will present one such example in the following section.

In summary, computational modeling is a powerful but complex technique for designing and studying systems. Building a good model can be

---

[1]The resistance of the air, called drag, is given by the equation $D = KrV^2A / 2.0$, where K is the coefficient of drag, r is the air density, V is the velocity of the object, and A is the reference area of the object. Now you can begin to see why computational models can quickly become so complex.

a difficult task that requires us to capture, in computational form, all the important factors that influence the behavior of a system. If we are able to successfully build such a model, then we have at our disposal a powerful tool for studying the behavior of that system. This is how a good deal of quantitative research is being done today. Simulation is also an interesting area of study within computer science itself. Researchers in this field create new techniques, both algorithms and special-purpose languages, that allow users to design and implement computer models more quickly and easily.

13.2.3 An Example of Model Building

As we mentioned at the end of the previous section, there are many ways to build a model, but most of them require mathematical techniques far beyond the scope of this text. In this section, we construct a model using a method that is relatively easy to understand and does not require a lot of complex mathematics. It is called **discrete event simulation**, and it is one of the most popular and widely used techniques for building computer models.

In a discrete event simulation, we do not model time as continuous, like the falling body model in the last section, but as *discrete.* That is, we model the behavior of a system only at an explicit and finite set of times. The moments we model are those times when an event takes place, an **event** being any activity that changes the state of our system. For example, if we are modeling the operation of a department store, an event might be a new customer entering the store, a customer purchasing an item, or a customer departing the building.

When we process an event, we change the state of the simulated system in the same way that the actual system would change if this event had occurred in real life. In the case of a department store, this might mean that when a customer arrives we add one to the number of customers currently in the store or, if a customer buys an item, we decrease the number of these items on the shelf. Furthermore, the processing of one event can cause new events to occur at some time in the future. For example, a customer coming into a store creates a later event related to that customer leaving the store. When we are finished processing one event, we move on to the next, skipping those times when nothing is happening—that is, when there are no events scheduled to occur.

Figure 13.2(a) shows system S and three events scheduled to occur within system S: event E_1 at time 9:00, event E_2 at time 9:04, and event E_3 at time 9:10. Because E_1 is the event currently being processed, the variable *current time*, which functions like a "simulation clock," has the value 9:00. Let's assume that E_1 causes a new event, E_4, to be created and scheduled for time 9:17. We add this new event to the list of all scheduled events. When we are finished processing event E_1, we remove it from the list and determine the next event scheduled to occur in system S, in this case E_2. We move *current time* ahead to 9:04, skipping the time period 9:01–9:03, because nothing of interest happens, and begin processing E_2. The new list of events scheduled for system S is shown in Figure 13.2(b).

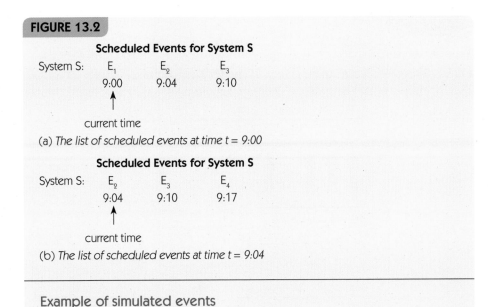

FIGURE 13.2

Scheduled Events for System S

System S: E_1 E_2 E_3
          9:00   9:04   9:10

↑

current time

(a) *The list of scheduled events at time t = 9:00*

Scheduled Events for System S

System S: E_2 E_3 E_4
          9:04   9:10   9:17

↑

current time

(b) *The list of scheduled events at time t = 9:04*

Example of simulated events

We repeat this sequence—process an event, remove it from the list, add newly created events to the list, move on to the next event—as long as desired. The variable *current time* keeps advancing as we process the events in strict time order. Typically the simulation is terminated when *current time* reaches some upper bound. For example, in a department store we might choose to run the model until closing time. When the simulation is complete, the program displays a set of results that characterizes the system's behavior and allows the user to examine these results at his or her leisure.

Let's apply this modeling technique to an actual problem. Assume that you have been hired as a consultant by the owner of a new fast-food restaurant, McBurgers, currently under construction. The owner wants to determine the proper number of checkout stations that will be needed in the new store. This is an important decision because if there are too few checkout stations, the lines will get long and customers will become irritated and leave. If there are too many checkout stations, money will be wasted paying for unnecessary construction costs, equipment, and personnel. Because you took a computer science class in school, you decide that the best way to advise your client is to construct a simulation model of the new restaurant and use this model to determine the optimal number of servers.

The system being simulated is shown in Figure 13.3. Customers enter the restaurant and wait in a single line for service. If any of the *N* servers is available, where *N* is an input value provided by the user, the first customer in line goes to that station, places an order, waits until the order is processed, pays, and departs. During that time, the server is busy and cannot help anyone else. When the server is finished with a customer, he or she can immediately begin serving the next person, if someone is in line. If no one is waiting, then the server waits until a new customer arrives.

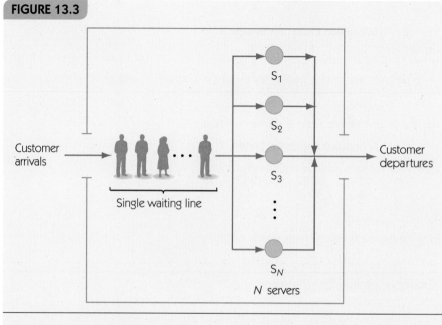

FIGURE 13.3

System to be modeled

To create this model, we must first identify the events that can change the state of our system and thus need to be included in the model. In this example, there are only two: (1) a new customer arriving and (2) an existing customer departing after receiving food and paying. An arrival changes the system because either the waiting line grows longer or an idle cashier becomes busy. A departure changes the system because the cashier serving that customer either begins serving a new customer or becomes idle because no one is in line.

For each of these two events, we must design an algorithm that describes exactly what happens to our system when that event occurs. Figure 13.4 shows the algorithm for the new customer arrival event.

Let's examine this algorithm in detail. When a new customer arrives, we record the time. The arrival time of each new customer is stored in a separate variable until that customer is served and departs. As we mentioned earlier, when the simulation is finished we want to display a set of results that allows the user to determine how well the system performed. The total time a customer spends in the restaurant (waiting time + service time) is a good example of this type of result. If this value is large, we are not doing a good job serving customers, and we need to increase the number of servers so that customers don't wait so long. A key part of any simulation model is collecting important data about the system so that we can understand and analyze its performance.

The next thing in our new customer arrival algorithm is to determine if there is an idle server. If not, the customer goes to the end of the waiting line (no special treatment here at McBurgers), and the length of the waiting line is increased by 1. If there is an idle server, then the customer goes directly

FIGURE 13.4

New customer arrival
    Record the time that this customer entered the restaurant
    Check if any one of the N servers $S_1, S_2, \ldots, S_N$ is currently idle
    If all of the servers are busy then
        Put this customer at the end of the waiting line
        Increase the length of the waiting line by 1
    Else (server S_i is idle)
        Mark that server S_i is now busy
        Determine how long it will take to serve this customer, call that value T_{serve}
        Schedule a customer departure event for (*current time* + T_{serve})
        Increase the total time that server S_i has worked by T_{serve}
End of new customer arrival

New customer arrival algorithm

to that server, who is then marked as busy. (*Note:* If more than one server is free, the customer can go to any one because our model assumes that all servers are identical. We could also construct a model in which not all servers are identical and some provide a special service.)

Now we must determine how much time is required to service this customer. This is a good example of what we termed a *stochastic*, or *random*, component of a simulation model. Exactly what a customer orders and how much time it takes to fill that order are random quantities whose exact values can never be known in advance. However, even though it behaves in a random fashion, it is possible that this value, called T_{serve} in Figure 13.4, follows a pattern called a statistical distribution, a mathematical equation specifying the probability that a random variable takes on a certain value. If we know this pattern, then the computer can generate a sequence of random numbers that follows this pattern, and this sequence will accurately model the time it takes to serve customers in real life.

How can we discover this pattern? One way is to know something about the statistical distribution of quantities that behave in a similar way. For example, if we know something about the distribution of service times for customers in a bank or a grocery store, then this information might help us understand the pattern of service times at our hamburger stand. Another way is to observe and collect data from an actual system similar to ours. For example, we could go to other fast-food restaurants and measure exactly how long it takes them to service their customers. If these restaurants are sufficiently similar to ours, then the McBurgers owner might be able to discover from this data the statistical distribution of the variable T_{serve}.

There are other ways to work with statistical distributions, but we will leave this topic to courses in statistics. In this example, we simply assume that the statistical distribution for the customer service time, T_{serve}, has been discovered and is shown in the graph in Figure 13.5.

FIGURE 13.5

Statistical distribution of customer service time

The graph in Figure 13.5 states that 5% of the time a customer is served in less than 1 minute; 15% of the time it takes 1–2 minutes; 40% of the time it takes 2–3 minutes; 30% of the time it takes 3–4 minutes; and, finally, 10% of the time it takes 4–5 minutes. It never requires more than 5 minutes to serve a customer. We can model this distribution using the algorithm shown in Figure 13.6.

First, we generate a random integer v that takes on one of the values 1, 2, 3, ... , 100 with equal likelihood. This is called a **uniform random number**. We now ask if v is between 1 and 5. Because there are five numbers in this range, and there were 100 numbers that could originally have been generated, the

FIGURE 13.6

Generate a uniform random integer value v between 1 and 100
If v is in the range 1–5, then
    Set T_{serve} to a uniform random number between 0.0 and 1.0
Else if v is in the range 6–20, then
    Set T_{serve} to a uniform random number between 1.0 and 2.0
Else if v is in the range 21–60, then
    Set T_{serve} to a uniform random number between 2.0 and 3.0
Else if v is in the range 61–90, then
    Set T_{serve} to a uniform random number between 3.0 and 4.0
Else
    Set T_{serve} to a uniform random number between 4.0 and 5.0

Algorithm for generating random numbers that follow the distribution given in Figure 13.5

answer to this question is yes 5% of the time. This is the same percent of time that customers spend from 0 to 1 minute being served. Therefore, we generate another uniform random value, this time a real number between 0.0 and 1.0, which is the value of T_{serve}, the customer service time.

If the original random value v is not between 1 and 5, we ask if it is between 6 and 20. There are 15 integers in this range, so the answer to this question is yes 15% of the time, exactly the fraction of time that customers spend 1–2 minutes being served. If the answer is yes, we generate a T_{serve} value that is in the range 1.0 to 2.0. This process is repeated for all possible values of service time.

Once the value of T_{serve} has been generated, we use this value to determine exactly when this customer leaves the store (*current time* + T_{serve}) as well as to update the total amount of time the server has spent serving customers. This last computation allows us to determine the percentage of time during the day that each server was busy.

The value assigned to T_{serve} using the algorithm of Figure 13.6 exactly matches the statistical distribution shown in Figure 13.5. If this graph is an accurate representation of customer service time, then our model is an accurate depiction of what happens in the real world. However, if the graph of Figure 13.5 is not an accurate representation of customer service time, then our model is incorrect and will produce wrong answers. This is a good example of the well-known computer science dictum garbage in, garbage out—the results you get out of a simulation model are only as good as the data and the assumptions put into the model.

We can now specify how to handle the second type of event contained in our model, which is customer departures. The algorithm to handle a customer leaving the restaurant is given in Figure 13.7.

When a customer is ready to leave, we determine the total time this customer spent in the restaurant. The variable *current time* represents the

FIGURE 13.7

Customer departure from server S_i
    Determine the total time that this customer spent in the restaurant
    If there is someone in line then
        Take the next customer out of line and decrease the waiting line size by one
        Determine how long this new customer will take to be served,
            and call that value T_{serve}
        Schedule a customer departure event for (*current time* + T_{serve})
        Increase the total time that server S_i has worked by T_{serve}
    Else
        Mark this server as idle
End customer departure

Algorithm for customer departure event

time now, which is the time of this customer's departure. We recorded the time this customer first arrived on Line 2 of Figure 13.4, and we can retrieve the contents of the variable storing that information. The difference between these two numbers is the total time this customer spent in the restaurant, including both waiting and service time. We use this result, averaged over all customers, to determine if we are providing an adequate level of service.

If there is another customer in line, the server begins serving that customer in exactly the same way as described earlier. If no one is waiting, then the server becomes idle and has nothing to do until a new customer arrives. (We don't want this to happen too often as the restaurant owner will be paying the salary of someone with little to do.)

We have now described the two main events that change our system: someone arriving and someone leaving the restaurant. The only thing left is to initialize our parameters and get the model started. To initialize the model, we must do the following four things:

- Set the current time to 0.0 (we begin our simulation at time 0).

- Set the waiting line size to 0 (no one is in line when the doors open).

- Get a value for N, the number of servers, and make them all idle.

- Determine the total number of customers to be served and exactly when they will arrive.

The last value—customer arrival times—are like the service times discussed earlier in that they are stochastic, or random, values that cannot be known in advance. We cannot possibly know exactly when each new customer will walk in the front door. However, if we know the statistical distribution of the time interval between the arrival of any two customers, then we can generate a set of random intervals, called $T_{interval}$, that allows us to accurately model our customer arrivals.

Assume we have a graph like Figure 13.5 that specifies the statistical distribution of the time interval that elapses between the arrivals of two successive customers. (That is, it might say something like 10% of the time two customers arrive within 0–15 seconds of each other, 20% of the time they arrive within 15–30 seconds of each other, and so on.) We schedule our first customer to arrive at time 0.0, just as the doors open. We then use an algorithm like the one in Figure 13.6 to generate a random value that matches the distribution of interarrival times. Call this value $T_{interval}$. This represents the amount of time that will elapse until the next customer arrives. Because the first customer arrived at time 0.0, we schedule the next one to arrive at $(0.0 + T_{interval}) = T_{interval}$. We repeat this for as many customers as desired, scheduling each one to arrive at $T_{interval}$ time units after the previous one. Our sequence of customer arrivals will look something like this:

The main program to run our McBurgers simulation model is given in Figure 13.8. It allows the user to provide two inputs: M, the total number of customers to model, and N, the number of servers. Each one of the M customer arrivals is handled by the arrival algorithm of Figure 13.4. Each arrival event generates a customer departure event that is handled by the departure algorithm of Figure 13.7. This simulation does not terminate at a specific point in time but, instead, when there are no more events to be processed—that is, when every customer who was scheduled to arrive has been served and has departed.

The last issue that we must address is how to implement the second-to-last line of Figure 13.8, the one that reads, "Print out a set of data that describes the behavior of the system." Looking back at Figure 13.1, we see

---

FIGURE 13.8

Main part of the simulation model

    Set *current time* to 0

    Set the waiting line size to 0

    Get an input value for N, the number of servers

    Set all N servers, $S_1, S_2, \ldots, S_N$ to idle

    Get an input value for M, the total number of customers

    Schedule M customer arrivals and put them on the list of events

        Each arrival occurs $T_{interval}$ time units after the previous one

    While there is still a scheduled event on the list do

        Get the next event on the list

        Move *current time* to the time of this event

        If this is a customer arrival event

            Execute the arrival algorithm of Figure 13.4

        Else

            Execute the departure algorithm of Figure 13.7

        Remove this event from the list of all scheduled events

    End of the loop

    Print out a set of data that describes the behavior of the system

Stop

The main algorithm of our simulation model

that one of the responsibilities of a simulation is to "collect data describing its behavior." Our model must collect data that accurately measures the performance of this McBurgers restaurant so that the new owner can configure it in a profitable manner *before* it is built. Therefore, we need to determine what data are required to meet this need. Often this cannot be done by the persons building the model because they are computer scientists and thoroughly unfamiliar with this application area. Instead, it is the *users* of a model who can best determine what data should be collected and displayed. In this case, the user is the restaurant owner. Thus, model building is often a cooperative effort between technical specialists in the area of software development and those knowledgeable about the system being modeled.

Let's assume that we have talked to the restaurant owner and determined that the information he or she most needs to know is the following:

- The average time that a customer spends in the restaurant, including both waiting in line and getting served

- The maximum length of the waiting line

- The percentage of time that servers are busy serving customers

From this data, the owner should be able to determine whether the system is functioning well. For example, if our model determines that a server is busy only 10% of the time (about 48 minutes in an 8-hour workday), we can probably reduce the number of servers without affecting service, saving a good deal in salary costs. On the other hand, if the average time that a customer spends in the restaurant is 1 hour or there are times when there are 100 people in line, then we had better increase the number of servers if we want to avoid bankruptcy (or riots)!

This model will likely be used in the interactive design approach first diagrammed in Figure 13.1. The owner will enter his or her best estimate for the arrival time and service time distributions and then select a value for N, the number of servers. The computer will run the simulation, processing all M customers, and then print the results, perhaps something like the following:

Servers	Average Waiting Time (min)	Maximum Line Length	Server Busy Percentage (%)
2	63.3	35	100.0

With only two servers, our customers waited on average more than one hour to be served, there were dozens of people in line, and both servers were busy every second of the day—not very good performance! The owner would certainly try to improve on this performance, perhaps by having 6 servers, rather than only 2. He or she resets the parameter N to 6 and reruns the model, which now produces the following:

Servers	Average Waiting Time (min)	Maximum Line Length	Server Busy Percentage (%)
6	2.75	1	43

Now the owner may have erred too far in the other direction. Our customers are being well served, waiting only a couple of minutes, and the line is tiny, never having more than a single person. However, on the average our six servers are busy only 43% of the time—meaning they are idle about 4.5 hours during an 8-hour workday. Could we provide the same high level of service to our customers with fewer servers? To answer this question, the owner might try rerunning the model with $N = 3$, 4, or 5, a compromise value between these two extremes. This is how a simulation model is used—run it, examine the results, and use these results to reconfigure the system so its performance is enhanced.

This completes the development of our McBurgers simulation, but is not the end of its usefulness. In the next Laboratory Experience, you are going to "play" with this model by selecting a range of values for customer arrival and service times. You then take on the role of the McBurgers owner and determine the optimal number of servers to use for the selected configuration. Working with a simulation in an interactive design environment demonstrates the enormous power and capabilities of computational models.

The restaurant modeled in this section is about as simple a system as we could present, yet it still took almost ten pages to describe its design. A computational model of a suspension bridge, "El Niño" Pacific Ocean currents, the human heart, or a strand of DNA would certainly be far more complex than the simulation of a hamburger joint! Real-world models are mathematically intricate, highly detailed, and difficult to build. However, if we are able to build such a model or if we have access to such a model, then we have a powerful tool that can significantly enhance our ability to do high-quality research and design.

Practice Problems

1. In the McBurgers new customer arrival algorithm, describe the consequences of accidentally omitting the instruction "Mark that server S_i is now busy."

2. In the McBurgers customer departure algorithm, describe the consequences of accidentally omitting the instruction "Mark this server as idle."

3. Suppose we try to simplify our model by assuming that every customer requires exactly two minutes of service to complete his or her purchase. How do you think this would affect the conclusions that we could draw from our model?

4. Are there other parameters that you might have included if you were building a model of a fast-food restaurant?

Laboratory Experience 18

In this Laboratory Experience, you will work with a simulation model of a McBurgers restaurant that is similar to the one presented in this section. You will play the role of the restaurant owner who is trying to determine the correct number of servers for a specific pattern of customer arrivals and service times. You will configure your restaurant, run the model, see how well you serviced your customers, and then reconfigure the restaurant to try to improve its performance and its profit. The software allows you to set parameters for (1) the total running time of the simulation, (2) the average service time of each customer, (3) the probability that a new customer will arrive, and (4) the number of servers. It will then run the model exactly as you have described and, upon completion, produce the following output: (1) the number of customers remaining in line when the simulation terminated, (2) the average time that a customer spent in the restaurant, and (3) the percentage of time that the cashier was busy over the entire simulation.

Your goal in this simulation is to determine the set of parameters that optimizes behavior of the overall system.

13.3 Running the Model and Visualizing Results

The McBurgers restaurant model developed in Section 13.2.3 is much simpler than real-world models for two reasons. First, it is computationally small. The process of running it and producing results does not require much in the way of hardware resources. For example, assume that we model $M = 1,000$ customers, a reasonable value for a large restaurant. Each customer generates one arrival event (Figure 13.4) and one departure event (Figure 13.7), for a total of 2,000 events that must be processed by the computer before the simulation is completed and the results displayed. The execution of these 2,000 events is a miniscule amount of work that could be handled by even the smallest laptop or tablet in just a few seconds or, more likely, fractions of a second. Most real-world models require much more computational work to produce their results.

For example, the U.S. Department of Energy's National Energy Research Scientific Computing Center (NERSC) at Lawrence Berkeley National Laboratory has developed a powerful new climate system model. Using this model, simulating one year of global climatic change requires about 10^{17} computations—one hundred thousand trillion operations. A single Von Neumann machine could not handle this almost unimaginably large amount of work.

A typical laptop executes roughly 2 billion instructions per second. At this rate, completing one year of simulated time in the model would require about one-and-a-half years of real time—we would not get our results until the actual time period being simulated had passed!

Massive models like this one can be executed only on the large-scale parallel machines described in Chapter 5. The NERSC climate model was executed on a massively parallel IBM-SP supercomputer containing 6,080 processors, with a peak computation rate of 6 teraflops, or 6 trillion operations per second. At this rate, one year of climatic change can be modeled in about five hours. Using a petaflop machine (1 quadrillion operations per second), the job could be finished in under two minutes!

These numbers are much more typical of the amount of work required by most real-world simulations. It is not unusual for a model to require 10^{15}, 10^{16}, 10^{17}, or more computations to produce a single result—amounts far beyond the capabilities of individual desktop machines. The increasing interest in building complex computational models is one of the main reasons behind the development of larger and more powerful supercomputers. For example, the massively parallel Japanese 'K' system mentioned in Chapter 3, which runs at a rate of 8.2 petaflops, executes computational models in the areas of petroleum exploration, climate modeling, and aircraft design.

The second reason why the McBurgers model in Section 13.2.3 is so unrealistic is that it produces only a tiny amount of output. After each run is complete, the model generates only three lines of output, such as those shown below and in the previous section:

Servers	Average Waiting Time (min)	Maximum Line Length	Server Busy Percentage (%)
6	2.75	1	43

Because the number of servers in a restaurant might range from one up to a couple of dozen, the total volume of output this model would ever produce is about 20–60 lines, less than a single page. With such a small amount of output, our model can display its results using a simple text format, as shown in the lines above. A user will have no difficulty reading and interpreting this output.

Unfortunately, most simulations do not produce a few dozen lines of output, but rather tens or hundreds of thousands of lines, perhaps even millions. For example, assume the NERSC climate model described earlier displayed the temperature, humidity, barometric pressure, wind velocity, and wind direction at 50-mile intervals over the surface of the Earth for every simulated day the model is run. After one year of simulated time, it will have produced roughly 500 million data values—about 10 million pages of output! If these values were displayed as text, it would overwhelm its users, who wouldn't have a clue how to deal with this mountain of paper.

Text, when it appears in such large amounts, does not lend itself to easy interpretation or understanding. The field of scientific visualization is concerned with the issue of how to visualize data in a way that highlights its important characteristics and simplifies its interpretation. This is an enormously important part of computational modeling because without it we would be able to construct models and execute them, but we would not be able to interpret their results.

The term *scientific visualization* is often treated as synonymous with the related term computer graphics, but there is an important difference. The field of computer graphics is concerned with the technical issues involved in information display. That is, it deals with the actual algorithms for rendering a screen image—light sources, shadows, hidden lines and surfaces, shading, contours, and perspective. (We will be discussing these operations in Section 16.2.) Scientific visualization, on the other hand, is concerned with how to display a large data set in a way that is most helpful to users and that maximizes its comprehension. It is concerned with issues such as *data presentation*, determining the optimal format for presenting data, *data extraction*, determining which values are important and should be included and which ones can safely be omitted, and *data manipulation*, converting the data to other forms or to different units that make the information easier to understand and interpret. Once we have decided exactly how we want to display the data, then a scientific visualization package typically uses a computer graphics package to render an image on the screen or the printer.

For example, assume we have built a computer model of the ocean tides at some point along the coast. Our model predicts the height of the tide every 30 seconds in a 24-hour day, based on such factors as lunar phase, wind speed, and wind direction. If this information is printed as text, it might look something like the following:

Time	Height (feet)
12:00:00 A.M.	43.78
12:00:30 A.M.	43.81
12:01:00 A.M.	43.84
12:01:30 A.M.	43.88
12:02:00 A.M.	43.92
12:02:30 A.M.	43.97
.	.
.	.
.	.
11:57:00 P.M.	45.08
11:57:30 P.M.	45.04
11:58:00 P.M.	45.01
11:58:30 P.M.	44.99
11:59:00 P.M.	44.97
11:59:30 P.M.	44.95

There are 2,880 lines of output, which at 60 lines per page would produce almost 50 printed pages. Trying to extract meaning or locate significant

FIGURE 13.9

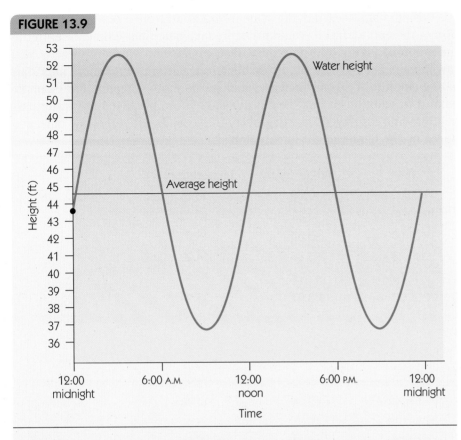

Using a two-dimensional graph to display output

features from these long columns of numbers would certainly be a formidable, not to mention boring, task.

What if, instead, we displayed these two columns of values as a two-dimensional graph of time versus height? The output could also include a horizontal line showing the average water height during this 24-hour period. This latter value is not part of the original output but can easily be computed from these values and included in the output—an example of a data manipulation carried out to enhance data interpretation. Now the output of our model might look something like the graph in Figure 13.9.

Using the graph in Figure 13.9, it is a lot quicker and easier to identify the interesting features of the model's output. For example,

- There appear to be two high tides and two low tides during this 24-hour time period.

- The high tide is about 8 feet above the average water level, whereas the low tide is about 8 feet below the average water level.

It is possible to extract the same information from a textual representation of the output, but it would probably take much more time. Interpreting the graph of Figure 13.9 is a great deal easier than working directly with raw numerical data. The use of visualizations becomes even more important as the amount of output increases and grows more complex. For example, what if in addition to tidal height our model also predicted the water temperature and displayed its value every 30 seconds. Now the raw data produced by the model might look like this:

Time	Height (feet)	Temperature (°C)
12:00:00 A.M.	43.78	15.03
12:00:30 A.M.	43.81	15.02
12:01:00 A.M.	43.84	15.01
12:01:30 A.M.	43.88	14.99
12:02:00 A.M.	43.92	14.97
12:02:30 A.M.	43.97	14.94
.	.	.
.	.	.
.	.	.
11:57:00 P.M.	45.08	14.95
11:57:30 P.M.	45.04	14.98
11:58:00 P.M.	45.01	15.00
11:58:30 P.M.	44.99	15.01
11:59:00 P.M.	44.97	15.03
11:59:30 P.M.	44.95	15.05

Now there are almost 6,000 numbers, and our task has become even more difficult as we try to understand both the behavior of the *two* variables, height and temperature, as well as any possible interactions between the two. Working directly with the raw data generated by the model is cumbersome. However, if the value of both variables were presented on a single graph, as shown in Figure 13.10, the interpretation would be much easier.

Looking at Figure 13.10, we can quickly observe that temperature seems to move in exactly the opposite direction as the tide, but delayed by a few minutes. That is, water temperature reaches its minimum value shortly after the tidal height has reached its maximum value, and vice versa. This is exactly the type of information that could be of help to a researcher. Without the graphical visualization in Figure 13.10, we may have overlooked this important fact.

The graphs in Figures 13.9 and 13.10 are both two-dimensional, but many real-world models study the behavior of three-dimensional objects, for example, an airplane wing, a gas cloud, or the Earth's surface.

FIGURE 13.10

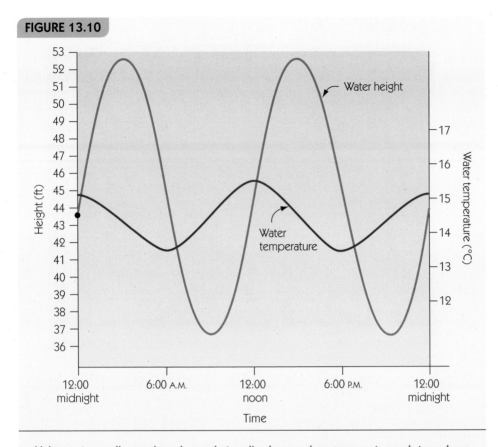

Using a two-dimensional graph to display and compare two data values

The results produced by these models are also three-dimensional, such as the spatial coordinates of a point on that airplane wing or on a gas molecule. Therefore, it is common for the output of a computational model to be displayed as a three-dimensional image rather than the two-dimensional graphs shown earlier. For example, Figure 13.11 shows the output from a model of a portion of the Earth's surface overlaid with colors to show the intensity of a forest fire at a particular moment in time. The hottest areas are shown in yellow and red, while cooler areas are displayed in blue and green. Such three-dimensional digital elevations make it easy to locate important topographical features, such as mountains, valleys, and rivers, and have many applications. This type of output could be extremely useful when, for example, planning the movement of equipment to fight the fire or directing airplanes on where to drop fire retardant chemicals.

As a second example, suppose that medical researchers are using a simulation model to study the behavior of the chemical compound methyl

FIGURE 13.11

Three-dimensional image of the Earth's surface with overlay showing status of a forest fire

Source: NASA

nitrite, CH_3NO_2, a potential carcinogen found in our air and drinking water. Assume that their molecular model produces the following textual output:

Molecule Number	Element	Location x	y	z	Bonded To
1	O	1.7	1.0	0.0	3, 4
2	O	3.0	0.0	0.0	3
3	N	2.6	0.3	1.0	1, 2
4	C	0.0	0.0	0.0	1, 5, 6, 7
5	H	−0.5	0.5	0.5	4
6	H	0.5	0.5	0.5	4
7	H	−0.5	−0.5	0.5	4

This is an accurate textual description of a methyl nitrite molecule. The output specifies the seven atoms in the molecule, the spatial (x, y, z) coordinates of the center of each atom, and the identity of all other atoms to which this one has a chemical bond. This is all the information required to understand the structure of this molecule. However, most of us would find it hard to form a mental image of what this molecule actually looks like using this table.

What if, instead, our model took this textual description of methyl nitrite and used it to create and display the three-dimensional image of Figure 13.12?

It is certainly a lot easier to work with the visualization in Figure 13.12 than with the original textual description. For example, if our model changed the shape or structure of this molecule, say by simulating a chemical reaction or the breaking of a chemical bond, we would be able to observe this change on our computer screen, significantly increasing our understanding of exactly what is happening. In the table-based representation, we would only see changing numerical values without any clue as to what these changes represent chemically or structurally.

The image in Figure 13.12 makes use of two other features found in many visualizations—color and scale. These characteristics allow us to display information in a way that makes the image more understandable by someone looking at the diagram. In this example, color represents the element type—blue for hydrogen, yellow for carbon, purple for oxygen, and red for nitrogen. The relative size of each sphere represents the relative size of each of the atoms.

The clever use of visual enhancements such as color and scale can make an enormous difference in how easy or hard it is to interpret the output of a computer model. For example, the image displayed in Figure 13.13 models the dispersion and height of tsunami waves following a massive earthquake near Japan.

In this example, color indicates projected wave heights across the Pacific Ocean. The largest wave heights, shown in purple, were expected near the earthquake epicenter off the Japanese coast. Progressively smaller waves are indicated in red, orange, and yellow. Using images like Figure 13.13, it is easy to see the areas likely to be most impacted and would help relief organizations determine where the greatest assistance might be needed. If, instead of these color-coded, three-dimensional images, we were given only

FIGURE 13.12

Three-dimensional model of a methyl nitrite molecule

FIGURE 13.13

Visualization of projected tsunami wave heights

Source: NOAA Center for Tsunami Research

page after page of numerical values, it would take much longer to extract this vital information. Here is an example where enhancing the comprehension of a model's output is not just for convenience but for saving lives!

Finally, we mention one of the most powerful and useful forms of scientific visualization—image animation. In many models, time (whether continuous or discrete) is one of the key variables, and we want to observe how the model's output changes over time. This could be the case, for example, with the forest fire model discussed earlier. The image in Figure 13.11 is a picture of the fire at one discrete instant in time. That may be of value, but what might be of even greater interest is how the fire moves and disperses as a function of time. Some questions we could answer using this time-varying model are: How long does it take for the hottest areas (yellow and red) to dissipate completely? What areas change more rapidly from hot to cool?

To answer these and similar questions, we need to generate not one image like Figure 13.11, but many, with each image showing the state of the system at a slightly later point in time. If we generate a sufficient number

FIGURE 13.14

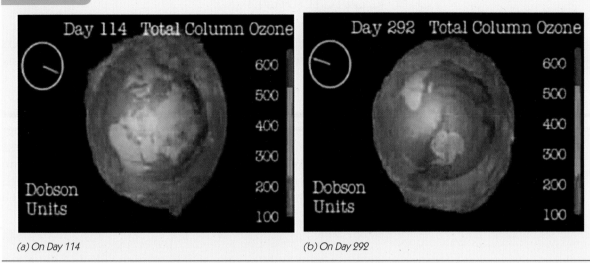

(a) On Day 114   (b) On Day 292

Use of animation to model ozone layers in the atmosphere
Source: Lloyd A. Treinish/IBM Thomas J. Watson Research Center

of these images, then we can display them rapidly in sequence, producing a visual animation of the system's behavior over time.

Obviously we cannot show an animation in this book, but Figure 13.14 shows two images (out of 365) from a program that models the total amount of ozone present in the Earth's atmosphere over a one-year period. The model computes the ozone levels for each day of the year and displays the results graphically, with green and blue representing acceptable ozone levels and red representing a dangerously low level. These 365 images can be displayed in sequence to produce a "movie" showing how the ozone level changes throughout the year.

The amount of output needed to produce these 365 images was probably in the hundreds of millions or billions of data values. If this volume of data were displayed as text, a user would be overwhelmed, and the truly important characteristics of the data would be buried deep within this mass of numbers, much like the proverbial "needle in a haystack." However, using the visualization techniques highlighted in this section—two- and three-dimensional graphics, color, scale, and animation—key features of the data, such as the presence of a significant ozone hole (the red area) over the Antarctic on day 292, can be quickly and easily located.

This is precisely why scientific visualization techniques are so important. It is not merely a desire to produce "pretty pictures," although, indeed, many of the images are artistically interesting. Instead, the goal is to take a massive data set and present it in a way that is more informative and more understandable for the user of that data. Without this understanding, there would be no reason to build computational models in the first place.

13.4 Conclusion

Computational modeling is a fascinating and highly complex subject, and one that will become even more important in the coming years as computers increase in power and researchers gain experience in designing and building models.

Constructing models of complex systems requires a deep understanding of both mathematics and statistics so, as we have mentioned a number of times, they can be rather difficult to build. However, even if you are not directly involved in *building* models, it is quite likely that you will *use* these types of models in your research, development, or design work. Simulation is affecting many fields of study. For example, in this chapter we looked at models drawn from physics (the falling body equations), economics (the

The Mother of All Computations!

Climatic changes occur slowly, often taking hundreds or thousands of years to complete. For example, the ice ages were periods when large areas of the Earth's surface were covered by glaciers. These individual ice ages were separated by intervals of thousands of years during which the Earth became warmer and the glaciers receded. To study global climate change, a researcher cannot look at data for only a few years. Instead, he or she must examine changes taking place over long periods of time.

To provide this type of data, scientists at the National Center for Atmospheric Research (NCAR) in Boulder, Colorado, used the NERSC global climate model described earlier to carry out a 1,000-year simulation of climatic changes on the surface of the Earth. NCAR used a 6,000+ processor IBM-SP supercomputer and started it running in late January 2002. This massive machine worked on the problem 24 hours a day, 7 days a week, modeling decade after decade, century after century of changes to the Earth's climate. Finally, on September 4, 2002, it finished its task. It had taken more than 200 days of uninterrupted computing and the execution of about a hundred billion billion (10^{20}) computations on a multimillion-dollar massively parallel machine to obtain the results!

Data from this simulation have been made available to the research community to further the study of changes to our climate and investigate such weather-related phenomena as global warming and "El Niño" ocean currents.

McBurgers simulation), chemistry (the molecular model of methyl nitrite), cartography (a map of the Earth's surface), meteorology (tides, climatic changes), and ecology (forest fire dispersion, ozone depletion). We could just as easily have selected examples from the fields of medicine, geology, biology, pharmacology, or urban planning. For those who work in scientific or quantitative fields like these, computational modeling is rapidly becoming one of the most important tools available to the researcher. It is also a vehicle for amusing and entertaining us through the creation of simulated fantasy worlds and alien planets where we can relax, explore, and play. We'll discuss this exciting new role of simulation in Chapter 16.

Even though simulation is an important scientific application, you are probably more familiar with the many uses of computers in the commercial sector—paying bills online, remotely accessing financial data, and buying and selling products on the Web. These commercial applications, often grouped together under the generic term *electronic commerce*, or *e-commerce*, will be discussed at length in Chapter 14.

EXERCISES

1. You are probably familiar with the idea of a two-dimensional spreadsheet, like the ones created in Microsoft Excel. Would you call this type of spreadsheet a "computational model"? State why or why not, and justify your answer.

2. Look up the definition of the terms *computer-aided design* (abbreviated CAD) and *computer-aided manufacturing* (CAM). Find out what they mean, how they are used, and how they relate to the ideas presented in this chapter.

3. Rather than using a general-purpose programming language like the ones discussed in Chapter 9, models are often constructed using *simulation languages* designed specifically for this application. (These languages fall into the category of "special-purpose languages" mentioned in Chapter 10.) Examples of simulation languages include:

- SIMULA
- GPSS (General Purpose System Simulation)
- Simscript

Read about one of these languages and discuss what features make it well suited for implementing simulation models.

4. In Section 13.2.2, we specified two inaccuracies in the equation describing a body falling under the influence of gravity: the problems of air resistance and the fact that the Earth is not a perfect sphere. Are there additional inaccuracies contained in this mathematical model? Do you think that these other factors should be included in our falling body model? Explain why you believe they do or do not need to be included.

5. In this chapter, we described a way to model a statistical distribution by using random numbers

generated by a computer. How do you think it is possible for a computer to generate a truly random number that successfully passes all tests for randomness? Read about random number generators and discuss the algorithms that they use.

6. In Section 13.2.3, we specified the statistical distribution for the service time in our McBurgers restaurant: 5% of customers were serviced in less than 1 minute, and so forth. Do you think this is an accurate distribution of service times in real-world take-out restaurants? Why or why not? If this distribution is not an accurate portrayal of the customer service time, what are the implications of this inaccuracy on our model?

7. Describe how the customer arrival and departure event algorithms (Figures 13.4, 13.7) and the main algorithm (Figure 13.8) of our McBurgers simulation would change if we changed the system in each of the following three ways:

   a. Instead of a single waiting line, we have N waiting lines, one for each of the N servers in the restaurant. That is, our model now behaves as shown:

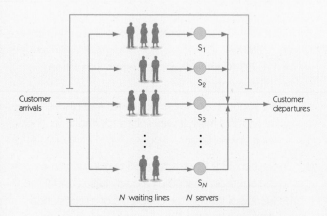

   b. The waiting line has a maximum length of MAX. If the length of the waiting line is currently less than MAX, then the customer gets into line in exactly the same way as in the current model. However, if the waiting line has a length equal to MAX, then the customer leaves the store without being served.

   c. Each customer is assigned a priority when first entering the store (a value from 1 to 10), and if there is no server currently available, the customer goes into the waiting line in priority order. That is, a customer gets into line ahead of all people with lower priority and behind everyone with an equal or higher priority.

8. In the McBurgers simulation, our model assumes that the arrival distribution of customers is the same throughout the entire day. Do you think this is a realistic assumption? If not, explain how you could modify the model to make it a better representation of customer arrivals in real life.

9. Do you think that inclusion of the following parameters in the McBurgers model would or would not increase the accuracy of the model and its ability to predict real-world behavior?

   a. Age of the customer
   b. Sex of the customer
   c. Height of the customer

10. Assume that you want to model a bus system in which passengers purchase tickets and travel from city A to one of four other cities, either B, C, D, or E. An important part of the model is determining to which city a specific passenger is traveling, a random variable. How might you go about creating a statistical distribution that accurately specifies to which of these four cities a passenger will buy a ticket and travel?

11. Do you think a computational model of elementary particles being created and destroyed by collisions in a high-speed accelerator would be discrete or continuous?

12. a. Assume our model requires 10^{14} computations to simulate one hour of activity. We run the program on a desktop computer with a computation speed of 800 MIPS. How long will it take to simulate one day of activity in the model?

    b. How fast a computer (in terms of MIPS) do we need to use if we want to complete the simulation of one day in five minutes of computing time?

13. We discussed the use of color and scale to enhance and highlight aspects of a data set being studied. In addition to these two features, suggest other ways to visually enhance the output of a model that will help to clarify its interpretation.

14. In this chapter, we focused our discussions primarily on the uses of modeling in the physical sciences, life sciences, economics, and engineering. However, the use of models is certainly not limited to these areas. Read about how simulation models are currently used to conduct research in the social sciences and humanities, such as the fields of anthropology, sociology, and political science. Write a report describing the uses of computational modeling in one of these fields.

15. Read about how simulation models are being used in your own specific field of study, and write a report on exactly what these models do and what type of research is being done using them.

CHALLENGE WORK

In this Challenge Exercise, you are going to build a computational model, much like the McBurgers simulation of Section 13.2.3. To do this, follow the same design steps that were used in this example, namely:

- Specify the events that can change the state of your system.
- For each event, specify an algorithm that shows how the system changes when this type of event occurs.
- Specify the main algorithm that will initialize your system, get the simulation started, and run the simulation until it has completed.

You do not need to specify your solution in a high-level programming language (unless you want to). Instead, you can write your algorithms using the pseudocode presented in Chapter 2 and shown in Figure 2.9.

The system that you are going to model is a small airport with a single runway that handles both takeoffs and landings. This system is diagrammed on the next page.

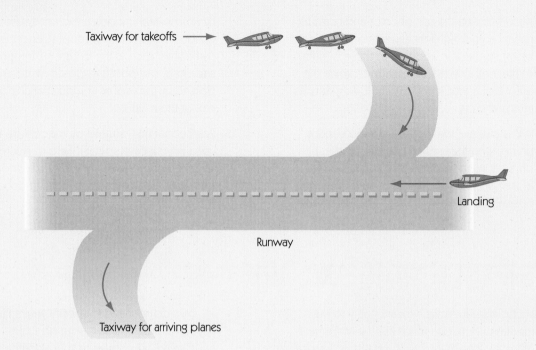

Taxiway for takeoffs →

Landing

Runway

Taxiway for arriving planes

All planes take off and land from right to left. In this model, departures are created, and these newly created flights taxi to the beginning of the runway, take off, and leave the system. Arrivals are created, and these new flights land, taxi off the far end of the runway, and leave the system. Only one plane at a time can use the runway, and because planes currently in the air may be low on fuel, arriving flights have priority to use the runway over departing flights. That is, if a flight is ready to depart and another flight is ready to land, the landing flight is the one that gets to use the runway and the departing flight must wait in line.

The purpose of this model is to determine, for a given rate of flight arrivals and departures, how long a plane must wait to take off or land and the maximum number of planes in the arrival and departure lines. This type of information would be of great help to a transportation engineer trying to decide whether a second runway will be needed as the airline traffic increases.

ADDITIONAL RESOURCES

CourseMate For additional print and/or online resources relevant to this chapter, visit the Computer Science CourseMate at login.cengagebrain.com.

Electronic Commerce and Databases

14.1 Introduction

As mentioned in Chapter 7, the Internet has been around for quite a while (since 1969), but it did not have a great impact on our everyday lives until the appearance of the World Wide Web in the early 1990s. Increasingly, the Web is our primary source of information about a variety of topics as well as a purveyor of goods and services from businesses "in the cloud."

These days, if you own just about any type of business, you really need to have a Web presence. For example,

- Your business provides a service, such as landscaping, that does not sell products directly to retail customers. But you use the Web for advertising—getting your name in front of the public, disseminating information on the services you provide, and convincing people to contact you or visit your place of business because you have superior services, knowledge, capabilities, and price.

- Your business provides a service for which follow-up information is important. For example, you are a shipping company and you use your Web site to allow customers to track their shipments.

- Your business provides a service that enables customers to engage in online transactions that are not retail sales. For example, you are a bank that allows customers to use the Web to view their current account balances and to transfer money between accounts.

- Your company sells products or materials to other companies rather than to the general public. You maintain a *B2B (business-to-business)* Web presence to streamline transactions between you as the seller and other businesses as buyers. Your goal is not only to advertise and attract new business customers, but also to cut down on transaction costs. (Note that the sales figures given in the Special Interest Box "Shopping on the Web" do not include these wholesale B2B transactions.)

- Your company is a retail business, and you maintain a *B2C (business-to-consumer)* Web site. You do this to advertise your products and to allow the general public to make online purchases.

In this chapter, we'll talk mostly about the last scenario—selling retail products to the general public. This is how most consumers interact with and experience the Web's commercial capabilities.

Assume that you run a retail rug business—let's call it "Rugs-For-You"—out of a traditional store, that is, a store with a physical building, display windows, aisles with merchandise, and salespeople. You have decided to expand your retail business into the e-commerce world, where financial transactions are conducted by electronic means over the Web. During the early stages of online commerce (the early and mid-1990s), this might have meant that a customer would fill out an order via the Web and submit it. The online order was printed out by the business at the other end, and this paper document was then processed much like any traditional purchase, including rekeying the order data for both the Shipping and Billing departments. The Web allowed the customer to initiate an order, but it had little or no role in filling the order, transferring funds, or restocking inventory.

This early approach to online commerce was cumbersome, inefficient, and error-prone. Today, businesses have moved away from this restricted model of online commerce to a total *e-business* concept where orders are processed, credit is verified, transactions are completed, debits are issued, the Shipping Department is alerted, and inventory is reduced, all electronically—at least in theory. The business may operate completely online, or it may also have a physical retail site. In the latter case, it uses the Web to complement and enhance its traditional "brick-and-mortar" business. This describes the e-business model you want to implement for your Rugs-For-You business. In addition to your traditional store, you have decided to establish a Web presence for your business where customers can come, view area rugs for sale, ask questions, make a selection, purchase their rug, and arrange to have it delivered to them, all in a quick, easy, and secure electronic environment.

In the next section, we'll look at some of the many considerations involved in such a decision. Some of these are technical; some are purely

Shopping on the Web

The Census Bureau of the U.S. Department of Commerce estimated e-commerce retail sales in the United States for the first quarter of 2010 to be $36.7 billion, an increase of 13% from the first quarter of 2008. The flattening in this growth curve no doubt is due to the economic downturn of 2008–2009, considered to be the worst since the Great Depression of the 1930s. In the first quarter of 2010, e-commerce sales accounted for 4.1% of total U.S. retail sales, an increase of about 20% over the 2008 figure for the same period.

There continues to be growth in the e-commerce retail sector, but clearly there is room for much more.

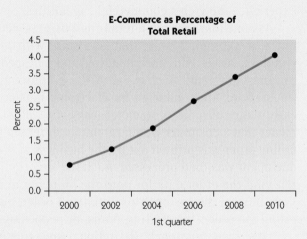

business; many are a combination of the two. Then we'll look more closely at databases, one of the most important features of the e-commerce world.

14.2 E-Commerce

In Chapter 10, we talked about HTML, the language used to build Web pages. As a small business owner, you might not know much about HTML, to say nothing of the many other technologies used in creating Web pages, such as XML. (See the Special Interest Box "Beyond HTML" in Chapter 10.) However, you can hire someone who knows these technologies, ask that person to put together some Web pages for your store, and presto, you're in e-business! But maybe not for long.

Opening an online store requires at least as much planning as building another physical store location—in fact, probably more, because it is a different medium in which to do business. Although it's possible to build Web pages in a virtual environment more quickly and cheaply than constructing a building, that doesn't mean you should charge ahead without the proper level of planning and forethought.

14.2.1 The Vision Thing

The first question you need to answer is: What is your vision for this new part of your overall commercial enterprise? Put another way: What is the business problem you are trying to solve? Do you want to:

- Broaden your customer base?

- Recapture customers you are losing to competitors with online stores?

- Better serve your existing customer base?

- Better integrate departments/functions within your existing business, so that the Shipping Department and the Accounting Department, for example, work off the same order form?

Any of these might be legitimate reasons for moving into e-commerce, but have you considered the risks involved with this decision?

- Will you just move your in-store customers online and achieve no overall gain?

- When you expose yourself to online competition, will you have something unique to offer?

- Does your existing customer base need or want anything that you don't or can't provide in your traditional business environment? What part of your existing customer base will never shop online?

- Are the employees in your Shipping and Accounting Departments in agreement with this idea, or do they feel threatened by change?

And we haven't even mentioned the costs involved with this decision:

- Do you have all the necessary hardware (computers), software, and infrastructure (network connectivity) to host a business Web site? If not, what will it cost you to acquire or lease them?

- Do you have the personnel and skills you need to build and maintain a Web site? If not, what will it cost to acquire new personnel or retrain existing personnel?

- Do you have the legal expertise onboard to manage issues such as (1) protecting your intellectual property; (2) navigating regulations, tariffs, and taxes in the many geographic regions where you will now be doing business (including perhaps overseas); and (3) legally handling customer data collected online? If not, what will it cost you to acquire this expertise?

- Do you know the potential costs of diverting resources away from your existing traditional business?

- Will you have adequate security to protect sensitive online data from hackers who may attempt to steal information such as credit card numbers?

Let's assume that you and your company officers have assessed the objectives, the risks, and the costs, and you feel that overall your bottom line will improve by going online. What should happen next?

14.2.2 Decisions, Decisions

Once you decide to move into the e-commerce arena, there are still many questions to be answered and decisions to be made. The first major decision is choosing between *in-house development* (doing the work within your own company) and *outsourcing* (hiring an outsider to do the work); in fact, this is not a single decision but a whole host of decisions.

First, the personnel issues: Are you going to use your existing staff to develop this e-business, either because they already have the necessary skills or because they will be retrained? Will you hire new personnel with the needed skills? Will you hire consultants who bring a good deal of expertise and will work with your people to get things up and running quickly? Or, alternately, will you turn the entire job over to an ASP (Application Service Provider) who, for a fee, will design your Web site and manage it/host it on an ongoing basis? The answers to these questions depend, of course, on the skills of your existing staff, how quickly you want your site to be up and running, the costs involved, and how much control you are willing to relinquish. Whoever is chosen to develop your Web site, it is important that business information about your company is made available and is used to shape all decisions along the way. In the end, your Web site should capture the "image" and provide the customer services of *your* company, not the company someone else may have in mind.

Similar questions follow regarding the hardware and software. You will need at least one Web server machine to host your Web site. You may need additional computers to store your customer database information, to support program development, to provide backup capabilities in case of hardware malfunctions, and to supply the appropriate network connections and security. Do you have these machines? Will you buy them? Will you lease space on someone else's commercial Web server? You will also need a good deal of new software, such as programs to process the customer orders that you hope will come pouring in; to interact with your accounting, shipping, and inventory control software; and to manage and store customer information. Will you use inexpensive, off-the-shelf software or

To the Cloud...

Cloud computing allows computing resources to exist anywhere with an Internet connection and still be easily accessible to the user. And these resources can expand and contract upon demand. Your business might start small and have minimal computer requirements. As your business grows, your cloud provider puts more computer assets at your disposal in a completely transparent way, that is, you need know nothing about this (at least not until you have to pay the bill). Similarly, if your business is seasonal, then after your busy season, your computing requirements go down and the pool of resources allocated for your use shrinks accordingly. This flexibility is much more efficient than buying computing resources that are underutilized much of the time or are insufficient to meet your growing needs.

more expensive packages that you can customize for your business needs? Will you use commercial software or open source software? (See "The Open Source Movement" Special Interest Box in Chapter 6.) Will your company develop its own proprietary software that can be modified whenever your business needs change? Of course, if you decide to turn everything over to an ASP, you will have little or no control over these hardware and software decisions.

14.2.3 Anatomy of a Transaction

What draws a customer to online shopping? The number-one attraction is probably *convenience*. Your online store is open 24 hours a day, 365 days a year. People can shop from the comfort of home, save time, and avoid the hassles of traffic. It is also easy to comparison shop merely by hopping from one Web site to another. But this also means that your competition is just a click away. Your goals are to:

- Draw potential customers to your site.

- Keep them there.

- Set up optimum conditions for them to complete a purchase.

Figure 14.1 illustrates the major components of an online purchase, which we have broken down into nine steps. Next, we'll elaborate on these steps, with an eye to the three goals just mentioned.

FIGURE 14.1

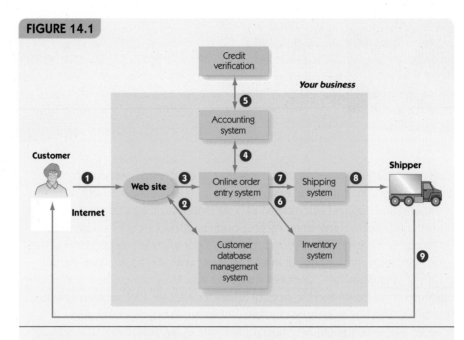

A typical online transaction in nine steps

Step 1: Getting There. How can you get customers to your Web site? Technically, once the customer knows the URL (Uniform Resource Locator), the process works exactly as described in Chapter 7. The customer hooks up to the Internet through his or her ISP (Internet Service Provider) and puts the URL into his or her Web browser. The browser works with the DNS (Domain Name System) to find the unique IP (Internet Protocol) address for this URL. Using this address, the TCP (Transport Control Protocol) routes a connection through the Internet from the customer's machine to the appropriate server. The browser uses this connection to send an HTTP GET message for the desired Web page, which is then transmitted from the Web server back to the browser and displayed on the user's screen, at which time the TCP/IP connection is broken. (All of this with a single click of the mouse button!)

But how does your potential customer learn your URL in the first place? There are many possibilities:

- *Conventional advertising*—You post your home page URL on flyers, in print and TV advertisements, on letterhead, and on any other traditional promotional materials you may produce.

- *Obvious domain name*—You want your domain name (your home page URL) to relate so closely to your business name that potential customers can easily guess it if they don't have it in front of them. Who wouldn't try *www.mcdonalds.com* to reach this well-known fast-food giant? Of course, Rugs-For-You might not be quite that well known. Domain names are registered by companies that are accredited for this purpose by ICANN (Internet Corporation for Assigned Names and

Numbers), a nonprofit corporation that took over the task of domain name management from the U.S. government in 1998. When a domain name is registered, it becomes part of the DNS so that Web users can find your IP address and get to your site. A list of accredited registrars can be obtained from *www.icann.org/registrars/accredited-list.html*, an information Web site maintained by ICANN. A number of Web sites allow you to determine whether a particular domain name has already been registered. In addition to registering your "real" domain name (*rugs-for-you.com*), you would be wise to register obvious spelling variants (*rugs-for-u.com*, *rugs-4-u.com*, etc.) if they are available, so that all roads lead to your Web site.

- *Search engine*—Potential customers may use an Internet search engine (such as Google, Yahoo, or Bing) to search for Web sites about products that you sell. For example, in response to a search using the words "rugs" and "retail sales", your company's Web site may turn up in the list of pages returned. You can also pay for a "sponsored link" so that a search on appropriate keywords will bring up links to your Web site in a prominent spot on the search engine's page or near the top of the list of search results.

- *Portal*—A portal is an entry-point Web page with links to other Web pages on some topic. It can be thought of as a starting point to learn about a particular subject, and it typically contains many helpful pointers to useful information on that subject. For example, *www.floorbiz.com* is a portal with links to retail stores selling rugs, carpet, tile, adhesives, padding, cleaning equipment, and so forth. This site also features links to information on flooring materials and manufacturers, news articles and press releases, upcoming conventions, and employment opportunities, as well as forums for bulletin board postings. The site also includes links to tips (e.g., how to maintain hardwood floors), leads for contractors to bid on floor installation jobs, and an opportunity to register to receive e-mail. You would certainly want to have a link to Rugs-For-You from this portal page, and you may even want to purchase a *banner ad* (a graphical ad, often with animation, placed in a prominent position on a Web page) so that anyone who goes to this portal sees the *rugs-for-you.com* link right away.

Step 2: Do I Know You? Regular customers at your traditional store are treated with special care. You might mail them promotional offers that you think will be of interest to them, and the salespeople know them when they walk into the store and greet them by name. You pay particular attention to their needs because, after all, return customers are the heart and soul of your business. How will your online store provide this type of personalized attention?

Some sites ask users to register and then log in when they revisit the site. These sites consult the database of registered customers and recall pertinent

A Rose by Any Other Name…

Cybersquatting is the practice of registering a domain name that uses the name or trademark of an existing business, with the intent to sell the name to that business at a profit or to capitalize on that name for some other purpose. A 1999 federal law called the Anti-Cybersquatting Consumer Protection Act (ACPA) makes cybersquatting illegal. A trademark owner claiming to be a victim of cybersquatting can file a suit under the ACPA. To have its claim upheld, a trademark owner must prove that it was the first to use the name or trademark for commercial purposes, that the name or trademark was distinctive at the time the domain name was first registered, that the domain name is the same as or sufficiently similar to the trademark as to cause confusion, and that the domain name registrant had a bad faith intent to profit from the trademark. A trademark owner who wins a suit can obtain the rights to the domain name and perhaps be awarded monetary damages up to $100,000.

ICANN also arbitrates cybersquatting disputes, with essentially the same criteria, but does not award any monetary damages. International disputes may be brought before the World Intellectual Property Organization (WIPO), a United Nations agency. Since beginning this practice in 1999, the WIPO has received over 20,000 cases concerning about 35,000 domain names. Over 90% of these cases were decided in favor of those who charged they were the victims of cybersquatting. A variant of cybersquatting, called *typosquatting*, takes advantage of typographical errors a user might make when typing a URL directly into the browser, as opposed to following a link, estimated to be about 15% of all Web traffic. For example, *www.rugs-for-you. com* might be entered as *www.rugs-for-you.org* (wrong top-level domain name), *www.rug-for-you.com* (spelling error), or *www.rusg-for-you.com* (transposition error). A company may have registered a few of these variations so that they link to the company's legitimate Web site, but there are many possibilities, some of which may be registered to typosquatters. If the user reaches a typosquatting site, the resulting Web page may contain anything from pornographic material to pay-per-click advertising links targeted to the user's interests, based on the likely site the user was trying to reach. Each click on such an ad link generates a small amount of revenue from the advertiser for the typosquatter, as well as for the ad network that brokered placement of the ad. Google—legitimately—makes its money by collecting a small sum for each click on an advertising link on its own Web pages. But in May 2008, a federal judge ruled that Google might be subject to suit for violation of the ACPA because it might post links to typosquatting pages that contain ads from which Google stands to profit, in its ad network capacity. This is an interesting case because Google is not the owner of the typosquatting domain names. As of mid-2011, this legal issue remained unresolved.

Microsoft estimates that on any given day there are 2,000 registered domain names that contain Microsoft trademark terms (e.g., *downloadvistaforwindows.com*) operated by cybersquatters seeking to profit from Microsoft intellectual property via pay-per-click online ads.

In June 2011, ICANN announced a new policy for "personalized" domain names. Top-level domain names, that is, the suffixes at the end of URLs, have been limited to two-character country codes plus the familiar .com, .org, .edu, and so forth. The new policy will allow for suffixes that are brand-specific or industry-specific names. Think "*www.mycoffee.starbucks*," for example. (Note that the application fee for these specialized domain names will be a hefty $185,000.) Proponents say this will benefit consumers and increase brand recognition; however, opponents see little value. But one thing seems certain—it will bring even more opportunities for cybersquatting.

information—for example, how the customer browsed the site previously, what pages the customer visited, where the customer lingered, what the customer bought, as well as more mundane information such as name and address. What the return customer sees is tailored to reflect this information.

Other sites that do not require a customer login still greet the customer with "Welcome, John," for example, and arrange a Web page with items tied to John's apparent interests, based on his last purchase. This type of Web site personalization can be accomplished by means of *cookies*. A cookie is a small text file that the Web server sends to the user's browser and that gets stored on the user's hard drive. It contains personal information about the user, such as name, address, time of visit, and what was looked at or bought. On the customer's next visit to that same site, the browser sends the cookie back to the server (along with the page request) so the server can create a customized page just for this shopper. This does more than merely create a friendly, personalized atmosphere. It also allows the server to record information for later use. For example, cookies enable a customer to put items into his or her online shopping cart and return at a later time to find them still there.

Transmission of Web pages between a client and server is *stateless*; that is, no information about this exchange is permanently retained by the server. Indeed, recall that the TCP/IP connection between the browser and Web server is (usually) broken once a Web page has been sent back to the browser. A totally new connection has to be established to access a different page or to return later to that same page. Without cookies, there is no association between the customer visiting one page and the same customer visiting another page, or between the same customer visiting the same page at different times. It's possible to configure a Web browser to not accept cookies, but cookies cannot execute on the client machine and are harmless. They just take up a little space.

You can provide incentives and benefits for return customers—product support for items already purchased, special promotions ("John, would you like some stain guard for that new rug you just bought? Click here for our special offer!"), free shipping, a clearly stated return policy (including the ability to return items to your traditional brick-and-mortar store if more convenient), and a chance to register complaints or ask questions online (to which you should pay attention and respond). And certainly you should provide a toll-free number where your customers can speak with a real, live person, although you don't want to make the number too prominent on your site because you are looking for your online business to free up staff, not burden them.

Online customers, both new and returning, can leave your site in the blink of an eye or, more precisely, the click of a mouse button. Your Web site must invite them in, entice them to stay, and make their path toward purchase so convenient that there is no reason not to buy from you. This is what makes designing a Web page so much more than just an HTML programming assignment! We'll talk more about Web page features in Section 14.2.4, but for now let's assume that a customer has successfully navigated your Web site, selected an item to purchase, and is ready for Step 3.

Step 3: Committing to an Online Purchase. Customers are understandably hesitant to transmit sensitive information such as their credit card number, or even their name and address, over the Web. Your site must provide a secure environment for transmitting this information, and that security comes in two pieces: encryption and authentication. *Encryption* encodes the data to be transmitted into a scrambled form, using a scheme agreed upon between the sender and the receiver. Although encryption provides for the secure transmission of data, this is of little use if the data are not being sent to the correct party. *Authentication* is the process of verifying the identity of the receiver of the data. In Step 3 of our online transaction process, the sender is the customer (actually the customer's Web browser) placing an order and sending confidential personal and financial information, and the receiver is the retailer's Web server. In Chapter 8, we discussed how the SSL (Secure Sockets Layer) and TLS (Transport Layer Security) protocols provide encryption and authentication for Web transactions. There we learned that the Web server can pass to the browser a certificate of authentication issued by a trusted third party such as VeriSign (*www.verisign.com*).

Because you decided to use VeriSign SSL software on your Web site, you can post a "VeriSign Secured" seal on your pages that users can click to verify that they are at the correct site. After all, they didn't walk into your physical place of business, so how do they know where they really are? The URL is *www.rugs-for-you.com*, and there are many pictures of rugs, but maybe it is simply a scam where the customer will send money but receive nothing in return. Spoofing is the practice of impersonating a legitimate site for the purposes of stealing money or stealing identity by collecting confidential information such as credit card numbers, names, and addresses. Clicking on your VeriSign seal might bring up a window with the information shown in part in Figure 14.2.

FIGURE 14.2

WWW.RUGS-FOR-YOU.COM is a VeriSign Secure Site

Security remains the primary concern of online consumers. The VeriSign Secure Site Program allows you to learn more about Web sites you visit before you submit any confidential information. Please verify that the information below is consistent with the site you are visiting.

Name: WWW.RUGS-FOR-YOU.COM   Status: Valid

Validity Period: 14-May-13 to 25-May-17

Server ID Information:

      Country = U.S.

      State = Ohio

      Locality = Cleveland

      Organization = Rugs-For-You, Inc.

      Common Name = www.rugs-for-you.com

If the information is correct, you may submit sensitive data (e.g., credit card numbers) to this site with the assurance that:

      This site has a VeriSign Secure Server ID.

All information sent to this site, if in an SSL session, is encrypted, protecting against disclosure to third parties.

Secure site assurance

Customers about to transmit sensitive information to your Web site are alerted by a message saying they are being transferred to a secure site. The corresponding Web page has the protocol heading *https*, rather than http, with the *s* signifying a site under the protection of SSL. Customers may also see a little lock graphic on the Web page to indicate a secure site, and the browser address bar may turn green. When they leave the site, they receive a message saying they are leaving a secure site.

Steps 4 and 5: Payment Processing. Let's assume that your customers will pay with credit cards, the most common online option. The online order form communicates with your accounting system (Step 4), which might verify the customer's credit and process this transaction with the credit company (Step 5) on the fly, that is, while the customer waits. This way, the customer can be alerted and given another chance to enter information if there is an error. In addition, you do not have to store the customer credit card number in your database, which reduces your security risk.

Another option is to collect information on the customer's order, including an e-mail address (Step 4), close the order process, and then evaluate the customer's credit and complete the transaction offline (Step 5). Once the transaction is completed, an e-mail confirmation is sent to the customer. To use this option, you must maintain customer credit card information.

Steps 6–9: Order Fulfillment. Once your customer's credit is approved, your order-entry system must alert your inventory system to decrement the number of items in stock by whatever quantity the user has purchased (Step 6) and must also contact your shipping system to arrange for shipping (Step 7). The shipping system works with the shipping company you use (Step 8) to pick up and deliver the purchase to the customer (Step 9).

14.2.4 Designing Your Web Site

Your Web site must be designed with your customers in mind. It has to be fresh and up to date, ever changing, and always displaying the latest product information. Department stores don't keep the same displays in their windows for months or years on end, and neither should you. One of your earliest decisions is your Web site *taxonomy*—how information is classified and organized so customers can easily find what they want. At *rugs-for-you. com*, you could organize your site by rug manufacturer, color, size, material, or rooms in the house. There are many options, and you must consider how your customers usually shop for their rugs.

Your customers should always know where they are on your Web site. As we mentioned in Chapter 7, hypertext allows a user to move easily from page to page by simply clicking a link. However, after a few clicks, it is easy to become totally lost and not know where you are or how to get back. A site map or a navigation bar can provide a high-level overview of your site architecture, plus make it easy to navigate (i.e., move from page to page) through the site. A good rule of thumb is that the customer should be able to get from any page in your Web site to any other page in four clicks or fewer. And although you want to encourage browsing, just as you do in your physical store, you also want customers to be able to find what they are looking for quickly, so your Web pages should include the ability to search the site for a specific item.

You need electronic "shopping carts" and order checkout forms. Keep in mind that customers want to feel in control (especially of their money!). Be sure that as customers step through the ordering process, they are always informed about the current order—items being ordered, quantity, price, and so on—and about what will happen with the next button click. It is also important to give customers the option to go back and change something or to clearly indicate that, following the next click, the order will be final and no further changes will be possible.

Give customers shipping options so that they can make the best trade-off between cost and speed of delivery. Send e-mail to confirm orders, and send follow-up e-mails when orders are shipped.

Display your privacy policy on the Web page. Tell your customers what personal information you collect, why this information is needed, how you will use it, whether you will share it and with whom you might share it, and how you will store and safeguard it. Also, understand what information you can legally collect, based on the regulations of the state or country of your target users.

You may also want to offer extras to your customers. Put up a *FAQ (frequently asked questions)* page and links to contact customer service, review new products, or connect with other customers. You can ask customers if they want to subscribe to an e-mail newsletter to alert them to the latest products (no spam, please), with the option to unsubscribe at any time. Give your customers a "suggestion box." Allow them to track their shipment through an order number. Post news and press releases about your business or products. And again, configure your site in a personalized way for return customers. All of these measures can help improve customer satisfaction, build customer relationships, and bring people back to your Web site time and time again. The suggestions and ideas listed above are part of your online *CRM (customer relationship management)* strategy.

At the same time that you want to cram all this content into your Web pages, your site must adhere to good design principles. It must look professional and uncluttered. Avoid glaring colors, flashing images, and annoying pop-up windows, although there could be a *judicious* use of animation or changing, tasteful images. Make good use of white space—it can draw attention to the items you want emphasized. All of your pages should have a consistent look and feel and a consistent set of navigation tools; this can be accomplished by designing a master template page from which all pages are derived. Be sure your company logo and/or slogan are part of this master template.

On the technical side, your Web pages should be designed to be displayed on many different machines with different operating systems and browsers (e.g., Internet Explorer, Safari, or Firefox). Not all browsers render every HTML element in exactly the same way. Users may run monitors at different screen resolutions and have widely varying communication speeds, from tens of thousands to tens of millions of bits per second. (See Section 7.2.1, "Communication Links.") Your Web design should use only those features that you know will work satisfactorily on virtually every machine and browser that your customers are likely to use. Offer features such as text-only options for users with slow connections. Adhere to ADA (Americans with Disabilities Act) requirements for Web accessibility (see the "Accessible Web Pages" Special Interest Box on the next page).

As you can see from our brief discussion, designing Web pages, or at least a successful set of commercial Web pages, is a difficult and complex task. It involves not only computer science skills (e.g., HTML, XML, HTTP, TCP/IP, networking, databases), but also a knowledge of such fields as art, graphics design, business, management, and consumer psychology, to name but a few. It is easy to create just any Web page, but much more difficult to create a really good one.

Finally, in addition to your own business Web site, consider having a presence on social networking sites. Create a Facebook page, post on Twitter and You Tube, and put links on your own Web site so people can easily find, follow, friend, watch, and tweet you. Keep your business message consistent through all these media. In addition, put links between these social networking sites to make it easy for people to move between sites and to reach your own Web site.

Accessible Web Pages

The Americans with Disabilities Act, signed into law in 1990, ensures equal opportunity in employment, government services, public facilities, and transportation for persons with disabilities. ADA has been interpreted to apply to Web page accessibility. In addition, Section 508 of the federal Rehabilitation Act mandated in 1998 that all U.S. federal agencies must make their Web pages accessible to people with disabilities.

One of the most common issues in Web page accessibility relates to images, charts, or photographs. Blind users or users with low vision have several assistive technologies available to them, such as speech synthesizers that speak text that appears on the screen or devices that translate text on the screen into touch-readable Braille. These technologies can only read text, so a visual element on a Web page needs a corresponding text tag in the HTML code for the image. The text tag should be as descriptive as possible. Here's an image that might appear on one of the *rugs-for-you.com* Web pages with its corresponding text tag as displayed by the browser.

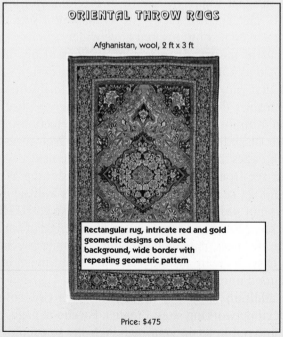

ORIENTAL THROW RUGS

Afghanistan, wool, 2 ft x 3 ft

Rectangular rug, intricate red and gold geometric designs on black background, wide border with repeating geometric pattern

Price: $475

Source: iStockphoto.com/Mehdi Farahmandfar

For those with hearing disabilities, if there is spoken information on a Web page, there should be an option to have those words displayed on the screen. If there is a telephone number for online assistance, there should also be an e-mail address or TTY phone number.

14.2.5 Behind the Scenes

Your business maintains a number of other computer applications in addition to your online order-entry system. In Figure 14.1, we saw that there are accounting, inventory control, and shipping systems as well as a customer database, and that's just to deal with customers. You also have systems that deal with your suppliers to manage orders, shipments, billing, and payments. Finally, you have personnel systems to deal with your employees—payroll, insurance, Social Security. Some of these systems may be brand-new and just installed (like your new Web site), whereas others may be legacy code that has been around for dozens of years.

Obviously, these systems are not all independent of one another, and some must collaborate quite closely. For example, your inventory control system must communicate with the supplier order system whenever you run low on an item and must restock it. Your accounting system needs to inform the customer database when a payment has been made. However, these systems may have been developed by different vendors (some functions may even be done by hand) and may run on different machines using totally different protocols and formats from those on your new Web site. Because of this, once the Web site is up and running, you may need to invest in middleware—software that allows separate, existing programs to communicate and work together seamlessly. These middleware packages do such things as translate between incompatible data representations, file formats, and network protocols to allow otherwise disparate systems to exchange information. This allows your new e-commerce application to access and/or transmit important business data to all other parts of your company. Think of middleware as a "translator" that allows for meaningful communications between, say, one businessperson who speaks just Chinese and another fluent only in Turkish.

Finally, as soon as you have your enterprise humming along smoothly as an e-commerce site, you will need an effective disaster recovery strategy. What are your plans for backing up critical data? What is your plan to keep

Practice Problems

1. Locate a portal page for at least one of the following topics: health care, environmental issues, basketball, higher education, and/or the steel industry.

2. Take a look at the Web site of a major online retailer such as Amazon.com, Apple.com, or Walmart.com and identify some characteristics of its site that you find helpful and some things that you might find annoying or troublesome.

The Price of Success

One happy thought is that your e-business might grow to be so successful that you have to scale up beyond your expectations. Amazon.com is one of the most successful e-businesses, and has expanded beyond its original bookselling role to include sales of toys, clothing, electronics, kitchen goods, housewares, home and garden items, and more.

July 21, 2007, marked the release of *Harry Potter and the Deathly Hallows*, the final book in the very popular Harry Potter series by author J. K. Rowling. On the day before it went on sale, Amazon.com had already received orders for 2.3 million books that had to be shipped out worldwide. Imagine the load this record-breaking sale placed on its online servers, back-office applications, and shippers! But even that volume paled in comparison to what Amazon faced on May 25, 2011, when it offered the new Lady Gaga album, *Born This Way*, for just 99 cents. The immediate and overwhelming response temporarily reduced even the massive Amazon server farm to a crawl, disappointing and angering music-loving customers. The following day, Amazon repeated the sale with the announcement that it was sorry for all the problems and saying "this time, we are ready for you!"

your online business open even when your server fails? Will you be able to survive a massive natural disaster? What will you do if a hacker breaks into your Web site and steals customer information? Without a plan, you are never more than one electrical storm, one malicious user, or one disk failure away from catastrophe.

By now you may have surmised that you need a lot of help to put together your successful e-business. You need network help, programming help, graphics design help, and legal advice, as well as input from those who know your business well.

14.2.6 Other Models

The e-commerce model we have been discussing is that of an online retailer selling products or services over the Web to the general public, but there are other models.

eBay. One of the most successful alternative e-commerce models is eBay, founded in 1995 and now a huge international business. Unlike the traditional retailer/customer relationship, eBay facilitates peer-to-peer relationships in an "auction" mode. Anyone can post an item to be sold at auction on eBay. The item must conform to eBay's policies (for example, it can't be a prescription drug, stolen property, or used cosmetics). Restrictions for this multinational company are aligned with regional or country laws. The seller selects the appropriate category for the item, writes a description, and includes shipping details and costs. The seller also sets the opening bid price. The duration of the bidding period is selected by the seller as a period of from 1 to 10 days. eBay collects a fee to list an item and a second fee if the item sells.

As a buyer on eBay, you see the current maximum bid for an item and the time left for bidding. You enter the maximum amount you are willing to pay, which is not revealed to the seller or to other bidders, and the system raises your bid just enough to make you the highest bidder, up to your maximum price. If the bidding exceeds your maximum price, you are notified that you have been outbid and you have an opportunity to enter a new maximum price. If the current maximum bid is yours and there is no further bidding, then you have purchased the item, possibly at a lower price than your maximum price. Safeguards are in place to protect both the buyer and the seller, for example, seller ratings, privacy policies, and standardized electronic payment mechanisms. A "fixed-price" selling option is also available.

Craigslist. Craigslist is an online classified ad site. Actually, it is a network of local sites for various cities or areas. Each such site gives postings for local items for sale, job opportunities, housing options, personal ads, discussion forums, and so on. Begun in 1995 as a modest list of San Francisco events circulated to friends of the founder, Craig Newmark, craigslist now has over 700 local sites in 70 countries. Craigslist users post about 50 million new classified ads each month, and the sites receive more than 20 billion page views per month. The craigslist Web page design is very simple—no banner ads, no flashing images, little use of color—and is quite straightforward to use. People post ads; other people respond. Users can flag postings for ads placed in the wrong category, ads that violate craigslist terms of use, or ads that are posted too frequently. Enough negative flags will cause removal of an ad. Unfortunately, there have been several cases of crimes committed and scams perpetrated based on contacts established through craigslist (the craigslist online community site now includes information about how to detect and avoid scams, *www.craigslist.org/about/scams*), but the overall effect is a sense of local community and people-to-people trust.

Groupon. Groupon has some similarities to craigslist, but is less peer-to-peer in nature. The name is a shortened form of "group coupon." Like craigslist, Groupon has many local sites and has grown at a phenomenal rate. Groupon's first site was launched in November 2008. In January 2010, it served 30 cities; by October 2010, there were over 250 sites worldwide. Here's how it works: A local business offers a coupon through Groupon for a great deal—on museum admission, a spa session, a restaurant meal, or whatever. The coupon offer is featured on the local Groupon site for a single day. The business specifies a minimum number of customers who must purchase the coupon. If that number is not met, the deal is off; no one gets a coupon and no one gets charged. If that minimum is met, the deal is on and additional customers can purchase the coupon. Coupons are e-mailed the next day to customers who purchased them. Groupon splits the coupon charge with the business, so the business spends no out-of-pocket money to advertise unless a minimum number of customers is already guaranteed. In addition, Groupon editors help make the one-day ads as attractive as possible (often with considerable humor). Groupon researches new areas for the most desirable local businesses to contact, and is rather selective about which businesses it will advertise. Groupon is also known for its customer service if, for some reason, there is a problem with the coupon when it is redeemed.

14.3 Databases

The management and organization of data have always been important problems. It is likely that a strong impetus for the development of written language was the need to record commercial transactions ("On this day Procrastinus traded Consensius 4 sheep for 7 barrels of olive oil"). From there, it is only a short step to recording inventories ("Procrastinus has 27 sheep"), wages paid, profits gained, and so on. As the volume of data grows, it becomes more difficult to keep track of all the facts, harder to extract useful information from a large collection of facts, and more difficult to relate one fact to another. With the 1890 U.S. census (Chapter 1), Herman Hollerith demonstrated the advantages that can accrue from mechanizing the storage and processing of large amounts of data.

We talked about the online customer database as part of your expansion into e-commerce, but databases are probably a key part of your business whether you have an online presence or not. You have a set of data to maintain about your employees (names, addresses, pay rates, Social Security numbers, etc.), another set of data to maintain about your suppliers (names, addresses, products, orders, etc.), and yet another set of data to maintain about your business itself (sales, expenses, taxes, etc.). Previously, such items of data were recorded by hand, but they are now maintained in electronic databases. The important thing about an electronic database is that it is more than a storehouse of individual data items; these items can easily be extracted, sorted, and even manipulated to reveal new information. To see how this works, let's examine the structure of a file containing data.

14.3.1 Data Organization

As we learned in Chapters 4 and 5, the most basic unit of data is a single *bit*, a value of 0 or 1. A single bit rarely conveys any meaningful information. Bits are combined into groups of eight called *bytes*; each byte can store the binary representation of a single character or a small integer number.

A byte is a single unit of addressable memory. A single byte is often too small to store meaningful information, so a group of bytes is used to represent a string of characters—say, the name of an employee in a company or a larger numerical value. Such a group of bytes is called a field. A collection of related fields—say, all the information about a single employee—is called a record, a term inherited from the pencil-and-paper concept of "keeping records." Related records—say, the records of all the employees in a single company—are kept in a data file. (*File* is another term inherited from the familiar *filing cabinet*.) And finally, related files make up a database. Thus,

> Bits combine to form bytes.
> Bytes combine to form fields.
> Fields combine to form records.
> Records combine to form files.
> Files combine to form databases.

Figure 14.3 shows this hierarchical organization of data elements. (This figure was drawn to look neat, but files in a database are almost never all the same size or "shape.")

Bits and bytes are too fine a level of detail for what we will discuss in this section. Also, for the moment, let's assume for simplicity that the database consists of only a single file. Figure 14.4 illustrates a single file made up of five records (the rows), each record composed of three fields (the columns). The various fields can hold different types of data. One field in each record might hold character strings; another field in each record might hold integer data.

Each record in a file contains information about an item in the "universe of discourse" that the file describes. In our example, we assume that the universe of discourse is the set of employees at Rugs-For-You and that each record corresponds to a single employee. An individual employee record, with six different fields, is shown in Figure 14.5. Here it is clear that the

FIGURE 14.3

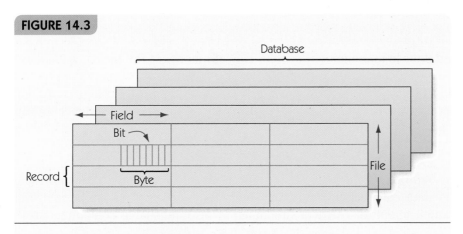

Data organization hierarchy

FIGURE 14.4

Records and fields in a single file

FIGURE 14.5

ID	LastName	FirstName	Birthdate	PayRate	HoursWorked
149	Takasano	Frederick	5/23/1986	$12.35	250

One record in the Rugs-For-You Employees file

LastName and *FirstName* fields hold character strings. The type of data being stored in the *ID* field is not clear to us as human beings from looking at the record; they could be numeric data, but because they are unlikely to be involved in computations, they could also be character string data. The data type must be specified when the file is created.

14.3.2 Database Management Systems

A **database management system (DBMS)** manages the files in a database.[1] We know that such files actually consist of collections of individual records. However, Edgar F. Codd (mentioned in Chapter 12 as a Turing Award winner for his work in database management systems) proposed the conceptual model of a file as simply a two-dimensional table. In this **relational database model**, the *Employees* file at Rugs-For-You would be represented by the *Employees* table of Figure 14.6.

With the change from records in a file to a conceptual table representing data come some changes in terminology. The table represents information about an *entity*, a fundamental distinguishable component in the

---

[1]Database examples and exercises in this chapter were run using Microsoft Access 2010.

FIGURE 14.6

Employees

ID	LastName	FirstName	Birthdate	PayRate	HoursWorked
116	Kay	Janet	3/29/1976	$16.60	94
123	Perreira	Francine	8/15/1989	$ 8.50	185
149	Takasano	Frederick	5/23/1986	$12.35	250
171	Kay	John	11/17/1974	$17.80	245
165	Honou	Morris	6/9/1993	$ 6.70	53

Employees table for Rugs-For-You

Rugs-For-You business—namely its employees. A row of the table contains data about one instance of this entity—that is, one employee—and the row is called a tuple (in Figure 14.6, each row is a 6-tuple, containing six pieces of information). How the tuples (rows) are ordered within the table is not important. Each category of information (*ID*, *FirstName*, and so on, in our example) is called an attribute. The heading above each column identifies an attribute. The table thus consists of tuples of attribute values. (In other words, in the relational model, files are thought of as tables, records as tuples, and fields as attributes.) A primary key is an attribute or combination of attributes that uniquely identifies a tuple. In our example, we are assuming that *ID* is a primary key; *ID* is underlined in the heading in Figure 14.6 to indicate that it is the primary key for this table. The Social Security number is often used as a primary key to uniquely identify tuples that involve people. Obviously, neither *LastName* nor *FirstName* can serve as a primary key—there are many people with the last name Smith and many people with a first name of Michael or Judith.

The computer's operating system functions as a basic file manager. As we learned in Chapter 6, the operating system contains commands to list all of the files on the hard drive, to copy or delete a file, to rename a file, and so forth. But a database management system, unlike a simple file manager, works at the level of individual fields in the individual records of the file; in more appropriate terminology, we should say that it works at the level of individual attribute values of individual tuples in the relational table. Given the *Employees* table of Figure 14.6, a database management system could be given the instruction shown here:

```
SELECT ID, LastName, FirstName, Birthdate, PayRate,
  HoursWorked
FROM Employees
WHERE ID = 123;
```

This command asks the system to retrieve all the information about the employee with ID 123. Because *ID* is the primary key, there can only be one such employee, and this is a relatively easy task. But the following request to locate all the information about an employee with a given last name,

```
SELECT ID, LastName, FirstName, Birthdate, PayRate,
   HoursWorked
FROM Employees
WHERE LastName = 'Perreira';
```

is done just as easily, even though the *LastName* attribute may not uniquely identify the tuple. If multiple employees in the table have the same name, all of the relevant entries will be returned.

If only some of the attributes are wanted, an instruction such as

```
SELECT LastName, PayRate
FROM Employees
WHERE LastName = 'Perreira';
```

produces just the last name and pay rate for the employee(s) with the given last name.

Database management systems usually require specialized *query languages* to enable the user or another application program to *query* (ask questions of) the database, in order to retrieve information. The three preceding SELECT examples are written in a language called SQL (Structured Query Language). We briefly discussed SQL in Chapter 10.

To appreciate the power of SQL, consider the following simple SQL queries for more complicated tasks:

```
SELECT *
FROM Employees
ORDER BY ID;
```

This query says to retrieve *all* of the attribute values (the asterisk is shorthand for listing all attributes) for all the tuples (because there is no further qualification) in the *Employees* table sorted in order by *ID*. Thus, we have effectively sorted the tuples in the relational table using a single command. This is a significant gain in productivity over the step-by-step process of comparing items and moving them around used by the sorting algorithms in Chapter 3. (Of course, what happens internally is that SQL invokes its own sorting algorithm, perhaps even one of those described in Chapter 3. However, the user is shielded from the details of this algorithm and is allowed to work at a more abstract level.) The query

```
SELECT *
FROM Employees
WHERE PayRate > 15.00;
```

gets all the tuples for employees above a certain pay rate. Here we've searched all the tuples on a particular attribute without having to specify the details, as we had to do when coding the sequential search or binary search algorithms of Chapter 3. Again, underneath this SQL command the system has invoked a sequential, binary, or other type of search algorithm, but we are insulated from this level of detail and allowed to think at a higher (and more productive) level of abstraction.

To manage a relational table, you must be able to add new tuples to the table (which is how the existing tuples got into the table in the first place), delete tuples from a table, and change information in an existing tuple. These tasks are easily handled by the SQL commands INSERT, DELETE, and UPDATE.

In order to explore further the power of a DBMS, let's expand our Rugs-For-You database to include a second relational table. The *InsurancePolicies* table shown in Figure 14.7 contains information on the insurance plan type and the date of issue of the policy for an employee with a given ID.

In the *InsurancePolicies* table, there is a *composite primary key* in that both *EmployeeID* and *PlanType* are needed to identify a tuple uniquely because a given employee may have more than one insurance plan (e.g., both health and disability insurance plans). Both attributes are underlined in the column headings in the figure, showing that they form a composite primary key. It is also true that an employee may have no plan; in Figure 14.7, there is no tuple with ID 116, although there is an employee with ID 116. Each value of *EmployeeID* in the *InsurancePolicies* table exists as an *ID* value in a tuple of the *Employees* table, where it is a primary key. Because of this, the *EmployeeID* attribute of the *InsurancePolicies* table is called a foreign key into the *Employees* table. This foreign key establishes the relationship that employees may have insurance plans.

The database management system can relate information between various tables through these key values—in our example, the linkage between the foreign key *EmployeeID* in the *InsurancePolicies* table and the primary key *ID* in the *Employees* table. Thus, the following query will give us information about Frederick Takasano's insurance plan, even though Frederick Takasano's name is not in the *InsurancePolicies* table:

```
SELECT LastName, FirstName, PlanType
FROM Employees, InsurancePolicies
WHERE LastName = 'Takasano'
AND FirstName = 'Frederick'
AND ID = EmployeeID;
```

FIGURE 14.7

InsurancePolicies

EmployeeID	PlanType	DateIssued
171	B2	10/18/1994
171	C1	6/21/2002
149	B2	8/16/2008
149	A1	5/23/2006
149	C2	12/18/2011

InsurancePolicies table for Rugs-For-You

The query is an instruction to retrieve the *LastName* and *FirstName* attributes from the *Employees* table and the *PlanType* attribute from the *InsurancePolicies* table by looking for the tuple with *LastName* attribute value "Takasano" and *FirstName* attribute value "Frederick" in the *Employees* table, and then finding the tuple(s) with the matching *EmployeeID* value in the *InsurancePolicies* table. (Here is the Boolean AND operation we encountered in Chapter 4 in our discussion on Boolean logic.) It is the last term in the WHERE clause of the query (the last line) that causes the two tables to be joined together by the match between primary key and foreign key. The result of the query is

```
Takasano Frederick B2
Takasano Frederick A1
Takasano Frederick C2
```

This query illustrates the use of three relational database operations:

- Project—Pick out certain attributes (columns) from a set of tuples. The

```
SELECT LastName, FirstName, PlanType
FROM Employees, InsurancePolicies
```

part of the query is doing a *project* operation.

- Restrict—Pick out tuples that meet a certain condition. The

```
WHERE LastName = 'Takasano'
AND FirstName = 'Frederick'
```

part of the query is doing a *restrict* operation.

- Join—Match tuples from two different relational tables using a common attribute. The

```
ID = EmployeeID
```

part of the query is doing a *join* operation.

The correspondence between primary keys and foreign keys is what establishes the relationships among various entities in a database and makes a *join* operation possible. The SQL command to create a table requires specification of the various attributes by name and data type, identification of the primary key, identification of any foreign keys, and identification of the tables into which these are foreign keys. This information is used to build the actual file that stores the data in the tuples.

We've now done a fairly complex query involving two different tables. It is easy to see how these ideas can be expanded to multiple tables, linked together by relationships represented by foreign keys and their corresponding primary keys. Figure 14.8 shows an expansion of the Rugs-For-You database to include a table called *InsurancePlans* that contains, for each type of insurance plan, a description of its coverage and its monthly cost.

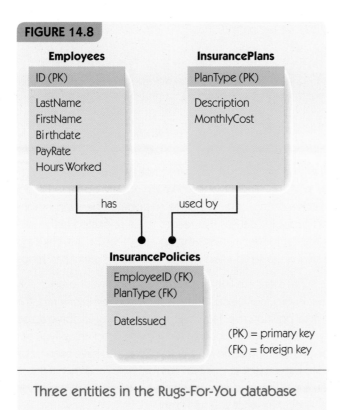

FIGURE 14.8

Employees

ID (PK)

LastName
FirstName
Birthdate
PayRate
Hours Worked

InsurancePlans

PlanType (PK)

Description
MonthlyCost

has   used by

InsurancePolicies

EmployeeID (FK)
PlanType (FK)

DateIssued

(PK) = primary key
(FK) = foreign key

Three entities in the Rugs-For-You database

PlanType is the primary key for this table. This makes *PlanType* in the *Insur-ancePolicies* table a foreign key into the *InsurancePlans* table, as shown in Figure 14.8. This linkage would allow us to write a query to find, for example, the monthly cost of Mr. Takasano's insurance (see Practice Problem 2 on page 683).

Using multiple tables in a single database reduces the amount of redundant information that must be stored. For example, a stand-alone insurance file for Rugs-For-You employees would probably have to include employee names as well as IDs. It also minimizes the amount of work required to maintain consistency in the data (if Francine Perreira gets married and changes her name, the name change need only be entered in one place). But most important of all, the database gives the user, or the user's application software, the ability to combine and manipulate data easily in ways that would be very difficult if the data were kept in separate and unrelated files.

As we have seen by looking at some queries, SQL is a very high-level language in which a single instruction is quite powerful. In terms of the language classifications of Chapter 10, it is also a nonprocedural language. A program written in SQL merely asks for something to be done (sort all tuples in some order, search all tuples to match some condition); it does not contain a specific sequence of instructions describing *how* it is to be done.

The Halloween Problem

The database Halloween Problem was named because it was first discovered on Halloween Day in 1976. Here's how it works: An update operation is done on a set of records that match a certain criterion. Once an update operation is done on a given record, the updated value causes that record to be relocated farther down in the set of records, where it once again meets the update criterion. It is once again updated, moved farther down, updated again … and the result is an infinite loop.

For example, assume there is a line of people, and you want everyone wearing a red shirt to move backward four places. If the first person is wearing red, then he or she must move back to position five. However, you are going to come across that same person when you take a look at position number five, and unless you have kept track you won't know if this is someone new or someone you have seen before. You will ask that person to move back to position number nine (and then thirteen, seventeen, etc.). When you are all done, everyone wearing a red shirt will be standing at the very end of the line—not at all what you had planned!

14.3.3 Other Considerations

Existing tuples in a relational database table can be modified or deleted, and new tuples can be added to a table. These operations must be done with care to be sure the data remains correct and consistent throughout the database. In database terminology, the *integrity* of the data must be preserved. There are three integrity rules that, if enforced during additions, modifications, or deletions, will help in this goal. The entity integrity rule says that no primary key value, or no component of a composite primary key value, can be missing ("null"). The reason is, if the primary key uniquely identifies a tuple, then a tuple with (part of) its primary key missing might not be uniquely identifiable. The data integrity rule specifies that values for a particular attribute must come from the appropriate category of information for that attribute. In the Rugs-For-You *InsurancePolicies* table, for example, any values for the *PlanType* attribute must be designations for valid plan types, and any values for the *DateIssued* must be valid dates. Finally, the referential integrity rule specifies that any value of a foreign key attribute in a given table must match a value in the corresponding primary keys of the related table. For example, we can't add a tuple to the *InsurancePolicies* table of the Rugs-For-You database with an *EmployeeID* value that does not exist in the *Employees* table. Most database systems enforce the integrity rules by default.

Performance issues definitely affect the user's satisfaction with a database management system; a slow response to a query is at best annoying and at worst unacceptable. Large files are maintained on disk in secondary storage rather than being brought in total into main memory. Accessing a record in the file involves at least one disk input/output (I/O) operation, which is a much slower process than accessing information stored in main memory, sometimes as much as three or four orders of magnitude slower.

In Chapter 5, we talked about the three components that contribute to reading an individual disk sector into memory or writing from memory to a disk sector: seek time (time to position the read/write head over the correct track on the disk), latency (time for the correct sector to rotate under the read/write head), and transfer time (time to read from or write to the entire sector). Organizing the way that records are stored on the disk can help to minimize the access time by reducing the number of disk I/O operations that must be done before finding the sector containing the desired record. For example, assume that we have a database that occupies 30 sectors on our disk, and there are 15 sectors per track. It would make the most sense to store the information on surface 0, track 0, sectors 0–14 and on surface 1, track 0, sectors 0–14. Using the same track on different surfaces means that the head does not have to move to a different track to obtain the data, and the seek time is always 0. A process called **disk defragmentation** improves access time by relocating separate pieces of a file that were originally stored randomly on the disk as space was available at the time so that they occupy contiguous storage.

Also, creating additional records to be stored along with the file, although consuming extra storage, can significantly reduce access time. This works much like a library catalog system. To access a book, the user first consults a smaller structure that is organized in a useful way (alphabetically), and that directs the user to the desired book. The smaller structure stored with the file may even be organized in a treelike manner that is a generalization of the tree structure we used in Chapter 3 to visualize the binary search. Following the branches of the tree can quickly lead to information about the location in the file of the record with a particular primary key value. A good DBMS incorporates the services of a sophisticated file manager to organize the disk files in an optimal way, in order to minimize access time to the records.

Distributed databases allow the physical data to reside at separate and independent locations that are electronically networked together. The user at site A makes a database query that needs access to data physically stored at site B. The database management system and the underlying network make the necessary links and connections to get the data from where it is currently stored to the node where it is needed. To the user, it looks like a

Think Big!

Who has the world's largest database? Many candidates come to mind—Google, Amazon, the Library of Congress... . But the winner, for the time being, is the World Data Center for Climate (WDCC) that runs in conjunction with the German Climate Computing Center. The WDCC's mission is to collect, examine, and disseminate data related to climate change on all time scales, particularly data from scientific climate modeling (see the discussion on climate modeling in Chapter 13).

The WDCC database has about 6 petabytes of "live" data available online to scientists from around the world! That's 6,000,000,000,000,000 bytes. A standard data DVD holds 4.7 GB, so this database represents the content of over 1.25 million DVDs. In addition, the supercomputer at the German Climate Computing Center (called Blizzard, and powered entirely by wind power) has access to 60 petabytes of stored magnetic tape data.

In the future, the idea of "the largest database" might be irrelevant. Distributed computing means that individual data centers may logically merge into one vast network of data accessible by anyone from anywhere. The World Data Center System consisting of 52 Centers (including the WDCC) in 12 countries is now reorganizing as part of the ICSU (International Council for Science) World Data System. Over time, the stand-alone World Data Centers plus other data centers will be merged into one gigantic globally distributed data system for scientific data.

single database on his or her own machine, except perhaps for increased access time when data have to travel across a network.

If a database management system can easily make connections among different files, and even among data stored at different locations, how difficult is it to electronically link information in the IRS database with information in the FBI database, the Social Security database, credit card databases, banking databases, and so on? Obviously, it would not be difficult, using the technology that we have described in this chapter. Building these types of massive, integrated government databases raises fewer technical questions than legal, political, social, and ethical ones. Remember that even the online customers of Rugs-For-You want assurances as to how their personal information is used. In general, issues of personal privacy and public safety are magnified enormously by the capabilities of networked databases. We'll discuss approaches to these and other related ethical issues in Chapter 17.

Practice Problems

1. Using the *Employees* table of Figure 14.6, what is the result of the following SQL query?

```
SELECT ID, PayRate
FROM Employees
WHERE LastName = 'Takasano';
```

2. Complete the following SQL query to find the monthly cost of Frederick Takasano's insurance; because *PlanType* is an attribute of both *InsurancePolicies* and *InsurancePlans*, we have to include the table name as well.

```
SELECT LastName, FirstName, _____
FROM Employees, InsurancePlans, InsurancePolicies
WHERE LastName = _____
AND ID = EmployeeID
AND InsurancePolicies.PlanType = _____;
```

3. Using the *InsurancePolicies* table of Figure 14.7, write an SQL query to find all the employee IDs for employees who have insurance plan type B2.

4. Assuming that no other changes are made to any of the three tables in the Rugs-For-You database, what integrity constraint is violated if the tuple with ID 171 is deleted from the *Employees* table?

Laboratory Experience 19

If you have a commercial database package available, you can work through the exercises in this Laboratory Experience using an expanded Rugs-For-You database. You will write SQL queries similar to the ones discussed in this section and will also learn how to use SQL to carry out some computations.

14.4 Conclusion

In this chapter, we've looked at e-commerce—an important application of computing. We've learned that there is much more involved in a retail Web business than simply creating a Web page and that technical areas of computer science such as information security, networking, and databases play a critical role. We've also seen new models of e-commerce that have become hugely popular.

In Chapter 15, we will look at another application of computer science, one that has long captured the public's attention through its depiction in science-fiction literature and movies—artificial intelligence.

EXERCISES

1. Find an example of what you consider an excellent retail Web site. Comment on:

   a. The use of color and white space.
   b. The ease of navigation.
   c. The taxonomy.
   d. Whether the site displays its privacy policy.
   e. Whether the site displays a security assurance.
   f. Your experience walking through the online purchase process (of course, cancel before you commit to the final purchase!). Are you in control and informed at each step?

2. Find an example of what you would consider a poor retail Web site. Use the same list as for Exercise 1 and note the differences you find.

3. Depending on your Web browser, you may be able to locate a folder or a file on your machine that contains cookies. Look through the folder or open the file. List references to three Web sites you have visited.

4. Using the *Employees* table of Figure 14.6, what is the result of the following SQL query?

   ```
   SELECT * FROM Employees
   WHERE HoursWorked < 100;
   ```

5. Write an SQL query that retrieves first and last names and pay rate, ordered by *PayRate*, from the *Employees* table of Figure 14.6.

6. Using the *Employees* table of Figure 14.6 and the *InsurancePolicies* table of Figure 14.7, what is the result of the following SQL query? (The # marks allow the date to be treated numerically.)

   ```
   SELECT ID, PlanType
   FROM Employees, InsurancePolicies
   WHERE Birthdate > #1/01/1980#
   AND ID = EmployeeID;
   ```

7. Using the *Employees* table of Figure 14.6 and the *InsurancePolicies* table of Figure 14.7, write an SQL query that retrieves first and last names, hours worked, and insurance plan types for all employees who have worked fewer than 100 hours.

8. Figure 14.8 describes the attributes in an *InsurancePlans* table. Write some possible tuples for this table.

9. Assuming the existence of an *InsurancePlans* table as described in Figure 14.8, write an SQL query that retrieves the employee first and last name, insurance plan type, and monthly cost for John Kay's insurance.

The following information applies to Exercises 10–14.

You are working for the ABC Clinic, a small medical clinic. The clinic would like to generate a reminder telephone call to clinic patients the day before their scheduled appointments. A vendor has a software application that will do this, given the appropriate data from the clinic database. You have been asked to investigate how to obtain the necessary data from the clinic's relational database. You are to begin with a small test database.

The following figure shows the entities in the clinic database, namely doctors, patients, and clinic appointments.

The following test data have been loaded into the tables. All fields are data type Text, i.e., the data are treated as character strings, except for AppDate and AppTime, which are type Date/Time.

Doctor

DoctorID	FirstName	LastName	Specialty
DO1	Vladimir	Yevgeny	Internal medicine
DO2	Nancy	Cooper	Internal medicine
DO3	Estelle	Villanueva	Dermatology
DO4	Anne	Davis	Gynecology
DO5	Michael	Roth	Pediatrics

Patient

PatientID	First Name	Last Name	Home Phone	Cell Phone
PA1	Craig	Martin	333-999-1212	333-410-9999
PA2	Gail	Perez	333-777-1212	333-410-7777
PA3	DuWayne	Martin	332-555-1212	332-317-1234
PA4	Gordon	Zhang	332-555-9999	332-217-4321

ClinicAppointment

Doctor ID	Patient ID	AppDate	AppTime	Reason
DO1	PA1	2/27/2013	11:30 AM	Infected finger
DO1	PA3	2/27/2013	10:30 AM	Chest pains
DO3	PA4	2/28/2013	1:30 PM	Poison ivy
DO4	PA2	2/28/2013	8:30 AM	Prenatal check

10. Write three SQL queries to display the full contents of each of the three tables.

11. Now you need to write a query to return the information used by the reminder program. The query needs to take a date and return the doctor's first and last name, the patient's first and last name and both phone numbers, and the appointment time, so it can produce a voice message of the form:

"<Patient's name> **has an appointment with doctor** <Doctor's name> **at** <Appointment time> **on** <Appointment date>."

Write the query to obtain data for all patients for February 28. (*Hint:* Your query will need two Join operations. Also, there are attributes in both the *Doctor* and *Patient* tables with the same names. You will need to qualify them with their table names, e.g., *Doctor.FirstName.*)

Show the results of your query.

12. Dr. Yevgeny has scheduled DuWayne Martin to return at the same time two days after his appointment on February 27 for another check on his chest pain. How can you add this record to the *ClinicAppointment* table? Be careful, there are a couple of subtle points to consider about scheduling this appointment. After you add this record, write the SQL query to display the resulting *ClinicAppointment* table, ordered by appointment date, then appointment time. Show the results of your query.

13. Someone has suggested that if the clinic is going to remind the patients, they should also remind the doctors. The query needs to take the doctor's ID and a date and return the doctor's first and last name and the appointment time so it can produce a voice message of the form:

"**Doctor** <Doctor's name>, **you have an appointment at** <Appointment time> **on** <Appointment date>."

Write the query to obtain data for all appointments for DoctorID D on 2/27/2013. Show the results of your query.

14. What would it take to allow the patient to call in, give his or her patient ID, select a date using the touch pad on the phone, and have the system tell him or her by voice the time of the appointment on the date specified along with the doctor's name? The query needs to take the date and PatientID and return the doctor's first and last name, the patient's first and last name, and the appointment time and date so it can produce a voice message of the form:

"<Patient's name> **has an appointment with** <Doctor's name> **on** <Appointment date> **at** <Appointment time>."

Write the query for PatientID PA3 on 2/29/2013. Show the results of your query.

CHALLENGE WORK

Make a list of all the databases (county, state, federal, school, credit card, bank, and so forth) that you think currently contain information about you. Investigate what laws or restrictions, if any, exist to protect your privacy. Then write a short paper on the additional legislation, at the county, state, or federal level, you believe is needed to protect consumer privacy, or write a newspaper editorial explaining why no further laws need to be passed.

ADDITIONAL RESOURCES

For additional print and/or online resources relevant to this chapter, visit the Computer Science CourseMate at login.cengagebrain.com.

Artificial Intelligence

15.1 Introduction

Artificial intelligence (AI) is the branch of computer science that explores techniques for incorporating aspects of intelligence into computer systems. This definition, however, raises more questions than it answers. What really is "intelligence"? Is it a uniquely human attribute? If a computer system exhibits behavior that we might characterize as intelligent, does that make it truly intelligent? What sorts of behaviors demonstrate intelligence?

Alan Turing, whose investigations into the fundamental nature of computation led to the Turing machine (Chapter 12), was also interested in artificial intelligence. In 1950, before the term *artificial intelligence* was coined, he proposed a test for intelligent behavior of machines. The Turing test allows a human to interrogate two entities, both hidden from the interrogator (Figure 15.1). One entity is a human and the other a machine (a computer). The interrogator can ask the entities questions and receive their responses. The communication is carried on in some form that does not alone reveal which entity is the computer; for example, the interrogator's questions could be typed on a keyboard and the responses printed out. If, as a result of this questioning, the interrogator is unable to determine which entity is the human and which the computer, then the computer has exhibited sufficiently human intelligence to pass the Turing test. This test does not explore the nature of human intelligence in a deep philosophical way; it merely says that if a machine exhibits behavior indistinguishable from that of a human, then how can we tell the difference—a question that has been explored more than once in science fiction.

In Chapter 13, we discussed models of physical phenomena (objects falling under the force of gravity, customers in a store). Artificial intelligence is the construction of computer models of human intelligence. Just as we learned in Chapter 13 that a model cannot capture all aspects of the system it represents, so artificial intelligence cannot capture all aspects of "intelligence." Although science fiction conjures scenarios of thinking computers controlling the world, the advances in artificial intelligence have been more modest. Nonetheless, artificial intelligence has produced practical results in natural language understanding, robotics, game playing, problem solving,

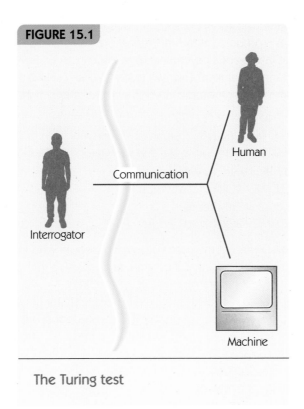

FIGURE 15.1

Human

Communication

Interrogator

Machine

The Turing test

machine learning, expert systems, pattern recognition, and other areas. And conversely, attempts to model intelligence within a computer have in turn made contributions to *cognitive science*, the study of how we as humans think and learn.

To Whom Am I Speaking?

The Loebner Prize Competition has been held annually since 1991. (You can read more about the prize on its home page, *www.loebner.net/Prizef/loebner-prize.html*.) This competition is essentially a Turing test. Dr. Hugh Loebner, a sociologist and inventor, has posted a $100,000 grand prize and a gold medal for the first computer program whose responses are indistinguishable from a human's. Though the grand prize remains unclaimed, a prize of $2,000 and a bronze medal is awarded each year to the computer program judged to be "most human" in that year's competition.

One of the most famous early AI experiments occurred in the laboratory of Professor Joseph Weizenbaum at MIT in 1966. A program named ELIZA conversed with people in the fashion of a psychotherapist, picking up on key words and echoing them back in a sentence. This was quite mechanical and there was no understanding involved. For example, an ELIZA conversation might go something like this:

> Human: I am not feeling well today.
> Computer: I AM SORRY TO HEAR THAT YOU ARE NOT FEELING WELL.
> Human: I had a fight with my wife.
> Computer: TELL ME ABOUT YOUR WIFE.
> Human: The house ate my zebra.
> Computer: TELL ME ABOUT YOUR ZEBRA.

Weizenbaum was horrified at the ease with which people who interacted with ELIZA became convinced that they were talking with a real person. Today, there are many "chatbot" programs available on the Web. The 2007 winning entry in the Loebner Prize Competition was Ultra Hal Assistant, a *chatbot* (from *chat*ter ro*bot*) program that can not only hold a conversation but remember and remind you of appointments, tell you the local weather report, give you the definition of a word, or do some Web searching for you. Ultra Hal also learns new things from conversations in which it engages. Not content to rest on past triumphs, Ultra Hal is now on Twitter and analyzes hundreds of thousands of publicly available tweets per day to increase its knowledge base (*www.zabaware.com/twitter.html*).

15.2 A Division of Labor

To understand better what artificial intelligence is all about, let's consider a division of task types. Humans can perform a great variety of tasks, but we'll divide them into three categories, representative but by no means exhaustive:

- *Computational tasks*

  - Adding a column of numbers

  - Sorting a list of numbers into numerical order

  - Searching for a given name in a list of names

  - Managing a payroll

  - Calculating trajectory adjustments for the space shuttle

- *Recognition tasks*

  - Recognizing your best friend

  - Understanding the spoken word

  - Finding the tennis ball in the grass in your backyard

- *Reasoning tasks*

  - Planning what to wear today

  - Deciding on the strategic direction a company should follow for the next 5 years

  - Running the triage center in a hospital emergency room after an earthquake

Algorithmic solutions exist for computational tasks (we devised algorithms for sorting and searching in the early chapters of this book). As humans, we can, in principle at least, follow these step-by-step instructions. Computational tasks are also tasks for which accurate answers must be found—sometimes very quickly—and that's where we as humans fall down. We make mistakes, we get bored, and we aren't very speedy. Computers are better (faster and more accurate) at performing computational tasks, provided they are given programs that correctly embody the algorithms. Throughout most of this book, with its emphasis on algorithms, we've been talking about procedures to solve computational tasks, how to write those procedures, how to get the computer to execute them, and so on.

Humans are better at recognition tasks. We should perhaps expand the name of this task type to sensory/recognition/motor-skills tasks because we receive information through our senses (primarily seeing and hearing), we recognize or "make sense of" the information we receive, and we often respond to the information with some sort of physical response that involves controlled movement. Although we wait until elementary school to learn how to add, an infant just a few weeks old, on seeing its mother's face, recognizes that face and smiles; soon that infant understands the spoken word. You spot the tennis ball in the yard even though it is green and nestled in among other green things (grass, dandelions). You register whether the tennis ball is close or far away, and you manipulate your legs and feet to propel you in the right direction.

How do we do these things? Traditional step-by-step procedural algorithms don't seem to apply, or if they do, we don't know what those algorithms are. Rather, it seems that we as humans succeed at these tasks by processing a huge amount of data and then matching the results against an even larger storehouse of data based on our past experiences. Consider the task of recognizing your best friend. You have, in effect, been shown a number of "pictures" of your friend's face that seem to be "burned into" your memory, along with pictures of the faces of everyone else you know well. When you see your friend, you sort through your mental picture file until you come to a match. It is a bit more complicated than that, however, because if you encounter your friend's sister, you might know who it is even though you have never met her before. If your friend has a different haircut or has started wearing glasses, you will most likely still recognize her or him, in spite of a changed appearance. You find not an exact match to one of the images in your mental picture file, but a close approximation. Approximation, unlike the exactitude required in computational tasks, is good enough. These complex recognition tasks that we find so easy are difficult for computers to perform, although facial detection (to aid in focusing when taking a photo) is now a feature of some digital cameras and facial recognition (to group photos by the people shown) appears in some photo management software as well as in programs used by law enforcement to identify criminals entering a building or boarding an airplane.

When humans perform reasoning tasks, they are also using a large storehouse of experience. This experience involves not just images but also cause-and-effect situations. You know that you should wear a coat when it's cold because you've experienced discomfort in cold weather when you didn't wear a coat. This could be considered "mere" commonsense reasoning, but getting a computer to mimic common sense, to say nothing of higher-order conceptual, planning, or reasoning tasks, is extremely challenging. There may be no "right" answer to such tasks, and the way humans arrive at their respective answers sometimes seems ambiguous or based at least in part on intuition, which may be just another name for knowledge or reasoning that we don't yet understand.

Figure 15.2 summarizes what we've outlined as the relative capabilities of humans and computers in these three types of tasks. Computers fall below humans where procedural algorithms either don't work or aren't known, and where there seems to be a high level of complexity and perhaps approximation or ambiguity. Artificial intelligence seeks ways to improve the computer's ability to perform recognition and reasoning tasks, and we'll look at artificial intelligence approaches in these two areas in the rest of this chapter. As mentioned earlier, however, both types of tasks seem to require a storehouse of information—images, memories, past experiences, and the like—for which we'll use the general term *knowledge*. Therefore, we'll first look at various approaches to representing this knowledge.

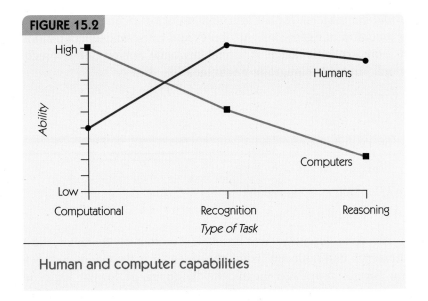

FIGURE 15.2

Human and computer capabilities

15.3 Knowledge Representation

We can consider knowledge about some topic as a body of facts or truths. For the computer to make use of that knowledge, there must be some representational form in which the knowledge is stored within the computer. (At the lowest level, of course, only 0s and 1s are stored within the computer, but strings of 0s and 1s are organized and interpreted at a higher level of abstraction—as integers or characters, for example.) For computational tasks, the relevant knowledge is often isolated numeric or textual items. This is the data that we've manipulated with procedural programs. What about more complex knowledge?

There are many workable representation schemes; let's consider four possibilities.

1. *Natural language*—A paragraph or a page of text that contains all the knowledge we are trying to capture is written in English, French, Spanish, or some other natural language. Here is an example:

   Spot is a brown dog and, like any dog, has four legs and a tail. Also like any dog, Spot is a mammal, which means Spot is warm-blooded.

   Note that although this representational form is text, it is text in a different sense from the character strings that are used in computational tasks. Here it is not simply the strings of characters that are important but also the meaning that those strings of characters convey. When reading a natural language paragraph, we use our understanding of the richness of the language's vocabulary to extract the meaning. Some researchers believe that the words we read or hear do not actually communicate meaning, but merely act as "triggers" to meanings stored in our brains.

2. *Formal language*—A formal language sacrifices richness of expression for precision of expression. Attributes and cause-and-effect relationships are more explicitly stated. A formal language version of the foregoing natural language paragraph might look like this:

> *Spot is a dog.*
>
> *Spot is brown.*
>
> *Every dog has four legs.*
>
> *Every dog has a tail.*
>
> *Every dog is a mammal.*
>
> *Every mammal is warm-blooded.*

The term *language* was used in Chapter 11 to mean the set of statements derivable by using the rules of a grammar. But here, the term formal language means the language of formal logic, usually expressed more symbolically than we have done in our example. In the usual notation of formal logic, we might use $dog(x)$ to symbolize that the symbolic entity x has the attribute of being a dog and $brown(x)$ to mean that x has the attribute of being brown. Similarly *four-legged*(x), *tail*(x), *mammal*(x), and *warm-blooded*(x) could symbolize that x has these various attributes. The specific entity Spot could be represented by S. Then $dog(S)$ would mean that Spot has the attribute of being a dog. Cause-and-effect relationships are translated into "if-then" statements. Thus, "Every dog has four legs" is equivalent to "For every x, if x is a dog, then x has four legs." An arrow symbolizes cause and effect (if-then); "If x is a dog, then x has four legs" would be written symbolically as

$$dog(x) \rightarrow four\text{-}legged(x)$$

To show that every x that has the dog property also has the four-legged property, we would use a *universal quantifier*, $(\forall x)$, which means "for every x." Therefore,

$$(\forall x)(dog(x) \rightarrow four\text{-}legged(x))$$

means "For every x, if x is a dog, then x has four legs" or "Every dog has four legs." Symbolically, the preceding six formal language statements become

Natural Language Statement	Symbolic Representation
Spot is a dog.	$dog(S)$
Spot is brown.	$brown(S)$
Every dog has four legs.	$(\forall x)(dog(x) \rightarrow four\text{-}legged(x))$
Every dog has a tail.	$(\forall x)(dog(x) \rightarrow tail(x))$
Every dog is a mammal.	$(\forall x)(dog(x) \rightarrow mammal(x))$
Every mammal is warm-blooded.	$(\forall x)(mammal(x) \rightarrow warm\text{-}blooded(x))$

The use of formal languages represents one of the major approaches to building artificial intelligence systems. Intelligent behavior is achieved by using symbols to represent knowledge and by manipulating these symbols according to well-defined rules. We'll see an example of this when we discuss expert systems later in this chapter.

3. *Pictorial*—Information can be stored in pictorial form as an image—a grid of pixels that have attributes of shading and color. Using this representation, we might have a picture of Spot, showing that he is brown and has four legs and a tail. We might have some additional labeling that says something like, This is Spot, the dog. This visual representation might contain additional knowledge about Spot's appearance that is not embodied in the natural language paragraph or the formal language statements, but it would also fail to capture the knowledge that Spot is a mammal and that mammals are warm-blooded. It also wouldn't tell us that all dogs have four legs and a tail. (After all, a photo of a three-legged dog does not tell us that all dogs have three legs.)

4. *Graphical*—Here, we are using the term *graphical* not in the sense of "visual" (we have already talked about pictorial representation) but in the mathematical sense of a graph with nodes and connecting arcs. Figure 15.3 is such a graph, also called a semantic net, for our dog example. In the terminology of object orientation that was a feature of the programming language(s) of Chapter 9, the rectangular nodes represent classes or objects, the oval nodes represent properties, and the arcs represent relationships. The "is a" relationship represents a subclass of a class that inherits properties from the parent class; "dog" is a subclass of "mammal," and any dog object inherits all the properties of mammals in general, such as being warm-blooded. Objects from

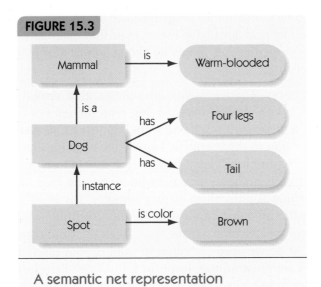

FIGURE 15.3

A semantic net representation

the dog class may also have properties of their own. The "instance" relationship shows that something is an object of a class; Spot is a particular object from the dog class and may have a unique property not necessarily shared by all dogs.

Any knowledge representation scheme that we select must have the following four characteristics:

1. *Adequacy*—The representation method must be adequate to capture all of the relevant knowledge. Because of its rich, expressive powers, a natural language representation will surely capture a lot of knowledge. However, it might be difficult to extract exactly what that knowledge is. You might have to wade through a lot of unnecessary verbiage, and you must also understand the nuances of meaning within the natural language. A formal language representation has the advantage of extracting the essentials.

2. *Efficiency*—We want the representational form to be minimalist, avoiding redundant information wherever possible. This means allowing some knowledge that is not explicitly represented to be inferred from the knowledge that is explicitly represented. In the preceding example, it is easy to infer from the natural language, the formal language, or the semantic net that because Spot is a dog, he has four legs and a tail and also is a mammal and, therefore, warm-blooded. This knowledge, as we have said, is not captured in the pictorial format. On the other hand, it would take a much longer natural language paragraph to describe all the additional knowledge about Spot that is captured in the picture.

3. *Extendability*—It should be relatively easy to extend the representation to include new knowledge. For example, the semantic net can easily be extended to tack on another "dog" instance. It would also be easy to capture the fact that dogs have two eyes or that mammals do not lay eggs; these properties can simply be plugged in as new ovals connected into the network.

4. *Appropriateness*—The representation scheme used should be appropriate for the knowledge domain being represented. For example, a pictorial representation scheme would appear to be the most appropriate way to represent the knowledge base for a problem dealing with recognition of visual images. We saw before that a pictorial representation is probably not appropriate for the kind of knowledge about Spot that is difficult to display visually. The level of granularity needed for the intended application might also influence the appropriateness of a particular scheme. Is a given pictorial representation sufficient, or do we need to "zoom in" and expose more detail? The appropriate representational form for knowledge therefore depends on the knowledge to be captured and on the type of task for which the knowledge is to be used.

Practice Problems

1. Write a natural language paragraph that describes the concept of a hamburger. Now draw a semantic net that incorporates the same knowledge as your natural language description. Which one is easier for you to produce?

2. Convert the following natural language statements to formal symbolic representation, using the properties sandwich(x), hamburger(x), grilledCheese(x), onBread(x), vegetarian(x):

   Every hamburger is a sandwich

   Every grilled cheese is a sandwich

   All sandwiches are on bread

   Every grilled cheese is vegetarian

15.4 Recognition Tasks

If artificial intelligence aims to make computers "think" like humans, then it is natural to investigate and perhaps attempt to mimic the way the human brain functions. It is estimated that the human brain contains about 10^{12} neurons (that's 1 trillion, or 1,000,000,000,000). Each *neuron* is a cell capable of receiving stimuli, in the form of electrochemical signals, from other neurons through its many *dendrites* (Figure 15.4). In turn, it can send stimuli

FIGURE 15.4

A neuron

to other neurons through its single *axon*. The axon of a neuron does not directly connect with the dendrites of other neurons; rather, it sends signals over small gaps called *synapses*. Some of the synapses appear to send the neuron activating stimuli, whereas others seem to send inhibiting stimuli. A single neuron collects all the stimuli passing through all the synapses around its dendrites. The neuron sums the activating (positive) and inhibiting (negative) stimuli it receives and compares the result with an internal "threshold" value. If the sum equals or exceeds the threshold value, then the neuron "fires," sending its own signal down its axon to affect other neurons.

Each neuron can be thought of as an extremely simple computational device with a single on/off output. The power of the human brain lies in the vast number of neurons, the many interconnections between them, and the activating/inhibiting nature of those connections. To borrow a term from computer science, the human brain uses a connectionist architecture, characterized by a large number of simple "processors" with multiple interconnections. This contrasts quite noticeably with the Von Neumann architecture discussed in Chapter 5 that is still the basis for most computers today. In that model, there are a small number (maybe only one) of very powerful processors with a limited number of interconnections between them.

In some areas of the brain, an individual neuron may collect signals from as many as 100,000 other neurons and send signals to an equally large number of other neurons. This extensive parallelism is evidently required because of the relatively slow time frame within which a neuron fires. In the human brain, neurons operate on a time scale of milliseconds (thousandths of a second), as opposed to the nanoseconds (billionths of a second) in which computer operations are measured, a difference of 6 orders of magnitude. In a human processing task that takes about 1/10 second (recognition of your friend's face), the number of steps that can be executed by a single neuron would be on the order of 100. (In the same time period a typical computer processor could perform about 100,000,000 operations.) To carry out the complexity of a recognition task, then, requires the parallel activities of a large number of neurons executing cooperatively within this short time frame. In addition, massive parallelism supplies redundancy so that information is not stored only in one place but is shared within the network of neurons. Thus, the deterioration of a limited number of single neurons (a process that happens constantly as biological cells wear out) does not cause a failure of the information processing capabilities of the network.

Artificial intelligence systems for recognition tasks have tried to mimic this connectionist approach. *Artificial neural networks*, usually just called neural networks, can be created by simulating individual neurons in hardware and connecting them in a massively parallel network of simple devices that act somewhat like biological neurons. (Recall our discussion in Chapter 5 of parallel processing and non–Von Neumann architectures.) Alternatively, the effect of a neural network may be simulated in software on an ordinary sequential-processing computer. In either case, each neuron has a threshold value, and its incoming lines carry weights that represent

FIGURE 15.5

One neuron with three inputs

stimuli. The neuron fires when the sum of the incoming weights equals or exceeds its threshold value; the input lines are activated via the firing of other neurons.

Figure 15.5 represents a neuron with a threshold value of 3 and three input lines with weights of 2, −1, and 2, respectively. If all three input lines are activated, the sum of the incoming signals is $2 + (−1) + 2 = 3$ and the neuron fires. It also fires if only lines 1 and 3 are activated because the sum of the incoming signals is then $2 + 2 = 4 > 3$. Any other combination of activated input lines cannot carry sufficient stimulation to fire the neuron. (Real, biological neurons fire with intensities that vary through a continuous range but, as usual, our simplified computer representation of such analog values uses a set of discrete values.)

Figure 15.6 depicts a neural net with an input layer and an output layer of neurons. An input value x_i is presented to neuron N_j in the input layer via a line with signal strength $x_i \times w_{ij}$. The values of x_i are usually binary (0 or 1), so that this line carries a signal of either 0 when x_i is 0, or the weight w_{ij} when x_i is 1. The weights to the input neurons, as well as the weights from the input layer to the output layer, can be positive, negative, or zero.

In the neural network shown in Figure 15.7, we have eliminated connections of weight 0. Here x_1 and x_2 have binary values of 0 or 1. If x_1 or x_2 or both have the value 1, then a signal of 1 is passed to one or both of the neurons in the input layer, causing one or both of them to fire, which causes the single neuron in the output layer to fire and produce an output of 1. If both x_1 and x_2 have the value 0, then neither neuron in the input layer fires, the single neuron in the output layer does not fire, and the network output is 0. This neural network is acting like an OR gate.

It turns out to be impossible to build such a network to represent the Boolean operation called exclusive OR, or XOR, whose truth table is shown in Figure 15.8. Here, the output is true (1) when one or the other input is true, but not when both are true. In Figure 15.9, no matter what values we give for the weights and thresholds, it is not possible to generate this behavior. If exactly one input signal of 1 is enough to fire the output neuron, which is the desired behavior, then two input signals of 1 can only increase the tendency for the output neuron to fire.

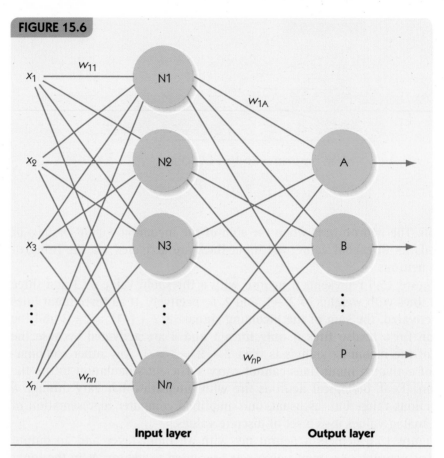

FIGURE 15.6

Neural network model

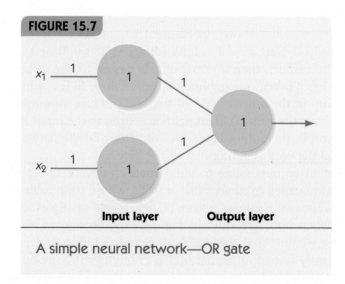

FIGURE 15.7

A simple neural network—OR gate

FIGURE 15.8

Inputs		Output
X_1	X_2	
0	0	0
1	0	1
0	1	1
1	1	0

The truth table for XOR

FIGURE 15.9

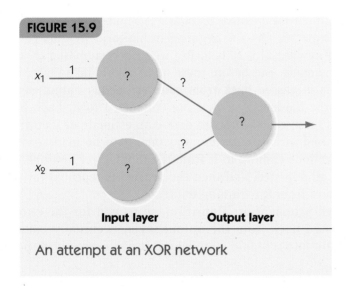

Input layer   Output layer

An attempt at an XOR network

To represent the XOR operation requires a "hidden layer" of neurons between the input and output layers (see the neural network for the Practice Problem at the end of this section). Neural networks with a hidden layer of neurons are useful for recognition tasks, where we want a certain pattern of output signals for a certain pattern of input signals. The XOR network, for example, recognizes when its two binary inputs do not agree.

Conventional computer processing works on a knowledge base where the information is stored as data in specific memory cells that can be accessed by the program as needed. In a neural network, both the knowledge representation and also the "programming" are stored in the network itself as the weights of the connections and the thresholds of the neurons. If you want to build a neural network that performs in a certain way, how do you determine these values? In a simple network, trial and error can produce a solution, but such is not the case for a network with thousands of neurons. Fortunately, the right answer doesn't have to be found the first time. Remember that neural networks are modeled on the human brain;

you learned to recognize your best friend through repeated "learning experiences" that modified your knowledge base until you came to associate certain features or characteristics with that individual.

Similarly, a neural network can learn from experience by modifying the weights on its connections (even making some connections "disappear" by assigning them 0 weights). A network can be given an initial set of weights and thresholds that is simply a first guess. The network is then presented with training data, for which the correct outputs are known. The actual output from the network is compared with the correct output for one set of input values from the training data. For those output neurons that produce correct values, their threshold values and the weights on their inputs do not change. Output neurons that produce erroneous values can err in one of two ways. If an output neuron fires when it is not supposed to, then the positive (excitatory) input values coming into it are adjusted downward, and the negative (inhibitory) weights coming into it are adjusted upward. If it fails to fire when it is supposed to, the opposite adjustment is made. But before these adjustments take place, information on the errors is passed back from each erroneous output neuron to the neurons in the hidden layer that are connected to it. Each hidden-layer neuron adds these error counts to derive an estimate of its own error. This estimate is used to calculate the adjustments to be made on the weights of the connections coming to it from the input-layer neurons. Finally, the weights are all adjusted, and then the process is repeated for the next set of input values from the training data.

This back propagation algorithm, so named for the error estimates that are passed back from the output layer, eventually causes the network to settle into a stable state where it can correctly respond, to any

Can You Hear Me Now?

In 1999, two biomedical engineers at the University of Southern California, Theodore Berger and Jim-Shih Liaw, created the Berger-Liaw Neural Network Speaker-Independent Speech Recognition System. This is a neural network that, after minimal training, can recognize words spoken by any individual. Furthermore, it can pick out individual words from a noisy background far better than a human listener can. Even more remarkable, this neural net uses only 11 neurons connected by 30 links. The key to the success of this neural net is that the researchers incorporated a temporal dimension; neurons do not all fire for the same time duration, nor in lockstep. A demonstration of this speech-recognition system can be found at *www.usc.edu/ext-relations/news_service/real/real_video.html*.

desired degree of accuracy, to all inputs in the training set. In effect, the successive changes in weights have reinforced good behavior and discouraged bad behavior (much as we train our pets) until the paths for good behavior are imprinted on the connections (as in Fido's brain). The network has "learned" what its connection weights should be, and its ability to recognize the training data is embedded somehow in the collective values of these weights. At the end of its training, the neural network is ready to go to work on new recognition problems that are similar to, but not the same as, the training data and for which the answers are unknown.

Neural networks have found their way into dozens of real-world applications. A few of these are handwriting recognition, speech recognition, recognizing patterns indicative of credit card fraud, recognizing bad credit risks for loans, predicting the odds of susceptibility to cancer, visual-recognition systems, segmenting magnetic resonance images in medicine, adapting mirror shapes for astronomical observations, and discovering the best routing algorithm in a large communications network (a problem we mentioned in Chapter 7). With the ever-lower cost of massively parallel networks, it appears that neural networks will continue to find new applications.

Laboratory Experience 20

In this Laboratory Experience, you will train a neural network simulator for a character-recognition task. You can choose one or more characters to present to a neural network's input layer and then train the network to correctly recognize these characters. After the network is trained, you can input garbled variations of these characters that are similar to, but not identical to, the training data characters and test the network's ability to correctly identify them. You can vary the level of "garbling" in the input to see at what point the network fails in its recognition task.

Practice Problems

1. If input line 1 is stimulated in the following neural network (and line 2 is not stimulated), will the output line fire? Explain.

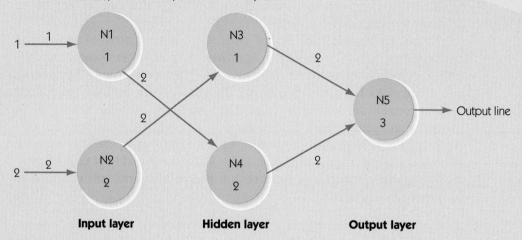

2. If the firing threshold on node N5 is changed from its current value of 3 to 5, under what conditions will it fire?

15.5 Reasoning Tasks

We noted that one of the characteristics of human reasoning seems to be the ability to draw on a large body of facts and past experience to come to a conclusion. In this section, we look at several ways in which artificial intelligence specialists try to get computers to emulate this characteristic.

15.5.1 Intelligent Searching

Earlier in this book, we presented two algorithms for searching—sequential search and binary search. These search algorithms look for a perfect match between a specific target value and an item in a list. The amount of work involved is $\Theta(n)$ for sequential search and $\Theta(\lg n)$ for binary search.

A *decision tree* for a search algorithm illustrates the possible next choices of items to search if the current item is not the target. In a sequential search, there is only one item to try next: the next item in the list. The decision tree for sequential search is linear, as shown in Figure 15.10. A decision tree for a binary search, such as the one shown in Figure 15.11, reflects the fact that if the current item is not the target, there are only two next choices: the

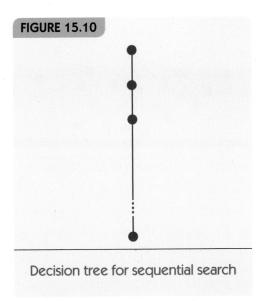

Decision tree for sequential search

Decision tree for binary search

midpoint of the sublist before this node or the midpoint of the sublist after this node. Furthermore, the binary search algorithm specifies which of the two nodes to try next.

The classical search problem benefits from two simplifications:

1. The search domain (the set of items being searched) is a linear list. At each point in the search, if the target is not found, the choice of where to look next is highly constrained.

2. We seek a perfect match, so the comparison of the target against the list item results in a binary decision—either they match or they do not.

Suppose, however, that condition 1 does not hold; the search domain is such that after any one node has been searched, there are a huge number of next choices to try, and there is no algorithm to dictate the next choice.

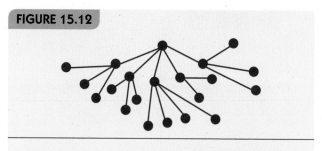

FIGURE 15.12

A state-space graph with exponential growth

Figure 15.12 attempts to portray this scenario. In the terminology of artificial intelligence, such a figure is called a state-space graph, and we seek to perform a state-space search to find a *solution path* through the graph. The idea is that each node of the graph represents a "state" of our problem, and we have some "goal state" or states in mind. For example, in a game of tic-tac-toe, our initial state is the empty game grid, and our goal state is a winning configuration. A solution path takes us from the initial state to a winning configuration, and the graph nodes along the way represent the intermediate configurations. In addition to finding a winning sequence of moves for a board game (tic-tac-toe, checkers, chess, and so forth), many other types of problems, such as finding the shortest path through a network or finding the most successful investment strategy in the stock market, fall into the state-space search category. In some of these problems, condition 2 of the classical search problem—that of seeking an exact match with a specified target value—is not present either. We simply want to acquire as many characteristics of the desired goal as possible, and we need some measure of when we are "close enough."

A *brute force* approach for a solution path traces all branches of the state-space graph so that all possible choices are tested and no test cases are repeated. This becomes a massive bookkeeping task because the number of branches grows exponentially. Given that time and computing resources are limited, an intelligent search needs to be employed. An intelligent search narrows the number of branches that must be tried and thereby puts a cap on the otherwise exponential growth of the problem. Intelligent searching involves applying some *heuristic* (which means, roughly, an "educated guess") to evaluate the differences between the present state and the goal state and to move us to a new state that minimizes those differences—namely, the state that maximizes our progress toward the goal state.

An intelligent chess-playing strategy, for example, is one that makes an appropriate first move and that, at each step, makes a move more likely than others to lead to a winning board configuration. Even a grand master of chess cannot pursue the brute force approach of mentally trying out all the possible next moves, all the possible moves following from each of those moves, and so on, for very many steps. (In Section 1.2, we showed that using a brute force approach, a computer would require a billion billion billion years to make its first move!) Intelligent searching is required. There must be a deep storehouse of experience that can be "consulted" on the basis of the present configuration of the board. A grandmaster-level player may need a mental database of around 50,000 of these board configurations, each with its associated information about the best next move.

Building a machine that can beat a human at chess was long thought to be a supreme test of artificial intelligence—machines that "think." Successfully playing chess, it was believed, surely epitomized logical reasoning, true "intelligence." Chess is difficult for humans. Yet, the rules for chess are straightforward; it is simply the size of the state-space that is overwhelming. As artificial intelligence researchers delved deeper into supposedly "simpler" problems such as visual recognition or natural language understanding— things we humans do easily—it became clear that these were the harder challenges for machines. Playing chess came to be viewed as the last of the "easy" hard problems.

15.5.2 Swarm Intelligence

Recall that the connectionist architecture—neural networks—draws its inspiration from nature, namely, the human brain. Another approach to achieving a desired end, *swarm intelligence*, also draws its inspiration from nature, modeling the behavior of, for example, a colony of ants. Each ant is an unsophisticated creature with limited capabilities, yet acting as a collective, an ant colony can accomplish remarkable tasks. Ants can find the shortest route from a nest to a food source, carry large items, emigrate as a colony from one location to another, and form bridges. An ant "communicates" with other ants by laying down a scent trail, called a *pheromone trail*; other ants follow this trail and reinforce its strength by laying down their own pheromones. Given a choice, ants have a higher probability of following the strongest pheromone trail. Hence, the ant that took the shortest path to food and returned to tell about it lays down a trail that other ants follow and reinforce faster than the trail laid down by an ant that took a longer path. Because pheromone trails evaporate quickly, the collective intelligence of the colony is constantly updated to respond to current conditions of its environment.

The swarm intelligence model captures this behavior. Computer scientists create algorithms that simulate the process of having simple agents (analogous to the ants) operate independently and follow each other's "trails" to find the most efficient routes. This algorithmic approach is called Ant Colony Optimization (ACO) and has been used commercially in vehicle routing, job scheduling, and sensing of biological or chemical contaminants. Research is under way to use such simple agents in telecommunications networks to avoid the complexity of a centralized control system to compute and distribute routing tables within a network.

ANTS in Space!

NASA's Goddard Space Flight Center is developing one of the most interesting applications of swarm intelligence. The ANTS (Autonomous NanoTechnology Swarm) project involves objects shaped like three-sided pyramids with a base (tetrahedrons). Called TETwalkers, these objects have a small motor at each vertex with connecting struts between motors. The motors can retract or extend the struts, thereby changing the center of gravity of the TETwalker and causing it to tumble over. Such tumblings, repeated over and over, are the method of locomotion for the TETwalker. Future versions of the TETwalker will be much smaller, and capable of being joined together in swarms.

NASA envisions using artificial intelligence to allow these swarms to make decisions and change shape as circumstances arise. For example, a swarm could configure itself as a snakelike body that slithers across the surface of a distant planet. When it finds something interesting to report, it can reconfigure itself to grow an antenna and transmit data back to Earth. Reconfiguration can also make the swarm resistant to damage—if a few TETwalkers are "injured," the swarm can just reconfigure itself to work around them.

This model TETwalker has toured all over the world. ANTS projects have involved collaborators among students and staff at more than 15 different colleges and universities. Go to *http://ants.gsfc.nasa.gov/features/ MeteorCraterSmall.mov* to watch a test of the TETwalker conducted in Meteor Crater in northern Arizona. For further information on TETwalkers, see *www.nasa.gov/vision/universe/ roboticexplorers/ants.html*.

Source: Courtesy of NASA

15.5.3 Intelligent Agents

Swarm intelligence rests in the colony as a whole, which seems to acquire "knowledge" that is greater than the sum of its parts. At the opposite end of the spectrum are intelligent agents. An intelligent agent is a form of software technology that is designed to interact collaboratively with a user somewhat in the mode of a personal assistant. Imagine that you have hired your own (human) personal assistant. In the beginning, you must tell your assistant what to do and how you want it done. Over time, however, your assistant comes to know more about you and soon can anticipate what tasks need to be done and how to perform them, what items to bring to your attention, and so forth. Your assistant becomes more valuable as he or she becomes more self-directed, always acting with your best interests in mind. You, in turn, put more and more trust in your assistant.

Like the human personal assistant, an intelligent agent does not merely wait for user commands but begins to initiate communication, take action, and perform tasks on its own on the basis of its increasing knowledge of your needs and preferences. Here are some examples that exist today:

- A personalized Web search engine that allows you to profile items of interest to you and then automatically delivers appropriate information from the Web. For example, you may request updated weather conditions for your geographic area, along with news items related to sports and European trade. At periodic time intervals, this *push technology* downloads your updated, personalized information to your screen (or cell phone) to be displayed whenever no other task is active.

- A more intelligent version of this personalized Web searcher that enables you to rate each article it sends you and then dynamically adjusts what it sends in the future as it learns about your preferences.

- An even more intelligent search agent that not only narrows down choices from topics you have chosen but can suggest new, related topics for you to explore. This is accomplished by having your agent communicate with similar agents on the Web, even when you are not online. If your agent knows of your interest in French cuisine, for example, it communicates with other agents to find those that represent users with the same interest. It may learn from these agents that many of their users are also interested in Cajun cooking. Your agent then judges whether these suggestions are coming from agents whose recommendations on the whole have been well received by you in the past. If so, it asks whether you also want information about Cajun cooking. If you do not agree to this proposal, your agent notes what agents made that suggestion and, on the next pass, gives less consideration to their ideas. The more agents that participate, the more accurate each one becomes at "understanding" the interests of its user.

- An online catalog sales company that uses an agent to monitor incoming orders and make suggestions. For example, a customer who orders a camera may be presented with a list of related accessories for sale, such as tripods and lens filters.

- A manufacturing plant that uses an intelligent agent to negotiate with suppliers on the price and scheduling of parts delivery to maximize efficiency of production.

Intelligent agent technology has been an area of interest in artificial intelligence for many years. However, intelligent agents need to display significantly greater learning capabilities and "common sense" before most users will trust them to make autonomous decisions regarding the allocation of time and money. Until then, they will be relegated to presenting suggestions to their human users. However, when a sufficient level of trust in intelligent agent technology has been achieved, and when human users are willing to allow their software to make independent decisions, we will begin to see such exciting new applications as:

- *Financial agents* that negotiate with one another over the Web for the sale and purchase of goods and services, using price/cost parameters set by the sellers and buyers

- *Travel and tourism agents* (electronic, not human) that book airline flights, rent automobiles, and make hotel reservations for you on the basis of your destination, schedule, price range, and preferences

- *Office manager agents* that screen incoming telephone calls and e-mail, putting meetings on their users' schedules, and drafting replies

15.5.4 Expert Systems

Although intelligent agents incorporate a body of knowledge to "filter" their choices and thereby appear to capture certain aspects of human reasoning, they still perform relatively limited tasks. Consider the more unstructured scenario of managing the triage center in a busy hospital emergency room. The person in charge draws on (1) past experience and training to recognize various medical conditions (which may involve many recognition subtasks), (2) understanding of those conditions and their probable consequences, and (3) knowledge about the hospital's capabilities and resources in general and at the moment. From this knowledge base, a chain of reasoning is followed that leads, for example, to a decision to treat patient A immediately in a particular fashion and to let patient B wait. We consider this to be evidence of quite general "logical reasoning" in humans.

Artificial intelligence simulates this kind of reasoning through the use of expert systems, also called *rule-based systems* or *knowledge-based systems*. (The latter term is a bit confusing because all "intelligent activity" rests on some base of knowledge.) An expert system attempts to mimic the human ability to engage pertinent facts and string them together in a logical fashion to reach some conclusion. An expert system must therefore contain these two components:

- A knowledge base—A set of facts about the subject matter

- An inference engine—A mechanism for selecting the relevant facts and for reasoning from them in a logical way

Note that the knowledge base contains facts about a *specific* subject domain to narrow the scope to a manageable size.

The facts in the knowledge base consist of certain simple assertions. For example, let's say that the domain of inquiry is U.S. presidents. Three simple assertions are

1. Lincoln was president during the Civil War.

2. Kennedy was president before Nixon.

3. FDR was president before Kennedy.

Another type of fact is a *rule*, a statement of the form *if ... then ...* , which says that whenever the clause following "if" is true, so is the clause following "then." For example, here are two rules that, taken together, define what it means for one president to precede another in office. In these rules, X, Y, and Z are variables.

I. If X was president before Y, then X precedes Y.

II. If X was president before Z and Z precedes Y, then X precedes Y.

Here we are using a formal language to represent the knowledge base.

What conclusions can be reached from this collection of three assertions and two rules? Assertion 2 says that Kennedy was president before Nixon. This matches the "if" clause of rule I, where X is Kennedy and Y is Nixon. From this, the "then" clause of rule I yields a new assertion, that Kennedy precedes Nixon, which we'll call assertion 4. Now assertion 3 says that FDR was president before Kennedy, and assertion 4 says that Kennedy precedes Nixon. This matches the "if" clause of rule II, where X is FDR, Z is Kennedy, and Y is Nixon. From this, the "then" clause of rule II yields a new assertion, that FDR precedes Nixon, which we'll call assertion 5. Hence,

4. Kennedy precedes Nixon.

5. FDR precedes Nixon.

are two new conclusions or assertions. These assertions were previously unknown and were obtained from what was known through a process of logical reasoning. The knowledge base has been extended. We could also say that the system has *learned* two new pieces of knowledge.

If this example sounds familiar, it is because it is part of the example we used in Chapter 10 to illustrate the logic programming language Prolog. Prolog provides one means of implementing an inference engine for an expert system.

The inference engine is basically using the following pattern of reasoning:

Given that the rule
  If A then B
and the fact
  A
are both in the knowledge base, then the fact
  B
can be inferred or concluded.

This reasoning process, as we noted in Chapter 10, goes by the Latin name of *modus ponens*, which means "method of assertion." It gives us a method for making new assertions. We humans use this deductive reasoning process all the time. However, it is also suitable for computerization because it is basically a matching algorithm that can be implemented by brute force trial and error. Systems like Prolog, however, apply some additional guidelines in their search for matches to speed up the process; that is, they employ a form of intelligent searching.

Inference engines for expert systems can proceed in several ways. *Forward chaining* begins with assertions and tries to match those assertions to the "if" clauses of rules, thereby generating new assertions. These may in turn be matched with "if" clauses, generating still more assertions. This is the process we used in our example. *Backward chaining* begins with a proposed conclusion and tries to match it with the "then" clauses of rules. It then looks at the corresponding "if" clauses and tries to match those with assertions, or with the "then" clauses of other rules. This process continues until all "if" clauses that arise have been successfully matched with assertions, in which case the proposed conclusion is justified, or until no match is possible, in which case the proposed conclusion is rejected. Backward chaining in our example says, Here's a hypothesis: FDR precedes Nixon, and the system works backward to justify this hypothesis.

In addition to the knowledge base and the inference engine, most rule-based systems also have an explanation facility. This allows the user to see the assertions and rules used in arriving at a conclusion, as a sort of check on the path of reasoning or for the user's own enlightenment.

Of course, a rule-based system about some particular domain is only as good as the assertions and rules that make up the knowledge base. The builder of such a system acquires the information for the knowledge base by consulting "experts" in the domain and mining their expertise. This process, called knowledge engineering, requires a great deal of interaction with the human expert, much of it in the domain environment. If the domain expert is the manager of a chemical processing plant, for example, a decision to "turn down valve A whenever the temperature in pipe P exceeds 235°F and valves B and C are both closed" may be such an ingrained behavior that the expert won't remember it as part of a question-and-answer session on "what you do on your job." It only emerges by on-site observation. For the hospital

Practice Problems

1. Given the assertion "Frank is bald" and the rule "If *X* is bald, then *X* is tall," what conclusion can be inferred? If Frank were known to be tall, would that necessarily imply that he was bald?

2. Given the assertion "Frank is not bald" and the rule "If *X* is bald, then *X* is tall," what conclusion can be inferred?

3. Given the assertion "Frank is bald" and the rule "If *X* is tall, then *X* is bald," what conclusion can be inferred?

4. Given the assertion "Frank is not bald" and the rule "If *X* is tall, then *X* is bald," what conclusion can be inferred?

example, one might need to follow people around in the emergency room, observe their decisions, and later question them on why those decisions were made. It is also possible to incorporate probabilities to model the thinking process, for example, "If the patient has fever and stomach pains, the probability of appendicitis is 73% and the probability of gall bladder problems is 27%, therefore I first check A and then B."

Expert systems have been implemented in many domains, including specific forms of medical diagnosis, computer chip design, monitoring of manufacturing processes, financial planning, purchasing decisions for retail stores, automotive troubleshooting, and diagnosis of failures in electronic systems. They will no doubt be even more commonplace in the future.

15.5.5 The Games We Play

These days, the world of video game playing draws many enthusiasts. We will explore some of the computer technologies that make video games possible in the next chapter. But here, we want to trace the progression of the "artificial intelligence" needed to have the computer play (rather than just display) a game.

Board Games. Almost everyone is familiar with the simple pencil-and-paper game of tic-tac-toe. Two players draw Xs and Os, respectively, in the squares of a 3 × 3 grid. The first player to draw three of his or her symbol in a row (vertically, horizontally, or diagonally) wins. While the "X" player is trying to build such a row, the "O" player is trying to block it, and vice versa. For example, if the current configuration looks like this:

then the "O" player should write an O in the middle square to block X's diagonal. The rules are pretty simple, making it a good children's game. For experienced players, most games will end in a draw.

Writing a computer program to play tic-tac-toe is fairly easy. (The first-ever computer game was tic-tac-toe, written for the EDSAC computer in 1952; it played perfect games against human opponents. The first computer program Bill Gates wrote, at the age of 13, played tic-tac-toe.) The state-space graph (see Section 15.5.1) for tic-tac-toe is relatively small. Because there are nine positions, each of which can contain X, O, or blank, at first it seems that there are 3^9 = 19,683 board configurations. However, many of these are essentiality the same. For example, a single X in a corner square with all other cells blank occurs four ways because there are four corners, but these are all rotations of the same thing, so this is really only one configuration. Eliminating these similarities, there are 765 distinct configurations. We want a solution path from the initially empty board to a winning configuration. A brute force approach is feasible. If we assume that each player can write in any vacant cell, that the game is terminated with any three-in-a-row symbol or a full grid, and that configurations that are essentially the same are ignored, there are 26,830 possible games (paths through the state space). By following the simple strategies of trying to make three in a row while trying to block your opponent, and concluding the game when the outcome is determined, the number of paths through the state space is much smaller—1145 games. These can be reviewed to find the winning paths.

Checkers is a board game with more complex rules than tic-tac-toe and a far larger state space; there are 5×10^{20} (500 billion billion) possible board configurations. The Chinook project, involving a group of computer scientists at the University of Alberta in Canada, headed by Professor Jonathan Schaeffer, began in 1989. This project was to develop a checkers-playing computer program. In 1992, an early version of Chinook competed in the World Checkers Championship against Dr. Marion Tinsley, the world champion who had won every tournament he had played in since 1950. The program lost this match but was the winner in a 1994 rematch. The *Guinness Book of World Records* in 1996 accorded Chinook the honor of being the first computer program to win a human world championship. In April 2007, it was announced that Chinook was finally perfected. From the standard starting positions used in tournament play, Chinook can never lose; the best a skilled opponent can achieve is a draw. Multiple computers—as many as 200 at a time—worked simultaneously to carry out the 10^{14} (100 trillion) computations needed to determine how Chinook should make its moves so that it never loses. You can play against a "reduced strength" version of Chinook at *http://webdocs.cs.ualberta.ca/~chinook/play/*.

The solutions to both tic-tac-toe and checkers are complete solutions— the "winning move" to make from any board position has been determined and has been built into the software. The game of chess is still more complex. As mentioned earlier, a computer that could play winning chess games was thought to be the pinnacle of artificial intelligence. In May 1997, international attention was focused on a historic chess match between world champion Garry Kasparov and the IBM chess-playing computer known as Deep Blue. (IBM has since built machines hundreds of times more powerful than Deep Blue, such as the 2004 Blue Gene/L, developed for biomolecular research. These machine names are a clever play on "Big Blue," IBM's nickname in the corporate world.) Kasparov and Deep Blue played neck and neck. Both relied on the respective strengths of their "species," Kasparov utilizing recognition and reasoning, and Deep Blue churning out its high-speed computations (Figure 15.13). In the final game, Kasparov lost the match by falling for a well-known trap. Kasparov's error, which was considered a major blunder for a player of his ability, probably reflected his weariness and the emotional strain of competing against an unexpectedly strong, utterly impassive foe. These human frailties, of course, were not shared by Deep Blue.

FIGURE 15.13

Garry Kasparov vs. Deep Blue
Source: P. Morgan/Reuters/Landov

Kasparov could evaluate up to three chess positions per second, or 540 in the 3 minutes allowed between moves; he selected which few positions to evaluate on the basis of his experience, study of successful strategies or tactical approaches, and intuition. Deep Blue could evaluate up to 200,000,000 chess positions per second, or 50 billion in 3 minutes, using its 512 communicating processors. But even Deep Blue could not pursue a true brute force approach of playing out to the bitter end every possible consequence of every potential move from a given configuration. Instead, its programmers provided a number of heuristics that helped "prune" the search tree to a manageable number of paths, in effect selecting what seemed to be the most promising moves.

The game of Go is an ancient Chinese board game played by two players using black-and-white stones placed on a (usually) 19 × 19 grid. Stones represent territory controlled by a player. Once put in place, they are never moved, but can be removed if "captured" by the opposing player. The object of the game is to control a maximum amount of territory. A stone surrounded by stones of the opposite color is subject to capture, which makes it advisable to keep your stones clustered closely together. But that defeats the object of increasing the territory you control. Although the rules of Go are simple, there is a great deal of strategy involved in successful play. Computer programs to play Go are not as far along as chess-playing programs. Obstacles to success include the large size of the grid and the number of pieces on the grid, the fact that pieces generally remain on the board, the fact that a player has a huge number of moves at his or her disposal at any time, and the fact that a given move could be good or bad depending on the intent of the player. Players are ranked in Go competitions at the *kyu* rank or the *dan* rank, with the *dan* rank considered the master rank, beginning with the lowest *dan* rank of 1. The first programs to attain low *dan*-level rankings appeared in 2009. But progress has been swift since then; in June 2011, a Go program called Zen19D, running on a 25-core machine, attained the rank of 5 *dan*, which is beginning to approach the top master level of 7 *dan*.

Quiz Games. *Jeopardy!* is a popular American television quiz show. The show draws an estimated 9 million viewers daily who watch Alex Trebek, the host since 1984, throw "answers" at three contestants, who have to supply the corresponding "question." *Jeopardy!* took a startling new turn when, in 2011, an IBM supercomputer was one of the three contestants. Named Watson, after IBM's founder Thomas Watson, the computer got off to a slow start, but over three days of competition, bested two previous *Jeopardy!* champions (Figure 15.14; see also the Special Interest Box, 'Now I Understand,' Said the Machine, in Chapter 11).

In Figure 15.14, the Watson avatar is glowing proudly. But behind the scenes is the real Watson, consisting of 90 IBM Power 750 servers, each with 32 core processors and up to 256 GB of RAM (Figure 15.15). When Watson gets the clue, processing algorithms analyze the clue and then run several different searches that can produce as many as 300–500 candidate answers.

FIGURE 15.14

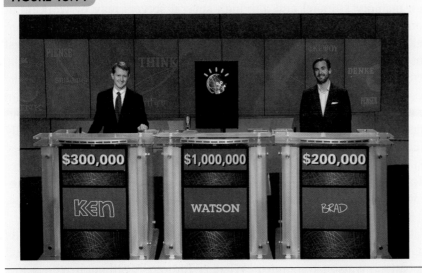

IBM's Watson beats its human opponents on *Jeopardy!*
Source: Jeopardy!/Landov

FIGURE 15.15

IBM's Watson supercomputer
Source: Courtesy of IBM

This phase uses heavy-duty computing resources (note the large amount of main memory storage) and although several servers may be working at once on the same clue, this is basically not a parallelized process. However, the next phase of "scoring" the candidate answers to decide on the best response is distributed across the cluster and done in parallel.

Certainly Watson has a huge database of facts at its disposal, but what the IBM researchers and their collaborators have accomplished is much more than a massive search process. Web search engines conduct massive searches, but they basically do word matching and then present you with a list of potentially relevant documents or other artifacts to sift through yourself, although they do vast statistical analyses to attempt to improve relevance. Watson analyzes clues fraught with vagaries of English language—puns, humor, rhyme, subtleties, riddles, irony, plays on words, and so forth—to understand their meaning. This is a far more formidable task than playing chess.

Watson is not infallible. With a category of "U.S. cities" and the clue "Its largest airport is named for a World War II hero; its second largest for a World War II battle," Watson responded "What is Toronto?", although with a low level of confidence in its answer.[1] But before you feel smug, consider Watson's correct response in the category of "edible rhyme time" and the clue "A long, tiresome speech delivered by a frothy pie topping." It has to recognize that the clue consists of two parts, a long tiresome speech and a frothy pie topping. It has to find potential answers for each part, and then apply the constraint that the two answers must rhyme. Can you answer this—in under three seconds?[2]

15.6 Robotics

The term *robot* implies a device, often humanlike in form, that has the ability to gather sensory information from its surroundings and to autonomously (i.e., without direct human instructions) perform mechanical actions of some sort in response. The term *robot* was used in a play written in 1921 by Czech author Karel Capek. The play was titled *R.U.R*, short for *Rossum's Universal Robots*. In the play, a scientist invents robots that perform simple repetitive tasks to help people but who take over the world when their human owners try to use them to fight wars. The word *robot* comes from the Czech word *robota*, meaning slavelike labor. Robots have been part of science fiction ever since—think C-3PO and R2-D2 in the *Star Wars* movies.

Fact has not yet caught up with science fiction, but today there are a surprising number of applications of robots. Here's a partial list of the uses to which robots are put in manufacturing, science, the military, medicine, and in the consumer marketplace:

- Assembling automobile parts

- Packaging food and drugs

---

[1] The correct response is "What is Chicago?"
[2] The correct response is "What is meringue harangue?"

- Placing and soldering wires in circuits

- Bomb disposal

- Welding

- Radiation and chemical spill detection

- Inspection of sewer lines and oil pipes

- Exploration (the Mars Rovers)

- Underwater salvage

- Microsurgery

- Wheelchair navigation

- Emergency search and rescue

- Vacuum cleaning

- Window washing

- Lawn mowing

- Home or commercial security sentry duty

Robots currently perform tasks that are too repetitive or dangerous for humans. Robots, of course, do not get bored, they can perform the same tasks with the same precision every time, and they can work in hostile environments.

Groups of robotic devices can act together to investigate wide-ranging geographic areas that, again, would be difficult for human workers. Scientists at the University of Washington in Seattle have built robotic "fish." Each fish is about 20 inches long, with the ability to flap its tail and two fins; using this propulsion and steering mechanism, the fish can swim in any direction and make tight turns. Communicating with each other using radio signals, the fish can swim together as a coordinated group or move independently. Such technology will eventually allow tracking of marine wildlife or assessment of environmental damage in the Earth's oceans.

Researchers at the Harvard Microrobotics Laboratory are perfecting a robotic "fly." Robotic flying insects are not just "small airplanes"—the flight dynamics of insects are much more complex because of an insect's ability to hover, fly in any direction, land on walls, and so forth. Once perfected, swarms of robotic insects could be released in a disaster area to search for survivors. Because of their size, they could penetrate hard-to-access areas of debris and transmit signals to (human or robotic) rescue workers. They could also be used for military espionage work (again, science fiction becoming reality).

Collecting data on the world's ice shelves, to study climate change, is the goal of researchers at the Georgia Institute of Technology and Pennsylvania State University. They have created small robotic "snowmobiles" called SnoMotes that will be able to travel autonomously over assigned terrain, take measurements, and report their findings. After an initial failure at building a rugged robot from scratch, the team turned to a toy snowmobile designed to operate in snow conditions and to withstand abuse by children. In addition to a camera, sensors, and computing equipment, the robot needs to be fitted with a heater to protect the electronic equipment in below-zero environments. Like the robotic fish, the SnoMotes will communicate with each other to decide which robot samples which location for the most efficient overall coverage.

More and more, however, robots are being developed to interact with humans in a less "robotic" and more "humanlike" way to perform tasks for the disabled, to watch over small children, and to entertain and provide companionship. Japan has an interest in developing "humanoid" robots to help care for its aging population.

One of the more well-known humanoid robots is ASIMO (Advanced Step in Innovative Mobility), built by Honda Motor Company, a Japanese corporation. As the name suggests, much of the focus of the design of this robot over earlier models was refinement of the robot's motion capabilities, extending the range of its arm movement and improving the smoothness and stability of its two-legged walking, including walking on uneven ground and navigating stairs. This jointed robot is designed to measure the forces acting on it at each step. If these forces get out of balance, threatening a fall, adjustments are made in the placement of the foot and the position of the torso to regain balance. One only has to watch a toddler learning to walk to see the challenges this represents. ASIMO's capabilities continue to be developed. ASIMO can open and close doors while passing through a doorway, guide office guests to a meeting room and serve refreshments on a tray, recognize when it needs recharging, and walk to the nearest recharging station and hook up to be recharged. ASIMO has even conducted the Detroit Symphony Orchestra in a concert for young people (Figure 15.16).

Research is ongoing in the field of robotics. Robotics involves the aspects of artificial intelligence we discussed earlier, namely recognition tasks and reasoning tasks. Through some sort of elementary vision, auditory, or tactile system, the robot must not only gather sensory information, but also filter out the possibly vast amount of data its surroundings might present to it to "recognize." That is, it must be able to make sense of the important features and discard the unimportant. Then the robot must make decisions—reason about—the information it has recognized to be able to take some action. There is also the additional challenge of the mechanics and electronics needed to make the robot respond physically.

Two strategies characterize robotics research. The **deliberative strategy** says that the robot must have an internal representation of its environment and that its actions in response to some stimuli are programmed into the

FIGURE 15.16

Honda's ASIMO conducting

Source: Courtesy of American Honda Motor Co., Inc.

robot based on this model of the environment. This strategy seems to reflect what we as humans think of as high-level cognitive reasoning—we have a mental model of our environment, we reflect on a stimulus from that environment, and make a reasoned decision about the next course of action. (This is a generalization of the expert system idea discussed earlier.) The reactive strategy uses heuristic algorithms to allow the robot to respond directly to stimuli from its environment without filtering through some line of reasoning based on its internal understanding of that environment. This stimulus-response approach seems to reflect human subconscious behavior—holding out our hands to protect ourselves during a fall, for example, or drawing back from a hot flame. Proponents of the deliberative strategy argue that a robot cannot react meaningfully without processing the stimulus and planning a reaction based on its internal representation of the environment. Proponents of the reactive strategy say that such a requirement is too restrictive and does not allow the robot to respond freely to any or all new stimuli it might encounter. Note that we as humans use both our conscious thought processes and our subconscious reactions in our everyday life, so a combination of these strategies may be the most successful approach.

Robots in the Operating Room

You are probably familiar with the use of hand gestures to communicate with video game consoles, used with the Wii Remote controller for the Nintendo game console and the Kinect device for the Microsoft Xbox 360 game console. Researchers see more serious uses to gesture-recognition technology. The photo here shows a graduate student at Purdue University using a prototype robotic scrub nurse that recognizes hand gestures directing it to give instruments as needed to the surgeon in a hospital operating room. Another use for hand-gesture recognition would allow the surgeon to direct a computer to display appropriate medical images during surgery. Both of these developments could improve operating room efficiency so that a patient would be in surgery for less time. The challenge is to build a system that recognizes legitimate hand-gesture commands and differentiates them from unintended motions by the surgeon. In fact, the hand-gesture recognition system being developed uses Kinect.

Source: Purdue University photo/Mark Simons

15.7 Conclusion

In this chapter, we have touched on three basic elements of artificial intelligence: knowledge representation, recognition problems, and reasoning problems. We've discussed common approaches to building artificial intelligence systems: symbolic manipulation (expert systems), connectionist architectures (neural networks), and genetic or evolutionary approaches (swarm intelligence). We have followed the progress of artificial intelligence in game playing and have also outlined some of the strategies and challenges in robotics design. Yet we have mentioned only a few of the many application areas of AI, a field that is finally beginning to realize its potential. Today we can use speech-recognition systems to control our telephones, appliances, and computers by talking to them, exploit face-recognition software to assist the police with their crime-solving responsibility, use a tablet PC with handwriting-recognition software, and ask a Web page to translate text from one language to another. In 20 years, artificial intelligence will be used in ways we have not even imagined today.

EXERCISES

1. Suppose that in a formal logic, *green*(*x*) means that *x* has the attribute of being green, *frog*(*x*) means that *x* has the attribute of being a bullfrog, and *J* stands for the specific entity Jeremiah. Translate the following formal statements into English:

   a. *frog*(*J*)

   b. $(\forall x)(frog(x) \rightarrow green(x))$

2. Draw a semantic net that incorporates the knowledge contained in the following paragraph:

   > If I had to describe what distinguishes a table from other pieces of furniture, I guess I would say it has to have four legs and a flat top. The legs, of course, hold up the top. Nancy's table is made of maple, but mine is bigger and is walnut.

3. a. Use an English-like formal language to represent the knowledge explicitly contained in the following semantic net:

b. Add to your list from Exercise 3a the knowledge that can be inferred from the semantic net.

4. In the following neural network, which event or events cause node N3 to fire?

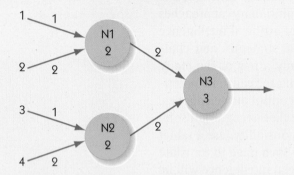

5. Assign weights and threshold values in the following neural network so that the output neuron fires only when x_1 and x_3 have the value 1 and x_2 has the value 0. Remember that weights can be negative.

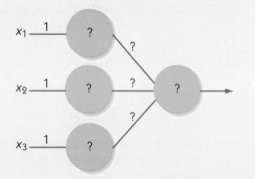

6. The truth table for the XOR operation is given in Figure 15.8. As noted in the text, a neural network for this operation requires a hidden layer of neurons. A partial solution to a neural network for XOR is shown at the bottom of this page. In this solution, all neurons have a threshold value of 1 and the inputs x_1 and x_2 are binary. Finish this network by finding weights for the connections and test that the resulting network implements the XOR operation. (*Hint:* All weights can be integer values.)

7. Find some literature or product information on a mobile device or tablet PC that allows pen-based handwritten entries. What sort of scheme does this system use for handwriting recognition? Does the system use a neural network? Does it require initial training on the user's handwriting?

8. Ant colonies are an example from nature of swarm intelligence. Find two other examples of swarm intelligence seen in nature.

9. You are a knowledge engineer and have been assigned the task of developing a knowledge base for an expert system to advise on mortgage loan applications. What are some sample questions you would ask the loan manager at a bank?

10. We described both forward chaining and backward chaining as techniques used by inference engines in rule-based systems. In Section 11.2.2, we described how a parser might analyze a programming statement to produce a parse tree. Does the method described in Chapter 11 correspond more closely to forward chaining or to backward chaining? Explain.

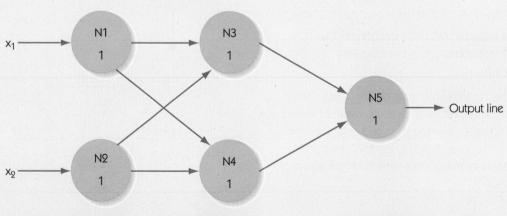

11. A rule-based system for writing the screenplays for mystery movies contains the following assertions and rules:

> The hero is a spy.
>
> The heroine is an interpreter.
>
> If the hero is a spy, then one scene should take place in Berlin and one in Paris.
>
> If the heroine is an interpreter, then the heroine must speak English.
>
> If the heroine is an interpreter, then the heroine must speak Russian.
>
> If one scene should take place in Berlin, then there can be no car chase.
>
> If there can be no car chase, then there can be no crash scene.

> If one scene should take place in Berlin, then the hero is European.
>
> If one scene should take place in Paris, then the hero must speak French.

Can the following assertion be inferred? Explain.

> The hero must speak French and there can be no crash scene.

12. In Exercise 11, is it possible to add the following assertion to the knowledge base? Why or why not?

> The hero is American.

13. If you studied Prolog in Chapter 10 and have a Prolog interpreter available, try implementing the rule-based system of Exercise 11 in Prolog.

CHALLENGE WORK

1. An argument called the Chinese Room argument (similar in many ways to the Turing test) challenges whether true artificial intelligence is even possible. This argument has provoked much discussion, and many replies that claim to refute it. Go to *http://plato.stanford.edu/entries/chinese-room* to see a summary of the Chinese Room argument and some of the replies.

   a. Describe the Chinese Room argument.

   b. Pick one of the replies and describe it. Does it seem to invalidate the Chinese Room argument?

2. A neural network is to be built that behaves according to the following truth table, which represents the Boolean AND operation. Input to the network consists of two binary signals; the single output line fires exactly when both input signals are 1.

Inputs		Output
x_1	x_2	
0	0	0
1	0	0
0	1	0
1	1	1

a. Find values for the missing weights and threshold values for the neurons in the following diagram that cause the network to behave properly.

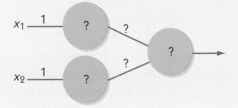

b. Because this is a relatively simple problem, it is easy to guess and come up with a combination of weights and threshold values that works. The solution is not unique; there are many combinations that produce the desired result. In a large network with many connections, it is impossible to find a solution by guessing. Instead, the network learns to find its own solution as it is repeatedly exercised on a set of training data. For networks with hidden layers, the back propagation algorithm can be used for training. For a general class of networks of the form shown in the next diagram, an easier training algorithm exists, as we will see. Note that in the diagram, the input signals are binary, and all neurons are assumed to have the same threshold value θ.

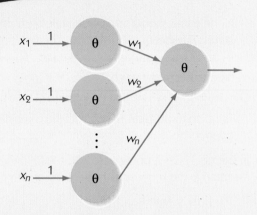

The following table sets up the notation needed to describe the training algorithm.

Symbol	Meaning
$x_1, x_2, \ldots$	Binary input values from the training set
y	The binary output value from the network
t	The target binary output value from the network for this set of input values
α	The "learning rate" for the network; a small positive value that controls how rapidly the weights change during training
$w_1, w_2, \ldots$	The current set of weights
θ	The current threshold value
$w_1', w_2', \ldots$	The next set of weights
θ'	The next threshold value

Initially, the network is given arbitrary values between 0 and 1 for the weights $w_1, w_2, \ldots$, and the threshold value θ. A set of input values $x_1, x_2, \ldots$ from the training data is then applied to the network. Because we are working with training data, the correct result t for this set of input values is known. The actual result from the network, y, is computed and compared with t. The difference between the two values is used to compute the next round of values for the weights and the threshold value, which are then tested on another set of values from the training data. This process is repeated until the weights and threshold value have settled into a combination for which the network behaves correctly on all of the training sets. The network is fully trained at this point.

Each new weight w_i' is computed from the previous weight by the formula

$$w_i' = w_i + \alpha (t - y) x_i \qquad \text{(A)}$$

and the new threshold value θ' is computed from the previous value by the formula

$$\theta' = \theta - \alpha (t - y) \qquad \text{(B)}$$

There are three cases to consider:

i. If the network behaved correctly for the current set of data—that is, if the computed output y equals the desired output t—then the quantity $\alpha(t - y)$ has the value 0, so when we use formulas (A) and (B), the new weights and threshold value will equal the old ones. The algorithm makes no adjustments for behavior that is already correct.

ii. If the output y is 0 when the target output t is 1, then the quantity $\alpha(t - y)$ has the value α, a small positive value. Each weight corresponding to an input x_i that was active in this computation (i.e., had the value 1) gets increased slightly by formula (A). This is because the output neuron didn't fire when we wanted it to, so we stimulate it with more weight coming into it. At the same time, we lower the threshold value by formula (B), again so as to stimulate the output neuron to fire.

iii. If the output y is 1 when the target output t is 0, then the quantity $\alpha(t - y)$ has the value $-\alpha$, a small negative value. Each weight corresponding to an input x_i that was active (i.e., had the value 1) gets decreased slightly by formula (A). This is because the output neuron fired when we didn't want it to, so we dampen it with less weight coming into it. At the same time, we raise the threshold value by formula (B), again so as to discourage the output neuron from firing.

We will use the training algorithm to train an AND network. The training set will be the four pairs of binary values for the AND truth table shown earlier. (Here, the training set is the entire set of possible input values; in most cases, a neural network is trained on some input values for which the answers are known and then is used to solve other input cases for which the answers are unknown.) For starting values, we choose (arbitrarily) $W_1 = 0.6$, $w_2 = 0.1$, $\theta = 0.5$, and $\alpha = 0.2$. The value of α stays fixed and should be chosen to be relatively small; otherwise, the corrections are too big and the values don't have a chance to settle into a solution. The initial picture of the network is therefore the following:

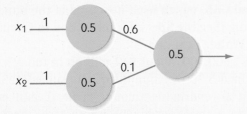

Note that with these choices we did not stumble on a solution because input values of $x_1 = 1$ and $x_2 = 0$ do not produce the correct result.

The table at the bottom of this page shows the first three training sessions. The current network behaves correctly for the first two cases ($x_1 = 0$ and $x_2 = 0$; $x_1 = 0$ and $x_2 = 1$), so no changes are made. For the third case ($x_1 = 1$ and $x_2 = 0$), an adjustment takes place in the weights and in the threshold value.

After these changes, the new network configuration looks like this:

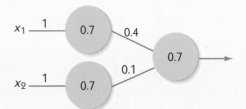

Continue the table from this point, cycling through the four sets of input pairs until the network produces correct answers for all four cases.

3. Pick one of the technologies discussed in this chapter (neural networks, swarm intelligence, intelligent agents, expert systems, game-playing machines, or robotics) and write a report on how it has been applied to a real-world product or problem.

w_1	w_2	θ	x_1	x_2	y	t	$\alpha(t-y)$	w_1'	w_2'	θ'
0.6	0.1	0.5	0	0	0	0	0	0.6	0.1	0.5
0.6	0.1	0.5	0	1	0	0	0	0.6	0.1	0.5
0.6	0.1	0.5	1	0	1	0	−0.2	0.4	0.1	0.7

ADDITIONAL RESOURCES

For additional print and/or online resources relevant to this chapter, visit the Computer Science CourseMate at login.cengagebrain.com.

Computer Graphics and Entertainment: Movies, Games, and Virtual Communities

16.1 Introduction

The first commercially marketed computer was the UNIVAC I, manufactured by Remington Rand. On March 31, 1952, the company delivered its first machine to the U.S. Census Bureau. Later systems went to the U.S. Army, the U.S. Air Force, the Atomic Energy Commission, U.S. Steel, General Electric, and CBS, which used it to predict the outcome of the 1952 presidential election. (See the Special Interest Box in Chapter 1 titled "Good Evening, This Is Walter Cronkite.")

In 1952, a UNIVAC I cost $1,500,000, about $12 million in today's dollars. It weighed 15 tons, contained 5,200 vacuum tubes, consumed 125,000 watts of electricity (generating an enormous amount of heat), and occupied floor space equal in size to a small apartment. These early machines were prohibitively expensive and required a massive financial investment in space, power, cooling, and support staff. Because of these costs, computers of the 1950s and early 1960s were only available to large organizations and only for what were deemed "important" purposes—classified military work, corporate research and development, or governmental policy analysis. The idea of using these systems for such frivolous pastimes as playing games or watching videos would have been unimaginable.

However, conditions changed dramatically in the late 1960s due to the development of transistors and integrated circuits, introduced in Chapter 4. Computers became more compact, more reliable, and much less costly. In 1965, Digital Equipment Corp. (DEC) rolled out the PDP-8, the world's first minicomputer, a term coined to describe a computer system that was smaller and less expensive than the unwieldy mainframes of the 1950s and early 1960s. A DEC PDP-8 minicomputer could be purchased for as little as $16,000 (about $100,000 in current dollars) and only took up as much space as two or three refrigerators.

Although still not cheap by today's standards, this lower price meant that computers were no longer accessible only to the military, government, and wealthy corporations; instead, they were now within the financial reach of colleges, universities, and small businesses. Some of the first computer games were created in the early 1970s by college students experimenting after hours to see what these new minicomputers were capable of doing. Games like Space Wars, Adventure, and Dungeons & Dragons were played on university computers, arcade machines, or custom-designed home consoles well before personal computers arrived on the scene.

In 1972, Nolen Bushnell, an electrical engineering graduate of the University of Utah, started a company called Atari (named after a board position in the game of Go), which released its first product in 1974, an arcade game called Pong. It was wildly successful and quickly became the most popular computer game in the country with 40,000 units sold nationwide and hundreds of thousands of players eager to stuff coins into a slot just for the privilege of playing a primitive electronic version of Ping-Pong, as shown in Figure 16.1. (It is amazing to see how far video game technology has progressed in just 40 years!)

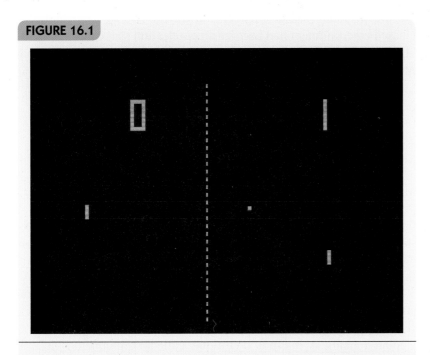

Pong—One of the first computer-based video games

In 1976, Atari produced a home version of Pong that allowed users to play on their televisions using a game console, complete with joysticks and on-screen scoring. It sold hundreds of thousands of units and became one of the most popular Christmas gifts of the late 1970s. Other games soon followed, and the decade of the late 1970s and early 1980s is termed the "golden period" of video arcade systems. By early 1982, Atari had become a $2 billion corporation and the fastest-growing company in the United States.

Using computers for entertainment, once considered frivolous and a complete waste of valuable scientific resources, had by the late 1970s become an important, not to mention financially lucrative, industry, and that growth has continued unabated. Today, computer-based entertainment is a $40–$60 billion industry employing tens of thousands of talented designers, artists, computer scientists, and engineers. Gamers stand in line for hours to purchase the latest and greatest video game releases. Hollywood spends massive amounts of money and manpower producing computer-generated images that amaze and enthrall, all in the hope of reaping hundreds of millions of dollars in movie ticket sales, DVD sales, and online streaming income. Virtual worlds enroll millions of subscribers who spend hours wandering imaginary spaces, joining online virtual communities, and making virtual friends.

Using information technology to amuse, fascinate, and frighten is no longer viewed as a waste of time, at least not by the millions who participate and play. Instead, it is now seen as an application that contributes significantly to the national economy and brings enjoyment to many people. Just as the Jeep and Hummer evolved from specialized military vehicles into passenger cars used for off-road fun and adventure, so too has the computer evolved from a research tool of the military, government, and universities to something available for our personal pleasure. By the start of the twenty-first century, computer-based entertainment had become an application that can stand alongside such traditionally "important" uses of computers as mathematical modeling (Chapter 13), electronic commerce (Chapter 14), and robotics (Chapter 15).

16.2 Computer-Generated Imagery (CGI)

16.2.1 Introduction to CGI

On March 2, 1933, a sellout audience at Radio City Music Hall in New York City was treated to the premiere of the science-fiction movie *King Kong*. This was the first feature-length film (rather than cartoon) to have its central character, in this case a giant gorilla, generated using animation. Animation had been used before in feature films, but only in a few short scenes or to animate minor characters. Because the movie's premiere occurred years before the appearance of the first commercial computer, Kong's movements were created using a manual technique called stop-motion animation. The special effects staff built a small-scale clay mock-up of the creature, positioned it, and snapped a single photograph, called a frame. Then they made a tiny change in the position of the model to represent its location a fraction of a second later and shot another frame. This process of "move the model, shoot a frame" was repeated thousands of times and, when the frames were shown in sequence without interruption, Kong appeared to come alive on screen. (This is similar to the "flip-book" style of animation in which pages of a notebook are filled with drawings and riffled to produce the effect of motion.) Stop-motion special effects were used in many fantasy, adventure, and science-fiction movies of the 1940s through 1970s.

Although it is possible to produce reasonably good images using either hand-drawn frames or stop-motion animation (*King Kong* was voted one of the 100 best films of all time by the American Film Institute), both of these techniques have serious limitations. Hand-drawing frames can be a painstakingly slow process, requiring dozens or even hundreds of highly skilled artists. The most notable problem with stop-motion techniques is the difficulty of repositioning a clay model with a sufficient degree of accuracy so that the model's movements do not appear jerky and artificial. At 30 frames per second (the standard rate for video; film uses 24), one hour of stop-motion animation requires 108,000 separate images, each of which must be manually positioned and photographed. The effort required can make this a painfully slow and expensive way to create special effects.

However, until the early 1990s, there were really no other choices. As we will soon learn, using a computer to produce realistic images requires enormous amounts of computational speed and power, and the mainframes of earlier decades were generally not up to the task. In addition, the algorithms used to create realistic human and animal replicas were in their infancy and not well understood. There were some early attempts to produce computer-animated movies—for example, *Tron* (1982) and *The Last Starfighter* (1984)—but the quality of that early work was rather poor, and most movie directors opted to stay with either stop-motion or hand-drawn animation to produce their special effects.

Two groundbreaking movies of the early 1990s quickly changed Hollywood's mind: *Terminator 2: Judgment Day* (1991) used a computer to create the T-100 Terminator character and the special effects used in action sequences. *Jurassic Park* (1993) used computers to create and animate the movie's dinosaurs and paste them seamlessly into the background of the frames. The quality of those early 1990s images was an order of magnitude improvement over what had been available just 8 to 10 years earlier. Both movies were huge financial as well as artistic successes, and they clearly demonstrated the rapidly improving capability of computer-generated imagery, usually referred to by its acronym CGI. By the mid-1990s, computer hardware could handle the massive computational demands required to create realistic three-dimensional images, and CGI software development had reached a point where its final product was as good as, if not better than, the manual output of human animators. By the beginning of the twenty-first century, CGI had become the method of choice for virtually all film and TV animation and special effects.

CGI has many advantages over manual techniques. It can produce extremely high-quality, lifelike images, called photorealistic animation, that are difficult to create using hand-drawn pictures or stop-motion models because of the high level of detail that is required. CGI can generate images that would be prohibitively expensive to produce manually, such as massive crowd scenes containing thousands of characters. Without CGI, directors would either have to hire thousands of extras, animate the scenes by hand, or produce thousands of miniature models, all of which would be quite costly and time-consuming. Computers can be used to produce scenes that would be dangerous if filmed using human subjects, such as car chases and explosions. Finally, CGI produces frames by using only a single animator and a single tool—the computer—instead of a large team of animators, model builders, directors, camera crew, and lighting staff. This can reduce costs and speed up the animation process.

Today, computer imaging is a multibillion-dollar industry, and the CGI budget for a wide-release feature film can easily exceed $40–$50 million. Furthermore, CGI techniques have moved well beyond the Hollywood sound stage and are now used in such fields as video gaming (discussed later in this chapter), computer software, scientific and medical imaging, television, advertising, flight simulation, and the production of still images for books and magazines.

Computer Horsepower

Industrial Light & Magic (ILM) is one of the largest visual effects companies in the world. It was founded by George Lucas in 1975 to produce special effects for his science-fiction movie *Star Wars*. ILM went on to do the CGI work for *Jurassic Park*, *Star Trek*, *Pirates of the Caribbean*, *Mission Impossible*, *Avatar*, *Iron Man*, *Transformers*, the *Harry Potter* series, and dozens of other well-known and highly profitable films. The company has won 15 Oscars for its outstanding visual effects work.

None of this would be possible, however, without an enormous amount of computing resources. At its California headquarters, ILM has the computational power equivalent of 15,000 home computers, and enough online storage to hold 5,000 trillion bytes of data. These systems are interconnected by a high-speed network capable of transmitting 12 trillion bits of information per second. This massive collection of equipment draws 2.4 million megawatts of power and is cooled by 32 air-conditioning units that require 25 tons of coolant to keep the building inhabitable—all of this computing power just to make sure that the alien Death Star spaceship looks realistic while you sit back and munch popcorn!

Although most of us are well aware that computers generate many of the images we see in the theater or on TV, few of us know how this is done. In the following section, we'll describe some of the fundamental algorithms used to produce computer-generated images.

16.2.2 How It's Done: The Graphics Pipeline

The production of high-quality computer-generated images is an enormously complex subject. In this short chapter, we cannot possibly do justice to its many facets and details. Instead, we introduce and describe a few of the fundamental operations required to generate and display images. Our goal is to provide a basic understanding of CGI techniques and an appreciation for the powerful computers and sophisticated algorithms required to carry out this difficult task.

There is a sequence of operations, termed the graphics pipeline, that must be completed successfully to produce a realistic three-dimensional image. There is no agreement on exactly which steps should or should not be included, and the number of distinct items in a pipeline diagram can vary from three to eight, depending on the type of image being produced and whether certain operations are grouped together or listed separately. The following sections describe the three stages shown in the simplified graphics pipeline of Figure 16.2: object modeling, object motion, and rendering and display. (Exercise 1 at the end of the chapter asks you to find other examples of a graphics pipeline diagram to determine which steps were omitted from the simplified version shown in Figure 16.2.)

FIGURE 16.2

A simplified three-stage graphics pipeline

16.2.3 Object Modeling

The first step in generating a realistic three-dimensional image is object modeling—the creation of a mathematical or computational model of a three-dimensional object that can be stored in the computer's memory and manipulated algorithmically. There are many approaches to object modeling, but one of the most well known and widely used is wireframe modeling. In this technique, the object's surface, but not its interior, is represented mathematically using a set of simple nonoverlapping polygons, usually triangles or rectangles.

For example, to create a scene containing a dolphin, we might start by inputting an image of that object. There are a number of ways to provide this input—an artist could draw a picture by hand, or we could scan an existing photograph. Next, using special CGI software and an algorithm called tessellation, the image is subdivided into a set of plane figures that completely covers its surface. An example of this tessellation process is shown in Figure 16.3, using triangles. Figure 16.3 also explains the reason behind the name of this technique. The polygonal outline on the surface, called a *polygon mesh*, produces a model that looks as if it were built from many thin pieces of wire.

Once the object's surface is tessellated, information about the individual polygons is stored in memory, usually in the form of a vertex list. This is a table giving the coordinates of each vertex on the object's surface and the identity of all other vertices to which this one is connected. In order to enter the proper (x, y, z) coordinates of each vertex, where z is the third axis,

FIGURE 16.3

Wireframe model of a dolphin (based on image in Wikipedia entry on polygon meshes)

coming out of the plane, we need to know the *origin* of the coordinate system, that is, the (0, 0, 0) reference point. For simplicity, one of the vertices is usually specified as the origin. It does not matter which point is chosen, as long as the computer knows its identity.

As an example, the four triangles in Figure 16.4(a), which represent a pyramid coming out of the page, might produce the vertex list shown in Figure 16.4(b) using vertex v_1 as the origin point.

The simple four-triangle tessellation shown in Figure 16.4(a) produced the vertex list of Figure 16.4(b) containing about three dozen pieces of information. Realistic objects such as the dolphin of Figure 16.3 can result in enormous tables that consume massive amounts of computer time to generate and huge amounts of memory to store. Furthermore, our dolphin may be only one of hundreds of objects (e.g., rocks, coral, algae, fish, water, sky) present in a single frame, all of which must be modeled and stored. You can now begin to understand the reasons why CGI places such huge processing and storage demands on a computer system.

16.2.4 Object Motion

After we have captured and stored a model of our object in a computational format, we can begin the next stage in the graphics pipeline of Figure 16.2— moving that object to its proper position in the next frame.

There are three types of **rigid motion** (motion that does not bend or deform an object): translation, rotation, and reflection. These three motions are illustrated in Figure 16.5.

FIGURE 16.4

	Vertex	x	y	z	Connected to
(Origin)	v_1	0	0	0	v_2, v_3, v_4
	v_2	0	1.0	0	v_1, v_4, v_5
	v_3	1.6	0	0	v_1, v_4, v_5
	v_4	0.7	0.5	0.5	v_1, v_2, v_3, v_5
	v_5	1.4	1.1	0	v_2, v_3, v_4

(b)

Simple tessellation and corresponding vertex list

Practice Problem

The following is a polygonal mesh representation of a two-dimensional drawing of a house created using tessellation:

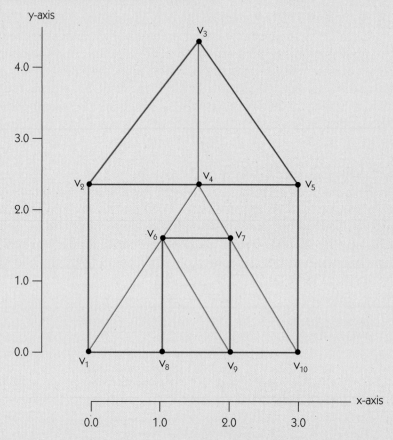

Using v_1 as the origin, show the vertex list generated by this wireframe model. (*Note:* Because this is a two-, rather than three-, dimensional model, the z entry in each column of Figure 16.4(b) would be 0.) How many distinct pieces of information are required to store the information about this model?

Translation, shown in Figure 16.5(a), is the lateral (up, down, right, left, and in 3D, in, out) movement of every point in an object by the same amount and in the same direction. Rotation, Figure 16.5(b), is the circular movement of an object around a fixed point or, in 3D, around a fixed axis, much as a merry-go-round horse revolves around the ride's central

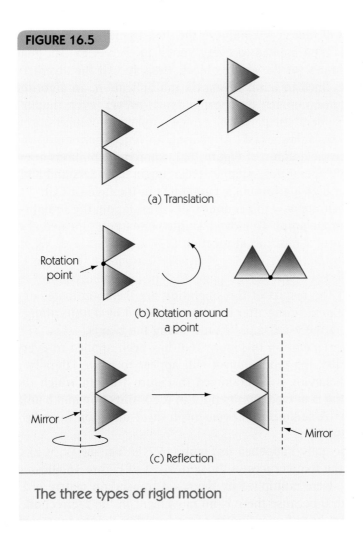

FIGURE 16.5

(a) Translation

Rotation point

(b) Rotation around a point

Mirror

Mirror

(c) Reflection

The three types of rigid motion

mechanism. Finally, reflection, Figure 16.5(c), produces a mirror image of an object such that every point in the reflected image is the same distance from the mirror as in the original object, but on the opposite side of the mirror.

The movement of an object from its location in one frame to its new location in the next is often described not by a single type of motion but a combination of two or more of these basic operations. For example, to model the motion of an airplane taking off and banking to the left, we might use translation to move the airplane forward and upward in space and rotation to model the turning operation. (*Note:* Some types of movement cannot be described using just these three operations. Motions that *deform* or *change* the shape of an object, such as scaling, squeezing, stretching, or ripping, are widely used in computer graphics, but they need additional operators not described here.)

To implement these three motions, we use a mathematical structure called a transformation matrix. When a vector containing the (x, y, z) coordinates of a single vertex point is multiplied by this matrix, the result is a new vector containing the translated, rotated, or reflected (x', y', z')

coordinates of that vertex point in the next frame. This same multiplication operation is then applied to every vertex in the vertex list, generating the new coordinates for the entire object. Thus, in CGI the abstract concept of motion is defined in terms of matrix multiplication, an algorithmic operation easily programmed on a computer. However, even though it may be easy to implement, the potentially huge number of multiplications can make this a time-consuming task. Animating an object containing thousands of vertices, like the dolphin of Figure 16.3, can require millions or even billions of arithmetic operations. Again, we can begin to understand and appreciate the need for high-performance computers in the field of CGI.

Let's illustrate how this is done using translation, the straight-line movement of a single point. To move a single vertex point located at coordinates (x, y, z) to a new position at location (x + a, y + b, z + c), we multiply the current coordinates by the 4 × 4 *translation matrix* shown in Figure 16.6. (See Section 8.3.2 starting on page 403 for an explanation of matrix multiplication.) The results of this operation are the coordinates of this vertex point in the next frame after it has been moved by *a* units along the x-axis, *b* units along the y-axis, and *c* units along the z-axis.

After the operation of Figure 16.6 has been applied to every vertex in the vertex list, the entire object will appear to move laterally as a single unit. This behavior is diagrammed in Figure 16.7, in which the object of Figure 16.4(a) is moved *a* units right in the x-direction and *b* units up in the y-direction. (Assume zero movement in the z-direction to make the picture easier to visualize.)

What actually happened in Figure 16.7 is that the (x, y, z) coordinates of each of the five vertices in the vertex list of Figure 16.4(b)—i.e., columns 2, 3, and 4—were multiplied by the 4 × 4 translation matrix in Figure 16.6, with *c* set to 0 because there is no movement in the z-direction. The newly generated (x′, y′, z′) coordinates of each vertex point are copied back into columns 2, 3, and 4 of the vertex list, replacing the old coordinates. Now, when this object is displayed in the next frame, it will be in its proper location. If we repeat this entire operation 30 times, moving the object a tiny amount each time (i.e., using small values for *a*, *b*, and *c*), then when these 30 frames are shown in sequence, the result will be one second of animated

FIGURE 16.6

$$\begin{bmatrix} 1 & 0 & 0 & a \\ 0 & 1 & 0 & b \\ 0 & 0 & 1 & c \\ 0 & 0 & 0 & 1 \end{bmatrix} \times \begin{bmatrix} x \\ y \\ z \\ 1 \end{bmatrix} = \begin{bmatrix} x + a \\ y + b \\ z + c \\ 1 \end{bmatrix}$$

Translation   Current vertex   New
matrix   coordinates   coordinates

Using matrix multiplication to implement object translation

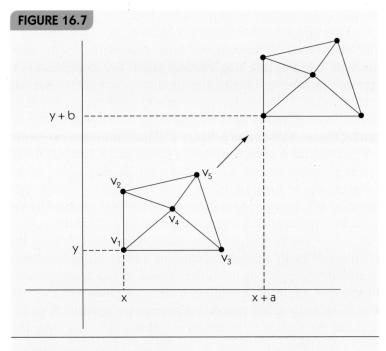

FIGURE 16.7

Example of a translation performed on the object
shown in Figure 16.4(a)

motion. Our eyes will not see 30 separate and distinct movements like those
in Figure 16.7, but one second of smooth, flowing motion.

Both rotation and reflection operations are implemented in a similar
way, but using the appropriate rotation or reflection matrix in place of the
translation matrix shown in Figure 16.6. (Exercises 7 and 8 at the end of the
chapter ask you to determine what these two matrices look like when working in two dimensions rather than three.)

One of the advantages of CGI over manual systems is that a computer
can perform many of the required operations without the assistance of a
human designer, greatly speeding up the animation process. For example,
assume the translation motion diagrammed in Figure 16.7 takes place over
one second. At 30 frames per second, the standard rate for video, an animator would need to generate 30 distinct frames to obtain the desired effect.
However, using a CGI technique called **keyframing**, a human animator only
needs to produce the first frame, containing the starting location of the
object; the last frame, containing the final location of the object; and the
elapsed time, in this case one second. Using this information, a computer
can automatically generate the 28 required intermediate frames, called
in-between frames or, more simply, *tweeners*. The computer adds 1/29th
of the distance between the object's location in the first and last frames to
the coordinates of the object in the current frame to position it correctly
for the next frame, because with N total frames, there are $N - 2$ in-between
frames and $N - 1$ time intervals. The work of the animator has been reduced

from creating 30 frames to creating two, the first and the last. This is a huge shift in workload from human being to computer.

In our discussions of motion, we have moved the entire object as a single entity in relation to a single origin point. For example, the polygon in Figure 16.7 moved up and to the right as a complete unit. However, sometimes we want to move different parts of an object in relation to different points or axes, rather than one, in order to achieve a specific effect. For example, Figure 16.8 shows a figure-8 object with two axes of rotation, labeled A and B, with A lying outside the object and B lying at the center of the right circle. (*Note:* Assume the axes of rotation are parallel to the z-axis and are coming out of the page.)

If we perform a rotation operation around axis B on just the rightmost circle, that circle rotates like a wheel around its axle. If we do a second rotation on the entire figure-8 object, this time using axis A, the figure-8 flies around A like the Earth around the sun. We will have created two distinct types of motion—one part of the object spinning like a wheel, while both parts of the object are flying around in a circle. We have achieved this complex set of motions by using two different points of control. A point or axis used to control the motion of an object is called a control point, also called an animation variable.

In an object like the dolphin of Figure 16.3, there may be dozens or hundreds of distinct control points that allow us to move the object's head, body, and tail in multiple ways. Similarly, if we are animating the image of a human face, we might want control points for the smiling and frowning movements of the mouth; a control point for the eyes to allow them to move independently; and control points for the head, to allow it to turn left and right as well as swivel up and down. It would not be unusual for an animated image of a human being to have as many as 500 separate control points, to allow it to move in many different ways, just as people are able to do in the real world.

16.2.5 Rendering and Display

We now have a polygon mesh composed of a set of plane figures, such as triangles, correctly positioned within the new frame after motion has taken place. The final step in the graphics pipeline of Figure 16.2 is rendering and

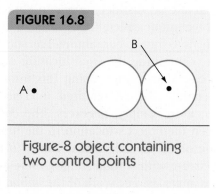

FIGURE 16.8

Figure-8 object containing
two control points

Practice Problem

Assume that you want to animate the lateral motion of a triangle from its current location, in which:

> vertex v_1 is at (0, 0, 0), vertex v_2 is at (1, 0, 0), and vertex v_3 is at (0.5, 1, 0) to a new location such that

> vertex v_1 is at (4, 2, 0), vertex v_2 is at (5, 2, 0), and vertex v_3 is at (4.5, 3, 0)

This movement is shown in the following diagram:

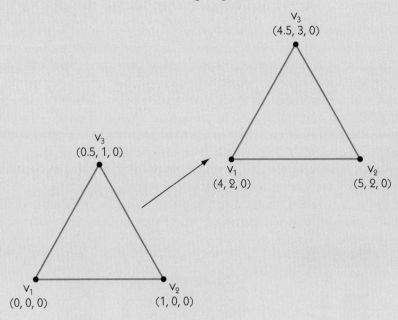

This motion will take two seconds to complete. Show the translation matrix that can be used to generate all the necessary in-between frames.

displaying the final image. **Rendering** means taking an object stored as a mathematical model, such as the vertex list of Figure 16.4(b), and converting it into a fully formed, visually pleasing three-dimensional image.

Rendering is a complex set of operations that often consumes the great majority of computer time required to produce an image. Some of the issues addressed during the rendering process are:

- *Lighting*—We specify the location and intensity of all light sources illuminating the image and determine the effect these light sources have on the final appearance.

- *Color shading*—We initially assign a single color or gray level to each vertex in the model and then blend those colors across the face of the polygon. We also determine if there are any modifications to the intensity or shade of that color due to the incidence of light falling on that plane.

- *Shadows*—We modify the color and brightness of each plane figure because of shadows cast on that plane by opaque objects.

- *Texture mapping*—In the first two stages of CGI, we assume that each plane is a homogeneous, detail-free surface. However, real surfaces like human skin or tree bark are far from homogeneous. Texture mapping allows us to add surface details (bumps, grain, indentations) to each of the plane figures.

- *Blur*—If an object is moving rapidly from one frame to the next, we may choose to blur the final image to represent that motion.

The operations just described (and many others not listed here) are carried out by CGI software running special-purpose rendering algorithms. Figure 16.9 shows a fully rendered color image generated from a polygon mesh representation of each object—glasses, pitcher, dice, ashtray, tiled walls, and table. This image clearly illustrates the many difficult issues that rendering software must deal with in producing a finished image—the color shading of the ashtray from bright green to almost black; the transparency of the glass objects, revealing objects located behind them; the opaqueness of the pitcher; shadows on the wall; reflection of light off the glass surfaces; and the complex texture on the bottom of the water glass.

Rendering a complex image like Figure 16.9 can be difficult and time consuming, especially when there are numerous objects and many light

FIGURE 16.9

Example of a fully rendered frame
Source: Courtesy Gilles Tran

sources. It would not be unusual for a computer, even a powerful one, to spend hours rendering a single frame such as Figure 16.9.

There are many different algorithms for carrying out the rendering operations just described, such as *rasterization* and *radiosity*, but the most common algorithm, by far, is **ray tracing**. In this approach, the computer determines the total amount and direction of light falling on each plane surface in the model's vertex list. For example, in Figure 16.10 there are three light sources illuminating triangle T, where T is a single triangle located on the object's surface. Light source A shines directly onto the surface of T. Light source B is blocked by an opaque object, so it does not contribute any direct light, although it does contribute some indirect lighting due to reflection off another surface. Light source C is partially, but not completely, blocked by an opaque object, so it contributes only a fraction of its potential light. The contributions of each light source are summed to determine the total amount and direction of light rays falling on the face of triangle T. This value, along with a knowledge of the object's orientation in space, determines the proper intensity, color shading, and brightness of that face so that it can be rendered in a visually appropriate manner.

Tracing the individual rays of light falling on every face of a model can be an extremely slow operation, especially if there are numerous light sources and we are rendering a "busy" object, such as leaves on a tree or strands of hair on a human head. For these special surfaces, CGI often uses algorithms designed to render just this one type of object.

FIGURE 16.10

Light source A

T

Light source B

Light source C

Three light sources illuminating triangle T

The end product of rendering is a fully colored and textured three-dimensional image ready for display. The final step in the process is changing that three-dimensional image into a two-dimensional one for display on a computer monitor, game console, or movie screen. This is a relatively simple step based on the position of each object in the frame, the location of the viewer, and some simple geometry. For example, Figure 16.11(a) contains three three-dimensional objects labeled A, B, and C, and a viewer whose position is indicated by the letter V. Knowing the three-dimensional coordinates of A, B, C, and V, we can determine that, from the perspective of point V, sphere B is totally obscured while pyramid C is partially obscured. This information can be used to produce a two-dimensional screen representation of what can be seen by a viewer from location V. This is shown in Figure 16.11(b).

16.2.6 The Future of CGI

High-quality CGI is one of the most computationally demanding applications of computers, and only in the last 15 or so years have processors become sufficiently powerful and memory units grown sufficiently large to

FIGURE 16.11

(a) Three-dimensional representation

(b) Two-dimensional representation

Converting an image to a two-dimensional representation

carry out the operations described in this section in a reasonable amount of time. However, as we learned in Chapter 5, parallel and multi-core computers are becoming far more common, and this increased level of parallelism is allowing computers to overcome Moore's law and continue to gain in speed, allowing for the production of far more detailed images. In addition, computer scientists are discovering newer and better algorithms for such common CGI operations as modeling, animation, and rendering. The future of CGI is bright, and it is quite likely that the next 40 years will see improvements in the quality of computer-generated imagery that may be as (or more) dramatic than the change from the primitive Pong game of Figure 16.1 to the elegant still life of Figure 16.9.

16.3 Video Gaming

The computer science issues involved in producing video games are much the same as those addressed by CGI because game images displayed on a laptop, tablet, or smartphone must still be modeled, animated, and rendered as described in the last section. However, there is one huge difference between CGI and video gaming that makes an enormous difference in how we approach and implement these two applications.

A movie is not an interactive environment. There is no change to the plot or action on the screen based on what the user is thinking or doing. If you watch a movie 10 times, you will see exactly the same images in exactly the same order 10 times. Therefore, movie animators can spend as much time as they want rendering each frame, even hours if necessary, because once each frame is completed, its content never changes and the order in which the frames are shown never changes. Simply put, a movie is a static environment that is created once and shown as often as desired.

On the other hand, a video game is a highly interactive environment. Using an input device such as a joystick, wireless controller, or finger tap, a user dynamically controls the action and makes instant decisions about what happens next—Should I shoot that alien? How hard should I swing this club? The content of the next frame depends on what the user does at this instant. Therefore, we cannot render all frames in advance because we don't know exactly how the objects will move or behave. When the game is in progress, we must generate the frames fast enough so that the action on the screen appears to happen at roughly the same rate as it would happen in the real world. For example, if I use my game controller to swing a virtual golf club, the screen image must immediately display the ball's proper flight based on the properties of the swing that I just made. If the processor cannot work that quickly, the action will be sluggish, and the game will be far less enjoyable to play.

The branch of computer graphics that studies methods for creating images at a rate matching that of the real world is called real-time graphics, and video gaming is an excellent example of a real-time application. This means that instead of having minutes or hours to render a frame, we have, at 30 frames per second, only 1/30th of a second to get the user's input, determine what took place, generate a new frame representing the result of that action, and display the final image. That is a severe time constraint, and because of this limitation, the operative principle in producing video game images is:

If necessary, sacrifice image quality for speed of display.

One of the most common techniques for increasing imaging speed, termed the **frame rate**, is to use a **GPU**, an acronym for **Graphics Processing Unit**. A GPU is an independent Von Neumann processor, much like those described in Chapter 5 and diagrammed in Figure 5.18. A GPU executes instructions in parallel with the CPU, the Central Processing Unit, and carries out all of the graphics operations described in this chapter—modeling, motion, rendering, and display. If there is no GPU, these operations must be handled by the CPU in addition to its many other responsibilities—running user programs, updating disks, handling input/output, and managing network connections.

With a GPU, all imaging responsibilities are off-loaded from the CPU to the GPU, and the two processors run in tandem, an excellent example of the multi-core parallelism introduced in Section 5.4. Because a GPU does not have to do general-purpose computing, only image processing, its instruction set can be optimized to perform the specific operations needed by CGI. These might include rendering and drawing triangles like those in the dolphin model of Figure 16.3 or searching two-dimensional matrices like the vertex list of Figure 16.4(b).

Typically, a GPU has its own dedicated random access memory where it stores the image data and which is separate from primary memory. The GPU along with this dedicated RAM, referred to as **video memory**, is located on a **video card**, also called a **graphics card**, and is connected to the main CPU and memory through a plug-in expansion slot or via the system bus. This architecture is diagrammed in Figure 16.12. The configuration shown in Figure 16.12 allows the GPU to access image data (e.g., vertex list, color information, location of light sources) from video memory without having to compete with, and be slowed down by, the CPU as it tries to access the primary memory. Today, the great majority of computer systems and video game consoles contain a dedicated video card and GPU architecture similar to the one shown in Figure 16.12. In fact, many systems today contain multiple graphics cards, each with multiple GPUs. For example, the Apple iPad 2 contains two separate graphics cards, each having two graphics processors. This higher level of parallelism is becoming common in newer systems.

Another way to achieve speedup in real-time graphics is to avoid the use of algorithms that, although they produce high-quality images, simply take too much time. An excellent example is the ray-tracing algorithm introduced in Section 16.2.5 and diagrammed in Figure 16.10. Following millions (or billions) of light rays from their source to an object's surface and any

FIGURE 16.12

Typical architecture of a GPU and video memory

subsequent reflections can produce truly lifelike images, such as the still life of Figure 16.9, but it can take minutes or hours to render a single frame. In a real-time environment, we don't have hours or minutes, only 1/30th of a second, to complete this task.

We can gain considerable speedup by rendering an entire plane (i.e., a single triangle) using a uniform color, shade, and texture. As was mentioned in the previous section, many rendering algorithms initially assign a uniform color and texture to each triangle but then blend and mix adjacent colors to create a smooth and pleasing color transition. We can eliminate this step and instead use a single color and texture for the entire face; subtle color differences or brightness changes within a single plane would not be allowed. This reduces our workload significantly, but it comes at the cost of a less lifelike image.

Another technique to speed up rendering and display is **culling**. Rather than rendering every plane in the wireframe model and then determining which planes are visible from the user's perspective, as diagrammed in Figure 16.11, we could turn those two operations around. First determine which planes can be seen from the user's point of view, based on location and opaqueness, and then render only those objects visible in the next frame, omitting all operations on hidden surfaces.

Finally, video gaming often makes use of a technique called **cut-ins**. These are fully modeled and fully rendered objects stored in a video library in video memory. These already prepared objects can be dropped into a frame as is, producing a significant speedup in frame creation. These cut-ins often include images of the main game characters as well as standard background objects—cars, castles, weapons—that appear in many of the frames.

The end result of these optimizations (and many others not mentioned here) is the ability to accept user input, determine what action should be taken in response to this input, and render and display a frame representing the game state after that action has been completed. And all of this in only 1/30th of a second!

Today the quality of a typical video game image does not approach the level achieved by high-quality, feature-film CGI because of the time constraints placed on real-time graphics. However, as processors grow faster and as higher degrees of multi-core parallelism (4, 8, 16 GPUs per system) become both technically and financially feasible, the quality of real-time video game images will certainly improve and perhaps begin to approach the level of the computer-generated imagery found in today's best feature films.

The Good, the Bad, and the Ugly

In the mid-nineteenth century, a British literary genre called "penny dreadfuls" was extremely popular among English teenagers. These cheap magazines, costing a penny, contained lurid tales and drawings of horror, sex, and violence. Respectable Victorians detested these publications and fought to censor them, claiming they warped the minds of young, impressionable British lads. This was one of the earliest attempts at censoring a style of youth culture deemed inappropriate and degrading by adults of that era.

Similar attempts at censorship have been repeated numerous times against other popular pastimes such as comic books, rock and roll, R- and X-rated movies, and rap music. Most recently, there has been a good deal of vocal opposition to modern video games.

There is no doubt that video games contain a good deal of controversial content—drug use, criminal behavior, sexual acts, violence, and strong language. In many cases, this extreme content forms the central theme of the game. For example, the primary goal of one popular game is to steal a car and run down pedestrians. A widely played video game includes the simulated shooting of police officers and the rape and murder of prostitutes. Another game involves violent gang activity between competing ethnic groups. These games often use a "first person shooter" format, in which the player views the activity through the eyes of the main character, actually pointing the gun and shooting the victims.

This is rough stuff and has led to public criticism of the video game industry from politicians, schools, parents, religious groups, and mental health organizations. To address these concerns, the industry has adopted a voluntary rating system, but it is strongly opposed to any additional forms of censorship. The game industry argues that adults should be free to play these games if they so desire, and that there are few scientific studies linking the playing of violent video games to real-world crime or changes in the personality or behavior of their players.

This controversy will no doubt continue to grow, as governments around the world have passed, or are considering, legislation to regulate or restrict the production and sale of violent video games.

16.4 Multiplayer Games and Virtual Communities

Most video games involve a small number of players, typically one to four. However, the last 10 years have seen the development of a new game genre called **massively multiplayer online games (MMOG)**. These games allow a large number of players, often thousands or tens of thousands, to interact, form groups, and compete against one another within a simulated virtual world.

The world in which the action takes place is created and managed by special computers called **game servers**. Depending on the game complexity and the number of players, there may be only one or two servers or many thousands. In an MMOG, the virtual world in which the game is played is *persistent*. This means the *server software* that creates the world is always running and always available, and it always maintains the current state of every player. This is unlike games that can be turned off and on at will, but that lose state information when turned off, and must be restarted from the beginning.

Users log on to the game server whenever they want, using *client software* running on their home computer, laptop, or smartphone. This client software may be either proprietary code purchased from the gaming company or a publicly available program such as a Web browser. Thus, the architecture of an MMOG, shown in Figure 16.13, is virtually identical to the client/server network model introduced and diagrammed in Chapter 7, Figure 7.20.

The development of an MMOG incorporates a number of important computer science–related research topics that have been discussed earlier in the text. For example, the three-dimensional images displayed on the

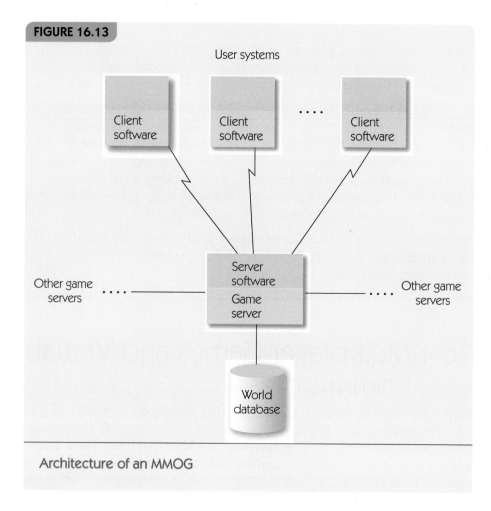

FIGURE 16.13

Architecture of an MMOG

user's computer employ all the real-time graphics algorithms discussed in the previous section, but with the added complexity and tighter time constraints caused by delays across the network. In addition to rendering the game images, designers of MMOG must also address and solve the following technical problems:

- *Registration management*—There may be tens of thousands of existing users at various points in the game, as well as thousands of new users joining every day. The responsibilities of the server software that manages this user base include ensuring that new users correctly join the community, saving the game state of existing users when they log off, and restoring that state when they log back on. This is similar to the "receptionist" responsibility of the operating system discussed in Section 6.4.1.

- *Client/server protocols*—In an MMOG, there are tens of thousands of users simultaneously accessing hundreds or thousands of game servers across multiple communication channels. The game designers must implement the network protocols that support this vast communications array. We discussed the topic of computer networks and protocols in Chapter 7.

- *Security*—An MMOG must keep track of each user's activity to ensure that his or her actions do not incorrectly or inappropriately affect the actions of other players. Furthermore, the system must ensure that all users adhere to the rules of the game and do not attempt to carry out illegal operations. The topic of computer security was discussed in Chapter 8.

- *Database design*—The world database of Figure 16.13 can be a truly massive structure holding trillions of bytes of data. The game designers are responsible for implementing this database and making sure that it can be accessed quickly enough to provide real-time response to user actions. Databases were introduced and described in Section 14.3.

Because of these many technical complexities, the cost of developing a sophisticated MMOG can run to tens of millions of dollars and take hundreds or thousands of person-years to design and implement.

When we think of the word *game*, we usually assume an environment based on competition, scoring, winners, and losers. However, a recent development in MMOG design is the concept of a noncompetitive MMOG, sometimes called a metaverse, short for *metauniverse*. This is a simulated virtual world, much like what we have just described, but where the goal is not to destroy your opponent or get the highest score. Instead, the purpose of entering this metaverse is simply to explore the virtual world, interact with other people in the world (often called "residents"), form communities of residents with similar interests, and create new economic entities that have (virtual) value. Players behave in this metaverse in many of the same ways they do in the real world—communicating, working, building, and moving around. There is no winning or losing in a noncompetitive MMOG, just the enjoyment of experiencing a new environment and meeting new people— not unlike traveling (for real) to a foreign country.

The most widely used and well-known metaverse is *Second Life*, a virtual world created by Linden Labs in 2003. Many of the items in this virtual world (houses, cars, clothing) are user-generated objects constructed by individuals or groups using a CGI modeling tool that allows residents to customize their virtual environment. (This tool performs the operations listed in the graphics pipeline diagram of Figure 16.2.) According to many of its residents, it is the collaborative and creative activities, not competition, that make *Second Life* so popular.

Second Life uses the client/server model diagrammed in Figure 16.13. The client software that provides access to the virtual world is a free, downloadable program called Second Life Viewer. Currently, there are several thousand server computers and over 100 trillion (10^{14}) bytes of data in the *Second Life* world database. However, even with this vast amount of computing power, the popularity and growth of *Second Life* is beginning to strain the computational resources of Linden Labs, making it difficult to keep up with the growth of its virtual world. (This problem is not unlike the problems encountered in rapidly growing real-world cities whose resources strain to keep up with an expanding population.)

Currently, there are approximately 21 million residents of *Second Life*, which would make it the 55th-largest country in the world (if it were a country), a little smaller than Australia but larger than Chile, the Netherlands, Ecuador, and Greece. At any instant in time, there are approximately 54,000 people logged on to *Second Life*, wandering through this virtual world, chatting with members of virtual communities, and creating virtual economic wealth.

16.5 Conclusion

Not that long ago, almost all input to a computer was textual. Communication with the operating system was via cryptic textual commands that were hard to remember and difficult to understand. The primary applications of the 1960s, 1970s, and 1980s were also textual—e-mail, word processing, databases, spreadsheets—and they often produced reams of incomprehensible textual output. The appearance of the first graphical user interfaces in the early 1980s demonstrated the power of visualization, using icons, windows, and buttons to enhance user understanding. By the early 1990s, graphics had moved into the scientific domain via charts, diagrams, and images that made it easier to interpret the output of scientific programs. (This was described in Chapter 13 and shown in Figures 13.11, 13.12, and 13.13.) Businesses began to use graphics in the form of *computer-aided design* (CAD) tools that gave architects and manufacturers the power to create and edit designs online. Soon visualization was being added to just about every popular application, such as the ability to insert images into documents or enhance JPEG photographs and attach them to e-mail.

But it is in the last 15 years that visualization has found one of its most compelling and exciting uses—the ability to amuse us, entertain us, and enhance our pleasure. The use of CGI in feature movies, TV, advertisements, and online videos is growing to the point where nearly every environment and action can be created on a computer and displayed in a photorealistic fashion. The use of interactive real-time graphics takes us beyond passive viewing of virtual worlds to letting us play in them, function in them, and even "live" in them.

As graphics processors and visualization algorithms grow faster and more sophisticated, and as parallel computing environments become even more common in laptops, tablets, and smartphones, the quality of computer-generated images will continue to improve, and the feeling of actually being inside a virtual world will grow more real. Perhaps the simulated-reality "holodeck" technology from the 1980s TV series *Star Trek: The Next Generation*, usually thought of as a comic book fantasy, is no longer an unattainable goal.

The Computer Will See You Now

Computer imaging can be used to amaze, enthrall, and entertain. It can also be used to diagnose, treat, and heal—applications that most of us would agree are far more important.

Medical imaging is a rapidly growing area of computer and biological science research in which computers and graphics software are used to produce highly accurate two- and three-dimensional images of the human body without surgery or other invasive procedures. The instrumentation that generates the image data may be X-ray, MRI, PET scans, or ultrasound. However, in all cases, the raw data would be useless for diagnostic purposes if they could not be converted into high-quality, lifelike images that can be examined and analyzed by health professionals. To do this, the initial data from these instruments become the input to a graphics pipeline similar to the one in Figure 16.2. This allows a computer to model, render, and display images in a photorealistic fashion. Today, medical imaging algorithms are helping physicians detect the early stages of breast cancer, perform delicate brain surgery, and track fetal development in the womb.

The algorithms that produce these medical visualizations are quite similar to, sometimes identical to, the algorithms originally developed to generate images of alien invaders, prehistoric dinosaurs, and virtual worlds. This is an excellent demonstration of the importance of basic scientific research—you never know where that work may lead, or to which fields it may ultimately make fundamental contributions.

16.6 Summary of Level 5

At the beginning of Level 5, "Applications," we said that we would be able to cover only a sampling of the important applications of computers. After looking at simulation and modeling, electronic commerce and databases, artificial intelligence, and computer graphics, we hope you will seek to learn more about application areas that interest you but that were not covered in detail here.

There is one more level to our story. With all the capabilities that exist today and that will be developed tomorrow, what is the larger picture of computer technology within society? What are the ethical, legal, and social consequences of these capabilities? What should we welcome? What should we monitor or regulate? Is there anything we should prohibit? (Some of these issues were raised earlier in the Special Interest Box in this chapter titled "The Good, the Bad, and the Ugly.") Are there any tools that can help us clarify thorny ethical decisions? Level 6 raises these questions in more detail, though, of course, it provides no definitive answers. Individuals, armed with adequate knowledge, must hammer out their own position on many of these complex social issues. This is one of the responsibilities that comes with our unprecedented opportunity to enjoy the benefits of computer technology.

EXERCISES

1. Locate sources describing the graphics pipeline of Figure 16.2 in greater detail. (A good place to start is the "Graphics Pipeline" entry at Wikipedia.org.) How many distinct steps are included in these versions of the pipeline? Which ones that are included were omitted in this chapter, and what operations do these missing steps perform? Write a report giving an overview of these more complete treatments of the sequence of steps involved in computer graphics.

2. Given the following triangular model of a two-dimensional object:

show what a vertex list representation of this model would look like. Because you are working in two dimensions rather than three, your vertex list will only have (x, y) coordinates rather than (x, y, z). Assume vertex v_1 is the origin.

3. a. Assume the matrix multiplication of Figure 16.6 requires a total of 28 arithmetic operations—floating-point additions and multiplications. If we want to move (i.e., translate) a wireframe representation of an object containing 100,000 vertex points, and if that motion takes 10 seconds to complete, how many arithmetic operations in total does a computer need to perform to implement that movement?

   b. If your GPU can execute 50 million floating-point operations per second, how long will it take the processor to complete this translation operation?

4. Assume a polygon mesh contains 250,000 vertices. If a single matrix multiplication requires 28 floating-point operations, how fast a GPU is needed (floating-point operations per second) to produce real-time graphics at the rate of 30 frames per second?

5. Here is the vertex list for a two-dimensional wireframe triangular model:

Vertex	x	y	Connected to
(Origin)	v1	0	0	v2, v3, v4
	v2	0	1	v1, v4
	v3	1	0	v1, v4, v5
	v4	1	1	v1, v2, v3, v5
	v5	1.6	0.5	v3, v4

Draw the two-dimensional figure modeled by this vertex list.

6. We want to animate the movement of the object in Exercise 2 from its current location at (0, 0, 0), the coordinates of v_1, to the point (3, 5, 0). The motion lasts for a total of 2 seconds. Show the translation matrix that accomplishes this motion. That is, show the matrix that, when reapplied 30 times each second for a total of 2 seconds, will produce the desired ending position.

7. Assume you are working in two, rather than three, dimensions. Determine the four entries of the 2 × 2 *rotation matrix* that will take a vertex point located at position (x, y) and rotate it clockwise around the origin by an angle ø. The rotation is shown here: (*Hint:* You will need to use some trigonometric functions to accomplish this.)

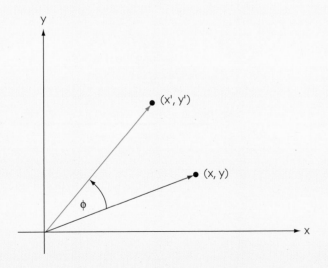

8. Again assume you are working in two, rather than three, dimensions. Determine the four entries of the 2 × 2 *reflection matrix* that takes a vertex point at position (x, y) and reflects it around the y-axis. That is, assume the mirror line in Figure 16.5(c) is the y-axis. This reflection operation is shown here:

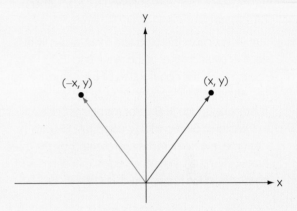

9. Shown here is an image of a human arm, from shoulder to hand. It has three control points labeled A, B, and C. Describe what type of motion might require the use of each of these three control points. Using these three control points, describe informally how you might animate the motion of an arm raising a glass held in the hand up to a figure's mouth.

10. Would a flight simulator package used to teach pilots to fly an airplane be a *real-time graphical environment*? Explain your answer.

11. The next diagram shows a single triangular face in the wireframe representation of an object. The three vertices of the triangle are labeled v_1, v_2, and v_3, and each has been assigned a color, either red, blue, or green.

    The vertex color is stored as a three-tuple, with each entry an integer in the range 0 to 255, representing the contribution of the components red, green, and blue, respectively. (*Note:* This is identical to the RGB color model introduced in Chapter 4, Section 4.2.2, page 169.) So, for example, the color red is represented by the three-tuple (255, 0, 0). Purple, an equal mix of red and blue, would be represented as (128, 0, 128).

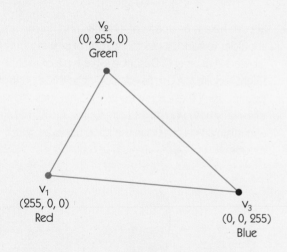

During the rendering phase, a computer must shade in the entire triangular face, according to the colors assigned to each of the three vertices. Describe an algorithm that would do color shading and blending of the triangular face in a visually attractive manner.

12. You are given the three-dimensional coordinates of a point P1 (x_1, y_1, z_1) and a point P2 (x_2, y_2, z_2). You are also given the coordinates of the location point of a viewer (x_v, y_v, z_v). You may assume that P1 and P2 are located on the same side of the viewer. Describe informally (you do not need to write out an algorithm) exactly how to determine if, from the point of view of the viewer, it is possible to see both points P1 and P2, or if one of these points is obstructed and not visible. In the latter case, describe how you can determine which is the occluded point.

13. The following diagram contains a circle of radius 1 with its center at the origin (0, 0). There is a mirror line parallel to the y-axis located at the point x = –2. For each of the following pairs of operations, show the final result after each of the two pairs of motions has been completed, one at a time:

a. Translate the circle along the x-axis by +2 units. Reflect the circle around the mirror line.

b. Reflect the circle around the mirror line. Translate the circle along the x-axis by +2 units.

c. Reflect the circle around the mirror line. Reflect the circle around the mirror line.

CHALLENGE WORK

In Section 16.2.5, we described only the most basic aspects of the rendering process. It is a far more complex topic than the elementary material presented in that one section. However, it is also the most critical and most difficult step in the overall imaging process. A wireframe model is not a finished image that could be displayed on a screen. It is the set of rendering algorithms that takes this primitive model and turns it into something both realistic and believable in its appearance.

Find sources of technical information on rendering and read about the steps involved in this visualization process. Specifically, read about some of these aspects of rendering that were not presented in this chapter:

- *Bump-mapping*—Creating small-scale bumps on the surface of an object

- *Fogging*—The dimming and dispersal of light as it passes through a partially obscure atmosphere

- *Refraction*—The bending of light associated with transparency

- *Indirect illumination*—Surfaces that are illuminated by light reflecting off other objects

- *Translucency*—The scattering of light as it passes through solid objects

- *Depth of field*—Objects that appear out of focus because they are too close to or too far from the object that is in focus

For one or more of these rendering topics, write a report that describes the algorithms used to address these issues.

ADDITIONAL RESOURCES

 For additional print and/or online resources relevant to this chapter, visit the Computer Science CourseMate at login.cengagebrain.com.

> Chapter 17 — Social Issues

Chapters 13, 14, 15, 16 — Applications

Chapters 9, 10, 11, 12 — The Software World

Chapters 6, 7, 8 — The Virtual Machine

Chapters 4, 5 — The Hardware World

Chapters 2, 3 — The Algorithmic Foundations of Computer Science

W e have now reached the highest and most abstract level in our discussion of computer science—the social, ethical, legal, and moral questions raised by the information-based technologies just presented. In this section, we are no longer interested solely in algorithms (Level 1), hardware (Level 2), virtual machines (Level 3), software (Level 4), or applications (Level 5). Instead, we investigate the impact, both good and bad, that these developments can have on business, government, society, and individuals. These concerns were not part of the original definition of computer science, and in the early days were often not included in the computer science curriculum but, instead, left to departments such as Philosophy, Religion, or Sociology to discuss and debate. However, as computing has become more pervasive, these social and ethical issues have become a critically important part of the study of computer science.

Making Decisions About Computers, Information, and Society

17.1 Introduction

Most of this book has focused on the technical issues of computing. For example, you have read about the mathematics of algorithmic efficiency (Chapter 3), the hardware implementation of computer systems (Chapters 4 and 5), building computer networks (Chapter 7), and software development (Chapters 9 and 10). However, in this chapter, we focus on the *human* issues lurking behind these technical details. We can't provide a comprehensive list of such issues; such a list would be way too long, and it is growing daily. Instead, we introduce skills that will help you to think and reason carefully when making personal decisions about computing. This chapter also discusses important societal issues related to information technology and personal privacy and points you toward resources to help you explore these issues in greater detail. Making critical decisions about computing technology is unavoidable. Increasingly, our society is being driven by the access to and the control of information. As citizens of our communities, our country, and the world, we want our decisions to be well informed and well reasoned.

Whenever humans make decisions about things they value, there are conflicts and trade-offs. The scholarly field of ethics has a long history of studying how to identify and resolve such conflicts, and we will borrow from several classical theories of ethics. In this chapter, we present a number of case studies built around complex ethical issues related to computing and information. For each case study, we present the issues as well as arguments used to support and oppose certain positions. We then describe methods that allow us to understand and evaluate these arguments in terms of their ethical implications. When you finish this chapter, you should have an increased appreciation for the complexities of human/computer interactions as well as an enhanced set of skills for thinking and reasoning about these interactions.

17.2 Case Studies

17.2.1 Case 1: The Story of MP3—Compression Codes, Musicians, and Money

In 1987, some scientists in Germany started working on an algorithm to compress digital files that store recorded music on CDs. Using a complex model of how humans perceive sound, the Fraunhofer Institute in Erlangen, Germany, devised a method with the rather ungainly title of Moving Picture Experts Group, Audio Layer III. This algorithm (or protocol) quickly got the nickname *MP3*.

We introduced MP3 in our discussion of the binary representation of sound in Section 4.2.2. In that section, we showed how the digital representation of audio information can produce massive and unwieldy data files. To reduce these files to a more manageable size, we compress them using a compression algorithm such as MP3, which allows various levels of compression. The more you compress the music data, the more sound quality you lose. A compression ratio (defined in Section 4.2.2) of 12 to 1 has become popular, with the resulting sound quality almost indistinguishable from a music CD that has not been compressed.

In 1989, the Fraunhofer Institute patented MP3 in Germany, and a few years later MP3 became an international standard. It might simply have become another technical detail known to only a few engineers had it not been for the World Wide Web and an army of young people enthusiastic about recorded music.

In 1997, Tomislav Uzelac, a software developer at Advanced Multimedia Products, created what is regarded as the first commercially viable MP3 playback program. Two students from the University of Utah, Justin Frankel and Dmitry Boldyrev, used Uzelac's player to develop a user-friendly Windows application called WinAmp that played MP3 music. WinAmp was offered for free on the Internet in 1998. Suddenly MP3 became *very* well known.

Prior to the release of WinAmp, there had been some sharing of digital music from copyrighted CDs. However, uncompressed sound files produced from traditional CDs were massive, and transferring these files using a 56 Kbps modem (the most widely used communication link on the Internet in the late 1990s) was slow and clumsy. But because MP3 sound files were so much smaller, and Internet connections were getting faster (especially in university computer labs), sharing MP3 music files became increasingly popular, and the people who make and sell music CDs became increasingly nervous.

In the spring of 1999, two Northeastern University students, Shawn Fanning and Sean Parker, created a file-sharing system that spread quickly over the Internet. The users of the system were mostly other university students, who had ready access to fast Internet connections and who were very interested in obtaining music files that other students were willing to share. Fanning and Parker called their system "Napster," and it became so popular that several universities noticed their campus networks were slowing to a crawl because of student MP3 downloads.

The Napster system is a wonderful example of how technical details about computing systems can have significant social effects. The Napster software set up what's called **peer-to-peer file sharing**. As diagrammed in Figure 17.1, Napster's software electronically "introduced" two users who are distant from Napster and from each other. Once Napster helped these users find each other electronically, the file sharing took place between the users, *not* through Napster. Although that sounds like an unimportant technical detail, this distinction turned out to be quite significant in the many court battles to follow.

On December 7, 1999, an organization of recording companies filed suit against Napster in U.S. District Court on grounds of copyright infringement.

FIGURE 17.1

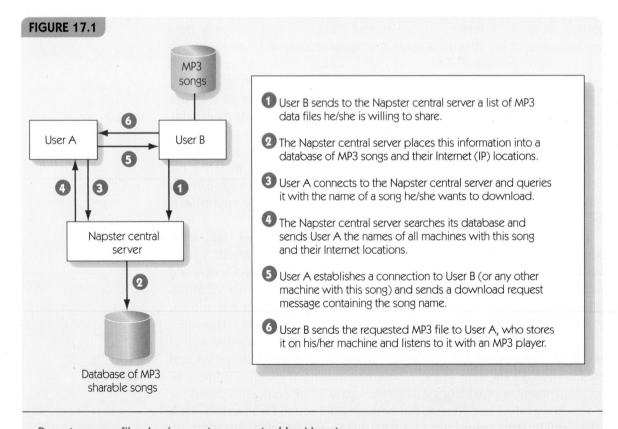

1. User B sends to the Napster central server a list of MP3 data files he/she is willing to share.

2. The Napster central server places this information into a database of MP3 songs and their Internet (IP) locations.

3. User A connects to the Napster central server and queries it with the name of a song he/she wants to download.

4. The Napster central server searches its database and sends User A the names of all machines with this song and their Internet locations.

5. User A establishes a connection to User B (or any other machine with this song) and sends a download request message containing the song name.

6. User B sends the requested MP3 file to User A, who stores it on his/her machine and listens to it with an MP3 player.

Peer-to-peer file sharing system created by Napster

During the highly publicized arguments that followed, the recording companies insisted that Napster was a conspiracy to encourage mass infringement of U.S. copyright law. By most accounts, the majority of MP3 music that Napster users "shared" was copyrighted, and most of the copyright holders objected to the copying of their music without royalty payments. Some artists wanted their music copied, but they were said to be in the minority.

Its supporters argued that the Napster system was merely acting as a common carrier, much like a telephone company. They claimed that Napster was simply providing information on songs and their location, and did not participate in the actual exchange of copyrighted information. They argued that Napster could not be held responsible for what peers (Users A and B) did with that information in the peer-to-peer file-sharing system depicted in Figure 17.1. In addition, Napster contended that peer-to-peer copying was very similar to a user making a backup copy of a file. It pointed out that copyright law allows a person who has purchased a recording in one format to transfer it to a different format as long as it is for personal use and is not resold. Napster claimed that both peers in each swap were transferring the file without any payment to each other or to Napster, and therefore the copying should be considered "fair use."

Eventually, Napster lost the case and subsequent appeals, and it ceased operating as a file-sharing site in 2001, although it did reopen as a commercial music downloading service. (In October 2011, the company's assets were purchased by Rhapsody, and the Napster name disappeared from the Web after a dozen tumultuous years.) However, new peer-to-peer file-sharing systems such as Kazaa sprang up on the Web, and illegal MP3 music sharing via the Internet continues, much to the chagrin of recording companies. Legal purchasing and downloading of MP3 (or similarly compressed) music has also become very popular. Apple's iTunes music store, in particular, accounts for more than 25% of music sales in the United States, and in early 2010 it sold its 10 billionth download. Movie file swapping, both legal and illegal, is also quite common, and taking copyrighted photographs off the Web for personal use is a regular occurrence. These file-swapping and photo-copying scenarios will no doubt continue, both on the Internet and in the courts; but for the rest of the discussion in this section, we concentrate on a question that isn't exactly a legal issue and isn't merely a technical computer science topic: Is it ethical to swap copyrighted MP3 music files?

Asking Ethical Questions. A legal question, we take to a judge. A technical question, we take to a scientist or an engineer. But who can help us with an ethical question? In this section, we look to ethicists for guidance about getting an answer to an ethical question.

We define ethics as the study of how to decide if something is morally right or wrong. A fundamental question in ethics is what criteria to use when "measuring" the rightness or wrongness of a particular act. Over the centuries, ethicists have championed different criteria and developed schools of thought about how to label an act as good or bad, better or worse. One of the most influential schools is called consequentialism. As the name implies, a consequentialist focuses on the consequences of an act to determine if the act is good or bad. If the consequences are on the whole good, then the act is good. If the consequences are mostly bad, then the act is bad. However, in focusing on the goodness of an act, we have to ask, "Good for whom?" For instance, in our MP3 example the copying is certainly good for people who get the free music. But, just as clearly, most music copyright holders are convinced that MP3 copying is bad.

The most well-known consequentialists are the utilitarians. Utilitarians answer the question "Good for whom?" with a hearty, "Good for everyone!" Imagine a cosmic calculator that is capable of adding up human happiness. **Utilitarianism** holds that a moment before an act takes place, the cosmic calculator adds up all human happiness and puts a happiness number into the variable HAPPINESS_BEFORE. Then the act occurs. We wait awhile, long enough for the consequences of the act to become visible; then we use our cosmic calculator again and put a second happiness total into the variable HAPPINESS_AFTER. According to a utilitarian, the act in question is "good" if

HAPPINESS_AFTER > HAPPINESS_BEFORE.

If

HAPPINESS_AFTER < HAPPINESS_BEFORE,

then the act is said to be "bad." (Just to satisfy the law of trichotomy, if HAPPINESS_AFTER = HAPPINESS_BEFORE, a careful utilitarian would declare the act to be ethically neutral.)

Of course, there is no cosmic calculator, and quantifying happiness is no easy task. Clearly, using the utilitarians' criterion requires subjective judgments. But making consequences count and ensuring that all people are taken into account when making an ethical judgment both seem like good ideas. So let's try out two short utilitarian arguments to explore whether mass copying of MP3 music files is right. First, we'll build a utilitarian argument that says such copying is OK, and then we'll build a second utilitarian argument that says such copying is not OK.

Utilitarian Argument #1: MP3 Copying Is OK. First, there are many more music listeners than there are music publishers. Music listeners are very pleased to get convenient, virtually free access to this music. Furthermore, music publishers should be pleased to get so much free publicity for their product. When radio stations play music, it's free to listeners, and many listeners go out and buy music that they've heard on the radio. The same thing happens to listeners who download MP3 files. That makes sense, because the music on a CD provides slightly better sound quality than MP3 music. Many also choose to buy legal copies, even though they do not need them, so that artists get paid. There is some market research that shows that MP3 downloading can increase the sale of music CDs. Opponents of MP3 sharing point out that overall music sales revenue has fallen dramatically since 1999, but this cannot be completely blamed on file sharing. During the CD era, people bought whole albums. Today music retailers like iTunes and

Death of a Dinosaur

The Virgin Megastores in New York City's Times Square and Union Square were the two largest music stores in the world, sprawling over 180,000 square feet of retail space and selling an estimated $55 million worth of recordings every year. Not only were they important economic engines for the entertainment industry, they were also popular gathering places for hard-core music lovers and emerging artists. Unfortunately, even megastores with massive sales volumes and huge financial backing are finding it difficult to compete with online music sites like iTunes and the ease of digital copying. "It's clear that the model of a large entertainment specialist working in a large retail space is not going to work in the future," said Simon Wright, the CEO of Virgin Entertainment Group, North America.

In February 2009, the Times Square store closed its doors for good, with the Union Square store following suit just four months later. In the words of a former Virgin employee, "The large retail music store is a dinosaur, and we all know what happened to them!"

Amazon.com encourage consumers to buy one song at a time, which has also hurt overall album sales.

Utilitarian Argument #2: MP3 Copying Is Not OK. Although some early research suggested that MP3 file copying may have initially encouraged CD buying, later research showed that overall retail music sales had declined rapidly. That's the real, long-term effect of widespread copying of copyrighted materials. The main reason that iTunes and Amazon sell one song at a time, instead of albums, is that this is the only way to compete with illegal MP3 file sharing. If the people who publish music can't make a fair profit, then less and less music will be published. Eventually, both music listeners and music publishers (including the people who make the music) will lose. In addition, copyright protection is the law. This widespread criminal activity will result in a widespread disrespect for the law in general, and that is a very dangerous consequence.

Hmmm. We have used an ethicist's idea, a utilitarian argument, to try to clarify the MP3 question. But instead of getting a clear answer to our question, you might be thinking we've only managed to make things more confusing. Both sides of this issue seem to have some reasonable points. How are we to decide between them?

Let's admit something up front: Deciding right and wrong is not always easy. If you want to do a binary search on a sorted array, there is a "plug-and-chug" algorithm that does the job quite nicely. Unfortunately, there isn't an all-purpose "ethics algorithm" that is guaranteed to provide a definitive answer to every ethical question. Still, we do have to make decisions about these issues, and we want to make those decisions on reasonable grounds, not just on whims or instinct.

Ethicists depend on what is called a dialectic to try to make better and better ethical decisions. In a dialectic, we move back and forth between different viewpoints, criticizing each and trying to learn from each. In a debate, one side is trying to win by undermining the opposition and building up the arguments for its position. Ideally, in a dialectic the ultimate goal is for both sides to "win" by moving closer to the truth from two different perspectives. It's perfectly OK for people engaged in a dialectic to change their minds; in fact, that's the point. By systematically reasoning about the issue, the back and forth of argument can bring all parties to a more well-reasoned and justified decision. There's never a guarantee that the two sides in a dialectic will arrive at identical positions (although that is possible). More often, the participants end the dialectic still disagreeing, but hopefully with a better understanding of the reasons why there are still disagreements.

In the spirit of a dialectic, let's examine the strengths and weaknesses of the two previous utilitarian arguments on the issue of MP3 copying. Both arguments cite evidence about music sales to bolster their position: People for MP3 copying claim that it increases the sales of music; people against the copying claim that it decreases overall music sales. This is an example of a difference in fact, not just a difference of opinion. If the effect of MP3 copying is, in fact, to increase music sales, then the "copying is OK" people have a strong argument; if the effect is instead to decrease sales, then the "copying is not OK" people have a strong argument. When the dialectic uncovers an empirical question at the heart of a disagreement, the smart move is to check the facts.

According to published statistics, worldwide music recording sales in 2003/2004 were down almost 8% from 2001/2002, and this downward trend has continued virtually unabated over the last decade. For example, in 2010 global revenues from the sale of recorded music fell another 8.4%. In the early days of Napster, sales were climbing; but as more and more files were downloaded for free, and as more and more MP3 hardware was sold, CD and album sales fell. Even with the introduction of iTunes, which makes legal downloading very easy, album sales have continued to decline. So it seems that, on this point, the MP3 opponents have a stronger argument. It often happens that consequences take a while to become visible, and that seems to be the case here.

Next, let's examine the other main point in support of MP3 copying: the happiness of legions of listeners at getting free music. The opponents of the copying again make an argument about short-term and long-term effects of copying: In the short run, listeners might get tremendous benefits; but in the long run, there may be far less music available for copying because artists and publishers will have far less incentive to create and disseminate music. This seems to make a certain amount of economic sense.

A third point raised by opponents of MP3 copying is the issue of illegality. The claim is that widespread disregard of copyright protections will have as a consequence widespread disrespect of the law, such as the illegal copying of movies, videos, or photographs from the Internet. This claim is harder to demonstrate empirically than the CD sales claim, so we're probably not going to be able to settle this with statistics. But MP3 advocates don't often claim that breaking the law will have particularly salutary effects, and we don't see many legitimate claims for anarchy.

The dialectic so far seems to favor banning MP3 copying, but there are a few interesting counterarguments. For example, some musicians (particularly relatively unknown ones) are great enthusiasts of MP3. These musicians have not yet been able to get recording contracts, so they use MP3 Internet file copying as a way to distribute and publicize their music as well as to generate interest in upcoming performances. For them, MP3 copying has positive consequences for both listeners and music makers. Advocates of MP3 copying also point out that only a small percentage of the money spent on legally purchased music goes to the artists. The rest of the money goes to the people who market the music. Some artists (including a few bands who have not achieved commercial success) have decided to give away their music on the Internet and make their money via live concerts. They are content to accept reduced sales of their albums if it means more people listen to their music, and hence come to their concerts.

Seen from this perspective, MP3 copying is merely the first wave of a new way of thinking about making and sharing music. This new way will favor music listeners and music makers who like to perform live. The new way will deemphasize the need for large publishing companies. Some people think that these are good directions, although, quite obviously, most music company executives don't agree.

Notice something technically interesting about the MP3 debate. If you buy a lightbulb, you are mostly paying for the materials and the manufacture of the bulb. When you buy a CD, very little of the cost has to do with the materials and manufacture of the disc; that costs only pennies per disc. You mostly pay for the *information* encoded on the disc, not the physical disc itself. That's why MP3 copying is so dangerous for music publishers—the information on the Internet bypasses the physical intermediary, and it was always the transfer of a physical form during which publishers made their money.

An ethical dialectic rarely has a clean stopping point. We can almost always make better and better arguments, and there are often strong points remaining on different sides of an argument. For example, we haven't discussed the fact that some MP3 music copying takes place using university and corporate computers (which may have faster Internet connections than home computers), and that such equipment usually isn't supposed to be used for such purposes. We'll leave that and other issues for you to pursue on your own. We will make some closing remarks on MP3 copying, but we don't think this is a final word on the issue, and we certainly don't want you to think so either.

The consequences of widespread disregard of the law seem troubling and are a strong argument against illegally copying copyrighted music or video. If the United States decides as a country that we are better off without copyrighted music, then the law should be changed. Until then, it seems unethical to encourage breaking the law that currently protects copyrighted music.

In response to this seeming deadlock, some music distributors have come up with new ways to sell music online. Apple's iTunes music store has shown that music consumers will opt for legal copying if the system is convenient and reasonably priced. Starting in 2012, Apple's iCloud will allow music studios to make money even from illegally downloaded MP3 files. iCloud will allow users to store their music in a "locker" on computers belonging to Apple, and then listen to that music on their phone or computer. If all music was purchased on iTunes, then the service is free. If not, users can pay a yearly fee to get access to their other songs, even those obtained illegally. Part of this yearly fee could be used to pay back music studios. (See the Special Interest Box titled "The Sound of Music.") Also, the Creative Commons License is a copyright approach that allows intellectual property creators to have more control over copyright specifications, while encouraging legal sharing of music, videos, texts, and other intellectual property.

Practice Problems

1. Talk to someone you know about copying MP3 files or commercial movies using the Internet. Ask this person to show you how he or she does it. Does the software used differentiate between music that is copyrighted and music that isn't copyrighted? Ask the person showing you how to copy the files if he or she has ever thought about the ethical implications.

2. Not every decision is an ethical one. For example, we usually don't think of choosing an ice cream flavor as being "good" or "bad." Write down 10 choices you have made in the past week. Then go back over the list and label each as ethical or not ethical. (*Note:* "Not ethical" is different from "unethical"; "not ethical" means there are no ethical issues involved.) After you've labeled all 10 choices, see if you can convince yourself to change your mind about one of the choices you labeled "not ethical."

3. To effectively build a utilitarian argument, we need to think of all the people who are affected by a decision. We call these people "stakeholders" in the decision. Choose one of the "ethical" choices you listed in Practice Problem 2. Now write down all the people or groups of people who are potentially affected, directly or indirectly, by your decision. Finally, list what each stakeholder may gain or lose from your decision.

The Sound of Music

Peer-to-peer music sharing became popular because it offered users virtually unlimited access to free music. Many computer scientists and ethicists thought that once people were accustomed to this, it would be virtually impossible to break them of the habit and charge for music. Steve Jobs and Apple Inc. did not believe this. Instead, they thought that if costs were reasonable and value-added services were provided (e.g., previewing, Billboard charts, audiobooks, movie trailers), people would be willing to pay for legal access to copyrighted music. In 2003, Apple went public with the iTunes music store, a paid online music downloading service for its new iPod MP3 player. The service started small with access limited to Mac OS X users and a few thousand songs on its playlist. However, it was an immediate success with more than 1 million downloads in the first week. It rapidly expanded to Windows machines as well as European and Asian users. Currently, the iTunes Music Store has the rights to hundreds of millions of songs and other audio materials. Obviously, those who did not think people would pay for online music after having free access were wrong. Perhaps the desire to act ethically is more deeply ingrained than we had thought.

When the service first launched, there was a great deal of concern that files purchased legally on iTunes would then be illegally shared over the Internet. To control dissemination of the music it sold, Apple used a proprietary digital rights management (DRM) software package called FairPlay. FairPlay digitally encrypts a song so it can only be played on Apple's iTunes and iPod systems, limits the number of times it can be burned onto a CD, and restricts the number of computers on which it can be played within a 24-hour period. For many years, every music download store (including Microsoft's Zune store, and the new Napster) used DRM systems. Since 2009, however, almost all music files sold through iTunes have been DRM-free.

17.2.2 Case 2: The Athens Affair—Privacy vs. Security

Modern telecommunications networks create significant problems for law enforcement. Over the past century, state and federal law enforcement officers have come to rely on the ability to set up "wiretaps," which allow them to intercept and record telephone conversations between suspected criminals. As phone technology has changed, however, it has become increasingly complicated to set up wiretaps.

In the past, an intercept might have literally involved tapping a wire, using a piece of hardware similar to the Y-connector you might use to plug two sets of headphones into a single MP3 player. Such hardware could be installed at the local exchange (where the wire from your house connects to the phone company), and a recording device could be set up to record all calls.

Today, however, more than 25% of U.S. households have no landline-based phone, and that percentage is growing rapidly. Instead, people are turning to cellular phone and Internet phone technology (known as Voice over Internet Protocol, or VoIP) for their voice communications. This has created major headaches for phone companies because it is no longer possible to tap a particular phone by simply hooking on to a particular wire in the local exchange. Cell phone calls can be made from anywhere, even from places where a person's phone company owns no cell towers. VoIP calls can be made from any place that the user can get an Internet connection, including the thousands of free wireless access points in cafés, libraries, and colleges. Phone companies now need complicated automated systems to follow a user from place to place, intercept his or her conversations, and forward them to law enforcement. Creating such lawful intercept (LI) systems is complicated and expensive.

Furthermore, to make sure that every phone call could be tapped, it is necessary for Internet Service Providers (ISPs) to get involved. It is not hard for law enforcement to partner with phone companies, because there are only one or two phone companies in each part of the country. With ISPs, however, there are sometimes hundreds operating within a single city. It is also necessary for makers of VoIP software to get involved. In Chapter 8, we learned about cryptography and the use of encryption to protect communications on the Internet. If VoIP providers choose to implement cryptography on their systems, then this could render wiretaps useless. Even though the police could listen in on the call, they would not be able to decrypt it, and it would sound like random pops and static.

In the mid-1990s, law enforcement officials saw these problems coming. They assumed (correctly) that smaller ISPs, VoIP software makers, and even some phone companies would not build LI systems unless required to. After all, building and operating the LI functionality would cost a lot of money. As a result, many countries, the United States included, passed laws requiring everyone involved with telecommunications to cooperate with law enforcement, and build LI capabilities into all of their systems.

Critics of LI worried that it would be a tempting target for computer hackers. Modern LI systems allow an authorized user to create a wiretap by filling in a few blanks in a computer program. It is no longer necessary to attach new hardware to create a wiretap. Because all phone calls now travel through computers as streams of data, that data can simply be copied and stored as it flows by. It is even possible to forward phone calls to another number, so every time a phone call is placed from a monitored number, the police officer's phone rings, and he or she can pick up and listen in on the call in real time. For spies this functionality would be tremendously attractive. What if you could listen in on every call the president makes, or to all the phone calls of finance ministers or heads of major corporations?

This is exactly what happened to government and industry figures in Greece in 2004. Persons unknown broke into the LI system for the major cellular phone vendor in Greece, and installed illegal wiretaps on over 100 important Greek business leaders and politicians, including the prime minister. From June 2004 through February 2005, hackers used the LI system to forward calls from tapped numbers to a series of "shadow phones," which allowed the hackers to listen in on conversations. This tapping was massive in scope, and went undetected for almost a year. More disturbingly, law enforcement officials still know next to nothing about who did this or why. Due to a series of errors by everyone involved in the investigation, important access logs (both digital and paper) were destroyed, and the hackers were tipped off that authorities were on to them.

For this case, we will focus on the ethical implications of the decision to require all Internet and telecom companies to participate in lawful intercept. How does the decision impact privacy? How does it impact security? We used utilitarian arguments to explore ethical questions about MP3 copying; but in this case study, we will use a different kind of argument, argument by analogy, to explore questions about lawful intercept.

Analogies are commonplace, and that's one of the reasons they can be a useful way to think about ethical concerns. Most people are familiar and comfortable with the idea of explaining something less well known by comparing it with something better known. "It tastes a little like chicken, but drier" is a pedestrian example of an analogy. But when we apply analogies to ethics, we need to be more careful about the analogies that we choose.

The power of an analogy is that it can transfer our understandings and intuitions about something well known to a situation or entity that is less well known. Sometimes that transfer is ethically appropriate, and sometimes it isn't. In a dialectic argument that uses analogies, there may be competing analogies presented; one analogy supports a particular view of the situation being discussed and the other analogy supports an opposing view of the exact same situation. In a productive dialectic using analogies, the participants in the discussion explore the strengths and weaknesses of each argument.

In any analogy between two "things," there are both similarities and differences. For example, someone might say "swimming is like riding a bike—once you learn it, you never forget." Clearly, swimming is not *exactly* like riding a bike. (Just try swimming on a driveway or riding a bike in a lake.) The point of this analogy is clear: The person making the analogy thinks that the similarity (you don't forget it once it has been learned) is most important to the current conversation.

Analogies serve several purposes in ethical reasoning. When an analogy fits well, it helps us take advantage of decisions we have made in the past because if two situations are sufficiently similar we can apply the solution for the original problem to the new one. If the analogy does not fit well, this also provides useful information. If we can precisely identify the mismatch in the analogy, this often highlights some ethically significant aspect of the case.

In our analysis of lawful intercept, we will consider two analogies that bear directly on privacy concerns raised by LI.

Analogy #1: Lawful Intercept Is Like Requiring Everyone to Record Their Face-to-Face Conversations. The first analogy focuses on Internet VoIP phone systems such as Skype, but most of our arguments apply equally well to cellular phone systems because they use very similar technologies. Here's an expression of the analogy:

> If you and I decide to go for a walk in the woods and just talk, no one in his right mind believes that we should be forced by the government to carry microphones along to record our conversation so that they can listen to it. Before all this technology came in, every conversation was private. —Phil Zimmermann in *Life on the Internet: Cyber Secrets* (PBS, 1996).

Using Analogy #1 to Analyze the Case. In this case, we can see some clear similarities between face-to-face communication and Internet phone calls. They are similar in that people want to communicate with each other, and that both types of communication are meant to include a limited number of people. In both types of communication, however, the actual audience may be larger than intended: In a voice conversation, people may be eavesdropping either by being physically close but unnoticed by the speakers, via a hidden microphone, or by a distant parabolic listening device. With VoIP, the conversation may be intercepted at any number of places along the electronic path between sender and receivers. If there is a system that makes it easy to listen in on private conversations, we might justifiably worry that law enforcement officials or hackers would abuse it. Both lawful intercept systems and the "carrying microphones" system in the analogy could be abused.

In U.S. society, private conversations are, by default, free from government intrusion. This is not an absolute right—court orders can be obtained by law enforcement to use technology that invades private physical conversations. But these are the exceptions that prove the rule. Unless law enforcement can demonstrate probable cause, they are not permitted to take extraordinary measures to listen in on private physical conversations.

In both cases (VoIP and face-to-face conversations), there is a trade-off between privacy and security. In the case of face-to-face conversation, our society has decided not to record all conversations all the time, but to allow law enforcement to record certain conversations if they can demonstrate that they need to do so.

The analogy implies that requiring lawful intercept for all Internet-phone equipment would be the same as requiring everyone to record all of their private conversations, and provide recordings to the government as needed. If lawful intercept capabilities were not built into VoIP hardware, law enforcement's powers would be the same as in the case of face-to-face conversation. Law enforcement could still get a warrant, and then physically eavesdrop on one end of the conversation. With sufficiently powerful microphones, they would be able to hear both ends of the conversation. The conclusion seems to be that lawful intercept should not be built into VoIP hardware.

Problems with Analogy #1. The conclusion we reached just now may conflict with your intuition about the case. Notice that the argument we made applies to normal phone tapping as well as tapping VoIP. We know that most people accept the need for the occasional use of regular phone taps, so this seems to indicate a problem with the analogy. Our analogy must have left out some ethically significant factor.

This demonstrates another powerful use of analogy, which is to discover which parts of the case are most ethically relevant. Sometimes, when you make an analogy, the answer does not match your intuition. This could be because your intuition is wrong, but it could also be because the analogy does not fit. If we can precisely describe how the analogy does not fit, this often identifies some ethically relevant part of the case that we had not considered. In this case, where is the mismatch in the analogy?

There are many reasonable criticisms of analogy #1, but one big problem is that it has only three significant parties: The two parties in the conversation plus the government. In the case of lawful intercept, there is a very significant fourth party, the telecommunications company. In the previous analogy, Zimmermann points out the absurdity of requiring individuals to record their own conversations and provide them to the government. But what if there was another party that was already well positioned to record any conversation? Could the government require that party to do so, and to hand over the recordings? This is exactly the case with Internet phone services. The Internet service provider is always in a position to record calls and provide them to the government. Our current analogy does not seem to shed any light on this. In our process of dialectic reasoning, this causes us to look for a different analogy that has this "middleman" feature built in.

Analogy #2: Lawful Intercept Is Like Suspicious Activity Reporting in Banking. There are two critical resources needed by criminals and terrorists that each require the help of a large corporation: means of communication and means of transferring and transporting money. U.S. banks are required to keep detailed records on all transactions and to notify the U.S. Department of the Treasury (through a Suspicious Activity Report, or SAR) whenever they detect unusual or suspicious transactions. This careful recordkeeping and monitoring is expensive, but it allows law enforcement to find links between suspects and to discover and defeat criminal networks. In the same way, phone calls are an excellent source of information about the relationships between people. Intercepting phone calls between suspected terrorists is necessary if we are to discover and prevent attacks.

Using Analogy #2 to Analyze the Case. This analogy seems to support the idea that telecommunication companies can be required to monitor phone usage and report certain data about suspicious activity. This would be consistent with the monitoring and reporting requirements placed on financial institutions. So, again, reasoning by analogy allows us to apply our solution to an old question (Should banks be forced to report suspicious activity?) to a new one (Should telecom companies be forced to report suspicious activity?).

What can we learn about lawful intercept from suspicious activity reporting? If you do a bit of research, you will discover that suspicious activity reporting differs in two very important ways from current lawful intercept systems. First, the suspicious activity report is initiated by the bank. The government does not get to continuously monitor what is going on in a bank. Instead, the bank is responsible for deciding what might constitute suspicious behavior, and if it sees suspicious behavior, to report it using the SAR form.

The SAR form is very simple, and this is the second major difference. It requires identifying information for those involved in the suspicious activity, and a written description of the activity. There is nothing in this that is comparable to completely recording a telephone call. The list of parties involved in the suspicious activity would be similar to listing the phone numbers or names of the people on the call. Listing the amount of the activity and the dates on which it took place would correspond to the times and dates on which phone calls took place, the lengths of the calls, and so on. But a financial transaction does not include the wealth of data that a phone call does, because a financial transaction is not a conversation.

So analogy #2 lends some support to the idea that we might require telecom companies to keep careful track of call records (who calls whom, when, and for how long), to monitor this information for suspicious patterns, and to report suspicious activities to the government or law enforcement. Like the previous analogy, it seems to contradict the idea that government/law enforcement should be allowed direct or unsupervised access to the data. It does not seem to tell us, directly, whether or not the telecom companies should be recording and storing the actual contents of calls.

Making a Decision. In most cases, just having a convincing analogy is not enough to be sure we are making the right decision. Even if an analogy appears to fit, there is always a good chance that we are overlooking some morally significant factor in the case that would invalidate the analogy. Analogies are tremendously useful, however, in brainstorming. The analogies help us identify the most morally significant factors of a case, and they help us identify potential solutions based on previous solutions to similar problems. Nonetheless, it is always wise to double-check a solution using other methods.

In this case, we will use a utilitarian approach to check potential solutions identified by our analogies. So far, we have three possible solutions on the table:

1. Require all VoIP systems to implement lawful intercept (as in the current law).

2. Do not require VoIP systems to implement lawful intercept or do any other reporting. Law enforcement will have to use physical eavesdropping, after getting a warrant (as suggested by analogy #1).

3. Require VoIP providers to monitor and report suspicious activities, but do not build the ability to record conversations into the system (as suggested by analogy #2).

First, we need to identify the interested parties, and how this decision might affect their happiness.

- *Those that make or operate VoIP systems*—Increased monitoring costs them money for building in the monitoring and for defending against privacy lawsuits.

- *Law enforcement officials and employees*—Increased monitoring saves them money because they do not have to do as much physical surveillance. This also allows them to catch more lawbreakers and do their jobs better.

- *Hackers*—Built-in lawful intercept provides them with greater opportunities for stealing (and selling) secrets, but increases their likelihood of being caught.

- *Nonhacker criminals*—Increased monitoring increases the likelihood that they will be caught or that their plots will be disrupted.

- *The public*—Increased monitoring means increased efficiency for law enforcement, saving tax money, and possibly increasing safety. It also, however, decreases privacy because it makes everyone's phone calls easier to tap, and possibly decreases safety by exposing the public to hacker attacks or to abuse by law enforcement officials.

We will start by making an assumption about the happiness of criminals. We will assume that any unhappiness that a criminal feels as a result of this decision is offset by an increase in happiness for others. In other words, we can ignore the hackers and criminals, and just focus on increasing the happiness of the other parties. This assumption is plausible because it points out that the criminals' happiness comes from hurting other people. If someone feels very happy because he or she stole some money, then the person he or she stole the money from probably feels less happy. Lots of other people also feel less happy because they hear about the theft, and this makes them fearful that they will also experience a theft.

For law enforcement, solution 1 (lawful intercept) is clearly the best. It gives them the most options and the most direct control over monitoring, at low cost compared with solution 2 (no monitoring). Keep in mind, however, that law enforcement officers are public employees. They are tasked with enforcing the laws and keeping people safe. This means that a police officer's change in happiness, due to this decision, will mostly reflect the change in happiness of the public as a whole. So, in the utilitarian analysis, we can also mostly set aside the happiness of the law enforcement officers. As long as we ensure that the public is happy, this should go a long way toward making law enforcement officers happy as well.

For VoIP providers, solution 2 (no monitoring) is clearly the best. Options 1 and 3 are probably about equally bad for them. Although solution 1 (lawful intercept) requires them to modify their systems significantly and opens them up to hackers, it requires much less manpower to operate than option 3 (suspicious event reporting), because option 3 would require humans to review cases, fill out forms, and interact with the police.

The stickiest part of this case, and the reason we will not be able to immediately come to a clear solution, is evaluating the effect on the public. Every option has pros and cons for the public. If we assume that the number of tax dollars going to law enforcement is held constant (so it is the same number in all three schemes), then option 2 (no monitoring) would result in a serious decrease in the effectiveness of the police. Option 1 (lawful intercept) might result in major abuses by hackers and rogue law enforcement officials, but then again it might not. Option 3 (suspicious event reporting) might also seriously decrease police effectiveness because they might really need the contents of the calls in order to prevent criminal schemes.

To reach a final decision on this case, we need to make a prediction about how much harm hackers and rogue law enforcement officials might do if we choose option 1, and weigh this against the loss of law enforcement capacity caused by options 2 and 3. To do this, we need a lot more information. This is the process that members of Congress went through when first drafting CALEA (the Communications Assistance for Law Enforcement Act, which created the lawful intercept requirement).

It may be a bit disappointing to spend so much time on a case without "solving" it, but the fact is that ethical decision making, done well, is very difficult. It takes a lot of time and careful work, just as any important problem does. In this section, however, we have learned about reasoning by analogy. This style of reasoning, by finding similar cases in the past and using them to reason about a new case, is fundamental to ethics and to law. We saw that analogy can be used as part of our dialectic to identify possible solutions to a problem. But we also saw that, in most cases, an analogy is not enough to justify an ethical decision. Once we identify possible solutions through analogies, we would be wise to go back and check our choice using other ethical theories.

Practice Problems

1. An important skill in using analogies is noticing both similarities and differences. This skill can be practiced. Think of a book and a Web site that contain essentially the same information. How are they alike? How are they different? Make a list of similarities and differences, at least 10 of each. Don't ignore the obvious, but don't limit yourself to the obvious either.

2. Imagine that your public library decides to go completely digital. The library now has a policy to phase out physical books and replace them with e-books, digital audiobooks, Web sites, and public access computers in the library. Using the list you made in Practice Problem 1, make another list of the people who would gain from this decision and a list of the people who would lose. Build a utilitarian argument either for or against the decision.

3. Some people think that the content of Internet sites should be regulated just as the content of radio and TV is, for example with rules regarding obscenity and the amount of advertising. Other people think that the content of Internet sites, like private phone conversations, should not be regulated. Is the analogy between Internet sites and radio and TV broadcasts more appropriate, or is the analogy between Internet sites and telephone conversations more appropriate? Justify your position.

17.2.3 Case 3: Hackers—Public Enemies or Gadflies?

During the Middle Ages, a "hacker" was someone who made hoes. In the seventeenth century, a hacker was a "lusty laborer" who enthusiastically wielded a hoe. But *hacker* has quite a different meaning today, far removed from its agricultural roots (see the Special Interest Box "How Hackers Became Crackers" in Chapter 8). Today, the term *hacker* is used in several different ways, but a common definition is someone who breaks into computer systems and launches Internet worms and viruses, or perpetrates other computer-related vandalism.

Not everyone sees hackers in this negative light, however. Some people view hackers as *social gadflies*, people who raise important, but irritating, questions about society. The ancient Greek philosopher Plato used the word *gadfly* to describe Socrates' relationship with the political establishment of their day. While most people agree that purposeless vandalism or outright theft through hacking is wrong, some of the activities categorized as "hacking" may constitute a public service, and several computer hackers have written books and articles about the ethics of computer hacking. In this section, we explore whether there is an ethical case to be made in support of computer hackers. To focus our discussion, we concentrate on a single type of hacking: gaining unauthorized access to someone else's computer system to obtain and publish secret information. This could be as simple as copying files from your company's private network and posting them on the Web, or as elaborate as breaking into a government installation using an Internet worm and circulating classified documents using an anonymization service to protect the hacker's identity.

These issues, which in the past were considered largely theoretical, have taken on particular urgency in recent years due to the founding of several organizations that specifically focus on information leaking as a form of hacktivism (that is, hacking that is intended as political activism). The two main groups discussed here are WikiLeaks and Anonymous.

WikiLeaks, which was launched in December 2006, is a site that specializes in protecting government and corporate whistle-blowers. Imagine that you discovered a document at your work that proved the company's leadership was engaged in significant unethical behavior. Furthermore, imagine that you decide you need to blow the whistle on this behavior. How would you go about it? In the past, one common route was to share the incriminating documents with an investigative journalist. The journalist acts as a firewall between you and the authorities; most journalists hold to a code of ethics that says that they will not identify their sources, even if it is clear that the source has committed a crime. Journalists sometimes go to prison rather than reveal their sources. The problem with this approach today is that it is very hard to share an electronic document with a journalist without leaving traces that law enforcement (or corporate security) officers can follow. Most journalists don't have the necessary computer security and hacking skills to actually safeguard the anonymity of their sources. WikiLeaks' goal is to provide exactly this kind of technical expertise. It provides a secure electronic drop box, and tips on how to submit documents that will prevent the leaker from being traced. WikiLeaks then provides the submitted documents to journalists. In the past, it has partnered with the *New York Times*, the *Guardian* (in the U.K.), and *Der Spiegel* (in Germany), among others. WikiLeaks has been involved in several major leaks:

- In April 2010, WikiLeaks published a video from a 2007 U.S. military action that shows the U.S. military firing on two employees of Reuters news service. The soldiers believed the two men were militants armed with a rocket-propelled grenade, but it was most likely a camera.

- In November 2010, WikiLeaks began to provide leaked U.S. diplomatic cables to various newspapers. The *Daily Mail* (a U.K. newspaper) and others have attributed the 2011 revolution in Tunisia, at least in part, to allegations of Tunisian government corruption contained in the diplomatic cables.

- WikiLeaks has published nearly a million confidential or secret U.S. government documents.

Though not hackers themselves, WikiLeaks employs people with the same skill set because they provide defenses against government and corporate hackers.

The hacker group Anonymous is much harder to describe. Anonymous is a group of hacktivists that seem primarily interested in freedom of speech. Even this characterization, however, is in dispute. WikiLeaks is easy to describe because it has a known public spokesman (Julian Assange), and a board of directors. WikiLeaks is part of an officially registered Icelandic corporation. Anonymous has no such official organizing body, or leader. In fact, its semiofficial logo is a suit with a question mark instead of a head, and members wear masks (all of them identical) when appearing in public. As a result, any hacker or activist can claim to be part of Anonymous, and there is no official spokesman to refute these claims. Among the best-known actions of Anonymous are:

- A December 2010 attack in retribution for financial sanctions against WikiLeaks. Several companies, including PayPal and MasterCard, have blacklisted WikiLeaks, preventing donors from using those systems to donate to WikiLeaks. Anonymous used denial-of-service attacks to disrupt the sites. (See the Special Interest Box, "Don't Mess with Amazon," in Chapter 8.)

- Attacks throughout the summer of 2011 that disrupted the government Web sites of Tunisia, Egypt, and Libya. These attacks were in retaliation for government censorship of the Internet, and meant to help support pro-democracy revolutions in those countries.

- Publication of e-mails stolen from Bank of America, security company HBGary Federal, and others.

Anonymous has also been accused of threatening the Westboro Baptist Church, a group known for protesting at the funerals of U.S. soldiers. Members of Anonymous have said that these charges are false, that they support all forms of free speech, even by people they disagree with. Due to the leaderless nature of Anonymous, however, clarity on what Anonymous has, and has not, done is hard to get.

We will examine the ethics of this kind of hacktivism, first using the two techniques we have already introduced, analogy and utilitarian analysis. Then we will introduce a third analysis technique, deontological ethics. In our analogy, we will focus on the first step of the process, breaking into a computer system to steal information. (This is sometimes called "cracking" to distinguish it from hacking in general.)

Analogy: Breaking into a Computer Is Like Breaking into Someone's House. Imagine that a burglar picks the lock on your back door, wanders around picking up valuables, and then escapes into the night undetected. When you find out you've been robbed, you feel outrage and fear. If computer hacking is ethically linked to burglary, then we will have an instinctive revulsion toward both.

Clearly there are similarities between burglars and hackers; in both cases, the intruders are there without our permission and (at least in most cases) without us being aware of their presence. In most homes and with most computers, the owners take some precautions to discourage unwanted visitors, precautions that must be overcome by the intruder. There are laws against both forms of intrusion, although the laws against physical break-ins are clearer and easier to enforce.

There are also differences between the intrusions. A burglar is likely to take something from your house, and that removal will deprive you of something. A hacker may look at things, and even copy things from your computer, but the hacker is less likely to remove or destroy things from your system. A hacker takes your intellectual property and privacy, and that is different from taking physical objects.

When someone breaks into a house, there is a palpable threat of violence. When a burglar is detected, things may turn nasty. This physical threat is not present in a computer break-in, although the information stolen may be personal and could lead to future physical threats. The physical degree of separation of a virtual break-in seems to be an ethically relevant distinction.

The analogy between a house break-in and a computer break-in helps us to clarify differences and similarities, both of which seem important in this case. Next we'll look at a pair of utilitarian arguments to extend the dialectic.

Utilitarian Argument: Costs and Benefits of Hacking. What is gained and lost when a computer is hacked? First, whoever owns the hacked computer loses some control over the information in that computer, and the hacker gains access to that information. Second, as a consequence of the break-in, there may be intentional or unintentional deletions or corruptions of data on the computer. These changes may be largely benign or may subsequently cause significant harm. Neither the hacker nor the person hacked can know with certainty the eventual consequences of these changes.

When computer system owners or system administrators discover that a system has been hacked, they often increase system security to reduce the probability of another successful intrusion. Some hackers claim that they provide a public service by alerting people to security holes in their systems. As long as the hacker doesn't hurt anything while "inside" the system, and especially if the hacker makes the intrusion obvious, then such hackers would argue that the consequence of the hacking is improved security against malicious hackers. An alternative consequential argument says that increased security wouldn't be necessary if hackers weren't such a threat.

This discussion illustrates two challenges when using a utilitarian argument in a dialectic about hacking:

1. It is sometimes hard to predict consequences with any accuracy.

2. There seems to be a distinction between "good hackers" (who are trying to act in the public interest) and "bad hackers" (who want to do damage or steal things for self-interested or pathological reasons).

These kinds of challenges arise in other discussions, and some people think they are difficult to overcome using a utilitarian argument. Let's try a different kind of ethical argument, a *deontological argument*, to try to meet these challenges in a different way.

Deontological Argument: Hacking with a Golden Heart. Utilitarian and other consequentialist arguments focus on the consequences of an act to determine if the act is ethical. Deontological arguments focus instead on the duties of the person acting and the way the act impinges on the rights of others.

The word deontology is from the Greek and means "the study of duty and obligation." Perhaps the most famous deontologist was the German philosopher Immanuel Kant (1724–1804). Kant wrestled eloquently (and at great length) about what duties we humans have to each other. He came up with "categorical imperatives" that characterized these duties. His second categorical imperative goes something like this:

> Never treat a fellow human merely as a means to an end.

To boil that down to a bumper sticker slogan, we might say, "Every human being deserves respect." Notice that the categorical imperative is really about your mental attitude toward the other person: Do you see him or her as a person, or just as the means to an end? Kant's deontological approach encourages us to consider the intent behind the action, not just the results of the action.

Let's try out a deontological perspective on our question about hacking. Is the act of hacking into another person's computer system inherently unethical? If we take some hackers at their word, their intent is not to harm the public. They characterize themselves as a foil against corporate and government abuse, and they characterize hacking as a form of investigative reporting, similar to the leaking of the Pentagon Papers. They also claim to want to help people discover security holes to protect against malevolent hackers.

Let's stipulate that hackers who break into other people's computers for personal gain are doing something unethical by any of the three arguments we've seen so far in this section (analogy, utilitarian, deontological). For the rest of this section, we concentrate on hackers who claim a benign if not benevolent intent to their computer break-ins.

First, we assume that "good hackers" are telling the truth when they claim to mean no harm to the public. (If some good hackers are lying about that, we'll reclassify them as "bad hackers" and focus on those hackers who are telling the truth.) Next, we'll explore how hackers describe the "goodness" of what they do. In his influential history of hacking, *Hackers: Heroes of the Computer Revolution*, Steven Levy[1] describes six components of what he calls the "hacker ethic." Here we focus on two:

1. "All Information Should Be Free"—Information sharing is a powerful positive good because it is not possible to make good decisions if important information is hidden. It is the ethical duty of hackers to facilitate access to information wherever possible.

---

[1] Levy, Steven. (2010). *Hackers: Heroes of the Computer Revolution.* http://shop.oreilly.com/product/0636920010227.do.

2. "Mistrust Authority—Promote Decentralization"—The rules and hierarchical management structures that characterize government and corporate bureaucracies mostly serve to prevent people from getting things done, rather than solving problems. Each hacker should act individually (or in very small groups) to do what he or she thinks is best, and ignore the rules.

We'll examine each of these ethical claims. In claim 1, the idea of sharing information looks pretty good at first glance. But it seems a bit less noble when we remember that much of the information that hackers share isn't *their* information, it's someone else's! It's one thing to share open source computer code (like Linux or OpenOffice.org) or the works of Shakespeare on the Web. It's quite another thing to share material whose copyright is legally still in force (like Lady Gaga's latest CD), or to share classified information that might impact national security. Unless hackers consciously make these kinds of distinctions (and many hackers do not), then the duty to respect other people isn't being met. In the case of WikiLeaks' releases of government documents, WikiLeaks collaborated with big newspapers to help determine which cables were safe to release, and which needed redactions to protect innocent people from harm. Some groups that release leaked documents simply release all documents without doing any such filtering.

The second claim has a similar weakness. Hackers might argue that the rules protecting electronic privacy are incorrect, and thus can be violated. They might argue that these rules exist because we expect electronic privacy, but it is our expectation of electronic privacy that is the problem, not their violation of that expectation. What's missing from the hackers' argument is why their ideas about information ("all information should be free") should take priority over the majority view ("some information should be private"), which forms the basis of the rules. Ethically, there's no problem with thinking and arguing that all information should be free, or to be suspicious of rules; there is a big problem, however, with acting on that belief in a way that treats people as a means to an end.

The preceding arguments won't convince most hackers, and you too might have some remaining questions about this issue. The sharing of information and resistance to authority are usually moral goods, and these values are part of the American identity. But the fact that these are ideals is not a slam-dunk ethical argument when applied to a specific act. Acts have both good and bad consequences, and utilitarians remind us that we have to weigh these consequences and think of them globally. Deontologists encourage us to remember that acts can be inherently good or bad outside the consequences, if they involve a right or duty, and to examine the intention behind an action. At the very least, the preceding brief analysis raises serious questions about the claims of the hacker ethic. In the following Practice Problems, you're invited to continue the dialectic about this ongoing controversy.

Practice Problems

1. There are times when you want someone to break into your house. For example, if your house is on fire, you probably won't object if firefighters use an ax on the front door. Can you think of other such situations? Try to make an argument based on an analogy between firefighters and hackers that supports the hacker ethic. Do you find this analogy convincing? Why or why not?

2. Sometimes we are invited to look into windows and to enter privately owned property. For example, stores spend money to make attractive windows to draw us in. What are some ethically significant differences between a store inviting us in and a computer being hacked? Focus on the issue of intent as you consider this question.

3. Some corporations and even government agencies have employed former hackers to improve security measures; the hackers test the security of the systems at the employing corporation or agency and report weaknesses. Consider the analogy of an auto manufacturer hiring a former auto thief to test how easy it might be to break into a new car model. Is this a reasonable analogy? Does it support the hacker ethic?

4. Some Internet chat rooms allow and even encourage people to remain anonymous. As people type to each other in real time, the people chatting are identified by fictitious "handles." Is this a good idea? Think of two reasons why such Internet anonymity may be a good thing and two reasons why it may be a bad thing.

17.2.4 Thinking Straight About Technology and Ethics

So far in this chapter, we've looked at three different cases using three different techniques: reasoning by analogy, utilitarian analysis, and deontological analysis. In this section, we suggest a "paramedic method" for computer ethics, and we invite you to practice that method on another case.

"Paramedic Ethics" for Technology. When you get sick, you often need medical help in a hurry. Paramedics aren't necessarily medical doctors, but they know quite a bit about how to help people, and they know who to ask when they aren't certain about a particularly puzzling case. We don't expect you to become a research ethicist by reading this chapter, but we hope you have started to gain some new skills: recognizing ethical questions regarding computing and reasoning carefully about answers to those questions.

Professional Codes of Conduct

Many professional organizations in the fields of computer science and electrical engineering have established codes of ethical behavior to provide guidelines for their members. These codes outline standards of behavior and conduct that typically include general imperatives such as avoiding harm to others and being honest, as well as more specific professional responsibilities and duties such as respecting intellectual property and protecting client privacy. Some of these organizations are:

- The Association for Computing Machinery (ACM) *www.acm.org*

- The Association of Information Technology Professionals (AITP) *www.aitp.org*

- Computer Professionals for Social Responsibility (CPSR) *www.cpsr.org*

- The Institute of Electrical and Electronics Engineers (IEEE) *www.ieee.org*

- The British Computer Society (BCS) *www.bcs.org*

In addition, ACM has published an article titled "Social responsibility and the CS student: How can I get involved?" that all students entering the field should read. It can be found at *http://xrds.acm.org/article.cfm?aid=332219*.

When you recognize an ethical problem, we think there are several important questions you should ask yourself:

1. Who are the stakeholders in this situation?

2. What does each stakeholder have to gain or lose? (This is the utilitarian step.)

3. What duties and responsibilities in this situation are important to the stakeholders? (This is the deontological step.)

4. Can you think of an analogous situation that doesn't involve computing? If so, does that analogous situation clarify the situation that does involve computing? (This is reasoning by analogy.)

5. Either make a decision or revisit the steps.

Before we illustrate how to apply these questions to a particular case, we need to announce a disclaimer. Unlike the formal algorithms studied earlier in this book, this "paramedic method" is not a step-by-step solution method, guaranteed to produce a result and then halt. Instead, it is an outline that can help guide you in a productive dialectic. That dialectic may be in your head or with others interested in the case. Either way, you want to think carefully and move toward a better understanding of the problem and toward better ethical solutions.

17.2.5 Case 4: Genetic Information and Medical Research

Many people believe that the Industrial Age is over and we are now living in the Information Age. In the last few years, human genetic information has taken center stage in scientific exploration. Computers are an integral part of this research and of the growing commerce connected to the human genome. Because this "new" information is contained in the cells of our bodies, the computerization of this information is simultaneously personal and mysterious. (Genetic information is not new because human genes have always encoded information, but our access to that information is new.) In our final case study, we explore a fictional case involving genetic information. We use the paramedic method outlined in the previous section to examine this case from several different perspectives.

Imagine that you are at your family doctor for a routine checkup. The doctor asks you to participate in a study of genetic diversity and disease by donating some skin cells for the study. The doctor informs you that your skin cells will be identified only by a randomly assigned number and your zip code. Should you donate your cells?

Step 1: Identify the Stakeholders. According to our paramedic method, the first question to ask is, "Who are the stakeholders?" Clearly the doctor and you are two stakeholders. But are these the only ones you should consider? Probably not. Unless the doctor is doing this study on her own (unlikely), there is someone else involved in this research. When you inquire, the doctor tells you that a pharmaceutical company is sponsoring the research and that it hopes to use the information gathered from around the country to identify genetic links to several diseases, some of them fatal. Now you've identified three more stakeholders: the pharmaceutical company (let's call the company PHARM CO), skin cell donors all over the country, and people who have or will have these genetic diseases. (There may be more stakeholders, but this list seems long enough for now.)

Step 2: What Is at Stake? Next, we ask what each stakeholder might gain or lose from our decision. If we say yes and donate our skin cells, then we will undergo some sort of procedure and lose a few cells; our doctor will participate more fully in the study; PHARM CO will get a larger database and may be able to develop new drugs; if the drugs are successful, then people with diseases may have new therapies. If we say no to the donation, then our doctor, PHARM CO, and patients will have a slightly smaller chance of success with the research.

Just thinking about these possible costs and benefits might lead to a few more questions. First, is the procedure for donating the cells dangerous? Your doctor assures you that the procedure is harmless and requires just a moment to scrape a tongue depressor lightly against your arm.

Probably, you also have questions about how your genetic information is going to be stored and processed. (Because you've almost finished this book, you have quite a bit of sophistication about computerized information!) A logical way to store this information would be to assign a randomly generated number for each donor in the study, perhaps linked to information your doctor already has. We might envision information like the following table, which includes the use of your Social Security number (SSN):

Random Number	SSN	Name	Zip Code	Gender	Doctor
10568322	532 12 3456	Joe Smith	45321	M	Goodgene
952990981	532 11 9503	Sue Jones	55416	F	Goodgene

The doctor has assured you that only the random number (from the first column) and the zip code (from the fourth column) will be associated with your genetic sample and the information derived from it. If we believe that the doctor will in good faith send only that information to PHARM CO, should you be confident that your privacy is assured? The answer is probably not. If a table such as the one just shown exists, then PHARM CO could potentially link the information it receives from your doctor back to you by gaining access to that table. At the very least, PHARM CO could likely find out the names and addresses of all the people who donated cells from a particular zip code, and there may not be many from your particular zip code. Furthermore, computerized files like our table have a habit of hanging around, in one form or another, for a long time unless they are explicitly and carefully deleted. Unless your doctor has been scrupulous about data deletion (including cleaning up any backups and the like), PHARM CO may indeed be able to track down your personal information if it becomes important for the company to do so. And we can envision situations in which PHARM CO might be eager to track you down; for example, your genetic information might reveal that your body has a resistance to a widespread disease.

You've also read in Chapter 7 some technical details about networks and communication over those networks. You know that information on the Internet can be intercepted at various points. Will your genetic information and/or the table described above be sent electronically to PHARM CO or anyone else? If so, will it be encrypted using the algorithms described in Chapter 8? Will access to the information be password protected?

A final question involves finances. Presumably, PHARM CO plans to make a profit from these drugs. Is anyone being paid for this research?

Let's assume that the doctor is being paid a nominal fee for collecting the samples, say $5 for each patient who donates cells. PHARM CO is paying for all the collection kits and for all the analysis. Because PHARM CO is paying for the research, the information collected and any information developed will belong to PHARM CO.

Step 3: Identify Duties and Responsibilities. Now that we have a clearer picture of possible costs and benefits, we'll move to the third step of the paramedic method: analyzing duties and responsibilities. Your doctor has a primary responsibility to do her best to treat you and protect your privacy. You have a duty to pay your bills promptly and to follow instructions that the doctor prescribes. PHARM CO is responsible for developing safe and useful drugs, and in return its customers pay for those drugs. In this research effort, PHARM CO is hoping that doctors will enlist volunteer patient donors, and in return PHARM CO is promising doctors a small fee for each patient who volunteers. Both your doctor and PHARM CO have promised to protect donors' privacy and are obligated to make a good faith effort to fulfill that promise.

Most of the responsibilities we've discussed so far are fairly straightforward and uncontroversial. There are other possible responsibilities that are less obvious and more controversial. We've already discussed intellectual property, the value of information, in the preceding MP3 case. Analogous to the music in that case study, this example also involves valuable information. What if your genetic information includes an important clue to the treatment of cancer or some other fatal disease? If PHARM CO develops an effective drug based on your genetic information, it stands to make billions of dollars. Should you get a royalty on the information in your genes? Does PHARM CO have a duty to share your genetic information and the information from others, or does its initial funding of this research give it proprietary control of that information?

Your doctor told you that only a random number and a zip code would identify your donated skin cells. This coding procedure seems to afford you some confidentiality, and that's a good thing. But you might also want to know why the zip code is required at all. Is geographic location part of the research, or is the zip code important for subsequent marketing of drugs? Is this study being done all over the world, only in the United States, or only in select zip codes in the United States? If it turns out your genetic information is particularly valuable, can the doctor give you assurances that your privacy will not be invaded? As we've seen previously, maintaining strict confidentiality would require a sophisticated protocol to make sure information could not be linked back to you and to protect information stored on computers and communicated over a network. Because both PHARM CO and your doctor want you to volunteer for this process, they have a duty to disclose these kinds of details before asking for your genetic information.

Another question is whether you have a duty to try to help cure disease in this case. If there is a chance for you to advance medicine by a simple donation process, is there an obligation for you to donate? In a situation like this, is altruism required?

Step 4: Think of Analogies. As we move through the paramedic method, the seemingly simple request for a few skin cells has taken on added depth and complexity. Ethical analysis often reveals a broader perspective than our first thoughts about a situation. Now let's move on to our final step in the paramedic method, reasoning by analogy. An important aspect of this case is the promise of confidentiality to donors. Another aspect of the case that emerged during the first steps is that two of the stakeholders are potentially gaining money, PHARM CO and the doctors. The other two stakeholders, you and patients who potentially will want the drugs developed, are not getting money now and may be paying later. To explore both the confidentiality and the financial aspects of donors and users of donations, we'll consider blood donations.

The Red Cross solicits blood donations. The Red Cross is concerned about the quality of the blood that it distributes. Therefore, when you give a blood donation, the blood is tested for certain diseases. If your donated blood turns out to be unusable, then your name is entered into a "deferred donor database" and you are prevented from giving blood. Clearly, the Red Cross cannot offer you complete confidentiality about your blood and any diseases it discovers in your donation. However, the Red Cross is sensitive to the issue of confidentiality. On the Web site *www.givelife2. org/donor/faq.asp#5*, the following appears on a FAQ (frequently asked questions) list:

> **Are the health history questions and my test results confidential?**
> Yes. The health history will be conducted by a trained professional in an individual booth arranged to preserve confidentiality. Your answers will be kept confidential, except where required by law. If your blood tests positive to any of the administered standard tests, you will receive confidential notification. The Red Cross maintains strict confidentiality of all blood donor records.

The Red Cross is a not-for-profit organization, but it incurs processing costs associated with collecting, testing, and distributing blood. To recover these processing costs, the Red Cross charges a reimbursement fee to hospitals that use the donated blood. The hospitals also incur operating costs, which appear on your hospital bill. One of the reasons that the Red Cross prefers volunteer donors is that it has been found that people who donate blood for altruistic reasons are the safest blood donors. Blood donation and skin cell donation (as proposed by your doctor) are similar in that the donors are volunteers, but the collectors and eventual users of the donated materials are paid. In both cases, it is something from donors' bodies that is being collected. And in both cases, the donors are asked to volunteer for altruistic reasons.

There are differences between the two situations. In the case of blood donation, the blood itself is the item of value, and both donor and collector are clear about what will happen with the blood. In the case of the skin cells, it is the genetic information in the cells that is of value, not the cells themselves. Also, PHARM CO is looking for something it might or might not find in your cells. If it finds valuable information,

PHARM CO stands to make a profit; if it doesn't find valuable information, it might take a loss on the project. The Red Cross and hospitals presumably won't make large profits on your blood, although they do charge for its use.

Let's examine another analogy: companies that solicit money for a charity. In this case, a for-profit company solicits donations from volunteers. Again, confidentiality is an issue. On the one hand, we expect that a charity will keep records that we can use to confirm our donation if the government audits our tax returns; on the other hand, there are many reasons why we might not want our history of donations to become public information.

On the issue of finances, a for-profit solicitation company takes a certain percentage of donations to pay for its costs in soliciting and processing the donations and then passes on the rest of the money to the charity. This process becomes ethically objectionable when the percentage of money that goes to the solicitor becomes comparatively large. If the soliciting company pockets 80% of the donations it collects and passes along only 20% to the charity, donors feel cheated. If the soliciting organization keeps only 2% of the donations and passes along 98% to the charity, most people would not object.

The charity solicitation scenario is similar to the skin cell donation in that volunteers are asked to donate by someone who has a financial interest in that donation. In both situations, the donors are asked to make the donation for altruistic reasons. In both cases, the amount of money given to the person in the middle (the solicitor or the doctor) seems ethically relevant, as does the control of information about donors. In all of the cases we've examined, this donor information is almost certainly in the form of computer files and therefore easy to store and distribute.

The scenarios are different in that the donation requested for charity is monetary, not physical. In the charity solicitation, only the solicitor is for-profit. In the skin cell donation, both the doctor and PHARM CO are for-profit entities, although the doctor is making just a little money and PHARM CO is both spending and hoping to make much larger sums.

Step 5: Make a Decision or Loop Through the Method Again. You've moved through the first four steps of the paramedic method and now you've developed a better understanding of the situation. If you have to make a decision right away (the doctor is waiting!), you can do so with a more reasoned response than before. But perhaps you have the luxury of thinking it over some more ("Doc, let me get back to you about the skin cell donation, OK?"). You might want time to ask a few more questions of the doctor or PHARM CO. You also might want to think about it more carefully on your own. In cases where the decision was potentially more critical to you or someone important to you, you might want to seek out help in making your decision. If you have the time, you could revisit earlier steps in the paramedic method.

Just to give this section some closure, let's imagine that the doctor wants you to decide about the donation while you're there at the office. ("The study is only going on for a few more days, and we wouldn't want you to have to come in again for such a trivial procedure.") We think that the analysis above would give you sufficient reasons to decline the invitation unless the doctor could give you more assurance about how PHARM CO was going to store and use your genetic information. On the one hand, helping find cures to serious diseases seems like a good thing, and the donation procedure sounds harmless. On the other hand, you haven't been given much assurance about how your genetic privacy will be maintained, and the financial interests of the other stakeholders might give you pause.

A thoughtful reader might or might not agree with that conclusion, but we hope any reader recognizes that this seemingly straightforward request has some surprisingly complex issues attached to it.

17.3 Personal Privacy and Social Networks

In the previous section, we examined four topics that demonstrate the relationship between computing and ethics: illegal music copying, surveillance, hacktivism, and medical privacy. We chose these topics not because they were necessarily the most important, but because they were useful in illustrating our four methods of reasoning about ethical cases: utilitarian analysis, reasoning by analogy, deontological analysis, and the paramedic method.

In this section, we turn to issues you might face in everyday life. The concerns raised in this chapter are "big issues," big in the sense of having the potential to cause enormous economic and political damage to a vast number of people—the cracking of military or governmental databases, the theft of vital financial or medical information. However, other than illegal music copying, most people will not be directly impacted by these problems. However, there are ethical and legal issues regarding computing of a somewhat "smaller" nature—smaller in the sense of impacting as few as a single individual, but the "smallness" of the apparent harm is misleading. To a person whose privacy has been invaded or who has been subjected to public ridicule and shame, these are certainly not small problems, and the consequences can be devastating.

Bullying is a problem that has been around for a long time—being verbally tormented or physically abused is something that Greek and Roman citizens probably had to deal with thousands of years ago. However, the growth of the Internet and social networking Web sites has allowed bullying and the violation of one's personal privacy to become much easier and far more virulent: Online taunting allows bullies to remain anonymous, gang up on victims in enormous numbers, harass victims in places they would normally be safe, such as the confines of their home, and have their hateful screeds live on in cyberspace long after they have been identified and deleted.

According to the Pew Foundation, about 93% of U.S. children and young adults regularly use the Internet and the Web, with the great majority accessing it on a daily, even hourly, basis. Some of the most popular destinations are social media sites such as Facebook, YouTube, Twitter, MySpace, chat rooms, forums, and blogs. These applications are a fun and convenient way to exchange messages, share stories and photographs, and keep in touch with friends and family; unfortunately, they are also a quick and easy way to spread personal information, malicious rumors, hate speech, and indecent images to a massive audience.

Cyberbullying is humiliating, taunting, threatening, or invading someone's privacy using the Internet, Web, or other type of electronic technology. Cyberbullying can take many forms, from posting hurtful and insulting messages, to leaking sensitive and embarrassing personal data, to online threats of violence and physical assault. One popular form of cyberbullying is *impersonation*. A bully, masquerading as the intended victim, posts provocative images or knowingly false messages on a social network, chat room, or blog. The intent is to destroy the victim's reputation and invite retaliation from offended individuals and groups. The post will often include a home address and cell phone number to make it easy for others to find and harass the targeted victim.

As in most high-tech fields, the enactment of state and federal statutes to deal with cyberbullying lags far behind its popularity and use. Although 34 states have enacted some form of law or school policy against cyberbullying, these laws often apply only to minors and only to behaviors committed on school property. Laws focusing on wider audiences, such as private communications between adults, have frequently been challenged and struck down in court for violating First Amendment rights of free speech, even speech that might be considered hurtful or embarrassing. In response, many cases have been prosecuted under other statutes, such as state or federal laws against fraud, bias, or making terroristic threats.

For example, in 2006, 13-year-old Megan Meier of St. Charles County, Missouri, who was being treated for depression, committed suicide after repeated harassment and persecution on the social networking site MySpace. The perpetrator was the 47-year-old mother of an ex-girlfriend posing online as a 16-year-old boy. The mother was not charged with cyberbullying but fraud under the 1986 U.S. Computer Fraud and Abuse Act, a law written with a totally different concern in mind—the hacking of financial and governmental computer systems. The jury returned a not guilty verdict, which led the state of Missouri to enact "Megan's Law," making it a felony to use the Internet or other electronic media to harass or frighten a child under the age of 17. In 2009, the first case testing the constitutionality of this new law was filed against a defendant for posting photos and personal information about a young girl in the Casual Encounters section of Craigslist, leading to numerous unwanted phone calls and e-mails of a sexual nature. In February 2011, a jury again returned a verdict of not guilty, saying the law as written was too vague in its definition of exactly what constitutes online harassment and the invasion of privacy.

In 2010, Tyler Clementi, an 18-year-old Rutgers University freshman, jumped to his death from the George Washington Bridge after a roommate used a hidden webcam to record his private sexual encounter with another man. The roommate then posted the video on the Internet, without Clementi's consent, even inviting Twitter followers to watch it online.

In April 2011, a grand jury indicted the roommate on 15 counts, including the transmission of sexual images of another person without his knowledge and bias intimidation, a hate crime, but not cyberbullying because at the time there was no state law addressing this issue. The suicide so stunned the Rutgers campus and the entire state that in November 2010 the New Jersey legislature passed, with only a single dissenting vote, a comprehensive anti-cyberbullying law.

It will likely be many years and many court cases before there is widespread agreement on exactly how to craft a law to deal effectively with the many types of cyberbullying, from the relatively harmless online taunts of young children ("You are stupid," "You have big ears") to the truly frightening threats of disturbed adults and violent sexual predators. These laws need to carefully balance the public's right to a free and unfettered exchange of ideas and opinions, even controversial ones, with the individual's right to control the publication and dissemination of personal information. The difficulty of writing such legislation was highlighted by the judge in the Craigslist case who said that laws addressing cyberbullying and the online invasion of privacy are so new there was virtually no precedent to guide him with proper jury instructions.

Another problem exacerbated by the rapid growth of social networks and online communications is sexting, the transmission of sexually explicit messages or images, usually via smartphones or tablet computers, between consenting individuals. Although the scale of the problem is a matter of debate, a recent survey conducted by a popular magazine of 1,000 girls between the ages of 12 and 20 revealed that about 20% had recently sent either sexually explicit text messages or nude/seminude images of themselves to friends via a mobile phone.

Like bullying, the consensual circulation of sexually explicit material is not a new phenomenon, and sharing "pin-up" pictures has been around since the 1890s. However, the popularity of digital cameras and smartphones, as well as their ubiquitous use by high school and college-age youth, has greatly inflamed the problem. Unlike images from digital cameras and smartphones, older, film-based photographs generally had to be processed by a third party. If the photos contained questionable sexual content, the involvement of print shop personnel could lead to an embarrassing situation or, in extreme cases, arrest and prosecution. This tended to put a natural damper on the practice of circulating such photos, a damper that no longer exists. To make matters even worse, smartphones can record and transmit not just still images but videos, which can be far more explicit.

Compounding the problem is the ease with which images and videos can be distributed to a huge audience via popular Web sites, often without the knowledge or approval of the person being recorded, as was the situation with the streaming video in the Tyler Clementi case. Relationships that an individual thought would last forever can quickly turn ugly and spiteful, resulting in the public distribution of messages and photographs that were originally shared in strict privacy. Social networking sites like Facebook, MySpace, and Twitter are enormous in scale (In 2010 Facebook was reported to have 750 million active users; Twitter about 175 million) and highly persistent, so once documents or images have been posted, there is virtually no way to get them all back and no way to ever know how many people have viewed them. Years or decades later, long after that indiscretion has been forgotten, these photographs can resurface to your everlasting shame and humiliation, not to mention loss of employment and irreparable damage to your reputation.

In June 2011, U.S. Rep. Anthony Weiner (NY) was forced to resign in disgrace when a link to sexually explicit photographs he had placed on the Web was accidently posted on his public Twitter account. Only a few months later, U.S. Rep. Louis Magazzu (NJ), a Democrat, had to resign when nude photos he sent in private to a female "friend" ended up on a Republican activist's Web site. It turns out that the friend was really an employee of a political rival.

It is not simply your reputation and employment that are at risk—there can be serious legal ramifications when one or both of the individuals involved in the image transmission are under 18. As with cyberbullying, state and federal laws have yet to determine how best to deal with the problem of sexting when the photographs are of minors, even if the transmission is consensual and private. In some states, this issue is dealt with under existing laws against the production and distribution of child pornography, an extremely serious felony that can lead to a long jail sentence and inclusion on the National Sex Offender Registry. For many, this seems like an overly harsh way to deal with the problem of individuals under 18 who send sexually explicit images of themselves to a boyfriend or girlfriend without any intent to sell or distribute the photos. In 2009, the American Civil Liberties Union (ACLU) filed suit against a Pennsylvania District Attorney who was threatening to file child pornography charges against a group of high school girls for posting risqué photos of themselves on a social networking site. The ACLU and the girls' parents won the initial case, but as of 2011 it is being appealed and the outcome is uncertain.

In response to this case, a number of states, including Connecticut, Ohio, Vermont, and New York, have reduced legal penalties for the *consensual* and *private* transmission of sexual images by those under the age of 18 from a felony to a misdemeanor. Many of these new laws also include mandatory educational and family counseling regarding the real and serious dangers associated with sexting, including encounters with sexual predators, and the humiliation and embarrassment caused by the unexpected distribution of these private photos, a situation that has resulted in numerous teen suicides.

Probably no court decision better exemplifies the legal trade-offs between the public nature of social networks and the individual's right to privacy than the 2009 California case *Moreno vs. Hanford Sentinel Inc.* A student at UC-Berkeley, returning during school break to her hometown of Coalinga, California, posted a story on MySpace ("Ode to Coalinga") containing extremely vitriolic and highly unflattering comments about her hometown and its residents. After six days, she deleted the article from her home page; but once an image or message has been posted in cyberspace, it is virtually impossible to control who is able to see it, how many people can copy it, and what can be done with it.

In this case, the offensive posting was viewed by the principal of Coalinga High School who forwarded it to the editor of the *Coalinga Record*, the local newspaper, which published it in full as a letter to the editor, including the author's full name. This led to death threats (a gunshot was fired into the family home), the closing of the father's business, and the family being forced to sell their home and move out of town in disgrace. The family sued the principal, the editor, and the newspaper's owners for invasion of privacy and emotional distress.

The California Court of Appeals ruled that the principal did not invade the young girl's privacy when he sent the article to the newspaper, and the newspaper did not violate her rights by publishing either the article or her full name, both of which had been available on MySpace. The court held that "[She] publicized her opinions about Coalinga by posting the Ode on myspace.com, a hugely popular Internet site. Her affirmative act made that article available to any person with a computer and thus opened it to the public eye. Under these circumstances, no reasonable person would have an expectation of privacy regarding the published material." What this decision is effectively saying is that any material posted to a popular Web site should, by definition, be considered public property, without legal protection against the invasion of privacy.

The best way to ensure personal privacy with regard to online information is simply to assume that any articles, facts, ideas, opinions, rants, photos, or videos you post on a social network may not remain private and, instead, may become widely read and distributed—"go viral" in Internet terminology. Therefore, if you don't want a large number of people to read something, *don't post it*. If you would be embarrassed or upset to have this information widely circulated (to parents, employers, teachers, neighbors), *don't post it*. If there is a chance this material could be considered libelous

Practice Problems

1. Should cyberbullying be made illegal, or should it be something handled (more informally) by parents, teachers, and the social networking companies? Use a utilitarian analysis, deontological analysis, or argument by analogy to justify your position.

2. Think forward to 15 years from now. You are Facebook friends (or whatever the equivalent will be in the future) with many of your coworkers. During a messy divorce proceeding, your coworker's ex-spouse posts old sexting messages, sent by the coworker, on Facebook, tagging them so that you and everyone else at work see the pictures. How should you react? What specific actions should you take, or not take, in response? What if you were the manager or owner of the business?

or defamatory and lead to future litigation, *don't post it*. If you are thinking about sending someone a private photo of a sexual nature, *don't do it*. To paraphrase a popular slogan for a Nevada city: "What happens on Facebook, does not necessarily stay on Facebook."

In the Internet age, personal privacy is no longer as simple as putting a lock on your diary and hiding the key. When you say something or show something on a social networking Web site, you are effectively sharing it with the world.

17.4 What We Covered and What We Did Not

We don't want to end this chapter without warning you that we've only scratched the surface of some of the ethical and legal issues involving technology, privacy, and society. In the chapter exercises, we'll invite you to look at some of the many controversies in these developing areas of applied ethics. And although we've discussed how to apply utilitarian ideas, deontological ideas, and analogies to computer ethics, we haven't even mentioned Rawlsian negotiation, virtue ethics, or any other number of ethical techniques. We also haven't explicitly mentioned "science and technology studies," though many of the themes we've described are included in that emerging scholarly field. Please examine the Additional Resources for this chapter if we've piqued your interest.

You may think that the paramedic method is too involved for your decisions, and perhaps just trying to remember how to spell *deontological* gives you a headache. But we hope you'll at least remember that technical decisions involve human values, whether we recognize it or not. And when you have to decide if something having to do with technology is right or wrong, we hope you remember to think carefully about consequences and duties. Computers give us tremendous power. Let's hope we learn to use the power well. Happy computing!

17.5 Summary of Level 6

In this last and highest level of abstraction in our study of computer science, we looked at several case studies involving computer technology and saw how even seemingly straightforward situations, when examined closely, reveal multiple facets of ethical implications. But more than the particular cases involved, this level provided some tools for coping with ethical decision making.

Because of the increasing capabilities of computers and their increasingly pervasive presence in our private and public lives, the path ahead will be filled with instances in which the use of computers, information, and technology will have ethical consequences. As private citizens and as members of society, we cannot avoid making decisions on such issues, because even doing nothing is a decision that has ethical consequences. Finally, ethical decision making seems to be a purely human responsibility, not one that our computers can help us with directly, at least not yet.

EXERCISES

1. Here are some issues that you may have noticed in the news, each of which involves the intertwining of technology and human values:

    Personal privacy when surfing the Web
    Software quality issues: How good is good enough?
    Licensing of software engineers
    The digital divide: The haves and have-nots of information
    U.S. Supreme Court ruling on virtual kiddie porn
    U.S. Supreme Court ruling on filters in public library Internet use
    U.S. Supreme Court ruling that children have the right to buy violent games
    Tracking terrorist and hate group Web sites
    Censoring information on the Web about making bombs
    Loss of jobs due to technology
    Computer algorithms for determining the risks of subprime mortgages
    Virtual reality as recreation
    Computer simulations in the courtroom
    E-mail spam and legislation to stop it
    Online education and cheating
    Surveillance cameras in public areas
    Face recognition to scan for terrorists at the Super Bowl
    FBI databases of criminals
    Web sites with convicted sex offenders' addresses
    Stolen credit card numbers posted on the Internet

    Sales taxes on Internet sales
    Computing for the disabled
    Open source software versus commercial software
    Remixing pictures or videos found on the Web to create art
    Term papers for sale on the Internet
    Internet-based plagiarism detection services
    States selling information compiled from drivers' licenses
    Database matching to find deadbeat parents
    Internet casino gambling
    Workplace monitoring using computers
    Legal rights for robots
    Smart bombs and other lethal robots
    Artificial intelligence devices for medical diagnosis
    DNA evidence in capital cases
    The increasing influence of Anonymous, LulzSec, and other hacker groups
    WikiLeaks' publication of secret U.S. diplomatic cables
    The e-mail of public figures, like Sarah Palin and Elena Kagan, being published
    Politicians' Twitter- and/or Craigslist-related "sex" scandals

a. *Practice creating analogies*—Pick three topics from the list shown here, or make up some topics of your own that involve technology and humans. For each topic, think of an analogous situation that does *not* involve computing. For example, if you picked "online education and cheating," an obvious analogy would be to consider face-to-face education and cheating. If you picked "personal privacy when surfing the Web," an analogy might be "personal privacy when checking out library books." When you've picked your three topics and your analogy for each, make a short list of how each analogy is like the topic and how the analogy is different from the topic.

b. *Practice finding stakeholders*—Pick your favorite topic from among the three topics you chose in Exercise 1a. For that topic, make a new list of all the significant stakeholders in the topic. (*Hint:* Remember that a stakeholder can be an individual, a group of individuals, a corporation, perhaps the environment, or any other entities you think are important in your topic.) For each stakeholder, list what the stakeholder most values in this situation.

It might help you to frame a specific question or propose a particular action related to the topic. For example, if your topic is "online education and cheating," you might propose the action, "online education should be suspended until online cheating can be better controlled" or "online education should include automated cheating detection." This narrowing of the topic sometimes simplifies the task of imagining what people value with respect to this issue.

c. *Practice identifying costs and benefits*—For each stakeholder you identified in Exercise 1b, list the possible costs and benefits in the situation you chose. In many cases, these are *potential* costs and benefits, things that might or might not happen. Sometimes the words *vulnerability* and *opportunity* can be more accurate than *cost* and *benefit* because of uncertainties in the situation.

d. *Practice looking for duties and responsibilities*—In the previous two parts, you identified some stakeholders. Let's use the letter *N* to stand for the number of stakeholders you identified. Now, make a two-dimensional table that has $N \times N$ cells. At the top of the table, label each column with one of your stakeholders. At the left of the table, copy the list of stakeholders, one for each row. If the stakeholders were {Fred, Ethel, Lucy}, then the table would look like this:

	Fred	Ethel	Lucy
Fred			Things that Fred owes Lucy
Ethel		Things that Ethel owes Ethel	
Lucy	Things that Lucy owes Fred		

Inside each cell, list any duties or responsibilities that the stakeholder on the left owes the stakeholder above. For example, three of the cells are marked in the sample table. Don't neglect the cells that describe duties people have to themselves.

2. *Pull it all together*—In Exercise 1, you looked at one topic in some detail. In this exercise, write a short paragraph about what you think is the right thing to do in the situation you selected. Justify your decision based on the analogy you developed, the costs and benefits you listed, and the duties in your table. After you've devised the best argument you can to show that you're right, write a short description of what you think is the best argument *against* your decision.

ADDITIONAL RESOURCES

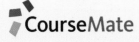 **CourseMate**   **For additional print and/or online resources relevant to this chapter, visit the Computer Science CourseMate at login.cengagebrain.com.**

Answers to Practice Problems

Chapter 2
Section 2.2.2

1. | Step | Operation |
| --- | --- |
| 1 | Get values for *x, y,* and *z* |
| 2 | Set the value of *average* to $(x + y + z)/3$ |
| 3 | Print the value of *average* |
| 4 | Stop |

2. | Step | Operation |
| --- | --- |
| 1 | Get a value for *r,* the radius of the circle |
| 2 | Set the value of *circumference* to $2 * \pi * r$ |
| 3 | Set the value of *area* to $\pi * r^2$ |
| 4 | Print the values of *circumference* and *area* |
| 5 | Stop |

3. | Step | Operation |
| --- | --- |
| 1 | Get values for *amount,* the amount of electricity used, and for *cost,* the cost per kilowatt-hour |
| 2 | Set the value of *subtotal* to *amount * cost* |
| 3 | Set the value of *tax* to $0.08 *$ *subtotal* |
| 4 | Set the value of *total* to *subtotal + tax* |
| 5 | Print the value of *total* |
| 6 | Stop |

4. | Step | Operation |
| --- | --- |
| 1 | Get values for *balance,* the current credit card balance, for *purchases,* the total dollar amount of new purchases, and for *payment,* the total dollar amount of all payments |
| 2 | Set the value of *unpaid* to *balance + purchases – payment* |
| 3 | Set the value of *interest* to *unpaid * 0.12* |
| 4 | Set the value of *newbalance* to *unpaid + interest* |
| 5 | Print the value of *newbalance* |
| 6 | Stop |

5. | Step | Operation |
| --- | --- |
| 1 | Get values for *length* and *width* in feet |
| 2 | Set the value of *length-in-yards* to *length*/3 |

3	Set the value of *width-in-yards* to *width*/3
4	Set the value of *area* to *length-in-yards* * *width-in-yards*
5	Set the value of *cost* to *area* * 23
6	Print the value of *cost*
7	Stop

Section 2.2.3

1. If $x \geq 0$ then

   Set the value of *y* to 1

   Else

   Set the value of *y* to 2

2. Get values for *x*, *y*, and *z*

   If $x > 0$ then

   Set the value of *average* to $(x + y + z)/3$

   Print the value of *average*

   Else

   Print the message 'Bad Data'

   Stop

3. Get values for *balance, purchases, payment*

   Set the value of *unpaid* to *balance* + *purchases* − *payment*

   If *unpaid* < 100 then

   Set the value of *interest* to *unpaid* * 0.08

   Else

   If *unpaid* ≤ 500 then

   Set the value of *interest* to *unpaid* * 0.12

   Else

   Set the value of *interest* to *unpaid* * 0.16

   Set the value of *newbalance* to *unpaid* + *interest*

   Print the value of *newbalance*

   Stop

4. Get a value for *x*

   While $x \neq 999$

   Set the value of *a* to x^2

   Set the value of *b* to $\sin(x)$

      Set the value of *c* to 1/*x*

      Print the values of *a, b,* and *c*

      Get a value for *x*

   End of the loop

   Stop

5. Get values for *length, width, price*

   Set the value of *length-in-yards* to *length*/3

   Set the value of *width-in-yards* to *width*/3

   Set the value of *area* to *length-in-yards * width-in-yards*

   Set the value of *cost* to *area * price*

   If *cost* ≤ 500 then

      Print the message 'You can afford this carpet'

   Else

      Print the message 'This carpet is too expensive'

   Stop

6. Add the following statement to the end of the solution, just before the Stop statement:

   (Assume that we have stored the cost of the carpet in the variable *cost*.)

   If (*cost* ≤ 250.0)

      Print the message 'This is a particularly good deal.'

Section 2.3.1

1. Initial values

a = 2	*b* = 4	*count* = 0	*product* = 0

After pass 1

a = 2	*b* = 4	*count* = 1	*product* = 2

After pass 2

a = 2	*b* = 4	*count* = 2	*product* = 4

After pass 3

a = 2	*b* = 4	*count* = 3	*product* = 6

After pass 4

a = 2	*b* = 4	*count* = 4	*product* = 8

2. Yes, the algorithm still works correctly. On Line 1, we input the two values *a* = 0, *b* = 0. On Line 2, the Boolean expression is true, so we set *product* = 0 and skip the entire else clause. The next line executed is "print the value of product" which outputs a 0, the correct answer to the problem 0×0.

3. case 1 ($a = -2, b = 4$):
The value of *product* will be –8, which is correct.

case 2 ($a = 2, b = -4$):
The value of *product* will be 0 (the while loop does not execute at all), which is incorrect.

4. The original algorithm fails when $b < 0$ because *count* is never less than b. If $b < 0$, change the value of b to $-b$, but set the value of a variable called *bnegative* to YES to remember that b was negative. After the product is computed, the sign of *product* will be incorrect if b was negative, so change the sign. Here is a pseudocode version that works for all integer values of a and b:

Get values for a and b

Set the value of bnegative to NO

If (either a = 0 or b = 0) then

   Set the value of product to 0

Else

   If b < 0 then

      Set the value of b to –b

      Set the value of bnegative to YES

   Set the value of count to 0

   Set the value of product to 0

   While (count < b) do

      Set the value of product to (product + a)

      Set the value of count to (count + 1)

   End of loop

   If (bnegative = YES) then

      Print the value of –product

   Else

      Print the value of product

Stop

5. It is a highly inefficient algorithm because of the number of steps required to find the answer. For example, to add $234 + 567$, we will have to repeat the addition of the value 234 to a running sum 567 separate times. When we do multiplication the "traditional" way that we learned in grade school, we have to carry out far fewer operations. (We will learn much more about how to evaluate the efficiency of algorithms in Chapter 3.)

Section 2.3.3

1. We would need to change Line 1 so that the algorithm would input one million names and numbers rather than 10,000. We would need to change Line 3 so that the loop would repeat a maximum of one million times rather than a maximum of 10,000. Actually, that is not a lot of change given that the problem is 100 times bigger. We only needed to change two lines. In fact, if the phone book were one billion names in length, we would only need to change the same two lines.

2.

Step	Operation
1	Get values for *NAME*, N_1, ..., N_{10000} and T_1, ..., T_{10000}
2	Set the value of *i* to 1 and the value of *Found* to NO
3	Do
4	If *NAME* is equal to the *i*th name on the list N_i then
5	Print the telephone number of that person, T_i
6	Set the value of *Found* to YES
	Else
7	Add 1 to the value of *i*
8	While (*Found* = NO) and ($i \leq 10000$)
9	If (*Found* = NO) then
10	Print the message 'Sorry, this person is not in the book'
11	Stop

3. You must change the operation on Line 7 from a greater-than (>) to a less-than (<) sign. That line will now read as follows:

    If A_i < *largest so far* then ...

    That is the only required change. However, to avoid confusion about what the algorithm is doing, you probably should also change the name of the variable *largest so far* to something like *smallest so far* on Lines 3, 7, 8, and 12. Otherwise, a casual reading of the algorithm might lead someone to think incorrectly that it is still an algorithm to find the largest value rather than the smallest.

4. If $n = 0$ (the list is empty), then there are no values for A_1, A_2, ... , A_n. In particular, setting the value of *largest so far* to A_1 gives a meaningless value to *largest so far*. The while loop will not execute at all because *i* has the value 2 and *n* has the value 0, so the condition $i \leq n$ is false. The algorithm will print out nonsense values for *largest so far* and *location*.

    The algorithm can be fixed by putting a conditional statement after Line 1. If $n = 0$, the algorithm should print a message that says the list is empty. The "else" case will be the rest of the current algorithm.

5. If $n = 1$, then *largest so far* is set to A_1, the only list element, and *location* is set to 1. Also *i* is set to 2, so the while loop will not execute because it is false that $i \leq n$ (i.e., it is false that $2 \leq 1$). The correct values of *largest so far* and *location* are printed.

6. Yes it would still work correctly in one sense—it would find the largest numerical value in the list. However, if two numbers were equal, this change would cause the algorithm to find the last occurrence of that number rather than the first. So the value of *largest so far* would not change but the value of *location* might be different.

Section 2.3.4

1. a. NAME = Adams

i	Operation	Found
1	Compare Adams to N_1, Smith. No match.	No
2	Compare Adams to N_2, Jones. No match.	No
3	Compare Adams to N_3, Adams. Match.	Yes

Output = 921-5281

    b. NAME = Schneider

i	Operation	Found
1	Compare Schneider to N_1, Smith. No match.	No
2	Compare Schneider to N_2, Jones. No match.	No
3	Compare Schneider to N_3, Adams. No match.	No
4	Compare Schneider to N_4, Doe. No match.	No

Output = Sorry, but the name is not in the directory.

2. $n = 7, A = 22, 18, 23, 17, 25, 30, 2$

Largest So Far	Location	i	Operation
22	1	2	Compare A_2 and *largest so far*. Is 18 > 22? No
22	1	3	Compare A_3 and *largest so far*. Is 23 > 22? Yes, so reset values
23	3	4	Compare A_4 and *largest so far*. Is 17 > 23? No
23	3	5	Compare A_5 and *largest so far*. Is 25 > 23? Yes, so reset values
25	5	6	Compare A_6 and *largest so far*. Is 30 > 25? Yes, so reset values
30	6	7	Compare A_7 and *largest so far*. Is 2 > 30? No

Output: Largest = 30. Location = 6.

3. Pattern = an $m = 2$. The pattern has 2 characters.
    Text = A man and a woman $n = 17$. The text has 17 characters.

k	i	Mismatch	Operation
1	1	No	Compare P_1, the "a", to T_1, the "A". No match.
		Yes	End of the check for a match at position 1 of the text.
2	1	No	Compare P_1, the "a", to T_2, the blank. No match.
		Yes	End of the check for a match at position 2 of the text.

3	1	No	Compare P_1, the "a", to T_3, the "m". No match.
		Yes	End of the check for a match at position 3 of the text.
4	1	No	Compare P_1, the "a", to T_4, the "a". Match.
4	2	No	Compare P_2, the "n", to T_5, the "n". Match.
4	3	No	i (3) is greater than m (2), so we exit the loop.

Output: There is a match at position 4

In a similar way, the program will produce the following two additional lines of output:

There is a match at position 7

There is a match at position 16

4. If $m > n$, then $n - m + 1 \le 0$. Because the value of k is set to 1 right before the outer while loop, the condition $k \le (n - m + 1)$ is false, the loop is not executed, and the algorithm terminates with no output.

5. If we had incorrectly initialized i to 0 rather than 1, the algorithm would halt with a fatal error on Line 8. In that line, we reference the variable P_i. If i is 0, this would be P_0, but there is no such value, as the pattern begins with the element P_1. This shows how important it is to be very careful about not only the "big issues" but the little details as well. Even a very tiny initialization error can cause an entire algorithm to fail.

Chapter 3
Section 3.2

The numbers from 1 to n, where n is even, can be grouped into $n/2$ pairs of the form

$1 + n = n + 1$

$2 + (n - 1) = n + 1$

$\ldots$

$n/2 + (n/2 + 1) = n + 1$

giving a sum of $(n/2)(n + 1)$. This formula gives the correct sum for all cases shown, whether n is even or odd.

Section 3.3.2

N	Best Case	Worst Case	Average Case
10	1	10	5
50	1	50	25
100	1	100	50
1,000	1	1,000	500
10,000	1	10,000	5,000
100,000	1	100,000	50,000

Section 3.3.3

1. a. 4, 8, 2, 6
       4, 6, 2, 8
       4, 2, 6, 8
       2, 4, 6, 8

   b. 12, 3, 6, 8, 2, 5, 7
       7, 3, 6, 8, 2, 5, 12
       7, 3, 6, 5, 2, 8, 12
       2, 3, 6, 5, 7, 8, 12
       2, 3, 5, 6, 7, 8, 12

   c. D, B, G, F, A, C, E, H
       D, B, E, F, A, C, G, H
       D, B, E, C, A, F, G, H
       D, B, A, C, E, F, G, H
       C, B, A, D, E, F, G, H
       A, B, C, D, E, F, G, H

2. This question can be answered using the formulas from Section 3.3.3:

    Number of comparisons $= \dfrac{1}{2} n^2 - \dfrac{1}{2} n$ Number of exchanges $= n$

    a. Comparisons: 6   Exchanges: 4
    b. Comparisons: 21   Exchanges: 7
    c. Comparisons: 28   Exchanges: 8

Section 3.3.4

The basic shape of the curve as n gets large is still n^2 because as n gets large, the n^2 term dominates the other two terms.

Section 3.4.1

1. *legit* = 3

2	4	1	1

2.

2	0	4	1

2	4	1

3. *legit* = 3

2	1	4	1

4. For example,

1	2	0	0

Section 3.4.2

1. Devi, Nathan, Grant

2. Devi, Nathan, Sue

3. If the data file is sorted numerically by SSN, then the binary search algorithm can be used. The worst case is 29 (2^{28} = 268,435,456 and 2^{29} = 536,870,912). If the data file is sorted alphabetically by the individual's last name, then as far as searching for a SSN is concerned, the file is unsorted. The sequential search algorithm must be used, with a worst case of 350,000,000.

Section 3.4.3

Pattern = AAAB; Text = AAAAAAAAA; m = 4; n = 9; $m \times n$ = 36; the exact number of comparisons is 4×6 = 24.

Section 3.5

1. 38 paths

2.

3. Algorithms of $\Theta(n^2)$ are polynomial algorithms because n is raised to a constant power. An algorithm of $\Theta(2^n)$ is an exponential algorithm. It is the nonconstant exponent that makes this value grow so quickly, as opposed to polynomial algorithms. An algorithm of $\Theta(n^n)$ would still be considered an exponential algorithm because its exponent is n. In fact, such an algorithm grows even faster than one of order 2^n because of the nonconstant base.

Chapter 4
Section 4.2.1

1. a. $10101000 = (1 \times 2^3) + (1 \times 2^5) + (1 \times 2^7)$
        $= 8 + 32 + 128$
        $= 168$ as an unsigned integer value

    b. $10101000 = (1 \times 2^3) + (1 \times 2^5)$
        $= 8 + 32$
        $= 40$

        This is the value of the magnitude portion of the number. The leftmost bit represents the sign bit. In this example, it is a 1, which is a negative sign.

        $= -40$ as a signed integer value

2. To answer this question, you need to represent the decimal value as a sum of powers of 2 and then convert that representation to binary.

    $99 = 64 + 32 + 2 + 1$
    $= 2^6 + 2^5 + 2^1 + 2^0$
    $= 1100011$

    However, this is only 7 bits and we need 8, so we must add one leading 0 to fill out the answer.

    $= 01100011$

3. The 10 bits would be represented as 9 bits for the magnitude and the leftmost bit for the sign. To represent the magnitude, we must rewrite 300 as the sum of powers of 2, as we did in the previous question.

    $300 = 256 + 32 + 8 + 4$
    $= 2^8 + 2^5 + 2^3 + 2^2$
    $= 100101100$ in 9 bits

    To make it a negative value, we must add a 1 bit (the negative sign) to the leftmost position of the number.

    $-300 = 1100101100$
    $254 = 128 + 64 + 32 + 16 + 8 + 4 + 2$
    $= 2^7 + 2^6 + 2^5 + 2^4 + 2^3 + 2^2 + 2^1$
    $= 011111110$ to 9 bits of accuracy for the magnitude

To make it a +254, we must add a 0 (the + sign) to the leftmost position of the number.

+254 = 0011111110

4. Because the leftmost digit is a 1, the number is negative. The magnitude is represented by the remaining 7 digits, 0010111, which is $1 + 2 + 4 + 16 = 23$. Thus, the number is -23.

5. Writing the numbers 0000 through 1111 around a circle, the positive values count up from 0000 and the negative numbers count down from 1111.
   a. +6 is 0110
   b. -3 is 1101

6.   1110   ← carry digit
      01110
   +01011
   ‾‾‾‾‾‾‾‾
     11001

7. a. To see what this value would look like in ASCII, we first look up the characters "X", "+", and "Y" in the ASCII conversion table to see what their internal representation is in decimal.

   "X" = 88
   "+" = 43
   "Y" = 89

   We then convert these decimal values to unsigned 8-bit binary values.

   "X" = 88 = 01011000
   "+" = 43 = 00101011
   "Y" = 89 = 01011001

   The internal representation of the three-character string 'X+Y' is formed by putting together all three of the preceding values, producing the following 24-bit string:

   010110000010101101011001

   which is how a computer stores 'X+Y' using ASCII encoding.

   b. From the Unicode tables,

   "X" = 0058
   "+" = 002B
   "Y" = 0059

   where these representations are in hexidecimal (base 16) form. In base 16, digits run from 0–F rather than 0–9 as in the decimal system. Translating these representations into decimal, we get

   $$\text{"X"} = 0 \times 16^3 + 0 \times 16^2 + 5 \times 16^1 + 8 \times 16^0$$
   $$= 80 + 8$$
   $$= 88$$

"+" $= 0 \times 16^3 + 0 \times 16^2 + 2 \times 16^1 + 11 \times 16^0$
$= 32 + 11$
$= 43$

"Y" $= 0 \times 16^3 + 0 \times 16^2 + 5 \times 16^1 + 9 \times 16^0$
$= 80 + 9$
$= 89$

These are the same decimal values as under ASCII encoding (Unicode for common characters agrees with ASCII encoding) but will be written in 16-bit binary form, with extra spaces for readability.

"X" $= 88 =$ 0000 0000 0101 1000
"+" $= 43 =$ 0000 0000 0010 1011
"Y" $= 89 =$ 0000 0000 0101 1001

Putting these together produces the following 48-bit string for 'X+Y':

0000 0000 0101 1000 0000 0000 0010 1011 0000 0000 0101 1001

8. a. $+0.25 = 0.01$ in binary
$= 0.1 \times 2^{-1}$ in scientific notation
so the mantissa is $+0.1$ and the exponent is -1.
$= 0 \underbrace{100000000}_{\text{mantissa}} \quad \underbrace{1\ 00001}_{\text{exponent}}$

   b. $-32\ 1/16 = -100000.0001$
$= -0.1000000001 \times 2^6$
$= 1 \underbrace{100000000}_{\text{mantissa}} \quad \underbrace{0\ 00110}_{\text{exponent}}$

Note that the last 1 in the mantissa was not stored because there was not enough room. The loss of accuracy that results from limiting the number of digits available is called a *truncation error*.

9.   1111   ← carry digits
     00001
    +01111
    ‾‾‾‾‾‾
     10000

Here $15 + 1 = -16$

10. You are adding the two values $+7$ and $+14$, which should produce the value $+21$. But when you add the two values together, you get 10101, which is a negative value because the leftmost digit is a 1. In fact, it is the value -5. What happened is that we got an *arithmetic overflow*. The value $+21$ is too big to represent in sign/magnitude with only five digits.

Section 4.2.2

1. 44,100 samples/second $\times$ 16 bits/sample $\times$ 3 minutes $\times$ 60 sec/minute
$= 127$ million bits

Compressed at a ratio of 4:1, this becomes about 32 million bits.

2. 66,000 samples/sec $\times$ 24 bits/sample $\times$ 180 seconds = 285,120,000 bits

3. 2,100,000 pixels $\times$ 24 bits/pixel = 50,400,000 bits or 6,300,000 bytes

4. To reduce 6,300,000 bytes to 1,000,000 bytes requires a compression ratio of almost 7:1.

   To reduce 6,300,000 bytes to 256,000 bytes requires a compression ratio of almost 25:1.

5. Compression ratio = original size / compressed size = 9.6/3 = 3.2

6. The fixed-length 4-bit representation of ALOHA requires 5 $\times$ 4 = 20 bits. Using the variable-length code requires the following:

A	L	O	H	A
00	1111111	0111	010	00

   which is a total of 18 bits. The compression ratio is 20/18 = 1.11.

Section 4.3.1

1. a. $(x = 1)$ AND $(y = 3)$
       True AND False
       False   The final answer is False.
    b. $(x < y)$ OR $(x > 1)$
       True OR False
       True   The final answer is True.
    c. NOT $[(x = 1)$ AND $(y = 2)]$
       NOT [True AND True]
       NOT [True]
       False   The final answer is False.

2.
A	B	C	((NOT A) AND B) OR C
F	F	F	F
F	F	T	T
F	T	F	T
F	T	T	T
T	F	F	F
T	F	T	T
T	T	F	F
T	T	T	T

3. $(x = 5)$ AND $(y = 11)$ OR $([x + y] = z)$
   True AND False OR True

   We now must make an assumption about which of the two logical operations to do first, the AND or the OR. If we assume the AND goes first, then we get

False OR True
True

If we assume that the OR goes first, then the expression would be evaluated as follows:

True AND True
True

In this case, the answer is the same, but we arrive at the answer in different ways.

4. $(x \geq 0)$ AND $(x \leq 100)$ AND $(y \geq 0)$ AND $(y \leq 100)$ AND $(\text{NOT}(x = y))$

5. NOT[$(score \geq 200)$ AND $(score \leq 800)$]

6. The expression (A OR B) OR (NOT A) is true for all values of A and B and, therefore, is never false. A Boolean expression that is always true is called a *tautology*.

Section 4.4.2

1. The four separate cases are

    $$\overline{a}\cdot\overline{b}\cdot\overline{c} \qquad \overline{a}\cdot b\cdot\overline{c} \qquad \overline{a}\cdot b\cdot c \qquad a\cdot b\cdot\overline{c}$$

    Combining them by using the OR operator produces the following Boolean expression:

    $$\overline{a}\cdot\overline{b}\cdot\overline{c} + \overline{a}\cdot b\cdot\overline{c} + \overline{a}\cdot b\cdot c + a\cdot b\cdot\overline{c}$$

    When this Boolean expression is represented as a Boolean diagram, it appears as follows:

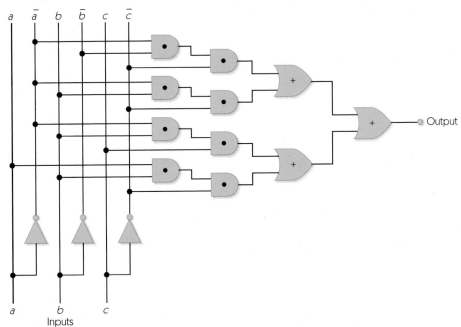

2. The Boolean expressions for the two cases are

    $\bar{a}\cdot b$

    $a\cdot\bar{b}$

    Combining these two by using the OR operator produces

    $\bar{a}\cdot b + a\cdot\bar{b}$

    Pictorially, the corresponding circuit diagram is

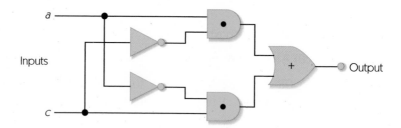

3. The Boolean expression for this is

    $\bar{a}\cdot\bar{b}\cdot\bar{c} + a\cdot b\cdot c$

    Pictorially, the corresponding circuit diagram is

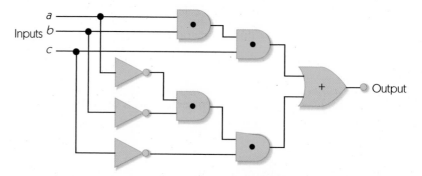

4. If we use the circuit construction algorithm described in this chapter, we produce the circuit: $\bar{a}\cdot\bar{b} + \bar{a}\cdot b$. When this expression is implemented as a logic circuit, it takes two NOT gates, two AND gates, and one OR gate for a total of five gates. However, looking carefully at the truth table, we see that the output is a 1 whenever a is a 0, and the output is a 0 whenever a is a 1. The output is not affected by the value of b. Thus, an equivalent circuit is $\bar{a}$, which takes only 1 gate—an improvement of 80%. This is a good example of how much optimization can improve a preliminary design, and how important it can be to the efficiency of a computer system.

Section 4.4.3

1. Each 1-CE circuit contains two NOT gates, two AND gates, and one OR gate. This will require $(2 \times 1) + (2 \times 3) + (1 \times 3) = 2 + 6 + 3 = 11$

transistors. The 32-bit compare-for-equality circuit of Figure 4.23 has the following components:

32 1-CE circuits = 32 × 11 = 352 transistors
31 AND gates = 31 × 3 = 93 transistors
Total = 352 + 93 = 445 transistors

2. Bit-compare $a > b$, where both a and b are 1 bit in length.

The truth table for this circuit would be as follows:

a	b	Output	
0	0	0	
0	1	0	
1	0	1	(because a is greater than b)
1	1	0	

There is only one case where there is a 1 bit in the output. It is in the third row and corresponds to the following Boolean expression:

$a \cdot \overline{b}$

We can skip Step 3 because with only one case, there is no combining of Boolean expressions. Thus, the circuit diagram for this circuit is

3. The truth table is already given, and again there is only one case with a 1 bit in the output. This occurs in the first row and corresponds to the Boolean expression

$\overline{a} \cdot \overline{b}$

Given this single subexpression, we can proceed immediately to draw the circuit diagram:

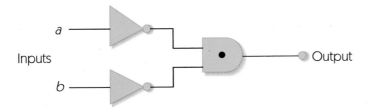

4. The truth table is already given. There are two cases with a 1 bit in the output, occurring in rows 1 and 4. The corresponding subexpressions are:

Case 1: $\overline{a} \cdot \overline{b}$

Case 2: $a \cdot b$

The final Boolean expression is $\overline{a} \cdot \overline{b} + a \cdot b$ and the circuit diagram is

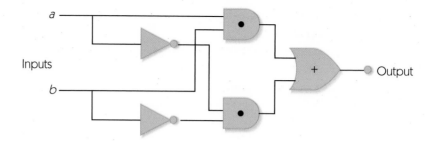

Chapter 5
Section 5.2.1

1. If the memory unit is a two-dimensional grid 1024 (2^{10}) by 1024 (2^{10}), then it contains a total of 1,048,576 (2^{20}) memory cells. We need a total of 20 bits to represent all the possible memory addresses, which range from 0 to $2^{20} - 1$.

2. Because there are $2^{10} = 1024$ row lines and $2^{10} = 1024$ column lines, we would need to send 10 (of the 20) bits in the MAR to the row decoder and 10 bits to the column decoder.

3. The instructions that are fetched from memory are usually much larger than 8 bits in size, often 16, or 32 bits. If the MDR were only 8 bits, then to fetch a 16-bit instruction we would have to go back to memory twice. If the instruction were 32 bits, then we would have to go back to memory four separate times. This would greatly slow down the fetch phase of the instruction cycle. The MDR should be at least as large as the largest instruction that we fetch.

4. Average access time $= (0.80 \times 10) + 0.20 \times (10 + 25) = 15$ nsec

5. Average access time $= (0.90 \times 10) + (0.10 \times (10 + 25)) = 9 + 3.5 = 12.5$ nsec

6. With a cache hit rate of 92%, the average access time is

   $(0.92 \times 10) + 0.08 \times (10 + 25) = 12$

7. For example: If we think that human memory consists of "cells" in which information is stored and from which it can be retrieved, then human memory does not seem to have the property of a uniform time to access every cell. "Short-term memories" seem to be more quickly accessible than long-term memories.

Section 5.2.2

1. The total number of characters (ch) is

   2 surfaces/disk $\times$ 50 tracks/surface $\times$ 20 sectors/track $\times$ 1024 ch/sector which is 2,048,000 characters on a single disk.

2. The seek time depends on the number of tracks over which the read head must move. This could range from 0, if the arm does not need to move, to a worst case of the arm having to move from the far inside track to the far outside track, a total of 49 tracks. The average, as stated in the problem, is a move across 20 tracks. The best-case rotational delay is 0, whereas the worst case is one complete revolution. The rotational speed is 2400 rev/min = 40 rev/sec = 25 msec/rev. On the average, we will wait about one-half a revolution. Finally, the transfer time is the same in all cases, the time it takes for one sector (1/20 of a track) to rotate under the read/write head, which is 1/20 rev * 25 msec/rev = 1.25 msec. Putting all this together in a table produces the following values for the time (in msec) required for each task:

	Best Case	Average Case	Worst Case
Seek time	0.0	20 * 0.4 = 8.0	49 * 0.4 = 19.6
Latency	0.0	0.5 * 25 = 12.5	1 * 25 = 25.0
Transfer	1.25	1.25	1.25
Total	1.25	21.75	45.85

3. The new rotational speed is 7200 rev/min = 120 rev/sec = 8.33 msec/rev. The seek time is unaffected by the rotational speed. The new average latency time is 0.5 rev * 8.33 msec/rev = 4.17 msec. The new transfer time is 1/20 rev * 8.33 msec/rev = 0.42 msec. The total average case time = 12.59 msec.

4. average seek time = 20 tracks $\times$ 0.2 msec/track = 4 msec
   average latency = 0.5 rev $\times$ 8.33 msec/rev = 4.17 msec
   transfer time = 1/20 rev $\times$ 8.33 msec = 0.42 msec

   So the average access time = 4 + 4.17 + 0.42 = 8.59 msec

5. If many pieces of the file are on the same track, then no movement of the read head arm is required and seek time is 0.

Section 5.2.4

Assuming that variables a, b, c, and d are stored in memory locations 100, 101, 102, and 103, respectively:

1.
Memory Location	Op Code	Address Field	Comment
50	LOAD	101	Register R now contains the value of b
51	ADD	102	R now contains the sum $b + c$
52	ADD	103	R now contains the sum $b + c + d$
53	STORE	100	And we store that sum into a

There are many other possible solutions to this and the following problems, depending on which instructions you choose to use. This solution uses the one-address format. The two- and three-address formats will lead to different sequences.

2.

Memory Location	Op Code	Address Field	Comment
50	LOAD	101	Register R contains the value of b
51	MULTIPLY	103	R now contains the product $b \times d$
52	STORE	101	b now has the value $b \times d$
53	LOAD	102	R contains the value of c
54	DIVIDE	103	R now contains the quotient c / d
55	STORE	103	d now has the value c / d
56	LOAD	101	Load the product $b \times d$ back into R
57	SUBTRACT	103	R now contains $(b \times d) - (c / d)$
58	STORE	100	Store the result into a

3.

Memory Location	Op Code	Address Field	Comment
50	LOAD	100	Register R now contains the value of a
51	SUBTRACT	104	R now contains the value $a - 1$
52	STORE	100	Store the result into a

4.

Memory Location	Op Code	Address Field	Comment
50	COMPARE	100, 101	Compare a and b and set condition codes
51	JUMPNEQ	54	If they are not equal, go to address 54
52	LOAD	103	Otherwise load R with the value of d
53	STORE	102	And store it into c
54			The next instruction begins here

5.

Memory Location	Op Code	Address Field	Comment
50	COMPARE	100, 101	Compare a and b and set condition codes
51	JUMPGT	55	Jump to address 55 if $a > b$
52	LOAD	103	Load R with the value of d
53	STORE	102	And store it into c
54	JUMP	58	Jump to address 58
55	LOAD	103	Load R with the value of d
56	ADD	103	R now contains $2d$
57	STORE	102	And store that result into c
58			The next instruction begins here

6.

Memory Location	Op Code	Address Field	Comment
50	LOAD	103	R contains the value d
51	STORE	100	And store it into a
52	COMPARE	100, 102	Compare a and c, set condition codes
53	JUMPGT	58	Jump to address 58 if $a > c$
54	LOAD	100	R now contains the (current) value of a
55	ADD	101	R now contains the value $a + b$
56	STORE	100	And store that sum into a
57	JUMP	52	Jump back to test loop condition again
58			The next instruction begins here

Chapter 6
Section 6.3.1

1. Initial values $R = 20$ memory location 80 = 43
memory location 81 = 97

Operation	Final Contents of Register R	Final Contents of Mem Loc 80	Final Contents of Mem Loc 81
a. LOAD 80	43	43	97
b. STORE 81	20	43	20
c. COMPARE 80	20 (and the GT indicator goes ON)	43	97
d. ADD 81	117	43	97
e. IN 80	20	Whatever value is entered by the user	97
f. OUT 81	20	43	97

2. Initial value memory location 50 = 4

Operation	Final Contents of Register R
a. LOAD 50	4
b. LOAD 4	A copy of the contents of memory cell 4.
c. LOAD L	Because L is equivalent to 50, this operation is equivalent to LOAD 50, which is the same as part (a).
d. LOAD L+1	A copy of the contents of memory cell 51. This operation means LOAD $(L + 1)$, which is equivalent to LOAD 51. LOAD $L + 1$ does arithmetic on addresses, not contents.

3. The HALT operation tells the CPU to stop program execution. If the program is organized as in Figure 6.6, then without the HALT instruction the CPU will fetch the data value stored in the next memory location after the last instruction and attempt to execute it. The .END pseudo-op tells the assembler to stop the translation process. The assembler is a piece of software that is acting on the source code, loaded into memory, as its "data"; without the .END pseudo-op, the assembler will try to translate whatever might be stored in memory after the last legitimate source code statement.

4. The first instruction will cause the memory location labeled L to be loaded into register R. Because L contains the data value +1, this will go into R, overwriting whatever was there previously. After completing one instruction, a processor will go on to the next one unless told to do otherwise—that is the essence of the Fetch/Decode/Execute cycle. Thus, the processor will next try to execute the "instruction" + 1. As we explained in the text, this will be incorrectly interpreted as the op code 0 and address field of 1, which is a LOAD 1. Thus, the value +1 in register R will be overwritten with the contents of memory location 1.

Section 6.3.2

1. a.
```
          INCREMENT X
              .
              .
              .
X:        .DATA       0
```
Another way to do the same thing is
```
          LOAD        X
          ADD         ONE
          STORE       X
              .
              .
              .
ONE:      .DATA       1
X:        .DATA       0
```

However, the first way is much more efficient. It takes two fewer instructions and one fewer DATA pseudo-op.

b.
```
          LOAD        X
          ADD         FIFTY
          STORE       X
```

.
.
.

FIFTY:	.DATA	50	
X:	.DATA	0	

c.

	LOAD	Y	--Load the value of Y into register R
	ADD	Z	--R now holds the sum (Y + Z)
	SUBTRACT	TWO	--R now holds (Y + Z – 2)
	STORE	X	--Store the result in X

.
.
.

X:	.DATA	0
Y:	.DATA	0
Z:	.DATA	0
TWO:	.DATA	2

d.

	LOAD	FIFTY	--R holds the constant 50
	COMPARE	X	
	JUMPGT	THEN	--if X > 50 go to label THEN
	IN	X	--input a new value
	JUMP	DONE	--and jump to done because we are --all finished
THEN:	OUT	X	
DONE:			--the next statement goes here

.
.
.

X:	.DATA	0
FIFTY:	.DATA	50

e.

	LOAD	ZERO	--Put 0 in R
	STORE	SUM	--Initialize SUM to 0
	STORE	I	--Initialize loop counter to 0
LOOP:	LOAD	FIFTY	--Put 50 in R
	COMPARE	I	
	JUMPEQ	DONE	--I equals 50, exit loop
	LOAD	SUM	--Put SUM in R
	ADD	I	--R now holds (SUM + I)
	STORE	SUM	--Store result in SUM
	INCREMENT	I	--Add 1 to I
	JUMP	LOOP	--end of loop body

```
        DONE:                                    --the next statement goes here
                 .
                 .
                 .
        I:       .DATA       0
        SUM:     .DATA       0
        ZERO:    .DATA       0
        FIFTY:   .DATA       50
2.               .BEGIN
                 IN          NUMBER      --get first number
        LOOP:    LOAD        ZERO
                 COMPARE     NUMBER      --see whether number < 0
                 JUMPLT      DONE        --the number is negative so
                                         --go to DONE
                 INCREMENT   COUNT       --it is nonnegative so
                                         --increment count
                 IN          NUMBER      --get next number
                 JUMP        LOOP        --and repeat the loop
        DONE:    OUT         COUNT       --print out the final count
                 HALT
        COUNT:   .DATA       0           --count of number of
                                         --nonnegative values
        ZERO:    .DATA       0           --the constant 0 used for
                                         --comparison
        NUMBER:  .DATA       0           --place to store the input
                                         --value
                 .END
3.               .BEGIN
                 IN          NUMBER      --get first number
        LOOP:    LOAD        ZERO
                 COMPARE     NUMBER      --see whether number < 0
                 JUMPLT      DONE        --the number is negative so
                                         --go to DONE
                 INCREMENT   COUNT       --number is nonnegative so
                                         --increment count
                 LOAD        HUNDRED
                 COMPARE     COUNT
                 JUMPEQ      DONE        --count = 100 so go to DONE
                 IN          NUMBER      --count < 100 so get next
                                         --number
                 JUMP        LOOP        --and repeat the loop
```

DONE:	OUT	COUNT	--count is either 100 or a
			--legitimate count of the less
			--than 100 nonnegative
			--numbers read, so print
			--count in either case
	HALT		
COUNT:	.DATA	0	--count of number of
			--nonnegative values
ZERO:	.DATA	0	--the constant 0 used for
			--comparison
NUMBER:	.DATA	0	--place to store the input
			--value
HUNDRED:	.DATA	100	--the constant 100
	.END		

4. The most important thing was that you were looking at a program that contained English words and familiar mathematical terminology. That made it much easier to understand what was going on and where the modifications were to be made. Also, the use of labels allowed you to make changes in the program without having to make changes to binary memory addresses.

Section 6.3.3

1.		.BEGIN		
		CLEAR	NEGCOUNT	--Step 1. Not really necessary
				--because
				--negcount is already set to 0
		LOAD	ONE	--Step 2. Set i to 1. Also not
				--really
		STORE	I	--necessary because i is
				--initialized to 1
	LOOP:	LOAD	FIFTY	--Step 3. Check whether $i > 50$
				--and if so
				--terminate the loop
		COMPARE	I	
		JUMPGT	ENDLOOP	
		IN	N	--Step 4. Read a value
		LOAD	ZERO	--Step 5. Increment
				--negcount if
		COMPARE	N	--N is less than zero
		JUMPGE	SKIP	
		INCREMENT	NEGCOUNT	

SKIP:	INCREMENT	I	--Step 6. Count one more --loop iteration
	JUMP	LOOP	--Step 7. and start the loop --over
ENDLOOP:	OUT	NEGCOUNT	--Step 8. Produce the final --answer
	HALT		--Step 9. and halt
NEGCOUNT:	.DATA	0	
I:	.DATA	1	
N:	.DATA	0	
ONE:	.DATA	1	
FIFTY:	.DATA	50	
ZERO:	.DATA	0	
	.END		

2. a. COMPARE = 0111   Y = decimal 10 = 0000 0000 1010
       instruction = 0111 0000 0000 1010

    b. JUMPNEQ = 1100   DONE = decimal 7 = 0000 0000 0111
       instruction = 1100 0000 0000 0111

    c. DECREMENT = 0110   LOOP = decimal 0 = 0000 0000 0000
       instruction = 0110 0000 0000 0000

3. LOOP is the address of an instruction (IN X), but decrement is treating it as though it were a piece of data and subtracting 1 from it. Thus, what this instruction is doing is "computing" (IN X) – 1, which is meaningless. However, the computer will be very happy to carry out this meaningless operation.

4. The address values that you come up with will depend entirely on your solution. The symbol table for the program in Practice Problem 1 would look like the following example. (*Note:* The solution assumes that each instruction occupies one memory location.)

Symbol	Address
LOOP	3
SKIP	11
ENDLOOP	13
NEGCOUNT	15
I	16
N	17
ONE	18
FIFTY	19
ZERO	20

5. No, it is not illegal, just highly misleading. You can label a piece of data with any name you want, but you should pick something that is helpful to the people who have to read and modify the program at some future time. By labeling the constant $+1$ with the symbolic name TWO, you will confuse and mislead the people looking at your code.

Section 6.4.1

1. If there is one chance in four that a program is blocked waiting for input/output, then there is a $(1/4) \times (1/4) = 1$ chance in 16 that both of the two programs in memory are simultaneously blocked waiting for I/O. Therefore, the processor will be busy 15/16, or about 94%, of the time. This is the processor utilization. If we increase the number of programs in memory to four, then the probability that all four of these programs are blocked at the same time waiting for I/O is $(1/4) \times (1/4) \times (1/4) \times (1/4) = 1$ chance in 256. Now the utilization of the processor is 255/256, or about 99.6%. We can see clearly now why it is helpful to have more programs in memory. It increases the likelihood that at least one program will always be ready to run.

2. Passwords are not secure because people often write them down on a piece of paper put in plain sight for all to see. Furthermore, when choosing passwords people will often pick something that can be easily guessed, like their child's name or birthday. You can reduce the risk of using passwords by requiring passwords to (1) be at least 8–10 characters in length, (2) include at least one special character like /$*&, and (3) not be something found in a dictionary. You can also use *personal information* rather than a memorized password. Personal information is a fact that you would know without having to write it down, but which an acquaintance or coworker would likely not know—maybe the name of your first pet or your maternal grandfather's first name.

Chapter 7
Section 7.2.1

1. The figure shows the representation of a binary signal using frequency modulation of a carrier wave.

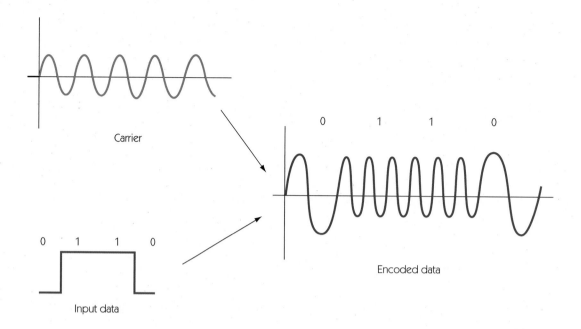

Carrier

Input data

Encoded data

2. The number of bits in the image is 1200 × 780 × 8 = 7,488,000. To transmit this in 1 second requires a transmission speed of 7,488,000 bps, or nearly 7.5 Mbps.

3. 1200 × 780 = 936,000 pixels × 8 bits/pixel = 7.488 million bits
7.488 million bits / 1 billion bits/sec = 0.007488 seconds or
7.48 milliseconds

Section 7.2.2

1. Collisions can occur in a ring topology because all nodes share the ring and a node may want to send a message just as a message from another node is passing by. In a star topology, collisions are avoided because each node has a direct line (via the hub node) to any other node.

2. Because the message is to be broadcast, there is no need to include a destination address. Each node reads the message.

3. Node A sends the message on LAN1, where every node receives it, but only bridge B1 keeps it. All other nodes discard it because it is not addressed to them. Bridge B1 removes the message from LAN1 and rebroadcasts it out on LAN2. Every node on LAN2 receives the message, but again, only bridge B2 keeps it. All others discard it. Bridge B2 knows that node B is located on LAN3, so it rebroadcasts the message on LAN3, where node B receives it, recognizes its own address, and removes the message from the network. The message has arrived at its intended destination.

4. The main security concern is that in an Ethernet-like bus topology every
    node receives a copy of every message sent. A node is supposed to look
    at the address field of the message to see if it is the desired recipient
    and, if not, discard that message. However, a malicious node could keep,
    read, and record every message on the network, even those that are not
    intended for it.

Section 7.3.2

1. A has resent M(3), presumably because B's ACK(3) message never
    reached A. When B receives the second copy of M(3), it should
    again send the ACK(3) to A but discard the message because it is a
    duplicate.

2. B should disassemble M(4) and check that it was correctly transmitted. If
    so, B should send an ACK(4) message to A; if not, B should discard the
    faulty message and wait for A to resend it.

3. B should disassemble M(5) and check that it was correctly transmitted. If
    so, B should send an ACK(5) message to A; if not, B should discard the
    faulty message and wait for A to resend it. Although this message has
    been received out of sequence (presumably because M(4) was lost), no
    special action is required at this time; B did not send an ACK(4) so
    A should in time resend M(4).

Section 7.3.3

1. There are four distinct paths from node A to node D, and their total
    weights are

ABCD	Weight = 16
ABFD	Weight = 14
AEFBCD	Weight = 25
AEFD	Weight = 15

    So the shortest path is ABFD, found by computing the weight of every
    possible path and then picking the smallest. This is essentially a "brute
    force" approach to the problem.

2. This approach would not work with larger graphs such as one with
    26 nodes and 50 links. The number of possible paths would grow much
    too large for us to enumerate and evaluate them all in a reasonable
    amount of time. We must use a more clever algorithm.

3. If the link connecting node F to node D fails, then the paths ABFD and
    AEFD will not work and their weights become "infinite." Of the two
    paths remaining, path ABCD with weight 16 now becomes the shortest
    path. No one link in the network will disconnect nodes A and D. We can
    see that clearly by noting that the two paths ABCD and AEFD do not

share any links in common. Therefore, if a link along one of these paths fails, we can use the other path.

4. Yes, the shortest path would change. The shortest path from A to E would now be the route AEFD with a cost of $4 + 2 + 7 = 13$ units. It had been ABFD with a cost of $3 + 4 + 7 = 14$ units.

Chapter 8
Section 8.2.1

Step 1:   chjbup5 $\rightarrow$ 3 8 10 2 21 16 5

Step 2: $3 + 8 + 10 + 2 + 21 + 16 + 5 = 65$

Step 3:   65 / 7 leaves a remainder of 2 ($65 = 9 \times 7$ with 2 left over)

Steps 4 and 5:   are identical to the example.

Section 8.3.2

1. STB NX YMJ MTZW

2. Because there are 26 letters in the alphabet, a shift of $s = 26$ encrypts each character as itself, so you should not trust the messenger.

Section 8.3.3

1. In the example, where $n = 21$ and $e = 5$, then $d = 5$ as well. To decode, compute

$$C^d = 17^5 = 1419857 = 67612 * 21 + 5 \rightarrow 5$$

Therefore the original numeric message was 5.

Chapter 10
Section 10.2.2

1. `ITIME .LE. 7`

2.
```
    IF  (X .LT. 3) THEN
        A = 2
    ELSE
        A = 1
        B = 3
    ENDIF
   30 . . .
```

Section 10.2.3

1. In Ada:
   ```
   outputNumber := inputNumber;
   sumOfValues  := sumOfValues + inputNumber;
   ```

   In C++, C#, or Java:
   ```
   outputNumber = inputNumber;
   sumOfValues = sumOfValues + inputNumber;
   ```

   In Python:
   ```
   outputNumber = inputNumber
   sumOfValues = sumOfValues + inputNumber
   ```

2. `MULTIPLY 2 TIMES RADIUS GIVING DIAMETER.`

Section 10.2.4

1. *Rate* refers to the contents of the memory cell called *Rate*; &*Rate* refers to the address of that cell.

2. 10

Section 10.2.5

The program prints the numbers from 1 through 10 on a single line with a blank space between them.

Section 10.2.6

`The answer is7`

Section 10.2.7

The Python version is
c. `print("Hello World")`

Section 10.2.8

The name entered in the text box will be displayed in the label.

Section 10.3.3

1. It results in the names of all vendors from Chicago.

2. These are the *times* that try **men's souls**

Section 10.4.1

1. a. `(2 3 4)`
   b. `5`

2. `(define (threeplus x)`
   `(+ 3 x))`

Section 10.4.2

1. No

2. X = jefferson

3. X = lincoln
   X = fdr
   X = kennedy
   X = nixon

Section 10.4.3

1. One processor could compute A + B while another computes C + D. A third processor could then take the two quantities A + B and C + D and compute their sum. Parallel processing uses a total of two time slots: one to simultaneously do the two additions A + B and C + D, then one to do the addition (A + B) + (C + D). Sequential processing would require a total of three time slots: (A + B), then (A + B) + C, then ((A + B) + C) + D.

2. One solution would be to have the input/output processor set a timer for the maximum possible response time from each of the search processors and if that time is exceeded, it reports that NAME was not found. This is not foolproof, because it could simply be that the communications link between the one processor that found NAME is broken, so it was unable to report back. A better solution would be to have each search processor report back to the input/output processor when it cannot find NAME; when the input/output processor has received that message from all 100 search processors, it would then report that NAME was not found.

Chapter 11

Section 11.2.1

1. a.

Token	Classification
x	1
=	3
x	1
+	4
1	2
;	6

b.

Token	Classification
if	8
(	10
a	1
+	4
b42	1
==	7
0	2
)	11
a	1
=	3
z	1
-	5
12	2
;	6

2. a. This would most likely be classified as three tokens: the name abc, the minus sign '-', and the name def. The reason is that a minus sign is rarely ever allowed to be part of a variable name.

   b. This would likely be classified as a single token with the name abc_def. In many programming languages, the underscore character is allowed to be part of a name to allow the different parts of the variable to stand out, for example, the names inches_per_yard or cost_per_square_meter.

   c. This would definitely be classified as two separate tokens –abc and def– because a space is always used to end one token and to identify the start of the next one.

3. A scanner is not involved in the determination of the legality or illegality of a programming language statement; that is done in the next two steps. A scanner is only concerned with finding and classifying tokens. So it would simply return the following six tokens:

Name	Classification
X	1
=	3
;	6
(	10
14	2
hello	1

Section 11.2.2 (Set 1)

1. <Boolean operator> ::= AND | OR | NOT

2. <identifier> ::= <first> <second>
<first> ::= i | j
<second> ::= <letter> | <digit> | Λ
<letter> ::= A | B | C | D | ... | Z
<digit> ::= 0 | 1 | 2 | ... | 9
<identifier> is the goal symbol

3. <expression> ::= (<var> <op> <var>)
<var> ::= x | y | z
<op> ::= < | == | >

4.

5. You eventually reach the point in the parse where you have the following sequence:

(<var> <op>)

which does not match the right-hand side of any rule, and the parse fails.

6. The first rule of Practice Problem 3 could be changed to

<expression> ::= (<var> <op> <var>) | <var> <op> <var>

Section 11.2.2 (Set 2)

1.

2.

3.

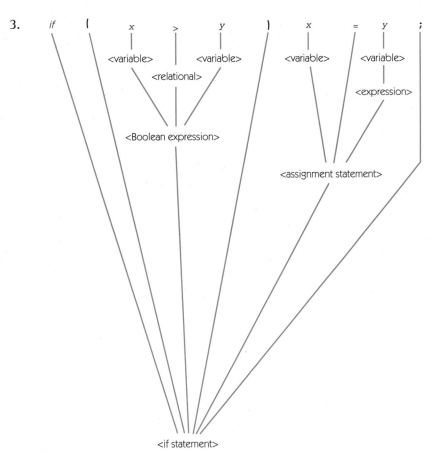

4. The language consists of all strings containing an arbitrary sequence of *a*s and *b*s of length 1 or more.

5. <goal> ::= <pair> | <pair> <goal>
   <pair> ::= AB

6. No, this grammar is not ambiguous. There are only four sentences that belong to the language defined by this grammar:

*a * c, a * d, b * c,* and *b * d*

and all of these sentences have only a single possible parse tree.

Section 11.2.3

The parse tree for this expression is

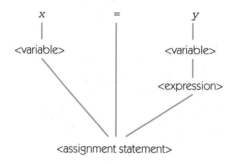

During the construction of this parse tree, you will build four semantic records: two for <variable>, one for <expression>, and one for <assignment statement>.

The code generated is

```
              LOAD      Y
              STORE     TEMP
              LOAD      TEMP
              STORE     X
              .
              .
              .
X:            .DATA     0
Y:            .DATA     0
TEMP:         .DATA     0
```

Chapter 12
Section 12.2

1. Piloting a boat, performing an operation, fighting a fire

2. Soil conditions, water supply, types of industrial waste. It could illustrate long-term effects of various waste disposal policies. If it were inaccurate, policies based on the model could be pursued that would result in environmental damage.

Section 12.3.2

1. $b\ 1\ 1\ 1\ b$
    $\uparrow$
    3

2. a. $b\ 1\ 0\ 1\ b$
        $\uparrow$
        2

    b. $b\ 1\ 1\ 1\ b$
        $\uparrow$
        2

    c. $b\ 1\ 1\ 1\ b$
        $\uparrow$
        2

    d. $b\ 0\ 1\ 1\ b$
        $\uparrow$
        1

3. $b\ 0\ 1\ 0\ b$

Section 12.5.1

1. It is not equivalent. There is no transition from State 1 for an input symbol of 0, and no transition from State 2 for an input symbol of 1.

2. The machine would halt immediately because there are no instructions for what to do when looking at a blank cell.

Section 12.5.2

1. a. $b\ 1\ 1\ 0\ 1\ 0\ b$

Section 12.5.4

1. $b\ 1\ 1\ 1\ 1\ b\ 1\ 1\ 1\ 1\ 1\ b$ becomes
    $b\ b\ b\ 1\ 1\ 1\ 1\ 1\ 1\ 1\ 1\ 1\ b$

2. $(1,1,1,1,R)$
    $(1,0,0,1,R)$
    $(1,b,1,2,R)$

Section 12.7

1. To prove that something is not true, assume that it is and arrive at a contradiction. The assumption must then be wrong.

Chapter 13
Section 13.2.3

1. Without this instruction, server S_i is servicing a newly arrived customer yet is still marked as idle; the next newly arrived customer could try to go to that server.

2. Without this instruction, server S_i has finished serving a customer and there are no customers waiting in line, but the next newly arrived customer will not try to be served by S_i.

3. It most likely would make the conclusions less valid and much less usable. The idea of every customer taking the same amount of time is unrealistic. Therefore, making this assumption would cause our model to be a very poor abstraction of the real system. If your assumptions are wrong, then there is a far greater likelihood that your conclusions will be wrong as well. (We called this "garbage in, garbage out" in the text.)

4. There are many other possibilities, but here are a few:
   a. The possibility of mechanical breakdowns. The model could be designed to include the occasional breakdown of a critical component (e.g., the French fryer) to study how the system responds to these types of unexpected events.
   b. Rather than say no customer ever takes more than 5 minutes to be served, the model could be designed to allow for an occasional massive order—someone purchasing 100 hamburgers—to see what happens to our waiting times when this unusual event occurs.
   c. Some servers could be used only for special orders, rather than have all servers be identical.

Chapter 14
Section 14.2.5

1. For example:
   www.webmd.com
   www.ci.austin.tx.us/environmental
   www.thebasketballportal.com
   www.petersons.com
   www.steelonthenet.com

2. As an alternative, students could be asked to compare two such sites.

Section 14.3.3

1. 149   12.35

2.
```
SELECT LastName, FirstName, MonthlyCost
FROM Employees, InsurancePlans, InsurancePolicies
WHERE LastName = 'Takasano'
AND ID = EmployeeID
AND InsurancePolicies.PlanType =
    InsurancePlans.PlanType;
```

3.
```
SELECT EmployeeID
FROM InsurancePolicies
WHERE PlanType = 'B2';
```

4. Referential integrity. Removing this tuple leaves the InsurancePolicies table with tuples that have EmployeeID foreign key values no longer existing as a primary key value in the Employees table.

Chapter 15
Section 15.3

1. For example, a hamburger is a kind of sandwich. As such, it comes between two pieces of bread, but it is hot. It must contain ground meat, but it may also have various condiments, such as mustard, ketchup, and a pickle.

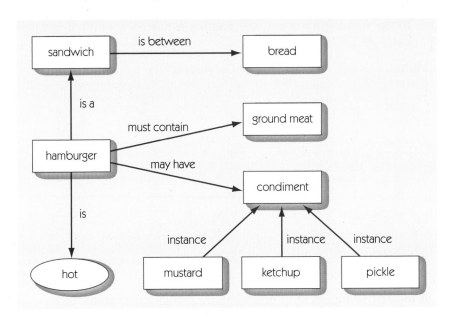

2. a. $(\forall x)(hamburger(x) \rightarrow sandwich(x))$
    b. $(\forall x)(grilledCheese(x) \rightarrow sandwich(x))$
    c. $(\forall x)(sandwich(x) \rightarrow onBread(x))$
    d. $(\forall x)(grilledCheese(x) \rightarrow vegetarian(x))$

Section 15.4

1. No. N1 and N4 fire, but N2 and N3 do not, so N5 does not.

2. It will never fire. The maximum incoming signal that node N5 can receive is $2 + 2 = 4$, which is not enough to make it fire if its threshold value is 5.

Section 15.5

1. Frank is tall. Knowing that Frank is tall does not necessarily mean that he is bald.

2. No conclusion can be inferred. Frank may or may not be tall.

3. No conclusion can be inferred. Frank may or may not be tall.

4. Frank is not tall (because if he were, he would be bald).

Chapter 16
Section 16.2.3

(*Note:* In the following answer, the *z* column has been omitted because it will contain all zeros.)

Vertex	x	y	Connected To	
V_1	0	0	V_2 V_6 V_8	(Origin)
V_2	0	2.4	V_1 V_3 V_4	
V_3	1.5	4.5	V_2 V_4 V_5	
V_4	1.5	2.4	V_2 V_3 V_5 V_6 V_7	
V_5	3	2.4	V_3 V_4 V_{10}	
V_6	1	1.7	V_1 V_4 V_7 V_8 V_9	
V_7	2	1.7	V_4 V_6 V_9 V_{10}	
V_8	1	0	V_1 V_6 V_9	
V_9	2	0	V_6 V_7 V_8 V_{10}	
V_{10}	3	0	V_5 V_7 V_9	

A total of 67 pieces of information are stored in the above table.

Section 16.2.4

Because the motion takes place over a period of two seconds, we need to produce a total of 60 frames, given that 30 frames/second is the standard frame rate for video. These 60 frames represent 59 time intervals. So in each of the 58 in-between frames we need to move the triangle 1/59th of the total distance from its position in the first frame to its position in the last frame. This information allows us to compute the translation matrix.

Total x-distance moved = 4 units.
a = 1/59 × 4 = 0.067796

Total y-distance moved = 2 units
b = 1/59 × 2 = 0.033898

Total z-distance moved = 0 units
c = 1/59 × 0 = 0

Now, using the model shown in Figure 16.6, we can say that the translation matrix required to perform the desired motion is as follows:

1	0	0	0.067796
0	1	0	0.033898
0	0	0	0
0	0	0	1

Index